Systems of Psycho

Donald K. Fromme

Systems of Psychotherapy

Dialectical Tensions and Integration

 Springer

Donald K. Fromme
Pacific University
School of Professional Psychology
222 SE 8th Ave.
Hillsboro, OR 97123
USA
dfromme1@yahoo.com

ISBN 978-1-4899-8698-6   ISBN 978-1-4419-7308-5-(eBook)
DOI 10.1007/978-1-4419-7308-5
Springer New York Dordrecht Heidelberg London

Springer is part of Springer Science+Business Media (www.springer.com)

Dedicated to my wife, Marie, for her encouragement, support, constancy, and love.

Preface

The author's principal thesis is that each of the existing therapeutic systems is based on a partial, incomplete picture of human functioning, problems, and change. Some focus narrowly on microcontextual factors affecting human problems; e.g., biomedical interventions typically focus on neurohormonal imbalances, while behavioral therapies focus on relatively small units of behavior and reinforcement contingencies. At the other extreme, macrocontextual approaches minimize the role of the person and focus on environmental factors: e.g., family therapies examine how problematic patterns of interaction evolve among family members over time, while ecosystemic therapies address the socioeconomic and cultural factors such as poverty and oppression that are at the heart of many problems that people have.

Other approaches cover still other factors located between these extremes that impact human problems. Although there is often significant overlap in the factors considered by different approaches, most are defined by an emphasis on just a few of the possible factors. Cognitive therapies note the importance of other factors, but nevertheless focus primarily on beliefs and reasoning. Similarly, experiential therapies focus on the emotions and psychodynamic therapies on early attachment experiences. Their inclusion of the individual's subjective experience and interpretation of events gives them a broader focus than the microcontextual approaches, but still that focus is partial.

Humanistic therapies are considered holistic and endeavor to understand clients in their own terms; but giving priority to internal, subjective experience means that a client's objective situation and behavior are given less consideration. Interpersonal therapies take note of the fact that human problems invariably involve other people and thus are more toward the macrocontextual pole in their focus on clients' relationships with significant others; once again, other important areas are given less importance.

As Chapter 1 discusses, therapy outcome research consistently shows therapy to be more effective than non-treatment. However, few differences are found in efficacy of different approaches, once experimenter allegiance and demand characteristics are controlled. The few differences that are found suggest that some approaches work better with some problems than others do; e.g., family therapy seems to work best for family-related problems. Perhaps in recognition that no one approach is equally helpful for all clients, most practicing clinicians now use more than one set of ideas or techniques in their work and identify themselves as eclectic or integrative.

The field of psychotherapy is currently experiencing an exciting explosion of new ideas and approaches. Traditional ideas about the nature of science and reality are being challenged by therapists espousing the ideas of postmodern philosophy. Postmodernists suggest that ideas about reality are constructions and could always be otherwise. They also emphasize the importance of language and culture in how people construct their views of the world. New, integrative therapies that provide broader, more inclusive conceptions of human problems are being proposed, with some already gaining strong empirical support for their use.

This text introduces readers to some of the debates fueling current developments in psychotherapy. It reviews the philosophical differences that separate different approaches and the ways each major therapeutic system has inspired integrative efforts. Rather than viewing the various systems as competitors, the focus is on what is uniquely valuable in each approach with an eye toward how those unique factors might eventually be combined into a comprehensive view of human functioning.

Chapter 1 discusses the philosophical and empirical debates that are spurring current developments in the field. Chapter 2 examines transtheoretical and common factors that are relevant to every therapeutic approach, including basic interviewing and assessment skills. Chapter 3 provides an introduction to psychopharmacology in the belief that every helping professional needs to understand how this essential tool can help clients with the most serious, debilitating problems. The approaches in Chapters 4–13 are organized according to their focus of intervention, moving from microcontextual to macrocontextual levels. Chapter 14 reviews important postmodern and integrative approaches that were not discussed earlier, while Chapter 15 is a first approximation of what a fully comprehensive, multilevel therapeutic approach might look like.

Because the author believes the therapeutic relationship to be the most important factor in outcomes, the term "client" is used throughout the book to emphasize that therapy is a process co-created by therapist and client. The one exception is Chapter 3 in which the medical model's use of the term "patient" seemed more appropriate. Third-person plural pronouns are used whenever possible.

Acknowledgments

The author owes a debt of gratitude to the following friends and colleagues who graciously read sections of this text and provided invaluable suggestions. Thanks to Genevieve Arnaut, Lorna Smith Benjamin, Steve Berman, Larry Beutler, Paul Feldman, Erik Fromme, Jason Fromme, Eva Dreikurs Ferguson, Miller (Rocky) Garrison, Eva Gold, Rhonda Goldman, Sandy Jenkins, Robert Julien, Michel Hersen, Dan McKitrick, Russ Miars, Cathy Miller, and Rick Warren.

Contents

About the Author

Donald K. Fromme is Professor Emeritus in the Department of Psychology at Oklahoma State University and also in the School of Professional Psychology at Pacific University, where he continues teaching part-time. He served as Director of the Psychological Service Center at both universities as well as Director of Intern Training at Pacific. He has also taught overseas with the University of Maryland University College on several occasions. During sabbaticals, he has taught at the University of Carabobo in Venezuela and the University of Exeter in England. In 1985–1986 he was a Senior Fulbright Research Fellow at the University of Rome. He has published research focusing on emotional communication, empathy, and the qualitative experience of being part of a step-family. He has also chaired 60 graduate theses and dissertations. Now retired, he previously maintained a part-time private practice together with his wife.

Chapter 1
The Dialectics of Psychotherapy: Philosophical and Empirical Debates

> *[T]he Dodo suddenly called out "The race is over!" and they all crowded round it, panting, and asking "But who has won?" This question the Dodo could not answer without a great deal of thought and it stood around for a long time with one finger pressed upon its forehead .... At last the Dodo said "Everybody has won, and all must have prizes."*
> (Alice's Adventures in Wonderland, *Lewis Carroll*, 1832–1898)

How does the beginning therapist go about choosing a therapeutic approach when there are over 400 different systems available (Karasu, 1992)? Researchers have repeatedly failed to find consistent differences in client outcomes even with therapeutic approaches based on very different assumptions and using varied interventions (Luborsky *et al.*, 2002; Shoham & Rohrbaugh, 1999; Wampold *et al.*, 1997). Lambert and Ogles' (2004) extensive literature review concluded: (a) therapy is superior to placebo or no treatment conditions and (b) all approaches are essentially equivalent when artifacts such as experimental demand characteristics and researcher's theoretical allegiance are controlled.

As early as 1936, Rosenzweig (2002) suggested that commonalities among therapeutic systems were more important than their differences. The success of this prediction led modern researchers to refer to outcome equivalence as the **Dodo Bird verdict**, following Rosenzweig's quotation from *Alice's Adventures in Wonderland*, "everybody has won, and all must have prizes."

Lambert and Ogles (2004) suggested three possible reasons for the Dodo Bird verdict:

1. Different therapies share *common factors*, such as a supportive relationship or instilling hope and expectation for change.
2. Different therapies achieve similar goals through different processes or *specific factors*: *e.g.*, each approach helps clients examine beliefs about the future in unique ways. As clients see problems in a new light, goals are clarified and they begin to see new ways to meet their needs (Beitman, Soth, & Bumby, 2005).
3. Current research methods fail to detect actual differences that exist among therapies.

D. K. Fromme, *Systems of Psychotherapy,*
DOI 10.1007/978-1-4419-7308-5_1, © Springer Science+Business Media, LLC 2011

Although attempts to improve research methods continue, it is not surprising that more therapists currently endorse integrative or eclectic combinations than classical approaches such as psychoanalytic, behavioral, or client-centered therapy (Prochaska & Norcross, 2007). The increasing realization that some approaches work better with certain clients than others has fostered integrative efforts to match therapeutic interventions with relevant client characteristics (Bedi, 2001; Norcross, Beutler, & Clarkin, 1998). Until recently, experienced practitioners were more likely to endorse integrative or eclectic positions than were beginners or academically based therapists. This trend appears to be changing as more academicians and training programs emphasize multiple, eclectic, or integrative approaches (Hoffman & Rosman, 2003; Lampropoulos & Dixon, 2007). One goal of this book is to describe the opportunities and challenges created when therapy systems or interventions are combined.

The reader who expects straightforward answers about how to practice psychotherapy is apt to be disappointed. Instead, skepticism, tolerance for ambiguity, and an appreciation of *dialectics* are necessary to bring together valid, competing viewpoints. Dialectics suggests that *dialog* among opposing points of view is the best way to understand a phenomenon. Dialectical reasoning (Hegel, 1830/1991) involves a dialog that contrasts one idea, a *thesis*, with an opposing idea, or *antithesis*. Every thesis implies an antithesis: *e.g.*, therapy clients both desire and resist change, perhaps fearing a negative outcome. Dialecticians believe that every thesis and antithesis contain elements that are "true" or at least "useful." Eventually, a *synthesis* of those elements may be created, such as "I want to change as long as I don't have to give up essential qualities of who I am." As understandings evolve, each synthesis becomes a new thesis that implies another antithesis, which leads to still another synthesis, and so on in a never-ending series. From a dialectic perspective, competition among systems of psychotherapy constitutes a series of theses and antitheses awaiting synthesis or integration.

The nature of knowledge, or *epistemology*, is itself a dialectic. For example, *scientific modernism*, historically dominant in the field of psychology, is increasingly being challenged by other perspectives. Instead of the modernist view that empirical research will eventually produce an accurate picture of reality, contemporary dialecticians take a *postmodern* view of knowledge: as different theories are constructed and debates become more sophisticated, there is always more than one way to describe events. Kuhn (1970) suggested that science advances as a result of *paradigm shifts* as theorists discover new ways to think about an area of interest. Earlier theories are seldom disproved, but simply left behind in the marketplace of competing ideas. The *scientific modernism/postmodernism* dialectic on whether there is more than one viable conception of reality may represent such a paradigm shift.

This chapter describes four principle dialectics that contribute to therapeutic proliferation:

1. The *scientific modernism/postmodernism* dialectic of competing philosophical assumptions;
2. The *eclectic/integrative* dialectic on how to integrate different approaches and interventions;

3. The *science/practice* dialectic, or *scientist-practitioner gap* on the difficulty of conducting well-designed research that is also relevant to real-life clinical settings;
4. The *microcontext/macrocontext* dialectic on what constitutes the best level of intervention (*e.g.*, psychopharmacology, cognitive-behavioral, humanistic, or social systems levels).

Not surprisingly, still other dialectics exist within these larger arenas.

Dialectical Tensions in Psychotherapy: Philosophical Assumptions

Psychologists have not been as concerned with the assumptions underlying their work as perhaps they might be. Many argue that philosophy detracts from science because it deals with unprovable assumptions. While philosophy can be abstract and seem remote from every day concerns, this view ignores the fact that the scientific method is itself based on unprovable assumptions about reality (*ontology*) and knowledge (*epistemology*). Many differences among therapeutic systems result from differing ontological assumptions about human nature and epistemological differences about how to evaluate the "truth" or "utility" of competing approaches.

Ontologies involve the constructs and causal relationships that describe an area of study. Aristotle's analysis of causality, unquestioned for two millennia, is now a source of debate. To understand a phenomenon, Aristotle believed we must identify four types of causes:

1. *Material*—e.g., water behaves differently than air;
2. *Efficient*—some force must act upon an object in order to set it in motion;
3. *Formal*—the shape or organization of an object in relation to its environment affects its motion;
4. *Final*—the purpose or goal of the object.

For example, water, but not air (material cause), can be poured (efficient) from a pitcher and will seek (final) the lowest level possible (formal) in its environment. Scientific modernism began by appropriately rejecting the anthropomorphism implicit in assigning purposes or intentions (final causes) to inanimate objects. Part of the behavioral/humanistic dialectic is whether or not human purposes should also be rejected as "anthropomorphic." Humanists note that anthropomorphism is not a valid criticism when discussing human intentions!

Epistemologies describe decision rules that determine whether an ontological statement is "true" or "useful." Epistemologies differ in whether they are *objective*—our senses provide a "true" depiction of reality; or *subjective*—it cannot be known whether or not our senses provide a true depiction of reality. Objectivist philosophers believe we can agree on the nature of reality because our senses are reliable guides to what is observed. Subjectivists counter that our senses and past experience interact to produce observations unique to each individual. The color, green, is not "out there," but instead is the way brains interpret light of a particular wave length. In addition, its emotional impact reflects past experience: *e.g.*, Fromme and O'Brien (1982) found that Pakistani students rated the color green, sacred to Islam, as more "joyful" than did American students. *Monistic* epistemologies assume that one model will eventually be found to accurately describe reality, while *pluralistic* epistemologies assume there are many ways of describing reality. The major therapeutic approaches reflect differing assumptions about knowledge and reality, which need to be considered when integrating therapeutic approaches.

The choice of a therapeutic system is a defining moment for every therapist. Often this choice reflects a therapist's training, rather than a thoughtful evaluation of an approach's assumptions. Philosophy clarifies epistemological assumptions about "truth," ontological assumptions about the nature of reality, and ethical assumptions about correct action. Discussions about the respective merits of different therapeutic approaches are often at cross-purposes if these assumptions are not made explicit. Therapeutic assumptions define what constitutes "data," what makes a conclusion valid, what the goals of therapy should be, and even the language used to describe goals, actions, and outcomes.

For example, behavioral therapists believe that as scientific modernism is empirically based, objective epistemology is the best way to evaluate the efficacy of therapeutic interventions. They focus on how consequences reinforce problem behavior, but have little interest in inner conflicts or broad theories of human nature. Empirical research decides which interventions are valid. *Patients* are *given empirically supported treatments* that *remove symptoms*. In contrast, humanistic therapists believe that the clients' subjective experience (*i.e.*, their pain and how they interpret events) is more real than an observer's "objective" reality. Humanists are concerned that the reality of an individual's experience is lost when objective measures involving many different people are combined statistically. They strive to understand problems from the perspective of the client, who is the ultimate authority on what is meaningful or problematic. Therapists *collaborate* with *clients* to *discover insights* that help *resolve problems in living*. The incompatibility of humanist and scientific modernist epistemologies helps explain why many humanists view scientific research as counterproductive and misleading. On the other hand, many behaviorists consider humanistic therapies to be "unscientific."

Epistemological assumptions about whether "truth" is *discovered* or *constructed* and ontological assumptions about the nature of reality are implicit in every therapeutic system. Table 1.1 describes four philosophical positions important for therapists: *scientific modernism, phenomenology, general systems theory,* and *postmodernism.*

Scientific modernism assumes *objective monism*: scientific explanation is *reductionistic*. It assumes a *single, empirically derived* model, *universally* applicable to all people, will eventually explain *objective, causal* relationships among *elements*

Table 1.1 Principle philosophical positions in psychotherapy systems

Philosophical position	Objectivism	Subjectivism
Monism	Scientific modernism	Phenomenology
Pluralism	General systems theory	Postmodernism

abstracted from reality. Explanations at higher levels of explanation will ultimately be *reducible* to lower levels: *e.g.*, social processes reduced to people's thoughts and beliefs; thoughts and beliefs to neural processes in the brain; and neural processes to biochemical interactions at neural synapses. Therapists help clients discover and correct the cause of their problems.

Systems theory also embraces an empirical epistemology, but rejects reductionism in favor of an *objective pluralism* that assumes different explanatory principles *emerge* at different levels of analysis: *i.e.*, different principles, *not reducible* to lower levels, are needed to explain events at each level. Each level influences every other level; *e.g.*, social and family processes affect an individual's intentions, which both affect and are affected by processes at cognitive, neural, and biochemical levels.

In contrast, phenomenology assumes *subjective monism*: each person has a *true self* that is revealed in dialogs with unbiased observers and reflects his or her own unique reality. The person's *full potential* is realized as the true self is actualized and replaces "*false*" selves that develop to meet others' expectations. Rather than causal analyses, therapists try to *describe* their client's reality in terms of his or her *unique, subjective meanings* or *values*.

Postmodernism's *subjective pluralism* rejects the idea of a "true" self and assumes people *construct* a variety of *possible selves*. Some postmodernists see no limits on the number of possible selves, but others suggest the number is constrained by experiential and cultural *contexts* such as the concepts available in the person's language. Instead of helping clients *discover* their "true" self, postmodern therapists help them *construct* an adaptive *self-narrative* that meets their needs.

Both systems theory and postmodernism emphasize the importance of *context*. A modernist cognitive therapist might see negative self-statements causing a woman's depression, while a systems theorist might focus on the context of her dysfunctional family. A phenomenological therapist might help her examine her feeling that life lacks meaning, while a postmodernist might help her address the ways a cultural "glass ceiling" limits opportunities for advancement in her profession. Table 1.2 summarizes some of the assumptions associated with various therapeutic approaches discussed in more detail in subsequent chapters.

Scientific Modernism

Scientific modernism reflects dominant *foundational* assumptions that seem so self-evident they are seldom examined critically. Slife (2004a) described five major assumptions:

1. *Objectivism*: Nature exists independently of observers and can be described without bias using the scientific method. Our senses provide a reliable guide to reality.
2. *Universalism*: Scientific explanations apply to all times, places, and situations, regardless of the contexts in which events occur.
3. *Atomism*: Scientific descriptions involve elements appropriate to each discipline, such as individual behaviors in psychology or atoms in chemistry.

4. *Materialism*: Every event involves observable objects set in motion by external forces.
5. *Hedonism*: People are motivated to maximize pleasure and minimize pain.

[These five assumptions] constrain not only what is thought to be the *desired outcome* of research and therapy, but also what is viewed as the *desired process*. The most desirable

Table 1.2 Philosophical assumptions associated with different therapeutic approaches

Approach	Ontological assumptions	Epistemological assumptions
Biomedical approaches	Organ or neurohormone (*material cause*) disease or mutation is the *efficient cause* of symptoms or dysregulated behavior	*Objective* (observable) data *re* physiology and symptom changes will eventually yield comprehensive (*monism*) explanations
Behavioral: operant approaches	*Material* stimuli are the *efficient* causes of responses; future responses become more likely when reinforced	*Objective* data describe S-R reinforcement patterns with increasingly comprehensive (*monism*) explanations of behavior
Cognitive approaches	Verbalization accurately reflects inner thoughts; changed thoughts are *efficient* causes of changed behaviors	Inferences about internal processes may be tested by *objective* data, with increasingly complete (*monistic*) theoretical explanations
Psychodynamic: psychopathology	Internalized childhood conflict→*efficient* cause of anxiety→ego defense→ symptom	Client report is internally consistent and congruent with theory (*subjective monism*)
Psychodynamic: treatment approaches	Insight into goal (*final*) of symptom or ego defense→no rational basis for anxiety→symptom reduction (*efficient*)	Consistent, congruent (*subjective monism*) client reports are followed by changes in symptoms and behavior (*objective monism*)
Humanistic approaches	The goals of behavior (*final*) reflect each individual's *unique* interpretation of his/ her experience, opportunities, and plans	Unbiased, empathic description, verified by the client→*holistic* view of each person's unique experience (*subjective monism*)
General systems theory	*Hierarchic* organization of dynamic systems yields *emergent* properties (*formal*) that are *regulated* by feedback loops (*efficient*)	*Objective* data reveal regulatory processes and explanations that invoke different principles (*pluralism*) at each hierarchic level
Postmodern: feminist approaches	Language, socio-historical constructions, and "accepted practice" limit (*formal*) choices (*final*) and cause problems (*efficient*)	Recognizing *social constructions* allows us to *deconstruct* current practice and create a more equitable reality (*subjective pluralism*)
Postmodern: narrative approaches	Unique experiences and choices (*final*)→either problem- or solution-rich narratives that describe each person's unique reality	Narratives that create more equitable and empowering solution-focused realities are desirable (*subjective pluralism*)

outcome for research and therapy is a generalizable (universalism) and observable (materialism) benefit (hedonism) to the individual client (atomism). The fifth assumption, objectivism, enters the picture by helping therapists and researchers to assume that this desired outcome is not itself laden with questionable values and biases (*i.e.*, it is "objective") (Slife, 2004a, p. 75).

It is important to remember that foundational assumptions are arbitrary and may limit full consideration of alternatives. Utility is the only test of their validity since assumptions cannot be proven. Modern science's achievements have been extremely useful by this measure, but there are debatable corollaries to its assumptions; *e.g.*, objectivism implies that science is value-free and unbiased. However, scientific modernism supports whatever social system or values currently exist when it assumes that social practices are "universal" instead of arbitrary human constructions.

For example, modern diagnostic practices define depression as pathological if it lasts over 6 months after bereavement. Queen Victoria mourned Prince Albert's death for 40 years and was praised for devotion to her husband's memory. Today, she would be given an antidepressant. Also, materialist or hedonist assumptions that reduce human problems to biochemical imbalances or inadequate reinforcement schedules allow little room for exploring spirituality or what constitutes a meaningful life. Atomism implies people are nothing more than the "sum of their constituent parts." Universalism suggests that context is of little importance, but many human problems are inextricably linked to their context: *e.g.*, the boy who misbehaves to deflect his parents from their marital conflict.

The limitations of foundational assumptions suggest a need to consider other possibilities, despite the proven utility of modernist approaches such as psychiatry or cognitive-behavioral therapy. The fact that "universal" principles do not work for every client is one basis for the perception of many practitioners that therapeutic research is irrelevant to their work, the *researcher-practitioner gap*. Scientific modernism's context-free principles may not always help specific individuals who have context-rich, real-life problems (Safran, 1998).

Because humanist, existential, psychodynamic, and postmodern therapists assume values and meanings are part of understanding a client's problems, they emphasize the individual's *unique* situation and aspirations. In contrast, empirically based modernist approaches, such as cognitive-behaviorism, emphasize interventions that are *generally* effective for most people. Although empirically supported treatments are important, they provide little guidance if their procedures fail with a "treatment-resistant" client. As a result, phenomenological approaches such as humanistic, existential, and psychodynamic therapy have remained important even though, until recently, they have lacked cognitive-behaviorism's level of empirical support.

Phenomenology

Phenomenological philosophers (*e.g.*, Husserl, 1931) criticize the objective emphasis of modernism and suggest that people respond to their subjective understanding of an event rather than the event itself. Knowledge is seen as *descriptive*, rather than *predictive*. A smile may have many meanings and is best understood by simply asking the one who is smiling. People usually report intentions accurately as long as listeners avoid distorting the message. On the other hand, people are seldom aware of the "causes" of their actions, which may be over-determined.

Humanistic client-centered, existential, or experiential therapists use nondirective methods to avoid bias in understanding clients. Instead of causes, they focus on goals and reasons. They view people *holistically*, believing that something is lost if people are reduced to their constituent parts. The goal is to understand the client's reality from the client's point of view. However, postmodernists criticize both humanists and behaviorists for focusing on the individual and neglecting the socio-historical contexts in which meanings are created and behavior occurs.

General Systems Theory

General systems theory is a useful integrative framework that addresses both behavioral contexts and goals. Hierarchically organized subsystems and suprasystems provide the context of self-regulating, goal-oriented processes that maintain the system's function and integrity. Developed by missile and computer scientists, systems theory may be generalized to *any* self-regulating system including social systems, families, systems of belief, or neural networks. It is also called *cybernetics*, from the Greek *kybernetes* meaning pilot, steersman, or governor. In contrast to the modernist ontology of a universe that is *static* until put in motion by external forces (*positive explanation/linear causality*), systems theory views the universe as constantly in *motion*. Systems theory examines why *self-regulating systems* resist change or move in one direction rather than another (*negative explanation/circular causality*). Positive explanations describe a linear relationship between antecedents (causes) and consequences (effects). In contrast, negative explanations describe constraints such as *feedback loops* (circular causality) that maintain stability: *e.g.*, just as thermostats limit temperature ranges, depression may regulate emotional distance by distracting a couple from marital conflict.

Reciprocal determinism (Bandura, 1986) reflects a convergence of modernism's linear causality and systems theory's circular causality. Both linear causality and reciprocal determinism assume positive explanation, while both reciprocal determinism and circular causality assume mutually causal relationships among environment, behavior, and person variables. The difference is that circular causality assumes negative explanation: that behavior *limits* and *is limited by* environmental constraints and personal abilities, beliefs, or goals. Figure 1.1 illustrates *hierarchical* relationships between two feedback loops in a circular causality model: social influences shape personal beliefs and goals, which govern behavior within environmental limits in a short-term loop. A long-term causal loop then describes how a behavior's environmental impact can shape social influences on beliefs about goals.

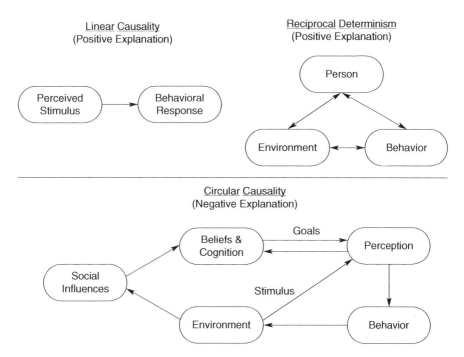

Fig. 1.1 Linear, reciprocal, and circular models of causality

Systems theory addresses two criticisms of scientific modernism: its inability to account for human intentionality and its neglect of contextual influences (universalism). Systems theory describes intentional behavior as actions that reduce perceived deviations from goals: *e.g.*, if therapists get feedback that treatment goals are not being met, they reduce deviations (achieve positive outcomes) by modifying their approach (Lutz, Martinovich, Howard, & Leon, 2002).

In systems theory, contextual influences are described by feedback loops among ecosystemic, societal, family, conceptual, behavioral, and biological system levels. Levels are organized *hierarchically*: Ecosystems (*e.g.*, political and economic systems) are comprised of smaller social systems such as interest groups and corporations that, in turn, are comprised of individuals who also belong to family systems. Together, these larger systems influence the beliefs and behaviors of individuals, while beliefs and thoughts influence and also reflect the activity of biochemical and neural systems. In general, higher-order systems establish the goals for lower-order systems. Success or failure of lower-order systems in achieving those goals then completes a feedback loop in which higher-order systems either adopt new strategies or move on to new goals; *e.g.*, families may set high academic goals for their children, but need to adopt remedial strategies or revise their expectations if the children fail to meet those standards.

Emergent principles govern processes at each level; *e.g.*, thoughts emerge from neural processes that limit what thoughts occur. However, thoughts are not mere neural epiphenomena and also reflect past and current experiences. Conversely, cognitive and emotional processes complete a feedback loop and influence neural activity: *e.g.*, thoughts about goal-directed activities help maintain optimal levels of neural activation, which is also influenced by brain biochemistry. Systems theory's ability to model this dialectic of subject and object is another reason for its adoption by many integrative theorists.

Postmodern Criticism and Philosophy

Modernist and systems theorists assume reality can in principle be accurately described (objectivism). Phenomenologists assume there is only one unbiased way to describe each person's reality (subjectivism). In contrast, postmodernists assume all phenomena, including subjective experiences, may be described in a number of equally plausible ways that change over time as language, meanings, and cultural practices evolve (subjective pluralism). Competing postmodern positions add still further dialectic tensions.

All postmodernists believe all claims to knowledge of reality are constructions that cannot be independently verified. Cultural or theoretical constructions determine what data are of interest and how they should be collected and interpreted. There is no independent way to verify the "truth" of scientific evidence other than pragmatic criteria. *Radical constructivists* suggest each person's unique learning history creates as many reality "maps" as there are people. *Social constructionists* differ in suggesting that ideas about reality are also limited by the evolution of language and social constructs: *e.g.*, many people now view homosexuality as a biological trait, not a choice.

Postmodern epistemologies, such as social constructionism, dialectics, and hermeneutics, suggest that "knowledge" is the product of ongoing social dialog. These groups all agree that the limits of language inevitably result in partial, pluralistic theories of reality. People need *some* map of reality, but also need to remember that maps reflect abstract concepts that never capture the totality of any actual situation. "Knowledge" is thus the sum of the competing constructions people use to understand their cultural practices and the world.

Critics (*e.g.*, Donnelly, 1984) note that constructionism's rejection of universal truths implies *cultural* or *moral relativism*, which could be used to justify harmful cultural practices such as female circumcision. However, it is necessary to distinguish between human rights and cultural mores: pain is real, but people may construe it in different ways. Postmodernists do not argue that reality has no consequences. A plane crash is quite real, but has different meanings for insurers, airline executives, and the families of victims. Such meanings are constructed and could be different. Problems are also real, but postmodern therapists help clients construe that reality in less problematic ways.

Dialectical constructionists (*e.g.*, Greenberg & Pascal-Leone, 2001) suggest reality also limits the number of meaningful or useful constructions. Constructions incongruent with reality are not apt to survive in the marketplace of ideas; *e.g.*, if empathy consistently improves the therapeutic alliance, then to suggest otherwise is not useful. Extensive research with different methods and populations supports empathy's effectiveness (Lambert & Ogles, 2004). Exceptions may still occur, however, as when accurate empathy threatens the teenager who uses being misunderstood to protect a fragile sense of autonomy. In general, contextual influences on problems should always be considered; *e.g.*, poverty may be a more important factor than inner conflicts for many clients.

Postmodern *hermeneutics* suggest that a culture's typical *practices* create still other limits on constructions. Interpretations made by researchers are "... *relative to their perspective*, but not *arbitrary*" (italics in original; Westermann, 2004, p. 132). Instead, they are constrained by historical and cultural practices including language, research methods, theories, and assumptions about the nature of knowledge and reality. Hermeneutic investigators interpret events in terms of the relationships that exist among people in a given historical, cultural, and situational context. Like phenomenologists, they try to understand the individual's unique meanings, but also focus on how socio-historical and relational contexts influence the person's problems, options, and choices.

Brent Slife (2004b) contrasts the *relational ontology* of hermeneutics with scientific modernism's *abstractionist ontology*. He believes the contextually rich information needed to understand a particular client's situation is lost if reality is analyzed into its constituent parts. Something is lost when problems are separated from the situation in which they occur, just as a sentence's meaning is not found in its separate words. This has important ethical and cultural implications. In cultures with modernist ontologies, identity derives from the individual's unique set of beliefs. Community and intimacy are created by shared beliefs and values, so that differences may be seen as a threat. Deviants learn to hide their differences, are persuaded to change, may be marginalized by peers (*e.g.*, school cliques), or may be diagnosed as mentally ill by authorities.

In contrast, cultures with relational ontologies define identity by the person's unique set of relationships in the community. Differences from peers are not viewed as threats, but as reasons for dialog and understanding the other's viewpoint. Conflict resolution skills develop because restricting dialog threatens the community. Intimacy is a celebration of *differences* with someone who is not a mere *reflection* of the self. Clearly, ontology, cultural mores, and ethical values are interwoven.

Relational ontologies suggest that events need to be understood in their social, political, and historical contexts, not in isolation (Pepper, 1942). Reducing an event to its constituent parts misses emergent properties such as its meaning for the participants. By ignoring contextual meanings of beliefs and events, foundational abstractionism maintains the status quo. It may be desirable to *deconstruct* established beliefs that help maintain social problems such as discrimination and sexism (Sexton & Griffin, 1997).

Deconstruction examines how social and historical contexts of a belief contributes to the advantage or disadvantage of different groups: *e.g.*, feminist and civil rights movements gained force only as disadvantaged groups questioned established views of gender, ethnicity, and sexual orientation. Therapists and researchers need to recognize the political impact of their actions: *e.g.*, what if a therapist helped Malcolm X resolve his "anger" problem, but ignored the prejudice that led to his resentment (Halleck, 1979). While some might applaud a treatment that reduced Malcolm X's disaffection with society, others might regret the loss of his political voice.

Defining abnormality in terms of differences from the norm reinforces the centrality of dominant groups and marginalizes people who differ (Foucault, 1967; Safran, 1998); *e.g.*, the American Psychiatric Association (APA, 2000) defines mental health as the absence of mental illness, a distinction that marginalizes people diagnosed as mentally ill. The APA only stopped designating homosexuality as a "disorder" after pressure by gay rights activists. A current example of marginalization may be the 5–6 million children annually treated with psychostimulant drugs for attention-deficit hyperactivity disorder (ADHD). The 700% increase in ADHD prescriptions during the 1990s (Marshall, 2000) raises the question whether this reflects an actual increase in ADHD cases, more pharmaceutical advertising, or more restrictive educational and familial contexts.

Hermeneutic, qualitative, and phenomenological research methods try to understand people in their own terms, rather than in comparison with others. Skeptical of language's ability to describe "objective" reality, postmodernists argue that people need to be understood in their cultural, political, and socio-historical context. In this view, the meanings, goals, and practices of scientific research are also a subject of interest. The socio-political consequences of scientific findings need to be considered: *e.g.*, uncritical acceptance of symptom-oriented, empirically supported treatments may restrict third party payment for useful treatments based on other standards. Although many clients respond well to symptom-focused therapies, "treatment-resistant" clients may need help at the level of relationships, values, or meanings, which can also create problems.

Dialectical Tensions in Psychotherapy Integration

Several factors have increased interest in psychotherapy integration. Economic pressure by Health Maintenance Organizations (HMOs) and needs for accountability have encouraged problem-focused, short-term therapies including integrative approaches. Given the Dodo Bird verdict (no one approach is superior to others), training programs are increasingly introducing students to a variety of approaches (Lampropoulos & Dixon, 2007). Paradoxically, integrative efforts, with many possible combinations of over 400 systems of therapy, have created even more proliferation.

However, preliminary evidence for integrative approaches is promising, especially for more challenging problems, but there is not yet sufficient research to state categorically they are more effective than traditional approaches (Schottenbauer, Glass, & Arnkoff, 2005). A dialectic exists between *integrating* two or more theories and *eclecticism*, which uses research to identify *what* intervention works best for *whom.* This dialectic asks if it is better to integrate approaches that may have incompatible assumptions or to combine interventions with the best research support.

Integrative Dialectics

Integrative theorists argue that science involves a theory *vs.* data dialectic. Without theory, there is no way to decide what should be studied or how to interpret the data. When combining theories, the integrationist's challenge is to reconcile incompatible assumptions; *e.g.*, behaviorist objectivism *vs.* humanist subjectivism. Since an objective view of someone else's inner experience is not possible, this dialectic of objective observation *vs.* the reporting of subjective experience is not easily reconciled. However, the incompatibility may be more apparent than real, since therapists use dialog to help clients resolve their problems. Behaviorists use dialog to teach clients how to modify symptomatic behavior, while humanists use dialog to help clients articulate inner experience and discover their own solutions. Ultimately, the dialectic is more about what is more effective for a particular client, directive or nondirective methods, than about irreconcilable assumptions.

Another dialectic contrasts *theoretical integration* with *assimilative integration*; *e.g.*, Wachtel (1977, 1987) integrates disparate theoretical systems, such as behavioral and psychodynamic therapies, while Messer (2003) assimilates interventions from other systems into a preferred theoretical position to ensure consistency in assumptions. Interventions from other approaches are only incorporated after considering how their meaning is transformed by the principal set of assumptions; *e.g.*, the meaning of two-chair role-play in experiential therapy is radically changed when it is used with interpersonal therapies. Instead of two-chair work that voices both sides of an inner conflict, interpersonal therapists ask clients to role-play both sides of an interpersonal conflict.

Safran (1998) suggests that incompatibility concerns reflect a modernist assumption of one "true" perspective, which disappears in a postmodern perspective:

> [F]undamental philosophical perspectives … cannot be integrated because they are by their very nature mutually exclusive …. [I]t is possible to move beyond the position of mutual exclusivity … if one has a superordinate worldview that views all worldviews as partial and inadequate in nature and recognizes the importance of viewing reality from the perspective of multiple lenses …. [I]ntegration can nevertheless proceed, through engaging in a dialectical process in which adherents of different worldviews discuss their relative positions in an open-minded way, ultimately leading to a broadening and elaborating of both perspectives (p. 265).

Postmodernists advocate for plurality in perspectives, since no one viewpoint ever captures the real world's full complexity. As Messer (2003) suggests, meanings shift when interventions are combined from systems with differing assumptions. The impact of borrowed interventions or of theory integration is best understood by clarifying the implications of underlying assumptions.

Eclectic Dialectics

Incompatibility is not a problem in atheoretical, eclectic approaches based on research-supported interventions. The dialectic here is between *common factors* that are part of every approach and *technical eclecticism*. Common factor therapists (*e.g.*, Garfield, 2003) foster a warm, empathic alliance with clients, provide new ways of thinking about problems, and use other factors common to all approaches. In technical eclecticism, empirically supported interventions are chosen to meet specific client needs. Another dialectic exists between discrete interventions, as with Lazarus' Multimodal Therapy (see Chap. 4) and general principles of intervention, as with Systematic Treatment Selection (see Chap. 2).

Multimodal Therapy (Lazarus,1967, 1971, 2005) focuses on client *problems*, assesses which of seven domains of experience is most affected (Behavior, Affect, Sensation, Imagery, Cognition, Interpersonal relations, and Drugs/biology), and then suggests empirically supported treatments: social skills training for behavioral problems, two-chair work for ambivalent emotions, relaxation for tension, *etc.* Systematic Treatment Selection (Beutler & Clarkin, 1990) focuses on research-supported intervention principles relating to client *characteristics*: *e.g.*, nondirective or self-directed interventions work better with autonomous clients, while directive approaches work better with compliant clients. Both are empirically based and avoid theorizing.

Garfield (2003) describes several disadvantages of not having a theoretical framework:

1. Science involves a dialectic tension between theory and data—without theory, data only tell us *when* to use an intervention, but not *why* it works so that adaptations can be made if a client does not respond as expected.
2. Empirically supported interventions acquire different meanings when divorced from their theoretical framework—*e.g.*, "two-chair work" addresses inner conflicts in experiential therapy and interpersonal conflict resolution in interpersonal approaches.
3. Helping clients develop some new "theory" or understanding of their problems is a common factor in all successful therapy regardless of approach.

Stricker (2005) suggests that a client's new "theory" only has to be plausible, not necessarily "true." There can be many useful ways to understand an event or problem.

Being atheoretical, eclecticists avoid the problem of combining incompatible assumptions. The tradeoff is that only technology is developed with no suggestion of why an intervention works. Eclectic approaches are nevertheless preferable to *syncretism*, where idiosyncratic therapist preferences determine interventions instead of theory or research findings (Norcross, 1990). When interventions are *ad hoc*, even technology becomes impossible as there is no basis for deciding what intervention was effective with which problem.

The Dialectics of Common vs. Specific Factors

Does the Dodo Bird verdict rule? Or do specific interventions improve outcomes in some situations? This is the common *vs.* specific factors dialectic. Rosenzweig (1936/2002) and Duncan *et al.*, (2009) suggest that common factors such as the therapeutic relationship, hope, client expectations, and interventions that overlap among different approaches are responsible for the effectiveness of psychotherapy. They doubt that differences among approaches will ever be found. Unfortunately, much like the Dodo bird that required a "great deal of thought" before deciding, researchers took almost 40 years to confirm Rosenzweig's hypothesis. Asay and Lambert's (1999) meta-analysis found four sources of outcome variance: client factors, common factors, expectancy or placebo, and specific factors. Extra-therapeutic client factors including motivation, resiliency, or social support accounted for 40% of the variance, common relationship factors such as an acceptance, empathy, and reality testing accounted for 30%, and placebo for 15%. Specific interventions only accounted for about 15% of outcome variance.

Although little evidence exists that specific factors improve outcomes for all clients, they may help with certain clients, problems, or situations: *e.g.*, behavior therapy is more effective with panic disorder, phobias, or childhood aggression; interpersonal and cognitive therapies with depression; and couples therapy with marital problems (Lambert & Ogles, 2004). These differential outcomes fuel continuing efforts to find more specific factors. Many therapists choose integrative or eclectic approaches as a way to improve therapy outcomes by explicitly combining research-supported common and specific factors (Norcross, 1986).

Common factors theorists assume the systematic application of demonstrated common factors will improve outcomes (Frank & Frank, 1991). The most important common factor is a positive relationship with a respected therapist who models novel, non-blaming ways of understanding the client's problem (Lambert & Ogles 2004). Clients are not *held* responsible for problems, only for cooperating with therapy. Responsibility for problems is externalized to minimize feelings of guilt and shame; *e.g.*, clients learn to view their problems as caused by reinforcement contingencies, biochemical imbalances, or childhood experiences.

Another dialectic exists between using *interventions* or *goals* as the basis for classifying common factors. Column headings in Table 1.3 describe Lambert and Ogles' (2004) classification of interventions in which *support* factors create a safe haven so clients can *learn* new skills that lead to new *actions* which solve problems. In contrast, Karasu (1986) uses goals such as affective experiencing, cognitive mastery and behavioral regulation instead of interventions to classify common factors. He suggests different therapeutic systems use different methods to achieve a particular goal: *e.g.*, psychoanalysts use free association to encourage affective experiencing, while Gestalt therapists use two-chair work; cognitive therapists foster cognitive mastery by challenging false beliefs, while existentialists help clients search for meaning; behaviorists foster behavioral regulation by teaching assertiveness, while humanists confront avoidance, and psychoanalysts help clients apply

Table 1.3 Common factors in psychotherapy outcome. (M. J. Lambert, *Bergin and Garfield's handbook of psychotherapy and behavior change*, 5th ed., p. 173, 2004, © Wiley. Reprinted with permission)

Support factors	Learning factors	Action factors
Catharsis	Advice	Behavioral regulation
Identification with therapist	Affective experiencing	Cognitive mastery
Mitigation of isolation	Assimilating problematic	Encouragement of facing
Positive relationship	experiences	fears
Reassurance	Cognitive learning	Taking risks
Release of tension	Corrective emotional experience	Mastery efforts
Structure	Feedback	Modeling
Therapeutic alliance	Insight	Practice
Therapist/client active	Rationale	Reality testing
participation	Exploration of internal frame of	Success experience
Therapist expertness	reference	Working through
Therapist warmth, respect,	Changing expectations for per-	
empathy, acceptance,	sonal effectiveness	
genuineness		
Trust		

insights to daily life. Because different interventions can have the same result, it may be that some interventions work better for some clients than for others.

The Dialectics of Intervention Levels: Microcontext to Macrocontext

One critical difference among interventions is whether they target very small or very large levels of change. The *microcontext/macrocontext* dialectic reflects interventions developed for a variety of populations. Microcontextual interventions at the molecular level of biochemistry may be needed to alleviate depressive or psychotic symptoms and facilitate the ability to cooperate with a psychosocial therapy. Since such clients may lack basic interpersonal or self-regulation skills, behavioral interventions may also be needed. Macrocontextual interventions at molar family or social system levels may then be needed to prevent relapse in stressful home or work situations. Other clients may need an intermediate, *holistic* intervention to resolve inner conflicts, develop supportive relationships, or create a more meaningful life.

Level of Intervention

To help seriously disturbed, hospitalized patients, therapists use microcontextual interventions such as psychopharmacology and cognitive-behavioral skills training. For clients diagnosed with a personality disorder, intermediate intervention levels such as psychodynamic analysis of early parent-child attachments may be help-ful. "YAVIS" (**Y**oung, **A**dult, **V**erbal, **I**ntelligent, and **S**uccessful) clients may ben-efit from a holistic client-centered, experiential, or existential focus, while child or marital problems are best addressed at more macrocontextual family levels. Multi-problem families may require macrocontextual ecosystemic interventions to nego-tiate government agency services in addressing socio-economic stressors, such as poverty or school problems.

Case Illustration

Hung Lanh (HL), the 16-year-old son of Vietnamese refugees, was referred to an out-patient clinic and diagnosed with panic disorder with agoraphobia by his fam-ily physician. HL was a "pre-menopausal" baby born after his parents had given up hope of having children. Before his first panic attack, HL's only illness had been mild symptoms of asthma. He was an honor student and a basketball star. His first panic attack came 2 months after a teammate suddenly died after practice from an undiagnosed heart defect. His team had lost a close game despite an exceptional effort on his part. In the locker room he had an asthma attack which began with difficulty in breathing and rapidly escalated to chest pains, pounding heart, light-headedness, nausea, and fears he was going to die. During the following 2 weeks he had several more panic attacks that occurred at unpredictable times. Physical examination revealed no apparent medical problems other than asthma and HL was placed on an antidepressant. HL had only two more panic episodes after the second week of medication, but continues to worry about dying, dropped from his basket-ball team, and finds it difficult to concentrate on studies. He would like to drop out of school, but continues at the insistence of his parents.

Despite his obvious talents, HL reports he has always felt like an outsider and has no close friends. Except for basketball, he has never had time for extra-cur-ricular activities since he is expected to help his parents at their family-owned res-taurant. Although supportive of his academic efforts, his parents view basketball as frivolous and only grudgingly permitted his playing. HL says that most people in the Vietnamese community consider it odd that he plays this sport. At the same time, classmates find him odd because he excels academically, goes home im-mediately after school or basketball, and does not join their activities. His team-mates provided a sense of camaraderie that he valued very much, but even they are perplexed that he does not join in after-game parties. He says classmates have taunted him for letting the school down since he quit the team. He would like to rejoin the team but is frightened of dying like his teammate. School has become a trial, both because of his classmate's reactions and because he finds it difficult to concentrate on his studies. He wants to drop out and just help with the family restaurant, but his parents insist that he completes his education and goes on to college. He also says it would bring shame to his family if he were to show weak-ness by dropping out.

Alternative Levels of Intervention

Although medication has helped the panic attacks, HL still has symptoms that could potentially be helped by interventions at any of the following levels:

- *Biomedical*: Varying the type or level of medication might reduce the remaining symptoms.
- *Behavioral*: Reduce anxiety using exposure to situations HL is currently avoiding—studies, sports, school, and interaction with classmates.
- *Cognitive*: Challenge unrealistic thoughts about death; explore alternative interpretations of panic symptoms.
- *Intrapsychic*: Explore conflict between HL's need for intimacy with others and his underlying sense of shame about being different.
- *Holistic/Personal/Experiential*: Help HL explore his feelings and wishes about classmates, parental expectations, cultural differences, and the death of his classmate.
- *Existential*: What does HL want from life; how can he find courage to confront his own death?
- *Interpersonal*: Teach HL how to inform classmates about his family obligations in a graceful manner; explore how best to respond to classmates' taunts; encourage joining other groups.
- *Family*: Encourage parents to allow HL more free time for outside activities; help them understand how important relationships with classmates can be; help them "normalize" sports activities as a valued part of the American experience.
- *Ecosystemic*: Explore how to increase informal interactions with classmates; explore ways HL is similar to classmates to decrease sense of difference; help HL see that many of his concerns reflect differences in cultures; have HL meet with members of Vietnamese community to dialog about tensions between their cultural heritage and American values.
- *Postmodern*: HL has created "problem-rich" narratives about his life; he needs a "solution-oriented" focus that builds on his abilities, strengths, and successes; help him celebrate his uniqueness and difference from other people.

These increasingly broader levels of intervention suggest a rationale for integrating therapeutic approaches and describe the organization of chapters in this book. It is unlikely that any one intervention level will help every client, while integrating several levels may be more likely to help a greater diversity of clients (Beutler, Consoli, & Lane, 2005; Feldman & Feldman, 2005).

The Dialectics of Psychotherapy Research

Little systematic empirical support existed for psychotherapy's efficacy before Carl Rogers' groundbreaking efforts (Rogers & Dymond, 1954), but support developed rapidly after the Health Maintenance Organization (HMO) act passed in 1973.

HMOs ushered in managed care with far-reaching effects on funding, research, and practice. HMOs encourage empirically based, brief treatments that have largely replaced long-term therapies such as psychoanalysis. Extensive outcome research now supports the overall efficacy of psychotherapy and suggests that nearly 80% of therapy clients function better than controls (Lambert & Ogles, 2004).

Three major dialectic tensions appear in psychotherapy research: 1. clinical *vs.* statistical significance; 2. outcome *vs.* process research; and 3. treatment *vs.* patient-focused research.

The clinical/statistical significance dialectic, or *researcher-practitioner gap*, reflects the fact that many practitioners make little use of the psychotherapy research literature. Ironically, attempts to improve research designs tend to reduce their clinical utility. Better research designs improve the interpretability of results: *e.g.*, monitoring the degree to which treatment manuals are followed ensures that it is the treatment and not extraneous variables that cause the observed effects. However, strict adherence to manuals has been shown to detract from the flexibility necessary to adapt therapy to an individual client's needs (Strupp & Anderson, 1997).

The outcome/process dialectic results from the difficulty of isolating variables that make a difference in outcome from all those found in an overall system of therapy. Instead of examining the entire system, process research evaluates the impact of relatively small processes on outcome: *e.g.*, research shows that accurate empathy is associated with positive outcomes (Elliott, Greenberg, & Lietauer, 2004). A recent development is the treatment- *vs.* patient-focus dialectic. Patient-focus research monitors the progress of individual clients instead of averaging treatment effects across an entire treatment sample: *e.g.*, Lutz (2003) found that informing therapists and clients about therapeutic progress significantly improves outcome, regardless of approach.

The Dialectics of Clinical vs. Statistical Significance

Practitioners often fail to see the relevance of psychotherapy research for their practice, other than reassurance about psychotherapy's overall efficacy. Asay, Lambert, Gregerson, and Goates (2002) suggest a number of reasons for the scientist-practitioner gap:

1. The Dodo Bird verdict provides no guidance for choosing a therapeutic approach.
2. Statistically significant group differences are often too small to guide clinical decisions.
3. Practitioners want advice on how best to respond to the needs of a particular individual.
4. Statistical differences do not tell if a treatment will work for a particular individual.

5. Without valid outcome measures, it is difficult to interpret even large group differences.
6. It is difficult to draw meaningful conclusions from studies that use different methods, client populations, or *ad hoc* outcome measures created for a single study.

On these last two points, Froyd and Lambert (1989) found that most outcome measures were created for just one study and lacked standardized norms or validation. Further, defining improvement in different ways gives different results: *e.g.*, *minimizing* psychotic symptoms would seem useful, but interventions that enhanced symptom *acceptance* were actually more effective at reducing re-hospitalization rates (Bach & Hayes, 2002). Even with clinically relevant valid measures, interpretation is difficult when studies use different methods and yield conflicting results. There are several approaches to these interpretive problems: 1. meta-analysis, 2. empirically supported treatments, and 3. evidence-based practice.

Meta-Analysis and Effect Size

Meta-analysis combines results from many studies with varied designs and populations. Combining results reduces biases associated with researcher allegiance and increases the generalizability of studies that individually lack adequate outcome measures or sample sizes. The weaknesses of individual studies are minimized by meta-analyses based on large numbers of studies with varied methods and outcome measures. Meta-analyses have consistently supported the effectiveness of psychotherapy (Lambert & Ogles, 2004).

Meta-analysis is based on Cohen's (1962) d-statistic. It calculates an average intervention *effect size* for included studies by dividing the mean difference between experimental and control groups by the pooled standard deviation. The d-statistic is a standard score with a mean of zero and a standard deviation of one. Small, medium, or large effect sizes are defined respectively as d's of 0.20, 0.50, or 0.80 (Cohen, 1977). A typical therapy outcome effect size of $d = 0.70$ indicates that the average therapy client is better off than 76% of control subjects (Lambert & Ogles, 2004).

Empirically Supported Treatments: Efficacy, Effectiveness, and Efficiency

Many researchers believe that improved research designs for *empirically supported treatments* (ESTs) will enhance clinical relevance. Needs for interpretable findings, accountability to HMOs, and clinical relevance create a unique set of competing demands. To meet these demands, Chambless and Hollon (1998) recommended that ESTs meet three criteria:

1. *Efficacy*: Randomized control trials that demonstrate the validity of the EST.
2. *Effectiveness*: The EST is useful with specified populations in applied clinical settings.
3. *Efficiency*: The EST is cost-effective relative to alternative interventions.

Unfortunately, most ESTs meet only the efficacy criterion. Shadish *et al.*'s (1997) meta-analysis of over 600 EST studies found only one that met their criteria for clinically relevant research. ESTs use *randomized control trials* (RCTs), subjects who present with only the targeted diagnosis, and monitor adherence to interventions specified by manuals. In an RCT, subjects with the targeted disorder are randomly assigned to treatment or control groups. These procedures ensure that the treatment causes the observed outcome, *internal validity*, and not some uncontrolled variable. A number of ESTs for anxiety and mood disorders have been adopted by therapists who prefer well-defined and well-supported methods. HMOs hope that ESTs will increase cost-efficiency by making it possible to use Masters-level technicians as therapists; doctoral level professionals would develop new ESTs, diagnose client problems, and supervise technicians. These procedures would help:

1. Enhance experimental replicability by training for procedural competency and adherence;
2. Monitor the integrity of therapists' procedural adherence so outcome differences may be attributed to interventions rather than qualities of the therapist;
3. Increase cost effectiveness by using technicians rather than doctoral level therapists; and
4. Compare the efficacy and, potentially, the cost effectiveness of different ESTs.

Unfortunately, the absence of EST effectiveness or efficiency data reduces *external validity* and contributes to the researcher-practitioner gap. Standardized treatment protocols and RCTs reduce therapist and client variability and ensure that observed differences reflect only the EST treatment protocol. However, such controls reduce external validity or real-world effectiveness, since manual adherence prevents therapists from trying alternatives when an EST does not work (Lueger, 2002). Instead, therapists become more defensive and authoritarian when adhering to a manual, as well as less approving, supportive, optimistic, and effective (Strupp & Anderson, 1997; Svartberg & Stiles,1992).

In contrast to an EST protocol, most practitioners tailor interventions to each client's unique requirements, which may involve several presenting problems that only become apparent as therapy progresses. Sanderson, DiNardo, Rapee, and Barlow (1990) found that 70% of anxiety disorder clients had at least one other diagnosis. By restricting samples to single-diagnosis clients, ESTs seldom address problems as severe or heterogeneous as those seen in clinical practice.

The scientist-practitioner gap results from narrowly focusing on treatment efficacy and failing to examine effectiveness or efficiency. Effectiveness studies use naturalistic designs to evaluate outcomes in realistic, uncontrolled clinical settings (Lutz, 2003); *e.g.*, in a large-sample questionnaire study, *Consumer's Report*, readers reported increasing benefits for longer treatment (Seligman, 1995). Efficiency studies compare ESTs with alternative approaches to evaluate possible cost-savings; *e.g.*, Cunningham, Bremmer, and Boyle (1995) compared group-based and individualized parent-training programs with wait-list controls. Group treatment was six times less costly and more effective than individualized treatment.

Despite rigorous research methods, ESTs have also failed to overturn the Dodo Bird verdict. A large-scale, multi-site, National Institute of Mental Health depression study (Elkins *et al.*, 1989) compared antidepressant, interpersonal, and cognitive behavior treatments with a placebo plus case management control group. Significant pre-post improvements were found for all treatment conditions, but there were few treatment differences. Similarly, Wampold *et al.* (1997) meta-analysis suggests ESTs are roughly equivalent in efficacy to other methods, showing an advantage on only a few specific outcome measures.

In reflecting on over 40 years experience reviewing the literature, David Orlinsky notes that, on the positive side, clinical outcome research now resembles Kuhn's description of normal science: "[It] has become devoted to incrementally and systematically working out the details of a general 'paradigm' that is widely accepted and largely unquestioned" (Orlinsky, 2006, p. 37). Orlinsky suggests that RCTs lose sight of clinical realities by viewing symptoms separately from the person, as self-contained phenomena that can be eliminated by correct treatment.

> The reality, as I see it, is that a person (a) is a *psychosomatic unity*, (b) evolving over time along a specific *life-course trajectory*, and (c) is a *subjective self* that is objectively connected with other subjective selves, (d) each of them being *active/responsive nodes in an intersubjective web* of community relationships and cultural patterns, a web in which those same patterns and relationships, (e) exert a formative influence on the psychosomatic development of persons ... [None] of these realities seems to me to be adequately addressed by the dominant paradigm or standard research model followed in most studies (Orlinsky, 2006, p. 39).

Evidence-Based Practice: A Statistical-Clinical Synthesis

Evidence-Based Practice (EBP) balances internal validity with external validity by including clinical judgments about when, how, and with whom research findings should be applied. The American Psychological Association Presidential Task Force (2006) defines EBP as "... the integration of the best available research with clinical expertise in the context of patient characteristics, culture, and preferences" (p. 273). Table 1.4 describes the range of research methods used in EBP in order of their increasing potential for generalization to broader questions.

An EBP also asks therapists to develop self-reflective and interpersonal skills, systematically use a theoretical rationale to individualize case formulation and plans, and assess and monitor client progress. Even if two clients have similar symptoms (*phenotype*), individualized plans are important since the prognosis and cause (*genotype*) may be affected by individual differences in family, ecosystemic, or developmental contexts. Differences in the meaning and function of similar symptoms may require very different interventions; *e.g.*, depression following bereavement may differ significantly from chronic depression. Interpreting such differences requires clinical judgment, something not captured in manuals. It is still to be determined, however, if EBP produces better outcomes than non-EBP interventions (Kanfer, 2008).

Table 1.4 Research methods considered in empirically based practice. (APA Presidential Task Force, Evidence-based practice in psychology. *American Psychologist, 61,* 274, 2006, © APA. Adapted with permission)

Research method	Applications
Clinical observations	Individual case studies are a source of innovation and useful hypotheses
Qualitative research	Describes subjective, lived experience of clients, such as being in therapy
Systematic case study	Aggregated case studies useful to compare individuals with similar problems
Single-case design	Establishes causal relationships in the context of an individual
Public health/ethnography	Monitors acceptance of treatments; maximizes use in given social contexts
Process-outcome research	Identifies mechanisms of change that are related to outcome
Effectiveness research	Assesses ecological (external) validity of interventions in naturalistic settings
ESTs and other RCTs	Describes causal relationships between interventions and outcomes
Meta-analyses	Integrates multiple studies; tests hypotheses; estimates effect sizes

Dialectics of Outcome vs. Process Research

Outcome research supports the overall efficacy of psychotherapy, but provides little guidance for an empirically based practice. It is difficult to determine which interventions among the many found in a particular approach are most important to outcome. Ideally, process research examines *what* treatment by *whom* is most effective for *this* individual with *that* specific problem (Paul, 1969). Unfortunately, research has yet to address all of these interactions simultaneously. Instead, most process research looks at how specific therapist, client, and intervention factors contribute to intermediate therapy goals and outcomes ranging from moment-to-moment impacts (*microprocesses*) to lifetime influences (*macroprocesses*).

Another process dialectic contrasts traditional *evidence-based* research and *practice-based* research. In top-down, evidence-based research, hypotheses are derived from theoretical considerations. In contrast, "[p]ractice-based research involves collecting evidence from routine settings and applying a range of methods, from the collection of large data sets using common measures to single case and case studies" (Hardy, 2007, p. 21). Questions that arise in practice settings serve as the bottom-up basis for both exploratory and hypothesis testing research.

Hardy (2007) found that, compared to unsuccessful clients, successful clients in cognitive-behavioral therapy reported a personal connection with their therapist (working alliance). Feeling understood, they made better use of therapeutic tools and developed a sense of competence. Alliance strains led to drop outs by the fourth session if therapists failed to respond sensitively to the client's experience or to the significance of a problem. Alliance strains suggest an *affirmation vs. criticism* dialectic: competent therapists affirm the validity of their client's experience, but also critically examine how they and their client contributed to the alliance strain (Safran & Muran, 2000).

It is important to involve clients in the process of therapy since their understanding of an intervention determines whether it has a positive or negative impact. Since clients may conceal hurt feelings, therapists need to explore possible misunderstandings or negative reactions. This is necessary because clients may be reluctant to volunteer negative reactions and therapists may not notice strains in the relationship. Therapists should avoid describing a client's role negatively and acknowledge their own contribution to a problem when the therapeutic alliance is strained.

Process Research

Orlinsky, Ronnestad, and Willutzki's (2004) meta-analytic review describes six empirically supported process variables common to all approaches (see Table 1.5).

Their process-outcome meta-analysis may be summarized as follows:

1. Clients should be screened and prepared with mutually agreed expectations about therapy.
2. Both client and therapist need to maintain a problem-oriented focus.
3. Transference or relationship issues are discussed when the alliance is strained, focusing on the therapist's contribution to the strain and the client's reactions to the intervention.
4. Interpretations, experiential confrontation, and paradoxical interventions are all useful, but client reactions and potential alliance strains should be explored.
5. Causal or transference interpretations should be reserved for less disturbed clients; more disturbed clients may benefit from interpretations of other people's actions and motives.
6. Strong therapeutic alliances result when clients perceive the therapist as empathic and credible, therapists perceive clients as actively communicating, and there is mutual liking.
7. Client cooperation, active engagement, and positive feelings for the therapist and therapy are important, but require close monitoring since therapist perceptions may not be accurate.
8. Client self-understanding is fostered by encouraging openness; treating defensiveness as an alliance strain may be more helpful than confrontation.
9. If progress is not observed after a few sessions, treatment plans should be revised.

Rogers' (1957) emphasis on relationship factors is supported by findings that the therapeutic alliance is the most important process variable in therapy. Negative outcomes occur when clients feel criticized *and* therapists do not acknowledge their contribution to the strain. Hilsenroth and Cromer (2007) describe interventions that enhance the therapeutic alliance, especially during the first few sessions. They recommend establishing a clear collaborative treatment frame in which results of a depth-oriented intake interview are explained in concrete language that relates clients' thoughts to their feelings. Assessment involves helping clients take the initia-

Table 1.5 Process variables related to positive therapeutic outcome. (After Orlinsky *et al.*, 2004)

Process variable	Therapy outcomes are improved when …
1. Treatment contract	1. Expectations are clear.
	2. Therapist and client agree on goals.
	3. Client is prepared for role.
	4. Client is actively involved in therapy.
	5. Client is screened for intervention "fit".
	6. Therapist suggests effective procedures.
2. Therapeutic operations	1. Focus is on client's problems and core relationships without disrupting defenses.
	2. Interpretation or emotional arousal leads to greater client self-understanding.
	3. Therapist and client agree on therapeutic approach.
	4. Paradoxical directives or experiential confrontations are used.
	5. Clients are positive and cooperative about therapeutic operations.
	6. Any arousal of negative feelings is resolved by session's end.
	7. Self-exploration occurs in experiential or dynamic, not behavioral therapy.
	8. Therapist notes alliance strains and takes responsibility for own contribution.
	9. Intervention impacts are explored and therapist doesn't rely on own perceptions.
3. Therapeutic alliance	Therapist and client like each other and work well together. This happens if the therapist sees the client as motivated, actively engaged in role, and communicating feelings; and if the client perceives the therapist as assured, engaged, and empathically attuned.
4. Self-relatedness	1. Client is open and non-defensive about experiencing or articulating feelings.
	2. Therapist genuineness and self-acceptance are perceived in experiential or dynamic; apparently not relevant to cognitive-behavioral or directive therapies.
5. Emotional/insight impact	1. Client, not therapist, believes something important happened in the session.
	2. Therapist has an overall sense of personal efficacy.
6. Sequential flow	1. Therapy duration is longer.
	2. Significantly large improvements occur after only a few sessions.

tive to clarify the source of their distress, identify cyclical interpersonal patterns, and actively explore these issues. It facilitates active exploration of feelings that arise both from discussion of the presenting problem and from the process of therapy. Therapists then provide feedback and explore the meaning of the assessment results to provide clients with new understandings and insight into their problem. Clients are educated about the nature of their symptoms and the treatment process and work collaboratively with the therapist to develop individualized treatment goals and tasks.

Microprocess Research and Process Markers

Microprocess research (*e.g.*, Sachse & Elliott, 2001) focuses on the impact of single interventions. Using transcripts of client-therapist-client (CTC) interactions, observers rate whether or not interventions encourage deeper exploration or integration of problematic experiences. The Depth of Processing Scale (Sachse & Elliott, 2001; see Table 1.6) rates CTC sequences on the degree of client experiential avoidance or therapist encouragement for resolution of problematic experiences. Clients may initially have difficulty processing feelings (level 1), but by mid-therapy the meaning of their experience should be integrated with their plans for the future (level 8). *Deepening* proposals occur when therapist interventions are rated at high-

Table 1.6 Depth of therapist proposal or client processing. (Adapted from Sachse & Elliott, 2001, p. 94)

1. No discernible processing of relevant content
2. Intellectualize—talks about issues impersonally, as if related to someone else
3. Report—non-evaluative, non-emotional descriptions of personal experiences or events
4. Assessment/evaluation—experience is evaluated, but impact on self not examined
5. Personal assessment—impact of experience on self is evaluated
6. Personal meanings—long term significance of experience for self is examined
7. Explication of relevant structures of meaning—significance for personal goals explored
8. Integration—experience is integrated into personal meanings with a sense of resolution

er levels than the client's initial comment. *Maintaining* proposals intervene at the same level and *flattening* proposals are rated below the client's level. The resultant depth of processing by the client is then rated to evaluate the intervention's effect.

An example of a *maintaining* proposal (level 3) would be to ask a client about the content of a reported argument with his wife. A deepening proposal would ask about the client's emotional response (level 5), while a flattening proposal would change the subject (Level 1). In general, deepening proposals increase client's depth of processing, while flattening proposals decrease processing depth (Sachse & Elliott, 2001). Because deepening interventions evoke anxiety, clients accept flattening more easily. Empathic understanding helps therapists adjust to a client's unique needs and encourage deeper processing of problematic experiences. A strong alliance and short, unambiguous interventions also help. Clients with somatic complaints are often inattentive to feelings and may need to learn how access inner experience. Sachse and Elliott (2001) emphasize the necessity for an active, directive stance in which therapists are *process-directive*, but allow therapy's *content* to be client-directed (Orlinsky *et al.*, 2004). The risk that a process-directive may strain the alliance reinforces the need to monitor how clients respond to interventions.

Leslie Greenberg's Emotionally Focused Therapy (EFT; Chap. 8) uses *process markers* that identify critical moments in therapy, guide case formulation, and direct moment-to-moment interventions. EFT research identifies interventions that encourage deeper exploration for each marker (Elliott, Watson, Goldman, & Green-

Table 1.7 Types of therapy process markers

1. *Micromarkers*: momentary processes; *e.g.*, poignant comments, rambling, incongruent statements, hesitancy, unusual vocal quality, distant, abstract language, or nonverbal signs of arousal or affect
2. *Characteristic Interpersonal Styles*: problems in relating to oneself and others, such as over- or under-responsibility, self-neglect, invalidating the feelings of self or others, hostility, over- or under-control, avoidance, or other patterns that reflect trauma or insecure attachment
3. *Mode of Engagement*: degree to which clients recognize and process their feelings rather than externalize, intellectualize, or somaticize them
4. *Major Task Markers*: statements that indicate struggles with distressing thoughts and feelings, puzzling reactions, intense negative feelings, unfinished business, or how to express feelings
5. *Treatment Foci Markers*: core thematic issues that develop as clients return session after session to the same issue or related problems

berg, 2004; see Table 1.7). Outcome research suggests that EFT produces very large overall effect sizes (Elliott & Greenberg, 2002).

The Dialectics of Treatment-Focused vs. Patient-Focused Research

Traditional *treatment-focused* research satisfies HMO accountability requirements and validates new techniques. It evaluates interventions that work for the average client, but not necessarily for every client. In contrast, *patient-focused research* uses repeated measures of intervention outcomes to monitor each client's rate of progress. Table 1.8 lists the computer model variables that predict the number of sessions typically needed to bring about expected changes in client scores. If scores lag behind expectations, then therapists can decide whether or not to change their intervention approach (Lutz, Martinovich, & Howard, 1999). Lambert *et al.*, (2002) found that rationally derived predictions based on the outcome questionnaire, OQ-45 (Lambert & Burlingame, 1996), identify clients at risk for failure more quickly and almost as accurately as the computer model. Feedback about expected *vs.* actual rates of progress helps therapists make timely revisions of treatment plans and motivates clients as they see their progress. This feedback increases

Table 1.8 Lutz *et al.* (1999) predictors of expected progress in treatment

1. Client ratings of subjective well-being
2. Current symptoms (DSM-IV, Axis I; American Psychiatric Association, 2000)
3. Measures of current life functioning
4. Global Assessment of Functioning (DSM-IV, Axis V)
5. Past use of therapy
6. Duration of problem
7. Treatment expectations

the effect size of outcomes compared to the usual reports for a therapeutic approach (Hawkins, Lambert, Vermeersch, Slade, & Tuttle, 2004).

In general, patient-focused, *dose-response* research (time needed to achieve positive results) shows that many clients make large changes early in treatment and smaller ones later on (Lutz *et al.*, 2002). Significant change is seen by the fifth session in 50% of clients with acute anxiety or depression. However, 14 sessions are needed for clients with chronic symptoms and 104 sessions for those with characterological symptoms (Kopta, Howard, Lowry, & Beutler, 1994). Clearly, symptom chronicity is a critical component of treatment planning.

Integrative Implications

The tension between therapeutic proliferation and integration reflects four principle dialectics: modernism/postmodernism; eclecticism/integration; microcontext/macrocontext levels; and clinical/statistical significance in research. Table 1.9 lists some of the factors that create therapeutic proliferation, including the difficulty of comparing approaches with incompatible assumptions and the failure to demonstrate overall superiority for any one therapy approach. Some may question the utility of integrative efforts that have, paradoxically, led to still more proliferation. Such criticism assumes that proliferation is a problem. But postmodernists suggest that multiple perspectives increase opportunities for fruitful dialog, that any one theory can provide only a partial map of reality. Theoretical proliferation ensures that more aspects of reality are mapped, while integration helps make those maps more coherent. Incompatibility concerns are less compelling when remembering that all theory is a construction based on unprovable assumptions. There is latitude for incompatible assumptions as long as

Table 1.9 Factors contributing to the proliferation of therapeutic approaches

 1. Ontological differences about the nature of reality and what should be investigated
 2. Epistemological differences about appropriate standards for evaluating outcomes
 3. Difficulty of synthesizing incompatible assumptions about reality and knowledge
 4. The Dodo Bird verdict: Absence of greater overall effectiveness for any approach
 5. Development of approaches based on experience with specific populations or problems
 6. Failure of any one approach to be equally effective with the full range of human problems
 7. Differential utility of interventions from micro- (biogenic) to macro-context (sociocultural) levels
 8. Competing approaches emphasize differences to demonstrate their superiority
 9. Communication among approaches is limited as each develops its own jargon and journals
10. Failure of behavioral or dynamic approaches to accommodate idea of client responsibility
11. Exponential ways of integrating over 400 systems creates even more approaches
12. Developing a unique approach increases a theorist's professional recognition
13. Managed care promotes short-term, problem-focused treatments

integrative models prove useful. As Chairman Mao proposed, "Let one thousand flowers bloom!"

Postmodernism is an integrative framework that sees modernist research as one of several powerful ways to support an argument. The apparent incompatibility of assumptions in subjective and objective approaches reflects a monistic, epistemological assumption of a universal reality that can be known empirically; but if all knowledge is a pluralistic construction, the impasse disappears. Postmodernism reflects a "both-and" logic rather than modernism's "either-or" logic. This suggests integrative therapies may use both subjective and objective frameworks to conceptualize a client's problems from the "inside-out" and the "outside-in." Therapists need to attend both to their clients' subjective experience as well as their objective behavior.

Outside-in, objective psychotherapists infer inner experience from observed behavior, while inside-out, subjective therapists rely on clients' reports about their inner experience. Rather than just one perspective, therapists need to maintain a dialectic tension, alternating between perspectives. It is just as well that the subjective and objective worlds are impossible to integrate completely. People might not really appreciate a "brave new world" where others have objective knowledge about their inner thoughts.

Critics who question the legitimacy of integrating approaches with incompatible assumptions have proposed atheoretical technical eclecticism as an alternative. The postmodern perspective suggests these concerns are not "true" incompatibilities, but reflect language and conceptual limitations. More troubling is eclecticism's lack of theoretical guidance for research and treatment planning. It is likely that eclecticism will serve as an intermediate step in which useful interventions are temporarily brought together before eventually being synthesized into a coherent theoretical framework. Systematic treatment selection principles that determine promising intervention levels relevant to particular clients may be useful starting point for this integration.

Therapies based on classical theories of personality and behavior help therapists adapt interventions to the client's unique situation, giving them an advantage over eclectic and many integrative approaches. General systems theory may also help conceptualize issues unique to a particular client's biogenic or cultural context. Although each person's experience is unique, many human needs and abilities are universal. Further, shared language and socio-historical contexts allow common themes to develop within various cultural groups. Modeling these commonalities in dynamic systems terms can provide ways to describe each client's unique experiences; e.g., a hierarchic systemic levels model can describe the various contextual influences on each client's unique situation, describing interactions from the biochemical to the ecosystemic level. Systems theory potentially can provide contextualized, empirically testable models of behavior, experience, and change. The subject-object divide may require parallel models for interactions among physical systems and how these are experienced subjectively by the individual.

Empirically based practice (EBP) uses the postmodern idea that randomized controlled trials are only one way to explore the utility of a treatment. EBP incorporates contextual influences and subjective experience by using qualitative research, case studies, and clinical judgment to adjust treatment planning to each client's unique situation. Empirical research can then be adapted to a client's unique qualities; *e.g.*, research suggests that transference interpretation is more helpful for clients with good ego strength than more disturbed clients.

In conclusion, evidence that different techniques work better with different clients has fueled efforts to integrate therapeutic systems. Parallel outside-in and inside-out techniques will always be needed since the subject/object divide precludes any ultimate therapeutic integration. Systems theory may usefully bridge modernist empirical emphases and post-modern contextual emphases. A comprehensive, contextualized view of problems and their resolution is likely to serve client needs better and may become the new "foundational" view. Preliminary evidence suggests therapy integration may significantly improve outcomes (Schottenbauer *et al.*, 2005).

Chapter One: Main Points

- The Dodo Bird verdict suggests no overall differences among therapeutic systems. Explanations include common factors such as a supportive relationship, new learning, and practicing new, adaptive behaviors. The Dodo Bird verdict has led to therapeutic integration combining two or more approaches and to technical eclecticism using research-supported, atheoretical interventions that work best with specific client issues or problems.
- Proliferation with over 400 different therapeutic systems in approaches has also increased integrative efforts, paradoxically resulting in still more therapeutic approaches. Therapeutic systems may be classified in terms of philosophical assumptions and intervention levels. Proliferation contributes to dialog and ensures that multiple perspectives are considered.
- Biomedical, behavioral, and cognitive approaches are based on Scientific Modernism. They assume an objective that universal theory of human change will eventually be developed in which principles from more molar, macroscopic levels may be reduced to those currently being studied at more molecular, microcontextual levels.
- Phenomenological humanist, experiential, and modern psychodynamic therapies assume that each person experiences reality in unique ways. Entering their world nonjudgmentally with empathy helps clients to discover the "true" self that reflects their own needs and to overcome problems based on a "false" self they created to meet others' needs.
- Interpersonal, family, and ecosystemic therapies, based on general systems theory, assume the therapist's job is to discover the feedback loops that maintain problems. Change occurs when old loops are interrupted or new ones are created. Emergent principles unique to each level of analysis of a problem are necessary to describe functioning from microscopic, biomedical levels to macrocontextual, ecosystemic levels.

- Integrative theorists often adopt general systems theory to model interactions among different levels of analysis and to model human intentionality. Integrationists are also drawn to the postmodern assumption that all knowledge is partial and constructed. This eliminates the philosophical problem of incompatible assumptions. The only postmodern criterion for a theory is its pragmatic utility in the marketplace of ideas.
- Therapies based on postmodern philosophy assume that all knowledge is constructed and could be constructed otherwise. Therapists help clients construct "solution-rich" narratives to replace "problem-rich" narratives about their lives.
- Manualized therapies (Empirically Supported Treatments or ESTs) clarify reasons for a treatment's efficacy by reducing extraneous sources of variance. They do not address complex, comorbid problems and have yet to demonstrate superior efficacy. A scientist-practitioner gap results from ESTs use of manuals and homogeneous subjects, which increases internal validity or interpretability, but decreases external validity or utility.
- Strategies to enhance clinical significance include effectiveness research, meta-analysis, and patient-focused research. Effectiveness emphasizes outcomes in everyday practice, calculating the percentage of clients achieving clinically significant outcomes. Meta-analysis uses effect size calculations that standardize scores across many different studies. This increases the overall similarity to clinical practice by integrating many studies with diverse methods, populations, and outcome measures. Patient-focused research compares actual with predicted rates of progress, allowing feedback that can improve therapy outcomes.
- Outcome-process research has identified useful interventions such as treatment contracts, focus on presenting problem(s), strengthening the therapeutic alliance, encouraging insight, deepening emotional processing, and enhancing client adaptive skills. Dependent upon the client's response, interpretation, experiential confrontation, paradoxical interventions, and therapist disclosure may also be helpful. Other factors that are significant include openness and self-acceptance by both therapist and client, client cooperation, and client perceptions of a positive session impact.
- Microprocess research relates client-therapist-client sequences to client processing depth and to in-session or overall outcomes. Therapists actively encourage the client to explore issues with short, unambiguous interventions, which results in deeper processing and positive outcomes. Markers, such as struggles with puzzling or negative feelings, have been related to intervention principles that help deepen exploration.

Further Reading

American Psychological Association Presidential Task Force. (2006). Evidence-based practice in psychology. *American Psychologist, 61,* 271–285.

Kazdin, A. E. (2008). Evidence-based treatment and practice: New opportunities to bridge clinical research and practice, enhance the knowledge base, and improve patient care. *American Psychologist, 63,* 146–159.

Lambert, M. J. (2004). *Bergin and Garfield's handbook of psychotherapy and behavior change* (5th ed.). New York: Wiley.

Norcross, J. C., & Goldfried, M. R. (Eds.). (2005). *Handbook of psychotherapy integration* (2nd ed.). New York: Oxford University Press.

Safran, J. D., & Messer, S. B. (1998). Psychotherapy integration: A postmodern critique. Ch. 13 in J. D. Safran (Ed.), *Widening the scope of cognitive therapy* (pp. 269–290). Northvale: Aronson.

Chapter 2
Transtheoretical Approaches: Treatment Planning and the Initial Interview

What *treatment, by* whom, *is most effective for this individual with that specific problem, under* which *set of circumstances, and* how *does it come about?*

(Paul, 1969, p. 111)

Researchers have yet to address every interaction suggested in Paul's question of what treatment works for whom, but transtheoretical approaches examine some of the permutations: Beutler, Consoli, and Lane (2005) focus on client characteristics, while Prochaska and DiClemente (2005) focus on a client's readiness for therapy. Both approaches agree integration should be at the level of intervention principles rather than techniques: *e.g.*, Prochaska and DiClemente suggest "that integration across a diversity of therapy systems most likely would occur at an intermediate level of analysis, between theory and techniques" (p. 148).

Intermediate levels of abstraction avoid incompatible theoretical assumptions and may be used with many people in many situations. The transtheoretical approach integrates research-supported common and specific factors to provide an empirically based framework tailored to fit individual client needs. This chapter discusses dialectical tensions in common factors and transtheoretical approaches to treatment planning, illustrates transtheoretical treatment planning, and concludes with a discussion of transtheoretical implications for integrative therapy.

The Dialectics of Transtheoretical Treatment Planning

James Prochaska's *Transtheoretical Model* (TTM) and Larry Beutler's *Systematic Treatment Selection* (STS) are empirically based practices developed from literature reviews and research examining their respective hypotheses. Rosen's (2000) meta-analysis found effect sizes ranging from $d = 0.70$–0.80 across 47 studies based on TTM principles suggesting it is at least as effective as other approaches. TTM focuses more on dynamic processes that affect a client's readiness for change, while STS focuses more on pre-existing client characteristics.

D. K. Fromme, *Systems of Psychotherapy*,
DOI 10.1007/978-1-4419-7308-5_2, © Springer Science+Business Media, LLC 2011

The Transtheoretical Model (TTM)

TTM identifies four transtheoretical *dimensions* of change (Prochaska & DiClemente, 1984, 2005; Prochaska & Norcross, 2002, 2007):

1. *Processes of Change*: These are the overt and covert activities that various therapy systems use to initiate change, such as consciousness-raising, catharsis, counterconditioning, contingency management, and reevaluation of the self or the environment.
2. *Stages of Change*: Clients make attitudinal, intentional, motivational, and behavioral changes as they move through the *precontemplative, contemplative, preparation, action*, and *maintenance* stages of readiness for change.
3. *Pros and Cons of Changing*: The relative pros and cons of changing undergo a shift as clients move through the stages. Cons outweigh pros in the *precontemplative* stage, become equivalent by the *contemplative* stage, and lose relevance by the *action* stage. Pros gain strength and motivation increases as clients move through the stages.
4. *Levels of Change*: More intensive intervention is required depending on whether problems are conscious or unconscious. Some problems are *symptomatic* responses to a difficult *situation*, but more complex problems may have nested levels: *e.g.*, *symptoms* may be supported by *maladaptive cognitions*, which create *interpersonal conflicts* that repeat childhood *family conflicts*, which were internalized in the form of *intrapersonal conflicts*.

Processes and Stages of Change

Most therapy systems emphasize only two or three of the ten intervention processes identified by TTM research; *e.g.*, although most systems use *consciousness raising* (interpretation, confrontation, or feedback), it is the principal psychoanalytic intervention. Dramatic relief and catharsis are also important in psychoanalysis, but are central for experiential therapies. Counterconditioning and contingency management are behavior therapy's principal interventions. TTM suggests using the full range of change processes as needed for different stages of change rather than just two or three processes.

Stages of change that indicate when different intervention principles may be useful have strong empirical support and has had a significant impact on the field. The following describes TTM's recommended *change processes* for the different stages of readiness for change (DiClemente, 2003; Prochaska & DiClemente, 1984):

1. *Precontemplation*: The client lacks awareness or has no plans to change. Therapy focuses on the relationship, providing *dramatic relief* from symptoms, and on *consciousness-raising*: (a) educating client about therapy, (b) addressing anxiety or shame about seeing a therapist, and (c) gently exploring reasons for treatment. Motivational interviewing (Miller & Rollnick, 2002; see Chap. 9) helps treatment-resistant, court-referred, or substance abuse clients move to the *contemplation* stage by focusing on the long-term consequences of their behavior.

2. *Contemplation*: Clients realize problems exist, are considering change, but have not yet made a commitment. *Reevaluating self, others*, and *the environment* helps clients discover patterns in antecedents, consequences, and recurrences of problems. They gain hope that change is possible as they understand how problems develop and are maintained. Psychodynamic or interpersonal therapy may be needed for complex, long-term *thematic* problems.
3. *Preparation*: Clients realize they can change by learning skills such as counter-conditioning, contingency management, and relaxation in this transitional stage. This *self-liberation* process helps clients determine goals for the *action* stage.
4. *Action*: Clients commit to behavioral, perceptual, or environmental changes and make at least one change. Increased self-efficacy lets them implement action-oriented processes such as *contingency management, stimulus control, counterconditioning*, or *experiential exercises*. They recognize patterns that signal possible relapse and develop prevention strategies.
5. *Maintenance*: Clients consolidate gains and work to prevent relapse. They understand relapse occurs only if they perceive lapses as failure and give up. By definition, *relapse* occurs only if clients exit the change process after a lapse. Booster sessions help prevent lapses from becoming relapses. Clients learn that progress is an ascending spiral as they lapse and recycle through the stages. Clients typically lapse to earlier stages and then move forward once again in a "helical" fashion through the stages until the next lapse occurs. New learning opportunities occur each cycle until they finally maintain their gains. Long-term chronic conditions, such as substance abuse, may cycle several times until the maintenance stage becomes progressively longer and lapses no longer occur.

Pros and Cons of Changing

This dimension reflects a dialectic as clients weigh the pain caused by their problems against fears of the unknown and the social stigmas of not solving one's own problems or being labeled "mentally ill." Hall and Rossi (2003) evaluated pro-to-con ratios and found that cons outweigh pros by 0.7 standard deviations during precontemplation. Not surprisingly, 40–50% of precontemplative clients terminate prematurely, but consciousness raising helps reduce that percentage. Pros and cons are equivalent by the contemplation stage, but pros outweigh cons by 0.7 standard deviations by the action stage. Clients are more likely to complete therapy if change processes are appropriate to their current stage of change (Prochaska *et al.*, 2001).

Levels of Change

This describes problem depth or complexity, ranging from *symptoms* or problematic situations to internalized conflicts that are recurring *themes* throughout the client's life.

TTM identifies five increasingly complex levels, each with recommended therapeutic approaches:

1. Symptom/Situational Problems .... Behavior Therapy; Exposure Therapy
2. Maladaptive Cognitions .... Adlerian Therapy; Cognitive-Behavioral
   Therapy
3. Current Interpersonal Conflicts .... Sullivanian Therapy; Interpersonal Therapy
4. Family/Systems Conflicts .... Strategic, Bowenian, and Structural Family
   Therapy
5. Intrapersonal Conflicts ....Psychoanalytic, Existential, and Gestalt Therapy

TTM also suggests that precontemplative clients will benefit from consciousness-raising approaches; *e.g.*, motivational interviewing, Adlerian, Sullivanian, or psychoanalytic therapy are, respectively, helpful for situational, maladaptive cognition, interpersonal conflict, or intrapersonal conflict. Strategic family therapy reframes family conflicts and does not require precontemplative clients to have insight into their problems. Adlerian, Bowenian, or existential therapies respectively help contemplative clients explore faulty beliefs, family conflicts, or intrapersonal conflicts. For clients at the action stage, TTM recommends behavior and exposure therapy for symptoms, cognitive therapy for maladaptive cognitions, interpersonal therapy for interpersonal conflicts, structural therapy for family conflicts, and Gestalt therapy for intrapersonal conflicts (Prochaska & Norcross, 2007).

Treatment Planning

Intervention processes shift in TTM treatment planning as the appropriate level of change is discovered and as clients move from one stage to the next.

Three strategies exist for choosing interventions as a function of level of change:

1. *Shifting Levels*: Initial interventions focus on symptom or situational change. If this does not work, therapists progressively shift to deeper levels until the client responds.
2. *Key Levels*: Interventions are targeted for a clearly indicated level; *e.g.*, family therapy is needed for parents in conflict over discipline for an out-of-control child.
3. *Maximum Impact*: With the most complex cases, interventions target multiple levels; *e.g.*, long-standing interpersonal conflicts that reflect family of origin problems and affect most areas of life have probably been internalized as intrapersonal conflicts. Symptoms and situations may be targeted for immediate relief and then used to raise awareness about patterns of maladaptive thoughts, interpersonal conflicts, or family of origin influences.

Therapists shift their approach to address the increased resistance to change that those results when clients discover they need to process problems at deeper levels.

Systematic Treatment Selection

Systematic Treatment Selection (STS; Beutler, 1983; 2000; Beutler & Clarkin, 1990; Beutler *et al.*, 2005) is based on literature searches and research about client characteristics that interact with different treatment approaches. STS's *Functional Impairment* and TTM's *Levels of Change* dimensions overlap, while STS's dimensions of *Coping Style, Resistance Level*, and *Distress* are distinctly different from the other TTM dimensions.

Functional Impairment

Functional Impairment combines two previously separate, but related STS factors, *Chronicity* and *Problem Complexity*, into a single dimension (Beutler *et al.*, 2005). Complexity is similar to TTM's Levels dimension. It ranges from short-term symptomatic responses to difficult situations to long-term thematic or trait-like problems. Thematic problems often cause family and friends to withdraw when their efforts fail to alleviate a recurring problem, resulting in low levels of social support for the client. As problems become chronic, they interfere with many areas of life and may involve comorbid, personality disorder diagnoses.

Functional impairment determines treatment frequency, duration, and intensity: *e.g.*, out-patient *vs.* in-patient settings, psychosocial *vs.* medico-somatic intervention, individual *vs.* group or family formats. STS prescribes short-term cognitive-behavioral therapies for acute symptomatic problems and long-term psychodynamic, interpersonal, or experiential therapies to uncover and resolve the core interpersonal or intrapsychic conflicts of chronic *thematic* problems (Beutler & Clarkin, 1990).

Global Assessment of Functioning (GAF) scores (American Psychiatric Association, 2000) are one way to evaluate functional impairment. Clients with GAF scores of 0–20 are a danger to self or others or are unable to care themselves and require hospitalization. Clients with GAF scores of 21–40 need supervised group home settings. They have significantly impaired reality testing or social functioning and may require pharmacological intervention especially at the lower levels. Behavioral or emotional stabilization, reality testing, social skills training, and after-care to ensure social support and medication compliance are typically needed (Hogarty *et al.*, 1991).

GAF scores of 41–60 reflect moderate to severe symptoms or impairment in social, occupational, or school functioning; *e.g.*, no friends, unable to keep a job, but basic self-care is intact. Clients are closely monitored to see if intensive intervention or medication is needed to reduce symptomatic distress. Therapy may include ecosystemic or family interventions as well as social skills training. Long-term interventions are often needed for associated thematic problems. GAF scores of 61–80 suggest mild, transient symptoms. Treatment length hinges on the degree to which symptoms are transient and situational (71–80 range) or more thematic and interpersonal (61–70 range). Clients with child or marital issues in the 61–80 range benefit from family therapy. GAF scores above 80 are in the normal range, but clients may need brief counseling to cope with a particularly difficult situation.

Coping Style

This dimension includes *internalizing, repressing, externalizing*, and *cyclic* styles of coping with problems (Beutler, 2000; Beutler & Clarkin, 1990; Beutler *et al.*, 2005). Internalizers attribute negative feelings and impulses to factors within their control, while idealizing others. The result is timidity, self-blame, and constricted emotional experiencing. Experiential therapy can help emotional constriction, anxiety, guilt, or shame, while insight-oriented, dynamic therapies are compatible with the internalizer's tendency toward introversion.

Repressors tend to be introverts who use selective inattention or denial to avoid threatening impulses or feelings (Beutler & Clarkin, 1990). Experiential therapies help direct attention toward cognitive and affective experiences, while psychodynamic therapy is useful if repressors are aware of early childhood memories. If not, here-and-now experiential therapy may help them gain better awareness of internalized childhood conflicts.

Externalizers rationalize impulsive, angry acting out by blaming others for their problems. Clients with paranoid tendencies project threatening impulses onto others and then act as if actually threatened. Externalizers need to become emotionally aware how they contribute to their problems in order to become less impulsive. Because they are not introspective, externalizers respond best to structured, action-oriented approaches such as cognitive-behavioral therapy.

Cyclic clients alternatively externalize threatening impulses or internalize guilt and withdraw if things go wrong. They either idealize or demonize self and others and are unable to see self or others as sometimes helpful and sometimes not. This coping style needs the structure of cognitive-behavior therapy or dialectical behavior therapy (Linehan, 1993a; see Chap. 14).

Resistance

STS views resistance in terms of Brehm's (1966) concept of reactance: to oppose a directive or restriction of freedom. Resistance is more familiar to clinicians and is the preferred term. Compliant clients respond well to directive therapies, but resistant clients require either paradoxical or nondirective interventions. Paradoxical, "win-win" interventions advise against "premature change" or encourage resistant clients to act symptomatically. Clients either abandon their symptoms or learn they can control them consciously.

If clients resist exploring thematic problems, therapists validate their need for autonomy and adopt a more nondirective stance. Once clients become aware of their resistance, therapists often can become more directive. In contrast, compliant or dependent clients usually respond well to directive cognitive-behavioral methods in learning how to be more assertive. Clients' coping styles and resistance defend against internal and external pressures. Coping styles tend to be more thematic or trait-like, while resistance can show both state and trait properties; *i.e.*, even compliant individuals sometimes resent being pressured by others. Table 2.1 describes how coping styles vary as a function of the client's resistance.

Table 2.1 Coping styles in high- and low-resistant clients

Coping style	High resistance	Low resistance
Internalization	*Compartmentalization*—attends only to unavoidable threats; *Affect Isolation*—ignores the emotional impact; *Rationalization*—denies seriousness of threat; *Intellectualization*—isolates emotions from insights. Explosive if unable to suppress emotions	*Ruminates* about personal failures; *Constricted Affect*—learns not to feel strongly; *Undoing*—makes amends for imagined/real wrongdoings; *Selective Inattention*—ignores uncomfortable impulses or situations
Repression	*Reaction Formation*—counters threats by focusing on opposite impulse→ naïve, easily distracted or overwhelmed coping; suicide a risk if unable to suppress emotions	*Displacement*—pays attention to less threatening thoughts→diffuse worries, as in generalized anxiety disorder
Externalization	*Extrapunitive*—harsh, judgmental responses to perceived threats; *Paranoid Projection*—requires nondirective or paradoxical strategy. *Somatic* symptoms may develop if client learns to inhibit externalized impulses	*Acts Out* or *Displaces* perceived threats onto safe targets; *Emotional Isolation*—many friends, few intimates; paradoxic directives and Socratic methods avoid passive-aggressive resistance
Cyclic Coping	*Sensitization*—intense focus on perceived threats elevates suicide risk as client cycles out of externalizing; common with histrionic/cyclothymic/borderline personality disorders	Impulsive *Acting Out* alternates cyclically with passive-aggressiveness, dysthymia, or somatization; *Rationalization* is common

Motivational Distress

STS invokes Yerkes and Dodson's Inverted-U Law (1908; see Fig. 2.1), which states that performance on a complex task increases up to an optimal point as arousal increases and then decreases with continuing arousal. Yerkes-Dodson's law suggests when to increase or decrease emotional arousal in therapy. Very high arousal

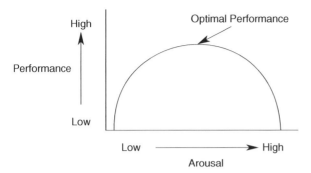

Fig. 2.1 Yerkes and Dodson (1908) inverted-U law for complex tasks

is destabilizing because it increases the probability that competing responses will interfere with complex task performance. Clients are overwhelmed and unable to maintain the focus needed to resolve emotionally arousing problems.

Arousal-induction uses confrontation or experiential methods to increase the motivation of clients with low symptom distress. Experiential methods help clients become more aware of their feelings and gain the information or motivation needed to act effectively. In contrast, *arousal-reduction* methods enable high-distress clients to concentrate on the therapy process (Beutler, 2000). Relaxation training, meditation, or cognitive-behavioral methods alleviate strong negative emotions such as anger, anxiety, or grief that interfere with adaptive functioning.

Despite their differences, both behavioral and experiential techniques help clients confront negative emotions. Behavioral exposure therapy helps clients confront feelings and extinguish maladaptive emotional responses. Similarly, experiential therapy helps clients learn they will not be overwhelmed if they "stay" with their negative feelings. This enables them to discover the source of their feelings and make an informed choice about how best to respond.

Arousal-inducing procedures, *e.g.*, directed fantasies, interpretation, confrontation, encounter with significant others, two-chair dialog, or silence (which can be very uncomfortable), are used with clients referred by the courts, schools, or family members whose motivation or symptom distress is typically low (Beutler & Clarkin, 1990). Motivational interviewing (Miller & Rollnick, 2002; see Chap. 9) may also help them confront the long-term aversive consequences of their actions. Substance-abusing clients need to experience the long-term effects and losses with a sense of immediacy to counter the short-term reinforcing effects of drugs or alcohol.

Arousal-reducing interventions are needed when symptomatic or emotional distress is so intense it interferes with the client's ability to focus in therapy. Arousal-reduction methods include reassurance, empathic reflection, teaching, meditation, relaxation, pleasant imagery, and helping clients express feelings. Counterconditioning or exposure to feared stimuli may be helpful. Highly resistant clients may paradoxically become agitated if directed to relax, but may relax if they have a choice of different relaxation methods or record relaxation instructions themselves.

Integrating the Transtheoretical Model and Systematic Treatment Selection

The STS model includes client characteristics not present in the TTM model, while TTM's Stages of Change dimension is not part of the STS model, although Beutler (2006) is working with John Norcross on this point. Figure 2.2 and Table 2.2 describe one way to add Stages of Change to STS dimensions for treatment planning. Figure 2.2 illustrates the combination of Functional Impairment (GAF scores) and Stages of Change: the left hand column lists GAF levels; the middle column lists mediating variables such as stages of change, danger to self, or lack of social support; and the right hand column suggests interventions for various combinations of functional impairment and stages of change. The top row of Fig. 2.2 suggests clients with substance abuse, suicide risk, or psychotic symptoms, who are a danger to self or others, need medication and hospitalization; if not at risk, they are referred to less restrictive settings. In the third row, clients with GAF scores between 41 and 60 who lack adequate social support may need day hospitalization, social skills training, or medication; if they have social support, consciousness raising increases precontemplative clients' motivation to change and explore how their problems are maintained. If clients are already at the contemplation stage, row five directs treatment planning to the Intervention Selection Table (Table 2.2). Finally, the bottom

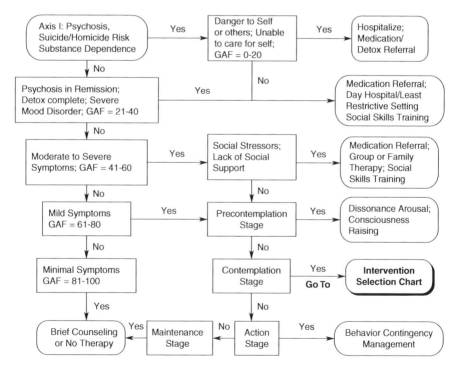

Fig. 2.2 Flow chart relating functional impairment and stages of change to interventions

Table 2.2 Intervention selection table for contemplative clients

If Problem is:	Low Distress, then goal is Arousal Induction				High Distress, then goal is Arousal Reduction			
If Problem is:	Thematic, then goal is Insight		Situational, then goal is Symptom Change		Thematic, then goal is Insight		Situational, then goal is Symptom Change	
If Resistance is:	Low, use Directive Therapy	High, use Nondirective Therapy	Low, use Directive Therapy	High, use Nondirective Therapy	Low, use Directive Therapy	High, use Nondirective Therapy	Low, use Directive Therapy	High, use Nondirective Therapy
Intervention Methods for *Internalizers*	Interpret resistance or transference; Directed imagery	Free association; Discuss painful memories; Question schemas	Thought-stopping; Covert practice	Paradoxic directives; Identify alternative assumptions; Self-monitor	Focusing; Support; Directed imagery; Dream interpretation	Reflect or restate; Explore schemas; Support; Dream interpretation	Identify automatic thoughts; Thought stopping; Covert practice	Self-monitor/restructure automatic thoughts; Hypnosis
Intervention Methods for *Externalizers*	Closed questions; Confrontation; Enact opposite behavior	Predict symptoms; Physical movement; Silence; Two-chair work	Closed questions; Directed imagery	Behavior contracts; Contingency management; Overt practice	Confront schemas; Practice self-statements; Direct instruction	Genograms; Redecision work; Paradoxic directive to not change	Counter-condition; Self-instruction; Relaxation	Role rehearsal; Relaxation training; Exposure; Contingency management

row recommends environmental contingency management for clients at the action stage and brief counseling or support for those at the maintenance stage.

The Intervention Selection Table (Table 2.2) relates interventions for clients at the contemplation stage to their motivational distress, problem complexity (functional impairment), resistance, and coping style. The left side of the table describes arousal induction methods for clients with *low distress*, while the right side describes arousal reduction methods for *high-distress* clients. In the table's second, problem complexity level, *thematic problem* columns combine TTMs interpersonal and intrapersonal conflict levels of change, while *situational problem* columns combine symptom-situational and maladaptive cognitions levels. As in TTM, treatment planning also incorporates family therapy when appropriate to the client's presenting problems. The table's third level reflects *low vs. high resistance*, while the final levels respectively describe interventions for *internalizers* or *externalizers* as a function of the variables in which they are nested. The following illustrates two possible treatment planning scenarios using this model.

Following STS recommendations, a client who shows little interest in the therapy process (*low distress*), has a history of problematic relationships (*thematic problem*), repeatedly questions suggestions (*high resistance*), and complains of depression and anxiety (*internalizer*) should respond best to free association or nondirective exploration of painful childhood memories. In contrast, the agitated (*high distress*) client who finds it difficult to concentrate (*situational problem*), is cooperative (*low resistance*), but very angry with her husband (*externalizer*) may be helped by self-instruction that reframes her marital problems as unrealistic expectations based on childhood experience: *e.g.*, "I get upset at my husband's silences because they remind me how my father's angry silences upset my mother." The model in Fig. 2.2 and Table 2.2 is a point of departure for combining specific factors to develop plans individualized to particular client traits. As in all treatment planning, the proposed techniques may not work for every client. The following section reviews how common factors are included in treatment planning.

Common Factors in Treatment Planning

In addition to common factors such as a supportive relationship and expectations for a positive outcome, managed care requirements focus initial therapeutic contacts on diagnostic interviews and treatment planning. A dialectic exists between the *spontaneity* needed for a positive therapeutic alliance and the *structure* needed to make a diagnosis and treatment plan. Therapists must set aside preconceived ideas to respond spontaneously to the client's immediate concerns, but also need to make diagnostic judgments and involve the client in treatment planning.

This tension is especially notable in humanistic therapies that suggest treatment planning interferes with the therapist's spontaneity. Therapists who respond with spontaneity and warmth provide clients with the corrective emotional experience of being cared for and taken seriously. However, treatment plans ensure a focus on the presenting problem, prevent digressions to side issues, and provide a concrete basis for collaboration. If treatment plans anticipate the client's core issues, then therapists can respond both spontaneously and thoughtfully as relevant issues arise in therapy; otherwise, the treatment plan may need revision.

Among other common factors, Orlinsky *et al.'s* (2004) literature review suggests outcomes improve if clients see their therapists as assured and expert in a consistent theoretical position. However, patient-focused research suggests that therapists need to try a new approach if clients fail to improve by the third session. Therapists need theoretical expertise, but also need to know when to abandon their approach. Bernstein (1992) suggests, "Critiques and affirmations are always tentative, fallible, open to further questioning" (p. 319). The need to question practices constantly is reinforced by *confirmatory bias* research demonstrating how people attend selectively to information congruent with existing beliefs. Downing (2004) summarizes the situation as follows:

> [C]onceptual systems introduce structure into what would otherwise be an overwhelmingly complex and chaotic experience. They allow us to manage and navigate an unpredictable world successfully. Yet they imbue perceptions, which may later turn out to be mistaken, with a sense of ultimate reality, and they invisibly eliminate alternative perceptions that may have their own value and usefulness (p. 127).

Treatment plans accordingly need criteria for deciding when a plan should be revised.

Patient-Focused Research

Patient-focused research provides such criteria and confirms the importance of monitoring client progress (Howard *et al.*, 1996; Kopta *et al.*, 1994). Clients motivation is enhanced if they see evidence of progress and therapists can make necessary changes if clients are not making expected progress (Lambert *et al.*, 2002). Wells, Burlingame, Lambert, and Hoag's (1996) developed feedback rules by comparing predicted *vs.* actual progress on the 45-item Outcome Questionnaire (*OQ-45*):

1. Clients who score in the out-patient range (*OQ-45* = 70–90) are making adequate progress after 2–4 sessions as long as no deterioration in their score occurs. If scores deteriorate 1–8 points, therapists should consider changing the treatment plan. Any greater deterioration in scores indicates a serious risk of premature termination or poor outcome. Improvement is clinically significant if scores increase by at least 14 points and treatment may be terminated successfully once clients' scores are within the normal range (less than 64).

2. Clients who score in the in-patient range (*OQ-4* > 90) after 2–4 sessions must improve at least 7 points since they are in great distress and therapy needs to have a significant early impact. With less progress, therapists should consider changing the treatment plan. Serious risk of negative outcome or premature termination is suggested by either deterioration or no change. Therapists should

seek consultation about changing the treatment plan. Again, improvement is significant if scores increase by 14 points or more and treatment may be terminated once clients' scores are less than 64.

Hawkins *et al.* (2004) found that feedback improved client retention and reduced the number of sessions needed for adequate progress. To avoid discouraging clients when giving negative feedback, therapists might say, "These scores suggest you may not be making the progress you had hoped or may even be considering terminating. Let's discuss such concerns so we can consider other ways to help." It is important to use objective measures of progress, since research has consistently shown clinical judgment to be unreliable (Garb, 2005; Meehl, 1954).

Planning and Assessment in Clinical Care: The PACC Approach

The PACC approach (Woody, Detweiler-Bedell, Teachman, & O'Hearn, 2003) is based on factors common in all theoretical orientations. While transtheoretical and patient-focused methods suggest useful therapeutic *processes*, PACC uses client collaboration to identify critical *content*. Clients are the experts on the content of their feelings and problems. The *process/content* dialectic suggests outcomes improve if clients see therapists as competent and therapy focuses on their core issues (Orlinsky *et al.*, 2004). PACC's three parts include listing problems, treatment plans, and periodic progress reviews. Plans are revised as problems are clarified, new issues are discovered, or if no change has occurred.

Problem List

As client stories unfold, therapists make a tentative list of problems and then seek client input on its accuracy (see Table 2.3). Once problems are described in concrete terms they seem less overwhelming than the abstract, global descriptions often used by clients. Also, problems are more easily solved if they are clearly defined, addressed one at a time, and core concerns separated from side issues. Stubborn, complex problems become less challenging if divided into several phases of treatment so that each seems less difficult. Helping clients see that problems can be "divided and conquered" facilitates optimism that they can overcome problems that previously seemed insurmountable.

Problems that interfere with therapy such as motivation, ambivalence, procrastination, or time management are included in the list as well as broader ecosystemic, cultural, or family problems. Eclectic models, *e.g.*, Lazarus' (1967) BASIC-ID model, can help ensure coverage of all the relevant areas. During the interview's last 10–15 minutes, clients collaborate in a review of the problem list, endorse the items they see as most important, and choose their treatment goals.

Table 2.3 Problem list for a substance abusing, depressed client

Problem list	Endorsed by client?
1. Alcohol and tranquilizer abuse	X
2. Court involvement related to DUII	X
3. Frequent arguments with family	X
4. Not confident of family's love	X
5. Ambivalence in role as father	
6. No role models for consistent and warm parenting	X
7. Frequent absences from work	X
8. Unstable work history	
9. Few social contacts	
10. No exercise	X
11. Suicidal ideation	X
12. Feeling depressed	X
13. Loneliness	X
14. Generalized anxiety	X
15. Fatigue	X
16. Insomnia	X
17. Eating too much between meals	
18. Weight gain	X
19. Feeling worthless	X
20. Feeling that life lacks meaning	X

Treatment Planning

Once problems are listed, they are grouped into categories and priorities are set: *e.g.*, Table 2.3 lists related problems (sadness, loneliness, anxiety, and feeling worthless) that might benefit from emotional self-regulation, cognitive, or experiential methods in therapy's initial phase. Collaborative planning balances easily attained goals that might enhance self-efficacy feelings with more difficult goals that might give greater relief.

Therapy begins with the highest priority problems, postponing the rest until later treatment phases. Clients motivation is enhanced as they see the value of working on subsets of concrete problems. A formal contract about the goals and approach of the initial phase of treatment ensures informed consent and makes a good conclusion to an intake session. Goals for later treatment phases are discussed in subsequent meetings if needed. Orlinsky *et al.* (2004) note that contracts:

1. Ensure informed consent;
2. Provide a guide to treatment that keeps a clear focus on client problems;
3. Help clients understand why a difficult or time-consuming procedure is necessary.

Dividing treatment into phases increases commitment to realistic time frames as clients realize that not everything gets better at once. It is important they understand the rationale for the suggested time frame to prevent discouragement and premature termination. Agreement about therapy's length is basic to "time-sensitive" therapy. Deadlines help both therapist and client work with greater focus and intensity. Decisions whether to terminate, extend the number of sessions, take a new approach, or refer to another therapist can be made once deadlines arrive.

Progress Review

As in patient-focused research, each PACC phase requires that a new conceptualization and strategy be developed should the initial approach not work. Each phase has its own *aims, measures, and strategies*:

1. Treatment *aims* are derived from the problem list and divided into easily achieved short-term goals. If sub-goals are achieved, client self-efficacy and motivation are enhanced; if not, changes need to be made in the treatment plan.
2. Standardized *measures* or individualized tests are given at 3–5-week intervals to monitor the degree to which sub-goals and overall aims are being achieved. The *Subjective Units of Distress Scale* (SUDS; Derogatis, 1994) may be used to rate levels of depression or anxiety experienced during the week. The OQ-45, used in patient-focused research, is a validated measure for overall symptom changes. Barriers that could interfere with completing tests are discussed as the contract is developed. Clients are told that repeated testing shows whether therapy is progressing or if new procedures may be needed.
3. Intervention *strategies* are based on a collaboratively developed conceptualization of the client's problems. Collaboration shows that therapists value their clients' concerns and input; it ensures informed consent, enhances motivation, and strengthens the therapeutic alliance.

Dialectical Tensions Between Client and Therapist During the Initial Interview

The therapeutic alliance is the heart of the client/therapist dialectic (Orlinsky *et al.*, 2004). Even before the first session, therapist and client are forming impressions about one another that may prove critical for therapy's eventual success. Both struggle with personal dialectics: therapists must resolve task *vs.* relationship-oriented tensions, while clients must resolve ambivalence about changing. Change requires clients to choose between problematic but familiar ways of relating to others and the unknown risks of new ways of relating with others. The client's dilemma pits hope for a better life against the costs of trusting a stranger, exploring painful topics, and making life changes with no guarantee that problems will be solved.

The dilemma for therapists is to build a working alliance based on respect, warmth, and trust in an inherently unequal relationship while asking clients to reveal intimate details. Therapists balance the risk of alliance strains against the need to help clients confront painful experiences. The structure *vs.* spontaneity dialectic adds another layer of complexity, since establishing rapport is not easily combined with the structured questioning needed for diagnostic and risk assessment.

The following section discusses common factors in therapeutic intake interviews.

Gathering Information While Establishing a Collaborative Relationship

Therapists have three goals that are frequently incompatible during an initial interview:

1. Establish a collaborative working alliance;
2. Allow clients to tell their story;
3. Gather diagnostic data for treatment planning and institutional requirements.

Listening to the client's story with genuine warmth and empathy fosters an active, collaborative alliance. In contrast, gathering information may require active, intrusive questioning that discourages active collaboration. Clients may feel interrogated if therapists focus only on gathering information.

Masi, Miller, and Olson (2003) found that 15–17% of potential clients miss the first session and another 26–30% drop out after the first or second session. One explanation may be that client ambivalence about therapy was not addressed during the initial phone contact or intake session. Considerable research suggests that first impressions predict outcomes in many areas (Ambady & Rosenthal, 1993; Caplan, 2005). It may be that first impressions are very accurate or that they bias subsequent outcome ratings, but clearly they are important.

Preparing for the Interview

The relationship begins with a phone call about appointment times, costs, insurance, *etc.* Therapists determine if any risk requires immediate attention and if the presenting problem is within their range of competence. They discuss who will be at the first session in the case of child, couple, or family problems. Because clients are always ambivalent, significant delays between initial phone contacts and the intake session increase the chance they will decide against coming. Asking clients to complete a personal data questionnaire beforehand will help reduce the questioning needed during the intake interview (see Appendix A).

Being on time respects the client and helps reveal any time management problems. If therapists begin or end late, it is hard to tell if a client has feelings of entitlement or is avoiding anxiety-provoking issues. Time management requires that therapists limit chit-chat delaying discussion of difficult issues. Rapport is usually enhanced more by professionalism and task-orientation than by chit-chat. One approach is to discuss weather or current affairs while escorting clients from the waiting room to the therapy office. The therapist waits for a pause and then sits down to signal the start of the session. Exceptions to strict time management may be needed if a life-threatening situation develops or for clients from cultures with a relaxed sense of time.

Beginning the Session

Clients are informed about their rights, limits to confidentiality, and the risk that problems could become intensified during therapy. Despite potentially threatening overtones, clients may appreciate the therapist's concern for their privacy in such an introduction. It is better to feel anxious early than betrayed by later, unexpected disclosures. Since therapists may have no idea *what* is a problem for *whom*. Benjamin (2006) suggests therapy begin with a neutral phrase focusing on motivation, "What do you need? What would help?" (p. 37).

The therapist's active, reflective listening builds rapport and gives clients the corrective emotional experience of being heard. Reflecting relevant points in their narrative encourages active participation and ensures a focus on significant problems. Inviting clients to tell their story in their own words with minimal interruptions reveals:

1. The specificity, coherence, and organization of their thoughts (*mental status*);
2. Preliminary information on their emotional regulation, typical mood, and coping style;
3. What is most salient among their immediate needs and concerns;
4. Whether their concerns are with themselves, with others, or with their environment;
5. Whether they internalize or externalize responsibility for their problems; and
6. Their readiness for change.

Gathering Information

Problems are often revealed in the way clients describe their concerns and relate to the therapist. The relationship reveals interpersonal and cognitive problems directly even if reports are distorted. Therapists may redirect the client's narrative by being curious about missing or incongruent elements. Asking "Why did you call last week instead of last month?" or "If I were a hidden camera, what would I have seen happening?" may clarify what precipitated their decision to seek help. How clients understand and try to solve their problem may reveal how it is maintained or exacerbated. Many problems, such as alcoholism, are often "solutions" that avoid negative feelings or other underlying problems.

Discussing times when problems were successfully resolved or avoided may suggest ways to solve problems (Miller, Hubble, & Duncan, 1996). Genograms (see Chap. 12) clarify important family and generational pressures. Therapists should also clarify the *ecosystemic* variables affecting their client's life. They might ask, "You've given me a good picture of what's happening at home, but I'm not sure about the big picture. Many people have problems with health, schools, the law, jobs, prejudice, and so on. Could you tell me how those things have affected you?"

Clients provide diagnostic information as they discuss their problems. Presenting problems are often replicated in the therapeutic relationship. Beginning therapists sometimes feel they must be a "friend" to establish a working alliance; but rapport develops naturally when information is gathered in a friendly, professional way that avoids constant questioning or interrogation. Table 2.4 describes ways to respond to problems that can occur in an interview. The key is to explore the reasons for the client's words or actions empathically, while maintaining good boundaries.

Table 2.4 Responding to common problems during an initial interview

Problem: client is …	Therapeutic responses
Taciturn; shy; withdrawn	Empathize with ambivalence and the difficulty of sharing private information; use open-ended questions
Over-talkative; rambling	Closed questions that reflect the most relevant concerns or comments
Court-mandated; uncooperative	Discuss confidentiality and limitations; develop common goals: *e.g.*, resolving court or parental concerns or shortening the length of treatment
Angry; hostile	Empathically explore cause and actual target of anger and past problems with anger expression; develop common goals: *e.g.*, to be treated more fairly
Asking about credentials	Provide relevant information; discuss concerns about therapist's competency
Asking about age or personal information	Acknowledge request, but first ascertain reason: *e.g.*, concerns *re* experience, discomfort with needing help, or cultural expectation for more personal relation
Making unreasonable requests	Give reason for refusal; empathize with frustration over denial and explore underlying needs to discover an acceptable alternative response
Threatening	Always arrange seating for easy exit; acknowledge client's feelings; disclose how threats make it difficult to help and explore underlying needs
Delusional	Test how firmly belief is held: "Is that really happening?" Do not challenge belief, but empathize and explore impact of belief, "Most people would be unhappy if they felt they were being spied on by neighbors."

Although client reports are essential, information not available to the client may be obtained from family members, records, or other professionals. Consulting with family or other helping professionals also develops the network that clients with chronic or ecosystemic problems may need. Consulting with the client's physician is essential if somatic symptoms are present.

Mental Status Examinations

Observation and conversation are often sufficient to assess mental status, neurological, or psychotic signs (see Table 2.5). Specific questions may also be neces-

Table 2.5 Mental status examination categories and information sources

Observation can evaluate:	Conversation can evaluate:
Cooperativeness	Concentration and attention
Hygiene and grooming	Memory for recent and remote events
State of consciousness (*alert; confused; lethargic*)	Speech clarity (*pressure of speech; neologisms; paraphasia or incoherence*)
Psychomotor behavior (*tremors; tics; repetitive movements; coordination*)	Thinking (*concreteness; fragmentation; perseveration; rambling; tangentiality—answers miss, but are "near by" the mark; circumstantiality—related but irrelevant details*)
	Orientation for time, place, and person
	Affect (*elated; depressed; hostile; flat; or exaggerated expression*)

sary: *e.g.*, "Do you ever hear voices of people who are not there?" Since asking about hallucinations may alienate some clients, this is usually done only if other neurological or psychotic signs are present. It is best to form hypotheses as a client's narrative unfolds. If diagnostic data are insufficient, then short follow-up questions can resolve uncertainties. This strategy resolves the spontaneity *vs.* structure dialectic by minimizing intrusive questions and maximizing opportunities for clients to tell their story. Othmer and Othmer (1994) provide a useful guide to diagnostic interviewing and mental status examination.

Personal data questionnaires (see Appendix A) gather demographic, occupational, legal, medical, and family information and help reduce feelings of interrogation during initial interviews. Questionnaires may yield information that suggests further testing, such as a history of seizures, head trauma, high fever, or exposure to toxins. Many clients reveal abuse, rape, or fears of "going crazy" in checklists that they would conceal in face-to-face interviews. Perceived strengths and weaknesses, expectations about therapy, and common problems such as sleep disturbance can also be explored this way.

Risk Assessment

Risk assessment is needed if a questionnaire or the interview reveals suicidal thoughts or attempts. Clients seldom lie when asked directly about suicidal thoughts even if they fail to volunteer this information. They may feel ashamed, but recognize it is a life or death question. Even if the questionnaire does not reveal suicidal thoughts, it is still necessary to question the client about thoughts of self-harm. Similar considerations apply to assessments of substance abuse. The SLAP mnemonic is frequently used in preliminary assessment of suicidal risk:

Suicidal ideation: "Have you ever considered taking your own life?" "Recently?"
Lethality of method: "Have you thought about what method you might use?"
Access to method: "Do you actually have the means to do it that way?"
Plan: "Have you made plans to follow through killing yourself?" "When?" "Any preparations?"

Risk is moderate if suicidal ideas are specific and the method is *either* lethal *or* accessible, but *not both*, in which case risk is high. If risk is moderate or high, or severe depressive symptoms are present, then more intensive assessment is indicated. Rudd and Joiner (1998) recommend the following line of questioning, while being sensitive to the client's emotional state during transitions:

1. *Predisposing variables*: "Can you tell me about your family, what your childhood and adolescent years were like? Were you ever the victim of physical, sexual, or emotional abuse, either by your parents, a family member, or anyone else? Was there violence of any type in your family? How did your parents discipline you? When and how? Have you ever been hospitalized for a psychiatric disturbance? When?"
2. *Precipitants or stressors*: "What triggered this crisis for you?" Look for any significant financial or interpersonal losses or problematic relationships at home or work. Address health issues by asking, "Have you had any health problems lately or any chronic pain?"
3. *Symptomatic presentation*: Anxiety or mood disorders—vegetative symptoms (appetite, sleep, or sexual disturbances). Assess severity, "On a scale from 1 to 10, with 1 being the best you've ever felt and 10 being such severe anxiety or depression you were unable to do anything, how would you rate yourself the past few days? Weeks? Months? Does anything give you relief?"
4. *Hopelessness*: "Have you felt hopeless lately … like things wouldn't get better?" "With 1 being optimistic and 10 being utterly hopeless things will ever get better, how would you rate yourself?"
5. *Nature of suicidal thinking*: This is the SLAP assessment discussed above; also assess for frequency, intensity, and duration of suicidal thoughts. Ask, "What has kept you from committing suicide up to this point?"
6. *Prior suicidal behavior; making preparations*: Determine frequency, context, lethality, and outcomes of prior attempts. "Did you think you would die?" "How did you get help—did you go to the hospital?" "Who discovered you?" "Did you try to avoid being discovered?" It is important to discover if any preparations are being made—rehearsals, letters to loved ones, insurance or will changes, arranging for pet care, or gathering the means to follow through.
7. *Impulsivity and self-control*: Assess for substance abuse. Also ask, "On a scale of 1 to 10 with 1 being in complete control and 10 being totally out of control, how would you rate yourself?" "Do you feel you can control your impulses to commit suicide?"
8. *Protective factors*: Social support—"Do you have family or friends available you can depend on and talk to? If not, why?" Also ask, "Do you have times when you feel more hopeful or optimistic? When? What is happening then?" "How have you responded to therapy in the past? Was it helpful? What was not helpful?"

If ideas, methods, or plans are vague and abstract, suicidal risk is low but regular follow-ups are needed, "I understand this is just a thought now, but may I check with you once in a while to see if things have changed?" Also ask "What has kept you from following through on these ideas?" This allows clients to think about reasons to stay alive and to identify protective factors. With moderate risk but no immediate plan, more intensive assessment is warranted. If this cannot be done immediately, an informal "no-harm" agreement is requested: "We need to discuss this further. Will you commit to calling this number if you feel more suicidal?" Risk level is severe and immediate intervention is needed if ideation, available method, and plan are all present. Table 2.6 summarizes factors affecting suicide risk levels and related interventions.

Table 2.6 Rudd and Joiner's (1998) suicide risk factors and suggested interventions

Level	Risk factors	Recommended interventions
No risk	No suicidal ideas	None required if ideation not present
Low	Ideas; no plan or intent; mild symptoms; good self-control; protective factors	Acknowledge hopelessness; client makes contact if thoughts become more intense; check monthly whether suicidal ideation still present or client is more optimistic
Moderate	Ideas; plan, but no intent; mild to moderate symptoms; good self-control; protective factors	Weekly appointments; careful monitoring; mobilize social support; informal agreement not to act on suicidal thoughts before discussing them in therapy
Severe	Ideas; plan and access; no intent; serious symptoms; self-control impaired; few protective factors	Twice weekly appointments; activate social support; restrict access to means; formal agreement regarding steps to take if suicidal impulses become overwhelming
Extreme	Same as with severe risk, but with stated intent	Hospitalization; also whenever the client expresses immediate intent, regardless of other factors

Severe or extreme risk clients should not leave the office until hospitalization is arranged or they commit *credibly* in writing to keep themselves safe and are not just avoiding hospitalization. Therapists can say, "I'm concerned to hear how seriously you're considering suicide. Can we make a commitment to keep you safe until we've had a chance to work on your concerns?" Commitment agreements should include the following steps (see Appendix B):

1. Procedure when suicidal impulses are hard to resist—*e.g.*, call friend, hotline, or therapist.
2. Phone numbers of significant others to call for support are posted on a refrigerator.
3. Ongoing contact with friends or family to strengthen support network.
4. Lethal methods such as guns or drugs are destroyed or given to someone trustworthy.
5. Therapists make answering service or call-forwarding arrangements, so their client can contact them directly or be directed to an emergency call service.

At extreme risk levels with expressed intentions to commit suicide, clients need immediate hospitalization. Therapists should lobby hard for voluntary hospitalization since the therapeutic alliance is often irreparably harmed by an involuntary commitment.

Substance Abuse Assessment

Since untreated substance abuse makes it difficult to work effectively with other problems, clients are always asked when they last had a drink or used prescription or "street" drugs. Answers about use during the past 24 hours need to be specific and concrete to prevent clients from minimizing the frequency or amount of usage. The "CAGE" questions are often used to screen drinking problems, but therapists should be aware that recent research suggests they are more sensitive to detecting alcohol abuse in older women than in other groups (Buhler, 2004). The CAGE questions are:

C. Have you ever felt you should *Cut* down on your drinking (substance use)?
A. Have people *Annoyed* you by criticizing your drinking (substance use)?
G. Have you ever felt *Guilty* about your drinking (substance use)?
E. Do you ever start the day with an *Eye-opener* to get rid of hangovers or steady your nerves?

The "FADES" questions assess diagnostic criteria for substance abuse or dependence and are used if clients endorse more than one CAGE item or show other signs of substance abuse:

Frequency of use: Never, 1–2 month, 1–2 week, 3–4 week, 5–6 week, daily?
Amount for each episode of drinks, pills, or "hits": 1, 2–3, 4–5, 6 or more?
Duration: How many months or years has the client used these drugs?
Effects of abuse: needed daily to function; inability to cut down; interference with occupational or social functioning; co-ordination/judgment impaired; loss of memory or control; black-outs; "lost" weekend benders; acting out (driving impaired, fights, or self harm)?
Symptoms of dependence: tolerance (increased use needed to achieve same effect) or *withdrawal* (shakes or malaise when not using)?

Heavy, long-term usage, serious consequences following abuse, or dependence symptoms all require that treatment planning consider whether detoxification is needed or if abstinence is a reasonable goal. Some clients with minor levels of abuse may succeed with "social drinking" as a goal (Humphreys & Klaw, 2001). Client motivation is reduced and other problems are exacerbated unless therapy addresses substance dependence or abuse. In general, clients are more motivated if they actively collaborate in setting goals and developing the therapeutic plan. The following case illustrates how an initial interview and transtheoretical treatment plan work together.

Case Illustration: Integrative Transtheoretical Treatment Planning

Background: Edna is a moderately obese, 42-year-old African-American woman, who is married with three children, aged 14–24. She complained of depression, chronic fatigue, insomnia, binge-eating, poor concentration, loss of interest in activities, thoughts of committing suicide, and expressed many physical concerns. She admitted occasional, vague thoughts of suicide, and said she often drank heavily to "drown my sorrows." She described a chaotic childhood with an alcoholic, physically abusive father. Edna became sexually active at age 13 and began drinking about the same age.

After a particularly brutal beating by her father, she dropped out of school at age 16, moved out of the home, and got a job as a waitress. She had a succession of stormy relationships, often involving violence by both parties when drinking. Her oldest daughter, estranged for 7 years, was born to one of these relationships. At age 29, she met her husband and they lived together several years before getting married. He is a machinist and a good provider, but they frequently argue, especially over sex. He also complains that she does not keep the house properly.

Edna admits she often starts arguments because she does not like their neighborhood, but says that he does not realize how ill she is, how hard it is for her to work, or how painful sex is for her. She has had repeated visits to the emergency room, complaining of abdominal pains, vague heart problems, and migraine headaches. She says her "mystery disease" baffles the doctors. She was well-oriented, but tended to externalize responsibility for her problems.

- *Diagnosis*: Axis I: Major depression (with somatization; low suicidal risk); Alcohol Abuse;
  Axis II: Personality Disorder, NOS (not otherwise specified), with borderline features;
  Axis III: Refer for medical examination for somatic complaints;
  Axis IV: Marital arguments; estrangement from daughter; lack of social support;
  Axis V: GAF=50
- *Problem List*:

  1. Depression: symptoms include chronic fatigue, insomnia, poor concentration, little interest in activities, thoughts of committing suicide
  2. Variety of physical complaints
  3. Binge-eating
  4. Alcohol abuse
  5. Marital conflict
  6. Estrangement from daughter
  7. Low levels of social support
  8. High crime, poor neighborhood

- *Case Conceptualization:* Edna's cyclic coping style reflects her history of abuse by her father and adolescent acting out. She impulsively acts out anger and then retreats guiltily into depression with somatic complaints, using alcohol to deaden her feelings. Deadening her feelings results in depression with her only relief being food and more drinking. Somatic complaints also reflect the chronic stress associated with an unsatisfactory life style and with living in a high crime district where it is difficult to develop adequate social support.

- *Treatment Plan: Phase 1*—Edna is at the precontemplative stage and not motivated for psychotherapy. Motivational interviewing will be used since she resists any suggestion her problems are not physical. The goal is to reach an agreement that therapy may help her cope with the many stressors in her life until the doctors can find a physical cure. Edna will be asked to sign a "Release of Information" form to request medical records of her past treatment for somatic complaints. Alcohol abuse complicates her cyclic coping with thematic problems and will be the initial focus of intervention. Relaxation training and positive imagery will provide an alternative means to self-soothe and regulate her sleep. The presence of suicidal ideation will be monitored closely should risk levels increase. Medication referral will be considered if her depression deepens or suicidal risk increases. Edna will be referred to Alcoholics Anonymous to address alcohol abuse and to expand her social support network. Weekly self-report measures will assess the working alliance. The Beck Depression Inventory (BDI) will be given at the 1st, 3rd, and then each subsequent 5th session. These measures will be reviewed with Edna to encourage active collaboration and assess whether symptomatic relief is occurring or if alternative interventions are necessary. *Phase 2*—After her drinking is reduced and she is contemplating change, dialectical behavior therapy will help Edna (a) learn emotional regulation; (b) provide support during crisis; and (c) address splits in her perceptions of herself and others as either all-good or all-bad. If needed, a third phase will address family and ecosystemic problems.

Integrative Implications

Transtheoretical approaches are empirically based practices that suggest interventions tailored to specific client characteristics, but they lack theoretical explanations *why* an intervention works in a particular situation. A comprehensive theory of personality and psychopathology such as proposed in Chap. 15 is needed to help therapists tailor interventions to an individual's needs. Theory can guide interventions and suggest new treatment approaches, which may be needed since no existing approach covers the full range of intervention levels. TTM's Levels of Change dimension comes close, lacking only the biomedical or ecosystemic levels of intervention.

The following suggests one way to conceptualize a comprehensive transtheoretical approach.

Case Conceptualization with an Integrative Transtheoretical Approach

Figure 2.3 follows the organization of chapters in this book and summarizes part of the model described in Chap. 15. It combines elements of Prochaska's TTM and Beutler's STS approaches. The top dimension of Fig. 2.3 incorporates STS's client variables, while the vertical dimension incorporates TTM's Stages of Change. The horizontal, *contextual focus* dimension resembles TTM's Levels of Change, but emphasizes the *breadth* of an intervention, rather than the latter's focus on intervention *depth*.

The major therapeutic systems are distinguished by a contextual focus, varying in breadth from molecular interventions in biomedical *microcontexts* to molar interventions in environmental or ecosystemic *macrocontexts*. Historically, therapists developed methods to work with a specific population; *e.g.*, symptomatic clients respond better to the contextual extremes of biomedical or environmental interventions, while more functionally impaired, thematic problems respond better to an intermediate, holistic focus that explores client problems in as much depth as necessary.

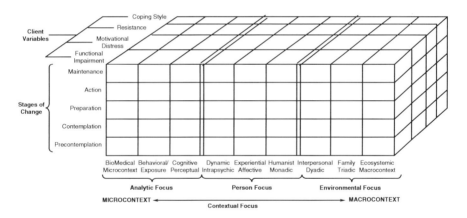

Fig. 2.3 Integrative transtheoretical case conceptualization model

Stages of Change and Client Variables

These two dimensions replicate similar factors in Prochaska's TTM and Beutler's STS approaches; however, no therapy system works for every stage of change client variable. As a result, many contextual focus cells in the model are blank. The model organizes treatment plans so that important variables are included: *e.g.*, biomedical or cognitive-behavioral approaches are indicated for the most functionally impaired clients, who may also require family and ecosystemic interventions. Humanistic, experiential, and psychodynamic approaches are ideally suited for precontemplative or contemplative clients, while cognitive-behavioral, interpersonal, or family and ecosystemic interventions may be useful during action and maintenance stages.

Short-term cognitive-behavioral therapies are most effective in treating symptomatic reactions to current or recent environmental stressors. In contrast, interpersonal or intrapsychic conflict themes that pervade many areas of the client's life usually require long-term treatment. This involves core interpersonal schemas that interfere with a client's ability to meet basic needs. Psychodynamic, interpersonal, experiential, or integrative therapy can help clients untangle the meaning of core schemas reflecting past experiences. Family therapy can interrupt interpersonal vicious circles that maintain problems; *e.g.*, families that learned to wait upon a child who reacts violently when demands are made. If such parents fail to recognize attempts at independent self-regulation, they may reinforce their child's dependency.

From Macro to Microcontexts

Macrocontextual, ecosystemic approaches focus on gender, ethnicity, and socioeconomic problems; family therapy focuses on family problems. Intermediate, holistic approaches such as existentialism explore life's goals and meaning. At microcontextual levels, cognitive-behavior therapy focuses on specific thoughts or environmental contingencies, while psychiatrists adjust biochemistry. A number of approaches may be found at each contextual level of Fig. 2.3; *e.g.*, postmodern narrative therapies intervene at cognitive or family levels, while postmodern relational approaches have much in common with modern psychodynamic and humanist approaches.

Although the book reverses this order for expositional purposes, treatment planning moves mostly from macrocontext to microcontext levels. Functional impairment determines whether or not clients require biomedical intervention. Thereafter, therapists evaluate ecosystemic, family, or interpersonal contexts, consider the person holistically, and end by analyzing contingencies in the presenting problem's microcontexts. Hypotheses are first developed to address sociocultural processes that precipitate or maintain problems. Family members, social workers, or teachers may be caught in a vicious circle and contribute to relapse if they fail to recognize the client's attempts to change. An ecosystemic focus also minimizes self-blame and invites collaboration by seeking external causes for problems. Clients are less likely to feel judged if problems are described as the result of environmental or historical family processes. Clients are not *held* responsible for their problems, but are expected to *take* responsibility for actively collaborating with treatment. In this dialectic, therapy externalizes responsibility for past problems, but expects clients to take responsibility for changing their current behavior or life situation.

In summary, every therapeutic system must resolve the competing needs of establishing a collaborative working alliance and meeting managed care requirements for diagnosis and treatment plans. Client self-harm and substance abuse risk must also be assessed. Current trends toward non-systematic eclecticism are likely to be replaced with systematic eclectic and integrative approaches as therapists recognize the unifying roles of transtheoretical and common factors. Current treatment approaches vary in focus along a continuum from biomedical to ecosystemic levels. One approach to integration is to plan interventions hierarchically from the macrocontext of ecosystemic interventions to the microcontext of environmental contingencies.

Chapter Two: Main Points

- A dialectic tension exists between needs both to establish a collaborative relationship and to collect diagnostic and treatment planning data. It is desirable to collect as much personal data as possible with questionnaires to minimize a question-and-answer format. Use of open-ended questions encourages client collaboration and allows therapists to observe how clients organize their thinking. Information about factors precipitating and maintaining problems is needed if not already provided.
- Screening for referral appropriateness and preliminary risk assessment is done by telephone before the first meeting. Office arrangements and scheduling need to maximize privacy and confidentially. Before beginning an initial intake, clients are informed about confidentiality and the procedures, risks, and advantages of treatment.
- Mental status examination evaluates whether serious neurological or psychotic problems exist. Semi-structured interviews or questionnaires provide more detailed information, if needed.
- Suicide risk levels determine the least restrictive environment for that client. Hospitalization is indicated when there is extreme risk (all risk factors, no protective factors), and may be necessary, preferably on a voluntary basis, for severe risk. Mild and moderate risk levels are generally managed on an out-patient basis, but with close monitoring and plans are made collaboratively in case risk levels increase. The SLAP procedure screens for risk of suicide or homicide and determines whether more intensive evaluation is needed. SLAP refers to *S*uicidal (homicidal) ideation, *L*ethal method, *A*ccess to method, and having a *P*lan to commit suicide.
- CAGE or FADES procedures assess substance abuse; CAGE refers to *C*utting down, *A*nnoyance at others' criticism, *G*uilt over usage, and *E*ye-openers to start the day.
- Treatment plans begin with a problem list developed collaboratively that groups and prioritizes related problems. Related problems are addressed sequentially in separate treatment phases. Dividing problems into small groups increases clients' confidence that each is doable.
- Outcome is improved by repeated problem measurement to assess client progress. Feedback by the third session either reinforces client efforts or allows the treatment plan to be modified.

- Flow charts help guide treatment planning. Systematic Treatment Selection dimensions include:

    1. *Functional impairment* is a combination of symptomatic *severity* and *discomfort*. Severity determines the location, length, duration, and mode of treatment; discomfort determines whether arousal-induction or reduction is needed.
    2. Acute *symptoms* are best addressed through brief cognitive-behavioral interventions. *Thematic* or long-standing interpersonal problems are best addressed with long-term approaches, such as psychodynamic, interpersonal, or experiential therapies.
    3. Clients who are *resistant* to suggestions respond better to collaborative, non-directive interventions, while compliant clients respond better to directive interventions.
    4. *Coping style* determines what intervention approach may be most helpful with long-term thematic problems. Clients who *externalize* responsibility or *cycle* between acting out and remorse are best helped by the structure of cognitive-behavioral approaches. Clients who *repress*, avoid awareness of threatening feelings, or *internalize* responsibility for problems are helped to explore their inner experience with a psychodynamic or experiential approach.

- The Transtheoretical Method *Stages of Change* dimensions include:

    1. *Precontemplation* stage—consciousness raising and motivational interviewing are needed.
    2. *Contemplation* stage—insight/experiential therapies help clients decide to change.
    3. *Preparation* stage—clients learn necessary skills to apply in next stage.
    4. *Action* stage—active practice and contingency management of new skills.
    5. *Maintenance* stage—relapse management: *e.g.*, lapses are relapses only if one gives up.

- Case conceptualizations focus on environmental, personal, and analytic contexts of the client's problems to decide whether to focus on environmental contingencies or core interpersonal schemas. They also help choose objective or subjective measures to assess client progress.

Further Reading

Beutler, L. E., & Clarkin, J. F. (1990). *Systematic treatment selection: Toward targeted therapeutic Interventions*. New York: Brunner.

Beutler, L. E., Consoli, A. J., & Lane, G. (2005). Systematic treatment selection and prescriptive psychotherapy. In J. C. Norcross & M. R. Goldfried (Eds.), *Handbook of psychotherapy integration* (2nd ed.). New York: Oxford University Press.

Othmer, E., & Othmer, S. C. (1994). *The clinical interview using DSM-IV: Vol. 1: Fundamentals*. Washington: American Psychiatric Press.

Prochaska, J. O., & DiClemente, C. C. (2005). The transtheoretical approach. In J. C. Norcross, & M. R. Goldfried, (Eds.), *Handbook of psychotherapy integration* (2nd ed.). New York: Oxford University Press.

Woody, S. R., Detweiler-Bedell, J., Teachman, B. A., & O'Hearn, T. (2003). *Treatment planning: Taking the guesswork out of clinical care.* New York: Guilford Press.

Chapter 3
Biomedical Approaches to Treatment

The words, mind, spirit, thought, sensibility, volition, life,
designate no entities and no things real, but only properties,
capacities, actions of the living substance, or results of entities,
which are based upon the material form of existence
Ludwig Büchner (*Force and Matter*, 1855/2007)

Are mental and emotional problems simply malfunctions of the body? Are mind and body separate phenomena as ontological dualists suggest? Or are the subjective experiences of the mind simply brain activities as ontological monists such as Büchner suggest? The mind-body dialectic has influenced modern thought in many ways. Most religions believe the mind or soul survives after the body's death. The legal system views the mind in control of the body and, before holding an individual responsible, considers whether an action was intentional. In contrast, many *medical model* theorists adopt the scientific modernist assumption that the mind is nothing more than the sum of its underlying biological processes. They view emotional or cognitive problems as biochemical processes that may be relieved by psychoactive drugs.

While drugs provide rapid relief for serious problems such as psychosis, major depression, or hyperactivity in children, some critics worry about side effects, residual symptoms, and over-prescription (*e.g.*, Marshall, 2000). Keen (1998) believes over-prescription is epidemic, driven by pharmaceutical advertising and the convenience of prescribing pills compared to time-intensive psychotherapies. More fundamentally, recent evidence suggests a circular causal relationship between mind and body; *e.g.*, Vestergaard-Poulsen *et al.* (2009) found that meditation increased gray matter density in the brainstem. Although thoughts are an activity of the brain, those thoughts can create physical alterations in the brain, a recursive, circular process.

Property dualism, which considers mind an *emergent* property of the brain's activity, is one resolution of the mind-body debate: there is just one ontological substance, the brain, but separate objective and subjective epistemologies are required to explain brain activity and the mind's thoughts. Brain activities realize the mind's intentions and goals, but a phenomenological epistemology is required to elucidate what those intentions or goals might be.

D. K. Fromme, *Systems of Psychotherapy*,
DOI 10.1007/978-1-4419-7308-5_3, © Springer Science+Business Media, LLC 2011

In practice, drugs give symptom relief and enable psychosocial interventions with seriously disturbed patients, but do not address life stressors that precipitate those symptoms. Research suggests psychosocial intervention is also needed to address the interpersonal problems that both cause and are affected by symptoms and to prevent relapse (*e.g.*, Hogarty *et al.*, 1991; Michalak & Lam, 2002; Scott, Palmer, Paykel, Teasdale, & Hayhurst, 2003). Drug side effects often increase patient non-compliance and increase relapse rates. Although psychotherapy is slower, it has few side effects and can reduce relapse rates. Integrating drug and psychosocial therapies is generally more effective than either mode separately (Petersen, 2006) and is recognized as the ideal mode of treatment by the Presidential Commission on Mental Health (U.S. Department of Health and Human Services, 2003).

Despite their advantages, integrated biomedical and psychosocial treatment plans are unfortunately not common; *e.g.*, general practitioners treated 86% of clients reporting mental health problems on their own (van Rijswijk, Borghuis, van de Lisdonk, Zitman, & van Weel, 2007). General practitioners typically prescribed antidepressants for depression complaints and benzodiazepines, a class of anxiolytic drugs that are no longer recommended, for anxiety. Few biomedical or psychosocial practitioners receive cross-discipline training, so the lack of collaboration is not surprising. One goal of this chapter is to begin this dialog and introduce psychosocial therapists to basic principles of biomedical intervention.

Dialectics of the Medical and Psychosocial Models

The medical model assumes that biological processes underlie psychological and physical symptoms that reflect specific disease syndromes. Once an appropriate syndrome is identified, empirically supported treatments correct the biological problem. Paul Erlich's 1910 demonstration that Salvarsan 606 (*arsphenamine*—the 606th compound tested) effectively killed the syphilitic spirochete was one of the medical model's greatest successes. Mental hospitals of this time were overloaded with patients with general paresis, a dementia of the last stages of syphilitic infection. Although dementia is irreversible, the drug prevented syphilis from developing to that stage. Salvarsan has been replaced by antibiotic drugs, which have largely eliminated general paresis.

Since then, the medical model has led to important advances in understanding and treating developmental, mood, anxiety, and psychotic disorders. In particular, knowledge about the effects of heredity and biochemistry on mood and behavior has led to a large group of psychoactive drugs. The medical model has also identified problems such as hypothyroidism that present with psychological symptoms. Meehl's (1962) diathesis-stress model of schizophrenia integrates the biomedical and psychosocial models and has proved useful in describing the development of many mental and emotional disorders (*e.g.*, Zuckerman, 1999).

The Diathesis-Stress Dialectic

Meehl (1962) hypothesized that *shizotaxic* genes determine an individual's *schizotype*; *e.g.*, normal, shy, schizoid, or vulnerable to developing *schizophrenia*. This vulnerability or *diathesis* reflects the degree to which schizotaxic genes are expressed in an individual. Meehl proposed that genes alone are insufficient to explain schizophrenia; a stressful environment is also needed to trigger the onset of schizophrenic episodes.

The diathesis-stress hypothesis is now well supported and has been applied to attentional, mood, and anxiety disorders among others (Zuckerman, 1999). The diathesis concept has been expanded to include other sources of vulnerability, such as predisposing personality factors or viral infection during pregnancy. Figure 3.1 illustrates a "dual-pathway" model, which describes how vulnerability for specific disorders can result from genetic combinations that shape both neural systems and personality. Social reinforcers and modeling also influence a person's resiliency and vulnerability to life stressors. The diathesis-stress model suggests that both biomedical and psychosocial interventions may be desirable for many problems.

Fig. 3.1 A dual-pathway diathesis-stress model of psychopathology. (Reprinted from *Vulnerability to psychopathology: A biosocial model*. By M. Zuckerman, p. 19. © 1999 by American Psychological Association. Used with permission.)

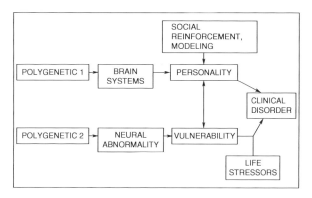

Psychosomatic Illness vs. Medical Illness with Psychological Symptoms

The ontological unity of body and mind is reflected in somatoform disorders (mind affects body) and a host of medical conditions with psychological symptoms (body affects mind). Table 3.1 presents some of the psychological symptoms that can disguise various underlying medical conditions and interfere with proper treatment if not diagnosed correctly. Conversely, somatoform disorders may reflect psychological problems primarily, but present with a wide range of physical symptoms, including pain, amnesia, paralysis, and sensory deficits such as blindness or deafness. Stress, unrealistic anxiety, and catastrophic interpretations of physical sensations are implicated in the development of somatoform symptoms (Mang, Weiss, & Schalke, 1993).

Table 3.1 Psychological symptoms that may appear in various medical conditions

Psychological symptom	Medical conditions sometimes associated with symptom
Depression	Adrenal Insufficiency; AIDS; Brain Tumor; Cancer; Cerebrovascular Stroke; Congestive Heart Failure; Cushing's Syndrome; Diabetes Mellitus; Epilepsy; Fibromyalgia; Hyperparathyroidism; Hyperthyroidism; Hypothyroidism; Kidney Failure; Klinefelter's Syndrome; Liver Failure; Lupus Erythematosus; Lyme Disease; Menier's Syndrome; Menopause; Migraine; Multiple Sclerosis; Obstructive Lung Disease; Parkinson's Disease; Pernicious Anemia; Post-Operative State; Premenstrual Syndrome; Rheumatoid Arthritis; Sickle-Cell Anemia; Sleep Apnea; Systemic Infection
Anxiety	Adrenal Insufficiency; AIDS; Cardiac Arrhythmia; Congestive Heart Failure; Cushing's Syndrome; Hyperparathyroidism; Hyperthyroidism; Lyme Disease; Menier's Syndrome; Menopause; Migraine; Myasthenia Gravis; Obstructive Lung Disease; Parkinson's Disease; Pneumonia; Post-Operative State; Premenstrual Syndrome; Pulmonary Blood Clot; Thiamine Deficiency
Irritability	Antidiuretic Syndrome; Cryptococcosis; Liver Failure; Menopause; Migraine; Pernicious Anemia; Premenstrual Syndrome; Sleep Apnea
Panic attacks	Congestive Heart Failure; Diabetes Mellitus; Hyperthyroidism; Menier's Syndrome; Mitral Valve Prolapse; Obstructive Lung Disease; Pneumonia
Agitation; Mania	Cerebrovascular Stroke; Hyperthyroidism; Multiple Sclerosis
Psychosis	Adrenal Insufficiency; AIDS; Antidiuretic Syndrome; Brain Tumor; Cryptococcosis; Cushing's Syndrome; Head Trauma; Hyperparathyroidism; Klinefelter's Syndrome; Lupus Erythematosus; Protein Malnutrition
Delirium	AIDS; Antidiuretic Syndrome; Brain Tumor; Cancer; Cardiac Arrhythmia; Congestive Heart Failure; Cryptococcosis; Cushing's Syndrome; Diabetes Mellitus; Head Trauma; Hypertensive Emergency; Hyperthyroidism; Liver Failure; Lupus Erythematosus; Obstructive Lung Disease; Pneumonia; Post-Operative State; Pulmonary Blood Clot; Systemic Infection; Thiamine Deficiency
Cognitive symptoms	Cerebrovascular Stroke; Cryptococcosis; Head Trauma; Hypothyroidism; Lyme Disease; Menier's Syndrome; Multiple Sclerosis; Myasthenia Gravis; Pernicious Anemia; Thiamine Deficiency
Personality change	Brain Tumor; Cerebrovascular Stroke; Hyperparathyroidism
Dementia	AIDS; Cerebrovascular Stroke; Hypothyroidism; Lupus Erythematosus; Neurocutaneous Disorder; Obstructive Lung Disease; Parkinson's Disease

Medical consultation is recommended to determine if somatoform symptoms reflect a medical disorder or compromised immune system (Irwin, 2008). Psychosocial interventions can alleviate symptoms that have no biological basis as in conversion reaction and stressors that compromise the immune system. Clarke's (2007) *They can't find anything wrong!* may help clients who resist psychosocial explanations for somatic complaints. Clients may also be encouraged to focus on symptom relief while awaiting a "permanent" medical cure. In general, therapists should be cautious in treating physical symptoms with psychosocial interventions and be ready to make a medical referral.

Psychopharmacology: A Conceptual Framework

Psychoactive drugs are the principal intervention used by psychiatrists and psychiatric nurse practitioners. However, primary care practitioners, who may have only 4–8 weeks of training in psychiatry, prescribe 60–83% of psychoactive drugs (LaVoie & Barone, 2006). Psychologists are now licensed in New Mexico and Louisiana and are seeking prescription privileges elsewhere to address shortages of psychiatrists and prescribing nurse practitioners. Since psychiatrists typically have only 10–15 minutes with a patient, the psychologist's 50-minute hour creates opportunities to combine biomedical and psychosocial interventions. Psychologists have time to evaluate side effects and medication efficacy, but may lack the necessary medical training. Some worry that the economic pressures that limit psychiatric practice could also limit the time psychologists have for psychosocial interventions. In lieu of practitioners with both skill sets, it is essential that both biomedical and psychosocial therapists have sufficient knowledge of each other's discipline to be able to communicate effectively and collaborate in planning interventions. The following sections provide an introduction to biomedical interventions and are intended to encourage psychosocial practitioners to continue to acquire the knowledge to communicate effectively with physicians.

Neurons and Synaptic Transmission

The diathesis-stress hypothesis helps integrate psychosocial and biomedical interventions by viewing psychological problems on a continuum rather than as a disease that is either present or absent; *e.g.*, vulnerability to schizophrenia is caused by combinations of genes that vary in the extent they are expressed in an individual. Other factors such as a viral infection during pregnancy may also contribute to the diathesis. As a result, the stress levels needed to precipitate a schizophrenic episode may be very low for some people and very high for others. Genetic vulnerabilities for psychological problems are expressed by neurohormonal dysregulation at neuronal synapses. Stress can then destabilize the regulation of neurohormones, cause emotional responses that exacerbate stress levels, and initiate a vicious circle that causes still further neurohormonal dysregulation. Psychoactive drugs help regulate synaptic processes and maintain neuronal health, while psychosocial interventions help alleviate the stressors that contribute to this vicious circle (Julien, Advocat, & Comaty, 2008).

Psychoactive drugs affect neurohormonal regulation of the transmission of electrochemical impulses across the neuronal synapse. Neurons have three main parts:

1. *Dendrites*—receive impulses from other neurons;
2. *Soma*—contains the DNA nucleus and the mitochondria that provide the cell's energy;
3. *Axons*—transmit impulses to subsequent neurons; longer axons have fatty *myelin sheaths*, which act as insulators and increase neural transmission speed.

Each neuron has hundreds of dendritic branches forming several thousand synapses with other neurons. With an average 10^{11} neurons in the adult brain, there are more than 10^{14} synapses. The number of possible interconnections among those 10^{14} synapses exceeds the estimated number of atoms in the universe, suggesting the brain has a good "reserve" capacity (Thompson, 1993).

Electrochemical neural impulses are measured in milliseconds compared to nanoseconds (one billionth second) for electricity in wires. Chemical processes that regulate the neuron's *action potential* or electrochemical impulse cause this reduction in speed. During a neuron's *resting potential*, the axon's interior is negatively charged and the synaptic space is positively charged. The neuron's resting potential or *polarity* is maintained by a semi-permeable membrane. Neurohormones control neuronal firing or *depolarization* by modulating the size of *ion channels* (axonal permeability) to either allow or prevent positive ions from entering the neuron and binding on *ionotropic receptors* (sites that attract ions). Stimulation causes momentary enlargement of ion channels in the axon, which allows sodium (Na+) ions to enter, *depolarizing* the resting potential, and moving the action potential along the neuron. Next, calcium (Ca^{2+}) ion channels open in the pre-synaptic end bulbs of the neuron and trigger release of *neurotransmitters* in the synaptic cleft. Figure 3.2 illustrates how a neuron, triggered by other neurons or sensory receptors, releases neurotransmitters that bind on the post-synaptic neuron's dendrite or cell body receptor sites. The neurotransmitters then affect the permeability of the post-synaptic neuron allowing Na+ ions to flow in, causing depolarization and onward transmission of action potentials.

During a *refractory period* in which the neuron is unable to fire, Na+ ions are pumped out of the neuron in exchange for potassium (K+) ions and various enzymes break down and recycle neurotransmitter hormones at the synapse. While ionotropic receptors respond quickly, *metabotropic* receptors work more slowly to regulate the overall rate of neuronal firing. Since neurons spontaneously fire all the time, stimulating a post-synaptic neuron only increases its *rate* of firing. If more *excitatory* than *inhibitory* synapses are stimulated, an *excitatory threshold* is passed and the neuron fires in an "all-or-none" fashion to transmit an incoming action potential onward. This is the nervous system's first level of interpreting the environment: the action potential is reached and depolarizes the neuron only if multiple neuronal networks stimulate hundreds of dendritic branches.

Fig. 3.2 Synaptic transmission. (Wikipedia, n.d.; retrieved 12/14/2009)

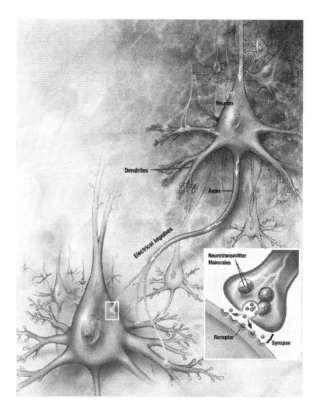

Pharmacokinetics

Pharmacokinetics describes how psychoactive drugs are processed, determining the level of psychoactive drugs in the bloodstream at any time. Drugs influence neurotransmitters through four pharmokinetic processes (Julien *et al.*, 2008):

1. *Absorption*—The method used to administer drugs affects their absorption in the blood stream.

    (a) *Oral*: intestinal mucosa absorb up to 75% of drug in 1–3 hours; only lipid (fat) soluble drugs pass brain barrier; convenient, slow action with time to correct if needed. But absorption rates are unpredictable; stomach acids destroy some of the drug, and may cause nausea.

    (b) *Rectal*: suppositories useful if patient is unable to swallow, unconscious, or vomiting; may irritate rectal membrane, and absorption rates are unpredictable.

    (c) *Skin absorption*: slow, predictable drug release with transdermal patches; useful for nicotine, angina, pain control, or hormones, but can irritate the skin.

    (d) *Injection*: provides precise dosages with rapid absorption in emergencies, but requires sterile conditions with risk for infections and little time to correct an unexpected reaction.

(e) *Inhaled*: rapid absorption in the lungs and transmission to the brain with intense effects, but subject to abuse; *e.g.*, "Laughing Gas" (Nitrous Oxide).

(f) *Mucous membrane*: rapid rate of absorption in nasal or oral mucosa; Lollipops are popular for treating addictions, but subject to abuse such as snorting crack or cocaine.

2. *Distribution*—Once absorbed, psychoactive drugs disperse in the bloodstream in minutes, but only small amounts contact appropriate receptor sites at any point in time. Distribution can be affected by the permeability of cell membranes, capillary walls, the placental barrier, or the blood-brain barrier where only small, lipid-soluble molecules can pass; *e.g.*, treatment of strokes, Alzheimer's, or other brain disorders hinges on finding ways around the blood-brain barrier that prevents passage of large, lipid-insoluble drugs. (Pardridge, 2003).

3. *Metabolism*—Drugs break down into *metabolites* that can have other effects or into waste products. Lipid-soluble, psychoactive drugs are usually broken down by enzymes in the liver.

4. *Elimination*—Metabolic waste-products are eliminated by the kidneys, lungs (alcohol breath), skin, and bile, with the largest amount eliminated in urine.

Prescribed dosages are generally poor indicators of bloodstream levels, especially for oral administration, since absorption, metabolic, and elimination rates vary widely from one person to the next. As a result, close monitoring of drug levels is needed. Once in the brain, metabolic and elimination rates determine a drug's *half-life*, the time required for drug levels in the bloodstream to drop by half (Julien *et al.*, 2008). A drug's half-life predicts the optimal dosage to maintain a steady-state plasma level, fluctuating in proportion to the drug's half-life and dosage intervals. A steady state is reached after about six half-lives, which is also the time needed for 98.4% of a drug to be eliminated and have no further effects after withdrawal. An optimal dosage ensures a therapeutic response without risking a toxic overdose.

Pharmacodynamics

"It is a basic principle of pharmacology that the pharmacological, physiological, or behavioral effects induced by a drug follow from their interaction with receptors" (Julien *et al.*, 2008, p. 38). *Agonist* drugs facilitate and *antagonist* drugs inhibit neurotransmitter actions. *Partial agonists* reduce risk of overstimulation by not producing maximal effects at post-synaptic receptor sites.

Psychoactive drugs affect neural synapses in one of three ways:

1. Their molecular shape and ionic charge mimics a neurotransmitter;
2. Increasing neurotransmitter levels by inhibiting reuptake into the neuron after depolarization;
3. Increasing or decreasing enzymes that metabolize the neurotransmitter.

For example, monoamine oxidase is an enzyme that breaks down norepinephrine and dopamine, but monoamine oxidase inhibitors (MAOIs) inhibit this action. As fewer neurotransmitters are metabolized, more are available at the neural synapse, which creates an antidepressant effect.

Dosage-response curves illustrate the effect of increasing dosages up to a drug's maximal *efficacy*. Figure 3.3 describes the increase in percentage of people with therapeutic and toxic responses for increasing blood plasma drug levels. A drug's *potency*, the amount needed to create a particular effect, is indicated by its position on the horizontal axis. The area in Fig. 3.3 labeled "therapeutic window" indicates dosage levels that maximize therapeutic effects, while minimizing toxic effects. Curves with steep slopes attain maximal efficacy with only a small dosage increase. When patient responses are averaged, slope *variability* describes individual differences in absorption, metabolism, and elimination of the drug. Dashed lines indicate the point at which 50% of experimental animals show a therapeutic effect (ED_{50}) or a lethal effect (LD_{50}). The right edge of Fig. 3.3's "therapeutic window" indicates the dosage level at which 99% of the experimental animals have a therapeutic response and 1% have a lethal response.

Fig. 3.3 Theoretical therapeutic and toxic dose response curves

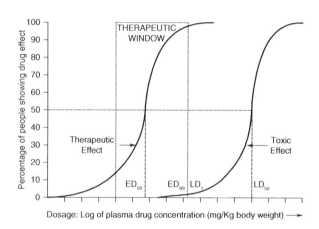

Julien *et al.* (2008) describe other considerations in deciding on appropriate dosage levels:

1. Side effects—may be expected, such as the sedative effects of tranquilizers, or unexpected, such as allergic reactions by sensitive individuals.
2. Drug interactions—may be additive as with alcohol, marijuana, and methamphetamine impairment of driving ability, or may influence metabolic rates of other drugs: *e.g.*, Tegretol (*carbamazepine*), an anticonvulsant, stimulates enzymes that break down many Selective Serotonin Reuptake Inhibitors (SSRIs), reducing their efficacy (*cross-tolerance*). On the other hand, Prozac (*fluoxetine*) inhibits enzymes, which increases the toxicity of a number of drugs including certain other antidepressant, antiasthmatic, antipsychotic drugs, or heart medications. Some of these effects could be lethal.

3. Tolerance—three processes can affect the efficacy of a drug:

   (a) *Metabolic tolerance*—some drugs increase hepatic (liver) metabolism, which reduces the drug's half-life and requires increased dosages to achieve the same effect;

   (b) *Cellular-adaptive tolerance*—homeostatic adaptation of neurons to high drug levels by reducing the number or sensitivity of available receptor sites;

   (c) *Behavioral conditioning*—environmental cues associated with drug administration elicit responses that mimic the drug's direct effects.

4. Dependence—typically accompanies tolerance; the drug is needed to prevent withdrawal symptoms. It is common in drugs of abuse, but also in therapeutic drugs such as SSRIs. Physical dependence is caused by homeostatic mechanisms that compensate for high levels of the drug; *e.g.*, by reducing related endogenous hormones.

Drugs that mimic endogenous neurotransmitters vary in potency as a function of how close their shape is to the receptor site; *e.g.*, methamphetamines are more potent than amphetamines because their shape is closer to that of norepinephrine and dopamine. Careful monitoring of drug use is essential given the variability in absorbing and metabolizing drugs, drug interactions or toxicity, and the potential for side effects and patient non-compliance.

The placebo response is a significant reminder of the mind-body relationship. Placebos such as touching, talking, or sugar pills have been shown to contribute as much as half of a drug's observed efficacy. Walsh, Seidman, Sysko, and Gould's (2002) review of 75 randomized studies found 22% of patients responding positively to placebos compared to 50% on antidepressants. They also found that placebo effects are growing as much as 7% each decade, which may reflect society's increasing belief in the efficacy of antidepressants.

Neurotransmitters

Table 3.2 describes central nervous system (CNS) neurotransmitters, problems that can occur, and psychoactive drugs developed to counteract those problems. Neurotransmitters act upon related neural pathways: acetylcholine on cholinergic pathways; dopamine on dopaminergic; serotonin on serotonergic, *etc.* Neurotransmitters may also modulate effects on other pathways or serve as metabolic precursors: *e.g.*, the neurotransmitter GABA inhibits glutamate receptors, while the enzyme *dopamine β-hydroxylase* converts dopamine into norepinephrine.

In addition to direct effects on related, neural pathway receptor sites, neurotransmitters are affected by a number of indirect effects:

• Dopamine is a metabolic precursor of norepinephrine.
• Neurotransmitters may affect pre-synaptic and post-synaptic receptor sites differently.

- Some affect neurotransmitter reabsorption or the availability of other neurotransmitters.
- Enzymes break down neurotransmitters, affecting their availability at the synapse.

Table 3.2 Neurotransmitter, CNS functions, CNS problems, and psychoactive drug treatments

Neurotransmitter	CNS functions	CNS problems	Drug treatments
Acetylcholine (ACl)	Learning, memory, and mood	Alzheimer's disease	*Donepezil HCl* (Aricept): cholinesterase inhibitor
Glutamate (Amino Acid)	Excitatory: Learning and memory	Seizures; mania; Alzheimer's disease; dementia	Lamotrigine inhibits toxic neuron excitation
Gamma amino-butyric acid (GABA-Amino)	Inhibits Glutamate: Cl ions into cell; Na+ out	Alcohol, tranquilizers are agonists → abuse; mania; epilepsy	Anxiolytics (antagonist): seizure; Valproate→mania
Norepinephrine (NE) (Catecholamine)	Excitatory: Mediates autonomic arousal	Stress hormone and anxiety; Low levels→depression	Tricyclics: NE agonists; anxiolytics: NE antagonists
Dopamine (Catecholamine)	Motor coordination; reward system; mood	Schizophrenia; drug addiction; Parkinson's disease	Clonidine (agonist); Antipsychotics (antagonist)
Serotonin (Indolamine)	Arousal, sleep and mood regulation	Depression; sleep; hallucinations; migraine; psychedelic drugs	Antidepressants: Tricyclics, SSRIs
Histamine	Sleep regulation; Immune system	Low in schizophrenic patients; vertigo; high in allergies	Antihistamines (antagonist); Betahistine HCl for vertigo

Various mechanisms maintain synaptic activity within functional levels by either up-regulating or down-regulating neurotransmitter levels:

- Pre-synaptic *autoreceptors* sense neurotransmitter levels and stimulate reuptake as needed.
- Unusually high or low levels change the number and sensitivity of post-synaptic receptor sites.
- *Glial* cells absorb excess levels for later release and prevent synapses activating one another.

Some psychoactive drugs are *agonists* that increase neurotransmitter availability by blocking reuptake of neurotransmitters into the pre-synaptic neuron or inhibiting enzymes that metabolize neurotransmitters. Other drugs are *antagonists* that compete with a neurotransmitter by blocking post-synaptic receptor sites. While knowledge of how neurotransmitters modulate each other's effects is rapidly growing, the ways their interactions affect behavior are still understood in only the most general terms. On the positive side, a number of psychoactive drugs have recently been developed that affect only specific enzymes or subsets of receptor sites, rather than indiscriminate effects on all of them; *e.g.*, Prozac increases serotonin levels only at 5-HT receptor sites and has fewer side effects than earlier classes of antidepressant drugs. By acting only on specific receptor sites, such drugs have fewer unintended effects.

Pharmacotherapy

During the past 50 years, psychoactive drugs have improved the quality of life for millions of people incapacitated by mental illness. They are especially useful for treating schizophrenia and severe mood disorders. This success sometimes leads to their overuse, but often they are still underused. They may be overused as short-term treatment of problems that respond better to psychotherapy or to combined interventions (LeFever, Arcona, & Antonuccio, 2003). At the same time, the Surgeon General reports that nearly two-thirds of people with diagnosable disorders fail to seek treatment even though 75% would benefit. Also, treatment of Hispanic- and African-Americans is half the rate for European-Americans (U.S. Department of Health and Human Services, 1999). Frank, Weihs, Minerva, and Lieberman's (1998) survey found that:

1. 20% of the population has a mental disorder in any one year;
2. Mental illness ranks second only to heart disease in the burden it creates for society;
3. One-third of patients seen by general practitioners have undiagnosed disorders, with 75% either anxiety or mood disorders.

Gilbody, Bower, Fletcher, Richards, and Sutton's (2006) meta-analysis of 37 studies covering 12,355 patients diagnosed with depression confirmed the value of collaborative care among case managers, physicians, and mental health professionals. Both short-term and long-term outcomes improved when compared to usual primary care. In the absence of a case manager, psychosocial therapists can provide useful case management by following steps outlined by Julien *et al.* (2008):

1. Take a medication history and monitor current drugs, reason they are taken, side effects, and compliance.
2. Determine if patients are non-compliant with medication due to its cost.
3. Determine if patients are non-compliant due to concerns about weight gain.
4. Determine if patients experience cognitive dysfunction, which may cause non-compliance or confusion that mimics dementia or delirium especially in young or elderly patients.
5. Communicate concerns and suggestions to the prescribing physician.

Side effects for each drug class are noted below in the various tables of psychoactive drugs.

Antidepressants

Treatment of anxiety and depression has evolved with the development of new drugs (Julien *et al.*, 2008):

1960s—anxiolytics are used to treat anxiety and antidepressants for depressive symptoms;

1970s–1980s—anxiolytics treat generalized anxiety, antidepressants treat depression, but specific anxiety disorders may be treated with either class of drug;

1990s—anxiolytics treat generalized anxiety, but antidepressants treat both depression and specific anxiety disorders;

2000s—antidepressants are now "first-line" treatments for all three classes of problems.

Although anxiety and depression have long been viewed separately, they are often comorbid and have significant symptom overlap. Both depressed and anxious patients make global, stable, and internalized attributions about the causes of negative events (Katerndahl, 2005). Anxious patients feel *helpless* to control outcomes, while depressed patients feel *hopeless* that a positive outcome is even possible (*e.g.*, Alloy, Kelly, Mineka, & Clements, 1990; Wise & Rosqvist, 2006).

Because *benzodiazepines*, an early anxiolytic drug class, increase synaptic levels of GABA, early thinking linked anxiety to GABA deficiencies in cortico-limbic neural receptors. Depression was linked to deficiencies in the monoamine neurotransmitters, serotonin and norepinephrine, since antidepressants increased their availability at cortico-hippocampal synapses. Currently, a diathesis-stress model is favored in which stress affects cortico-hippocampal neuronal health as well as neurotransmitter levels (Duman, Heninger, & Nestler, 1997). Stress decreases the *brain-derived neurotropic factors* (BDNF) that help maintain neuronal health. Antidepressant drugs and electroconvulsive therapy appear to increase both monoamine and BDNF levels (Sheldon, 2000). Sairanen, Lucas, Ernfors, Castrén, and Castrén (2005) suggest that BDNF induces *neurogenesis* of new hippocampal neurons over a period of 2–3 weeks. This model provides one explanation for the gap after treatment with antidepressants between increased levels of synaptic monoamines, which occur within hours and observed changes in mood, which takes 2–3 weeks.

The efficacy of antidepressants has recently been questioned. Turner, Matthews, Linardatos, Tell, and Rosenthal (2008) found a reporting bias in 74 outcome studies: while 94% of published studies reported positive results, when unreported studies were included in a new meta-analysis only 51% showed small to moderate positive effect sizes. Kirsch, Moore, Scoboria, and Nicholls (2002) found only a slight advantage for six widely used antidepressants when compared to placebo control groups. However, these results may reflect the restricted range of subjects found in most efficacy studies; *e.g.*, Kirsch *et al.* (2008) found greater improvement with drugs compared to placebos for subjects with more severe levels of initial depression.

Sequenced Treatment Alternatives to Relieve Depression (STAR-D; Gilmer & Kemp, 2006; Insel, 2008) is a promising effectiveness research program that resembles actual clinical practice, with patients trying different antidepressants until one is found that helps or is better tolerated. After 12 weeks of the first antidepressant, only 30% of depressed patients were in remission and over half were unable to tolerate side effects. When given alternatives, from 18 to 39% non-responders achieved remission. Even more were helped when further alternatives were tried.

Table 3.3 Antidepressant drugs. (Adapted from *A primer of drug action*, 11th ed., pp. 206–207; 432–433. By R. M. Julien, C. D. Advokat, & J. E. Comaty. © 2008 by Worth Publishers. Used with permission.)

Drug name: generic (trade)	Usual daily dosage range (in mg)	Elimination half-life (hrs.)	Anticholinergic activity[a]	Sedation	Cognitive impairment	Weight gain	Generic available (Yes/No)
Tricyclic compounds							
Imipramine (Tofranil)	150–300	10–20	Moderate	Moderate	Moderate	0–Low	Yes
Desipramine (Norpramin)	150–300	12–75	Low	Low	Moderate	0–Low	Yes
Trimipramine (Surmontil)	100–300	8–20	Moderate	High	Moderate	0–Low	Yes
Protriptyline (Vivactil)	15–40	55–125	Low	Moderate	Moderate	0–Low	Yes
Nortriptyline (Aventil, Pamelor)	75–125	15–35	Moderate	Low	Low	0–Low	Yes
Amitryptilne (Elavil)	100–300	20–35	High	High	Moderate	0–Low	Yes
Doxepin (Sinequan, Adapin)	150–300	8–24	High	High	Moderate	0–Low	Yes
Clomim-pramine (Anafranil)	150–250	19–37	Low	Low	Moderate	0–Low	Yes
Second generation: atypicals							
Amoxapine (Asendin)[b]	150–400	8–10	Low	Moderate	Low	0–Low	Yes
Maprotiline (Ludiomil)	150–225	27–58	Moderate	High	Low	0–Low	Yes
Trazadone (Desyrel)	150–400	6–13	Moderate	Low	Low–Mod.	0–Low	Yes
Buproprion-XR[c] (Wellbutrin-XR[c])	150–400	8–14	Low	Low	0	0	Yes
Venlafaxine-XR[c] (Effexor-XR[c])	75–350	3–11	None	Low	Low	0	Yes
Selective serotonin reuptake inhibitors							
Fluoxetine (Prozac)	20–80	4–96	None	Low	0–Low	Low	Yes
Sertaline (Zoloft)	50–200	26	None	Low	0	Low	Yes
Paroxetine (Paxil)	20–50	24	None	Low	0	Low	Yes
Citalopram (Celexa)	10–60	33	None	Low	0	Low	Yes
Fluvoxamine (Luvox)	50–300	15	None	Low	0	Low	Yes
Escitalopram (Lexapro)	5–20	2–5	None	Low	0	Low	Yes

Table 3.3 (continued)

Drug name: generic (trade)	Usual daily dosage range (in mg)	Elimination half-life (hrs.)	Anticholinergic activity[a]	Sedation	Cognitive impairment	Weight gain	Generic available (Yes/No)
Dual-action antidepressants							
Mirtazapine (Remeron)	15–45	20–40	High	Low	Low	Low-Mod.	Yes
Duloxetine (Cymbalta)	20–80	11–16	Low	Low	0	0	No
MAO inhibitors: irreversible							
Phenelzine (Nardil)	30–90	2–4[d]	None	Low	Low	0	Yes
Tranylcypromine (Parnate)	20–60	1–3[d]	None	Low	Low	0	Yes
Selegiline Patch (Emsam)	6–12	18–25	None	Low	Low	0	No
Selective norepinephrine reuptake inhibitor							
Atomoxetine (Strattera)	60–120	5	None	Low	Low	0	No

[a] Anticholinergic side effects include dry mouth, blurred vision, tachycardia, urinary retention, and constipation
[b] Also has antipsychotic effects due to blockage of dopamine receptors
[c] Available in standard formulation (XR) and time-release (XL); Prozac available in 90-mg time-release weekly dosage
[d] Half-life does not correlate with clinical effect

Tricyclic Antidepressants (TCAs)

The overall efficacy of different antidepressant classes is about the same, but some patients respond better to one class of drug than to others. Patient response, side effects, and cost typically determine which drug class is chosen for a particular patient (See Table 3.3). TCAs were developed first and are available in much less costly generic forms than other types of antidepressant. *Imipramine* was the first and is often used in comparing the relative efficacy of new drugs. TCAs have four different effects:

1. They block the pre-synaptic norepinephrine reuptake transporter.
2. They block the pre-synaptic serotonin reuptake transporter.
3. They block post-synaptic histamine receptors.
4. They block post-synaptic acetylcholine receptors (Julien *et al.*, 2008, p. 208).

The first two effects are antidepressant, but the latter two result in unwanted side effects. Although many patients develop tolerance for antihistamine and anticholinergic effects, TCAs can impair attention, motor speed, dexterity, and memory functions especially in children and the elderly. Antihistamine and anticholinergic effects include drowsiness, confusion, blurred vision, dry mouth, urinary retention, and increased heart rate. The sedative side effects may prove beneficial for patients with an agitated depression or who have impaired sleep. TCAs are usually taken just before bedtime in view of their sedative and cognitive effects. High TCA dosages may affect cardiac function lethally, a consideration if suicidal ideation is present. To minimize the risk of toxic overdose, only limited supplies of TCAs are usually prescribed.

TCAs improve mood, physical activity, appetite, and sleep patterns in depressed patients, while reducing morbid ruminations. They help about one-third of patients who fail to respond to other antidepressants. Their analgesic properties are useful in treating chronic pain disorders, including migraine, neuropathic pain from shingles or diabetes, low back pain, and chronic fatigue. Although TCAs cross the placental barrier, there is no evidence they harm the fetus. They are also not a risk for substance abuse since they have no euphoric effect on non-depressed individuals. Their main disadvantages are the potential for lethal overdoses and side effects that are not as well tolerated as those of other antidepressant drug classes.

Monoamine Oxidase Inhibitors (MAOIs)

As the title suggests, MAOIs inhibit enzymes that break down the monoamines, norepinephrine and serotonin. They also inhibit the breakdown of dopamine, which can have potentially fatal interactions with adrenalin-like drugs (nasal sprays or cold-medicines) or foods with *tyramine* (many cheeses, wines, beer, liver and some beans). MAOIs have fallen out of favor even though careful dietary monitoring can minimize this risk and they lack the anticholinergic and antihistamine side effects of TCAs. *Selegiline* (Eldapril), a new, slow-release transdermal patch, eliminates dangerous drug interactions and has led to renewed interest in MAOIs, especially for treatment-resistant depression. MAOIs may help elderly, treatment-resistant patients, patients with atypical or masked depression, or with anxiety, panic, hypochondria, anorexia, bulimia, dysthymia, or bipolar symptoms (Julien *et al.*, 2008).

Atypical Antidepressants

Atypical antidepressants have molecular structures similar to TCAs, but have less sedative and anticholinergic effects. *Amoxapine* has a tetracyclic structure that strongly inhibits reuptake of norepinephrine, while weakly inhibiting reuptake of serotonin. It is used for anxious or agitated depression, but requires close monitoring since it also blocks post-synaptic dopamine receptors causing Parkinsonian tremors and risk for lethal overdoses. *Trazadone's* (Desyrel) unique chemical structure acts more quickly than other antidepressants, taking 2–5 weeks to achieve its maximal effect. It has fewer anticholinergic side effects than TCAs and is less likely to be lethal in overdose. Prolonged painful penile erection, *priapism*, is a possible side effect that causes impotence and infertility if not treated promptly. Why *trazadone* works is unknown as it has only a slight effect on norepinephrine or serotonin reuptake. It is used mostly to aid sleep since drowsiness is its most common side effect.

Buproprion (Wellbutrin) blocks reuptake of dopamine and norepinephrine, but not serotonin. It has both antidepressant and anticraving effects and is used for nicotine dependence. Combined with SSRIs, it augments antidepressant effects. Some patients are helped since it may reduce sexual side effects and help them lose weight. It is used with bipolar depression and is less likely to induce manic episodes at high dosage levels than other atypicals. It sometimes helps attention deficit hyperactivity disorder (ADHD), but side effects may include anxiety, tremor, restlessness, insomnia, panic, seizures, or psychosis.

Clomipramine (Anafranil) is a *mixed serotonin-norepinephrine reuptake inhibitor*, effective with panic and phobic disorders and 40–75% of OCD patients. Its structure and side effects are similar to TCAs and so is not as well tolerated as other antidepressants. *Venlafaxine* (Effexor) is also a *mixed serotonin-norepinephrine reuptake inhibitor* with a minor dopamine reuptake effect. It has a favorable side effect and drug interaction profile, has analgesic properties, and can be useful in treating major depression or chronic pain with comorbid anxiety and depression. Care should be taken for patients at risk for bipolar depression, as it may precipitate a manic reaction.

Selective Serotonin Reuptake Inhibitors (SSRIs)

SSRIs selectively block serotonin reuptake at pre-synaptic sites, but do not affect post-synaptic sites or other neurotransmitters. As a result, SSRIs lack the sedative and anticholinergic side effects of TCAs. SSRIs inhibit serotonin reuptake at three different receptor sites: $5\text{-}HT_1$, $5\text{-}HT_2$, and $5\text{-}HT_3$. Antidepressant effects are associated with action at the $5\text{-}HT_1$ site, but $5\text{-}HT_2$ activation causes anxiety, insomnia, agitation, and sexual dysfunction, and $5\text{-}HT_3$ activation causes nausea.

SSRIs have four potentially problematic side effects (Julien *et al.*, 2008):

1. Sexual dysfunction—80% of patients have orgasm, erection, desire, and/or arousal problems.
2. Serotonin syndrome (Lane & Baldwin, 1997)—high dosage or interaction with serotonergic drugs may cause cognitive (confusion, hypomania), autonomic (tachycardia, hypertension, fever, chills, diarrhea, sweating), behavioral (agitation, restlessness), and neuromuscular symptoms (myoclonic muscle twitches, ataxia, increased reflexes). Visual hallucinations have been reported. This syndrome is sometimes confused with bipolar or brain damage disorders.
3. Serotonin withdrawal syndrome (Schatzberg *et al.*, 1997)—withdrawal symptoms often occur a few days after stopping medication, persist for several weeks, and can include psychological (anxiety, agitation, irritability) and somatic symptoms including:

    (a) Disequilibria (dizziness, vertigo, ataxia)
    (b) Gastrointestinal symptoms (nausea, vomiting, diarrhea)
    (c) Flu-like symptoms (fatigue, chills, aches and pains)
    (d) Sensory disturbances (parethesia, sensation of electric shock)
    (e) Sleep disturbances (insomnia, vivid dreams)

4. Pregnancy and breast-feeding—effects are unclear, but ingestion in late pregnancy can cause serotonin withdrawal symptoms in newborns; breast-feeding leads to non-problematic SSRI levels in infants (1–3% of maternal levels), but SSRIs are indicated for post-partum depression.

SSRIs are desirable because overdoses are not fatal and side effects are usually tolerated, which leads to better compliance by patients than those taking TCAs. SSRIs are recommended for anxiety disorders as well as depression. Patients need to stay on SSRIs at least 2 months, since symptoms may take 4–6 weeks to improve. Among popular SSRIs, *Fluoxetine* (Prozac) may be combined with the antipsychotic *olanzapine* to treat bipolar depressive episodes. *Sertraline* (Zoloft) and *paroxetine* (Paxil, Pexeva) are effective in treating anxiety disorders, but have greater risk for serotonergic side effects. *Citalopram* (Celexa) appears to have a slightly quicker onset than other SSRIs and may help moderate alcohol use, but large doses may induce cardiac irregularities, seizures, and (rarely) death.

Dual-Action Antidepressants

These drugs inhibit reuptake of both norepinephrine and serotonin, while minimizing serotonergic side effects. *Mirtazepine* (Remeron) is effective with depression, anxiety, somatization, and insomnia. It releases serotonin pre-synaptically and blockades histamine, 5-HT$_2$, and 5-HT$_3$ receptor sites, minimizing SSRI-related side effects. It should not be combined with CNS depressants or alcohol due to drowsiness side effects. Increased appetite and weight gain are also side effects. *Duloxetine* (Cymbalta) also blockades 5-HT$_2$ and 5-HT$_3$ sites, but not histamine receptors. The result is an effective antidepressant with moderate side effects. It is also effective with anxiety and chronic pain. *Milnacipran* (Savella) has a similar profile, but may have a quicker antidepressant effect. Both *duloxetine* and *milnacipran* are effective in the treatment of fibromyalgia. Serotonin reuptake inhibition helps depression, while inhibition of norepinephrine reuptake most likely helps chronic pain.

Other Antidepressant Interventions

Recent antidepressants include *atomoxine* (Strattera) and *reboxetine* (Vestra, Edronax), which are Selective Norepinephrine Reuptake Inhibitors (SNRIs). By acting primarily in the prefrontal cortex, they avoid the potential for abuse of CNS stimulants. Research suggests *atomoxine* is also effective with ADHD, while *reboxetine* is useful for treating patients with seasonal affective disorder, panic disorder, and to control the weight gain side effects of certain antipsychotic drugs.

In Pagnin, de Queiroz, Piini, and Cassano's (2004) meta-analysis of 13 studies, Electro-Convulsive Therapy (ECT) proved more effective than antidepressants (79% *vs.* 54% patients improved). From 6 to 12 ECT treatments over 3–4 weeks are given to patients who fail to respond to drugs. Modern techniques are much safer than earlier methods that could lead to brain damage or broken bones. Today, muscle relaxants prevent bone breakage, while brief low voltage pulses are applied to the nondominant hemisphere instead of the whole brain. ECT works more quickly than antidepressant drugs and is effective for patients who are suicidal or have manic or psychotic symptoms. Like drugs, ECT increases sensitivity of post-synaptic serotonin receptors. Unlike drugs, it increases dopamine and norepinephrine levels by decreasing autoreceptor sensitivity. ECT also temporarily slows EEG activity, which correlates with clinical improvement. Following ECT, patients show few side effects except amnesia for the experience and a brief period of mild confusion. Usually, they are then placed on maintenance levels of antidepressant drugs. ECT is a hospital procedure, however, and its cost precludes its use as a first-line intervention.

Mood Stabilizers

Bipolar disorder affects about 5% of the population with 20–25% of untreated patients committing suicide, reducing life span by 9 years; only one-third receive treatment. Mood stabilizers stimulate proteins that support neurogenesis and neuronal health and restore patient mood to normal levels (Hashimoto *et al.*, 2002). Antidepressants can precipitate manic episodes and should not be the sole treatment for bipolar depression. Combined psychosocial and medication therapies appear most effective, with one-year recovery rates of 64.4% compared to 51.5% for medication alone. Patients also became well 110 days earlier, on average (Miklowitz *et al.*, 2007). Treatment has three goals:

1. Stabilize acute mania, mixed, and depressive symptoms;
2. Avoid switches from mania to depression or depression to mania caused by antidepressants;
3. Prevent relapse (Keck & Susman, 2003).

Sachs (2003) recommends empirically supported (category A) mood stabilizers to manage mild-to-moderate manic or depressive symptoms or for maintenance. Mood stabilizers are combined with atypical antipsychotics for moderate to severe manic symptoms, and with standard antidepressants for moderate to severe depressive symptoms. Mood stabilizers include lithium and anticonvulsant drugs. Lithium has the broadest therapeutic effect, but its side effects reduce compliance and hamper its use: 28% discontinue, 38% continue but experience relapse, and only 23% continue medication and avoid relapse (Maj, Pirozzi, Magliano, & Bartoli, 1998). In contrast, anticonvulsants and atypical antipsychotics are better tolerated and generally safer (see Table 3.4). Sachs, Grossman, Ghaemi, Okamoto, and Bowden (2002) found that combining antipsychotics and mood stabilizers resulted in fewer drop-outs and reduced acute manic symptoms more than mood stabilizers alone.

Lithium's neural actions are uncertain, but Hashimoto *et al.* (2002) suggest it may have neuroprotective effects. Large individual differences in lithium absorption mean frequent blood tests are needed, which increases patient non-compliance. Lithium blood plasma levels are effective between 0.5–0.7 milliequivalents/liter (mEq/l). Above 1.0 mEq/l, problematic side effects include weight gain (30% obesity rates), gastrointestinal, and neurological symptoms such as impaired concentration and cognition. Severe side effects occur at levels above 2.0 mEq/l and become lethal above 2.5 mEq/l. Pregnant or breast-feeding women should not take lithium. Table 3.4 describes the evidence (Sachs, 2003), serum or dosage levels, and common side effects for drugs used in treating bipolar disorder.

In addition to treating seizure disorders, anticonvulsants are mood regulators that reduce neural excitation and enhance neuronal health. They are used to reduce lithium dosages and its side effects, or if lithium proves ineffective or leads to non-compliance. Since birth defects are a risk, anticonvulsants must be monitored closely with pregnant women. V*alproic acid* (Depakote), a GABA agonist, is effective with acute manic, mixed state, rapid-cycling, and schizoaffective disorders, as well as aggression and agitation, especially in children. It may be used with lithium-resistant patients or combined with antipsychotics to control manic symptoms (Sachs *et al.*, 2002).

Carbamazepine (Tegretol) combined with lithium is effective for bipolar symptoms, but its use is limited by potentially severe side effects (*e.g.*, reduced white blood cells). *Oxcarbazepine* (Trileptal) is equally effective and appears safer. *Lamotrigine* (Lamictal) is used for rapid-cycling episodes, bipolar depression, and for long-term maintenance or prevention of bipolar symptoms. In contrast to most other anticonvulsants, it improves cognitive functioning, but there is risk of a potentially fatal skin rash. *Gabapentin* (Neurontin) is more effective for anxiety or neuropathic pain, but is an adjunctive treatment for patients who fail to respond to other mood

Table 3.4 Bipolar mood stabilizer evidence quality. (Adapted from *A primer of drug action*, 11th ed., p. 434. By R. M. Julien, C. D. Advokat, & J. E. Comaty. © 2008 by Worth Publishers. Used with permission.)

Generic (trade) name	Acute mania/mixed	Mood stabilizer	Acute bipolar depression	Serum[a] level or dosage	Half-life (hrs.)	Weight gain	Cognitive impairment	Generic available
Lithium (e.g., Eskalith)	++	++	++	0.6–1.5	12–27	High	High	Yes
Anticonvulsants								
Valproic acid (Depakote)	++	++	0	30–100	5–20	Medium	Medium	Yes
Carbamazepine (Tegretol)	++	++	0	4–10+	18–20	Low	Low	Yes
Lamotrigine (Lamictal)	−	++	++	1–5	33	None	None	Yes
Gabapentin (Neurontin)	−	0	0	—[b]	5–7	Low	Low	Yes
Topiramate (Topamax)	0	0	0	—[c]	21	None	Mid-high	No
Atypical Antipsychotics				Dosages (mg)				
Aripiprazole (Abilify)	++	0	0	15–30	75–94	None	None	No
Haloperidol (Haldol)	++	0	0	2–40	12–36 (3 weeks)[d]	Low	Low	Yes
Olanzapine (Zyprexa)	++	0	0	5–20	27–38	High	Low	No
Risperidone (Risperdal)	++	0	0	4–16	3 (27)[e]	Medium	Low	No
Quetiapine (Seroquel)	++	0	0	150–400	6	Low	None	No
Ziprasidone (Geodon)	++	0	0	60–160	6	None	None	No

++ = Supported by randomized controlled trials
+ = Other research support
0 = Lacks research support
− = Negative research support
[a] Lithium levels expressed in mEq/l; anticonvulsant levels in mcg/ml; atypical antipsychotic dosages in mg
[b] Serum monitoring may not be necessary
[c] Not yet established
[d] Injectable form, Haldol Decanoate, has 3-week half-life; useful with non-compliant patients
[e] Active metabolite half-life is 27 hours; long-lasting injectable form, Risperdal Consta, is available

stabilizers. *Topiramate* (Topamax) is also an adjunctive treatment that can offset weight gains caused by other drugs. Interestingly, Marengell *et al.* (2006) report mixed support for *Omega-3 Fatty Acids*, available over-the-counter, as adjunct and maintenance treatments for manic symptoms.

Atypical antipsychotics, *e.g.*, *aripiprazole* (Abilify) and *resperidone* (Risperdal) are first-line interventions for manic symptoms. *Olanzapine* (Zyprexa) is also used for bipolar depression. Antidepressant drugs are sometimes combined with mood stabilizers to prevent "manic flips," but Sachs *et al.* (2007) found they add little benefit compared to mood stabilizers and recommend more research into their use for bipolar depression.

Antipsychotic Drugs

The first class of antipsychotic drugs, phenothiazines, reduced hospitalizations for psychosis in the United States from over 500,000 in 1955 to 220,000 in 1983. Phenothiazines ameliorate *positive* symptoms of schizophrenia such as bizarre ideation, delusions, and hallucinations, which allows patients to return to the community. They do not help *negative* symptoms of blunted affect, apathy, loss of motivation, or social withdrawal and outpatient care is required. Unfortunately, inadequate outpatient care levels have led to schizophrenic patients flooding the prison system and accounting for about half of all homeless people (Julien *et al.*, 2008).

The hypothesis that excessive dopamine levels cause schizophrenia stemmed from the antipsychotic effect of the phenothiazine class of drugs, which block dopamine D_2 receptors in the limbic system. However, blockades of D_2 receptors in the basal ganglia and brain stem as well as acetylcholine, histamine, and norepinephrine receptors also produce side effects (see Table 3.5). Phenothiazines are called *neuroleptics* because they take control of neurons in the brain's *extrapyramidal system* (motor pathways between the cortex and the brain stem and basal ganglia), causing Parkinsonian symptoms. High dosages of phenothiazines cause uncomfortable neuroleptic

Table 3.5 Phenothiazine side effects on different neurotransmitter systems

System	Phenothiazine side effects
Cholinergic	Dry mouth, blurred vision, constipation, urinary retention, tachycardia
Histamine	Sedation, antiemetic (antinausea, prevents vomiting)
Norepinephrine	Sedation, hypotension (low blood pressure)
Dopaminergic:	
Hypothalamic-pituitary axis	Appetite suppression, thirst, sexual arousal, temperature regulation; induces lactation in females—breast enlargement in males
Brain stem	Suppression of behavioral arousal (indifference to external stimuli)
Basal ganglia	Akathisia (anxiety, restlessness, pacing, repetitive purposeless actions); Dystonia (muscle spasms, bizarre postures of limbs, trunk, face, and tongue); Neuroleptic Parkinsonism (resting tremor, rigidity of limbs, reduced activity); Tardive dyskinesia (irreversible involuntary movements of face, trunk, and limbs); Neuroleptic Malignant Syndrome (rare, but potentially lethal condition)

and cholinergic side effects, leading to non-compliance and high relapse rates. Neuroleptic inhibition of behavioral arousal also reduces patient interest in the outside world and exacerbates negative symptoms. *Tardive dyskinesia*, irreversible involuntary movements caused by phenothiazines, limits their use as a maintenance drug.

Phenothiazines are often combined with anticholinergic, antihistamine, antiparkinsonian, or antiadrenergic drugs to counteract side effects. Alternatives with fewer extrapyramidal side effects have also been developed. Table 3.6 lists commonly prescribed antipsychotic drugs, each with slightly different dosage, efficacy, and side-effect profiles. *Transitional* antipsychotics, developed before the *atypicals*, are structurally different from the phenothiazines, but also act upon dopamine D_2 receptors with similar effectiveness and side-effect profiles.

Atypical antipsychotics treat negative as well as positive symptoms with few neuroleptic side effects and are also effective for bipolar and schizoaffective disorders. They are "atypical" because they block serotonin 5-HT_2 receptors as well as D_2 receptors, which may account for their efficacy in reducing negative symptoms and Parkinsonian symptoms. Some atypicals affect GABA and glutamate receptors, expanding and complicating attempts to unravel the underlying causes of schizophrenia (Javitt & Coyle, 2004). Currently, research is focusing on slow-acting, metabotropic receptors that modulate glutamate activity (see Singer, 2004).

Phenothiazines, transitional, and some atypical antipsychotic drugs are now available in affordable generic forms. Today, phenothiazines are generally given only to patients who fail to respond to atypical drugs; however, even more expensive atypicals are cost-effective compared to the cost of not treating schizophrenia. *Clozapine*, first introduced in 1990, requires monitoring for sudden potentially fatal decreases in white blood cell counts, *agranulocytosis*, and it can have severe withdrawal symptoms. Developed later, *risperidone* and *olanzapine* are safer and equally effective with negative and positive symptoms. They are also used to treat autism and pervasive developmental disorders. Their main limitations are possible weight gains and Type-2 diabetes.

Quetiapine may be combined with SSRIs to treat aggression and obsessive-compulsive disorder. It is effective in treating anxiety and sleep disorders and has been used to help prisoners tolerate confinement. *Ziprasidone* has both antidepressant and antipsychotic effects and is widely used in an injectable form for rapid control of agitation. *Aripiprazole* (Abilify), a third generation antipsychotic, acts as a *partial agonist* at serotonin 5-HT(1A) and pre-synaptic dopamine D2 sites and as an antagonist at post-synaptic D2 and serotonin 5-HT(2A) sites. It has few side effects and is effective for mood, positive, and negative symptoms of schizophrenia. As a partial agonist, it keeps D_2 receptor dopamine within functional levels: keeping levels from being too low enhances cognitive functioning and keeping them from being too high reduces positive symptoms.

Analgesics

The two main classes of pain-relieving drugs are nonsteroidal analgesic anti-inflammatory drugs (NSAIDs), *e.g.*, aspirin, acting mostly in the peripheral nervous

Table 3.6 Antipsychotic drugs. (Adapted from *A primer of drug action*, 11th ed., pp. 304; 436. By R. M. Julien, C. D. Advokat, & J. E. Comaty. © 2008 by Worth Publishers. Used with permission.)

Chemical classification	Drug name: generic (trade)	Dosage[a]	Sedation	Autonomic effects[b]	Involuntary movement	Weight gain	Cognitive impairment
Phenothiazine	*Chlorpromazine* (Thorazine)[c]	50–800	High	High	Medium	Low	Medium
	Fluphenazine (Prolixin)[c,d]	3–45	Low	Low	High	Low	Low
	Trifluoperazine (Stelazine)[c]	2–40	Medium	Low	High	Low	Medium
	Perphenazine (Trilafon)[c]	8–60	Low	Low	High	Low	Low
	Mesoridazine (Serentil)	50–500	High	Medium	Low	Low	Medium
	Thioridazine (Mellaril)[c]	15–800	High	Medium	High	Low	Medium
Thioxanthene	*Thiothixene* (Navane)[c]	10–60	Low	Low	High	Low	Low
Butyrophenone	*Haloperidol* (Haldol)[c,d]	2–40	Low	Low	Very high	Low	Low
Miscellaneous	*Loxapine* (Loxitane)[c]	50–250	Medium	Low	Medium	Low	Low
	Molindone (Moban)	20–225	Medium	Medium	Medium	Low	Low
	Pimozide (Orap)	1–10	Low	Low	Medium	Low	Low
New generation or atypical drugs	*Clozapine* (Clozaril)[c,e]	300–900	Medium	Medium	Low	High	Low
	Risperidone (Risperdal)[f]	4–16	Medium	Low	Low–Med	Medium	Low
	Olanzapine (Zyprexa)	5–20	Medium	Low	Low	High	Low
	Quetiapine (Seroquel)	150–400	Medium	Low	Low	Low	None
	Ziprasidone (Geodon)	60–160	Low	Low	Low	None	None
	Aripiprazole (Abilify)	15–30	Low	Low	Low	None	None

[a] Usual daily oral dosage range (in mg)

[b] Autonomic side effects include dry mouth, blurred vision, constipation, urinary retention, and reduced blood pressure

[c] Generic version is available

[d] Dose required to achieve efficacy of 100 mg chlorpromazine

[e] White blood cell count must be monitored since *agranulocytosis* is a risk

[f] Available in time-release IM format

system, and opioids, *e.g.*, morphine, acting in the central nervous system. Antide-pressants, *e.g.*, *amitriptyline* or *duloxetine HCl* (Cymbalta), and anticonvulsants, *e.g.*, *carbamazepine* or *gabapentin*, are used to treat neuropathic or chronic pain. NSAIDs block the synthesis and release of *prostaglandin*, a hormone that responds to infection or trauma with increased blood clotting, inflammation, and pain.

Opioid drugs, *e.g.*, morphine and synthetic derivatives such as *dihydromorphi-none* (Dilaudid) or *oxycodone* (OxyContin), mimic the actions of *endorphins*, en-dogenous morphine-related hormones, released by the hypothalamus and pituitary gland. Endorphins modulate the perception of pain by binding on opioid receptors located mostly in the brain, but also in the spinal cord and peripheral sites. Opioid drugs act in several ways: activating inhibitory GABA- or endorphin-secreting neu-rons to modulate spinal neuron responsivity; activating inhibitory neurons that de-scend from the brainstem to the spinal cord; and reducing glutamate levels (Julien *et al.*, 2008). *Methadone*, with both opioid and NMDA properties that reduce side effects, is used to treat opiate addictions. It is increasingly used as an analgesic because it is much cheaper than OxyContin or Dilaudid and its long, 56-hour half-life extends the period during which it is effective. However, the long half-life also means it takes longer to become effective, which can lead to lethal overdoses if patients become impatient and try to hurry methadone effects by taking more.

Tolerance, withdrawal effects, and potential for abuse have led to a debate whether or not opioids should be limited to short-term use for trauma or surgery. Research now suggests opioids may be used effectively for chronic pain if patients are screened for potential abuse and monitored for problems of tolerance or dependence (Nichol-son & Passik, 2007; Rowbotham *et al.*, 2003). In general, a stepwise strategy should be used in pain management, first trying NSAIDs, next antidepressants that affect norepinephrine levels, then anticonvulsants such as *gabapentin*, and finally opioids, if the others prove ineffective (Loeser, Butler, Chapman, & Turk, 2001).

Anxiolytics

Barbiturates, *e.g.*, *phenobarbital*, are used for seizure disorders, anxiety, and in-somnia. Barbiturates and other CNS depressants, *e.g.*, alcohol, are glutamate antag-onists or GABA agonists. Low dosages suppress behavioral inhibition and reduce anxiety, while high dosages are sedatives and induce sleep. *Benzodiazepines*, which are less likely to be fatal in overdoses, have largely replaced them. Benzodiazepine drugs act upon $GABA_A$ receptor agonists in the limbic system and have varied half-lives (Julien *et al.*, 2008, p. 174):

- 2.5–12 hours half-life—*temazepam* (Restoril), *triazolam* (Halcion), *alprazolam* (Xanax);
- 15–30 hours half-life—*lorazepam* (Ativan), *clonazepam* (Klonopin), *quazepam* (Dormalin);
- 60 hours half-life—*diazepam* (Valium), *chlordiazepolide* (Librium), *chloraz-epate* (Tranxene).

Side effects include sedation, ataxia, lethargy, motor and cognitive impairment, and amnesia. The elderly metabolize benzodiazepines slowly, especially long-acting types, and thus are at more risk for a reversible dementia. "Roofies" (Rohypnol) are the notorious date-rape drug. Although less lethal than barbiturates, *benzodiazepine* overdoses may be fatal if combined with alcohol and long-term use may lead to dependency. *Flumazenil* (Romazicon), a $GABA_A$ antagonist is used for overdoses. SSRIs are more effective in treating anxiety disorders and are safer and less likely to be abused (Reinblatt & Riddle, 2007). Short-term benzodiazepine use can provide immediate relief for anxiety or agitation during alcohol withdrawal or acute panic attacks. They are also used on a short-term basis to treat insomnia, but there are other, less problematic drugs.

Several nonbenzodiazepine drugs have been introduced recently that bind selectively to the $GABA_{1A}$ receptor. *Zolpidem* (Ambien) is a sedative with a short half-life of 2–2.5 hours, similar in effect to Halcion. *Zaleplon* (Sonata) and *zopiclone* (Imovane) have even shorter half-lives, less than 1 hour, and are largely eliminated from the body after 4 hours, which makes them safer for driving the next morning. This group of drugs is preferred to benzodiazepines as sleep aids since they reduce the likelihood of "insomnia rebound" or dependency. *Buspirone* (BuSpar), a serotonergic anxiolytic, is a weak agonist at the $5-HT_{1A}$ receptor with both antidepressant and anxiolytic properties and few side effects. Its primary drawback is the length of time needed for anxiolytic effects compared to the nearly immediate effects of benzodiazepines.

Pharmacotherapy with the Elderly and with Children

Zito *et al.* (2003) note that rates of psychotropic drug prescriptions for youths has reached levels comparable to those for adults, despite limited research on its efficacy until quite recently. The assumption has been that adult research can be extrapolated by adjusting dosages to accommodate differences in body weight (Emslie *et al.*, 1997). However, recent child research programs are now addressing this lack: e.g., the TADS Team (2007) found that combined antidepressant and psychosocial treatments are effective with youths.

Research is also limited on appropriate use of drugs with the elderly. Julien *et al.* (2008) suggest "it is wise to 'start low and go slow'" (p. 391) since aging differences in metabolic rates that prolong drug half-lives can make drugs effective at lower levels for older patients. Drug side effects or interactions should be ruled out before a dementia diagnosis is given, especially in older patients with multiple prescriptions. Overuse of anticholinergic or sedative-hypnotic drugs in the elderly, especially benzodiazipenes, can cause confusion, incoordination, and falling. Conversely, depression and anxiety disorders often remain undiagnosed and untreated (Julien *et al.*, 2008).

Geriatric Psychopharmacology

Drug treatments for the elderly may be overused (*e.g.*, benzodiazepines), underused (*e.g.*, antidepressants), or inappropriately used. Bregnhøj, Thirstrup, Kristensen, Bjerrum, and Sonne (2007) found that general practitioners gave 94% of their sample of 212 elderly patients a total of 640 inappropriate medications, including ineffective drugs, incorrect dosages or durations, or drugs with adverse drug or disease/condition interactions. Drugs most commonly misused were those for peptic ulcer, hypnotics, antidepressants, anti-asthmatics, and cardiovascular or anti-inflammatory medications. Laroche, Charmes, Nouaille, Picard, and Merle (2006) found that 66% of their sample of 2,018 patients received inappropriate medications, with 10% showing adverse drug reactions. Steinman *et al.* (2006) found rates over 60% inappropriate drug use in elderly patients taking over eight prescriptions. Problematic drug classes included opiates, benzodiazepines, anticholinergics (*e.g.*, tricyclics), antihistamines, muscle relaxants, and simultaneous use of two drugs from the same class. Clearly, making a medication list and eliminating inappropriate drugs is essential. Sedative-hypnotic drugs, *e.g.*, benzodiazepines, are especially problematic for the elderly and frequently produce symptoms of dementia and motor incoordination. Detailed lists of problematic drugs and drug/condition interactions may be found in Fick *et al.* (2003).

Although combined SSRI and psychosocial interventions are clearly effective (*e.g.*, Hunkeler *et al.*, 2006), only 8% of depressed seniors seek professional help. Undertreatment results in adults over 65 years having the highest suicide rate of any age groups, accounting for 20% of all suicides in the United States. Depression that presents as somatic complaints or as signs of dementia in the elderly is often misconstrued. Dementia or Parkinson's Disease (PD) can also mask depression: *e.g.*, depression is comorbid in 40–60% of PD patients. Patients are more likely to receive help for PD symptoms, which are more distinctive than many signs of depression. Non-sedating, SSRI antidepressants are used for comorbid depression, while other interventions treat PD. Tricyclics are avoided due to their anticholinergic properties. Fortunately, active research efforts are now underway for Parkinson's disease and Alzheimer's disease.

PD affects 0–1.0% of people aged 65–69, with 1–3% affected by the age of 80. Dopamine depletion in basal ganglia neurons causes several typical PD symptoms (Julien *et al.*, 2008):

1. Bradykinesia (slowness; reduced movement);
2. Muscle rigidity;
3. Resting tremors that usually lessen during voluntary movements;
4. Impaired postural balance and gait with increased risk of falling; and
5. After 5–10 years, if untreated, rigidity and mobility loss may prevent self-care.

Three principal interventions are used:

1. Dopamine replacement with *levodopa* (L-dopa);
2. D_3 dopaminergic receptor agonists—*pramipexole* (Mirapex) and *ropinirole* (Ropark);

3. MAO-B inhibitors (selective for basal ganglia)—*selegiline* (Emsam Transdermal Patch).

Since dopamine cannot pass the blood-brain barrier, its precursor L-dopa is used, but is largely metabolized before crossing the barrier. *Carbidopa + levidopa* (Sinemet) inhibit about 75% of the metabolizing enzyme, which increases L-dopa's therapeutic efficacy and reduces side effects. Adding *entacopone* to this combination (Stalevo) further enhances L-dopa's efficacy by inhibiting dopamine degradation and prolonging neuronal synthesis and storage of dopamine. L-dopa is used mainly in late-stage Parkinsonism since its efficacy declines over time.

The dopamine receptor agonists, *pramipexole* (Mirapex) and *ropinirole* (Requip), help during early and middle stages by stimulating post-synaptic D_3 receptors directly and avoiding problems associated with dopamine metabolism. These prolong L-dopa's effectiveness in the earlier stages of PD and are also useful in later stages when dopamine neurons may be largely missing. Side effects include dizziness, nausea, hallucinations, and either somnolence or insomnia. Another approach is *selegiline* (Emsam), an MAO-B inhibitor that selectively and irreversibly inhibits the enzyme that breaks down dopamine in the basal ganglia. This preserves remaining dopamine, prolongs L-dopa's efficacy during PD's early and middle stages, and may have neuroprotective value. Transdermal patches administer low dosages, eliminating the need for dietary restrictions and helping comorbid or treatment-resistant depression. Another MAO-B inhibitor, *rasagiline* (Azilect) is now available that also appears to be neuroprotective (Guay, 2006).

Approximately 40% of late-stage PD patients develop dementia or Alzheimer's disease (AD). It is important to distinguish early-stage PD frontal lobe deficits reversible by L-Dopa from irreversible dementias. Both AD and PD-related dementias usually involve loss of short-term memory, slowed responses, and poor concentration and initiative. AD may also present with aphasia, apraxia, and agnosia, reflecting loss of both cortical and sub-cortical functions.

AD is thought to result from neuronal loss caused by a build-up of *neurofibrillary tangles* and *amyloid plaques*, especially in temporo-hippocampal and frontal areas of the brain. AD affects 1% of adults between ages 65–69, with rates doubling every 5 years up to 40–50% of 95-year-olds. Progressive cognitive decline, behavioral changes, loss of independence, and, eventually death, usually occur within 10 years of the onset of symptoms.

Acetylcholinesterase inhibitors (AChE-Is) may help mild to moderate cases, while more severe cases are treated with a glutaminergic NMDA receptor antagonist, *memantine* (Namenda). *Donepezil* (Aricept), *rivastigimine* (Excelon), and *galantamine* (Reminyl) are AChE-Is that increase acetylcholine levels and improve cognitive functions. Peripheral cholinergic side effects include nausea, diarrhea, cramps, and anorexia. *Memantine* is thought to block activity at the N-Methyl-D-Aspartate (NMDA) receptor site and protect against neurotoxic glutamergic over-stimulation. High *memantine* levels can produce amnesia, but lower levels enhance neuronal health and memory with minimal side effects. Because it has a different mode of action, *memantine* may be safely combined with an AChE-I drug to treat moderate or severe AD cases (Mobius, 2003).

Ballard *et al*. (2009) found that the common use of antipsychotics to control agitation, delusions, and aggressive behavior in late-stage AD patients can cause further cognitive decline and may have fatal consequences. Patients on antipsychotic medications were more likely than placebo controls to die within the following 12 months and at 36 months, the survival rate was 30% *vs.* 59%. More helpful are psychosocial interventions that assist caretakers in managing problem behaviors. Caretakers of patients with dementia or other chronic, debilitating illnesses require support to cope with the stress of constant monitoring needed to prevent falls or wandering and to attend to bodily functions for patients unable to care for themselves.

Caretakers may be family members with limited support structures or understanding of the patient's conditions or needs. In treating dementia, the goals are to prevent caretaker burn-out and to delay institutionalization as long as possible. These goals are best achieved by combining drug interventions with psychoeducational support: *e.g.*, Belle *et al*. (2006) and Vickrey *et al*. (2006) report reduced depression and improved caretaker quality of life with relatively short-term interventions. These programs focused on education about the nature of the disease, self-care, stress management, safety, coping with problem behaviors, and enhancing social and emotional support structures. Respite from "24/7" caregiving is essential!

Pediatric Psychopharmacology

Undertreatment, over-treatment, and inappropriate treatments affect children as well as elderly patients. Adequate treatment to contain costs and improve quality of life is especially critical for children with a lifetime ahead of them. Half of all serious adult psychiatric disorders begin by age 14, anxiety disorders as early as 11 (Kessler *et al.*, 2005). Because depression, anxiety, and impulse-control disorders are often misconstrued as "normal" adolescent moodiness, insecurity, and impulsiveness, delays in seeking services range from 6–8 years for mood disorders to 9–23 years for anxiety disorders. Delayed recognition of problems is seen most often in poorly educated, married, minority men (Wang *et al.*, 2005).

With 14–25% of children needing mental services, less than two-thirds actually receive them even though early intervention could prevent a childhood disorder from developing into a chronic adult disorder (*e.g.*, Costello, Copeland, Cowell, & Keeler, 2007). Paradoxically, despite serious undertreatment, psychotropic drug use with children has nearly reached adult levels over the past 15 years (Zito *et al.*, 2003). Unfortunately, drugs are often the only treatment offered despite consistent research showing the superiority of combined therapies: *e.g.*, psychotherapy and SSRIs are consistently recommended for child and adolescent depression (Asarnow *et al.*, 2009; Cheung *et al.*, 2007; TADS Team, 2007).

Although SSRIs are more effective for anxiety disorders, benzodiazepines continue to be used for adolescent anxiety disorders despite side effects of sedation, aggression, irritability, and behavioral dyscontrol (Seidel & Walkup, 2006). Benzodiazepines are subject to abuse and can cause withdrawal symptoms if stopped suddenly. Autistic children also respond to psychosocial therapies when combined with atypical antipsychotics. Stimulants reduce hyperactivity and irritability in autistic children, but sometimes exacerbate irritability, cause insomnia, or precipitate aggression (McDougle, Stigler, & Posey, 2003). Perhaps due to high comorbidity for ADHD, impulsive and aggressive conduct disordered children respond well to stimulants, atypical antipsychotics, or anticonvulsant mood stabilizers combined with psychotherapy (Steiner, Saxena, & Chang, 2003).

Children diagnosed with ADHD are overly boisterous, constantly "on the go," fidgety, easily distracted, forgetful, impulsive, and avoid tasks requiring sustained attention. The *7R* gene associated with ADHD is correlated with sensation-seeking, quick reactions to challenges, and is common in groups with a history of migration; *e.g.*, it is found in 60% of South Americans *vs.* 1% of more stable Asian groups (Sohn, 2002). Children with ADHD have no attention span problems when playing exciting computer games, suggesting ADHD traits may be adaptive for a nomadic, hunter-gatherer society, but problematic in today's sedentary, structured classroom. The 7-fold to 14-fold increase between 1987 and 1996 in amphetamines prescribed for youth (Zito *et al.*, 2003) may reflect a cultural mismatch rather than a "disease" process.

Unfortunately, ADHD-related problems can disrupt classrooms and lead to rejection by other children and to academic failure. The result is high comorbidity of ADHD with conduct, anxiety, and mood disorders. Biederman (2004) found that 40–60% of ADHD children remain symptomatic in adulthood, with five-fold increased risks for substance abuse and nine-fold for incarceration. ADHD is associated with reduced dopaminergic activity in the prefrontal cortex and the basal ganglia striatum, areas that control executive functions, movement, impulse inhibition, working memory, reward, and learning (Ernst, Zametkin, Matochik, Jons, & Cohen, 1998; Krause, Dresel, Krause, Kung, & Tatsch, 2000). As a result, children with ADHD may choose immediate rather than long-term rewards.

Reduced dopaminergic activity is experienced subjectively as boredom. CNS stimulants are paradoxically calming, because children do not need to regulate cortical arousal with sensation-seeking activities. Stimulants such as *amphetamines* and *methylphenidate* (Ritalin) improve behavior and academic performance and reduce substance abuse and delinquency in 60–80% of children correctly diagnosed with ADHD (Julien *et al.*, 2008). Adderall XR, a time-release formula, effective at lower doses, lasts longer and prevents ADHD symptoms from waxing and waning.

Although Szatmari's (1992) large-scale review suggests 4–6% of children meet diagnostic criteria for ADHD, parent/teacher ratings show a range from 22 to 57% (Werry & Quay, 1971). Such elevated rates highlight risks that ADHD diagnoses may be used to justify medication when better classroom management or parenting techniques are needed. LeFever, Arcona, and Antonuccio (2003) note a 700% increase in psychostimulant use during the 1990s and conclude:

> [ADHD] is not universally overdiagnosed; however, for some U.S. communities there is evidence of substantial ADHD overdiagnosis, adverse educational outcomes among children treated for the disorder, and suboptimal management of childhood behavior problems (p. 49).

Current guidelines suggest that behavioral therapy should be used if drug interventions prove unsatisfactory (American Academy of Child and Adolescent Psychiatry, 2007).

Substance Abuse

Volkow, Fowler, Wang, and Swanson (2004) suggest that people who abuse drugs may have a *reward deficiency syndrome* and are self-medicating low levels of dopamine. Drugs of abuse target dopaminergic reward structures modulated by opioid (endorphin), cannabinoid, NMDA glutamate, and GABA receptors. Opiate and cannabinoid drugs increase endorphin synthesis and release, creating a relaxed, euphoric state; in addition, alcohol also inhibits glutamate and increases GABA release. Over time, homeostatic processes decrease receptor site numbers, restore neurohormones to original levels, and create dependence.

Addiction and withdrawal involve different areas of the brain: the dopaminergic reward system, from the midbrain *ventral tegmental area* to the *medial forebrain bundle* and *nucleus accumbens* and on to the *prefrontal cortex*, mediates addiction, while the midbrain *periventricular gray* pain system mediates withdrawal (Bozarth & Wise, 1984). Although uncomfortable, most addicts withdraw successfully, sometimes to reduce *tolerance*, the amount needed to produce the desired effect. Treatment must then address relapses created by craving and drug-related cues.

Learning occurs when people make *errors in prediction* and the unexpected happens (Schultz, 2002). Once experience becomes predictable, dopaminergic rewards are not needed to maintain behavior: *learned tolerance* develops as repeated experiences reinforce cues associated with drug use and dopamine release shifts from the drug itself to antecedent cues. Stress or drug paraphernalia lead to cravings that increase the likelihood of relapse. Withdrawal is only the first step in treatment of chronic substance abuse. Ongoing management is required both for the life problems caused by drugs and to prevent relapse.

Four strategies are used to treat substance abuse:

1. *Agonist* strategies replace the abused drug with one having fewer negative consequences;
2. *Antagonist* strategies reduce the rewarding effects of the abused drug;
3. *Aversive* strategies pair the drug with unpleasant experiences to reduce reward effects;
4. *Antidrug vaccines* stimulate the immune system to degrade the drug before it takes effect.

Table 3.7 summarizes strategies used in treating various drugs of abuse. Because drugs of abuse target the dopamine reward system, withdrawal causes a reward deficiency syndrome. Agonists that mimic dopaminergic drugs, *e.g.*, methadone or nicotine patches, prevent withdrawal symptoms, but are also addictive. However, learned tolerance cues are minimized with prescribed drugs, which may help motivated patients through withdrawal, especially if supported by psychotherapy or

Table 3.7 Drug treatment strategies for different classes of substance abuse

Type of treatment	Abused substance	Drug of treatment	Receptor action site	Side effects
Agonist	Alcohol	Benzodiazepine	GABA	Dependence, overdose
	Nicotine	Nicotine gum/patch	ACh-nicotinic	Dependence
	Nicotine	Buproprion	Monoamines	Overstimulation/insomnia
	Cocaine	Buproprion	Monoamines	Overstimulation/insomnia
	Cocaine	Methylphenidate	Monoamines	Nervousness/insomnia
	Cocaine	gamma-vinyl GABA[a]	GABA$_2$	Hives/confusion/seizure
	Methamphet-amine	Buproprion	Monoamines	Overstimulation/insomnia
	Opiates	Methadone	Opioid	Narcotic/allergy/dizziness
	Opiates	Buprenorphin[b] (Subotex)	K-Opioid	Narcotic/allergy/dizziness
Antagonist	Alcohol/Opiates	Naltrexone	Opioid	Nausea/headache/dizziness
	Alcohol	γ-hydroxy-butyr-ate	NMDA Glutamate	Subject to abuse
	Alcohol	Acamprosate (Campral)[c]	NMDA Glutamate	Allergies/tachy-cardia
Aversive	Alcohol	Disulfram (Antabuse)	Acetaldehyde	Acetaldehyde syn-drome/fatigue/funny taste
Vaccines	Cocaine and other stimulants	In development	Antibodies bind drug	Decreases reward-ing effects; long lasting

[a] Anticonvulsant that reduces craving for alcohol, nicotine, cocaine, benzodiazepines, or opiates (under study)
[b] Partial agonist
[c] Also acts as a GABA$_A$ agonist

a 12-step group. Instead of mimicking drug effects, *buproprion* (Wellbutrin) and *gamma-vinyl GABA* (Vigabatrin) directly reduce feelings of craving, which also helps people who are dieting. Antagonist and aversive strategies both interfere with drug rewards, but require motivated patients willing to remain in treatment. Less dependent on motivation is a current search for a vaccine that stimulates the immune system to degrade drugs of abuse before they have an effect. Animal research has found one long-lasting vaccine that reduces cocaine levels by 80% (Carrera et al., 1995).

The Epidemiologic Catchment Area Study (Regier et al., 1990) found that 29% of patients with mental disorders also met criteria for substance abuse. Conversely, comorbid mental disorders were present in 37% of those with alcohol disorders and

53% of those with other substance abuse disorders. Interpersonal, emotional, and vocational problems are common even in those without a comorbid diagnosis. The diathesis-stress model suggests that genetic deficiencies of dopaminergic reward and insecure attachments to early caregivers create vulnerability to peer pressure and media messages. Substance abuse is likely if the intrinsic rewards of drug experimentation also relieve life stressors. However, still more stress is created in a vicious circle as drug abuse leads to estrangement from family and social support, to job insecurity, and to criminal activity to raise money to buy drugs.

Drugs provide intrinsic rewards that clients, especially dual-diagnosis patients, use to self-medicate and solve their problems. The immediacy of rewarding effects makes drugs hard to ignore, adds to pre-existing impulse-control problems, and distracts clients from their long-term negative consequences. Sustaining the motivation to make long-term life changes is perhaps the most difficult step in treating substance abuse. Motivational Interviewing (Chap. 9) and Acceptance and Commitment Therapy (Chap. 14) address motivation by emphasizing how substance abuse interferes with realizing long-term goals and values. Twelve-step programs such as Alcoholics Anonymous (AA) and Narcotics Anonymous (NA) suggest alcoholics must first "hit bottom." They emphasize the spiritual and emotional toll drugs have taken on the patient's life. Once patients commit to abstinence, psychopharmacological interventions assist in withdrawal.

Patients need education about the differences between a lapse (using the drug again) and a relapse (giving up abstinence because it's "hopeless"). Because cravings can last a year or more, family education and long-term support groups such as AA or NA are needed to prevent relapse. Prevention efforts are preferable to treatment; *e.g.*, cigarette smoking rates, which declined from 42% to 21% between 1965 and 2006 (Center for Disease Control, 2007). Three factors were relevant in that decline:

1. Only adults could legally purchase cigarettes;
2. Legislation restricted advertising and media placement of cigarettes;
3. Extensive educational programs such as Surgeon General warnings on packaging emphasized the health risks of smoking.

Legalizing drugs is obviously controversial, but could have benefits as well as risks. Current *supply-reduction* strategies paradoxically serve as price supports for drug cartels, while *demand-reduction* strategies ("Just say no!") have proved inadequate. Legalization is a *harm-reduction* strategy that could impact drug-related crime much as Prohibition's repeal did in the 1930s. Making drugs affordable at treatment facilities could encourage entry into treatment programs, reduce HIV infections from shared needles, and reduce deaths due to variations in drug purities.

The Dutch harm-reduction strategy had many of these benefits, but unfortunately also led to an influx of drug users from around the world and to increased crime rates (de Koning & de Kwant, 2002). For harm-reduction to work in America, it may be necessary to limit programs to citizens.

Harm-reduction strategies of drug education and media limitation should initially target legal drugs of abuse such as alcohol and prescription drugs. As with cigarette

smoking, alcohol abuse may be decreased by requiring the media to stop glamor-
izing drinking, and teaching children about the dangers of alcohol abuse and how to
resist peer pressure. The dangers of combining prescription drugs and alcohol need
to be publicized and controls placed on the over-prescription of opioids, antidepressants, and benzodiazepines. A recent report found that three times as many died
from abusing psychoactive prescription drugs, compared to all illicit drugs (Florida
Department of Law Enforcement, 2008). Legal opioids (methadone, Vicodin, and
OxyContin) were most dangerous, followed by benzodiazepines, especially if taken
with alcohol. The Substance Abuse and Mental Health Administration (2008) reported that 16.3 million Americans over the age of 12 abused psychoactive prescription drugs during 2006, with 49.8 million abusing them at some point in their
lives. Comparable figures for abuse of illicit drugs, excluding cannabinoids, were
10.4 million people during 2006 and 62.5 million during their lifetime.

Integrative Implications

Pharmacological intervention is an essential component in treating serious psychological disorders. It provides patients quick relief from symptoms that interfere with their daily functioning and ability to cooperate with psychosocial treatment. Medical model successes have encouraged physicians and patients to expect
quick, low-cost relief with drugs. However, managed-care limits and patient-loads
mean that drugs may be the only treatment offered, particularly for general practitioners' patients, 20% of whom present with mental health complaints (Gilbody
et al., 2006). Few general practitioners have the time or training to diagnose mental
disorders or to monitor treatment compliance and efficacy. The result is a combination of over-prescription and undertreatment: *e.g.*, Lehman *et al.* (1998) found most
schizophrenic patients had appropriate antipsychotic medication, but less than half
received psychosocial interventions and less than half with comorbid depression
received antidepressant medications. Undertreatment was even more pronounced
in urban areas.

Psychosocial therapists see patients on a regular basis and have the diagnostic
training that allows them to monitor treatment efficacy and compliance. If trained
in psychopharmacology, they are in a position to recognize problematic drug interactions, side effects, or non-compliance, and to recommend a different drug if
an initial medication is ineffective. They are also able to address life stressors that
both precipitate and result from psychological problems. The diathesis-stress model
suggests a need for biomedical intervention to give symptom relief and disrupt the
vicious circle of stress→neuronal dysfunction→symptoms→stress. However, psychosocial interventions are also needed to address the sources and consequences
of stress and symptoms: to help patients address immediate life problems, create
adequate support structures, and learn new strategies to relate to others and cope
with stress.

Combined biomedical and psychosocial interventions are particularly needed in
treating the most serious problems such as schizophrenia. As an example of what
could be done given adequate resources, the following section describes approaches

developed by Gerard Hogarty and his colleagues for the treatment of schizophrenia. Their approach demonstrates what could be done for schizophrenic patients, but seldom is, and provides a model that could be adapted in many ways for the treatment of other serious psychological disorders.

Integrative Therapy for Schizophrenia

Hogarty (2002) developed *Personal Therapy* (PT), an individualized approach that helps patients manage stressors, medication, and residual symptoms, and recognize early, prodromal signs of relapse. Hogarty *et al.* (1997) compared patients receiving medication who were given PT, supportive, or family therapy. At the three-year follow-up, effect sizes were 0.93 for the PT group and 0.57 for the supportive and family therapy groups. Both relapse rates and personal functioning were improved.

PT is divided into three phases, corresponding to the patient's level of recovery and coping skills. Four distinct skill sets are taught:

1. *Internal coping* begins by identifying which life events and interpersonal contexts are perceived as stressful by the patient. Reviews of past psychotic episodes identify the patient's unique constellation of prodromal responses to stress. Past coping strategies are identified as helpful future strategies. Patients become aware of their "march of symptoms" as they move to PT's intermediate phase; *e.g.*, stressors lead to minor behavior changes (weak prodromal signs), to major behavior changes (strong prodromal signs), to minor psychotic symptoms, and finally to a psychotic episode. Patients learn to self-manage and interrupt this sequence with breathing and relaxation techniques. Relaxation and guided imagery skills help control negative affect and are generalized into home and community settings in PT's advanced phase.

2. *Social skills*: During PT's initial phase, patients learn to use appropriate eye contact, nonverbal, and paralinguistic behavior in managing stressful interactions. They also learn to: (a) avoid more challenging roles until basic skills are learned; (b) leave situations tactfully before being overwhelmed; (c) modify behaviors that elicit negative reactions—swearing, playing the TV too loud; and (d) interact positively with others—to express appreciation, show interest, and give compliments. PT's intermediate phase adds practice in social perception and assertion skills such as "I" language in low stress situations. In PT's advanced phase, self-instruction, conflict resolution, and management of criticism are practiced in the community.

3. *Resumption of responsibility* for basic hygiene and personal care is encouraged during PT's initial phase once acute symptoms are stabilized. Routines develop the anxiety tolerance needed to take on more important social and vocational roles. PT's intermediate phase adds household chores, while its advanced phase orchestrates resumption of social and vocational roles. Patients who are easily overwhelmed by anxiety or fear of failure or lack motivation learn to sequence tasks in small steps. Patients who attempt roles before being ready are reminded

of their vulnerability to stress and encouraged to resume social and vocational activities on a part-time basis.

4. *Pursuit of social and vocational goals*: PT's ultimate goal is to help patients self-manage their symptoms and resume an active, rewarding social and vocational life. They need to cope with anxieties over reintegrating into society and to recognize and manage prodromal signs, cope with stressful situations, and interact appropriately in ordinary social situations. An analysis of strengths and weaknesses, prior job skills and experience, and work place realities suggests strategies for re-entry into community and vocational activities. Realistic goals are set and patients are counseled how to respond to questions about their illness and gaps in their employment record. They practice favorable self-presentation, communicating the desired message, redirecting questions, taking the other's perspective, listening, and being supportive to others. *In vivo*, practical real-world experiences are generated whenever possible.

During PT's initial phase of 6–9 months, patients and families receive information on the nature of schizophrenia, the role of stress and prodromal signs, and how psychosocial and medication intervention interact to control symptoms. Throughout, the metacommunication is:

1. Schizophrenia is a brain disorder, not a moral or character failure;
2. Research continues to clarify the physiological basis of schizophrenia;
3. Physiological vulnerability leaves the brain sensitive to stressors, unless carefully negotiated;
4. Symptom recovery and stability are possible with new medications and interventions.

In addition, medication is carefully titrated to maximize therapeutic effects and minimize side effects. Patients need to be stabilized with the minimal dosage, have at least a 30-minute attention span, and exhibit no positive symptoms before moving on to PT's intermediate phase.

Once acute symptoms are well-managed, PT's 9–12 month intermediate phase tailors coping strategies to each patient's specific symptoms, vulnerabilities, and circumstances. Psychoeducation groups provide an overview of PT principles and identify stress markers that predict prodromal symptoms. Patients learn relaxation and social perception strategies to control prodromal signs of emotional or behavioral dysregulation. The goal is to help patients accept their disability and compensate for their vulnerability and residual symptoms.

Patients enter PT's 9–15 month advanced phase once they understand how vulnerability to stressors leads to relapse and learn skills to manage feelings of distress such deep breathing and recognition of prodromal signs. They learn to manage residual symptoms that might prevent their resumption of social and vocational roles. Cognitive organization, motivation, social comfort, and the stress of responding to other's needs or demands are typical problems. PT's last stage concludes by helping patients become involved in the community.

Cognitive Enhancement Therapy (CET) is helpful for patients who have significant residual schizophrenic symptoms, or deficits in perspective-taking, interpersonal problem-solving, or communication (Hogarty & Flesher, 1999b). Hogarty & Flesher (1999a) suggest these deficits reflect a concrete cognitive style characteristic of prepubertal children instead of an abstract, adult style. Patients with residual symptoms rely on rules such as "Share if you want people to like you" rather than attending to the *gist* of conversational contexts. Unable to abstract the gist of complex interactions, they become overwhelmed trying to follow each thread of a social exchange. They are easily distracted and their responses become irrelevant, tangential, or miss the point.

The goal of CET is active, *gistful* processing of unrehearsed social situations rather than passive, serial cognitive processing: *metacognitive* skills of context appraisal and perspective-taking rather than lower-order skills such as voice tone and volume, eye contact, and saying "no." Patients readily accept descriptions of their problems as attention or memory deficits, which encourages collaboration in developing treatment plans such as:

Problem: Following conversations
Short-term Goal: To get the main point in family conversations
Long-term Goal: To get the main point in conversations outside my home
Strategies:

(a) Practice getting the gist from reading brief stories.
(b) Remember key words.
(c) Try to forget unimportant details.
(d) Use the memory software.
(e) Try to focus on at least one gist in a conversation (Hogarty & Flesher, 1999b, p. 698).

Computer programs, originally designed for neurological rehabilitation, help patients develop attention, memory, and problem-solving skills. Patients collaborate in pairs with one following the program and one maintaining records and critiquing their partner's performance: *e.g.*, Bracy's (1986) Memory II program addresses cognitive flexibility, abstracting, categorizing, and decision-making. Patients categorize 20-word lists into four categories of which two are readily apparent (living *vs.* non-living) and two not so apparent (raw *vs.* fabricated materials). Therapists provide verbal cues and reinforcers, adjust exercise difficulty levels to maintain patient motivation, and fade their coaching as patients gain expertise. Patients gain feelings of mastery and growth as they ascertain the gist of word groups and learn to tolerate ambiguity as they form hypotheses about categories. Pairs of patients join in social cognition groups to observe and help one another "think on their feet" and communicate the gist of newspaper editorials or create "telegraphic" gistful summaries of interpersonal problems and how to solve them.

Case Illustration

Bennet, Davalos, Green, and Rial (1999) used an approach similar to Personal Therapy in the case of Ms. B (ethnicity not specified), which is summarized below.

- *History and Background*: Ms. B was a homeless woman in her late 40s, diagnosed with schizophrenia. She was hospitalized for 2 years since staff was concerned about her ability to live independently and lack of family support. She was involuntarily hospitalized after refusing shelter during a blizzard and exhibiting paranoid ideation, bizarre behavior, and inability to care for herself. Other than dental problems and an eye fungus when hospitalized, Ms. B had no history of medical problems or of substance abuse. She had finished 2 years of college and worked on an assembly line in her 20s before her functioning began to deteriorate. She then relied on various social agencies and collected cans for deposit money to support herself.
  Neuropsychological examination revealed normal functioning, except for primary cognitive deficits in planning, problem-solving, and expressive verbal fluency. This made it difficult for her to live independently or cope with unpredictable or unfamiliar events. Initially on *fluphenazine* and *risperidone*, she was switched to *olanzapine* and *benztropine mesylate* (Cogentin), an anticonvulsant. This medication controlled most positive and negative symptoms, but she still resisted changes or novelty in her routine. When confronted with the possibility of moving, her functioning regressed with poor self-care, hoarding, and compulsive behavior.

- *Diagnosis*:

  Axis I: Schizophrenia, chronic undifferentiated type in partial remission
  Axis II: No diagnosis
  Axis III: No diagnosis
  Axis IV: Lack of social support; unemployment; homelessness
  Axis V: GAF = 5 (before hospitalization); 35 (Current)

- *Conceptualization*: When confronted with change, Ms. B's cognitive deficits in planning and problem-solving result in regression, which prevents living in a non-institutional setting.

- *Treatment*: Ms. B received 20 group sessions, 2–3 per week, of training in executive skills with the Brainwave-R program (Malia, Bewick, Raymond, & Bennett, 1997). Goals included:

  1. Review need for Cogentin since anticonvulsants should not be needed for *olanzapine*.
  2. Planning and problem-solving strategies—learn to apply organizational principles to:

     (a) Establish new routines;
     (b) List and order steps needed to perform tasks;

    (c) Break problems into small units;

    (d) Simplify information used to solve them.

  3. Cognitive flexibility principles:

    (a) Examine problems from different points of view;

    (b) Scheduling—incorporate time needed to complete tasks into planning;

    (c) Gather and select information needed to solve problems.

  4. Self-awareness: consider needs and desired goals and generalize to novel situations.

- *Outcome*: Ms. B improved her problem-solving skills, assisted independent living plans, and became less frustrated when making requests. She recognized that, being unable to drive, she would need lodging near a bus route. She still uses public services, but is semi-independent, and manages cleaning, cooking, and meal planning in her new home.
- *Discussion*: Ms. B illustrates the value of integrative psychosocial and psychopharmacological interventions for even severely impaired patients. She is now ready for PT's advanced phase. She still requires assistance to prepare for re-entry into the work force and to develop social support in her community.

Chapter Three: Main Points

- Emergent dualism suggests that the mind is an emergent property of the brain. Although mind and brain are just one ontological substance, both objective and subjective epistemologies are needed to describe the different principles that govern the functioning of the mind and brain.
- Meehl's (1962) diathesis-stress hypothesis provides an integrative framework for biomedical and psychological factors in emotional disorders and their treatment. Genetic, perinatal, and personality factors create a diathesis or vulnerability for developing a disorder, which develops only after people are stressed. Both biomedical and psychosocial interventions are necessary to address both sides of this dialectic.
- The mind-body interaction means that medical disorders often have psychological symptoms while psychological disorders may have physical (somatoform) symptoms.
- The biomedical diathesis for a psychological disorder involves dysregulated neurohormones (neurotransmitters) at the neural synapse. Psychoactive drugs regulate neurohormonal levels.
- The body's absorption, distribution, metabolism, and elimination of drugs determine their half-life. Drugs reach a steady state in the bloodstream after six half-lives, which is also the time needed for their effects to dissipate.
- Psychoactive drugs regulate neurotransmitter levels at synaptic receptor sites by affecting enzymes that metabolize neurohormones, by occupying neurohormone

receptor sites in a "lock-and-key" fashion, or by inhibiting neuronal reuptake of neurotransmitters.

- There are six considerations in determining an effective dosage level for a drug:
  1. Efficacy—dosage level that has intended effect on 50% of experimental animals (ED_{50});
  2. Toxicity—dosage level with lethal effects on 50% of experimental animals (LD_{50});
  3. Side effects—*e.g.*, the sedative effects of tranquilizers, or unexpected allergic reactions;
  4. Drug interactions—additive effects of alcohol, marijuana, or methamphetamine may impair driving ability, influence metabolic rates of other drugs, or be lethal;
  5. Tolerance—three processes may reduce a drug's efficacy and require increased dosages:

     (a) *Metabolic tolerance*—increased hepatic (liver) metabolism reduces drug's half-life;

     (b) *Cellular-adaptive tolerance*—homeostatic reduction of receptor site numbers or sensitivity;

     (c) *Behavioral conditioning*—cues associated with taking drugs elicit a response even in the absence of drugs;

  6. Dependence—homeostasis reduces endogenous hormones to compensate for high drug levels, which can then cause uncomfortable withdrawal symptoms.

- Treatments for affective disorders regulate neurotransmitters and increase neuronal health. Antidepressants and mood regulators for bipolar disorder include:
  1. Tricyclic serotonin and norepinephrine levels for their antidepressant effects, but also increase histamine and acetylcholine levels with side effects that reduce patient compliance.
  2. MAO-Is decrease enzymes that break down monoamines, increase norepinephrine and serotonin levels, but can interact lethally with certain foods and drugs. New, safer forms are used for anxiety, bipolar, and eating disorders.
  3. Selective Serotonin Reuptake Inhibitors avoid the tricyclic side effects, but affect sexuality and, occasionally have serious side effects, generally, they are well tolerated.
  4. Atypical antidepressants retain tricyclic antidepressant effects, while minimizing their side effects. They are well tolerated and *buproprion* is also effective treating addictive cravings.
  5. Dual-action antidepressants target norepinephrine and serotonin and have few side effects.
  6. Electroconvulsive therapy, applied in brief pulses at low voltages to one hemisphere, works quickly, effectively, and safely for patients who fail to respond to medication.

7. Mood-stabilizers and prophylactics for bipolar disorder include lithium and anticonvulsants Antipsychotics are also used to control manic and psychotic symptoms.

- Phenothiazines are antipsychotic drugs that block limbic system dopamine D_2 receptors, but also affect the basal ganglia causing extrapyramidal symptoms. Atypical antipsychotics are more selective and have fewer side effects, making patient compliance less of a problem.
- Drug treatment for children and the elderly is often based on inadequate research. Exceptions include stimulants that treat attention deficit and hyperactivity disorder, but are sometimes used to control children's behavior. Parkinsonism is treated by drugs that increase basal ganglia dopamine levels, while symptoms of Alzheimer's Disease are helped by drugs that increase levels of acetylcholine or decrease glutamate.
- Nonsteroidal analgesics (*e.g.*, aspirin) and opioids are treatments for acute pain. For chronic pain, anticonvulsants and tricyclics are helpful.
- *Benzodiazepines* give rapid relief for insomnia, acute anxiety, or panic, but create dependency and are toxic if combined with alcohol. SSRIs are preferred for anxiety disorders.
- Addictive drugs target the dopamine reward system; homeostatic mechanisms reduce number of receptors, which causes increased tolerance, dependence, and withdrawal symptoms. Cues associated with drug use result in cravings that contribute to treatment relapse.
- Of the four strategies for treating substance abuse, the first three require motivated patients:

  1. Agonist—replaces abused drug with one having fewer negative consequences.
  2. Antagonist—treats with drug that reduces the abused drug's rewarding effects.
  3. Aversive—reduces rewards by pairing drug with unpleasant experiences.
  4. Vaccine—stimulates immune system to degrade drug before it takes effect.

- Integration of biomedical and psychosocial interventions addresses withdrawal, motivation, comorbid disorders, and problems secondary to substance abuse. Social support and 12-step programs are helpful.
- Supply-reduction (Prohibition) and demand-reduction (Just say No!) programs are ineffective in controlling substance abuse. A harm-reduction strategy, similar to that developed for cigarettes, that limits advertising and educates children about drug risks is needed.
- Hogarty's Personal Therapy is an effective integration of biomedical and psychosocial therapy that helps schizophrenic patients recognize prodromal signs and manage medication, stress, and residual symptoms. Cognitive enhancement therapy uses computer programs and groups to teach patients how to access the "gist" of complex social interactions and avoid tangentiality.

Further Reading

Hogarty, G. E. (2002). *Personal therapy for schizophrenia and related disorders: A guide to individualized treatment*. New York: Guilford Press.

Julien, R. M., Advokat, C. D., & Comaty, J. E. (2008). *A primer of drug action* (11th ed.). New York: Worth Publishers.

Morrison, J. (1997). *When psychological problems mask medical disorders: A guide for psychotherapists*. New York: Guilford Press.

Chapter 4
Behavioral Interventions

Give me a dozen healthy infants, well formed, and my own specified world to bring them up in and I'll guarantee to take any one at random and train him to become any type of specialist I might select—doctor, lawyer, artist, merchant-chief and yes, even beggar man and thief, regardless of his talents, penchants, tendencies, abilities, vocations, and race of his ancestors

J. B. Watson (1924/1930, p. 104)

Do human problems and potentials reflect inborn biological characteristics, or are they a product of an individual's environment? To what extent are they a characteristic of the person as opposed to a result of environmental influences? Watson's radical behaviorism asserts that children are a *tabula rasa*: their behavior can be modified as desired by controlling the environment. The mind is viewed as an unnecessary explanatory concept (objective monism) and this view dominated psychological thought from the 1930s to the 1960s. Today, it exists in dialectic tension with the cognitive thesis that the concepts of mind and mental schemas are also necessary to explain personality and behavioral consistencies across situations (see Chap. 5). Both behavioral and cognitive ideas are important for psychotherapy integration since most theorists now agree that human problems and their remediation involve learned concepts and behaviors (*e.g.*, Alford & Beck, 1997).

Behavioral and cognitive therapies share the medical model's modernist emphasis on empirical validation and on manualized treatments to treat disorders as specified in the *Diagnostic and Statistical Manual* (4th ed.; American Psychiatric Association, 2000). Only a few of the many interventions that have been developed are summarized below. Barlow (2007) and Leahy and Holland (2000) provide manualized interventions for most major diagnostic problems. By and large, behaviorists have focused on *first-order changes* of maladaptive symptoms, behaviors, or verbalizations. This constitutes a dialectic with other therapeutic approaches that emphasize *second-order change* of underlying conflicts or maladaptive cognitive-emotional schemas.

D. K. Fromme, *Systems of Psychotherapy,*
DOI 10.1007/978-1-4419-7308-5_4, © Springer Science+Business Media, LLC 2011

Conceptual Framework

Behavioral therapies assume that human problems result from learning maladaptive ways to respond to the environment. There are four distinct types of learning:

1. *Classical* or *associative conditioning*. A neutral *conditioned stimulus* (CS), repeatedly paired with an *unconditioned stimulus* (UCS), will come to evoke a *conditioned response* (CR) that resembles the UCS's *unconditioned response* (UCR). This enables subjects to predict important events. Exposure to the CS, when not paired with the UCS, teaches the subject that the CS no longer predicts the UCS and is the basis for exposure therapy. The "classical" example is Pavlov's dogs that salivated when a bell tone signaled the arrival of food.
2. *Operant* or *instrumental conditioning*. Subjects learn which responses produce rewards or *reinforcers* when appropriate *discriminative stimuli* or *cues* are present. A reinforcer is any consequence that increases the response's probability. Subjects discontinue the reinforced behavior (*extinction*) when reinforcers are removed. If toddlers whine to gain parental attention, withholding reinforcing attention extinguishes instrumental responses of whining.
3. *Vicarious* or *observational learning* (*modeling and imitation*) occurs when a subject observes a *model* receive reinforcement for behaving in a particular way: *e.g.*, Bandura (1965a) found that children were more likely to imitate adult models striking a Bobo the Clown doll when the model was rewarded than when scolded. Modeling is used in vicarious exposure therapy or to prepare a client for other exposure techniques. Snake phobics who observe a model handling a snake show reduced levels of anxiety. Modeling complex social skills (social learning) such as assertiveness is also part of social skills training and psychoeducation.
4. *Verbal learning*. Language is used to teach how to interpret or respond appropriately in problematic situations. It is part of all therapeutic approaches and is the basis of cognitive and narrative therapies. Behaviorally oriented therapists treat verbal behavior as operants. For example, Donald Meichenbaum (1977) treats speech as an operant skill. He models self-talk to help children bring impulsive behavior under verbal control. Cognitive therapists help clients challenge self-defeating beliefs and discover more constructive alternatives.

The behavior therapies comprise a very large number of techniques and approaches that may be classified by the type of learning emphasized. Although these terms are sometimes used interchangeably, it is useful to describe classical conditioning approaches as *behavior therapy*, operant approaches as *behavior modification*, modeling or social learning as *cognitive behavior modification*, and verbal learning as *cognitive therapy*. Increasingly, clinicians incorporate several or all of the different learning types. This chapter reviews exposure-based behavior therapies, operant-based behavior modification, cognitive behavior modification, and integrative approaches. Chapter 5 covers the cognitive therapies.

Exposure-Based Behavior Therapies

Exposure therapies are based on O. Hobart Mowrer's (1950) *two-factor* theory. Two-factor theory suggests that anxiety, dissociation, or somatization symptoms result from a combination of classical and instrumental avoidance conditioning. Problems occur when a neutral stimulus is associated with a noxious unconditioned stimulus to produce fear and anxiety. Avoidance of this feared cue is then reinforced by reductions in classically conditioned anxiety: *e.g.*, punishing a child's self-assertion can provoke anxiety; children learn to contain this anxiety by avoiding self-assertion and instead learn to appeal to others to meet their basic needs. This sequence is never extinguished, since self-assertion is consistently avoided.

Appropriate self-assertion by adults may also be punished sometimes, resulting in an intermittent reinforcement schedule that makes avoidance even more difficult to extinguish. Repeated self-assertion with no punishment will be needed to eliminate avoidance. Two-factor theory guides exposure interventions for a variety of symptoms. Meta-analytic studies suggest exposure has moderate efficacy for specific phobias (Klein, Zitrin, Woerner, & Ross, 1983) and for obsessive-compulsive disorders if combined with response prevention of the compulsion (Abramowitz, 1996). Exposure therapy is the treatment of choice for posttraumatic stress disorder (Foa & Meadows, 1997) and for panic disorder with agoraphobia (Cox, Endler, Lee, & Swinson, 1992). The dialectic tension in exposure therapy is between graduated (*e.g.*, systematic desensitization) or sustained, intense (flooding) exposure to anxiety-inducing stimuli.

Systematic Desensitization (Reciprocal Inhibition)

Exposure therapies, first developed by Wolpe (1958), are effective with a wide variety of anxiety symptoms (DeRueis & Crits-Christoph, 1998; Spiegler & Guevremont, 2003). Wolpe believed that fear or anxiety may be extinguished by reversing the conditions described in two-factor theory: a graded hierarchy of feared situations is *counterconditioned* to responses incompatible with anxiety such as relaxation or assertiveness. This new response *reciprocally inhibits* avoidance since the client cannot be both anxious and relaxed at the same time. Research now suggests exposure is critical, while counterconditioning and relaxation mostly prepare clients for anxiety-provoking experiences (Wilson & Davison, 1971). Critics suggest relaxation actually prevents anxiety from occurring, defeating the idea of exposure. Exposure may be better combined with social skills training such as assertiveness. Combining exposure with cognitive challenges to beliefs that support anxiety and avoidance has proven particularly effective (Resick & Schnicke, 1993). There are several exposure techniques.

Graduated *in vivo exposure* to a feared object is the most widely used technique. Simple phobias, *e.g.*, of animals, heights, or enclosed spaces, may be resolved by approaching and confronting feared situations directly. Social phobias are confronted first by role plays and then by engaging in increasingly challenging situations. *Interoceptive exposure* is used for fears associated with bodily sensations such as panic disorders or hypochondriasis. Panic disorder may be understood as a fear of fear-related cues such as accelerated heart rate or shortened breath. Producing such symptoms intentionally on a treadmill helps clients realize these are not signs of a heart attack. *Virtual reality exposure* has successfully treated fears of heights, flying, driving, and spiders with computer simulations (Emmelkamp, Krijn, Hulsbosch, deVries, Schuemie, & van der Mast, 2002).

Although not as effective as other approaches, Wolpe's *imaginal exposure* technique is useful when *in vivo* exposure is difficult to arrange: *e.g.*, confronting traumatic memories. It is the obvious approach when thoughts or impulses are feared, as in obsessive-compulsive disorder. Imagery helps extinguish intrusive thoughts as long as the compulsive ritual used to ward off obsessive ideation is prevented: *e.g.*, a *checker* may become anxious wondering if the gas stove has been turned off. Preventing checking exposes clients to the anxiety elicited by the worry. If unable to prevent a ritual such as hand washing, clients are asked to delay the response as long as possible and the interval is then gradually lengthened. Response prevention is also used with other compulsive problems, such as bulimia nervosa (Bulik, Sullivan, Carter, McIntosh, & Joyce, 1998) or alcohol usage (Rankin, Hodgson, & Stockwell, 1983). For example, clients would be asked to confront impulses to purge or drink without acting on them.

Wolpe's (1958) *exposure hierarchy* is helpful when clients are reluctant to confront their fears. Clients and therapists collaboratively develop a list of 10–15 fearful scenes ranging from easily confronted situations to very difficult ones. The feared cues are then confronted, either in imagination or *in vivo*, starting with the easiest. Associated anxieties are extinguished as clients successfully confront their fears. Increasing self-confidence allows clients to confront more challenging situations as they progress through the fear hierarchy. As mentioned earlier, Wolpe also teaches relaxation in association with anxiety provoking cues. Subjective Units of Distress Scales (SUDS) or Avoidance ratings may be used to measure anxiety or avoidance levels and to gauge the client's progress. Clients rate the degree of anxiety associated with various feared situations on a "fear thermometer" with SUDS units ranging from 0 (completely relaxed, or no anxiety) to 100 (overwhelming anxiety). Avoidance ratings range from 0 (no need to avoid) to 100 (overwhelming urge to avoid). SUDS and Avoidance ratings tend to correlate, so both are not always needed. An intermediate scene may need to be interpolated if clients experience difficulty moving from one imagined situation to the next; *e.g.*, another scene may be needed to bridge the avoidance distance between situations 3 and 4 in Table 3.1.

Relaxation techniques (*e.g.*, Jacobsen, 1938) are still widely used for self-soothing and emotional regulation (Hyman, Feldman, Harris, Levin, & Mallory, 1989), but now are often integrated with other procedures. They are also an effective stand-alone procedure for managing emotional distress. In Jacobsen's procedures, clients lie on their backs with shoes off, breathe deeply and slowly, and tense muscle groups moving from the feet to the calves, thighs, hips, stomach, back, and on to the hands, arms, shoulders, neck, and face. Clients tense for 5–7 seconds and then relax with two repetitions for each group. As clients subvocalize "tense" while tens-

Table 3.1 Imaginal exposure hierarchy for a young man's anxieties about dating

Feared situation	SUDS	Avoidance
1. Girl remarks how boring and uninteresting date is and leaves for home	100	100
2. Girl comments unfavorably on client's appearance and behavior	90	90
3. Girl looks bored and does not bother to respond to conversational gambit	75	80
4. Girl criticizes choice of restaurant and evening's entertainment	70	65
5. Girl acts cold, distant and indifferent when picked up	65	60
6. Client driving to date, thinking about all that might go wrong	55	50
7. Girl accepts date; client worries it will be a disaster	40	40
8. Calling a girl for a date and being turned down	25	30
9. Picking up phone to call about a date and thinking about being rejected	15	20
10. Thinking about asking girl out for a date and being rejected	5	15
11. Listening to music	0	0

ing and "relax" or "calm" while relaxing, they become more aware of their bodily tension. Clients practice twice each day, eventually learning to self-monitor cues of tension or anxiety and relax before tension occurs.

Diaphragm breathing is a simple, widely used relaxation technique. Clients learn to use deep breathing when stressed instead of increasing anxiety with shallow breathing (Borkovec & Newman, 1998). Since hyperventilation exacerbates panic symptoms by increasing O_2 blood levels, clients *rebreathe* into cupped hands or a paper bag to control symptoms by increasing CO_2 blood levels. Relaxation can be enhanced by instructing clients to imagine a quiet, secure, and pleasant scene. *Panic control therapy* (Craske & Barlow, 2001) integrates psychoeducation, rebreathing, and cognitive therapy with *in vivo* and interoceptive exposure to treat panic disorders.

Antony and Swinson's (2000) review of exposure therapies concluded:

1. Exposure that is *predictable* and under the client's *control* works best. Client understanding of rationale and collaboration on procedures is essential.
2. Long exposures up to 2 hours are more effective than short durations of 30 minutes. Allowing time for fear responses to decrease avoids reinforcing fears of associated cues.
3. Fear intensity must be strong enough to induce anxiety, but not overwhelm. During the procedure, clear communication is needed to prevent excessive levels of distress.
4. *Massed* practice is more effective than *distributed* practice. Daily sessions are more effective than an equivalent number of weekly sessions. If daily therapy sessions are not feasible, then homework assignments become critical.
5. Varying the contexts and stimuli used for exposure helps generalize fear reduction.
6. Removing distractions during exposures prevents avoidance and maintains the client's focus on anxiety cues.

Eye Movement Desensitization and Reprocessing (EMDR)

EMDR does not emphasize gradual exposure. It is used to treat posttraumatic stress disorder, phobias, grief, and somatic disorders (Shapiro, 1995, 2001). Controversy persists over its training methods and the mechanisms proposed for its effects (*e.g.*, Rosen, Lohr, McNally, & Herbert, 2000). There is also concern that evidence for EMDR is based mostly on case studies, self-reports, and therapist evaluations that do not meet accepted standards for behavior therapies (Spiegler & Guevremont, 2003). Nevertheless, recent meta-analyses suggest EMDR is as effective as other exposure-based treatments (Chambless, 1998; Davidson & Parker, 2001).

Shapiro suggests that inducing "bilateral neurophysiological stimulation" of the brain with activities such as back-and-forth eye movements, similar to rapid eye movement (REM) sleep, desensitizes and reprograms trauma-related memories. The similarity of EMDR's procedures to hypnotic induction techniques suggests they may instead enhance suggestibility and placebo effects. Clients are assessed for levels of social support and tolerance for distress and referred elsewhere if these are not strong. If selected, clients are given EMDR's rationale during the *preparation* phase of treatment. Metaphors help clients maintain a working distance to gain mastery as traumatic memories are recalled: *e.g.*, "Imagine watching the scenes of a movie. As you watch, just imagine that it is your traumatic memory that you are observing on the screen." Clients' self-soothing is assessed and they are taught relaxation procedures if needed.

Treatment then involves four procedures, followed sequentially during each of three 90–120 minutes sessions (Shapiro, 2001):

1. *Assessment.* Clients pick either the earliest or the worst traumatic memory for the day's work. Next they choose a negative thought or idea that expresses a negative self-concept in relation to the trauma. A rape victim might say "I'm not clean" or "I can't let myself get close to a man ever again." The client is asked to replace the negative thought with a positive one, such as "I have nothing to feel guilty about." This thought is then rated on a *Validity of Cognition* (VOC) scale, with 1 = completely false and 7 = completely true. Typical VOC ratings of positive thoughts are in the 1–3 range at the beginning of therapy. Clients are asked to rate their feelings while thinking about the chosen traumatic memory and related negative thoughts. SUDS ratings for the negative memory range from 0 = no distress to 10 = highest distress imaginable. Typical ratings are initially from 5 to 10.

2. *Desensitization.* Clients are asked to recall the traumatic memory and associated thoughts. They are asked to notice their feelings as the eye movement procedure is done. Clients track the therapist's finger as their therapist rapidly moves it back and forth, about 12–14 in. in front of the client's eyes. A "set" is 15–30 back-and-forth eye movements. After each set, clients are told to "blank it out" and "take a deep breath." The therapist then asks "What comes up for you?" or "What do you experience now?" and prompt clients to continue expressing their feelings. Support or empathy is avoided as these may distract from desensitization. Instead, once clients express their feelings and rate their distress, the thera-

pist begins another repetition or set. Desensitization continues until SUDS levels reach 0 or 1, or until the session ends.

3. *Installation.* Once SUDS levels are reduced, clients are in a position to consider more adaptive self-views. The therapeutic task is to *install* the competing, positive self-cognition. The original memory is linked with the positive thought during further eye movement procedures. Clients are asked to describe their feelings and make VOC ratings after each set. Every effort is made to allow clients to think positively about themselves with little or no assistance from the therapist. If client self-references do not spontaneously become more positive, then the therapist may use *interweaving* to reframe client comments positively. When VOC ratings reach 6–7, positive thoughts are viewed as installed. These procedures are repeated as long as traumatic memories require reprocessing.

4. *Equilibrium.* At the end of each session, therapists ensure that clients regain emotional equilibrium with self-soothing, relaxation, and positive self-statements. Clients are sent home instructed to maintain a diary of distressing thoughts, dreams, and images that occur during the week. They are reminded to use self-soothing and relaxation as needed.

Flooding and Implosive Therapies

Flooding and implosive therapies involve massed, intense evocations of feared cues, which require a strong therapeutic alliance. Clients must trust the therapist to prevent bad outcomes and be willing to subject themselves to intense levels of anxiety. Both client and therapist need to tolerate high levels of client distress. On the positive side, Shapiro and Shapiro's (1982) meta-analysis of 10 studies suggests that flooding approaches are very effective in reducing fears. Monitoring ensures that imagery induces intense levels of arousal and exposure continues until clients are fully desensitized and are no longer anxious. After several sessions of exposure to the point clients can no longer sustain their emotional arousal, the association between feared cues and anxiety is extinguished. *Flooding* focuses on consciously expressed fears, while *implosive therapy* (Stampfl, 1976) helps clients confront hypothesized psychodynamic conflicts. In this approach, therapists evoke anxiety with vivid descriptions of conflicts between instinctual impulses and internalized prohibitions.

For example, Stampfl demonstrated the treatment of a young woman who complained both of intense fears of cockroaches and of anxieties related to her sexual relationship with her boyfriend. Stampfl hypothesized a dynamic connection between these anxieties and constructed scenarios to evoke anxiety in both areas. In one scenario, she was covered by roaches and could feel the scratching of their legs as they crawled over her body, mouth, and vagina. As the session progressed, Stampfl had the client imagine making love to her boyfriend as he metamorphosed into a giant cockroach, kissing her with his mandibles. Clearly, clients must have trust both in the therapist and the rationale for this procedure. To prevent retraumatizing, implosive and flooding sessions are open-ended and stop only when the client no longer shows signs of anxiety. Signs of avoidance and anxiety are monitored to maintain the client's confrontation with anxiety cues. Signs of anxiety signal the therapist to intensify the vividness of the scenario. Signs of avoidance behavior must first be countered, and then the therapist must push the client even harder.

Acceptance or Mindfulness-Based Interventions

Acceptance or mindfulness-based interventions (Baer, 2003) are another method to help clients tolerate anxiety-inducing thoughts or impulses. Acceptance methods are based on Buddhist mindfulness traditions that encourage full awareness of both inner and outer experiences. Buddhists learn to let go of the need to have their experience be something other than it actually is. Suffering results not so much from pain itself, but rather from *fear* of pain and the struggle to avoid it. Mastering fear eliminates avoidance and boosts self-confidence.

Case Illustration: Exposure Techniques

The following case uses several techniques in treating obsessive-compulsive disorder:

- *History*: Janey is a 26-year-old, single, Asian-American woman, who lives alone and works as a dental office receptionist. For the past 4 months, she has been compelled to check repeatedly that all windows and doors to her first-floor apartment are locked before leaving for work. She has been late on several occasions and now rises an hour earlier than usual to complete her checking routine. She is concerned that her routine is getting longer. She was late to work twice recently and was told her job is in jeopardy. She is embarrassed to tell anyone about her compulsive checking as she believes it is totally irrational. She worries she may be losing her mind since she has never had any break-ins. But when she tries to leave without checking that everything is locked, she becomes panicky, with shaking, nausea, difficulty breathing, racing heart, and faintness. These symptoms are alleviated as soon as she resumes her routine of checking.

  Although she reports no other health problem, she has been very lonely and unhappy since breaking up with her boyfriend with whom she lived for 5 years. He left her for another woman and made cutting remarks when she tried to convince him to stay with her. She says this humiliation shook her self-confidence very badly. She is now frightened of even thinking about dating again. Janey dropped out of college to help support the boyfriend's education and now sees very little future for herself. She acted surprised when asked if her symptoms and the break-up might be connected, but agreed they could be related. She describes her family as traditional and ashamed of her "loose" behavior. She has had little contact with her parents or older brother during the past 5 years. She says she has never had but one or two friends at a time, has few outside interests, stays at home except for shopping and work, and indicates it is a hassle to get out of the apartment. She denies substance use, saying even one glass of wine makes her tipsy.

- *Diagnosis*:
  Axis I—Obsessive-Compulsive Disorder;
  Axis II—no diagnosis;
  Axis III—no other medical condition;
  Axis IV—estranged from family; lack of social support; symptoms threaten job;
  Axis V—GAF=65.
- *Conceptualization*: Janey experiences moderate symptoms and is in significant distress and motivated. Her symptoms are of recent origin, with premorbid functioning in the normal range. She seems ready to comply with a directive approach in addressing symptoms. Relief from checking rituals and panic attacks may allow her to address her problems with family, work, and socializing on her own or those issues may be postponed to a later phase of treatment.
- *Plan*:
  1. *Assessment.* Develop baseline measures by asking Janey to keep a diary recording the frequency and duration of checking behavior. Administer the OQ-45 to ascertain overall level of symptoms. Provide rationale and obtain agreement for proposed interventions and homework discussed during intake.
  2. *Interventions.*
     Week 1: Relaxation, breathing, and imagery training to self-soothe and minimize symptoms of panic attacks when leaving home; thought-stopping (yelling "Stop!!") to control anxiety-inducing thoughts when leaving the house. Discuss enjoyable activities to help get Janey out of the house, meet people, and increase social support. Discuss what reinforcers Janey would like to give herself as she reduces ritual time or leaves home more frequently. Homework: record time spent checking; practice thought-stopping, relaxation, and imagery each time she leaves home.
     Week 2: 90 minutes—Imaginal exposure to all the things that might happen if a door or window were unlocked. Repeat homework assignments when leaving home and diary of time checking.
     Week 3: 2-hours home visit—*In vivo* exposure during repeated trials leaving house with doors and windows unlocked. Prevent checking and support relaxation/imagery when leaving house.
     Continue homework as before.
  3. *Re-assess.* Week 4, review OQ-45 and weekly diaries for progress. Discuss progress, need for more sessions, or change in interventions. If no progress after third week, consider option that compulsive behavior may be functional. It may help her avoid negative feelings about her boyfriend, his treatment of her, and/or the emotional cutoff from her family.
  4. *Later phases of intervention.* Collaboratively explore targets for further interventions; problem-solving skills training as needed to help her reunite with her family.

Operant-Based Behavior Modification

Everyone has engaged in questionable behavior at one time or another. If rewarded, that behavior is likely to be repeated. Behavior modifiers suggest that abnormal, antisocial, or merely eccentric behaviors are responses to environmental cues and reinforcers. Children who receive positive attention only when sick may develop into adults with hypochondriacal symptoms that are reinforced by a doctors' attention. However, it is not necessary to understand how symptoms develop in order to treat hypochondriasis. Therapists need only remove ongoing reinforcers and encourage more adaptive responses to the cues (*discriminative stimuli*) that trigger symptoms.

Three operant principles are used to modify problematic behavior:

1. Control discriminative stimuli;
2. Eliminate reinforcers (extinction);
3. Countercondition responses incompatible with the problem behavior.

Meta-analyses consistently show effect sizes from 0.8 to >1.0 for operant methods (*e.g.*, Shapiro & Shapiro, 1982). Three other procedures help modify complex behaviors and address the problem that operant interventions may extinguish and fail to generalize outside the treatment setting once reinforcers are no longer provided:

1. *Shaping* of complex behaviors by reinforcing approximations may be necessary;
2. *Chaining* the components of complex behaviors, learned separately and then linked together;
3. *Reinforcement fading* prevents extinction of new behaviors by gradually increasing intervals between reinforcements (*intermittent reinforcement schedule*).

Applied Behavioral Analysis

Applied behavioral analysis is illustrated in the operant principles governing the behavior of a child who resists going to bed on time. First, a *baseline* is taken of the time elapsed between reminders (*discriminative stimuli*, S_D) to get ready and the child actually being tucked in bed (*latency*). Next, bedtime routine is *shaped* by setting weekly targets of being in bed by the average bedtime latency for the previous week. This is an easily attainable target and children typically agree to it with little fuss. Shaping occurs as the prior week's average latency is met or exceeded, thus reducing the current week's average. When targets are met, they may be *reinforced* by tokens the child can trade for desired activities, such as 15 minutes of game time during a quiet period. Once an acceptable latency period has been maintained consistently, reinforcers are *faded*: *e.g.*, as long as bedtime latency is within 2 minutes of limits, the child's access to the video game becomes non-contingent on bedtime routine. Social reinforcers such as favorable parental comments on the child's newly gained maturity in going to bed may be substituted for the tokens and then faded as well. Instead of a power struggle, bedtime becomes an opportunity for bonding and building the child's self-esteem.

Reinforcement

Rewards, such as praise for achieving a goal, are often *positive* reinforcers (R^+, something is given). Ending an aversive contingency, such as a child's time-out, may serve as a *negative* reinforcer (R^-, something is taken away). Reinforcers are often identified after the fact as it is difficult to predict what will be effective. Rewards and punishments operate in complex, unpredictable ways and cannot simply be equated with positive and negative reinforcers. Food rewards may lose their reinforcement value as satiation occurs. Punishment may encourage a child to behave; but this is a short-term effect and parents often discover that misbehavior resumes once they are out of sight. The attention involved in punishing misbehavior can be positively reinforcing and escalate misbehavior into a power struggle: if children discover they can outlast their parents, tantrums may be reinforced.

The parent, rather than misbehavior, may be associated with punishment. Punishment can induce fear, avoidance, and model aggressive behavior (Miltenberger, 2008). Because it has few positive, long-term influences on voluntary actions, behaviorists typically limit punishment to treatment of intractable, serious problems such as self-injurious behavior: *e.g.*, giving a mild electric shock when a neurologically compromised child bangs his/her head (Iwata, Dorsey, Slifer, Bauman, & Richman, 1982/1994). It is generally more useful for clients to learn what to do, rather than what *not* to do. For this reason, *functional analysis*, the careful assessment of intrinsic or extrinsic reinforcers that maintain self-injurious or aggressive behavior, is preferred (see case illustration below). It has fewer ethical and practical problems and has led to positive results even with severely impaired individuals (Pelios, Morren, Tesch, & Axelrod, 1999).

Considerable attention has focused on how to identify reinforcers since they are hard to predict and an important influence on voluntary behavior. Deci and Ryan (1985) distinguish between intrinsic and extrinsic reinforcers and found that extrinsic rewards, such as money, candy, or privileges, undermine intrinsic motivation; *e.g.*, children read more books if given extrinsic rewards, but their reading levels actually drop *below* baselines when rewards are removed (also see Deci, Koestner, & Ryan, 1999). Cognitive dissonance theory (Festinger, 1957) suggests they learned to view reading as an effort requiring a reward, rather than a pleasure. A plan is needed to avoid loss of intrinsic motivation if extrinsic reinforcers are used in treatment.

Naturally occurring, intrinsic, or social reinforcers that occur immediately after a response are more effective than those that occur after a delay. If long-term consequences are too remote to affect problem behavior, as in substance abuse, motivational interviewing (see Chap. 9) can help clients become more aware of the long-term effects of their behavior in their life. Grandma's rule, "First the spinach, then the ice cream" can help discover naturally occurring reinforcers. Premack (1965) puts it more technically, "High frequency behavior reinforces low frequency behavior;" *e.g.*, opportunities to read will reinforce children who read a lot, but not non-readers, while games reinforce game players, but not those who seldom play.

Assessment

Careful assessment of the factors that influence and maintain the presenting problem is a key feature of all behavioral therapies. Interventions are tailored to each client's unique situation by defining the presenting problem in concrete, measurable terms. Measurement aids planning and evaluation of therapy and provides feedback on the client's progress. Slow progress signals that different intervention strategies should be considered, not that treatment is a failure. Perhaps behaviorism's most important contribution to other therapeutic approaches has been the idea of using feedback measures to direct and modify interventions as needed.

Behavioral assessment (Nelson & Hayes, 1986) notes the contingencies among Stimulus-Organism-Response-Consequence (SORC) components, which are monitored and influenced to help clients learn more adaptive behavior. SORC analysis begins by specifying the *discriminative stimuli* (S_D) present when problems occur; *e.g.*, if arguments regularly precede binge-eating, then learning to resolve conflict and engage in activities incompatible with eating should be part of the treatment plan. If binge eating occurs after an argument only if the client has been drinking, an *organismic* factor, then drinking patterns must also be addressed. Baseline measures of binge-eating frequency, amount, and duration (*response*) assess intervention effectiveness. Finally, the response *consequences* that reinforce and maintain problem behavior are modified; *e.g.*, family education may be necessary if binges lead to attention and over-concern by the client's family.

With complex problems, a SORC analysis may reflect only one element in a *behavioral chain* of SORCs. The consequences of one SORC sequence may serve as a *cue-producing* response or discriminative stimulus for the next SORC. It's a matter of *punctuation*, whether cue-producing responses are treated as stimuli or as responses in developing a treatment plan. Many interpersonal conflicts can be viewed as SORC chains with one person's response serving as an S_D for the partner and vice versa; *e.g.*, a wife's childhood abuse history can turn the tilting of her husband's head into an S_D signifying imminent attack. This misperception leads her to act defensively, a cue-producing response her husband interprets as rejection. A continuing vicious circle of miscommunication can then leave both parties feeling victimized.

Functional Analysis

Functional Analysis is a SORC analysis that goes beyond simple observation or reports from clients or caretakers. Clinicians perform experiments that empirically determine relevant S_Ds and R^+s. A case study by Jones and Friman (1999) illustrates functional analysis and the use of multiple measures to evaluate the effects of exposure. Mike, a 14-year-old middle school resident at Boys' Town, was referred by his principal due to the interference of his insect phobia with his academic performance. Teachers were concerned that the other boys' teasing and shouting "Look out! There's a bug!" made it difficult for Mike to concentrate. Jones and Friman took multiple base-line measures to determine whether the effective cue was the actual presence of bugs or if it was Mike's belief that bugs were present. Their response criterion was the number of math problems Mike could solve in 4-minutes trials with crickets present. They showed him three crickets purchased from a pet store and discovered that telling Mike bugs were present depressed his performance initially. However, within 4–5 trials his performance approached levels when he was told none were present. Next, an *in vivo* approach hierarchy let Mike move from just holding the crickets in a jar to allowing them to crawl on his bare arm for a minute. Despite his ability to approach and handle the crickets, his math performance continued to suffer during sessions 10–15. However, Mike's math performance improved, even in the presence of crickets, when exposure was combined with tokens that were exchanged for candy, videos, *etc.*, during sessions 16–18. This level was maintained during extinction and reacquisition trials in sessions 19–28. Three points are noteworthy:

1. Teachers were wrong in thinking Mike was distracted by teasing about bugs being present;
2. Exposure alone enabled Mike to handle crickets, but their presence still interfered with his math performance;
3. Functional analysis discovered that the effective S_D was the actual presence of bugs. This made it possible to focus on procedures to address Mike's real problem, which was being distracted by the bugs from his academic work, not his fear of bugs.

A number of measures are used in SORC analyses, each with its own advantages:

1. *Physiological measures* require training and equipment, but are used with many health-related problems; *e.g.*, sleep disorders require information about sleep stages, restlessness, dreaming, *etc.* Such information helps classify disorders and guide treatment planning.
2. *Direct observation* may be necessary, *e.g.*, the frequency of out-of-seat behavior of a hyperactive child or how far an agoraphobic client can move from the home. As a result, school or home visits are more common among behavior therapists than other approaches. Direct observations in the therapist's office, *behavioral approach* tests, are often used with simple phobias together with SUDS ratings

of distress levels. Unfortunately, people are reactive and tend to behave differently when observed directly. Low-frequency behaviors, *e.g.*, anger outbursts or sexual problems, are not easily accessible to direct observation and may require role plays or enactments. A couple might be asked to role-play a situation that previously resulted in serious conflict. Panic attack symptoms can be simulated by asking clients to hyperventilate, to spin around, or to exercise on a treadmill.

3. *Diaries* or self-monitoring forms are used to measure problems that are not easily observed directly; *e.g.*, clients may be asked to keep a daily SORC diary to track arguments or sexual problems. Barlow and Craske (2000) published a form for reporting the sequence, type, intensity, and duration of symptoms during a panic attack. Clients then record any situational or thought triggers ($S_{D}s$).

4. *Tests and checklists* that measure anxiety, dissociative, depressive, or interpersonal problems are used by therapists of many different orientations to track progress in treating relevant symptoms. Examples include the Child Behavior Checklist (Achenbach, 1992), Beck Depression Inventory (Beck, Steer, & Brown, 1996), Beck Anxiety Inventory (Beck, Epstein, Brown, & Steer, 1988), and Beck Hopelessness Inventory (Beck, Weissman, Lester, & Trexler, 1974).

5. *Structured* or *semi-structured clinical interviews* develop problem lists and assess clients' experience of their problems and overall situation. Interviewers with different interview styles may develop quite different pictures of clients using unstructured interview formats. Most behaviorists prefer structuring to gain more reliable information. However, fully structured interviews do not allow follow-up questions when client misconstrue the question or answer ambiguously. As a result, semi-structured interviews that do so are preferred; *e.g.*, the Structured Clinical Interview for DSM-IV (SCID-IV; First, Spitzer, Gibbon, & Williams, 1996).

The SCID-IV is widely used for diagnoses, but takes about 2 hours to administer. In general, manualized interventions rely on semi-structured interviews and validated self-report measures.

In contrast, individualized behavioral approaches usually rely on interviews or direct observation.

Contingency Management Procedures

The basic assumption of operant interventions or *contingency management* is that behavior is governed by its consequences. Rewards and punishments motivate and reinforce behavior. People seek rewards and avoid punishments, which strengthens associations among discriminative stimuli ($S_{D}s$), operant responses, and reinforcers. As noted before, operant interventions involve some combination of managing cues, contingencies, or counterconditioning adaptive responses. If assessment indicates a lack of progress with an intervention strategy, then functional analysis and choosing another promising intervention proceed until one proves effective. Sherman (1973) summarizes the six steps of contingency management as follows:

1. *Operationalize target behavior.* Problems are operationally defined by frequency, duration, intensity, or latency measures, preferably in situations where they occur; *e.g.*, hyperactivity might be operationalized as the number of times a boy leaves his seat without permission.
2. *Identify behavioral objectives.* Which behaviors need to increase or decrease? Could an incompatible behavior replace behavior that needs to be decreased? What are acceptable outcome levels? The hyperactive boy's intermediate goal might be to decrease the mean frequency of leaving his seat each hour, ultimately to leave his seat only with permission.
3. *Develop behavioral measures and baselines.* Operant interventions begin with a SORC assessment of antecedent cues, organismic correlates, targeted response, and reinforcing consequences. Multiple baseline measures of frequency, intensity, or problem duration assess progress, *e.g.*, both out-of-seat frequencies and in-seat duration may be useful measures of hyperactivity; non-targeted behaviors such as frequency of teacher reminders may be included as controls to compare with the target behavior. The hyperactive boy may leave his seat more often when seated next to a window. Different seating arrangements might help control distracting cues. Assessment of organismic factors, *e.g.*, adequate breakfast, sleeping patterns, or need for medication. By measuring both in-seat time and the frequency of leaving without permission, other cues may be noticed, *e.g.*, that he stays in his seat during geography lessons. Consequences such as teacher reprimands or classmate laughter are evaluated as possible reinforcers.
4. *Conduct naturalistic observations.* SORC assessment is conducted in the client's natural environment when possible. The therapist ideally would observe the hyperactive boy in the classroom or perhaps enlist a teacher's aide.
5. *Modify existing contingencies.* Exposure to discriminative cues and unwanted reinforcers is reduced: the hyperactive boy is seated away from the window and 5-minutes time-outs in a quiet space minimize classmate attention for out-of-seat activities. Who gives what reinforcer when for desired behavior is specified. Reinforcers for meeting "in-seat" goals might be opportunities to help the teacher collect papers, clean chalk-boards, or gain access to another desired activity. Couples in counseling can make lists of rewards to give each other for meeting desired goals such as letting the partner know if one will be late.
6. *Monitor the results.* Intervention effects are assessed by comparing the targeted response with baseline measures. The treatment plan is changed if progress is not being made and treatment is terminated once goals are reached. Seeing progress on a chart may prove reinforcing for the hyperactive boy. Involving him in the design of the program also helps balance the power differential; *e.g.*, he might be asked to choose preferred reinforcers from a list. The child learns that he is not the "problem," but that he, his teacher, and his therapist are all working together to solve a problem that concerns everyone.

Paradoxically, contingency management accounts for both the success and the limits of operant techniques. The dialectic tension is between *other-management* and *self-management* of environmental contingencies: either the therapist has control of the environment or the client must be willing and able to self-manage reinforcers. Self-management is generally preferred since controlling another's environment raises ethical and practical considerations: ethically, other management reflects the therapist's greater power; practically, therapists may have very little control over environmental contingencies. The need for environmental control of contingencies has limited use of operant techniques primarily to help parents manage children or administrators to manage behaviors in institutions such as schools, prisons, or hospitals. Corporate managers also use contingency management to increase productivity.

Token Economies

Institutions such as prisons, mental hospitals, or schools for the developmentally disabled are often not very rewarding places to be. Reinforcers, such as grounds privileges, entertainment, or staff attention, tend to be provided non-contingently or after a problem occurs: "problem" residents receive staff attention. *Token economies* are a way to counter such tendencies. Token reinforcers are given for following rules or completing treatment or educational goals and exchanged later for extra privileges, snacks, soft drinks, or television access. Residents obtain tokens given by staff immediately upon successfully achieving treatment goals. Ayllon and Azrin (1968) describe how a state hospital solved towel shortages using tokens for each towel turned in on laundry day. One patient had become very adept at hiding towels, but turned in several hundred towels once the new contingency was announced.

Token economies are effective in helping institutions manage the behavior of even highly disturbed individuals, but response-reinforcer contingencies should be clearly understood by both staff and residents (Ayllon & Azrin, 1968). To be effective, the staff must be trained, motivated, and monitored to ensure reinforcers are given consistently. Untrained staff may misconstrue how reinforcers work and try to control negative behavior by withholding or taking back tokens. This encourages power struggles and creates an aversive rather than a cooperative environment.

Even well-administered token programs do better managing behavior than treating psychiatric problems. Residents may fail to use newly acquired skills after leaving the institution unless helped to generalize their skills after release. Also, many hospital residents or prison inmates may already have relevant skills and follow rules only to make their institutional stay more pleasant. Token economies are more desirable than punitive controls to encourage cooperation with the staff, but this should not be confused with rehabilitation.

Operant techniques work well with children partly because they want the parental approval that implicitly accompanies tangible reinforcers and partly because their problem behavior often reflects a lack of appropriate skills. When children, hospital patients, or developmentally disabled residents lack skills, token economies help motivate adherence to remedial programs. Response generalization can then be facilitated by fading reinforcers and practicing the new skills in a variety of contexts. With prison inmates or psychiatric patients who already possess such skills, the problem is to encourage their application outside the institution. Motivational interviewing (see Chap. 9) is useful in helping them discover personal, long-term advantages in committing to change.

Aversive Contingency Management

Although punitive techniques can have problematic effects, there are exceptions. Many autistic or brain-damaged patients require institutionalization to control repetitive, stereotyped, self-injurious behavior. "Headbangers" repeatedly bang their heads against a wall with sufficient force to cause concussion or other injury. Self-injurious behavior is reduced after only a few, moderately painful electric shocks are administered (Lovaas & Favell, 1987). Bucher and Lovaas (1968) used a short series of electric shocks to eliminate self-pummeling in a schizophrenic boy who struck himself nearly 3,000 times during a 90-minutes baseline period when not restrained. Ethical concerns about using electric shock appear balanced by its effectiveness in reducing more serious self-harm when it is not used.

To ensure effectiveness, several precautions are observed. Shocks are given calmly, early in the behavioral sequence, and with just enough intensity to influence the behavior. They should also be given on a continuous schedule in as many different situations as possible to encourage generalization. When cues that trigger a self-injurious sequence are identified, counterconditioning is used to associate the cues with more adaptive, competing responses.

Covert sensitization is an aversive technique effective in treating motivated clients with impulse disorders such as alcoholism or pedophilia. Cautela and Kearney (1993) first taught relaxation skills to a motivated pedophile and then asked him to imagine approaching a boy to whom he was attracted. Next he was asked to imagine becoming very nauseated as he thought about asking the boy up to his apartment: to feel acid regurgitating and vomiting over himself and the boy just as he began to speak to the boy. It was suggested that he was very embarrassed by people staring, but began to feel better as he turned away to return to his apartment. After a shower he felt clean again, relaxed, and good about himself. Clients may also be asked to repeat such exercises as homework and actually induce vomiting at the appropriate time. *Disulfram* (Antabuse), described in Chap. 3, is another aversive technique often used with court-ordered or motivated alcoholics that cause extreme nausea if alcohol is consumed. If coupled with therapy, the motivated client can be helped stop drinking (Martin, Clapp, Alfers, & Beresford, 2004). Without motivation, however, they simply learn not to drink when taking Antabuse.

Therapist Contingency Management

Therapist controlled reinforcers have several applications. (DeShazer, 1994; see Chap. 14) suggests that therapist attention is often contingently associated with *problem-saturated* narratives. His *solution-focused* therapy instead selectively focuses on *solution-saturated* narratives that emphasize client strengths rather than weaknesses. Therapists unconsciously use attention as a social reinforcer in other approaches: experiential therapists' interest in emotional behavior increases their client focus on feelings; psychodynamic therapists' attention to dreams or sexual concerns increases the likelihood that clients will discuss dreams and sexual matters. More explicitly, behavior therapists make contracts: *e.g.*, a client might be asked to deposit $100 and then earn the money back through achieving behavioral goals or adherence to the treatment program (Harris & Bruner, 1971). If goals are not met, an interesting response-cost variation on this technique is to have clients contribute the money to a political party they do *not* favor.

Couple's Contingency Contracts

Behavior exchange theory (Jacobson & Margolin, 1979) asks couples to decide what behavior they would like to see from their partner. Next, they decide what their partner might do to reward such behavior. In *contingent contracting*, they agree explicitly upon the consequences for any desired behavior; *e.g.*, partners may agree to exchange helping around the house for more intimate conversations. If this feels too materialistic, then *noncontingent contracts* may be used. Each agrees to perform some action from their partner's wish list during the coming week, but its timing is to be a surprise. This introduces greater spontaneity and ensures more positive interactions in the relationship.

Contingency Self-Management

This useful application of operant techniques requires active, motivated clients who persist with homework assignments. Clients learn to identify SORC contingencies, measure and graph problem behavior, establish baseline levels, set realistic goals, and develop a list of reinforcers to give themselves. Environmental and social supports that help maintain changed behaviors are identified. Clients are then coached how to trouble-shoot any problems they encounter. If the initial approach is not working, the therapist helps them design a new intervention. Obese clients might be taught to limit the variety of cues associated with eating: to always eat in one place, take small portions, use small plates to make portions seem larger, and get up from the table if they want seconds. Compliance could be reinforced by "mad" money or allowing oneself some (non-food) treats. Similarly, money usually spent on smoking can be set aside for healthier reinforcers during smoking cessation programs. Watson and Tharp (1997) describe four steps in self-directed change:

1. Select goals that are measurable, attainable, positive, and significant for the person.
2. Translate goals into specific target behaviors that can be increased or decreased.

3. Systematically self-monitor Antecedent-Behavior-Consequence sequences using a behavioral diary.
4. Develop a plan for change, that includes self-monitoring to evaluate progress and that reinforces progress.

Parental Contingency Management

Parents learn to manage their children's behavior positively using operant techniques. Watson and Tharp's (1997) four steps are also appropriate in this context. In an interesting switch, older children have been taught to modify their parents' behavior: *e.g.*, children can reinforce reductions in parental nagging or increases in positive talk by doing household chores contingently. Children gain a sense of self-efficacy and become rather excited as they graph parental "progress" and parents like the "changes" in their child's behavior!

Case Illustration: Functional Analysis of Behavior

Piazza *et al.* (1998) demonstrated the application of functional analysis in the treatment of three neurologically impaired children with severe communication impairment and diagnosed with *pica*, the ingestion of inedible objects. Contingency management procedures are useful with such clients since their environments may be modified without using speech. Piazza and colleagues used several different experiments with each of the children to determine what reinforcers were functional for each child. The case of Brandy is illustrative of a careful functional analysis:

- *Background.* Brandy is a 17-year-old female (ethnicity not specified) with Cornelia de Lange syndrome, a rare genetic condition marked by microcephaly, distinctive facial features, physical abnormalities, autism, and severe retardation. Her communication is limited to signs indicating "please," "eat," and "drink." She was hospitalized five times to remove objects from her stomach and esophagus, including keys, rocks, crayons, and coins. Her parents often offer her cola drinks to encourage her to spit out objects. Her mother notes that supervision of Brandy is very difficult, given the presence of five siblings ranging in age from 3 to 15 years old.
- *Diagnosis*:
  Axis I: Pica; Autistic Disorder;
  Axis II: Mental Retardation, Severe;
  Axis III; Cornelia de Lange syndrome;
  Axis IV: Family stressed by need for constant observation;
  Axis V: GAF = 15.
- *Conceptualization (Functional Analysis)*: Experimental sessions were held in play rooms "baited" with objects the medical team deemed safe for ingestion, including paper, birthday candles, uncooked beans and pasta, and rice sticks. Pica baselines were observed during 10-minutes play sessions in the first experi-

ment. Experimental conditions similar to her home environment tested hypotheses about possible discriminative cues and reinforcers:

1. Social *attention* as a reinforcer—a verbal reprimand "Don't do that!" was given if pica occurred.
2. Pica as escape from *demands*—Brandy was given sequential verbal, gestural, and physical prompts to complete pre-academic and self-care tasks; the "escape" was removal of task materials for 30 seconds if pica occurred.
3. Intrinsic reinforcement—a 30-minutes *alone* condition determined if extrinsic rewards were necessary.
4. Need for stimulation—stimulation was facilitated by *play* with preferred toys and non-contingent attention.
5. Cola as a reinforcer—one-ounce cola drinks were provided when pica occurred.

Observed pica rates for the five conditions, from highest to lowest, were *cola, alone, attention, play*, and *demands*. The results suggest that intrinsic or extrinsic reinforcers are important, but low rates in the *play* and *demands* conditions argue against Brandy using pica to self-regulate overall stimulation levels. Sensory qualities associated with possible intrinsic reinforcement were assessed in experiment 2 as pica levels were still high in the *alone* condition.

Pica rates in a room baited with ingestible objects were observed during 20 five-minute sessions to compare oral and other types of sensory stimulation. Brandy was given food and a rubber toy for oral stimulation and items such as a mirror, musical toy, or massager in the visual, auditory, or tactile stimulation conditions. Oral stimulation pica rates were 0.2/minute mostly with the rubber toy *vs.* 1.8/minute for non-oral stimulation. In later experiments, she showed the lowest rates of pica with firm, textured foods, when compared with soft, gelatinous foods. With her most favored foods, such as carrot sticks or sugar-free lollipops, pica was reduced to zero. Reducing pica to zero was particularly important for treatment planning, given the difficulties Brandy's parents reported with her supervision.

- Analysis: These results indicate that oral stimulation was an important reinforcer in the *alone* condition. However, the earlier findings suggested that *attention* or *cola* drinks might also be involved. Thus, more experiments were conducted in which receiving cola drinks or social attention were either non-contingent or made contingent upon the occurrence of pica. These results indicated that pica rates were dramatically higher when either attention or cola was given. Because Brandy preferred textured foods, it was inferred that cola was extrinsically reinforcing, independent of its oral stimulation value. However, non-contingent attention rates were not zero, suggesting that intrinsic oral stimulation was also reinforcing. Thus, intervention should make Brandy's favorite textured foods and cola available on a non-contingent basis.
- *Intervention Plan*: Brandy's parents will be shown how attention, cola, and intrinsic reinforcers all help maintain her pica. They will be instructed to provide Brandy safe, oral stimulation with continuous access to her favorite textured foods, including carrot sticks, sugar-free lollipops, bread-sticks, and a teething

ring. Finally, attention and colas will no longer be contingent upon the occurrence of pica, but given instead at appropriate times, non-contingently on the pica.

Behavioral Activation

Behavioral activation is frequently used with depressed individuals. Depression is viewed as a vicious circle: client expectations that nothing positive will ever happen result in a loss of energy, reduction of activities that could lead to positive experiences, and a depressed mood. Anticipating fewer rewards reinforces depressing expectations with still further reductions in activity, and so on. Even basic housekeeping or self-care may become irregular. Instead of extinguishing negative feelings as in exposure therapy, behavioral activation aims to increase positive feelings by helping clients increase activities with potentially positive outcomes.

Behavioral activation encourages clients to maximize intrinsically reinforcing activities or offer opportunities for social reinforcement (Jacobson, Martell, & Dimidjian, 2001). Clients keep a diary of activities and their duration, and rate any associated feelings of mastery or pleasure. The diary also records whether activities were planned or spontaneous, rewarding or unpleasant, monotonous or interesting, or accompanied by ruminations. This baseline is then compared against activities that used to be enjoyable, but now occur infrequently. Clients also explore any activities that might be enjoyable, but have never been tried. The various lists are compared to determine which unpleasant activities might be reduced and which pleasurable ones might be increased. Clients choose some pleasurable activities to try each day during the coming week. They predict degree of pleasure they anticipate and then complete a weekly activity schedule. During the next session, predicted pleasure ratings are compared with the week's actual ratings.

If client predictions prove too pessimistic (*negative fortune telling*), the negative attributions are challenged with cognitive interventions. Regular routines for meals, bed-time, *etc.*, are encouraged. In addition, training in being mindful of negative experiences is substituted for rumination or complaints. Homework compliance is encouraged by:

1. Ensuring that clients understand the approach and agree to specific assignments;
2. Addressing environment factors, such as significant others, that might block compliance;
3. Doing assignments in session if necessary;
4. Phone reminders during the week that are gradually faded.

To help prevent relapse, clients are taught to identify and avoid environmental cues that have triggered or maintained their depression in the past.

Case Illustration: Behavioral Activation (Adapted from Jacobson et al., 2001)

- *Background*: Steve, a 35-year-old European-American businessman, became depressed after his wife learned of his affair with his current partner and divorced him. Steve ruminates over his financial difficulties following the divorce. His resultant irritability causes conflict with his significant other and growing alienation from his children and co-workers. He is also in conflict with his ex-wife over parenting issues. Although work has been his one source of satisfaction, depression interferes with this as well. Increasingly, Steve is waking unrested and depressed, calls in sick, and ruminates on how bad things are. Although getting to work is increasingly difficult, he feels satisfaction with his efforts once there. His daily routines of getting up, getting dressed, having breakfast, and going to work are significantly disrupted. Typically, he does not bother to dress on days he stays home and just sits on the sofa feeling irritable and worrying. His Beck Depression Inventory (BDI) score of 40 is quite high.
- *Diagnosis*:
  Axis I—Major Depression;
  Axis II—No Diagnosis;
  Axis III—No Diagnosis;
  Axis IV—Recent divorce; financial difficulties; parenting and relational conflicts;
  Axis V—GAF=55.
- *Problem List*: 1. Depressed, irritable mood; 2. Financial problems; 3. Irregular routines; 4. Irregular work attendance; 5. Conflict with partner; 6. Conflict with ex-wife *re* parenting; 7. Decreased contact with children.
- *Case Conceptualization*: Steve has experienced reduced pleasure in life, following the stress of divorce and reduced financial resources. He has begun a pattern of avoidance and irritability that drives away others. This further reduces opportunities for positive reinforcement and exacerbates his depression and irritability. To counter this downward spiral, Steve must become more actively involved in activities that are intrinsically rewarding. He needs to see this pattern and make a commitment to engage more in enjoyable activities.
- *Intervention Plan*:
  Week 1. A list of enjoyable activities will be developed. Steve will keep an activity log monitoring the degree of mastery and pleasure associated with each activity. The log will include triggers, his reactions, and the consequences for each activity (*e.g.*, avoidance, depression, irritation, environmental response, *etc.*). He will select a pleasurable activity he is confident he can perform during the next week. It is expected that most pleasurable ratings will occur on days at work or when engaging in a chosen activity. Less pleasurable ratings are predicted for days at home.
  Week 2. If this prediction is verified to Steve's satisfaction, he will be encouraged to increase the number of days he reports for work until he reaches full-time. He will also be encouraged gradually to increase the number of pleasurable

activities attempted. As he gains more pleasure and sense of mastery in his life, it is predicted that his BDI scores and the degree of conflict with his partner, wife, and co-workers will decrease.

Week 3. The BDI will be administered and Steve will be asked about the degree of daily conflict with his partner, wife, and co-workers. If problems do not show a downward trend, possible changes in the treatment plan will be discussed. If initial successes are achieved, then Phase II of the treatment plan may begin once BDI scores are in the normal range.

Phase I would be expected to take about three more weeks.

Phase II *(Weeks 7–9).* Steve will learn conflict resolution skills to help him cooperate in his co-parenting responsibilities with his ex-wife. Parenting skills training will be added to increase the frequency and quality of his time with his children.

Cognitive Behavior Modification Approaches

Cognitive behavior modification includes related approaches that consider thoughts to be a verbal behavior modifiable by exposure, operant, and modeling principles, rather than challenging faulty cognitions as done in cognitive therapy (Chap. 5). They often use psychoeducation groups and emphasize skills such as assertiveness, communication, stopping obsessive or intrusive thoughts, problem-solving, behavioral activation, self-instruction, and stress inoculation.

Psychoeducation and Social Skills Training

Psychoeducation with large groups is a cost-effective method to teach clients how to change behavior and thoughts. It is useful for groups of clients that share uncomplicated symptomatic, as opposed to thematic complaints. Lectures on the nature and causes of target symptoms are supplemented with workshop activities and small group practice of skills to manage or control symptoms. Clients learn by observing other class members during skill practices as teachers give feedback to individuals on their performance; *e.g.,* clients with snake phobias learn to relax while observing the teacher handle a snake, followed by class members approaching and handling the snake. Psychoeducation can also help clients change life styles by learning to reduce stress, exercise, stop smoking, cope with chronic illness, prevent substance abuse relapse, comply with medical treatment programs, or adopt sexually responsible behavior. Psychoeducation is part of every approach since therapists need to explain risks and provide a rationale for therapy procedures. As discussed in Chap. 1, client understanding and agreement about the procedures of therapy is essential for a good therapeutic alliance and therapeutic outcome. The group format is also well suited to social skills training, providing opportunities to practice group and dyadic skills with other participants and is widely used to teach parenting and couple's communication skills (see Chap. 12). Participants gain new perspectives as they provide each other feedback on their skills. Therapists may also role play social skills with client as part of individual therapy.

Social Learning Programs (SLPs)

SLPs combine psychoeducation and social learning with token economy programs to address generalization and treatment adherence in institutional settings such as psychiatric hospitals or forensic settings (Menditto, 2002; Paul & Lentz 1977; Paul, Stuve, & Menditto, 1997). Residents learn adaptive social skills to replace deviant, bizarre, or aggressive behavior, while the staff receives ongoing consultation and training to help create a positive social environment for residents. SLP treatment is divided into levels that individualize programs for residents whose abilities range from bizarre or violent behavior to adaptive and constructive behavior. At lower levels, SLP programs give residents tokens for following simple instructions, decreasing bizarre verbalizations, or avoiding physical aggression. *Response cost*, the loss of tokens, occurs only with serious lapses such as violent outbursts. Adaptive behavior is shaped in this way until tokens are faded using non-contingent reinforcement.

As residents master a level, they are moved to less restrictive environments: different hospital units, minimum-security units, or half-way houses. Succeeding SLP levels involve treatment plans with more demanding goals for adaptive, appropriate, and socially skillful behavior. Administrators monitor staff compliance with time-sample observations of interactions with residents and how they handle low-incidence behaviors such as assault. Senior staff then provide feedback and training based on observations of the staff's verbal and nonverbal interactions with residents; *e.g.*, if they implement treatment contingencies in positive ways. Program administrators meet regularly with staff to review resident progress, update treatment plans as needed, and consider whether residents are ready to move to the next treatment level.

Paul and his associates have reported positive outcomes in preliminary research. Severely disturbed patients, averaging 17 years of hospitalization, showed improvement after introduction of SLP practices (Paul & Menditto, 1992). Fewer than 11% remained on antipsychotic medication and 25% functioned at normal levels. All but 3% were discharged, either completely (11%) or to sheltered living and work settings. At 18-month follow-up, fewer than 3% were rehospitalized, This dramatic improvement over typical hospitalization outcomes suggests that SLPs may be very cost-effective when compared with "treatment as usual."

Assertiveness Training

Wolpe (1958) first introduced assertiveness training as a skill incompatible with anxiety. Assertiveness psychoeducation groups are designed for shy, overly inhibited, and compliant individuals who let themselves be exploited by others or find it difficult to express their feelings. The assumption is that everyone has the right to express their feelings in a respectful manner. The ultimate goal of assertiveness training is the ability to choose whether or not to be assertive about legitimate needs. Clients are taught that assertion is not aggression. They learn to be sensitive to other's feelings when stating opinions or asking that needs be met. Cognitive interventions challenge faulty thinking or self-defeating, negative self-statements.

Assertiveness is broken down into sub-skills eventually chained into an integrated response. Sub-skills include desensitizing anxiety about assertiveness, speaking in a louder voice, learning appropriate eye contact and nonverbal behavior, and using *I-language*. I-language expresses the client's views and feelings in simple, non-defensive terms. It expresses needs as positive requests that avoid blaming the other person; *e.g.*, "I'd like to know when you're going to be late for dinner, so I can plan accordingly." Clients also learn active listening skills that show understanding of the other person's feelings and concerns in simple, direct terms; *e.g.*, "I know it's hard to plan dinner if you don't know when I'll be home." Therapists model communication skills for clients to practice with one another. The therapist and other group members suggest ways to improve performances and give positive feedback for each other's successes.

Thought-Stopping

Thought-stopping helps clients manage intrusive, ruminative thoughts, impulses, or images that occur in disorders such as PTSD or OCD. Clients recall the thought and then yell "STOP!!!" as loud as they can. The usual result is that the thought is interrupted. Clients practice this each time the intrusive thought occurs, gradually fading the volume of "STOP!" until it is sub-vocalized. They may also be asked to imagine a "stop sign" as they are saying the word, gradually fading to just the image. When ruminations such as "Maybe I'm going crazy" are present, covert assertion may be helpful. Clients are told to follow "STOP!" with a rational counterassertion: "Stop! Forget that nonsense! I'm perfectly normal! Everyone has thoughts they can't get out of their heads sometimes. I'm just worrying too much" (Rimm & Masters, 1974).

Problem-Solving

Designed for clients with dependency or self-efficacy difficulties, the first step evaluates any attributional biases that might interfere with effective problem-solving:

1. *Minimizing*: "It doesn't really bother me that she's divorcing me."
2. *Externalizing responsibility*: "Things would be fine if she wouldn't complain so much."

3. *Internalizing responsibility*: "He'd be less interested in other women if I were more attractive."
4. *Global attributions*: "I'll just fail at this like everything else in my life."
5. *Stable attributions*: "It doesn't matter what I do, it's never going to get any better."

Attributional biases may need to be addressed with psychoeducation or cognitive restructuring (Chap. 5) before problem-solving training begins. Clients need to recognize how they use automatic attributions before beginning training in the four stages of problem-solving (Nezu & Nezu, 1989; Nezu, Nezu, & Lombardo, 2004):

1. *Problem definition*: Clients often see problems in vague, global terms and confound several issues. They need to define problems in concrete terms, break them down into separate parts, form realistic goals, and recognize obstacles such as how others view the problem.
2. *Generate alternatives*: Therapist and client brainstorm a comprehensive list of solutions, regardless of how impractical they may seem at first.
3. *Decision making*: A "cost-benefit" analysis anticipates positive and negative consequences for each of the resulting ideas. Clients then compare and choose the best alternative.
4. *Solution implementation and verification*: Clients carry out the plan and observe its effects. Therapists help trouble-shoot any difficulties in implementation. If necessary, clients return to the brainstorming list and attempt the next best solution.

Self-Instructional Training

Self-instructional training helps children with attention deficits, hyperactivity, aggressiveness, or other impulse problems (Meichenbaum, 1977). It is based on Luria's (1961) three stages describing how children develop voluntary control over their behavior:

1. Parent's verbal commands control the child's behavior;
2. Children overtly imitate these speech patterns in directing their own behavior;
3. Overt verbal control of the child's behavior gradually shifts to covert speech.

Meichenbaum (1977) teaches children to repeat instructions out loud during training sessions. Parents watch and learn how to help with homework. He models solving tasks such as puzzles and describes the steps he takes, why he selects some alternatives and rejects others until the task is finished. Children then try the same task as Meichenbaum talks them through the problem-solving steps. He discusses the pros and cons of each move until the child is successful. Children then try the problem again, speaking aloud to themselves. Eventually, they repeat it with whispers and finally with covert speech. Children learn to slow down and think about the task requirements before acting as they repeat procedures across various tasks and settings. They also learn to correct themselves after mistakes without becoming angry or frustrated. Note that verbal learning is treated here as a skill that can be applied to a wide variety of situations.

Stress Inoculation

Meichenbaum (1986, 1996) uses psychoeducation methods to teach adults to anticipate, prevent, and solve problems by following three steps:

1. *Conceptualize the problem.* Clients learn how to conceptualize, anticipate, and address potential problems.
2. *Try on the conceptualization.* Clients explore and consolidate their understanding by imagining scenarios in which they try out the problem-solving approach.
3. *Modify cognitions and produce new behaviors.* Global, stable, and internal attributions of anticipated failure are challenged. Clients learn to modify internal dialogues and complete homework using their new problem-solving skills.

With this last step, stress inoculation begins to resemble the cognitive therapies (Chap. 5). Although stress inoculation involves cognitive principles, cognitions are treated as skills; *e.g.*, clients identify actual and potential stressors in their lives and learn the skill of viewing them as challenges rather than as stressors.

Lazarus' BASIC-ID Multimodal Therapy

Arnold Lazarus (1967), an early proponent of technical eclecticism, suggested therapists ignore theoretical incompatibilities among approaches and rely instead on systematic application of empirically verified treatments. Lazarus' *BASIC-ID* or *multimodal therapy* provides a framework that describes interventions for different areas where problems can occur (see Table 3.2). The BASIC-ID acronym provides a format that ensures all problem areas are reviewed and suggests which interventions are most likely to help.

Table 3.2 Lazarus' multimodal therapy: BASIC-ID interventions

Problem area	Suggested interventions
Behavior	Reinforcement; punishment; extinction; counterconditioning
Affect	Acknowledge, clarify, reflect feelings; abreaction (exposure)
Sensation	Tension release; sensory pleasuring
Imagery	Coping images; change in self-image
Cognition	Cognitive restructuring; heightening awareness; education
Interpersonal relations	Modeling; social skill/assertiveness training; disperse collusions
Drugs/biology	Treat substance abuse or medical illness; exercise; diet; medication

Integrative Implications

Behavioral approaches are particularly well suited to symptomatic, as opposed to thematic interventions. Operant therapists have developed idiographic measures and interventions tailored for nearly every imaginable situation. Behavioral interventions are especially useful working with children, nonverbal, developmentally delayed, or psychotic clients, and managing behavior in institutions. Although dialectical tensions have existed among the four types of learning, the field is now more integrative. Classical, operant, vicarious, and verbal learning methods have been integrated in Lazarus' BASIC-ID approach and Meichenbaum's cognitive behavior modification (CBM), which treats cognition or verbalizations as operants. Dialectic tensions continue between CBM's view of cognition as an operant and cognitive therapy's focus on the *meaning* of verbal behavior (See Chap. 5). Instead of shaping the client's self-talk or environment, cognitive therapists challenge the client's maladaptive internal schemas and understanding of events. However, cognitive therapists frequently integrate cognitive and behavioral interventions also, while behavioral therapists increasingly challenge maladaptive beliefs or attributional biases.

Three behavioral emphases are critical for integrative therapies: It is important to:

1. Recognize that learning underlies change in every psychosocial therapy;
2. Consider the unique qualities of each client's immediate environment;
3. Define problems in concrete terms that can be monitored to evaluate client progress.

As later chapters describe, postmodern emphases on how contexts influence meanings parallel behavioral emphases on environmental contexts or contingencies. Whether as a separate approach with a wealth of techniques or integrated with other approaches, behaviorists have had a major impact upon the field of psychotherapy.

Chapter Four: Main Points

- Behavioral approaches share a modernist philosophy of rational empiricism. They emphasize learning, active interventions, and environmental, rather than person factors. They are committed to empirically validated procedures.
- Anxiety symptoms may be addressed by relaxation and breathing training and/or exposure therapy. Collaboratively developed exposure hierarchies confront anxiety provoking cues with imagery, virtual reality, *in vivo*, or interoceptive cues (*e.g.*, spinning to become dizzy).
- Exposure is most effective if it is controlled by the client and lasts long enough for the fear to decrease. Exposure intensity should induce fear, but not overwhelm the client. It is varied across situations and cues to maximize generaliza-

tion. Success is measured in terms of the presenting problem, not just greater comfort levels or closer approach.

- Implosive therapy and flooding show large effect sizes using intense, extended exposure to anxiety cues until fears are reduced. Implosion exposes clients to cues associated with psychodynamic conflicts. Flooding exposes clients to overt anxiety cues.
- Eye Movement Desensitization and Reprocessing uses back-and-forth finger movement to stimulate corresponding eye movements. Supposedly, associated neurological activities aid in reprocessing traumatic memories or other anxiety producing cues. Exposure during recall of memories and cognitive relabeling of traumatic experiences is helpful, while eye movement procedures may increase client suggestibility.
- Operant therapies modify problematic overt and covert behavior by (a) controlling the discriminative stimuli that elicit the behavior, (b) eliminating the behavior's reinforcers, and (c) counterconditioning behaviors incompatible with the problem.
- Applied behavior analysis examines the SORC sequence to determine which factors maintain problems. Functional analysis uses experiments to analyze which reinforcers or cues are most influential.
- The SORC model assesses situation cues, organismic state, and response consequences to conceptualize how best to modify problematic responses.
- Measurement approaches include physiological measures, client ratings (SUDS or SORC diaries), self-report tests, behavioral observation and semi-structured interviews. Problems are specified concretely and frequencies, duration, and intensity are noted.
- Social skills or other complex behaviors are taught by chaining simple SORC sequences. Other techniques include shaping or rewarding successive approximations, and fading reinforcers and varying behavioral contexts to enhance response generalization.
- Intrinsic reinforcers are preferred over extrinsic reinforcers, which may reduce intrinsic motivation. Premack's principle helps discover possible reinforcers: "High frequency behaviors reinforce low frequency behavior." Social reinforcers in the natural environment help ensure response generalization.
- Reinforcement contingency control by institutional staff helps manage aggressive or bizarre behavior. Aversive control or negative reinforcement is used to control self-abusive behavior (head-banging). Covert sensitization is used with motivated impulse disorder clients. Antabuse helps alcoholic clients by causing nausea when alcohol is ingested.
- Negotiated contracts administered by the therapist or by partners manage reinforcement contingencies in couple's therapy. Therapists may use selective attention to influence client narratives. Parents may use operant principles in lieu of more punitive parenting.
- Motivated clients use self-management to define behavioral goals, complete behavioral diaries, identify SORC contingencies, devise interventions, and reinforce targeted goals.

- Behavioral activation helps depressed clients identify simple, pleasurable activities to break out of the vicious circle of reduced pleasure in activities, reduced activity levels, and subsequent reduction in opportunities for obtaining environmental rewards.
- Psychoeducation teaches self-management, including medication compliance, parenting, exercise, communication, problem-solving, assertiveness, stress reduction, or social skills.
- Mindfulness adapts Buddhist meditation to help clients become aware of inner and outer experiences without judging, labeling, or trying to manage their experience. This helps self-soothe and provide exposure to extinguish fears.
- Thought stopping controls unwanted thoughts or impulses as clients yell "STOP!" and eventually fade this to a sub-vocalization. Covert assertion, *e.g.*, "Forget that nonsense! Everyone has intrusive thoughts!" counters negative cognitions, *e.g.*, "Am I going crazy?"
- Self-instructional training for children is based on Luria's idea that behavior moves from being controlled by others' talk, to self-talk, to covert self-talk. New behaviors are first modeled, while the therapist makes appropriate behavior-directing comments. Children then imitate and gradually fade from talking out loud to whispering and to covert speech.
- Lazarus BASIC-ID eclectic approach suggests the best type of intervention for Behavior, Affect, Symptom, Imagery, Cognition, Interpersonal, or Drugs/biological problem areas.
- Behaviorists have contributed three important integrative ideas: (a) learning is the basis of all psychosocial therapy; (b) assess the immediate context of problems; and (c) define problems concretely to enable monitoring and to change approach if needed.

Further Reading

Association for Behavioral and Cognitive Therapies (ABCT). Website: www.abct.org.
Barlow, D. H. (Ed.). (2007). *Clinical handbook of psychological disorders: A step-by-step treatment manual*. New York: Guilford Press.
Leahy, R. L., & Holland, S. J. (2000). *Treatment plans and interventions for depression and anxiety disorders*. New York: Guilford Press.
Miltenberger, R. G. (2008). *Behavior modification: Principles and procedures*, (4th ed.). Belmont: Brooks/Cole.
Nezu, A. M., Nezu, C. M., & Lombardo, E. (2004). *Cognitive-behavioral case formulation and treatment design: A problem-solving approach*. New York: Springer Publishing.
Spiegler, M. D., & Guevremont, D. C. (2003). *Contemporary behavior therapy*, (4th ed.). Pacific Grove: Brooks/Cole.

Videos

American Psychological Association Systems of Psychotherapy Series (2007).

- Cognitive-Behavioral Therapy With Donald Meichenbaum
- Multimodal Therapy With Arnold Lazarus
- Problem Solving Therapy with Albert and Christine Nezu

Chapter 5
Cognitive Approaches

We are disturbed not by events, but by the views which we take of them.

Epictetus (Greek philosopher, 55–135 CE)

What is reality? Do events in the real world determine a person's actions as behaviorists suggest? Or is it the perception of those events as suggested by Epictetus? This dialectic is apparent in the tension between cognitive therapy's scientific modernist epistemology and its constructivist phenomenological assumptions about the ontology of change. On the one hand, cognitive therapists subscribe to objective empiricism, but on the other hand, they challenge the client's belief system in order to construct new phenomenal realities.

Theorists such as Albert Bandura (1965a,b) recognized that classical and operant conditioning models did not adequately explain verbal learning and behavior. Complex client problems were addressed more directly by phenomenological therapies than by behavioral therapies. Two theorists, Michael Mahoney (1996) and Donald Meichenbaum (1977, 1992) illustrate the evolution of cognitive therapy from its behavioral roots to its current postmodern, integrative, and constructivist position. The first step was cognitive behavior modification, treating verbal behavior as operants or as discriminative cues (Mahoney, 1971; Meichenbaum, 1969). The next was to view what clients say as an objective manifestation of their subjective experience: if clients are able to talk about a problem objectively, they should be able to solve it on their own. In the last step, clients are asked to examine existing biases to construct a more useful belief system. At each step, new procedures have been integrated with existing techniques, to form *cognitive behavior therapy*, the most widely adopted integrative therapy.

Rational Emotive Behavioral Therapy

Albert Ellis' (1962, 1990, 1995, 2003) phenomenological, constructivist approach derives from Epictetus' philosophy. The earliest cognitive approach, it has been termed *directive, rational-emotive*, and most recently, *rational-emotive and*

D. K. Fromme, *Systems of Psychotherapy*,
DOI 10.1007/978-1-4419-7308-5_5, © Springer Science+Business Media, LLC 2011

cognitive-behavioral therapy (RECBT) as Ellis' thinking converged with other cognitive-behavioral theorists. Ellis suggests that although an experience may be unpleasant, emotional disturbance results from interpreting it as terrible, horrible, or something that cannot be survived. RECBT therapists challenge the client's "irrational" thoughts and assign homework to practice behavior based on "rational" thoughts.

Conceptual Framework

The *ABCs* of thinking are *Antecedents, Beliefs*, and *Consequences* (Ellis, 1991):

A. Antecedent events are evaluated by;
B. Beliefs about the meaning of the events;
C. Consequent emotions or behaviors are a response to B, not A.

If beliefs are *rational*, then adaptive, measured emotional and behavior responses follow. If they are *irrational*, then emotional and behavioral responses will be maladaptive. Ellis (2003) describes three classes of common irrational beliefs (that lead to maladaptive consequences):

1. I absolutely *must* perform outstandingly well and win the approval or love of significant others under practically all conditions and at all times. If I fail, that is awful and I am an incompetent, bad, unworthy person, who will probably always fail and deserves to suffer (leads to anxiety, panic, depression, despair, and feelings of worthlessness).
2. People *must* treat me nicely at all times. If they do not, they are unworthy, rotten people. They will always treat me badly and should be punished for acting so terribly (leads to anger, rage, fury, and vindictiveness).
3. Things *must* be safe, hassle-free, and enjoyable all the time. If not, it is horrible, awful, and I cannot bear it. Life is impossible and hardly worth living (leads to self-pity, frustration, anger, discomfort, intolerance, depression, procrastination, and avoidance).

The common factor in these beliefs is that they are absolute demands, like those of young children. Wants, preferences, and desires become absolute "needs" that cannot be deferred or denied. These rigid, dogmatic beliefs (*musturbatory thinking*) are expressed by verbs such as *must, should, ought to, have to*, and *got to* (Ellis, 1991). They reflect a *tyranny of shoulds* that can result in obsessively blaming the self and others if irrational beliefs are not realized. They are emotionally draining, and interfere with learning new ideas. They lead to vague, bizarre, boring communication that interferes with intimacy or sexuality and creates interpersonal conflict.

RECBT challenges musturbatory thinking and encourages rational beliefs such as:

1. I have human limitations, just as other people do. I feel best when I am involved with helping others or projects outside myself; when I focus on self-respect and loving instead of worrying about being loved.

2. People sometimes behave stupidly, ignorantly, or neurotically. This does not make them rotten; they need my understanding, not my censure.
3. If conditions are bad, dangerous, or not as I like, perhaps I can change them. If not, it is better to accept the inevitable and not expect things to be other than they are. I need to remember that my desires, such as for sex, are preferences, not needs.

The goal is to help clients realize they have control over destructive emotions if they choose to work at changing the musturbatory hypotheses they use that create them.

RECBT has consistently emphasized the role of cognition in emotional and behavioral problems and a humanistic view that encourages people to accept themselves as they are, rather than trying to live up to other's expectations. It focuses on beliefs that *maintain* problems, but has little interest in how those beliefs were originally acquired. As the approach has evolved, it has left behind earlier psychoanalytic and behavioral conditioning ideas and places more emphasis on biological components of the emotions. The variety of cognitive, behavioral, imagery, and emotive interventions that RECBT uses has also significantly increased.

Intervention Techniques

Ellis agrees with Carl Rogers that clients deserve unconditional acceptance, but challenges their irrational ideas at every opportunity. The ABCs of irrational beliefs are followed by the DEFs of intervention (Ellis, 1991). RECBT therapists:

D. *Dispute* irrational beliefs when clients act in self-defeating ways; as these beliefs are refuted,
E. *Effective new philosophies* are developed that result in new,
F. *Feelings*.

Ellis considers RECBT humanistic since it encourages choice and action, based upon the client's own beliefs. It is also directive with the therapist disputing maladaptive beliefs and consequent actions or feelings. The three *Ds* encourage clients to dispute their own irrational ideas:

Detect—recognize absolute, musturbatory thinking as *self-defeating*.
Debate—question beliefs logically and empirically and reject those not supported by reality.
Discriminate—after repeated debates, clients recognize irrational ideas as they occur and are not affected by them.

Ellis (1999) suggests that a philosophical restructuring of beliefs occurs as clients learn:

1. They are largely responsible for creating their own emotional problems;
2. They have the ability to change these disturbances significantly;
3. That emotional problems stem largely from irrational ideas;
4. To perceive clearly how their beliefs are irrational;

5. To value disputing such beliefs;
6. To work hard to counteract dysfunctional beliefs with painful consequences; and
7. To continue addressing dysfunctional attitudes, behaviors, and consequences throughout life.

A psychoeducational perspective is favored over an intense therapist-client transference relationship. Therapists are expert coaches who help clients understand how:

1. They have incorporated irrational shoulds, oughts, and musts into their thinking;
2. They keep emotional disturbance alive by indoctrinating themselves with irrational ideas;
3. To dispute and abandon their irrational ideas and modify their thinking; and
4. To develop a new, more rational philosophy.

Ellis (1999) uses humor and logical analysis to illustrate how irrationality causes emotional and behavioral disturbance. Clients are taught to observe and apply the scientific method in their thinking to minimize irrational ideas and illogical deductions. They collaborate in designing homework to practice these skills and to carry out positive actions that induce emotional and attitudinal change. Success with homework is checked and problems examined for irrational thinking. A shy young man might first be asked to make lists of musturbatory or catastrophic thinking. In later weeks he might be asked to strike up a conversation with three young women, with no pressure at first to become more involved.

Emotive techniques include unconditional acceptance, forceful and vigorous intervention, modeling and role-playing, and exercises that attack self-devaluing or shame in the client; *e.g.*, clients might be asked to do something awkward intentionally, such as wearing mismatched clothing. They could then observe the validity of their expectation that others would mock them, and if so, to question whether this affected who they really are. RECBT practitioners also borrow behavioral techniques freely as needed, including self-management, contingency management, exposure techniques, relaxation, and real-life homework assignments. Lyons and Woods' (1971) meta-analysis of over 70 RECBT outcome studies found an average effect size of 0.95.

Cognitive Therapy

Aaron Beck's *Cognitive Therapy* (CT) is perhaps the most influential cognitive approach. Like RECBT, his approach is directive, active, structured, present-focused, and time-limited. CT also emphasizes recognizing and changing maladaptive thoughts and beliefs, but Beck focuses more on internalized representations or *cognitive schemas* of the self, the world, and the future: the *cognitive triad*. Originally developed to treat depression (Beck, 1967), CT is now used with a variety of problems, including anxiety and personality disorders (Beck, Emery, & Greenberg,

1985; Beck & Freeman, 1990). CT assumptions (Reinecke & Freeman, 2003) include:

1. The way people construe events affects how they feel and behave. Cognition, emotion, behavior, and events in the world reciprocally determine one another.
2. Construal is active and ongoing; it gives meaning to events in relation to goals or values and creates the individual's *personal environment*.
3. Belief systems give an idiosyncratic, personal meaning to events and selectively bias memory and what is perceived or overlooked; beliefs guide behavior and define whether events are perceived as stressful or challenging.
4. Events construed as stressors activate overlearned, maladaptive coping responses that "feed forward" to reinforce the belief system or *cognitive schema* and maintain the stress construal.
5. *Cognitive specificity* hypothesizes that the specific content of maladaptive cognitive schemas accounts for differences among clinical disorders and emotional states.
6. Introspection allows access to the inner experience, dialog, and assumptions of a cognitive schema; it reveals these meanings with no need for interpretation by a therapist.

CT assumes that cognitive schemas or belief and meaning systems determine behavior. Cognitive schemas involve perceptions, memories, expectations, values, emotions, goals, and our plans for action, whether conscious or not. They are implicit in the resulting behavior and may enter awareness in the form of *automatic thoughts* or following introspection.

Conceptual Framework

Beck (1963) originally suggested that depression reflects a cognitive triad of distorted, negative schemas about the self, the world, and the future. Depressed individuals have negative views of each of these components, seeing themselves as flawed and unable to meet their needs, others as rejecting and uncaring, and the future as bleak. *Cognitive specificity* suggests that different symptomatic and thematic problems reflect differences in the content of client views of the self, the world, and the future. For example, anxious individuals perceive the world as threatening and themselves as not competent to cope with these threats. Different anxiety disorders are thought to reflect different types of threat, while personality disorders are thought to reflect still other specific contents and processes involving the cognitive triad.

Schemas

Schemas are prototypes or generalized expectancies about the self in relation to others and the world. Schemas comprise neural networks that constitute the memories and emotions associated with meaningful or repetitive experiences. External events related to goals or resembling the original experience activate relevant portions of the network. The resulting schema-environment dialectic guides goal attainment and gives meaning to the individual's experience. New experiences are *assimilated* into schemas that are most similar to the ongoing situation (Piaget, 1952/1963). As a result, perceptions of events are biased toward aspects of an experience congruent with a schema, while incongruent information is ignored. This stabilizes experience, but also diminishes the person's ability to adapt to changing circumstances. *Accommodation* occurs if a schema is too incongruent with current experience to be assimilated, resulting in modifications or new schemas. Cognitive therapy exposes clients to incongruent experiences or uses nonjudgmental mindfulness (Baer, 2003) to modify schemas and minimize their biasing influence on ongoing experience.

Cognitive therapists view learning as an epigenetic "evolution of meaning" in which new experiences build upon and modify existing cognitive schemas, rather than the reinforcement of stimulus-response associations (Kegan, 1982). This is the difference between the verbal learning of complex conceptual networks and operant or classical conditioning, and also the difference between Meichenbaum's (1986) cognitive behavior modification and Beck's (1967) cognitive therapy. Evolution of meaning occurs only with verbal learning. However, care should be taken not to draw overly rigid distinctions, since both verbal learning and conditioning processes can add elements to the overall structure of a cognitive schema.

Cognitive Distortions

Maladaptive schemas reflect an evolution of relationship meanings that may have been adaptive during childhood, but now create difficulties. Such schemas result in *automatic thoughts* that clients apply to many situations without testing their logic or validity. Table 5.1 summarizes Beck's analysis of cognitive distortions and the clinical disorders that often follow (Beck, Rush, Shaw, & Emery, 1979; Beck & Freeman, 1990). These distortions occur in every type of disorder, but are especially common in the disorders noted in Table 5.1. Automatic thoughts are viewed as untested, rather than irrational; *e.g.*, the "standard model" of depression suggests depressed clients make *depressogenic assumptions* (Beck *et al.*, 1979). They:

1. Hold rigid, negative beliefs about self-worth and overvalue outcomes that make them vulnerable to depression;
2. Become depressed when social or environmental factors preclude valued outcomes;
3. Believe they are unlovable and/or helpless;
4. Respond to stress or personal loss with these beliefs;
5. Either have a *sociotropic personality style* in which loss of valued relationships signals lack of personal worth, or an *autonomous personality style* in which failure to accomplish valued goals signals lack of personal worth.

Table 5.1 Cognitive distortions that lead to disorders

Cognitive error	Example of assumption	Possible disorder
Dichotomous thinking	Things are all good or all bad, black or white	Borderline; OCD
"Should" statements	I should visit my family every time I am invited	Obsessive-compulsive
Overgeneralization	If it is true in one situation, then it is universal	Depression
Magnify/minimize	If I had studied even harder, I would have gotten an A	Depression
Selective abstraction	This is what is important, forget anything else	Depression
Hyper-responsibility	I am responsible for everything going wrong	Depression
Self-references	Everyone notices my failures	Depression
Mind reading	They probably think I am incompetent	Avoidant/paranoid PD
Personalization	I know they are laughing at me	Avoidant/paranoid PD
Emotional reasoning	I am upset, something is terribly wrong	Anxiety disorders
Catastrophizing	If I fail this test, my life is over	Anxiety disorders

In general, there is good support for the importance of cognitive distortions mediating human problems. Reinecke and Rogers (2001) found that dysfunctional attitudes mediate between insecure attachment styles and depression. Similarly, Alloy *et al.*'s (2000) large, prospective study compared never-depressed individuals who scored either high or low on dysfunctional attitude measures. Their results supported cognitive theory: 17% of high scorers developed major depression over the following 2 years, but only 1% of low scorers became depressed.

Cognitive-Behavioral Interventions

Early cognitive therapists were trained in empirical and behavioral methods and simply assimilated new cognitive interventions into existing behavioral repertoires. Examples of methods retained by cognitive therapists include behavioral activation, self-monitoring, and scheduling activities. DeRubeis, Tang, and Beck (2001) suggest that *behavioral activation* and self-managed reward contingencies can increase activity levels for depressed clients and improve their sense of self-efficacy and pleasure in daily activities. In *self-monitoring*, clients keep diaries that rate the moods associated with their activities: *e.g.*, a 0–100 scale where 0 is the worst they have ever felt and 100 is the best. Degree of mastery or pleasure in the associated activities may also be recorded. Diaries help therapists understand how clients spend their time and provide baselines to evaluate outcomes. They can also explore selective recall of events and often surprise clients, who may not realize how much time is devoted to nonrewarding activities.

Anxiety, depression, and interpersonal problems all interfere with having a rich, rewarding life. Diaries make this clear to clients, while *activity scheduling* provides a structure that helps increase rewarding activities. Scheduling bypasses procrastination, indecisiveness, or avoidance and tests the common belief of clients that there is no time for rewarding activities. Experiences that evoke good or bad strong feelings are useful starting points for scheduling activities to increase positive feelings and limit negative ones. Three types of activities are scheduled:

1. Activities associated with pleasure or mastery that were revealed by self-monitoring;
2. Activities that were rewarding in the past, but have been avoided since symptoms developed;
3. New activities collaboratively negotiated as likely to be pleasurable or informative.

Therapists help clients anticipate and overcome scheduling obstacles or barriers, or revise the schedule if necessary. If a client has negative thoughts about an activity, then empirical tests of their validity are scheduled. Complex, difficult tasks are broken down into sub-goals, or *graded* so that easier tasks are attempted first. If clients fail to complete homework, then the reasons for noncompliance are explored. Perhaps the therapist was overzealous and can model apologizing and taking responsibility. If noncompliance reflects past failures by the client, then associated negative beliefs, thoughts, or situational obstacles can be discussed using cognitive therapy.

Cognitive Therapy

Cognitive therapists believe it is essential to establish a collaborative, trusting relationship with the client. Therapists create a sense of discovery while guiding the exploration of the origins of beliefs and the meaning of traumatic events. A close, warm relationship is especially needed to explore automatic "transference" reactions when clients with chronic disorders try to avoid exploring unexpected shifts in narratives or nonverbal expression, saying it is unimportant. A basic CT principle is to explore all automatic thoughts and reactions, including those activated by the therapeutic relationship.

Beck and Freeman (1990) suggest noncollaboration is often a problem of motivation or skill rather than "negative transference" or "resistance." They describe a number of possibilities:

1. Clients lack collaborative skills, which is why they have interpersonal problems.
2. Therapists lack experience with chronic problems and need skills to develop collaboration.
3. Environment (*e.g.*, family) interferes with reinforcement or performance of adaptive behavior.
4. Client beliefs ("too difficult" or "I'm incompetent") interfere with collaboration.

5. Catastrophic beliefs about the effect of change on others interfere with client collaboration.
6. Clients fear the stigma or unknown consequences of therapy on their identity.
7. Therapist has a "blind spot" and shares a dysfunctional client belief.
8. Clients are not socialized into the client role and do not understand what is expected.
9. Client finds it hard to renounce secondary gains from dysfunctional behavior.
10. Interventions are poorly timed and clients fail to see how they are relevant to their problems.
11. Clients referred by others (*e.g.*, courts) lack motivation and see problems externally caused.
12. Rigid, obsessive, or paranoid clients question therapist goals and resist collaboration.
13. Pressure of current problem makes it hard for impulsive clients to focus on long-term issues.
14. Therapeutic goals may be set unrealistically high or low, causing lack of motivation or failure.
15. Frustration occurs if progress is not seen on mutually developed goals and procedures.
16. Lack of explicit, clearly stated goals and baselines prevents the evaluation of progress.

As this list suggests, problems in therapeutic collaboration may be due to therapist or external factors as well as client issues. When noncollaboration occurs, therapists should first scrutinize their own contribution such as failing to follow procedures or sharing a blind spot with the client. If therapist and external factors are not the problem, then noncollaboration most likely reflects dysfunctional client beliefs that are a necessary beginning point for CT exploration.

The *Dysfunctional Thought Record* (DTR) is used to identify automatic thoughts either alone or in conjunction with a behavioral diary. It records the essential elements of CT emotion theory: the situation, the evoked emotion, and the automatic thought or belief that led to that emotional outcome. Clients also are encouraged to counter a maladaptive belief with a more adaptive response. Therapists ensure that clients understand what the words "emotions" or "feelings" mean, can judge the intensity of their feelings, and can differentiate among different types of emotions. Once clients reliably report situations, thoughts, and feelings, the therapist helps them examine the validity of their automatic thoughts.

Differences between the client's DTR ratings of belief in automatic *vs.* alternative, rational thoughts, and the effect of alternative thoughts on subsequent ratings of emotions indicate just how challenging it may be for clients to revise their thoughts. Therapists use the ratings to evaluate how questioning impacts on automatic thoughts. If there is little impact, something has been missed and the client's belief has not successfully been challenged. The *downward arrow* technique described below is then used to challenge the belief. Therapists check the clients' understanding of the DTR, explore the meaning of automatic thoughts in greater depth, and measure progress. Between sessions, the client's homework assignment is to use the DTR to challenge automatic thoughts as they occur.

Exploring Automatic Thoughts

Therapists explore automatic thoughts by asking:

1. "What is the evidence for and against this belief?"
2. "What are alternative interpretations of the event or situation?" and
3. "What are the belief's implications, if it is correct?"

Initially, clients are apt to present "surface" beliefs connected only loosely to core schemas. Instead of immediately looking for evidence regarding the belief, therapists first assess core beliefs. The *downward arrow* technique helps clients move past derivative beliefs and uncover underlying core meanings. If a client says, "I know he thinks I'm just a little mouse," the downward arrow question would be, "If that were true, what would it mean to you?" If the client responds, "He'll never want to marry me," the therapist could use the arrow again, "And if he doesn't marry you, what would that mean?" If the client answers "I'm so unlovable, no one will ever want me," this is closer to a core schema and the therapist can question the evidence, alternatives, and implications for the belief. It may be necessary to alternate between downward arrow and exploratory questions, before core schemas are clearly identified.

As core beliefs are explored, cognitive distortions are likely to be discovered. The cognitive specificity hypothesis lets therapists make an informed guess about what errors are present, by examining the client's symptomatic complaints (see Table 5.1); *e.g.*, depressed clients' distortions may not be immediately apparent. The Dysfunctional Attitude Scale (Weissman & Beck, 1978) can also identify dysfunctional core schemas. It has nine factors, which, except for factor 8, reflect cognitive distortions that require further exploration:

1. Vulnerability: "Whenever I take a chance or risk, I am only looking for trouble."
2. Approval: "My value as a person depends greatly on what others think of me."
3. Perfectionism: "My life is wasted unless I am a success."
4. Need to please: "It is best to give up your own interests in order to please other people."
5. Imperatives: "I should be happy all the time."
6. Need to impress: "I should try to impress people if I want them to like me."
7. Avoidance of weakness: "If a person asks for help, it's a sign of weakness."
8. Control of emotions: "Criticism need not upset the person who receives the criticism."
9. Disapproval: "It is awful to be disapproved of by people important to you."

Cognitive therapists use *Socratic questioning* of problematic cognitive distortions to help clients discover answers on their own. Categories of Socratic questions include:

1. Clarify: "What exactly did you mean by that last statement? Can you give me an example?"
2. Assumptions: "Why do you think this happened? Can you explain your reasoning?"
3. Perspective: "What else could explain this? What might your partner think about it?"
4. Evidence: "How do you know? How might you test that idea?"
5. Implications: "What would happen next? How does that affect your partner?"
6. Meta-questions: "Why do you think I asked that question?"

Therapists balance leading clients (*e.g.*, to look more closely during the downward arrow) with allowing clients to discover for themselves. It is important not to lead so directly that only one possible answer is available. Therapists avoid suggesting a particular meaning, but rather help clients uncover meanings and core schemas on their own. This feature maximizes therapeutic collaboration in exploring problems, generating solutions, and is useful for resistant clients. DeRubeis *et al.* (2001) suggest that therapists review session tapes for declarative statements and closed questions to see if these could have been framed in a more useful, Socratic fashion.

Case Formulation in Cognitive Therapy

After collecting demographic data, therapists collaborate with clients to develop a *problem list* of current difficulties in concrete, operational terms. The list is kept between five and eight items, since significant redundancy is likely if lists exceed ten items. Problems are specified quantitatively in terms of frequency, intensity, and duration. Socratic questions and the downward arrow help clients discover underlying core beliefs including situations that activate dysfunctional beliefs. As core beliefs are uncovered, they are compared with the DTR and the case formulation is revised in the light of new information. The heart of case formulation is the *working hypothesis*, which ties together the *problem list, core beliefs,* and *activating* situations. Biological and behavioral hypotheses are also included when deemed relevant. Historical factors that explain the *origins* of dysfunctional core beliefs may also be included. The *treatment plan* is then derived from the case formulation with concrete, measurable treatment *goals* and sub-goals derived from the problem list. *Interventions* should flow logically from the working hypothesis, be focused on behavioral or cognitive changes (both if needed) and address *obstacles* to treatment. The following illustrates the categories Persons and Tompkins (1997) use in CT case formulation.

Case Illustration

- *Identifying Information*: Sam is a 30-year-old, married Asian-American lawyer, who identifies with the Anglo culture. He has no children and is an assistant in a large legal firm.

- *Problem List*:
    1. Depressed mood, most days for over 2 years.
    2. Job performance ratings were not as high as hoped.
    3. He is not being given important assignments.
    4. Sam has trouble getting to sleep at night.
    5. He worries a lot about his job and prospects for the future.
    6. Marriage is characterized by bickering.
    7. Sam feels trapped in a loveless marriage.

- *Core Beliefs*:

    "I'm not as smart as my colleagues."
    "Anyone I'm attracted to wouldn't be attracted to me."
    "Unless I succeed in my profession, I'm a failure."
    "No one who is competent likes a person who is a failure."

- *Precipitants and Activating Situations*: If Sam finds that no challenging assignments have been given to him at work, he ruminates over his job and rejection by colleagues and superiors. In school, he worried about what his classmates and teachers thought about him. With his wife, any indication that she is not as intelligent or poised as his female colleagues causes him to become irritable and critical of her, which leads to arguments and sleeping apart. Critical comments or signs that others are ignoring him are strong activating events.

- *Working Hypothesis*: Sam's core beliefs reflect a deep sense of inferiority. He compensates by trying to be superior to those around him. His depression reflects an autonomous personality style. Minimization and selective abstraction prevent recognition of his successes or positive qualities in his wife. "Shoulds" drive him to high standards and it feels catastrophic if they are unattainable. Despite objective success, he is vigilant for signs of disapproval, which he anticipates and maximizes. His depression and rumination interfere with his work and if he is fired, his deepest fears will be confirmed. He fails to relate to his wife as a person, believing her lack of sophistication causes others to see his underlying inadequacy.

- *Origins*: Sam's parents were boat people, who immigrated to the U.S., worked at menial jobs, and made sacrifices to ensure Sam completed his education and fulfilled their dreams of success. They emphasized Sam's Asian heritage, letting him know of his obligation to his ancestors by demonstrating his superiority. Sam struggled throughout his schooling, and he was shamed by his parents for not living up to their standards when his marks were poor. Through hard work, Sam did eventually succeed in school, graduated in the upper half of his law class, and obtained a well-paying position with a large law firm.

- *Treatment Plan*:
    - *Goals*:
        1. Reduce Sam's chronic feelings of depression.
        2. Reduce time ruminating at work and increase productivity.
        3. Reduce sleep latency time.
        4. Replace automatic thoughts facilitating Sam's worries with alternative constructions.

5. Reduce arguments with wife, and increase frequency of positive interactions.

– *Interventions*:
1. Monitor depressive symptom levels using Beck's Depression Inventory.
2. Teach thought stopping to disrupt rumination and replace with positive imagery.
3. Teach relaxation or, if Sam prefers, mindfulness meditation to assist sleeping.
4. Cognitive restructuring of core beliefs using Thought Records in session and as homework. Sam will "thought stop," record entries, and construct alternative beliefs, when he starts to ruminate or feel angry or critical toward his wife.
5. Socratic questioning will help Sam become more aware of cognitive distortions.
6. Sam will build a warmer relationship with his wife by doing at least one thing each day that he believes she would appreciate and by noticing one thing each day that she does that he finds admirable.

– *Predicted Obstacles to Treatment*:
1. Sam may be reluctant to discuss lapses in recording automatic thoughts or responding positively to his wife for fear the therapist will see him as a failure.
2. Sam may be uncomfortable with a collaborative stance, wanting "expert guidance;" cultural aspects of this discomfort and their relation to core beliefs will be discussed.
3. Lack of progress toward treatment goals may be experienced as failure and result in premature termination.
4. Sam may minimize real progress as insufficient or not up to others' standards.

Schema Therapy

Although CT is effective for clients with acute symptoms, more characterological, thematic problems have not responded well to traditional cognitive-behavioral therapy: *e.g.*, over 60% of depressed clients respond favorably at the end of treatment, but the relapse rate at 1 year is about 30% (Young, Weinberger, & Beck, 2001). Recognizing these limitations, Beck and his associates (Beck & Beck, 2005; Beck & Freeman, 1990) have updated the CT approach to address thematic problems. Jeffrey Young's schema therapy integrates CT with psychodynamic and emotion-focused therapies (1990, 1999; Young, Klosko, & Weishaar, 2003). In contrast to CT, schema therapy emphasizes the origins of maladaptive behavior in attachment theory terms (Bowlby, 1973, 1982), which implicates unresponsive caregiving for an infant's needs for safety and security. These *early maladaptive schemas* bypass conscious, verbal processing with rapid, automatic emotional responses that are less likely to be modified by conscious, verbal methods.

Conceptual Framework

Young *et al.* (2003) argue that cognitive therapists make several assumptions that may not be warranted when working with treatment resistant populations. They may assume that:

1. Clients are motivated to comply with treatment recommendations;
2. Clients can engage in a collaborative relationship;
3. Clients can observe and report their thoughts and feelings;
4. Thoughts and feelings can be changed by reasoning, experimentation, and repetition; and
5. Symptoms and problems are easily defined, observable, and circumscribed.

Schema therapy assumes therapy will be long-term and explores the childhood origins of the client's maladaptive interpersonal schemas. *Early maladaptive schemas* are defined as memories, emotions, cognitions, and bodily sensations related to pervasive, dysfunctional patterns of self and other relationships, developed during childhood or adolescence (Young *et al.*, 2003).

These schemas reflect a child's unmet core needs for secure attachment, autonomy, play and spontaneity, freedom to express needs or feelings, and realistic limits and self-control. Even though most schemas reflect childhood experiences, *conditional* schemas can develop later after repeated failures at coping with a problem; *e.g.*, a subjugation schema might result from a belief that submission to a controlling partner can prevent abandonment. Cues that activate a schema initiate a fast, emotional response mediated by the brain's amygdala system, which bypasses conscious processing (LeDoux, 1996). Since this response occurs prior to conscious awareness, schema therapy uses experiential methods to supplement traditional CT interventions.

Schema Domains

Factor analysis suggests that Schema Therapy's 18 maladaptive schemas can be grouped into five domains (Schmidt, Joiner, Young, & Telch, 1995):

1. *Disconnection/Rejection.* These clients fear that needs for safety, nurturance, and love will not be met. This leads to one or more of the following schemas:

   - *Abandonment*, if the parents were unstable.
   - *Mistrust*, if the parents were abusive.
   - *Emotional deprivation*, if the parents were cold.
   - *Defective*, if the parents were rejecting.
   - *Alienation*, if the parents were isolated from the outside world.

2. *Impaired Autonomy/Performance.* These clients find it difficult to differentiate from their family of origin and function independently in the world. Their parents

were either overprotective or provided very little care, undermining efforts to perform autonomously. This leads to:

- *Dependent/incompetence*—passivity and helplessness in handling everyday responsibilities.
- *Vulnerability to harm/illness*—catastrophic fears (medical, going crazy, accidents, or crime).
- *Enmeshment/undeveloped self*—fusion with significant others, lack of personal direction.
- *Failure*—beliefs that they lack talent, intelligence, or attractiveness and will ultimately fail.

3. *Impaired Limits.* These clients lack self-discipline and respect for the rights of others. They are overindulged and may be selfish, irresponsible, or narcissistic. This leads to:

- *Entitlement/grandiosity*—expectations of special privileges and not being bound by rules of reciprocity; demanding, dominating, and lacking empathy or respect for others.
- *Insufficient self-control/self-discipline*—inability to tolerate frustration and achieve goals; avoids discomfort, conflict, and responsibility; difficulty regulating emotions and impulses.

4. *Other-Directedness.* These clients give priority to others' needs to gain approval, maintain emotional connection, or avoid retaliation. They are unaware of their own needs and feelings, due to parental acceptance being conditional on approved behavior. This leads to:

- *Subjugation*—suppressing needs or feelings for fear of retaliation, anger, or abandonment. Although eager to please and compliant, they build up resentments over time and exhibit passive-aggressive behavior, psychosomatic symptoms, or temper outbursts.
- *Self-sacrifice*—focusing on the needs of others who are seen as suffering or needier. They may support negative behavior, *e.g.*, substance abuse, in misguided attempts to protect significant others from the consequences of their actions.
- *Approval/recognition seeking*—preoccupation with status and appearances. Self-esteem is dependent upon the reactions of others, which may result in inauthenticity.

5. *Overvigilance/Inhibition.* These clients were taught that life is dangerous and that one must be vigilant and self-controlled to prevent disaster from occurring. They suppress spontaneity and pleasure in order to maintain strict adherence to rules. This leads to:

- *Negativity/pessimism*—focusing on potentially catastrophic outcomes; worried, complaining, indecisive, and fearful of mistakes.
- *Emotional inhibition*—cold rationality suppresses anger, playfulness, vulnerability, or feelings.

- *Unrelenting standards/hypercriticalness*—perfectionism, rigid rules, and constant struggle to live up to unrealistic, internalized standards result in inability to experience pleasure and impaired self-esteem, relationships, or health.
- *Punitiveness*—anger, intolerance, and punitiveness toward those who do not live up to standards, including the self; does not consider human frailties or external reasons for failure.

For any combination of schemas, clients may use any of three *coping responses*:

1. Surrender (freeze in response to threat)—attempt to master by recapitulating the schema;
2. Avoidance (flight in response to threat)—avoid situations that elicit strong feelings or needs;
3. Overcompensation (fight in response to threat)—enact the opposite of the schema.

Since clients may use multiple ways of coping with any one schema, coping is not considered part of a schema; *e.g.*, a client diagnosed with paranoid personality disorder may simultaneously *surrender* to a punitiveness schema and treat others harshly, *overcompensate* a defectiveness/shame schema by being critical or rejecting of others, and *avoid* vulnerability in a mistrust/abuse schema by being secretive.

Young *et al.* (2003) suggest, "[E]ach patient is viewed as having a unique profile, including several schemas and coping responses, each present at different levels of strength ... rather than as one single Axis II category" (p. 37). While schemas tend to be stable and difficult to change, coping responses are highly variable. This may explain the problems of comorbidity and reliability in DSM-IV Axis II diagnoses: personality disorders are classified in terms of observable and variable coping responses, rather than stable, underlying schemas (Young & Gluhoski, 1996).

Schema Modes

While schemas are relatively enduring, *schema modes* are "moment-to-moment emotional states and coping responses—adaptive and maladaptive" (Young *et al.*, 2003, p. 37)—to situational triggers. As life events unfold, people *flip* from one schema mode to another with concurrent changes in affect. There are ten schema modes, grouped in four categories:

1. *Child* (vulnerable, angry, impulsive/undisciplined, or happy modes);
2. *Dysfunctional coping* (compliant surrenderer, detached protector, or overcompensator);
3. *Dysfunctional parent* (punitive or demanding modes);
4. *Healthy adult* mode.

For example, a helpless, frightened, and sad vulnerable child mode may activate emotional deprivation, abandonment, and vulnerability schemas. Schema therapy helps the healthy adult mode regulate dysfunctional modes. Dysfunctional schema modes are dissociated self-states not fully integrated into a coherent self. Degrees of dissociation vary from fully integrated, conscious functioning to fully dissociated functioning in dissociative identity disorders. Modes also differ to the degree they are mild or extreme, rigid or flexible, and pure or a blend of several modes.

Intervention in Schema Therapy

Schema therapy is divided into two phases: 1. assessment and education, and 2. change. During assessment and education, clients learn to identify schemas and recognize how coping styles perpetuate schemas. During the change phase, a mixture of cognitive, experiential, behavioral, and interpersonal strategies help clients interrupt this cycle of schema perpetuation.

Schema Assessment and Education Phase

The assessment phase goal is to develop a case conceptualization of how early maladaptive schemas and coping styles developed from dysfunctional childhood and adolescent interpersonal experiences. Five sessions (or more for avoidant or overcompensating clients) are usually needed for this phase. Assessment begins by deciding if schema therapy is appropriate for the client. It may be inappropriate for clients in crisis, or who have psychotic symptoms, moderate to severe substance abuse, or an acute, relatively severe Axis I diagnosis, or if the presenting problem is situational and not related to long-term patterns.

Hypotheses about schemas and coping styles are derived from a number of information sources, including presenting problems, interview behavior, reports of dysfunctional life patterns, and enactments of schemas during imagery exercises. Questionnaires may be used, *e.g.*, Young (1995) *Compensation Inventory*, Young (1994) *Parenting Inventory, Young Schema Questionnaire*, (Young & Brown, 1990, 2001), or the *Young-Rygh Avoidance Inventory* (Young & Rygh, 1994). Hypotheses are evaluated by cross-checking across different types of information and by the client's emotional resonance with the formulation.

Assessment includes a focused life history that tracks the current problem back through time as far as possible. Hypotheses about schemas and coping styles are developed in collaboration with the client based on repeated patterns of triggering events, thoughts, feelings, and actions or symptoms. Family history, parenting style, relationships with significant others, traumatic events, and possible biomedical or temperamental factors are explored for their role in the development of schemas and coping responses. This process also allows therapists to begin educating clients about the role of coping styles in perpetuating maladaptive schemas. As clients relate to the therapist, schema activation will very likely produce strong feelings about the therapist and influence the quality of the relationship. As this occurs, the therapist asks the client to remember other relationships that have created similar feelings and outcomes; *e.g.*, if the client feels trapped by the therapist's questions, this may reflect earlier traumatic experiences.

Directed imagery is an experiential technique used by schema therapists during both the assessment and the change phases. In addition to other assessment goals, imagery can help identify schema triggers, link schemas to presenting problems, and help the client experience schema-related emotions. Clients are given the rationale for directed imagery, asked to close their eyes, imagine being in a safe place, and allow pictorial images to surface (not words or thoughts). Once clients report an image, therapists help them describe it in vivid, emotionally real detail. They are then asked to remember an upsetting childhood scene with parents or other significant figures. Clients are asked to express the thoughts, feelings, and needs that arise as they interact with the imagined others. Once the images become vivid, clients are directed to imagine a scene from their current life that is emotionally similar to the childhood scene. Again, they are asked to express their thoughts, feelings, and needs to the current significant other in this imagined scene.

After returning to a "safe place," therapists help clients examine their images to identify childhood origins of schemas and relate these to current problems. Because imagery work can be powerful, it is done early in a session to allow time for adequate exploration and resolution of any distress. Variations in imagery include starting with a current, upsetting situation and working backward, or asking clients to imagine a symptom; *e.g.*, "Can you picture an image of your back when you're in pain? What does it look like? What is the pain saying?" (Young *et al.*, 2003, p. 81). Some clients are only able to produce vague images during imagery work. Therapists address this schema avoidance with a rationale for the exercise. They may also use soothing imagery, conduct a dialog with the client's avoidant side, teach relaxation or mindfulness, or use anxiolytic medication. Photos can be used if clients have difficulty imagining themselves as children. The therapist then asks about the child's thoughts, feelings, needs, and what is going to happen.

While diagnosis offers clues about schemas, it is important to remember that nearly any schema can result in nearly any diagnosis. Similar childhood experiences can create very different schemas or modify earlier schemas, dependent upon significant other relationships. Punitive parenting that causes defectiveness/shame schemas in some children might be ameliorated in others by a resilient temperament or nurturing grandparents. Identifying schemas accurately is essential, since very different therapeutic strategies may be needed for different schemas; *e.g.*, repeated requests for advice may reflect a dependence schema and the therapist may need to help the client become more self-reliant; but if an emotional deprivation schema is present, the therapist needs to reparent and provide nurturance and guidance. Expectations for self-reliance for this second client would just recreate earlier patterns of emotional inaccessibility by significant others. Similarly, the calm detachment of an avoidant coping style may resemble normal behavior; but calmness that reflects denial of basic needs must be confronted.

The Change Phase

Schema therapy's change phase goals include bonding, emotional regulation, schema mode change, and autonomy. Four change principles are important:

1. The therapy relationship, especially empathic confrontation and limited reparenting,
2. Cognitive restructuring and education,
3. Experiential imagery and dialog work,
4. Behavioral pattern breaking.

The Therapy Relationship

After establishing rapport and identifying schemas during assessment, therapists use *empathic confrontation* (*reality testing*) and *limited reparenting* to help clients challenge their schemas and develop more adaptive coping responses. Empathic confrontation helps clients recognize and modify the way their schemas influence the therapeutic relationship. Limited reparenting meets the client's appropriate needs for secure attachment, expression of needs and feelings, autonomy and competence, spontaneity and play, and realistic limits. It gives them the *corrective emotional experience* (Alexander & French, 1946) of a secure base so they can explore the attachment problems that created the maladaptive schemas (Bowlby, 1973, 1982).

Therapist reactions are an important resource for both schema assessment and change; *e.g.*, clients with an emotional inhibition schema often induce feelings of boredom. Therapists need to recognize when their reactions are appropriate and when they reflect the therapist's own schemas. Therapist schemas may be problematic in a number of ways:

1. Client schemas trigger the therapist's schema: "I'd really hoped to have a more mature, experienced therapist" may trigger the beginning therapist's defectiveness schema.
2. Therapist schemas prevent appropriate responses to client needs: Therapists with emotional inhibition schemas may find it difficult to provide the warmth needed for limited reparenting of clients with emotional deprivation schemas.
3. Therapists over-identify with clients who have similar schemas: If both share abandonment schemas, the therapist's boundaries may be overwhelmed by grief over the client's pain. This could reinforce the client's distorted perceptions and inadequate reality testing.
4. Client emotions trigger therapist avoidance: A client who is critical to overcompensate for a defectiveness schema may overwhelm therapists with a subjugation schema, which leads to a vicious circle of criticize-defend-criticize.
5. Client schemas trigger overcompensation by the therapist: A therapist with a defectiveness schema might overcompensate and criticize a client with an entitlement schema.

6. Clients are used to meet the therapist's schema-driven needs: A therapist with an emotional deprivation schema elicits nurturance from a self-sacrificing client.

Therapists must balance empathy and confrontation: they must encourage change, while acknowledging its difficulty and the reasons why the client developed the schema in the first place. This is essential when therapy itself triggers a schema. Therapists first ask open-ended questions to elicit the client's feelings and point of view, "What do you feel like doing? What did I do to trigger this urge? Has anyone ever made you feel this way in the past? What schema may have been triggered?" They next validate the client's feelings as understandable and apologize if anything hurtful was said or done. Once clients feel understood, therapists may self-disclose their own reactions and perceptions. The goal is to help clients test their perceptions against reality and to consider alternative explanations for them.

Limited reparenting appropriately meets client needs for nurturance, autonomy, limits, or self-expression. Reparenting is "limited" in that therapists provide temporary support so clients can safely confront the painful history of a maladaptive schema. Reparenting differs for clients who ask personal questions, depending on whether the request reflects an undeveloped, enmeshed self or an emotional deprivation schema. Emotionally deprived clients need openness and warmth, while enmeshed clients need limits. Openness reinforces an enmeshed client's disregard for boundaries, but counters the emotionally deprived client's belief that others are emotionally unavailable. Similarly, clients with abandonment schemas may require additional sessions to feel secure, but clients with entitlement/grandiosity schemas need clear limits.

Reparenting needs differ as a function of schema types. In general, therapists should meet the attachment and nurturance needs of clients with schemas in the disconnection/rejection domain. These clients lacked stable, trustworthy attachment figures during development, so therapists meet these needs until the client's healthy adult mode can provide self-nurturance and acceptance. Clients with schemas in the impaired autonomy and performance domain have not experienced success as a result of their own efforts and need structure and limits in order to differentiate from others. Therapists meet this need by showing confidence that the client will cope successfully. Clients with schemas in the impaired limits domain need structure and limits and have never learned the discipline necessary to succeed. Therapists model appropriate self-control and discipline, set limits, and support clients as they become more self-directed and emotionally connected. Clients with schemas in the other-directing domain learned that acceptance by others is conditional on meeting external standards and so they also need to learn to be self-directing and accepting. Therapists are nondirective, but reinforce clients as they act independently and assert themselves. Overvigilance/inhibition domain schemas reflect unrealistic values, standards, and concerns internalized from attachment models. Therapists model optimistic spontaneity, acceptance of self and others, and a balance of internal and external standards. Playfulness is modeled, encouraged, and reinforced.

Cognitive strategies

Schema therapy resembles Beck's cognitive approach (Beck & Freeman, 1990) in emphasizing the therapist's active guidance of therapy. Both approaches use cognitive and behavioral strategies to help clients test schemas and cognitions against reality. Both ask clients to collaborate as equals in developing case conceptualizations and emphasize homework and education about the therapeutic model and coping strategies. However, schema therapy begins with core schemas and then links these to surface-level thoughts, instead of Beck's top-down approach moving from automatic thoughts to basic beliefs. Schema therapy's bottom-up approach shifts attention from current problems to lifelong interpersonal patterns. More time is devoted to identifying schemas, modes, and coping styles, and less to testing the validity of surface beliefs. As a result, schema therapy is less structured than Beck's cognitive approach and is more likely to move between the past and the present or from one schema to another. Another important difference is the degree to which experiential imagery is emphasized.

The goal of cognitive intervention is to strengthen the "healthy adult" mode so clients can dispute maladaptive schemas. Therapists align themselves with the client using empathic confrontation to examine the evidence for a schema and to consider alternative explanations. Clients are encouraged to have a debate between their maladaptive schema mode and their healthy adult mode to evaluate the pros and cons of their coping style. Because clients have little experience articulating their healthy side, the therapist may need to role play arguments against the schema. Clients then create "flash cards" that summarize healthy responses to schema triggers. Young et al. (2003) describe a client with mistrust and defectiveness schemas who wrote a flash card summary to confront his anxiety about meeting women at social gatherings. In it, he noted his worries that women are untrustworthy and might not find him attractive reflected schema-based feelings toward his mother. He then countered his fears with a more realistic self-appraisal and concluded, "… I must approach this woman, even though I feel nervous, because it's the only way to get my emotional needs met" (Young et al., 2003, p. 106).

After learning to use flash cards, clients advance to "schema diaries." Clients complete blank forms when they recognize a schema has been triggered that includes the trigger and the resulting emotions, thoughts, and actual behaviors. They then relate their experience to their knowledge of their schemas, describe a more healthy view that includes realistic concerns, and consider how they initially overreacted. They then conclude with what would be a healthy response. Young et al. (2003) describe Emily's diary, whose subjugation schema enabled staff members to make administrative decisions for her. Emily described her fear of being confronted by a subordinate, Jane, who requested a meeting. She related her fear to feeling subjugated to her father to avoid his anger. She countered her fear noting she did not know what Jane wanted, but could end the meeting if Jane, who realistically is intimidating, became disrespectful. She noted her overreaction in assuming Jane had a complaint and, if so, that she could not handle it. She then chose to meet and find out what Jane actually wanted. Although Emily succeeded, schema-based feelings do not always change just because thoughts and actions have been modified. Experiential strategies are then necessary to alter those feelings.

Experiential strategies

The five steps in implementing imagery change interventions are:

1. Provide a rationale,
2. Begin with imagery of a safe place,
3. Use imagery linking past significant relationships and experiences to current problems,
4. Return to images of a safe place, and
5. Relate the imagery to the client's early maladaptive schemas.

Imagery is reintroduced in the change phase after clients become adept at challenging schemas with flash cards. Imagery helps clients confront feared situations in their imagination to overcome avoidant patterns. Imagery dialogs with significant others in the present and from childhood help clients express anger about unmet needs. Schema mode imagery work allows a "healthy adult" to support the "vulnerable child" whose needs were not met by a "dysfunctional parent." Expressing anger toward dysfunctional parts of the self helps externalize critical, controlling, depriving, or rejecting voices. This can be reinforced by having clients write a letter expressing their feelings to their parents, but not necessarily to send the letter. As clients gain distance from schemas, they can begin grieving over inadequate childhood nurturing. They begin to reparent themselves, develop more realistic expectations for the future, and accept the past.

Imagery work is especially helpful to reparent clients with disconnection/rejection domain schemas. During imagery, therapists ask permission to enter the image and speak to the vulnerable child. They provide appropriate reparenting for the vulnerable child and then help the client's healthy adult provide that reparenting. This is illustrated in an interview with Hector, whose abandonment and mistrust/abuse schemas reflect a history of foster placements after his mother was hospitalized with schizophrenia. As this segment begins, the therapist asks Hector to imagine himself as a child in the foster homes. Hector imagines sitting on a strange bed with his brother, feeling too scared and mistrustful to talk with the therapist (in the imagery).

Therapist: Why doesn't Little Hector trust me? What's he afraid I'm going to do?
Client: He thinks you're going to hurt him.
Therapist: How does he think I'd hurt him?
Client: He thinks you're going to be mean to him and make fun of him.
Therapist: Do you agree with him? Do you think that's how I would really treat him? That I would be mean to him and make fun of him?
Client: [*pause*] No.

Therapist:	Well, then, could you tell that to him? Could you tell him that I'm a good person who's been good to you and that I won't hurt him? [*continues to seek permission to speak directly with vulnerable child, until client agrees*]
Therapist:	Can you see me now in the image? Can you see me kneeling next to the bed so I can talk to Little Hector? [*begins reparenting*]
Client:	Yes.
Therapist:	Can you talk to me in the image as Little Hector and tell me what you're feeling?
Client:	I'm feeling scared. I don't like it here. I want my mother. I want to go home.
Therapist:	What do you want from me?
Client:	I want you to stay with me. Maybe to hold me.
Therapist:	How about if I sit next to you in the image and put my arm around you? How would that be?
Client:	Good. That's good.
Therapist:	[*in the image*] I'll stay here with you. I'll take care of you. I won't leave you. [*after determining the vulnerable child's needs, the therapist meets them in imagery*]
Therapist:	I want you to bring yourself into the image as an adult. Imagine that you are there in the image as an adult, and you see Little Hector, and you see the room and your little brother there with you. Can you see it? [*accessing client's healthy adult*]
Client:	Uh-huh.
Therapist:	Could you talk to Little Hector? Could you try to help him feel better?
Client:	[*to Little Hector*] I can see this is really hard for you. You're really scared. Do you want to talk about it? Why don't you just come over here with me, and we'll be together for a while.
Therapist:	And how does Little Hector feel when he hears that?
Client:	He feels better, like someone's there for him. [*client's healthy adult meets the vulnerable child's needs; may be a useful skill in later sessions*]
Therapist:	You seem distant and a little sad today.
Client:	Yeah.
Therapist:	What's going on? Do you know why?
Client:	No. I don't know why.
Therapist:	Can we do an exercise to find out? Could you close your eyes and picture Little Hector? Could you picture him here right now and tell me what you see?
Client:	I see him curled up into a ball. He's scared.
Therapist:	What's he scared about?
Client:	He's scared Ashley's [*current relationship*] going to leave him.

(Reprinted from *Schema therapy: A practitioner's guide*, by J. E. Young, J. S. Klosko, & M. E. Weishaar, pp. 131–133. © 2003 by Guilford. Used with permission).

As this last exchange suggests, clients who are out of touch with their vulnerable child are often unaware of their feelings. Their detached protector mode protects them from imagined hurts by keeping feelings out of awareness. Sometimes just giving clients permission to wait until images or feelings arise is sufficient. Alternatively, entering a dialog with the detached protector may help. In the case of traumatic memories, the client may need a greater sense of control. This is done by agreeing on signals clients can use to interrupt the imagery and return to a safe place. If clients remain unable to access their emotional experience, it may help to use one or more sessions to address trauma, emphasize relaxation and imagery of safe places, and focus on the client's physical sensations or "felt body experience" (discussed in Chap. 8).

Behavioral pattern breaking

Behavioral pattern breaking helps avoid relapse once clients learn how schemas affect their lives and have begun to challenge them through imagery. During this final phase of schema therapy, behavioral techniques target self-defeating coping styles. Clients are ready for this phase once they recognize maladaptive schemas and triggers as they occur, understand their childhood origins, and can defeat the schema during imagery dialogs.

Therapists and clients collaboratively identify problematic sequences of self-defeating behavior and their triggers and revise initial case conceptualizations with information gathered during earlier sessions. They then address motivation for change and prioritize goals by linking problematic behaviors to childhood origins and reviewing the pros and cons of their continuance. The goal is to help clients forgive rather than blame themselves for problems. Flash cards help clients identify relevant schemas, triggers and sequences of self-defeating behavior, more realistic interpretations of problem situations, and desired healthy behaviors. Clients practice healthy behaviors in role plays and in imagery before attempting them in homework. Homework assignments are concrete and specific, "This week I'm going to ask my boss if I can take my vacation at the end of May. Just before asking him, I'm going to read my flash card, and then visualize asking him, just the way I planned it. Afterward, I'll write down what happened, how I felt, what I was thinking, what I did, and what my boss did" (Young et al., 2003, p. 164).

Prior homework assignments are reviewed during therapy to address any barriers to completion. Once barriers such as fear of the consequences of changing are understood, dialogs between the block (perhaps the "dysfunctional parent") and the "healthy adult" help clients overcome the emotional constriction. A new flash card is developed and the homework is reassigned. If motivation is a problem, leaving the therapist a phone message about a success or some other mutually selected reinforcer can be used. In extreme cases, a break from therapy may be suggested until the client feels ready to attempt behavioral change.

Schema Mode Work

This unique intervention was developed after other techniques failed to help severely disturbed narcissistic and borderline clients. It is currently used with any client if therapy is blocked or the therapist feels that mode work would be helpful, *as* with self-punitive or self-critical clients. There are seven steps to schema mode work:

1. *Identify and label the client's modes*—Collaboratively identify appropriate labels for different modes that occur repeatedly in session. A "detached protector" might be the "workaholic," or a "vulnerable child" the "lonely child." Therapists can then ask the client to identify a current schema mode; *e.g.*, a "spoiled child" that appears when the client is bored.
2. *Explore the origin and adaptive value of the mode in childhood*—Clients are helped to understand and empathize with a mode once they discover its childhood function.
3. *Link maladaptive modes to current problems and symptoms*—As clients understand how a mode influences their current problem, they become motivated to work in therapy.
4. *Demonstrate the advantages of modifying a mode when it interferes with another mode*—Dialogs in role play or imagery illustrate the costs of a dominant mode; *e.g.*, a detached protector who keeps the vulnerable child "safe" through self-sacrifice.
5. *Access the vulnerable child through imagery*—Imagery is especially useful with suppressed vulnerable child modes; but significant levels of empathic confrontation may also be needed to help clients become fully aware of this mode.
6. *Conduct dialogs among the modes*—Therapists model a healthy adult mode that nurtures, protects, sets limits for the vulnerable child mode, and confronts maladaptive coping or dysfunctional parent modes. Clients assume the healthy adult mode when they are ready.
7. *Help client generalize mode work to outside life situations*—Clients use homework to break behavioral patterns, recognize their own needs and feelings, and relate to others in more emotionally fulfilling ways.

Case Illustration: Schema Therapy (Summarized from Young et al., 2003, pp. 66–67)

- **Background:** Annette G. was referred by her therapist, Rachel W., for consultation with Dr. Young. Annette is 26 years old, single, Caucasian woman who lives alone in a Manhattan apartment and works as a receptionist. She has been seen by Rachel for 6 months, receiving cognitive-behavioral and schema therapy for her long-term depression and alcohol abuse. She is also attending

Alcoholics Anonymous. She has been unable to hold a steady job, finding it difficult to complete boring or repetitive tasks. She also reports a history of drifting dating inappropriate men and being able to get close to a boyfriend. She feels lonely and emotionally disconnected from other people and uses drinking and parties to cope with her depression and feeling of emptiness. She has gained self-awareness in therapy, but is still depressed and continues to abuse alcohol. She says she should have protected her mother from her father's violent temper, but never received nurturance or protection herself. Her mother was needy and helpless, unable to respond to attempts to seek warmth or closeness, her father was frightening, and neither provided discipline nor limits on her behavior.

- **Therapy Relationship over Past 6 Months:** The therapist described Annette as engaged in therapy, but often acting tough and not admitting any strong attachment or neediness. She does not like imagery exercises, written homework, or talking about painful feelings.
- **Diagnosis:**
  Axis I—Dysthymic disorder; alcohol abuse
  Axis II—Personality disorder, not otherwise specified
  Axis III—No diagnosis
  Axis IV—Lack of primary support group; lacks stable employment or personal relationships
  Axis V—GAF=52
- **Problem List and Linked Schemas:**

  1. Depression: emotional deprivation, defectiveness, self-sacrifice
  2. Alcohol abuse: coping for emotional deprivation, mistrust/abuse, defectiveness
  3. Relational problems: emotional deprivation, mistrust/abuse, defectiveness, self-sacrifice
  4. Work problems: insufficient self-control/self-discipline, entitlement/grandiosity

- **Case Conceptualization:** Annette's schema triggers appear to be fears of intimacy when she starts to get close to a boyfriend, feeling lonely or bored, or having to think about her problems and therapy. Cognitive distortions include beliefs that no one will ever be there for her, she is fundamentally defective for being so needy, men are unpredictable and explosive, and she should be able to do what she wants rather than dull, boring things. Her schema modes include a Detached Protector (Tough Annette), a Lonely, Frightened Child (Little Annette), and a Spoiled Annette. She uses several coping mechanisms and *surrenders* to: defectiveness by not asking for nurturance; self-sacrifice by trying to take care of mother and expecting little in return; and mistrust/abuse by not showing vulnerability. She *avoids*: emotional deprivation with alcohol and seeking novelty; mistrust/abuse by avoiding intimacy with men; defectiveness by avoiding painful feelings. She *overcompensates* by being "tough" despite feeling vulnerable and needy.

- **Treatment Plan:**

  1. *Therapeutic Relationship*—The preponderance of disconnection/rejection schemas requires significant limited reparenting to give Annette consistent nurturance, strength, guidance, and safety. Nurturance and support are also needed to counter her self-sacrifice schema. She will need empathic confrontation when her impaired performance/insufficient self-discipline schemas are activated (Spoiled Annette).

  2. *Cognitive Strategies*—Black and white thinking in most schema modes requires empathic confrontation. Experiments will test both self-sacrifice schema perceptions of others as needy or helpless and impaired performance/ insufficient self-discipline schema perceptions that interpersonal reciprocity is unnecessary. Pros and cons of acting tough, using alcohol, and not asking for nurturance will be examined with dialogs between schema and healthy adult modes. Triggers and problematic sequences will be identified and used to complete schema diaries and construct flash cards.

  3. *Experiential Strategies*—Role play modeling of "healthy adult" will confront "Tough Annette's" protection of "Little Annette" with its subsequent self-sacrifice and emotional constriction. "Spoiled Annette's" inability to sustain effort or relationships will be explored in the context of imagery about the lack of parental discipline in Annette's childhood.

  4. *Schema Mode Work*—"Tough Annette," "Little Annette," and "Spoiled Annette" modes will be identified and related to Annette's history and current life situation. Imagery will help access the "Little Annette" mode and support her needs for nurturance and protection.

  5. *Behavioral Pattern Breaking*—Schema triggers that lead to problematic modes such as "Spoiled Annette" will be identified on flash cards and contrasted with more realistic interpretations; *e.g.*, "one has to give in order to receive." Role plays using flash cards to confront real-life situations will prepare Annette for homework, such as responding to urges to quit when she feels bored. When depressed feelings or avoidance of emotional needs trigger urges for drinking, she will practice relaxation and contacting her AA sponsor.

Table 5.2, below, summarizes Young, *et al.*'s (2003) discussion of relational, cognitive, experiential, behavioral, and schema mode intervention goals for each of the 18 schemas.

Integrative Implications

Cognitive therapy's contributions toward therapeutic integration include:

1. Bridging the gap between scientific modernism and phenomenology with empirical methods that explore the dialectic of thought and action;
2. Developing useful, highly structured methods for modifying dysfunctional thoughts;

Table 5.2 Client schemas and associated goals and treatment strategies

Schema	Treatment goals: strategies
Abandonment/ instability	Therapist is transitional figure in developing stable object relation-ships: Limited reparenting is gradually replaced with stable significant other; catastrophizing cognitions are challenged; unstable childhood experiences confronted in imagery; clients learn to walk away from unstable relationships, relinquish jealous control of significant others, and tolerate being alone.
Mistrust/abuse	Therapist establishes trust through an emotionally safe relationship: Use of imagery gradually confronts abuse and client expresses affect strangulated at the time; anger helps empower and reduce self-blame; clients learn to recognize a spectrum of trust-worthiness, to set appropriate limits, and to increase intimacy; tests of trustworthiness are relinquished.
Emotional deprivation	Therapist provides nurturance, strength, and guidance to help clients express needs and feelings: Imagery contacts "lonely child" to express anger and pain over unmet needs; therapist models "healthy adult" comforting and assists client's self-nurturance; black and white thinking is challenged; clients helped to choose nurturing friends and ask for what they need.
Defectiveness/shame	Therapist affirmation increases client self-esteem and reduces self-devaluation: Critical *vs.* healthy self dialogs challenge significance of flaws and highlight assets; imagery with "healthy adult" comforting "rejected child" helps to express anger at parental criticism; clients learn to set limits with critical others and respond with own perspective, rather than counter-attack.
Social isolation /alienation	Decrease feelings of difference and improve current peer group relationships: Focus on similarities with others and joining groups that share their differences; challenge thoughts that prevent joining or intimacy; imagery to vent anger at being excluded by peers.
Dependence/incom-petence	Competence and independence fostered by not reinforcing help-lessness: Gradual exposure to anxiety when acting and making decisions independently; challenge negative thoughts; imagery, flashcards and relaxation support homework confronting anxiety-arousing situations.
Vulnerability to harm or illness	Probability of catastrophe decreased and coping increased by confronting clients to long-term costs of phobic life pattern: "Healthy adult" assists "frightened child" to endure anxiety during gradual exposure to feared situations; catastrophic thoughts challenged.
Enmeshment/undevel-oped self	Spontaneous self-expression supported by clear boundaries: Similarities/differences with parent are explored via dialogs between enmeshed and fused self-aspects; imagery explores times when clients felt different from parent and how an autonomous life would be; homework explores intrinsically valued activities and relationships with friends that support autonomy.
Failure	Skills, confidence, and realistic self-appraisal modeled by therapist's pursuit of clear goals despite setbacks: Realistic aspirations and barriers are identified through exploration of past success and failure; imagery helps clients express anger at those who discouraged them and reattribute failure; homework replaces maladaptive coping with graded tasks for desired goals.

Table 5.2 (continued)

Schema	Treatment goals: strategies
Entitlement/grandi-osity	Therapeutic limits support interpersonal reciprocity and equality: Entitlement's problems are highlighted to increase motivation; appropriate self-appraisal, assertiveness, empathy, and awareness of impact on others help improve relationships with others; parental indulgence and its impact are confronted in imagery; entitlement in session is empathically confronted.
Insufficient self-control/discipline	Limits support impulse control, frustration tolerance, and long-term goal focus: Homework gradually increases organization and ability to perform routine tasks; clients learn to think before acting on impulse; "healthy adult" imagery helps "undisciplined child" exert self-control.
Subjugation	Nondirective support helps clients accept their right to have needs met: Related fears tested by behavioral experiments; imagery expresses anger and assertion toward controlling parent and explores own needs/preferences; clients select noncontrolling, responsive partners.
Self-sacrifice	Therapist nurturance helps client's accept their right to have needs met: Fragility and neediness of others is challenged; imagery supports anger and grief over parental deprivation; clients practice tracking and balancing what they give others with what they receive.
Recognition and/or approval seeking	Empathic confrontation of approval seeking helps clients recognize and act on own preferences: Pros and cons of seeking approval *vs.* self-express are explored; imagery helps discover what "vulnerable child" really needed when seeking approval; clients learn to tolerate disapproval.
Negativity/pessimism	Validate past losses and avoid reinforcing complaints and negativity to focus on needs and reduce rumination: Negativity and distortions tested against evidence, and alternatives explored in dialogs with imagery of "healthy, optimistic adult" expressing anger at "negative parent's" deflation of "happy child's" enthusiasm; response prevention/scheduled "worry time" reduces hypervigilance.
Emotional inhibition	Modeling and imagery expressing emotion in relations with significant others supports spontaneity and expression: "Healthy adult" helps "inhibited child" confront "inhibiting parent;" pros/cons of expression are reviewed; graded homework with self-expression in dance, sports, *etc.*
Unrelenting standards/ hypercriticalness	Modeling and empathic confrontation of rigid demands increases ability to play and self-other acceptance: Considering pros and cons of a spectrum of performance challenges perfectionism; imagery expresses anger at "demanding parent" or at perfectionistic side; schedules limit work time and allows for play; homework of gradually attempting less and setting lower standards.
Punitiveness	Modeling compassion for self/others helps clients learn to forgive: Pros/cons of punishment and dialogs between punishing and forgiving sides highlights costs of punishment; imagery helps clients externalize punitive voice; forgiveness practiced when punitive urges occur.

3. Validating the integration of cognitive and behavioral methods;
4. Expanding the cognitive schema concept to emphasize the influence of early childhood experiences and attachment in guiding interpersonal actions;
5. Using Piaget's assimilation-accommodation concepts to explain how schemas develop through experience provides a bridge to psychodynamic developmental theory;
6. Increasing emphasis on the therapeutic relationship.

Critics often point to incompatible assumptions as a reason for rejecting integrative efforts. Nowhere is this incompatibility more apparent than in the divide between subjective and objective therapeutic approaches. It is certainly impossible to know another's thoughts directly, but cognitive therapists have shown that behavior changes when clients' verbal reports about their thoughts change. This has led to extensive validation of a broad array of interventions that integrate cognitive and behavioral techniques.

Recently, cognitive therapists such as Beck and Beck (2000) and Young *et al.* (2003) have expanded the concept of a schema to emphasize its emotional components and include the influence of early attachments. In particular, they have been influenced by Piaget's theory of development, which suggests that new experiences are assimilated into existing schemas unless they are too dissimilar. In that case, an accommodation is made and the schema is either modified or a new one is formed. These developments align cognitive approaches more closely with psychodynamic theory's emphasis on developmental processes, another basis for therapeutic integration. Similarly, the increasing emphasis on relationship issues by cognitive therapists such as Safran and Muran (2000) and Young *et al.* (2003) creates still another basis for integration with psychodynamic and also interpersonal and experiential approaches.

Chapter Five: Main Points

- Cognitive therapies bridge the gap between modernist and phenomenological approaches by suggesting that people respond to beliefs, rather than events themselves, and that therapy can use verbal reports of those beliefs to examine how thoughts affect behavior. This has led to an empirically based integrative therapy: cognitive-behavioral therapy in its various forms.
- The ABCs of RECBT propose that *Antecedent* events are interpreted according to the individual's *Beliefs*, which then determine the *Consequences* of the event.
- Adaptive behavior results from *rational* beliefs that produce positive consequences, while maladaptive behavior results from *irrational* beliefs that produce negative consequences.
- *Irrational beliefs* tend to be dogmatic absolute, and reflect demandingness. What are actually preferences are seen as needs that cannot be denied or deferred.

Albert Ellis refers to them as the *tyranny of the shoulds* or as *musturbatory thinking*.

- Treatment involves the DEFs of RECBT: Therapists *Dispute* irrational beliefs; as clients are persuaded to reject their irrational beliefs, they are able to develop an *Effective* new philosophy, which results in more positive *Feelings*.
- Clients are taught to *Detect, Debate*, and *Discriminate* irrational ideas until they no longer drive maladaptive responses. The therapist serves as an expert coach to help clients see how irrational ideas keep emotional disturbances alive, to debate these ideas, and develop a more effective philosophy.
- Cognitive therapy is active, collaborative, structured, present-focused, and time-limited. It uses Socratic questions to challenge dysfunctional ideas rather than persuasion. It also focuses on modifying the core schemas that underlie dysfunctional thoughts, rather than modifying surface thoughts.
- *Schemas* are internalized representations of the cognitive, affective, intentional, and action tendencies associated with a person's developmental experiences. The *cognitive triad* refers to schemas that reflect the individual's beliefs about the self, the world, and the future.
- The *cognitive specificity hypothesis* holds that different diagnostic groups have specific sets of beliefs regarding the cognitive triad. Depressed individuals have negative perceptions in all three areas; they see themselves as flawed, others as rejecting and uncaring, and the future as bleak. In contrast, anxious individuals perceive themselves as not competent to deal with a threatening world.
- Maladaptive schemas reflect an understanding of the world that may have been accurate when first formed in childhood, but is no longer adaptive in an adult world. Some *cognitive distortions* associated with such schemas include dichotomous thinking, overgeneralization, magnification/minimization, personalization, emotional reasoning, and catastrophizing. Different distortions may occur with different diagnostic problems.
- Schemas tend to *assimilate* new information into existing structures, rather than change or create new schemas to *accommodate* incongruent information. This causes an *assimilative bias*: to attend selectively to information that confirms the schema and ignores the incongruent information. Thoughts resulting from an assimilative bias without being tested for accuracy or utility are termed automatic thoughts.
- Cognitive therapy, based on verbal learning principles, focuses on the evolution of meanings reflected in cognitive schemas. It may be contrasted with behavioral therapy, based on classical and operant conditioning principles, which can influence language or behavior, but are not directly related to the development of meaning.
- Cognitive therapy borrows behavioral interventions such as scheduling activities (to help reveal underlying cognitive distortions), behavioral activation, and self-monitoring.
- Cognitive distortions are monitored with the *Daily Record of Dysfunctional Thoughts* (DTR), also used to identify precipitating events and challenge resultant thoughts. The DTR serves as an outcome measure, as homework, and as a

focus for Socratic inquiry. Clients rate the degree to which they believe in dysfunctional beliefs or any alternatives they generate.

- The *downward arrow* is used to move from surface thoughts to core dysfunctional schemas. For example, "If that statement were true, what would it mean?" Repeating such questions invites clients to examine deeper meanings and assumptions embedded in their statements.
- Once *automatic thoughts* are described in core schema terms, Socratic questioning explores three areas: "What is the evidence for and against this belief?" "What alternative explanations exist for the event?" "What are the implications of your belief, if it is correct?"
- Cognitive therapy treatment plans begin with a problem list that suggests goals. They identify dysfunctional core beliefs and situations that precipitate the client's problems. A case conceptualization then suggests useful interventions and possible obstacles to treatment.
- Schema therapy addresses long-standing, treatment-resistant, thematic problems. It focuses on childhood attachment issues that create *early maladaptive schemas* that are not in conscious awareness and not easily addressed by Socratic questioning.
- Five *domains* of early maladaptive schemas have been identified: Disconnection/Rejection; Impaired Autonomy and Performance; Impaired Limits; Other-Directedness; Overvigilance and Inhibition. While maladaptive schemas are relatively stable, clients respond to them with one or more relatively unstable *coping styles*: Surrender, Avoidance, or Overcompensation. The instability of traditional diagnoses may be attributed to their focus on observable coping styles rather than stable maladaptive schemas.
- An *assessment and education* phase develops a case conceptualization and helps clients identify and re-experience dysfunctional life patterns related to schemas and coping styles.
- The *change* phase challenges maladaptive schemas and uses a variety of interventions to explore more adaptive coping:

  - *Relational*: repeated *empathic confrontation* of schema-driven patterns as they occur outside of therapy and in the relationship lets clients explore healthier coping; *limited reparenting* provides support, unavailable in early attachments, to challenge maladaptive schemas.
  - *Cognitive*: Homework to explore new ways to act include *Flashcards* to summarize schemas and coping styles and *diaries* of schemas, triggers, emotions, automatic thoughts *vs.* alternatives, realistic concerns *vs.* overreactions, and actual *vs.* healthy behavior.
  - *Experiential: Imagery* lets clients safely re-experience problematic relationships, past and present, and imagine alternative ways of responding.
  - *Behavioral: Pattern-breaking* targets dysfunctional coping styles—goals are prioritized, links between childhood and current problems clarified, and homework with flashcards and diaries explore alternative ways of responding in interpersonal relationships.

- *Schema modes* reflect four categories of moment-to-moment coping with schemas: *child* (vulnerable, angry, impulsive, undisciplined, or happy), *dysfunctional coping* (compliant surrenderer, detached protector, or overcompensator), *dysfunctional parent* (punitive or demanding), and *healthy adult* modes.
- Mode work is used when other methods fail: 1. Identify and label the client's modes; 2. Explore their childhood origins and adaptive value; 3. Link modes to current problems; 4. Show advantage of changing a dysfunctional mode; 5. Access "vulnerable child" through imagery; 6. Conduct "dialogs" among the modes; 7. Help client generalize mode work with homework outside of therapy.
- Cognitive therapy's contributions toward therapeutic integration include: 1. bridging the gap between scientific modernism and phenomenology; 2. developing structured methods for modifying dysfunctional thoughts; 3. integrating cognitive and behavioral methods; 4. expanding the schema concept to emphasize the influence of early childhood attachment experiences; 5. bridging the gap with other approaches with Piaget's developmental concepts; and 6. an increased emphasis on the therapeutic relationship.

Further Reading

Beck, A. T., & Beck, J. S. (2005). *Cognitive therapy for challenging problems: What to do when the basics don't work*. New York: Guilford Press.

Beck, A. T., & Freeman, A. (1990) *Cognitive therapy of personality disorders*. New York: Guilford Press.

Beck, A. T., Rush, A., Shaw, B., & Emery, G. (1979). *Cognitive therapy of depression*. New York: Guilford Press.

Ellis, A. (1991). The revised ABCs of rational-emotive therapy. *Journal of Rational-Emotive and Cognitive-Behavior Therapy, 9,* 139–172.

Young, J. E., Klosko, J. S., & Weishaar, M. E. (2003). *Schema therapy: A practitioner's guide*. New York: Guilford Press.

Websites

Albert Ellis Institute. Website: www.rebt.org
Beck Institute for Cognitive Therapy and Research: www.beckinstitute.org
Schema Therapy Institute: www.schematherapy.com

Videos

American Psychological Association Systems of Psychotherapy Series (2007).
- Cognitive Therapy with Judith Beck
- Schema Therapy with Jeffrey Young

Chapter 6
Psychoanalytic Approaches

> *Our normal waking consciousness, rational consciousness*
> *as we call it, is but one special type of consciousness, whilst*
> *all about it, parted from it by the filmiest of screens, there lie*
> *potential forms of consciousness entirely different.*
> W. James (1902/2002, from "Mysticism," lectures 16–17)

To what degree is human behavior governed by rational, conscious processes as opposed to unconscious processes as suggested by William James? Historically, cognitive-behaviorists emphasize rationality, while psychoanalysts emphasize irrational, unconscious determinants. A synthesis of these dialectic polarities is developing as cognitive therapists (*e.g.*, Young, Klosko, & Weishaar 2003) focus on unconscious schemas, while many analysts now give greater emphasis to conscious processes (*e.g.*, Aron, 2001). Unconscious motives, first described in Joseph Breuer and Sigmund Freud's (1893–1895/1955) *Studies in Hysteria*, led to modern ideas about psychopathology. Breuer and Freud proposed that conversion symptoms result from a wish to forget painful memories: *e.g.*, once hypnosis helped their patient, Anna O., remember painful childhood experiences, her symptoms disappeared. Later, Freud found that talking freely about early traumatic memories was more reliable and effective than hypnosis, the first "talking" therapy.

Freudian psychoanalysis focuses on helping clients become aware of the unconscious determinants of their behavior. It agrees with the medical model that mental illness is caused by processes within an individual (psychological rather than biological), which can be alleviated by appropriate treatment; *i.e.*, uncovering the unconscious determinants of symptoms. Freud's deterministic bias led him to de-emphasize conscious reasoning as a way to explain behavior. Later, ego analysts such as Erik Erikson, Heinz Hartmann, and Ernst Kris explained much of everyday behavior using conscious reasoning, but still viewed symptoms as an unconscious process. Contemporary object relations analysts (see Chap. 7) have replaced Freud's *monadic* emphasis on processes operating within individuals with a *dyadic* focus. They focus on internalized representations of early relationships and give greater emphasis to the therapeutic relationship in bringing unconscious conflicts and wishes into awareness to help clients overcome their problems.

D. K. Fromme, *Systems of Psychotherapy,*
DOI 10.1007/978-1-4419-7308-5_6, © Springer Science+Business Media, LLC 2011

Psychoanalysis

Freud was influenced by modernist epistemology, which looks for a prior cause for every phenomenon. This led to his assumption of *psychic determinism*: internal processes, such as unconscious wishes, determine even trivial or "mistaken" actions; *e.g.*, Freud described dreams as the "royal road to the unconscious" in which each aspect of a dream reflects wishes, defenses, or other causal processes operating outside the person's awareness. Slips of the tongue and neurotic symptoms are also examples of motivated processes that operate outside of awareness.

A dialectic tension exists between the assumption of psychic determinism and the methods Freud used to uncover unconscious wishes. Freud's theory of personality and psychopathology is essentially deterministic, but he used phenomenological methods to help clients bring unconscious materials into awareness. The tension between these opposing principles allowed Freud to create perhaps the most complete theory of human behavior yet developed. He bridged the subject-object divide by suggesting that psychoanalysis can decode unconscious wishes by interpreting the functions served by behavior in a particular context; *e.g.*, self-appointed censors of pornographic materials may gain partial gratification of sexual wishes, while simultaneously demonstrating their disapproval. Although interpretations do not meet modern scientific standards, they may provide useful hypotheses if the problem's context is considered as is done in hermeneutic interpretation.

Freud's Instinctual Drive Theory

Freud replaced hypnosis as a method of uncovering "lost" memories with *free association*, which asks clients to say whatever comes to mind in their "stream of consciousness." He was struck by the frequency of incest and sexual abuse reported by clients, which led to his *traumatic* or *seduction* theory of neurosis. However, in correspondence with his mentor, Wilhelm Fliess, Freud suggested four reasons for rejecting seduction theory (1897/1954, pp. 215–217):

1. High improbability of nearly universal sexual abuse of children by their fathers;
2. Failure of such revelations to produce lasting change in symptoms;
3. Realization that fantasy and reality are not distinguished by the unconscious;
4. No infantile seduction is revealed when unconscious contents flood awareness in psychosis.

Masson (1984) suggested more personal reasons for Freud to abandon his seduction theory. Masson cites the professional community's rejection of his descriptions of near universal childhood seduction and the possibility that Fliess sexually abused his own son and dissuaded Freud from this theory. If seduction does not actually happen, then Freud wondered if his female clients' stories reflected unconscious wishes for sexual intimacy with the father. Such socially unacceptable wishes are *repressed* and kept unconscious. Freud's rejection of the seduction hypothesis and his pervasive influence prevented several generations of therapists from realizing that abuse may have very unfortunate consequences and is not always a fantasy (Russell, 1986).

After Freud abandoned seduction theory, he spent 2 years in self-analysis of his own childhood wishes for intimacy with his mother and resentment of his father's intimacy with her. His self-analysis led to the ideas that sexuality and aggression are universal instincts that motivate all behavior and every child has sexual feelings toward the opposite-sex parent and aggressive feelings toward the same-sex parents: the *Oedipus Complex* for boys and the *Electra Complex* for girls. These feelings are repressed because they are unacceptable. Neurosis or other forms of mental illness then result if Oedipal feelings are not adequately resolved.

Structural Theory

Freud hypothesized that irrational elements of symptoms, slips of the tongue, or dreams are *compromises* between wishes and the social proprieties that make them unacceptable. Anna O. felt it was less scandalous to imagine she was pregnant by Breuer than to admit to sexual wishes about him. An imagined pregnancy gave partial gratification to her sexual wishes and kept them out of awareness (*primary gain*) and also gained Breuer's attention (*secondary gain*). At first, Freud divided personality into *conscious*, *preconscious*, and *unconscious* regions. The preconscious contained memories and wishes that could easily enter into awareness. He later elaborated his unconscious motivation theory with a *structural* theory of hypothetical constructs: the *id* reflects instinctual wishes; the *superego*, internalized parental and societal standards that keep id impulses in check; and the *ego*, or rational processes that mediate between reality and id-superego conflicts. Figure 6.1 illustrates the lack of clear demarcation between components in the combined structural model in

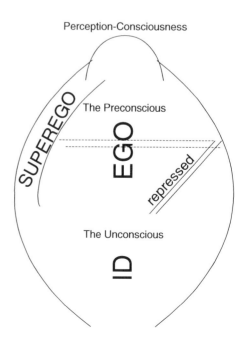

Fig. 6.1 Structural model of personality. (Freud, 1933, p. 111)

which the unconscious is the most important component. Freud (1933) emphasized that the boundaries between these components are permeable. While the id generally relies on the ego in dealing with the external world, it may sometimes do so on its own. Similarly, psychoanalysis or introspection may bring normally unconscious id impulses and wishes into awareness.

In structural theory, the id is governed by the *pleasure principle* in which *primary processes* of immediate gratification explain irrational behavior: *e.g.*, fantasies of desired objects that are not limited by reality. In contrast, the ego's *reality principle* is constrained by reality and *secondary processes* of reason and logic. Infants gradually invest (*cathect*) instinctual energy or *libido* into the ego's secondary processes. Libidinal cathexes create ego representations of the world (*object relations*) that then let infants use secondary processes to gain real rather than fantasized gratification of wishes. Development moves from fantasy to reality, from primary to secondary processes. Object relations are basically childhood schemas that encode interpersonal relationship patterns: *e.g.*, generalized expectations about others' trustworthiness or the self's lovability. The dialectic of pleasure *vs.* reality principles creates a *dynamic* relationship between id and superego in which dreams, slips of the tongue, and symptoms are the ego's compromise solutions of conflict between the id's unconscious wishes and the superego's internalized fear of social censure.

Freud believed that instincts have a bodily *source*, an *impetus* or motivating tension, a tension-reducing *aim*, and an *object* or means of reducing the tension: *e.g.*, hunger creates pangs that can be relieved by suckling the breast. Instinctual needs create wishes that are gratified either by primary processes of fantasy (imagining the breast) or secondary processes (nursing). Freud originally conceived of sexual libido, a life instinct, as the principle motivating force, but the horrors of World War I led him to propose an aggressive death instinct, *Thanatos*, as a second motive. The death instinct was never as fully developed or as widely accepted as libidinal theory, but aggression is generally regarded as an important instinct in its own right.

Psychosexual Developmental Stage Theory and Psychopathology

Psychosexual development stage theory completes Freud's overall model of the structure of personality and psychopathology. He believed that different *erogenous zones* serve to gratify the child's libidinal wishes as a child matures; *e.g.*, in the *oral* stage infants internalize representations of the gratifying object, the mother's breast, after repeated experiences of nursing. Fantasizing *internalized representations* of the desired object allows partial gratification until mother becomes available. Normal development is fostered by the optimal gratification and frustration of libidinal wishes. Over-indulgence leads to *positive fixations*, internalized object representations that are over-idealized, while harsh denial of wish gratification (*e.g.*, sudden weaning) leads to *negative fixations* and negative object representations: *e.g.*, seeing others as unworthy of trust.

Fixations create anxiety managed by *ego defenses*, primary process mechanisms that deny or *repress* indulged or frustrated wishes. If anxiety overwhelms ego defenses, *regression* to earlier developmental stages occurs and symptoms form to allow partial gratification of repressed wishes. Ego defenses include *projection* of unacceptable wishes onto others, *displacement* of instinctual wishes toward safer targets, and others described below.

During the *oral stage*, from birth to about 18 months, nursing, sucking, and other forms of oral stimulation dominate the infant's gratification of libidinal urges. Harsh or indulgent treatment in the first half of this period, the *oral dependence* stage, leads to fixations that can result in helpless, passive-dependent behavior later in life. In the second half of this period, the *oral aggressive* stage, the child may bite or otherwise act aggressively in response to weaning or separation from mother. Fixations at this stage can result in later patterns of passive-aggressive behavior.

As the anal sphincter matures, libidinal gratification of this erogenous zone ushers in the *anal expulsive* stage, which overlaps the oral stage and comes to the fore after weaning. Fixation at this stage gives the child another way to express aggression by having "accidents." Angry, disorganized life styles or accident proneness may result from fixation at this stage. The *anal retentive* stage begins as toilet training teaches the child the importance of controlling, retaining, and holding on to feces. Freud hypothesized that fixation at this stage is associated with obsessive-compulsive personality traits later in life.

The genitals become the primary erogenous zone by about 4 years of age and usher in the *phallic* stage. Children discover self-stimulation, are fascinated with differences between boys and girls, and have some beginning notions about sexuality and reproduction. Freud's use of the term, phallic, reflects the primacy of the male experience in his thinking, and also suggests that a child's sexuality is not a mature, heterosexual or *genital* sexuality. Freud focused primarily on the boy's situation, noting that the little boy typically wants to "marry" his mother when he grows up and actively seeks intimate contact with her. Freud suggested this may provoke fears of a negative response by the father, who becomes a frightening rival for the mother's affections. This overall sequence is termed the *Oedipal Complex*, after the mythical Greek king who murdered his father and married his mother.

The boy's Oedipal Complex is eventually resolved by displacing aggressive feelings and fears onto his penis, the focus of libidinal urges and the source of his problems. The child fears loss of his penis, *castration anxiety*, which has created such ambivalent feelings. These are eventually resolved by repressing sexual feelings, renouncing the mother, and by *identification with the aggressor*, his father. The superego develops as the boy internalizes his father's values and ideals at age six or seven, the end of the phallic stage. If the Oedipus Complex is not adequately resolved, the superego may fail to develop or become overly punitive and restrictive. The lack of a superego or conscience characterizes antisocial personality disorders, while a punitive superego leads to neurotic conflicts between instinctual wishes and ego defenses and to symptoms.

Freud used the term *Electra Complex* to describe the girl's dilemma, the lack of a penis, or *penis envy*. She turns to her father searching for a penis, competes with mother for his affections, and resolves her ambivalence toward mother by identifying with her. Freud believed penis envy to be less intense than castration anxiety, so that women do not incorporate their mothers' values as completely as men do with their fathers, which leads to a "weakened superego." Freud's ideas reflect late nineteenth-century, middle-class values that feminist theorists, among others, view as sexist and unconvincing. Horney (1970) suggested it was not the penis that women envy, but the relative advantages men enjoy in Western society. In fact, Freud treated the Electra Complex more as an afterthought than as a central part of his theory. His willingness to discuss sexuality openly, however, contributed to the evolution of more egalitarian ideas about gender and sexuality in Western society.

The Oedipus Complex is resolved by renouncing sexual feelings for the opposite-sexed parent and identification with the same-sexed parent. This begins the *latency* stage with libidinal strivings *sublimated* into learning about the world and becoming as powerful and desirable as the same-sexed parent. Hence, the interest that 6- to 12-year-old children take in super-heroes and movie stars. Latency lasts until the Oedipal resolution is disrupted by puberty's hormonal surge and the onset of the mature, *genital* stage in which adolescents experiment with heterosexual behavior. Freud defined successful adjustment as sufficient freedom from symptoms and behavior governed by primary processes, so individuals are free to "love and work." After the latency stage, problems are caused by stressors that trigger regression to an earlier stage of fixation.

Psychoanalytic Treatment

Initially, Breuer and Freud (1893–1895) used hypnotic suggestion to induce and to remove hysterical symptoms, which they understood to be a "reminiscence" of repressed, traumatic experiences, especially sexual abuse. However, Breuer found that Anna O. often spontaneously fell into a semi-trance state, speaking of traumatic experiences, such as her father's death, when her symptoms first developed. As Anna recalled specific traumatic events, her symptoms were relieved: *e.g.*, her inability to drink water disappeared after she recalled being disgusted by a dog drinking from a glass. This convinced Breuer that symptoms are meaningful, and that talking about an original trauma leads to a curative, *emotional catharsis* (Breuer & Freud, 1893–1895).

Freud found that hypnosis was not always effective. When symptoms were removed after hypnotic recall, new symptoms often appeared *(symptom substitution)*. He discovered that therapy was more successful, if symptoms were linked to their underlying symbolic meaning. This helped him understand that symptoms symbolically disguise the meaning of threatening ideas or wishes as a defense. He also found that simply suggesting the client would remember "something" helped those who had difficulty being hypnotized recall "forgotten" experiences. Freud's discovery of the *free association* method followed from the advice by a favorite author on creative writing and a client's demand that he stop asking questions and let her talk.

Psychoanalysis begins by establishing a *working alliance*. Other than fees and schedules (2–4 hours per week for several years), free association is the primary injunction given to clients in analysis: they are asked to say everything that comes to mind, regardless of how inappropriate, silly, illogical, embarrassing, or trivial it may seem. The analyst's position behind a couch facilitates free association by helping clients relax and removing the distraction of the analyst's reactions to what is said. As analysts listen to a client's associations and dreams, themes emerge that reflect the hidden meanings of forbidden wishes, disguised by the client's ego's defenses. *Interpreting* hidden meanings helps clients become aware of wishes and remove the need for ego defenses.

Interpretation can lead to *insight* and *emotional catharsis*, so clients no longer need to keep repressed wishes or conflict out of awareness. However, they may have difficulty in free associating or accepting an interpretation's validity. Freud named this difficulty, *resistance*, which led to his discovery of ego defenses. Interpretation of resistance is a necessary preliminary to the interpretation of underlying wishes. Freud captures the essence of psychoanalysis, as well as most other therapies, in the following:

> In psychoanalytic treatment nothing happens but an exchange of words between the patient and the physician. The patient talks, tells of his past experiences and present impressions, complains, and expresses his wishes and emotions. The physician listens, attempts to direct the patient's thought-processes, reminds him, forces his attention in certain directions, gives him explanations, and observes the reactions of understanding or denial thus evoked. (Freud, 1924/1953, p. 21)

Anna O. also contributed to the discovery that clients may *transfer* wishes and fantasies from their original childhood sources onto the analyst. During treatment, she developed sexual feelings toward Breuer that were kept from awareness by her belief she was pregnant by him. Transference is frequently sexualized as with Anna O., but may also reflect aggressive Oedipal wishes; *e.g.*, the client who becomes competitive with a same-sexed analyst. Freud suggested that transferences reflect repressed, primitive wishes that are transferred inappropriately onto current relationships, disguised by ego defenses and neurotic symptoms. Transference "cures" sometimes occur as therapeutic relationships intensify and clients transfer repressed wishes onto the analyst. Because the analyst is accepting toward such wishes, the need for ego defenses diminishes and symptoms may be temporarily alleviated. This acceptance also reduces resistance and the client's need to defend against interpretations of wishes. The middle phase of psychoanalysis helps clients understand and *work through* the meanings associated with resistance and transference reactions.

Freud also became aware of equally irrational, primary process reactions and wishes toward his clients. He believed that *countertransference* was counterproductive to his preferred stance of *neutrality* or *evenly hovering attention* toward clients. Analysts undergo analysis themselves to avoid having countertransference bias their interpretations and to provide a *tabula rasa* or blank slate on which clients transfer conflicts and forbidden wishes. Transference reflects what social psychology terms an *assimilative bias*: new experiences are assimilated into existing cognitive schemas and evidence is interpreted in ways that maintain initial beliefs (Lord, Ross, & Lepper, 1979). People overlook differences and respond as if they were in the original situation: *e.g.*, clients assimilate the intimate experience of the therapeutic relationship into object representations of childhood intimacies and respond as if the therapist was their parent.

The *termination* phase of psychoanalysis involves *working through* transference reactions so that client actions are based on the reality principle rather than the pleasure principle. As Freud put it, "Where Id was, Ego must be!" (Freud, 1933, p. 80). Clients begin to accept their wishes and find more realistic ways to realize them as they become aware of ego defenses and transferences. The object of psychoanalysis is not just symptom removal, but to reconstruct the client's personality from one dominated by primary processes to one dominated by secondary processes. Reconstruction is never perfect and irrational wishes and behaviors are unavoidable, but the balance may be shifted from maladaptive to relatively adaptive adjustments to reality. As analysis approaches termination, regression may occur as clients realize they will no longer have the analyst as a stable part of their environment. Therefore, termination is discussed well before the actual date to work through any regression and help clients face the world independently.

Ego Analytic Theory

Because psychoanalysis typically involves 2–4 weekly sessions for several years, there have been efforts to make therapy more accessible to the average person with less costly, brief intervention strategies (*e.g.*, Alexander & French, 1946). Some follow Freud's ideas fairly closely, and some transform them into distinctly different models. What is constant across many of these approaches is the psychoanalytic focus on resistance and transference. Interpersonal and relational therapists, discussed in later chapters, question whether therapeutic neutrality is possible and take a post-modern view of relationships as co-constructed. Ego analysts stay closer to Freud's original vision but suggest that not all ego and secondary processes have instinctual origins. Freud emphasized the id and primary processes in determining how people cope with the world. He viewed the ego as essentially a mechanism for mediating conflicts among instinct, social realities, and the individual's internalized values or superego. Ego analysts believe that human creativity is something more than the sublimation of sexual or aggressive impulses: they propose that the ego has its own "energies" that are the basis of creativity and problem-solving.

Anna Freud

Freud's youngest daughter, Anna, was his standard-bearer and retained his emphasis on the primacy of id instincts as determinants of behavior, but also extended the focus on independent ego processes her father began toward the end of his career. Freud (1923) first proposed that the ego is partly independent of the id, with a desexualized libido that is invested in cognitive processes, such as thinking and judgment. Anna worked mostly with children and was particularly interested in how they developed their ability to master life problems. During the World War II blitz of London, she helped children cope with separation from their families after they were moved to safety in the English countryside. Anna observed directly how children learn to cope with life stressors in contrast to her father's reconstruction of childhood experiences from adult reports.

Her interest in how children learn to cope with reality led her to propose six additional *lines of ego development* in the mastery of psychosexual tasks (Freud, 1965):

1. From dependency to emotional self-reliance;
2. From eroticized nursing to self-regulated eating habits;
3. From pleasures of releasing bowels or wetting to voluntary endorsement of cleanliness, basic rules of hygiene and personal care, and bowel and bladder control;
4. From dysregulated aggression to delay of dangerous wishes;
5. From narcissistic egocentricity to desire for companionship with peers who have their own needs;
6. From pleasurable self-stimulation to pleasure in achievements, games, and sports.

Anna Freud recognized that children's play reveals instinctual wishes and ego defenses and is a more appropriate method for treating children's disorders than free association. In addition to play therapy, she organized and extended her father's conceptions of ego defense into a more structured system of her own. Table 6.1 describes her typology of ego defenses and variants.

Table 6.1 A. Freud's (1936/1966) ego defense typology. (Adapted from *Beneath the mask: An introduction to theories of personality*, 7th ed., pp. 214–215. By C. F. Monte & R. F. Sollod. © 2003 by Wiley. Used with permission)

Defense mechanism	Definition and characteristics	Illustration
1. *Repression* (motivated forgetting)	Threatening impulses, ideas, or memories are removed involuntarily from awareness. Repression or denial underlies the other ego defenses	Girl feels guilty over sexual impulses and "blocks" on her boyfriend's name as she introduces him to her family
1A. *Denial* (motivated negation)	Blocking awareness of *external* events, when these are related symbolically or associatively to threatening impulses. Dangers "out there" are negated	Widow continues to set the table for her deceased husband; fantasizes about conversations with him
2. *Asceticism* (renunciation of needs)	Character style defense against being overwhelmed by sexual impulses→denial of pleasures of sex, food, *etc.*	Anorexia, fad diets, extreme exercise programs all may be attempts to control impulses

Table 6.1 (continued)

Defense mechanism	Definition and characteristics	Illustration
3. *Projection* (displacement outward)	Attributing unacceptable impulses, wishes, or thoughts to another, rendering the impulses "ego-alien" or not part of the self	Husband, tempted to be unfaithful, becomes suspicious of his wife's fidelity
3A. *Altruistic surrender* (sacrifice self)	Vicarious gratification of needs by identifying with another's satisfactions. May sacrifice own ambitions to allow other to succeed. Type of projection	Employee, too timid to assert own rights, becomes a militant, assertive advocate for a colleague
3B. *Displacement* (redirection of impulse)	Redirection of impulses, typically aggressive, onto a less threatening target than the appropriate one	Girl envies brother's childhood relation with mother, angry toward other older women
4. *Turning-Against-Self* (Self-as-Object or target)	Redirection of aggressive impulses toward self, rather than appropriate target→guilt, masochistic feelings of inadequacy, and depression	Woman in 3B turns hatred of mother inward, becomes passive, self-accusing, feels inferior, surrendering
5. *Reaction formation* (believing the opposite)	Transforming unacceptable impulses into their opposite, more acceptable forms: "The lady doth protest too much." Hate into love; love into hate	Child angry with her mother becomes worried for her safety, that some harm might befall her
5A. *Reversal* (active into passive)	Impulse transformed from expressing a wish into being the recipient: similar to reaction formation or turning against the self	Sadistic impulses may become masochistic, with the self as the target of the sexualized aggressive wish
6. *Sublimation* (socially acceptable substitute for wish)	Transformation of an impulse into a socially acceptable, productive form	Retired soldier becomes a policeman, preferring more dangerous assignments
7. *Introjection* (taking within)	Incorporating into one's own beliefs or behavior the characteristics of some external object or person	An adolescent adopts the traits, mannerisms, and speech of an admired teacher
7A. *Identification-with-the-Aggressor*	Adopting the traits, values, or mannerisms of a feared person; Oedipal resolution	Hostage syndrome: feeling protective of captors
8. *Isolation* (stripping emotion or meaning from impulse)	Unacceptable impulses are retained in awareness but divested of connecting ideas that would give them meaning	Angry child chants "One, two, step on a crack and break your mother's back." Obsessions
9. *Undoing* (magical cancellations)	Magical gestures or rituals that cancel the unacceptable impulse, once the ritual has been performed	Child is very careful not to step on any sidewalk cracks. Compulsions
10. *Regression* (developmental retreat)	Not a defense, but a primitivization of behavior in the face of stress: return to earlier modes of coping when confronted with anxiety	Separated from mother for the first time by hospitalization, Timmy begins soiling pants and sucking thumb again

Erik Erikson

Trained by Anna Freud, Erik Erikson retained her emphasis on the conflict between instinct and internalized social prohibitions as determinants of behavior. He
also worked primarily with children and was interested in how the ego develops
in relationship to the external world. Building on Freud's (1923) idea that some
libidinal energy is cathected by the ego, Erikson suggested that *psychosocial* skills
develop in parallel with the psychosexual stages. Psychosocial skills build *epige-
netically* upon previously learned skills: each skill is a necessary prerequisite for the
next developmental task as children mature, while difficulties in mastering earlier
skills create difficulties in later stages. The first five psychosocial stages parallel
Freud's psychosexual stages (see Table 6.2). But where Freud saw psychosexual
development ending in adolescence with the genital stage, Erikson conceived psychosocial development as continuing throughout the lifespan.

Increasingly challenging psychosocial tasks must be mastered as children mature. Each stage involves a crisis in which positive and negative elements of each
task must be balanced (Erikson, 1950, 1968). Ideally, children achieve a positive
balance of expecting needs will be met, tempered by realizing that obstacles may
need to be overcome. If accomplishments are balanced positively, the individual
acquires a *virtue* or ego strength for that stage that positively influences subsequent
development. However, a negative balance creates a *malignancy* or ego weakness
that can impede development at later stages.

Erikson also proposed a *ritualization/ritualism* dialectic that corresponds to the
concept of an interpersonal schema. Ritualizations define which behaviors are socially acceptable and create the moral foundation on which personal identity and a
sense of right and wrong is formed. Repetition and social reinforcement transform
play into behavioral patterns that coordinate personal goals with community norms.
However, if the developmental balance is negative, ritualisms cause people to act in
thoughtless, stereotyped ways that alienate others.

Erikson anticipated attachment theory (Bowlby, 1982) by suggesting responsive
caregivers promote *trust* that problems will be resolved and needs eventually met,

Table 6.2 Erikson's (1950, 1977, 1978) psychosocial stages of development

Age	Stage/crisis	Virtue	Malignancy	Ritualization/ritualism
Infancy	Trust/mistrust	Hope/faith	Fear/withdrawal	Numinous/idolism
Toddler	Autonomy/shame	Will	Doubt/compulsion	Judicious/legalism
Preschool	Initiative/guilt	Purpose	Ruthlessness/inhibition	Authenticity/imperson-ation
School age	Industry/inferi-ority	Competence	Incompetence/inertia	Formality/formalism
Adoles-cence	Identity/role confusion	Fidelity	Uncertainty/fanaticism	Ideology/totalism
Young adult	Intimacy/isolation	Love	Promiscuity	Affiliative/elitism
Mature adult	Generativity/stagnation	Care	Selfishness	Generational/authoritism
Old age	Integrity/despair	Wisdom	Meaninglessness	Integral/sapientism

while *mistrust* results from caregivers unresponsive to infant needs. Mistrust should temper optimism with caution, but for the virtue of *hope* to emerge, the overall balance should favor trust. A negative balance results in a malignancy of *fear* or *withdrawal* that colors subsequent development and the child's interactions with others. A *numinous* (hallowed) ritualization of experiencing mother develops from repeated, positive experiences with the caregiver. This is similar to *idealization*, an object-relations concept discussed in Chap. 7. *Idolism*, the corresponding ritualism, distorts reverence for mother into narcissistic adulation and undifferentiated dependence on the mother. Idolism is similar to Margaret Mahler's concept of *symbiosis*, discussed below.

An *autonomy vs. shame and doubt* dialectic results as children discover their ability to influence events, but experience shame when outcomes are negative. If the experiential balance is positive, children temper the virtue of *will*, a determination to exercise free choice, with willingness to accept limits. If the balance is negative, excessive shame leads to the malignancy of *self-doubt* or *compulsivity*. The ritualization of this stage is *judiciousness*, the ability to discriminate between good and bad as limits are tested and outcomes observed. A ritualism of *legalism* occurs, if children learn to avoid punishment by acting on the letter, but not the spirit of parental injunctions and fail to internalize a sense of right *vs.* wrong.

Preschoolers' increased mobility, use of language, and capacity to imagine the outcome of an action trigger the developmental crisis of *initiative vs. guilt*. Initiative reflects their growing capacity to plan and act intentionally, which occurs as they resolve the Oedipal Complex and internalize parental values and standards of conduct. A positive balance between impulsive action and guilt when standards are violated results in the virtue of *purpose*, the courage to envisage and pursue goals despite obstacles. A negative balance results either in a malignant self-concept of *unworthiness* and *inhibition*, or in reaction, *ruthlessness*. Children experiment with positive and negative goals in role-plays and dramatizations. The ritualization of *authenticity* results, if they experience guilt for negatively sanctioned activities without being overwhelmed. Authenticity develops when children choose congenial roles and coping strategies that let them become the person they want to be. If they lack a sense of guilt, however, the *impersonation* ritualism results: children take on roles, but have neither any criterion for choosing nor any anxiety over negative outcomes, which may lead to characteristics of an antisocial personality.

Children begin school in the *industry vs. inferiority* stage, which broadens their mastery of the environment. The virtue of *competency* enhances children's desire to succeed as skills expand, but failure leads to the malignancy of *incompetency* or *inertia*, and they may fail to identify with a competent model. *Formality* is a ritualization that helps children move from play to work, from games to cooperation and competition, and from free imagination to duty. Children learn the proper *forms* of adult responsibilities and activities. *Formalism* is the ritualism in which work is routine and meaningless, because children learn techniques, but not the purpose or meaning of adult activities.

Perhaps Erikson's most influential contribution was his description of the adolescent *identity formation vs. role confusion* stage. Adolescence is a socially sanctioned

Table 6.3 Adolescent
identity formation

		Adequate experimentation occurs?	
		Yes	No
Adolescent makes	Yes	Identity formation	Foreclosure
commitment?	No	Moratorium	Identity diffusion

period of experimentation and consolidation of social roles learned in earlier stages. Marcia (1980) described how role experimentation affects identity formation (see Table 6.3). Adequate experimentation followed by commitment leads to *identity formation*. If commitment to a particular identity is made with no opportunity to experiment, as in an early marriage, *foreclosure* is the result. *Moratorium* reflects continued role exploration without commitment (extended adolescence), while *identity diffusion* results, if neither role exploration nor commitment to a personal identity occurs.

If adolescents reject negative identities, Erikson suggests a healthy identity is formed with the virtue of *fidelity*, the ability to sustain loyalty to community and loved ones. Identity diffusion leads to the malignancy of *uncertainty* in which adolescents lack core convictions about their role in life. Graduation, marriage ceremonies, or other *rites of passage* are ritualizations that help adolescents commit to an *ideology* or world view. The unthinking, uncritical commitments of foreclosure lead to the ritualisms of *fanaticism* or *totalism*.

A clear sense of identity enables "I-Thou" relationships (Buber, 1976) in which young adults commit to *intimate* relationships with others; role confusion results in *isolation*. The virtue is *love*, while the malignancy is *promiscuity*, a reflection of the individual's inability to make commitments to another person. Love's ritualization is *affiliation*, which refers to an uninhibited capacity to share ideas, feelings, and activities with honesty and integrity with a wide range of friends. The ritualism is *elitism* or *narcissistic sharing* with an exclusive group.

Maturity's developmental crisis is *generativity vs. stagnation*: a concern for generations to come *vs.* existential meaninglessness that results from disconnection with the next generation. The virtue of generativity is to *care* for what is generated through love without feeling obliged. The malignant outcome is *selfishness*, a lack of connection. A *generational* ritualization describes the mature adult's willingness to accept responsibility and assert authority. Societal support for this ritualization is shown in the commandment "Honor thy father and thy mother" (Deuteronomy 5:16). The associated ritualism is *authoritism*, an unwarranted, self-serving seizure of authority.

People who successfully traverse these steps to maturity achieve *ego integrity* and do not *despair* over missed opportunities, infirmities of aging, or death's approach. The virtue, *wisdom*, is a "detached concern with life itself, in the face of death itself" (Erikson, 1964, p. 134). This mastery of fear in the face of death is the ultimate gift one can give to children: "Healthy children will not fear life if their elders have integrity enough not to fear death" (Erikson, 1950, p. 269). The ritualization of this stage is an *integral* ego that consolidates the achievements of the previous seven stages into an awareness of new ideas, new meanings, and the new generation that results from life's accomplishments: it is the ego's reach for immortality. The associated ritualism is *sapientism*, or pretending to a wisdom one does not have.

In its original form, psychoanalysis presented a pessimistic, even tragic view of human nature. Erikson provides a more balanced view by focusing on the ego's creative, problem-solving abilities. His model provides a comprehensive view of both healthy and unhealthy development, paving the way for a theory of ego functions that are not dependent on libidinal energies.

The Conflict-Free Sphere of Ego Function: Hartmann, Mahler, and White

Hartmann (1939/1958) was the first ego analyst to break with Freud to suggest the ego has innate energies and capacities not borrowed from libidinal energies: *the conflict-free sphere of ego function*. He proposed that ego functions such as perception, cognition, memory, and learning are more than instinctual sublimations: *e.g.*, Rembrandt's portraits reflect a creative mastery of his craft, not just a sublimation of anal-expulsive urges. *Primary ego autonomy* refers to innate ego functions such as memory and learning, but Hartmann also recognized *secondary ego autonomy* in which ego functions develop from sublimated instinctual conflicts. Skills that develop to meet instinctual needs, *e.g.*, food or shelter, may become *functionally autonomous* and provide gratification independently of their original purpose. In Hartmann's view, the ego has four tasks:

1. Balance the individual's actions with the external world's physical and social realities;
2. Balance the expression and satisfaction of competing instinctual demands;
3. Balance ego, id, and superego requirements;
4. Balance its own competing goals and aims.

The ego's ability to integrate these competing demands with successful, real world actions is the basis of a rational, adaptive mastery of life.

Mahler (1968) worked primarily with autistic and psychotic children whose problems become evident long before Freud's model might account for them. Accordingly, she examined ego development in children during the first 2 years of life. She suggested that newborns possess a strong *stimulus barrier* to protect against overstimulation during the first month of life. This *normal autism* phase is characterized by the child's minimal responsiveness to the external world. Although she may have under-estimated the infant's degree of awareness (*e.g.*, Stern, 1985), it is true that newborns spend much time sleeping or dozing except when hungry or in pain. During the next 2–4 months, the *normal symbiosis* phase, infants are unable to discriminate clearly between their mother's and their own actions. Mothers differ in the degree they interact with their babies with genuine enjoyment or with anxiety or indifference. Mahler refers to these interactions as the *symbiotic organizers of psychological birth.*

If babies experience responsive handling, they begin to notice differences between their environment and themselves, the difference in sensations between sucking a nipple or a thumb. Unresponsive handling interferes with noticing such differences, because the baby is focusing instead upon its discomfort. Babies next begin the process of *separation-individuation* as they differentiate between good *vs.* bad experiences and self *vs.* other experiences.

Mahler describes four subphases in learning to separate and individuate:

1. *Differentiation and development of the body image* (5–9 months) as babies learn to differentiate between their own body and actions and those of others. Stranger anxiety develops as babies form a rudimentary sense of self.
2. *Practicing* (10–14 months) as babies learn how to be separate as they become more mobile and learn to explore the world, still staying close to mother. Attachment research documents how babies now react quite differently to separation (*e.g.*, Ainsworth, Blehar, Waters, & Wall, 1978).
3. *Rapprochement* (14–24 months) as increased cognitive and language abilities help toddlers tolerate their growing awareness of separateness. A *rapprochement crisis* frequently occurs at about 18 months, as children increasingly recognize wishing "doesn't make it so," and they become especially anxious over separations. Darting away and dashing back are typical as are rapid mood swings, tantrums, whining, and clinging (ushering in the terrible two's!).
4. *Consolidation of Individuality* (2nd–3rd year): a stable image of self and others, *emotional object constancy*, develops as the child develops *object permanence* (Piaget, 1952/1963) and realizes that objects (and people) still exist even though they may be out of sight.

By the second or third year, language skills and internalized schemas of self, mother, and the environment are developed sufficiently that children can tolerate extended periods of separation. Mahler suggests that childhood psychosis is caused by the child's failure to use the mother as an aid in responding to the world (secondary autism), or from failure to separate from symbiotic fusion with the mother. Mahler demonstrated that the roots of ego strength, identity, and conflict resolution occur much earlier than Freud had thought and she is an important transition figure in the development of object relations theory (Monte & Sollod, 2003; see Chap. 7).

Robert White, the last of the ego analysts considered here, is notable for his theory of ego motivation, independent but interacting with instinctual drives that influence the development of the psychosexual stages. White postulated *effectance motivation*, an ego motive for competence or mastery, based on research findings that behavior is sometimes reinforced by increased internal stimulation instead of reduction of instinctual drives; *e.g.*, Berlyne (1960) found that monkeys will learn complex behaviors just to have their curiosity satisfied. White suggests it is difficult not to consider that mastery of the environment is at least part of the motivation when children play 6 hours at a time. Table 6.4 describes White's (1960) extension

Table 6.4 White's (1960) effectance motivation and the psychosexual stages

Stage	Additional competencies of White's model
Oral	Sensorimotor play to explore bodily and environmental objects; learning to influence caregivers to maximize care and minimize neglect; self-mastery over gratification delays
Anal	Locomotion and negativism to assert autonomy; toilet training as a venue to learn willfulness, orderliness, and parsimony in mastering environment demands
Phallic	Expanded mobility, language, and imagination help master world and build self-confidence; imaginative play imitates adult roles and develops interpersonal role competencies
Latency	Competency in social, gender, and "chum" role relationships; school, chores, and games help in learning real-world skills; learning to subordinate own needs to coordinate with others' activities
Genital	Consolidate past competencies into a sense of identity; prepare to choose vocational roles; begin to date for social and sexual gratification

of Freud's stages to include competency skills that meet effectance rather than in-stinctual needs.

Brief Psychodynamic Psychotherapy

Alexander and French (1946) made the then radical suggestion that not all cli-ents require long-term treatment. Their *psychodynamic psychotherapy* reduced the time and cost of traditional psychoanalysis by asking analysts to be responsive and direct rather than to present a "blank slate." A genuine encounter with the therapist provides clients with a *corrective emotional* experience that …:

> … reexpose[s] the patient, under more favourable circumstances, to emotional situations which he could not handle in the past. The patient, in order to be helped, must undergo a corrective emotional experience suitable to repair the traumatic influence of previous expe-riences. It is of secondary importance whether this corrective experience takes place during treatment in the transference relationship or parallel with the treatment in the daily life of the patient (Alexander & French, 1946, p. 66).

A supportive, non-judgmental relationship lets clients respond to the analyst more realistically as they work through the childhood memories of vulnerability that emerge during treatment.

Modern approaches that deviate from traditional psychoanalysis, but still focus on internal conflicts, are described as psychodynamic therapies. Psychodynamic therapists agree that internal representations of unresolved childhood conflicts cre-ate interpersonal problems later in life, result in symptoms, and surface in therapy as transference or countertransference reactions. Ego defense and transference inter-pretations are still used, but the therapeutic relationship is now seen as more central to change, especially in object relations approaches (see Chap. 7). Following the lead of the ego analysts, most psychodynamic therapists believe that behavior is af-fected by rational processes as well as the instinctual drives of sex and aggression.

Brief Psychodynamic Intervention and Treatment Planning

Managed care encouraged psychodynamic therapists, as well as others, to develop brief, empirically supported intervention protocols. This has been difficult since psychodynamic therapies rely heavily on phenomenological procedures that are hard to define objectively such as ego defense interpretations. In recent years, however, a number of empirically testable, psychodynamic protocols have been developed (Eels, 1997). One of the earliest, empirically supported approaches is the Core Conflictual Relationship Theme (CCRT) method developed by Luborsky (1997; Luborsky & Crits-Christoph, 1998).

CCRTs are both a research tool and a method for clinical case formulation. Reliable scoring methods for transcripts of client narratives are used to identify recurring conflictual relationship themes. The Revised Central Relationship Questionnaire (CRQ-R; McCarthy, Gibbons, & Barber, 2008) is derived from CCRT research and is more clinically useful since CCRT scoring is time-consuming and difficult. A CCRT or CRQ-R theme has three components: 1. a wish (toward others or the self; 2. responses of others; and 3. response of the self. Table 6.5 describes the factors (with subscales in parentheses) identified by McCarthy *et al.* (2008).

Wishes and responses can occur in different combinations; *e.g.*, a wish to be sexual could receive either a sexual or a hurtful response and make the person feel intimate or avoidant. Treatment plans are developed around the most commonly endorsed themes. Therapists then help clients identify relevant thematic components as they occur in order to:

1. Decrease the theme's narrative pervasiveness (Luborsky & Crits-Christoph, 1998);
2. Increase benefits received from therapy (Luborsky & Crits-Christoph, 1998);
3. Increase client mastery of central relational problems, as reflected in therapy outcome (Grenyer & Luborsky, 1996).

Therapists only interpret thematic components when clients appear ready to assimilate them. They ask clients to describe their experience of core conflicts more fully

Table 6.5 Central relationship factors and subscales

Wish	Response of other	Response of self
Be hurtful (distant, domineering, hostile)	Is hurtful (distant, domineering, hostile, uncontrollable)	Am domineering
Be independent	Is independent	Am autonomous (independent, successful)
Be intimate (close, loved, recognized, secure, supportive, trusted)	Is loving	Am intimate (close, supportive, valued)
Be sexual	Is sexual	Am sexual
Be submissive	Is submissive	Am nonconfrontational
		Am avoidant (ambivalent, anxious, disliked, distant, submissive)

and relate themes to presenting complaints. They emphasize the wish and the other's response, which are the components most strongly associated with outcome.

Case Illustration: Core Conflictual Relationship Theme Method

Daymond is a handsome, muscular, 32-year-old African-American man, referred by an emergency room doctor after his homosexual partner had summoned a crisis-response team. Daymond was enraged after an argument and later became suicidally depressed, threatening to shoot his partner and himself. Daymond was on his bed crying when the crisis team arrived. He did not resist as they disarmed and transported him to the hospital. The doctor placed Daymond on a Selective Serotonin Reuptake Inhibitor and discharged him upon assurance that he felt better, was willing to surrender his weapon, and would seek out-patient therapy.

Daymond appeared for treatment 4 days later, wearing an Armani suit and heavy gold jewelry. He appeared jovial and dismissed the earlier episode as an over-reaction by his partner with whom he was staying only for monetary reasons. He said he was ready to leave, as his partner would not be able to keep up once Daymond leaves his car sales job and goes into business on his own. Daymond was vague about his business plans when questioned, but said that he had connections with the "big money" men and expected one of them would recognize his obvious talents and bankroll him.

Daymond said his father left shortly after his birth, but his mother was very devoted to him during his early years. She impressed on him that they were special people who had fallen on hard times due to his father's desertion. He said he quickly learned that the other children in school were jealous of his abilities and that he did not really need anyone but himself. He found his teachers boring and inferior and began using drugs with older boys who he considered "cool." His mother never forgave him after he was arrested for selling drugs during his sophomore year in high school and was placed on probation. He said he was pretty angry at the time, but then realized he really did not need her either and certainly was not going to make the same mistake twice. Dropping out of school, he supported himself for several years as a male prostitute until an encounter in which he was severely beaten. This led to working out with weights at the YMCA, while taking a series of odd jobs. Daymond found the compliments on his muscle definition very satisfying and he became something of a guru to beginning weight-lifters, working for a time as a personal trainer.

When asked about therapy, Daymond thought he could benefit from anger management as he really did not like being taken to the hospital by the crisis team. He becomes angry if people disrespect him or do not take him as seriously as they should. He said it was frustrating his partner does not realize Daymond could have anyone he wants; otherwise, he would not criticize Daymond's buying a few things to keep looking good. When asked about the suicidal threats, Daymond said it just hurts so much when he is really angry that he "loses" it. He said he does not really need therapy as he would never really harm himself or anyone else. However, the interviewer might learn a lot from Daymond as he has had a very interesting life and has a lot to offer.

- Diagnosis: Axis I—No diagnosis; Axis II—Narcissistic personality disorder; Axis III—No diagnosis; Axis IV—No psychosocial stressors; Axis V—GAF = 52 (Unable to sustain stable intimate relationships).
- Case Conceptualization: Daymond has a borderline adjustment with a phallic fixation and strong narcissistic traits. He views himself in grandiose terms with little empathy for others. He wishes for love, respect and admiration from others, but is enraged and hurtful if they are insufficiently appreciative (splitting defense). He also shows splitting in his self-reaction, vacillating between denying any need for others (autonomy) and avoidance. His relationships mirror his mother's encouragement of a sense of superiority (so others *can* be loving) and not needing others (fearing hurt from others who are uncontrollable). His emotional response to rejection or criticism also reflects the loss of the only significant loving figure in his life when his mother rejected him after his probation for selling drugs.
- Plan:

    1. Negotiate length of therapy—preferably 20 sessions, as Daymond's issues are complex.
    2. Problem list: anger, loss of control, ability to respond constructively to criticism.
    3. CCRT: wish-split between to be intimate—loved, recognized, and be hurtful—dominant; response of other-split between is loving *vs.* is hurtful—uncontrollable; response of self-split between am intimate—valued *vs.* am avoidant—anxious and disliked.
    4. Assessments: continuous assessment of CCRT frequency in Daymond's narratives; weekly assessment with the Working Alliance Inventory (WAI; Horvath & Greenberg, 1989) to monitor continued investment in therapy.
    5. Phase 1 interventions: Provide secure holding environment that gives Daymond a corrective emotional experience; empathize with Daymond's situation to encourage exploration of associated thoughts and test his readiness to examine CCRT's.
    6. Phase 2 interventions: encourage Daymond to examine CCRT components as they occur in narratives or in the therapy relationship; ensure he is ready and does not feel criticized.
    7. Possible obstacles: Daymond expects therapist to reflect respect and admiration; perceived lapses may trigger premature termination; hence, weekly review of WAI for problems.
    8. Monthly assessment of progress in addressing CCRT's; review for presence of other important CCRT components.

Integrative Implications

Cognitive-behaviorists have criticized psychodynamic therapies for their non-scientific focus on intrapsychic processes that are not easy to verify empirically. Ironically, most cognitive-behavior therapists choose psychodynamic therapists when seeking therapy for themselves (Lazarus, 1971). Lazarus notes that cognitive-behavior therapists usually focus on symptomatic complaints rather than the meaning of a problem. This is both the strength and the weakness of cognitive-behavioral therapies, just as a focus on the unique meanings of problems is the strength and weakness of psychodynamic approaches. Today, empirically based approaches such as Luborsky's CCRT method also answer criticisms that psychodynamic therapies are not scientific.

As the only conceptual framework available for over half a century, psychodynamic theorists produced a rich dialectic of competing views about human nature. The current chapter is only an introduction to the psychodynamic literature. Chapter 7 discusses the development by object relations theorists of Mahler's emphasis on early attachment; interpersonal and family relationships are discussed in Chaps. 10 and 11; and Chap. 14 examines postmodern intersubjective views and the co-creation of new realities in treatment. Psychodynamic therapy's future is encouraging, both for research showing equivalence in therapeutic outcomes with other systems (Lambert & Ogles, 2004) and its influence in the development of integrative therapies.

Integrative therapies typically combine existing approaches, but make little effort to integrate the underlying theories of personality and psychopathology. As the most comprehensive current model of human functioning, psychodynamic theory provides a useful starting point for integrative efforts; *e.g.*, the integration of cognitive and psychodynamic approaches may be facilitated by parallels between cognitive schemas and internalized object relations or CCRTs. Traditionally, psychodynamic theory emphasized unconscious processes, while cognitive theory emphasized conscious processes in forming and retrieving cognitive schemas or internalized representations. This distinction becomes less important as cognitive theorists, such as Jeffrey Young, emphasize unconscious schemas and psychodynamic theorists attend more to conscious processes.

There are also important parallels providing a basis for integration between the developmental theories of Freud and Erikson and Piaget's (1952/1963) theory of cognitive development. The major dialectic has been whether development occurs in stages or is gradual. Many cognitive-behaviorists assume development is gradual rather than moving in distinct stages as Piaget or Freud suggest. Even if cognitive and social skills develop gradually, however, a clear qualitative difference exists between children before and after language develops. Qualitative differences also appear in the transition from Piaget's sensorimotor to pre-operational stage: schemas develop that represent objects when they are out of sight, allowing children to develop more differentiated schemas of other's trustworthiness and their own lovability or ability to act autonomously. Nearly all theorists agree adult behavior is

Table 6.6 Piaget's cognitive tasks compared with Freud and Erikson's developmental stages

Age	Piaget's stage	Cognitive task	Freud	Erikson
Infancy	Sensorimotor	Object permanence language	Oral	Trust/mistrust
Toddler			Anal	Autonomy/shame
Preschool	Pre-operational	Conservation	Phallic	Initiative/guilt
School age	Concrete operations	Logic; causality	Latency	Industry/inferiority
Adolescence	Formal operations	Abstract thought	Genital	Identity/role confusion
Young adult				Intimacy/isolation
Mature adult				Generativity/stagnation
Old age				Integrity/despair

influenced by childhood learning that is not always adaptive later in life. Table 6.6 describes some of these parallels.

The world of pre-operational children is magical, in part, because they have only a limited grasp of causality or how objects can be transformed and still *conserve* essential properties such as mass, volume, or number. They have difficulty attending simultaneously to two aspects of a situation: a ball of clay rolled into a cigar shape may now seem larger to them because it is longer. The transition to concrete operations and logical reasoning occurs once the child is able to attend to both width and length and recognize that mass and volume are conserved, despite the clay's transformation. This new ability to attend to two things simultaneously allows children to relate cause to effect and to take the initiative relating intentions to goals; *e.g.*, Oedipal wishes to possess the opposite-sex parent. Logical thinking makes formal education possible and begins Erikson's industry stage as children see how plans can realize desired goals.

Children at the formal operations stage are able to attend to three things simultaneously rather than just two. This allows them to think about what is *possible*, as well as what is real, to think about their identity in terms of whom they want to be. Abstract thought allows adolescents to imagine how other people might experience a situation differently, which permits greater empathy and intimacy with others. Similarly, abstract thought and the capacity to think about possibilities lets the person in Erikson's generativity stage evaluate and form plans to meet the needs of a situation.

A final area that may contribute to an integrative model of personality and psychopathology is the similarity of interpersonal needs identified by Erikson (*e.g.*, trust and autonomy) and White (effectance) with those identified by self-determination theory (SDT; Deci & Ryan, 1985, 1991, 2000). SDT research suggests three universal, interpersonal needs: intimacy, autonomy, and competence. Well-being is diminished if these needs are not met. Chapter 15 will argue that new psychosocial skills acquired during successive stages of cognitive development help children meet these needs in increasingly sophisticated ways.

Chapter Six: Main Points

- Freud's theory of *psychic determinism* suggests that even accidental behaviors are determined by *unconscious* conflicts between the *id's libidinal instincts* of sex and aggression and the demands of reality and the *superego's* internalized societal demands. The *ego* develops from libidinal energies to coordinate these determinants of behavior.
- The id is governed by the *pleasure principle* with a *primary process* logic in which fantasy provides immediate gratification with no reality constraints. The ego governs behavior using the *reality principle*, which uses the *secondary processes* of reason and logic. Id instincts are the bodily *source* of *wishes* that *aim* to reduce instinctual tensions through *objects* that gratify the wish. *Ego defenses*, such as *repression, displacement, projection, and regression* help protect the ego from being overwhelmed if id, superego, or reality demands are too great.
- During *psychosexual development* over-gratification or under-gratification of instinctual needs produce *positive* or *negative fixations* at the *oral, anal, or phallic stages* that later in life can cause *psychoneurosis*. Resolution of the *Oedipal Complex* (*Electra Complex* for girls) is critical: children become jealous and wish to displace the same-sexed parent's intimacy with the opposite-sexed parent. Resolution occurs when the child *identifies with the aggressor* and internalizes the perceived values of the same-sexed parent. During *latency*, psychosexual urges are held in check until re-awakened by puberty, which ushers in the *genital* stage.
- Analysts treat neurotic symptoms by interpreting the client's *free associations* or *dreams*. This brings underlying primary process wishes and unconscious conflict into awareness. Lying on a couch and free association cause clients to regress and *transfer* internalized childhood wishes and conflicts onto the analyst. Analysts interpret *transference* and *resistance* to interpretations or free association directives before attempting to interpret conflicts or primary processes.
- Ego analysts suggest the ego has energies independent of id instincts. They focus more on how the ego learns to cope with reality than traditional psychoanalysts. Heinz Hartmann suggested a *conflict-free sphere of ego function*, while Robert White proposed *effectance* as an independent ego motive that moves people to master their environment at each stage of development.
- Anna Freud systematized her father's ideas about ego defenses, while Margaret Mahler described *separation-individuation* as infants learn to discriminate between the self and mother. She suggested that failure to *differentiate* adequately and then re-establish a *rapprochement* or connection with the mother was associated with severe pathology and poor reality-testing. Erik Erikson proposed an eight-stage, life span development of *psychosocial tasks*: *trust, autonomy, initiative, industry, identity, intimacy, generativity,* and *integrity. Malignancies* or *ritualisms* may interfere with adult functioning if individuals fail to master these tasks. *Epigenetic* development occurs as early accomplishments determine how children progress with later tasks.

- Luborsky's CCRT method is a brief, empirically verified, psychodynamic therapy. Therapists use the Revised Central Relationship Questionnaire to determine the client's most prevalent themes of *wishes, responses of the other*, and *responses of the self.* These themes provide a focus for interpretations of the client's narratives. Research suggests the CCRT method is associated with positive therapeutic outcomes.

- Psychoanalytic therapy provides a rich conceptual framework for understanding personality and psychopathology that is missing in most integrative therapies. Parallels among psychosexual, psychosocial, and Piaget's cognitive developmental stages that may explain how maladaptive schemas or CCRTs form may further integrative efforts. Also of interest are parallels between developmental tasks identified by Erikson and White and basic interpersonal needs identified by self-determination theory. Well-being is adversely affected if people do not develop skills to meet the basic needs of intimacy, autonomy, and competence.

Further Reading

Alexander, J. F., & French, T. (1946). *Psychoanalytic therapy*. New York: Ronald Press.
Erikson, E. H. (1950). *Childhood and society*. New York: Norton.
Freud, A. (1936/1966). *The ego and mechanisms of defense* (Rev. ed.). *The writings of Anna Freud* (Vol. 2). New York: International Universities Press.
Freud, S. (1924/1953). *A general introduction to psychoanalysis*. New York: Permabooks.
Freud, S. (1933). *New introductory lectures on psychoanalysis*. New York: Norton.
Luborsky, L., & Crits-Christoph, P. (1998). *Understanding transference: The core conflictual relational theme method*. Washington, DC: American Psychological Association.
Piaget, J. (1952/1963). *The origins of intelligence in children*. New York: Norton.
Ryan, R. M., & Deci, E. L. (2000). Self-determination theory and the facilitation of intrinsic motivation, social development and well-being. *American Psychologist, 55*, 68–78.

Videotape

American Psychological Association Systems of Psychotherapy Videotape Series. Psychoanalytic therapy with Nancy McWilliams (2008).

Chapter 7
Psychodynamic Approaches: Object Relations and Self Theory

The clew of our destiny, wander where we will, lies at the cradle foot.
Jean Paul Friedrich Richter (German novelist, 1763–1825)

Does personality develop from the inevitable conflict of primitive instincts and societal prohibitions? Or from the quality of early caregiving as Richter implies in the above quotation? Which has greater influence: the earliest years of childhood or later years, ending with Freud's Oedipal period? Are people passively influenced by forces beyond their control, or do they actively influence their destiny? Is it possible for analysts to remain neutral or do analysts and clients inevitably influence one another? These dialectic tensions mark the evolution of psychoanalysis from Freud through the ego analysts to object relations theory. Still further dialectic tensions are covered in later chapters: *e.g.*, internalized representations *vs.* the ongoing co-construction of problematic relationships in interpersonal (Chaps. 10 and 11) and intersubjective psychodynamic approaches (Chap. 14).

Object relations theorists have strongly influenced modern psychodynamic practice with their emphases on early interpersonal experience and actively influencing one's destiny. They suggest transference and countertransference are not only inevitable in therapy, but provide clues to the nature of the client's internal representational world and interpersonal problems. Object relations theory shares the ego analytic focus on healthy, creative functioning, but de-emphasizes Freud's three-part model of id instincts, ego, and superego. Personality is no longer described as a conflict between id and superego, but as a struggle to fulfill one's ambitions. Object relations theory also focuses less on neurosis and more on borderline or psychotic functioning. Many object relations theorists still view instinctual drives and the Oedipus Complex as valid concepts, but most give equal or greater importance to interpersonal relations, empathy, initiative, and adaptation to environmental demands. Kohut (1977) suggests children must learn from early interpersonal relationships to see themselves as an independent center of initiative before they are able to experience Oedipal longings for the opposite-sexed parent. Kohut still sees a poorly resolved Oedipus Complex causing neurosis, but sees early relationship problems with caregivers as causing personality disorders and borderline or psychotic symptoms.

D. K. Fromme, *Systems of Psychotherapy,*
DOI 10.1007/978-1-4419-7308-5_7, © Springer Science+Business Media, LLC 2011

Object Relations Theory

Object relations refer to internalized representations of the self in relationship to others. Freud used the term *object* to describe the child's internal representation of things that satisfy wishes. The term, object relations, emphasizes that infants act toward people much as they do anything that meets their needs, including *part-objects* such as the breast. Object relations theory differs from Freud in its focus on the subjective meanings of the client's inner world of internalized object relations as opposed to unconscious wishes or defenses; *e.g.*, Fairbairn (1952) suggests the "libido is object-seeking, not pleasure-seeking" (p. 82). Behavior is directed more toward human contact than toward gratifying sexual or aggressive wishes. Object relations theory also differs from Freud in suggesting personality disorders reflect problems in infant-caregiver attachment during the first 2–3 years of life. Neuroses are still seen as related to poor resolution of the Oedipal Complex.

Freud (1917/1957) first described object relations as a means of continuing to receive gratification by internalizing an image of a loved one after a loss. The idea was not seen as a central concept, however, until Klein's (1935/1975; 1957/1975) proposal that object relations exist from birth onward. She believed attachment results, not from oral gratification, but from introjecting positive caregiver qualities into an undifferentiated "good object" that maintains the infant's integrity in the face of distress. If a caregiver is neglectful or hurtful, those qualities are internalized as a separate, unrelated "bad object." Separation from the bad object, or *splitting*, then allows the infant to focus on self-soothing fantasies about the good object.

Conceptual Framework

Splitting and Projective Identification

Klein's (1935/1975) idea that infants split objects into all-good or all-bad is a central concept in object relations theory. Splitting is the earliest ego defense, becoming apparent as infants learn to discriminate between self and other. During this separation-differentiation stage, infants have yet to develop the cognitive capacity to assimilate good and bad traits into a single object. They rely heavily on their representation of a *good-mother* to feel safe and meet their needs, and attribute lapses in sensitivity or kindness to a *bad-mother*. During a tantrum, the toddler is simply not able to recall that mother has been kind in the past: she is all-bad. The good-mother is *idealized*, while the bad-mother is *devalued*.

Similarly, aggressive behaviors or fantasies, incompatible with a child's developing sense of self, must be attributed to a *bad-me* to preserve a fragile *good-me*. As the child's sense of self-in-relation-to-others develops, enraged feelings threaten the relationship with the good-mother and are attributed to the bad-me after the emotional storm has passed. After such episodes, children wish to restore their sense of a good-me and repair their relationship with the mother they previously wished to destroy. Projecting split-off bad feelings so they seem part of mother restores the child's sense of good-me, but some remorse and guilt remain. This strategy creates complications when toddlers self-soothe by introjecting mother's strength and calmness, which also re-incorporates the bad feelings. Klein called this process *projective identification*: projecting self-content onto others, then taking it back by identifying with the other. Identification with projected idealized qualities creates a greater sense of worth, but identification with hostile projections backfires as guilt-inducing feelings and fantasies are re-incorporated.

In a warm, supportive relationship, remnants of guilt and remorse feelings help encourage a more differentiated view of self and others: children understand they are generally good, but sometimes bad, just as mother is generally nurturing and good, but sometimes depriving and bad. Initially, wishes and fantasies are as threatening as real actions; but as children integrate good and bad aspects into more complex object representations, they begin to discriminate between fantasy and reality. In the context of abusive, neglectful, or over-protective caretaking, however, the integration of good and bad objects and the discrimination between reality and fantasy may be poorly developed.

Under conditions of stress, adults with undifferentiated views of self and other or reality and fantasy demonstrate the splitting and poor reality-testing characteristic of borderline and psychotic functioning. Hamilton (1989) presented the case of Ms. B, a 35-year-old woman, who described the paradox of projective identification as follows:

> I can't have a relationship with a man for more than a few months because I see the man as so wonderful that I begin to feel empty. Then it's like I have to become him, get into him somehow to be valuable and feel good about myself (p. 1554).

She was unable to experience her own worth except as an idealized projection in another person. She then needed to identify with the other person to cope with the resulting emptiness.

While Klein focused on how projective identification affects internalized objects, other theorists examined its impact on interpersonal relationships. Winnicott (1949) and Kernberg (1965) describe how projective identification can turn into a self-fulfilling prophesy. Projected impulses are accompanied by subtle communications that influence others to behave in ways that confirm the projection. People who project angry feeling onto others may then act fearfully toward them. Others eventually resent this unwarranted attitude, but their anger only confirms the original projection. Ideally, parents or therapists *contain* these projected feelings without reacting defensively and beginning a vicious circle (Bion, 1962).

Projective Identification Illustration

Henry (2007) describes how interlocking vicious circles of projective identifications reinforced problems in the family of T, an out-of-control, physically aggressive, 9-year-old boy. Henry initially viewed T's rage and acting-out as a "hypervigilant reaction to his mother's abusive behavior … secondary to her anger toward her abusive father. [T's father was] a 'good-hearted person' who was unable to protect T from the unreasonable hostility of his wife" (p. 447). Following this interpretation, Henry empathized with T's anger at mother for being too harsh and father not protecting him, acknowledging that his behavior was an understandable response to a painful home situation. He referred both parents to individual therapy and in parent guidance sessions urged mother to "envision T as something other than a young sociopath" and to transfer most of her limit-setting to the father. Father was urged to maintain a united front and back up mother's limit-setting. Unfortunately, neither was able to comply with these suggestions. T's acting-out escalated at home and he became disruptive in therapy. Henry became aware of his countertransference when he recognized his relief at T's eventual hospitalization for suicidal ideation.

After an interim of unsuccessful treatment by another therapist, Henry re-conceptualized T's hostility as a projection of his overwhelming feelings onto mother. Unable to contain T's rage, she was ineffective in setting limits, which led to an escalation of angry feelings. T's anger and name-calling when she set limits created self-doubts, defended against with counterattacks that projected her self-criticism back onto T. Their mutual rage allowed T's father to project his own guilty rage onto both of them, allowing him to withdraw and preserve his self-image as a benevolent peacemaker. As a result he was also ineffective at setting limits and covertly supported T's aggression by openly disagreeing with his wife's parenting style. Henry was also drawn in; he worried he was too harsh and also became ineffective at setting limits.

With this new conceptualization, Henry realized that empathically suggesting someone else was the "bad one" failed to contain T's anger. It only encouraged T to escalate efforts at projecting his feelings outward. Even if partly correct, such interpretations only intensified the guilt and shame associated with T's unwanted bad-me state. Consequently, Henry (2007) consulted with the parents to help them contain T's rage, telling the father …

> … if anyone was going to be a tyrant in the home, I would want it to be him, not the boy. If his boy hated him momentarily for setting a limit and would tantrum excessively, the father should firmly state his commitment to his limit. His boy was intimidating him, and he was afraid. "Better that he be afraid of you," I stated to him. I assured him that he could handle this kind of authority much more than his son (I was taking a leap of faith here; p. 451).

He advised T's mother to avoid being defensive and ignore accusations of being mean and hateful. She was warned that this could escalate, but she should stay firm and nondefensive. She was encouraged to accept her own hateful feelings as a normal reaction, with no need to counterattack. If she still lost her temper, she could make a short, genuine apology, but avoid feeling hopeless or resentful. With consistent support in these efforts, T gradually became less aggressive and disruptive at home, although some struggles still occurred at school.

Attachment and Separation

Instead of relying on adult recollections, object relations theorists generally follow Margaret Mahler's example of directly observing children. Mahler (1968) suggested a *symbiotic* relationship, which ensures needs are met, forms at about 2 months of age between mother and child. This period determines the quality of *attachment* developing between mother and child and has profound effects on later development (Bowlby, 1982; see Integrative Implications below). From about 5–7 months to about 2 years of age, infants begin to differentiate self from others by tentatively separating and anxiously returning to their caregiver. Peek-a-boo games strengthen developing object representations and help them learn that objects continue to exist even if out of sight. Conversely, insecure attachment leads to anxiety or anger upon separation and can interfere with self-other differentiation (Bowlby, 1973).

During this period, children *split* representations of mother, self, or part-objects into good-mother/bad-mother, good-me/bad-me, or good breast/bad breast to manage anxiety caused by separations or nonresponsive caretaking. Splitting interferes with the integration of object representations of self, other, and self-in-relation-to-other, creating problems later in life. By age three, self and other objects are differentiated and the child begins to integrate the good and bad aspects of self and other (Mahler, 1968). The task for the toddler is to integrate good-me/bad-me into a self that is usually good and sometimes angry, while integrating the good-mother/bad-mother into a mother who is usually available and responsive, but sometimes not.

Holding Environments and Transitional Objects

Influenced by attachment theory, Winnicott (1965) held that *good-enough mothering* creates a *holding environment* that helps infants contain separation anxieties and avoid being overwhelmed. Good-enough mothering provides occasional challenges that encourage differentiation of self from other when needs are not immediately met. Holding refers to cradling, comforting, meeting physical needs, and responding appropriately to the child's actions with delight or limit-setting. Fortunately, new mothers experience a few weeks of heightened sensitivity or *primary maternal preoccupation* that helps them respond empathically to their newborn's needs.

Winnicott believed newborns represent an unintegrated set of potentials, unable to distinguish self from other objects. *Integration* begins as babies repeatedly experience need satisfaction and appropriate physical and emotional cuddling or holding. As children interact with the world, repetitions result in object representations of increasingly integrated sequences. *Personalization*, the sense of a differentiated physical self, develops as children experience how touching the self, other objects, and being touched by others creates different feelings. Unresponsive holding environments can create *depersonalization* in which people feel they are not "in their body" or their body is not under their control.

Realization is a third development that occurs when reality acts in unexpected ways or if needs and wishes go unmet sometimes. An early sense of *omnipotence* as wishes are magically fulfilled gradually gives way to reality testing if children experience good-enough, imperfect mothering and every wish is not immediately gratified. *Transitional objects*, such as favorite blankets or toys, provide a sense of comfort in mother's absence and help children separate and individuate without becoming overwhelmed.

If depression or emotional unavailability precludes good-enough mothering, children are enraged when needs are not met and fear abandonment. With repetition, children develop a *false self*, a mask that hides the child's actual feelings and needs in order to curb being overwhelmed by their rage. False self performances preserve essential relationships and the child's *true self* at the cost of spontaneity and a sense of being alive in the world. Winnicott (1965) classifies adjustment according to the degree the true self is hidden by the false self (see Table 7.1).

At the false self's most maladaptive level, the *mask*, people hide their true self and eventually meet situations that require spontaneity beyond their abilities, which can result in decompensation. At the moderately maladaptive *caregiver* level, the true self is kept as a secret, potential self; only minimal spontaneity is possible in the absence of an adequate holding environment. At the minimally adaptive *defender* level, the true self may be shared if the individual perceives a safe environment, but suicidal ideation may result if the hope of finding such a haven is lost. At moderately adaptive *imitator* levels, people lead a successful, but non-spontaneous life, so the individual may never fully realize what is missing. Humility and modesty necessary for social success characterize the adaptive, *facilitator* false self. Winnicott's treatment approach provides a responsive, caring holding environment that helps clients hear interpretations when they present a false self.

Table 7.1 Winnicott's levels of false self organization. (Reprinted from *Beneath the mask: An introduction to theories of personality* (p. 293, 7th ed.). By C. F. Monte & R. F. Sollod, © 2003 by Wiley. Used with permission)

False self	True self	Consequence
Extremely maladaptive: *mask*	Completely hidden beneath an utterly compliant false self	False self fails when life demands a whole spontaneous person
Moderately maladaptive: *caregiver*	Permitted secret life, regarded as potential self	Preservation of individual in abnormal environments. Minimal spontaneity, aliveness
Minimally adaptive: *defender*	Waits for safe/desirable conditions to reveal true self	Possible suicide if hope for safe conditions is lost; little aliveness
Moderately adaptive: *imitator*	Identifies with caring or productive objects as models	Successful life, but without realness, aliveness
Adaptive: *facilitator*	Normal socialization for politeness and self-restraint	Humility, modesty, social success

Self Theory

Kohut (1971) believed interpersonal needs provided a better explanation than drive theory for ambitions and ideals, which form well before instincts would be regulated during resolution of the Oedipal Complex. This belief was reinforced by his clients whose fears were about losing a nurturing love-object rather than castration anxiety. Kohut's clients developed either *idealizing* or *mirroring* transferences: his clients either idealized him as "all-good" or sought his admiration for their wonderful attributes. In idealizing transferences, self-esteem is enhanced and bad feelings avoided by fusion with a perfect object. In mirroring transferences, the self is experienced directly as perfect as long as the other reflects admiration.

Kohut (1971) described these transferences as an undifferentiated *Selfobject* in which clients experience others as an extension and part of the self, which they control like their own body. Selfobjects are people or objects that help the self regulate affect and feel whole and competent, but cause frustration if not there when needed. Imaginary Selfobjects help manage frustration until real Selfobjects become available, but problems occur if fantasy takes the place of reality. Kohut described three interpersonal needs that Selfobjects serve: the need in idealizing transferences for an *idealized omnipotent* figure; *grandiose-exhibitionistic* needs satisfied by mirroring transferences; and a *twinship* or *alter-ego* need to be like others who serve as Selfobjects until the child develops a differentiated, competent self.

Kohut (1977) replaced instinctual drive theory with the concept of a *bipolar nuclear self* that arbitrates tensions arising from opposing poles of interpersonal needs: *ambitions* and *ideals*. Nuclear ambitions are the child's learned desire for the caregiving *Selfobject's* mirroring and recognition of their developing competency. Nuclear ideals reflect later developing idealized goals based on the Selfobject's power and ability to soothe. The person is driven by ambition to strive for ideal goals: mediating tensions between these two poles are *basic talents and skills*, which condition the person's actual choices about life pursuits.

Kohut inferred these developments from working with narcissistically injured clients, whose anxieties stemmed from traumatic fears of losing the Selfobject: the all-powerful, all-good, nurturing parent introjected before children are able to distinguish clearly between self and other. In mirroring transferences, clients fuse with their therapist to once more enjoy the *absolute narcissism* of basking in all-powerful, all-good Selfobject's delight and joy in them. Therapist approval recreates this grandiose self that contains all that is good and splits off all that is bad. In idealizing transferences, clients merge with an idealized therapist who is all-good and all-powerful, and similarly take joy and sustenance from the therapist's acceptance and empathy.

Kohut (1984) suggests that narcissistic injuries distort the child's development of a cohesive, differentiated self and lead to one of four types of Selfobject failures:

1. *Understimulated self:* If a Selfobject is seriously unresponsive to the child's mirroring and idealizing needs, the self loses liveliness and spontaneity. To regain that sense of vitality, the child may turn to artificial forms of stimulation later in

life, seeking excitement in substance abuse, promiscuity, compulsive gambling, or other extreme forms of behavior. Because these experiences are transient, the person feels even more alienated and becomes a compulsive sensation-seeker.

2. *Fragmenting self*: If a Selfobject inflicts a particularly humiliating narcissistic injury at a vulnerable stage, the child may experience the self as unintegrated, uncoordinated, and lacking cohesion. Somatization and hypochondriacal complaints result when individuals experience the self as sickened, weakened, and at the mercy of external forces.

3. *Overstimulated self*: If a Selfobject overstimulates grandiose, omnipotent fantasies, unrealistically exaggerated ambitions and ideals may later create overwhelming anxiety that inhibits children from testing their abilities. They may try both to avoid scrutiny and to merge with idealized others, causing ambivalence and threatening a loss of self.

4. *Overburdened self*: When Selfobjects do not allow anxious or upset children to merge with their strength and calmness, the overburdened, developing self lacks the ability to soothe itself. The world is then a frightening, dangerous place, with most experiences appearing overwhelming and frightening.

Kohut's treatment goal is to integrate fragmented nuclear ambitions and ideals into a unified, purposive self that uses its talents and skills to achieve meaningful, self-directed goals. Therapists must abandon the classical position of therapeutic neutrality to respond to idealizing or mirroring transferences. Instead, they make themselves known, *empathically* mirroring respect and appreciation for their client. There is more emphasis on empathizing with unmet narcissistic needs and less on interpretation. Having needs met provides a corrective emotional experience that helps clients internalize the therapist's strength and develop a more cohesive self. Kohut's emphasis on empathically promoting a purposive, integrated self represents a significant rapprochement between psychodynamic and humanistic approaches.

Diagnosis and Treatment Planning in Psychodynamic Psychotherapy

Kernberg (1984), an object relations theorist who continued to incorporate drive theory in his work, considered the effects of self-other differentiation on personality organization more important than symptoms. He classified disorders in terms of neurotic, borderline, or psychotic levels of ego organization. People with fused self-object boundaries are unclear whether thoughts and actions are controlled by the self or by others. They have problems in reality testing and are classified as having a psychotic level of ego organization.

In *borderline disorders*, confusing swings in affect and behavior reflect the client's defensive splitting and alternately idealizing and devaluing self and others. A combination of significant trauma, excessive anger, and a weakened ego cause borderline clients to exhibit poor impulse control, poor tolerance of anxiety, extreme mood swings, and disturbed, chaotic object relations. Ego weakness is indicated by inadequate sublimation of impulses and anxiety, which causes poor anxiety tolerance and impulse control (Kernberg, 1984). Clients are unable to maintain an integrated view of self or other, if their own or others' actions prove hurtful. The resultant splitting leads to aggression directed inwards in the form of suicidal or parasuicidal behavior or outward in extreme physical or verbal aggression.

In contrast to clients with psychotic or borderline symptoms, clients with neurotic symptoms have well-differentiated self-other boundaries, integrated self and other object representations, and tolerate ambivalent feelings more easily. In the following section, Trimboli and Farr (2000) make treatment recommendations for each of these levels of functioning and also consider the role of oral, anal, or phallic fixations. This inclusion of drive theory makes their approach more similar to that of Kernberg's than to Winnicott or Kohut.

Treatment Planning

In general, psychodynamic therapists are phenomenologists who try to enter the client's subjective world. As noted previously, this stance is incompatible with the objective stance needed to provide the diagnoses and treatment plans required by insurance companies. Most psychodynamic therapists also object in principle to the DSM-IVs diagnostic reliance on observable symptoms or behavior instead of underlying etiology. They note that similar behaviors can have different meanings for different people or for the same person in different situations, while different behaviors may have similar meanings. The *Psychodynamic Diagnostic Manual* (PDM Task Force, 2006) is the most comprehensive effort to date to develop a diagnostic system based on underlying personality patterns, rather than overt symptoms. Although promising, it is too recent to have had much impact on the field as yet.

Although less comprehensive, Trimboli and Farr (2000) provide an accessible approach to psychodynamic treatment planning that considers three principal client factors:

1. Level of ego organization—Clients with …

   (a) *Neurotic* symptoms have good self-other boundaries and reality testing, but also have areas of rigidity and insecurity in relating to others; they suffer from guilt or shame;

   (b) *Borderline* symptoms have reasonable reality testing, but *split* good and bad aspects of self or others, which leads to unstable relationship patterns; they worry about separation, betrayal, and abandonment and have a diffuse identity or sense of self;

   (c) *Psychotic* symptoms have impaired reality testing, confusing their thoughts and actions with those of others; they experience feelings of engulfment, annihilation, or loss of self.

2. Client's *character style* results from psychosexual fixation at one of the following stages:

   (a) Oral (0–18 months): dependent—monadic focus on the self, "What about *my*
       needs?"
   (b) Anal (18–36 months): rigid, compulsive—dyadic focus, "*I* want to control/
       dominate *you*."
   (c) Phallic (3–6 years): competitive, jealous—triadic focus, "*I* want *who*, or
       what, you have."

3. Client's *level of adaptive functioning* as a function of level of ego organization:

   (a) *Adaptive*: minimal fixations or symptoms; balance of self and other
       concerns;

       i. Neurotic: symptom-free, "normal" healthy self-assertion;
       ii. Borderline: ego-syntonic self-absorption and exploitation of others;
       iii. Psychotic: ego-syntonic isolation and guarded or avoidant behavior.

   (b) *Partially impaired with mild to moderate anxiety (related character style)*:

       i. Neurotic: depressive (oral), obsessive (anal), or hysterical (phallic)
          symptoms;
       ii. Borderline: intensified ruthlessness and self-protective behavior;
       iii. Psychotic: increased paranoid guardedness and suspiciousness.

   (c) *Fully impaired* (oral, anal, or phallic character styles, respectively, are
       listed):

       i. Neurotic: severe depressive, obsessive-compulsive, or hysterical symp-
          toms;
       ii. Borderline: borderline, sadistic/antisocial, or narcissistic/histrionic per-
           sonality disorder;
       iii. Psychotic: psychotic depression, paranoid delusions, or bipolar (hysteri-
            cal) disorder.

In general, character style is more relevant for neurotic levels of ego organization
and adaptive functioning is more relevant for psychotic organization. Both factors are considered for borderline ego organization. Symptoms of full impairment
should be addressed early to help involve the client in the therapy process. Note that
for object relations theorists, borderline has a broader meaning than in the DSM-IV:
Borderline ego organization refers to the way repeated splitting interferes with interpersonal relationships. Object relations theorists group narcissistic, histrionic, and
antisocial personality disorders with borderline personality disorders since splitting
is a central defense for each of these.

Levels of Ego Organization

The first step in treatment planning is to determine the client's level of ego
organization: neurotic, borderline, or psychotic. People with a neurotic organi-

zation have an "… inner experience of continuity of self through time" (Mc-Williams, 1994, p. 54). An integrated identity helps neurotic individuals subli-mate and resolve contradictory instinctual impulses. They also use repression to maintain intact reality testing and defend against feelings of guilt or shame. In contrast, clients with borderline organization have a diffuse, impoverished sense of self with few channels for sublimation and use splitting to defend against the fear that failure may lead to rejection or abandonment. Anxiety from instinctual impulses causes them to act in ways that make it hard for others to be empathic (Kernberg, 1986).

Clients with borderline or psychotic organization have difficulty integrating con-tradictions if someone they idealize behaves poorly. The resultant *splitting* of self or others as all-good or all-bad results in impulsive, inflexible reactions to the chang-ing circumstances of interpersonal relationships. For clients with psychotic organi-zation, this impaired sense of self and others leads to impaired reality testing. The boundaries between thoughts and perceptions of others' actions are blurred, leading to delusions of thought control or persecution by others. Instinctual sublimation is replaced with primary process gratification of impulses either in fantasy or through acting out. Psychotic organization is shown by splitting, a diffuse sense of identity, regression over fears of annihilation, engulfment, or loss of self, and impaired real-ity testing.

Character Style and Treatment Planning

Character style is the main consideration for treating clients with neurotic ego organization since they generally function adaptively and can participate actively in their treatment. Character style is also relevant for clients with borderline ego orga-nization, but lower levels of adaptive functioning require a greater focus on forming a working therapeutic alliance. Adaptive functioning and establishing a therapeutic relationship are the critical variables for clients with psychotic ego organization, although character style may affect symptomatic content: *e.g.*, oral dependency and delusions of fusion or emptiness; anal control and delusions of persecution; or phal-lic striving and delusions of grandeur. However, the focus of treatment is on the relationship and impaired functioning rather than character style.

For clients with neurotic ego organization, the goal is to gain insight about ego defenses that maintain their symptoms and drive others away (see Table 7.2). Inter-ventions for achieving such goals are discussed in the section below on psychody-namic interventions. Clients are able to resolve conflicts as defenses are neutralized and their superego becomes less constrictive. Goals for clients with oral dependency problems include being more active, less self-focused, and more aware of other's needs. Goals for clients with anal over-control problems include confronting in-tellectualization defenses, superego prohibitions against emotional expression, and passivity. Goals for clients with phallic competitiveness involve increased aware-ness of how emotional expression and repression are used to avoid guilt or shame about sexual wishes.

Table 7.2 Treatment planning for the neurotic level of ego development. (F. Trimboli & K. L. Farr, A psychodynamic guide for essential treatment planning. *Psychoanalytic Psychology, 17,* 350, 2000. American Psychological Association. Adapted with permission)

Character style	Dynamic/diagnostic considerations	Treatment considerations
All styles	Superego prohibition of id impulses prevents anxiety, but intensifies ego defenses and leads to symptoms	Neutralize ego defenses and ease prohibitive superego; understand how symptoms are maintained and create interpersonal distance; resolve neurotic conflict
Oral fixation	Self focus; lacks empathy; depression; dependency	Encourage empathy; address passivity secondary to fear that aggression will drive away the source of gratification
Anal fixation	Control/dominance/aggression; obsessive-compulsive disorder	Confront intellectualization/doubting and explore/access emotions; address passivity/prohibitions against anger
Phallic fixation (Oedipal)	Competition/jealousy; guilt/shame; hysterical conversion; phobias	Confront defensive use of emotionality; explore repressed wishes or guilt/shame over sexual and competitive feelings

Character Style and Adaptive Functioning in Treatment Planning

Both character style and level of adaptive functioning are important in the treatment of clients with borderline ego organization. These clients see self and others as all-good or all-bad, think in either/or terms, and act out impulsively, which leads to unstable relationships. Table 7.3 describes goals for clients with borderline organization with different character styles and adaptive functioning.

Many treatment goals apply to every character style, such as the need to monitor and address possible harmful acting-out in impulsive, easily upset clients. Therapists provide a nurturing, supportive, structured *holding environment* to help clients regulate emotional extremes (Winnicott, 1986). Interpretations are made tentatively about interpersonal or acting-out crises. Defensive splitting that could disrupt the therapeutic alliance is then explored. Interpretation of character style issues is secondary, but understanding their influences may help therapists respond appropriately to underlying issues.

Kernberg (1986) discussed treatment issues for adaptive, partially impaired and fully impaired borderline ego organization. Treatment for clients at adaptive levels focuses on the type of fixation as with neurotically organized clients since acting out risks are minimal. With partial impairment, the emphasis is on creating a holding environment, while full impairment requires supportive therapy including medication, hospitalization, or assistance in dealing with real-life issues. Borderline ego organization with oral fixation is characterized by self-absorbed, exploitive relationships, poor boundaries, and impulsivity. Engulfing transferences and self-

Table 7.3 Treatment goals for factors in borderline ego development. (Adapted from F. Trimboli & K. L. Farr, A psychodynamic guide for essential treatment planning. *Psychoanalytic Psychology, 17,* 351, 2000. American Psychological Association. Used with permission)

Level of functioning	Character style		
	Oral	Anal	Phallic
Adaptive functioning (these individuals rarely seek treatment)	Goals for all styles: further ego development through promotion of object constancy and skill building; maintain consistency and therapeutic boundaries; confront splitting; nurture and support whatever semblance of higher level defensive functioning is exhibited; examine antecedents and consequences to acting out; teach alternatives		
Partially impaired (or individuals who function adaptively, but are stressed)	Goals for all styles; be alert to intense engulfing transference; attend to tendency toward self-destruction	Goals for all styles; be alert to aggression as manifestation of transference; if necessary, protect society	Goals for all styles; be alert to idealization as primary mode of resistance
Fully impaired (may need to treat as psychotic: pacify, stabilize, and support)	Goals for all styles; confront appetitive instability; may need to protect patient and society	Goals for all styles; confront aggression; if necessary, protect society	Goals for all styles; anticipate and resolve idealization

destructive behavior may be expected. For anal fixation, sadomasochistic, antisocial traits are common, and aggression is likely to be directed toward the therapist. Narcissistic or histrionic personality disorders are associated with phallic fixation; therapists should expect clients to be self-absorbed and have little empathy for others. Mirroring and idealizing transference are likely.

Table 7.4 describes treatment planning for clients with psychotic organization in which adaptive level of functioning is more important and coping style is less so. Individuals with an *adaptive* level of psychotic organization may be able to function in the outside world, with only minor reality disturbances of daily functioning. They may have circumscribed delusions, but do not usually seek help on their own. Their behavior is odd and does not encourage interaction.

A diffuse self-identity, splitting defenses, and poor anxiety tolerance and impulse control are typical for adaptive levels of psychotic ego organization. For all levels, supportive out-patient therapy focusing on social support and stabilizing situational stressors is indicated. For *partially impaired* individuals, therapists support reality testing by helping clients discriminate between their own thoughts and what the therapist is actually doing. Partial hospitalization or a supportive living situation and medication may be needed to stabilize ego defenses, so clients can function more independently. *Fully impaired* clients require immediate hospitalization with medication and a structured, supportive milieu to help stabilize symptoms and strengthen ego defenses.

Table 7.4 Treatment planning for the psychotic level of ego development. (Adapted from F. Trimboli & K. L. Farr, A psychodynamic guide for essential treatment planning. *Psychoanalytic Psychology, 17,* 352, 2000. American Psychological Association. Used with permission)

Adaptive functioning	Dynamic/diagnostic considerations	Treatment considerations
All levels (style is of minor importance)	Diffuse identity; no anxiety tolerance/impulse control; splitting	Stabilize, support, case management, assess for medication; focus on supporting weak ego
Adaptive level	Rarely seek treatment; guarded; odd; danger of decompensation	Stay supportive/resist exploring and uncovering; address situational stressors/social support/family expressed emotion
Partially impaired	Impaired reality testing; paranoid guardedness and suspiciousness	Reinstate/reinforce defensive functioning; assess need to change home/work setting; active self-disclosure of therapist's thoughts/feelings to preclude fantasy-based transference projections
Fully impaired	Impaired reality testing; loss of self; engulfment; annihilation; schizophrenia; paranoia; bipolar	Hospitalization and medication; structure and support through hospital milieu

Psychodynamic Intervention Issues

As in traditional psychoanalysis, psychodynamic therapists expect that encouraging the client's optimal functioning in work, love, and play will eventually lead to symptom reduction (Curtis & Hirsch, 2003). They are more likely to accept limited client goals, however, and take a less authoritative stance in making interpretations. Clients are understandably interested in symptom reduction, and priority is given to behavior that threatens life or the continuance of therapy such as substance abuse. Object relations therapists encourage curiosity, tolerance of ambiguity and strong feelings, increased self-reflection, disembedding from the past, mourning for lost opportunities, and exploring possible meanings for one's life. They believe that a neutral therapeutic stance is not possible and may disclose their feelings about what occurs in therapy. Warmth and empathy are emphasized, but effort is made not to be too gratifying as clients need the freedom to express negative as well as vulnerable feelings toward the therapist.

Differences among psychodynamic approaches reflect a dialectic about the nature of transference and countertransference. Although they all recognize the mutual influence of client and therapist, they differ in the particulars. Interpersonal therapists (Chap. 11) attend to countertransference feelings as they are elicited by the client. If they are confident their feelings are not their own issues, they may explore the meaning of the behavior that evoked the therapist's emotional response. This is referred to as *concurrent countertransference* and may be contrasted with *concordant countertransference* in which the client's *projective identification* induces therapist behavior congruent with the client's projected feelings or impulses (Klein, 1957/1975). Winnicott (1964) de-emphasizes transferential processes and instead has therapists provide a holding environment to *contain* transference feelings until clients can tolerate them. Kohut (1984) also de-emphasizes *empathic attunement* to the client's subjective experience in the belief that a focus on concurrent countertransference is distancing from immersion in the client's world. Both Winnicott and Kohut move still further away from the traditional analyst's role as an objective, neutral observer and closer to the intersubjective approach (Chap. 14) in which objectivity is seen as impossible. Rather than an expert stance, intersubjective analysts encourage clients to join their curiosity about the sources of difficulties, strong feelings, or problems that arise during the relationship. There is no claim to expert knowledge, as the client is seen as the final arbiter of what is meaningful for the client.

There is also great variability among traditional and object relations analysts with respect to the emphasis on early childhood experiences, current life experiences, and the therapeutic relationship. Generally, traditional analysts give more weight to early experiences, while object relations analysts focus more on how those childhood experiences influence the therapeutic relationship. Analysts of all varieties tend to think in *idiographic* rather than *nomothetic* terms, attempting to understand clients in terms of their unique experiences rather than in comparison with others. This reflects the historical lack of interest in empirical research by psychodynamic theorists, although psychodynamic approaches fare as well as others in outcome studies. Research has been hampered by the difficulty of translating many psychodynamic concepts into operational terms. There is research support for some of the ego defenses, but that for repression as defined by Freud is questionable (Westen, 1998). The idiographic emphasis is also revealed in the lack of attention given by many analysts to diagnostic categories, other than the broad distinctions of neurotic, borderline, and psychotic levels of ego organization. However, recent demands for accountability in clinical practice have encouraged more interest in research on brief forms of psychodynamic interaction (*e.g.*, Luborsky, 1997).

Case Illustration: Psychodynamic Therapy (Summarized from McWilliams, 2004, pp. 219–259)

Nancy McWilliams' *Guide to psychodynamic therapy* recounts her work with Donna, whose 10-year treatment illustrates many of the dynamics and interventions previously discussed:

- **Presenting Problems**: When first seen by Dr, McWilliams, Donna was a 23-year-old college student, diagnosed with chronic, undifferentiated schizophrenia. At age 16, her lesbian lover, with whom she shared quasi-delusional fantasies about rock stars, was hospitalized for schizophrenia. Donna's condition also deteriorated despite unsuccessful treatment at several agencies with short-term interventions, benzodiazepine and antipsychotic drugs, and two hospitalizations. She was sexually promiscuous, abused multiple drugs, cut herself on the wrists and arms, and once carved DAD on her leg when angry with him. She made homicidal threats, attacked others physically when irritated, and became disorganized and somewhat delusional in her thinking when stressed. She talked compulsively, chain-smoked, bit her nails and obsessed that she might have breast cancer. Since McWilliams did not routinely screen for eating disorders 35 years ago, she only discovered Donna's bulimia 5 years into treatment. As a condition of her college financial aid, Donna was mandated for treatment, but was uncooperative and abusive toward her therapists.

- *Initial Impressions*: McWilliams saw Donna as an attractive, overweight woman with an intimidating air of desperately intense hostility. Donna's thinking was initially tangential, paranoid, and concrete with inappropriate affect, which led to a diagnosis of schizophrenia. Later, it appeared these deficits were a regressive disorganization due to overwhelming anxiety in the interview, rather than psychotic ego organization.

- *History and Background*: Donna's father was a wealthy contractor with connections to organized crime who was more invested in his work and extramarital affairs than his family. He was frightening and sexually abusive and Donna would lock herself in her room to avoid him. Her mother called her "a liar and a pervert" when Donna reported the abuse. Her mother suffered long-lasting, psychotic, post-partum depressions after Donna's birth and her sister's and brother's births, respectively 7 and 12 years later. Her mother was unable to give adequate care, leaving the children unattended for hours, wet and crying. Donna was once cut by her mother during an enraged dissociated state. The maternal grandmother provided some support, but was not always available. Donna was expected to care for her siblings during her mother's depressions, but did so with resentment. She reported a chaotic childhood in which she abused animals, had battles over eating, felt no one cared for her other than her grandmother, feared abandonment, and was traumatized by separations. Despite poor concentration, a belligerent attitude, and association with nonconformist peers, she made mostly B's in school. She idealized her Girl Scout leader, who gave Donna emotional support but later committed suicide, cutting her throat. She reported first being out of control and suicidal when her parents divorced during her teens and Donna began her Lesbian relationship with the friend later hospitalized for schizophrenia. Her bulimia, self-cutting, substance abuse, and attacks on others began at this time.

- *Diagnosis*:
  Axis I—Polysubstance dependence
  Axis II—Borderline personality disorder (with suicidal ideation and self-cutting)
  Axis III—No diagnosis
  Axis IV—Problems with primary support group
  Axis V—GAF=35

- *Conceptualization*: Donna learned to use splitting to defend against neglect and abuse. As a result, her introjected Selfobject includes a constant threat that prevents stable object relations. She sees most other people as dangerous, idealizing the few people who have provided some consistent emotional support. She appears anally fixated with a paranoid, sadomasochistic character style. Her functioning is partially impaired with borderline ego organization, but mild stressors such as psychiatric interviews induce regression to full impairment. Her central conflict was to "feel engulfed and controlled when close, and devastatingly abandoned when given some space" (McWilliams, 2004, p. 227). Helpful or kind actions by others reminded her of wished-for nurturance from her mother, but also elicited memories of abuse by both parents. Projective identification located her rage in others to protect her split-off "good-me." She would then respond abusively to her self-created external threat just as her introjected abusive models did. In effect, this tested the kindness of others to see if it is real or only a mask for the betrayal she expected. A vicious circle followed as those trying to help were enraged by her belittling or physical attacks on them. Her self-destructive behavior was overdetermined by factors such as remorse over her outbursts, her identification with abusive models (who cut both themselves and Donna), and the attention it gained even when she mistreated others.

• *Early Course of Treatment*: Not surprisingly, Donna developed a negative transference toward McWilliams, was critical and verbally abusive, asked many personal questions, and questioned her training and orientation. Questions were answered fully and frankly on the rationale that paranoid individuals need feedback about accurate observations to feel less crazy and to correct the inaccuracies of misconstrued observations. McWilliams' strategy was to create a holding environment in which attacks were acknowledged but not interpreted since that could be perceived as a counterattack. Following Pine's (1985) advice of "striking when the iron is cold," she supported Donna's need to control her exposure in therapy by not interpreting premature session departures until Donna was able to stay for a whole session. Donna rejected most interpretations in the first year until McWilliams suggested she "seemed to have a core problem with closeness and distance, and she readily agreed" (p. 227). Donna's anxiety about revealing that much led her to miss the next session, despite regular attendance up to that point. Boundaries and limits were an issue. After being told about an upcoming vacation, Donna started cutting herself and having suicidal thoughts. She signed in for a 72-hours emergency hospitalization, but then decided she wanted to be released right away and was told she needed McWilliam's permission. When told she needed to keep her commitment and would be seen after discharge, Donna responded with her typical verbal abuse. Later, she acknowledged her secret appreciation that she was expected to accept the consequences of her actions as an adult.

• *Later Course of Treatment*: After 2 years of treatment, Donna developed more trust in McWilliams, vacillating between idealizing and devaluing transferences. She continued to see other caregivers negatively, but reduced her cutting, medication, and use of street drugs. Daily routines became more stable, she lost some weight, and she was more open and less tangential in therapy. She was more interested in exploring unconscious motives than in acting them out and became open to the possibility of change. Her father also died about this time and

4 months later she announced her intention to marry. Recognizing that she would not easily accept advice, McWilliams shared her dilemma with Donna:

I imagine you know that as your therapist, I'm supposed to raise questions and press you to examine any decision that seems impulsive to me. But I have a feeling that wouldn't feel very helpful to you. "You're absolutely right," she responded. "Don't say a word." She went on to explain that if I were to register even a whiff of objection, and then the relationship were to fail, it would be too humiliating for her to admit this to me and get my help at that point (2004, pp. 229–230).

Despite occasional verbal and physical abuse toward her husband, the marriage lasted several years and provided a continuity previously lacking in her life. At the anniversary of her father's death she became severely depressed, which McWilliams interpreted as a move from paranoid sensitivity into an ability to mourn, Klein's (1935/1975) *depressive position*. Despite recovering from this episode with Valium (before the advent of SSRIs) and therapy, Donna was still too paranoid and unstable to sustain employment. In her fourth year of treatment, she entered a sadomasochistic relationship with a biker with self-harming actions such as bondage, penetration with sharp objects, burning her nipples, and culminating in a superficial cutting of the throat. McWilliams notes that today she would have intervened more aggressively, but at that time was afraid that confrontation would make the situation worse. On one occasion Donna felt misunderstood in session, went to the bathroom, and cut her wrist. Unable to follow McWilliams' suggestion to express her feeling in words, Donna left in a rage only to call later that night afraid she had destroyed the therapeutic relationship. The following sessions were devoted to exploring Donna's self-punitive behavior and there were no more serious recurrences. By the end of treatment, Donna was able to inhibit automatic responses, self-observe her feelings and motives, and act appropriately. Her relationship with her family improved and she was able to respond to relationship difficulties with minimal support from therapy. Presenting problems of addiction, sexual risk-taking, self-cutting, paranoia, suicidality, homicidality, bulimia, and compulsions were either eliminated or significantly reduced.

Integrating Psychodynamic and Behavioral Therapy

Wachtel's (1977, 1987) *Cyclical Psychodynamic* assimilates behavioral and systems theory into an essentially psychodynamic approach. Wachtel, Kruk, and McKinney (2005; see Table 7.5) suggest that psychodynamic and behavioral strengths and weaknesses complement one another so their combination should provide a more complete system of therapy.

Behavioral emphases on active intervention and contingencies complement psychodynamic emphases on insight and early experience. Wachtel argues that both psychodynamic and modern cognitive-behavioral approaches rely too much on insight and cognitive processes to bring about change. He suggests instead that

Table 7.5 Strengths and weaknesses of the psychodynamic approach

Strengths	Weaknesses
Emphasis on the unconscious	Overemphasis on early experience *vs.* ongoing experience
Emphasis on inner conflict	Overemphasis on insight and cognitive processing
Importance of therapy relationship	Lack of clarity about the change process or "working through"
Transference of conflict to relationships	Insufficient attention to role of social skill deficits
Interpersonal focus (*e.g.*, Sullivan)	Discourages active intervention by therapist
Emphasis on ego defense and self-deception	Insufficient attention to situational influences
Guidelines for recognizing defenses	Lack of emphasis on research

action-oriented behavioral interventions attend more closely to the client's ongoing experience and provide corrective emotional experiences (Alexander & French, 1946). On the other hand, he suggests that behaviorists give insufficient attention to inner conflict, relational issues, and unconscious processes such as the ego defenses. Although no research has evaluated outcomes with Wachtel's approach, its basic tenets are grounded in research. Cyclical Psychodynamics' popularity reflects both its research basis and the fact that it is one of the earliest, most comprehensive integrative systems.

Conceptual Framework: Cyclical Psychodynamics

Wachtel *et al.* (2005) note that psychodynamic and behavioral approaches have contrasting linear views of causality, which are only partial explanations of human behavior: the *inside-out* psychodynamic view holds that unconscious inner conflicts cause behavior, while the *outside-in* behavioral view holds that external situations cause inner experiences. Wachtel *et al.* (2005) adopt a circular causality or systems perspective that integrates these linear views: "events that have a causal impact on our behavior are very frequently themselves a *function* of our behavior as well" (p. 344). Just as situations impact expectations, expectations impact situations in a *cyclical* fashion—expectations lead to:

1. Choosing to be in situations perceived as more desirable than others;
2. Acting in ways that encourage others to react according to expectations;
3. Biasing perceptions to confirm expectations about a situation (*confirmation bias*).

For example, Swann and Read (1981) found that people attend selectively to information that confirms their self-view, whether positive or negative. Confirmatory biases are stronger than self-enhancing biases, which may explain why clients find it difficult to change their self-concept. Information that contradicts the self-concept is either not noticed or is discredited in some way. Attempts to reassure a client with a poor self-concept may instead elicit thoughts that the therapist does not really understand how badly the client has let others down.

Wachtel *et al.* (2005) discuss how *vicious* and *virtuous circles* create self-fulfilling prophecies: *e.g.*, a man drinks to forget problems at work and in his marriage, but finds drinking exacerbates his problems. Snyder (1982) documented how vicious circles maintain ethnic and sexual prejudice. In contrast, Rosenthal and Jacobson's (1968) classic study illustrates the virtuous circle. Elementary school teachers were told that intelligence tests would predict which of their students would be "late bloomers," showing improved academic performance during the year. Several children from each class were then randomly selected and their teachers told they were likely to be "late bloomers." Later intelligence testing showed that this prophecy was fulfilled, perhaps because the teachers' new expectations led them to respond differently to targeted children. Frank and Frank (1991) suggest that placebo effects result from self-fulfilling prophecies or virtuous circles: *i.e.*, as clients, family, and friends begin to expect positive changes, they respond to each other in ways that support that hope.

A number of steps in cyclical processes and their treatment may be identified:

1. Children may learn to be anxious in situations, especially interpersonal ones, that would not be threatening for an adult; ego defenses then develop that help children avoid their anxieties, but also prevent them from confronting their fears in order to extinguish them.
2. Avoidance prevents clients from learning the social skills needed to negotiate anxiety-provoking experiences successfully, thus reinforcing anxieties about such situations.
3. Transference occurs when clients respond defensively to anxiety-provoking situations in therapy that resemble earlier negative experiences; transference reflects characteristics of the current relationship as well as of early relationships.
4. As transference creates problems in the therapeutic relationship that resemble presenting problems, interpretations interrupt the vicious cycle of anxiety-defense-anxiety, allowing extinction to occur; however Wachtel suggests action-oriented behavioral interventions may be more effective in extinguishing anxiety.
5. With increased confidence in confronting issues clients have previously ignored, a virtuous circle develops as they confront still other issues and gain still more confidence.

Wachtel adopts the psychodynamic emphasis on the therapeutic relationship as a means to reveal the client's unconscious conflicts, interpersonal problems, and defenses. He sometimes sees significant others to gain additional perspectives on the client's life and relies heavily on behavioral interventions to intervene in problem areas the client has avoided.

Wachtel suggests that repeated extinction trials of avoidance responses provide a "corrective emotional experience" (Alexander & French, 1946). However, motivation is a key factor in helping clients disrupt vicious circles and disconfirm the firmly held core beliefs of self-fulfilling prophecies: *e.g.*, Darley, Fleming, Hilton, and Swann (1988) found that subjects only asked questions necessary to disconfirm prior expectations if the outcome was important to them. The therapeutic relationship is critical in helping clients sustain the necessary effort. Problematic core beliefs must be repeatedly disconfirmed to overcome self-confirming biases and the tendency of the client's significant others to respond on the basis of old expectancies.

Wachtel's clients often present with characterological problems that can take years rather than weeks to remediate. Nevertheless, rapid change is seen as desirable and may occur with clients whose symptoms are circumscribed such as those in the following case.

Case Illustration (Summarized from Wachtel et al., 2005, pp. 347–354)

John N. is a well-known and respected professional who failed his licensing exam five times, even though some of his own work was included in the exam. John's self-diagnosis was "test anxiety." John's parents were members of a status-conscious Boston family who demanded not only that he excel, but that he seem to do so with little effort. This information was obtained only after Wachtel noted John's discomfort as a client and repeated efforts to impress him with his stature. Wachtel then wondered if John's parents were very status conscious, which was quickly acknowledged and helped him to relax. John was subsequently able to confront both his resentment over being tested and belief that the test should be effortless for him, and also his humiliation over his repeated failures:

- *Diagnosis*:
  Axis I—Anxiety Disorder NOS (Test Anxiety);
  Axis II—No diagnosis;
  Axis III—No diagnosis;
  Axis IV—Failed licensing exam;
  Axis V—GAF = 70 (Despite overall high functioning, symptom is seriously affecting his occupation)
- *Conceptualization*: Although John overtly rejected his parents' concerns about status, he grew up trying to meet their expectations and still tries to make his successes appear effortless. By framing this as John's parent's concerns, Wachtel enabled John to confront his efforts to please his parents and not question his attempts to be more egalitarian. John was caught in a vicious circle in which he felt it beneath his dignity to prepare seriously for the examination. The humiliation of repeated failure did not alter this process, but did cause high levels of anxiety which further depressed his ability to perform. Exposure for extinction focused on both the test situation and John's ambivalence about studying seriously.

• *Course of Therapy*: Insight helped John see the necessity for studying for the exam. As he became aware of the feelings that led him to dismiss preparation as beneath his dignity, he was motivated to include preparation for the exam in his anxiety hierarchy. As exposure imagery moved from studying for the exam to appearing at the exam site, new feelings were elicited. He recognized that the indignity of having his identity checked and being pushed at the door by other test-takers was even stronger than his anxiety. Further insight into childhood origins of wanting both to study more and study less than others led to work on imagery of "just being one of the crowd." John was then able to develop a better sense of the actual preparation that was needed.

Imagery about approaching the exam room door also brought forth his discomfort at confronting the same guard who had seen him take the test so often before. Imagining saying "good morning" instead of trying to sneak past the guard helped overcome this anxiety. When John imagined visiting the test room and touching the desks and walls the day before the exam, he spontaneously reported an image of the room as a morgue and the desks with graves covering a battlefield. This image left him feeling overcome and impotent. Wachtel asked "if he could picture himself as firm and hard, ready to do battle" (p. 349), leaving it ambiguous whether he was referring to an erection or general toughness. John's spontaneous image was of holding a huge sword, taking on a dragon. He saw this image as a reflection of previous discussions on "treating the exam as a worthy opponent."

Upon returning to test room imagery the next session, John reported feeling anxious, as if a large panther were behind him. Wachtel interpreted this as a symbol of John's power and aggression that was a threat as long as it was out of sight. Whether accurate or not, John's anxiety receded as Wachtel elaborated the panther as a metaphor for strength, meticulous purpose, and respect for one's prey or adversary. This metaphor helped John to relax and imagine himself as a panther resting and licking his fur. Because the panther knew his ability, he was able to experience any challenge without overt aggression. When imagining taking the test later, John spontaneously imagined the pencil as the panther's claw. He successfully passed his licensing exam during his next attempt.

• *Comment*: This case illustrates how psychodynamic and behavioral principles transform one another when combined. Interpreting childhood influences on symptoms and reactions to imagery both motivated John and directed the focus of the imagery to internalized conflicts. The imagery also resulted in a more directed focus than usually found in dynamic therapy and stimulated images that led to new insights. Wachtel notes that the seamlessness of this mutual influence in John's case was closer to the ideal of cyclical psychodynamic therapy than is sometimes achieved. It was more narrowly focused and John was more creative in his use of imagery than is typical. The case illustrates Wachtel's concern for language: by ascribing problems to *parental* attitudes that continued to have influence, John was able to take responsibility for his actions without diminishing his already shaky self-esteem.

Integrative Implications

New research protocols support the efficacy of the psychodynamic approach (*e.g.*, Luborsky, 1997; Luborsky & Crits-Christoph, 1998). Shedler (2010) reviews several meta-analyses of outcomes and concludes, "Effect sizes for psychodynamic therapy are as large as those reported for other therapies that have been actively promoted as 'empirically supported' and 'evidence-based'" (p. 98). Still other research suggests that the therapeutic relationship may be more important than interpretation in facilitating change (Orlinsky, Ronnestad, & Willutzki, 2004). Such research is revitalizing psychodynamic psychotherapy and is contributing to its becoming "… much more eclectic, abbreviated, and specifically targeted" (Lambert, Garfield, & Bergin, 2004, p. 812). Wachtel *et al.'s* (2005) use of action-oriented behavioral and experiential interventions to supplement interpretation and provide a corrective emotional experience is one example of this evolving process. As the movement toward integrative therapies develops, it will undoubtedly include the essential psychodynamic concepts of unconscious conflicts and ego defenses as a focus of intervention, especially for long-term thematic problems.

Wachtel *et al.* (2005) note the usefulness of the psychodynamic emphasis on ego defenses and the unconscious, especially for understanding thematic or characterological problems. Their interpretation of "working through" as repeated extinction trials for anxiety-evoking cues clarifies the therapy process and helps bridge the integration of psychodynamic and behavioral therapies. That integration is strengthened by the idea that the inside-out psychodynamic emphasis and the outside-in behavioral emphasis are two halves of a systemic circular causal process. A significant body of research also supports the object relations emphasis on early attachment and provides further empirical support for psychodynamic theory. A short introduction to attachment research follows since it has significantly influenced several of the integrative, experiential, and family therapies described in later chapters.

Attachment Research

Harlow and Harlow's classic (1966) surrogate mother study demonstrated the object relations principle that attachment develops from infant-maternal interaction rather than from the drive gratification of nursing. They found that infant monkeys, separated from their mothers, spent nearly all their time clinging to a warm, terry-cloth surrogate mother, and made only quick forays to nurse at a wire surrogate that provided milk. Mary Ainsworth's *strange situation* paradigm (Ainsworth, Blehar, Waters, and Wall (1978) has stimulated substantial research that supports a second object relations principle that responsive caregiving facilitates secure attachment and mental health. This research shows that attachment develops from long-term, two-way interactions of caregiver and child and has lasting impacts. Fortunately, problems caused by insecure attachment may still be corrected by supportive relationships later in life.

Patterns of Attachment

Ainsworth's experimental situation measures the level of secure attachment exhibited by toddlers when separated from their mother and left with a researcher in the strange situation of a laboratory playroom. Toddlers show four attachment patterns: secure, anxious-avoidant, anxious-resistant, and disorganized/disoriented (Main & Solomon, 1990). Figure 7.1 illustrates how Bartholomew's (1990) dimensional analysis of security and warmth in attachment interacts with the dimensions of parental responsiveness and supportiveness (*e.g.*, Isabella, 1993; Main & Hesse, 1990; and Sroufe, 1988). Bartholomew suggests that attachment patterns reflect differences in children's security and the degree of support they expect when stressed. A structured environment and caregiving that meets children's needs helps them be confident and act independently when separated. Children enjoy being close to caregivers who are warm and emotionally supportive.

Most children develop *secure* attachments in warm, responsive environments that give them confidence to explore their worlds without undue anxiety when separated from mother. The most toxic condition occurs when parenting is neither responsive nor warm. If caregivers are rejecting, neglectful, or abusive, infants are in the intolerable situation of being frightened of the attachment figure on whom they are totally dependent. This creates an approach-avoidance conflict and a *disorganized, disoriented* attachment with a deer-in-the-headlights child who is fearful, dazed, or acts in contradictory ways: *e.g.*, approaches caregiver while looking away.

If caregivers provide only support or only warmth, children fare better but still have problems: *e.g.*, parents who respond conscientiously to a child's needs, but are too depressed to enjoy the interaction or show warmth. Unless protected by a resilient temperament, an *anxious-avoidant* attachment results that leaves children

Parenting Style	Affectionate and Emotionally Supportive	Emotionally Distant and Nonsupportive	
	Confident Behavior		
Consistently Structured Interactions With Mutuality And Synchronicity	**Secure Attachment** Parent is base for exploring world; Readily separates; Responds to strangers in parent's presence; Easily comforted; Seeks contact on reunion	**Anxious Avoidant** Ignores caregiver; Readily separates and actively avoids parent on return: turns away, ignores, or combines proximity with avoidance signs; Little emotional sharing; Comfortable with strangers; Explores on own	
Close Behavior			Distant Behavior
Inconsistent, Nonresponsive, And Unstructured Interactions	**Anxious-Resistant or Ambivalent Attachment** Preoccupied; Poverty of exploration; Difficulty in reconnecting after separating; cries, resists, or is passive; Wary of novelty	**Disorganized/Disoriented** Fearful; Conflicted, contradictory behavior: contentment mixed with extreme anger; Fearful approach; May appear dazed/confused; Doesn't complete movements; Freezes; Odd mannerisms	
	Worried Behavior		

Fig. 7.1 Parental warmth, responsivity, and associated attachment patterns

closed and overly self-sufficient. They are able to explore the world independently without anxiety, but have little interest in the caregiver when reunited. Conversely, emotionally needy parents might give affection to their child, but be too self-absorbed to respond appropriately to the child's needs. This combination can result in an *anxious-resistant* attachment in which children anxiously resist separation. It is also called an *anxious-ambivalent* attachment, since anger over separation may lead to aggression toward the parent. Hazan and Shaver (1987) found analogous patterns in adults with 25% describing their relationship with others in avoidant terms and 19% in anxious-ambivalent terms.

Lyons-Ruth (2008) suggests that children are instinctively prepared to form attachments both to provide a sense of safety and to coordinate attention with their caregiver to salient parts of the environment. Between 12 and 18 months, coordinated attention helps toddlers develop a *theory of mind* in which they recognize "the parent as an independent agent in relation to the self, an agent who is a potential source both of pleasurable joint directions and of misaligned and distressing interactions" (p. 214). As babies learn to represent the self-in-relation-to-others, their attachment pattern affects the strategies they use to evoke their caregiver's attention when feeling threatened (Main & Hesse, 1990):

- *Securely attached* babies simply express their distress to elicit an appropriate response;
- *Insecure/avoidant* babies suppress expression of attachment behavior to maintain access to caregivers uncomfortable with closeness or unable to express warmth;
- *Insecure/ambivalent* babies express distress even if there is no obvious threat to ensure that their inconsistent caregiver remains available to respond;
- *Disorganized* babies are initially unable to develop a coherent strategy, given the lack of warmth or responsive caregiving. Main and Cassidy (1988), however, found that 6-year-olds develop controlling stances: either hostile control that forces a response or caregiving control that solicits reciprocation.

Attachment and Problems in Living

Increasing evidence suggests that early insecure attachment is a risk factor for later problems such as borderline or antisocial personality and anxiety or dissociative disorders (Cassidy & Mohr, 2001; Lyons-Ruth, 2008). Disorganized attachments are strongly associated with later, severe psychopathology even when corrective experiences intervene. Other risk factors include unresolved loss of a parent, trauma, or babies born with difficult temperaments: *e.g.*, a colicky baby that is easily upset and hard to console can make it difficult for even a conscientious mother to respond adequately to the baby's needs. Parenting style appears to interact with biological factors such as infant *temperament*, which appears particularly important in defining what constitutes sensitive, responsive parenting.

Temperament is the *phenotypic* result of interactions of genetic, intrauterine experience, and other birth factors, such as the effects of premature delivery or illness.

Thomas and Chess (1977) identified a number of neonatal, temperamental characteristics that influence later development. They classified infants as *easy, slow-to-warm-up*, or *difficult* (easily upset and hard to soothe). Parenting style differences are relatively unimportant in responding to an easy baby's needs, but slow-to-warm-up babies need extra warmth and difficult babies need both structure and warmth to develop secure attachments (*e.g.*, Vaughan & Bost, 2002).

The Adult Attachment Inventory (George, Kaplan, & Main, 1996) is an unstructured interview that examines attachment memories of loss, separation, feeling loved, or rejection. Its categories reflect a continuation of childhood patterns: *secure/autonomous, dismissing of attachment, preoccupied with attachment*, and *unresolved*, people who do not satisfactorily resolve attachment-related childhood trauma or loss. Not surprisingly, dismissing adults have difficulty making commitments to others, preoccupied adults have poor boundaries and are overly dependent, but neither group is at increased risk for diagnosable psychiatric problems.

In contrast, adults with unresolved attachment issues may show confusion, dissociation, and incoherence similar to the disorganized child. They may have difficulty in reasoning about their loss or abuse. They may have difficulty believing the attachment figure is dead, believe they were responsible for the death, worry the dead person is somehow manipulating their mind, confuse their identity with the dead person, or show other signs of disorientation; *e.g.*, the mother of a disorganized infant had earlier responded in a straightforward manner, but entered a trance-like, dissociated state of awareness when asked to describe a cousin's death:

> She was young, she was lovely, she was dearly beloved by all who knew her and who witnessed her as she was torn from us by that most dreaded of diseases, tuberculosis. And then, like a flower torn from the ground at its moment of splendor, she was taken from us in that most terrible moment of her death. The sounds of the weeping, the smell of the flowers, her mother in her black dress cast across her daughter's coffin, I remember it still (Main & Goldwyn, 1998, p. 104).

Unresolved adult attachment patterns are correlated with prior interpersonal traumas including assault, rape, and physical abuse (Mickelson, Kessler, & Shaver, 1997) and with later anxiety and borderline personality disorders (Fonagy *et al.*, 1995). van IJzendoorn, Schuengel, and Bakermans-Kranenburg's (1999) meta-analysis reported an effect size of 0.31 in the association between an adult's unresolved attachment and their infant's disorganization, which suggests attachment problems can be transmitted from one generation to the next. Fortunately, object relations are sufficiently flexible that problematic attachment patterns may be modified by later influences of other family members, teachers, neighbors, or therapists (Levy *et al.*, 2006).

Chapter Seven: Main Points

- *Object relations* theorists view early attachment as critical for later ego development. Donald Winnicott emphasizes the importance of mothers providing a *holding environment* to protect the infant from being overwhelmed by anxiety.

He noted that *transitional objects* such as favored blankets help children learn to self-soothe when the mother is absent.

- Otto Kernberg suggests children must develop unified *object representations* of the mother and of the self that integrate both good and bad interactions. Infants defend against anxiety by *splitting* object representations into an anxious, unresponsive *bad-mother* who differs from the *good-mother* who is reassuring and responsive. *Borderline ego organization* occurs if the child is unable to integrate this split in object representations.

- Heinz Kohut's *bipolar nuclear self* theory is based on his work with clients who experienced narcissistic injuries during early development: *e.g.*, the failure of parents to take delight and *mirror* joy in the infant's abilities interferes the development of *nuclear ambitions*, while an inability to *idealize* the parent and share in their strength affects the formation of *nuclear ideals*. Failure to integrate the poles of nuclear ambitions and ideals results in:

1. An *understimulated self* that acts out to seek excitement;
2. A *fragmenting self* that is sickly and weak;
3. An *overstimulated self* that avoids scrutiny and idealizes others; or
4. An *overburdened self* that views the world as frightening and overwhelming.

The therapist's *empathic attunement* allows *mirroring and idealizing transferences* to develop, which can provide a corrective experience.

- Psychodynamic treatment planning examines three dimensions:

1. Ego organization level—*neurotic, borderline, or psychotic*;
2. Character style—*oral, anal, or phallic fixation*; and
3. Adaptive functioning level—*adaptive, partially impaired, or fully impaired*.

Character style is most important for neurotic ego organization, while level of adaptive functioning determines appropriate interventions for psychotic functioning. All three dimensions are considered for borderline organization: interpreting character style is most important for those clients with adaptive functioning, while fully impaired clients require supportive therapy to stabilize their defenses; partially impaired clients need an extended *holding environment* before character style ego defenses and conflicts are addressed.

- Cyclical Psychodynamics assimilates behavioral techniques into its approach assuming that action-oriented interventions provide a more effective corrective emotional experience than interpretations do. Symptoms reflect a vicious circle in which problematic childhood interactions are recreated in the client's current life. However, ego defenses keep the anxiety associated with such situations out of awareness and prevent clients from confronting and mastering their fears. The goal of intervention is to expose the client to situations that recall such interactions and extinguish the associated anxiety.

- Psychodynamic therapy is undergoing significant changes driven in part by new research protocols and evidence that relational factors are more important than interpretations in helping clients change. It is more eclectic and focuses on specific, short-term outcomes.

- Attachment research strongly supports the object relations emphasis on early childhood experiences and is an important consideration for integrative therapies. Security of childhood attachments is affected by temperament and by parental warmth and responsiveness to the child's needs. Insecure attachments can persist and are associated with adult problems.

Further Reading

McWilliams, N. (1994). *Psychoanalytic diagnosis: Understanding personality structure in the clinical process*. New York: Guilford Press.
McWilliams, N. (2004). *Psychoanalytic psychotherapy: A practitioner's guide*. New York: Guilford Press.
Wachtel, P. L., Kruk, J. C., & McKinney, M. K. (2003). Cyclical psychodynamics and integrative psychodynamic psychotherapy. In J. C. Norcross & M. R. Goldfried (Eds.), *Handbook of psychotherapy integration* (pp. 335–370). New York: Oxford University Press.

Videos

Integrative Relational Psychotherapy with Paul L. Wachtel, Part of the American Psychological Association Systems of Psychotherapy Series. http://www.apa.org/pubs/videos/4310793.aspx.
Object Relations Therapy with Jill Saverge Scharff, Part of Psychotherapy.net Psychotherapy with the Experts Series. http://www.psycotherapy.net/video/Scharff_Object_Relations_Therapy.

Chapter 8
Humanism: Experiential Approaches

People are only influenced in the direction in which they want to go, and influence consists largely in making them conscious of their wishes to proceed in that direction.
T. S. Eliot (American Poet, 1888–1965)

Is change caused by outside influences or something that comes from within the person? Humanistic therapies take the phenomenological perspective that people choose to change rather than the scientific modernist perspective that change always reflects an external cause. The ability to choose is the basis of the human potential for growth or *self-actualization.* People consciously evaluate ideas and opportunities available in the environment, and after reflection, choose to act in ways they believe will meet their needs. This creative process involves risk-taking, new skills, and growth in the face of the uncertain outcome for any action.

With choice comes responsibility. People are responsible for how they choose to act and how they choose to interpret a situation. This usually serves both the individual's and society's needs, but as social creatures, people sometimes distort perceptions, ignore needs, or avoid taking responsibility in misguided efforts to gain others' acceptance. Humanists view these processes as the reason people have problems in living. Because each person's choices create a unique reality, humanists avoid diagnostic categories or manualized therapies designed for groups of people. Symptoms reflect unmet needs and distorted perceptions that are resolved only as clients become aware of unexamined aspects of their experience. The therapist's role is to establish a collaborative relationship in which clients feel free to explore their inner experience and make informed choices about desired changes in their lives.

The therapist's responsibility is limited to creating a safe, supportive environment by being fully present, nonjudgmental, and empathic. Treatment planning is de-emphasized. Not surprisingly, there are significant dialectical tensions between humanistic and cognitive-behavioral theorists given their differences in assumptions about human nature and change. Table 8.1 details some of these tensions. Experiential therapists agree with other humanists about the importance of phenomenology, choice, and responsibility. However, many experiential therapists adopt a postmodern pluralism that assumes there are many useful ways of construing the self and the

D. K. Fromme, *Systems of Psychotherapy,*
DOI 10.1007/978-1-4419-7308-5_8, © Springer Science+Business Media, LLC 2011

Table 8.1 Comparison of cognitive-behavioral and humanistic therapies

Cognitive-behavioral therapies	Humanistic therapies
Scientific modernist objective epistemology	Phenomenological subjective epistemology
Behavior determined by external forces	Actions freely chosen to meet needs or achieve goals
Universal principles apply to everyone	Unique experiences yield unique perceptions of reality
Reductionistic analysis of problems	Holistic, empathic description of client experience
Problems result from heredity/environment	Problems arise from meeting others', not one's own needs
Problems may be grouped diagnostically	Problems are unique to each person's situation
Change follows new learning	Change results from actualizing inner growth potential
Therapist is authority on how to change	Client is ultimate authority about his/her experience
Therapist responsible for change	Client responsible for change; therapy is a collaboration
Research-supported treatment planning	Therapist is spontaneous, fully present, and empathic
Focus on symptom removal	Focus on here-and-now experience, choices and growth
Teach new skills; eliminate negative feelings	Clients discover solutions; create new meanings
Emotions may be a "problem"	Emotions motivate and indicate what is important

human condition. This creates another dialectic with the phenomenological subjective monism of person-centered approaches (see Chap. 9); *e.g.,* Rogers' concept of a "true self." This chapter focuses instead on the pluralistic approaches of experiential therapies. Gestalt therapy, developed by Perls (1947) is one of the earliest, most important experiential approaches.

Dialectic Tensions in Gestalt Therapy

Contemporary Gestalt approaches are based on three linked philosophical positions:

1. *Phenomenology*—As humanists, Gestalt therapists empathically enter the client's experiential field and avoid imposing their own values, beliefs, or ideas as they reflect, describe, and help clients clarify and articulate their experience.
2. *Field Theory*—The client's experience reflects dialectic tensions in a phenomenal field that includes current needs or goals, past experiences, and environmental opportunities. This results in a *figure/ground* dialectic as elements relevant to current needs emerge from the phenomenal field's background to become a central figure of attention. A cycle of figural formation and destruction occurs as old needs are met and new needs lead to new figures.
3. *Dialog*—The therapeutic alliance requires therapists to be fully present in a here-and-now, *I-Thou* relationship (Buber, 1976) that respects the other person's

humanity. This modern emphasis on a collaborative relationship (*e.g.*, Polster, 1995) contrasts with Perls' (1947) more charismatic, directive style of relating to clients. In both approaches, therapists set aside their own theories or beliefs and avoid explanations or interpretations. Instead, they accept clients as they are and validate their experiences as meaningful. As therapists describe what they observe in the relationship, clients become aware of previously unavailable experiences and are able to act more creatively in the moment.

A Gestalt is an organized whole with emergent properties that are more than the sum of the parts. It forms automatically as individuals attend to relevant parts of their experience and the environment. Gestalt therapists believe that people form effective Gestalts and solve problems by attending to their experience and environmental opportunities that are relevant to their needs. Consequently, modern Gestalt therapists de-emphasize the "expert" role and instead help clients become fully aware of their potential to grow and to solve their own problems. They help clients focus on experiences that are out of awareness by observing what happens at the *contact-boundary* between person and environment: the point at which experience happens.

Gestalt therapists focus on the dialectic tension between experience and action. They view "negative" emotions as important information about necessary actions. Gestalt therapists help clients contact and explore the implications of their experience rather than desensitizing them to negative affect as is done in cognitive-behavioral therapy. They may suggest action-oriented experiments to help clients maintain their focus on uncomfortable feelings.

The emphasis on action reflects Ferenczi's (1952) belief that activities can complement insight and help uncover repressed impulses or memories. Moreno's (1946) psychodrama also de-emphasizes insight and intellectual understanding and instead stages dramatic recreations of problematic interactions. Clients play themselves, while other clients or therapeutic assistants play the roles of the significant others in the problem situation. While psychodrama is still used by some therapists, its greatest influence has been on the role-playing techniques used in Gestalt and other experiential therapies.

Classical Gestalt psychology (*e.g.*, Kohler, 1959) also influenced Gestalt therapy by showing that awareness is an active construal of the environment, not just a passive replication. Particularly important is the way aspects of the environment become figural and emerge from the ground in response to interests, needs, or goals. Other influences include field theory (Lewin, 1948) and Husserl's (1931) phenomenology. Reich's (1949) concept of *character armor* led to Gestalt therapy's emphasis on nonverbal expression and incongruities between verbal and nonverbal communication.

Perls' Classical Gestalt Approach: Conceptual Framework

Perls (1947, 1969, 1970; Perls, Hefferline, & Goodman, 1951) believed that the information necessary to act effectively in a situation is found at the *contact-boundary* between experience and relevant parts of the environment. A Gestalt is a dialectic formed by experiential awareness interacting with introspection, insight, and deliberate thought to create effective action. His oft-quoted phrase, "Lose your mind and come to your senses," has led to criticism of Perls as anti-intellectual. However, his position may also be understood as a counterpoint to Freud's over-emphasis on insight as a change process.

The interaction between what is "out there" and what is significant, meaningful, or important to the person determines what becomes figural in any situation. A Gestalt then forms to link awareness of needs and opportunities in the environment with a plan of action and the motivation to enact that plan. Awareness and action constitute a dialectic that creates a Gestalt that meets the person's needs with what is presently available in the environment. *Unfinished business* results when external or internal forces (*e.g.*, anxiety) interfere with the perceptions or actions needed to complete a Gestalt. Incomplete Gestalts distract the person until tasks are completed: *e.g.*, Zeigarnik's (1927) subjects spontaneously resumed rather boring tasks that were interrupted even though this was not even suggested to them.

Perls' Theory of Psychopathology

Perls (1970) was influenced by the modernist views of his time and developed a theory of neurosis despite a mostly atheoretical approach rejecting labels. He proposed that children may reach an *impasse* or *stuck point* if parents withdraw support before children are able to support themselves. They may then develop *catastrophic expectations* and learn to inhibit independent behavior for fear of punishment or withdrawal of parental love. They make a *creative adjustment* to environmental requirements and limit their awareness of associated needs, wishes, or aspects of themselves. This may prevent full contact developing between needs and awareness of the environment and result in *unfinished business* or *incomplete* Gestalts. Children may develop indirect, *phony* strategies that get needs met by others, but also reduce awareness and interfere with the ability to meet their own needs; *e.g.*, they may act *as if* they were ignorant, disabled, or "above" having sexual feelings.

Perls suggests that clients create boundaries that prevent contact or awareness to defend against unacceptable experiences. If applied rigidly or too often, boundaries become a short-term, problematic solution to a crisis. Therapists help clients examine how their defenses prevent Gestalts from forming by keeping threatening experiences out of awareness. Polster and Polster (1973) described five defenses that prevent experiential contact:

1. *Introjection*—This is a necessary process by which children incorporate parental models for coping with the world. In adults, it may create a naïve, "undigested" acceptance of others' opinions, beliefs, or standards that is not integrated with the client's prior experience or needs. Introjects are not integrated into a Gestalt

as an integral part of the client's self. Instead they create introjected inner *voices* that create polarities: *e.g.*, a critical *top dog vs.* an *underdog* who acts in incompetent, forgetful, stupid, or lazy ways. A passive-aggressive underdog may eventually defeat the top dog but at the price of interfering with Gestalt formation. Therapists can ask the client to use pairs of sentences beginning "You believe ..." and "I believe ..." to help clients differentiate between their own and another's experience: *e.g.*, "You believe I should study law," *vs.* "I believe I'd rather follow my love for music."

2. *Projection*—In order to understand things, people assume that others experience the world in ways similar to themselves. Problems arise if unacceptable aspects of self-awareness are seen as alien, coming from someone else. Clients see others as hostile instead of owning their anger. While projection allows them to avoid responsibility for unacceptable feelings or actions, they also lose the ability to act appropriately to resolve problems that inevitably arise with other people. Therapists can help clients reown projected experiences by asking them to imagine that they own the projected impulse; *e.g.*, "Let's try to understand your boss. If you were somehow him, what would make you so critical of an employee?"

3. *Retroflection*—Clients redirect acts, thoughts, wishes, feelings, or impulses about others back upon themselves; *e.g.*, being angry with themselves instead of people who injure them. Sustained retroflection prevents meaningful contact with others, but may adaptively prevent impulsive actions if used selectively. Muscular rigidity and stiff, awkward movements or posture are signs of retroflected impulses. Therapists can ask such clients to look inward and focus on their physical and emotional experience.

4. *Deflection*—Clients minimize strong feelings and avoid serious conflicts by using abstraction, humor, politeness, intellectualizing, or distraction to diminish contact with their experience. Overuse prevents intimate contact with others and makes the person seem distant or dull. Therapists should remark on deflections and then be prepared for strong feelings to emerge.

5. *Confluence*—Clients minimize conflict by minimizing differences with others. Contact with one's actual experience is lost by imagining it to be the same as the other person's. Clients who are "pleasers" and do not make their true feelings known may become resentful when others express strong feelings and violate the implicit "contract" not to rock the boat. Clients become more aware of their experience if asked, "What do *you* want (feel), right now?"

Perls' Approach to Therapeutic Intervention

Reflecting his charismatic style, Perls adopted an expert stance and was more confrontational than most modern Gestalt therapists. Perls typically demonstrated Gestalt methods in workshops in which volunteers took the "hot seat" as the center of attention. Perls' goal was always to help clients become fully aware of their experience in the *here-and-now* and of their power to choose, to shed phony roles, and to take responsibility for their own actions. His usual approach was to confront incongruities in verbal and non-verbal expression and notice other signs of blocked awareness such as muscular rigidity, tension, or constrictions of voice or movement.

Experiments to help clients access avoided experiences are essential in Perls' approach. They are not technique-driven, but develop from the therapeutic moment to increase client awareness. Common elements in people's problems have nevertheless led to a repertoire of useful experiments: *e.g.*, if clients blame their parents for a problem, Perls might ask them to enact their parents' roles and *play the projection*. In *two-chair work*, clients become aware of polarities in their personality by playing alternate roles such as punitive top-dog *vs.* guilty under-dog. To address *unfinished business*, *e.g.*, unresolved feelings toward an absent parent, clients are asked to imagine expressing their feelings as that person sits in an *empty chair*. *Reversals* elicit hidden polarities by asking clients to act the opposite of their usual way. In contrast to Moreno's theatrical approach, a client enacts all of the roles in an exercise (Levitsky & Perls, 1970). In group therapy *rehearsals*, clients share their thinking or rehearse how they play social roles, *e.g.*, being a patient, while other members serve as an audience and provide feedback.

Repetition or *exaggeration* help clients experience warded-off feelings more intensely. One client, whose whiny voice failed to elicit the desired sympathy from the group, was asked to go around the group requesting "something" from each member.

> As he went around the room doing his pleading bit, through the exaggeration and the accented focus he came clearly into touch with his own tone of voice. When he came to full sense of himself as beggar, Ben started to laugh … realizing … [p]eople could listen without having to give him the exorbitant hand-out (Polster & Polster, 1973, p. 151).

Clients are asked to end a statement about themselves with "*… and I take responsibility for it*" to help them experience their ability to choose. Clients who distance themselves from responsibility with *It-talk* or *You-talk* are asked to use *I-talk* to own their experience: "*I* have difficulty communicating with my mother," instead of "*It*'s hard to get through to my mother."

Perls believed that manifest dream content reflected projected parts of client experiences. Gestalt *dream work* has clients play the roles of each part of the dream, including inanimate elements. In one workshop, an individual reported a dream of walking on a mountain path. When asked to play the role of the "path," he became very animated and expressed feelings of being "walked all over." Perls was careful not to interpret meanings, believing interpretation to be one-upsmanship, suggesting the therapist's theory is better at discerning meanings than the client's experience. When clients avoid implicit feelings or messages, "*May I feed you a sentence?*" is used to make their experience explicit. Perls believed clients find it easier to reject suggestions inconsistent with their experience using this method than they might with an interpretation.

A Contemporary Relational Gestalt Approach (Erving Polster)

Three characteristics make contemporary Gestalt therapy a postmodern approach:

1. *Contextualism*—experiential contact with the immediate environment creates meaning;
2. *Constructionism*—meaning is created through dialog (Gold & Zahm, 2008; Jacobs, 1989; Perls, 1976; Polster, 1987; Polster, 1987; Yontef, 1993; Zahm & Gold, 2002); and
3. *Pluralism*—*e.g.*, "... there is no 'real' self, hidden by surface experience, but rather a community of selves that vie for ascendancy" (Polster, 1995, p. 5).

This pluralism contrasts with the widely held monistic belief that a socialized "false" self conceals one's "real" self (Miller, 1986; Ogden, 1986; Rogers, 1951; Winnicott, 1972).

Other theorists refer to the "community of selves" as voices, self-states, self-other introjects, or interpersonal schemas. The various selves are created as Gestalts form during significant experiences. *Essential* selves reflect enduring, compelling experiences that are more central to the individual's sense of identity than other, less compelling *member* selves. Together, they make the person's full range of experience available to meet the opportunities and demands present in the environment. Polster compares the coordination of the community of selves with the voices of musical counterpoint: "Some are complementary, others dissonant, but all contribute to the integrity and richness of the entire piece of music" (1995, p. 5). Each voice retains its individuality in contrapuntal music, but is integrated by the listener into a rich, musical whole. Similarly, relevant selves respond to different, momentary aspects of a situation, but are integrated by the individual into an emergent Gestalt. Polster expands Perls' concept of top dog/under dog polarities to include as many voices or selves as are present in the moment.

Polster's (1995) community of selves is similar to Rummelhart, Smolensky, McClelland, and Hinton's (1986) suggestion that schemas are *emergent properties* of neuronal network interactions, whose connections are weighted by repeated activation or experience. As various situations are encountered, relevant connections among neuronal networks activate schemas (selves) that guide our actions. Problems occur when connections are inhibited (selves are suppressed) and people are unable to use their full range of knowledge and experience to resolve a situation. The contemporary Gestalt emphasis upon the therapeutic relationship also nurtures dialog among the client's selves or voices. The community of selves reflects a dynamic process in which change and new, emergent selves are possible in every moment. Instead of an autonomous, static "real" self, there are dynamic relational selves or selves-in-context (Enns, 2004). Selves are *parts* of the person, internalized as schemas (or object relations), created in relationships with others, and evoked by the demands and opportunities present in the situation.

Conceptual Framework: Community of Selves

Boundaries, created by introjection, projection, retroflection, deflection, and confluence, are problematic if they are impermeable. However, Polster (1995) emphasizes they are essential for contact as well as for separation. After contact with the environment is resolved, there is a withdrawal while the Gestalt is completed and the experience is integrated into the community of selves. Integration is facilitated by the introjection triad of *contact, configuration*, and *tailoring*. Polster defines healthy introjection "… as spontaneous receptivity, unimpeded by the deliberative faculties of the mind" (1995, p. 31). Contact is the momentary merger and loss of boundaries between self and other, the basis for empathy in the mature individual. Self-other boundaries are also blurred when either infants or needy individuals introject another's strength for support they are unable to give themselves. Only this last example of introjection is problematic.

Configuration is a construal of the environment that enhances the internal consistency of the community of selves. Experiences sufficiently similar to an existing self are assimilated directly. Dissimilar experiences that are harmonious with the community are configured as a unique self. Less congruent experiences may require *tailoring*. Tailoring involves reconstrual of novel experiences to be compatible with the community of selves (*e.g., confirmation bias*, Wason, 1960; *belief bias*, Oakhill, Garnham, & Johnson-Baird, 1990).

As individuals mature and develop competence, tailoring may also involve creating situations more congruent with the community of selves: *e.g.*, gaining the education necessary to realize a desire to be an architect. Tailoring allows people to maintain a sense of self-coherence, unity, and harmony even in situations incongruent with their prior experience. If an introjection is inadequately configured or tailored, the resulting dissonance may prevent that internalized self from making full contact with subsequent experiences. Therapy helps clients tailor introjected selves to make them more compatible with the community of selves.

Intervention in Relational Gestalt Psychotherapy

Polster (1995) suggests "… that regulation of attention is a key source of distortions in a person's self formation process and that the renewal and redirection of attention are key focuses of all therapy" (p. 63). Narrowly focused attention on irrelevant details results in anxiety, obsessive-compulsive, or paranoid symptoms, while an overly broad focus misses important details as in histrionic symptoms (Shapiro, 1956; Wachtel, 1967). Problems result if attention is redirected to avoid negative emotions. A common goal of all therapies is to help clients attend to important experience; *e.g.*, reinforcers focus attention on effective behavior and psychoanalysis confronts warded-off impulses. An attentional focus is explicit in relational Gestalt therapy.

A principal aim of Gestalt therapy is to help clients attend to warded-off experiences. The therapist's interest in the contact-boundary helps clients focus on avoided areas of experience. This is challenging if clients make themselves seem uninteresting; but even boring clients become fascinating if therapists are interested in what they do to seem uninteresting. Therapists who are interested in clients as they are help clients be more interested in themselves and more self-accepting. Directing attention to avoided areas of experience increases client awareness of previously inaccessible resources and options. Polster (1995) notes that redirection is contrary to the classical Gestalt emphasis on self-discovery, but believes guided learning is also effective. Clients need not discover everything on their own, but a redirection should be timed sensitively to avoid disrupting a developing Gestalt or the client's own efforts.

Clients experience "stuckness" when a static, essential self tailors dynamic sequences of experiences to avoid change. Postmodernism suggests essential selves are "static" because they are narratives people tell about themselves. In order to change narratives, clients need to focus on how events constantly unfold in their lives, especially in the therapeutic relationship. Particular attention is paid to incongruous sequences of verbal and nonverbal behavior that reflect member selves responding to different aspects of an event. Sequential experiences can reflect moment-to-moment changes in feelings, needs, or goals, or depending on the situation, movement from one life stage to the next. A continuous, fluid sequence of experience is required for Gestalt formation and resolution. The goal of therapy is to connect isolated moments into continuous experiencing rather than the psychodynamic goal of insight relating the meanings of previously isolated events.

Polster (1995) describes a dialectic of *loose* and *tight* sequences that guide the therapist's activity. Initially, clients experience events in loose, disjointed sequences with gaps between cause and effect. The *storylines* they construct about their experiences are similarly disjointed and lack coherence. As therapists focus on the sequential connections of successive moments, clients begin to experience how later experiences follow from earlier moments. A sense of inevitability develops as they become aware of momentary and life span connections. An absorbing "of course" feeling occurs as clients configure experiences into a new, emergent self. Resulting storylines are not truly inevitable since many different stories could be developed from each experiential sequence. Therapists need to be sensitive to the client's experience since incongruent comments can derail the sense of inevitability of a developing Gestalt.

In the loose *vs.* tight sequence dialectic, looseness allows clients to explore a developing theme at a comfortable pace. A creative search for and acceptance of experiences at the edges of the client's awareness are encouraged by loose associations (*e.g.*, free association). Loose and tight sequences constitute a dialectic in which clients first become more open to all aspects of their experience and then form sequential connections and construct a coherent storyline that completes the Gestalt. This creates a more encompassing, adaptable essential self that is able to move beyond earlier feelings of stuckness.

232 8 Humanism: Experiential Approaches

Although sequential storylines energize and organize selves, their content derives from contact, awareness, and action:

[T]he contact we have with other people tells us whether we are good or bad, careless or careful, loved or not loved …. The selves that form from these events, feelings, and meanings are the result of simple experiences of the things people say or do to us. Thus in the therapeutic reconstruction of selves, the therapist aims for new experiences of contact so that they will become composed into new selves, better connected with actual experiences and better integrated (Polster, 1995, p. 132).

The self is *realized* as contact with others shapes the person's awareness, understanding, and action. A meaningful contact-awareness-action cycle results in a new self.

Contact implies boundaries. Polster and Polster (1973) identify six types of boundaries:

1. *Body*—physical sensations are allowed or denied awareness; *e.g.*, intellectualizing people tend to ignore sensations below the neck;
2. *Familiarity*—only well-known, comfortable aspects of the environment are noted;
3. *Expressive*—voice or movement may be expressive, constricted, or exaggerated;
4. *Exposure*—the degree to which a person is willing to be open or known to others;
5. *Values*—valued, interesting activities are allowed, but necessary, devalued activities are avoided;
6. *"I"-boundaries*—a superordinate category that defines the limits of self-expression or self-exposure; limits on parts of the body or environment the person is willing to contact.

People are comfortable and effective when environmental contacts are within I-boundaries. Novel actions, ideas, values, settings, memories, or people outside these boundaries create excitement in which contact results in growth or in problems if contact is avoided.

Rigid I-boundaries avoid new experiences and increase the predictability of a client's life, but also prevent the excitement and liveliness that accompany growth and learning. Couples have problems if one person moves beyond comfortable I-boundary levels to contact someone whose I-boundaries prevent that contact. It may be difficult from a third-party perspective to decide who is having the most difficulty. One person is rigidly cut-off, while the other's excitement at moving beyond comfortable I-boundaries is transformed into anxiety. In either case, the environmental contact necessary to allow Gestalt formation is disrupted resulting in *unfinished business*. If the contact episode is sustained, a Gestalt will form that incorporates prior experience and allows each person to grow and respond appropriately.

Polster (1995) believes that Gestalt theorists over-emphasize the role of contact, while theorists such as Kohut (1977) and Rogers (1951) over-emphasize empathy. His *Relational* Gestalt Therapy emphasizes a contact-empathy dialectic in which empathic understanding is effective only to the extent that therapists make full experiential contact with their client. Contact is also found in the relationship between con artists and their marks, but lacks therapeutic empathy. Therapeutic contact only occurs in the context of an empathic understanding of the client that includes an experience of "we-ness" or *mutuality*. Mutuality happens if permeable therapist and client I-boundaries permit an *I-Thou merger* of selves in which the other's needs, wishes, and feelings become as personal and meaningful as one's own (Buber, 1976).

For infants, merger is an introjection of the mother's strength and calmness to provide support for the infant's developing sense of self. For adults, merger involves a dialectic between intimacy and autonomy needs. I-boundaries must be sufficiently permeable to allow the intimacy of an I-thou relationship, yet also allow sufficient separation to maintain a sense of autonomy and identity. Polster (1995) describes this relationship as "… like breathing in and breathing out" (p. 196). If boundaries are overly rigid and impermeable, attempts to merge lead either to loss of identity or separation and loss of intimacy. Sensitivity to client I-boundaries and tolerance for separateness or merger enables empathic contact and change. Clients are able to accept previously subordinated selves when empathic contact shows the therapist understands and accepts those subordinated experiences.

Growth and change occur as clients contact inner and outer experiences and accept their member selves. Therapists need to accept unexpected changes and support the excitement that results from the client's expanding awareness as new selves form and old selves expand. Lack of support can transform the developing excitement into anxiety, reduce environmental contact, and subordinate the emerging self. Subordinated selves continue to react to the environment even when out of awareness. Actions that are out of awareness may be impulsive and interfere with the intentional actions of dominant selves. This is why Gestalt therapists use experiments to help clients experience their actions consciously; *e.g.*, asking clients to repeat or emphasize actions or to engage in role-plays that bring subordinated selves into awareness.

Gestalt experiments emerge from the therapeutic moment, as when a therapist asks a soft-voiced client to speak as loudly as possible and examine the resultant feelings. A significant repertoire of experiments has been developed by Gestalt therapists over the years (Stevens, 1971). More recently, emotionally focused, process-experiential therapy uses therapeutic *process markers* to suggest experiments that encourage deeper experiential exploration.

Emotionally Focused Therapy: Bridging the Researcher-Practitioner Gap

Since each person is unique, many experiential theorists question the utility of therapy research. However, Leslie Greenberg's Emotionally Focused Therapy (EFT) is empirically based and assumes people may make similar responses in similar situations (Elliott, Watson, Goldman, & Greenberg, 2004). Elliott, Greenberg, and Lietaer (2004) reported a mean effect size of 1.26 in a meta-analysis of 18 process-outcome studies, suggesting EFT is as least as effective as other approaches. In a "head-to-head" meta-analysis of six studies, they found EFT more effective ($d = 0.55$) than non-experiential, cognitive-behavioral approaches.

Rice and Greenberg (1984) isolated key *therapeutic markers* that identify critical moments in therapy, guide case formulation, and direct moment-to-moment interventions as clients experience difficult or puzzling emotions. They examined triads of client-therapist-client (CTC) exchanges to see which interventions *deepen* the client's level of experiential processing on the client/therapist Processing Proposal scale (Sachse & Elliott, 2001; see Table 1.7). Based on this research, EFT has identified effective interventions from Gestalt, cognitive, client-centered, and interpersonal approaches.

Conceptual Framework: Emotionally Focused Therapy

Client-therapist process research shows that clients do better when therapists direct the process of exploring problematic experiences and so EFT differs from client-centered therapy in being *process-directive*; it is nondirective for the *content* of therapy and also emphasizes the therapeutic relationship (Elliott *et al.*, 2004). Research on CTC interactions has identified relationship and task principles that facilitate therapeutic outcomes (Greenberg, Rice, & Elliott, 1993). Relationship principles, which always take precedence over task principles, include:

1. *Empathic Attunement*—therapists set aside preconceived ideas, emotionally attune to the client's experience, and focus on experiences that seem important to the client.
2. *Therapeutic Bond*—therapists create an authentic, emotionally meaningful relationship with appropriate self-disclosure, empathy, caring, trust, unconditional acceptance, and presence.
3. *Task Collaboration*—a collaborative, "non-expert" exploration of relationship strains and experiential teaching lead to a strong alliance and agreement on therapeutic goals and tasks.

Task principles include:

1. *Experiential Processing*—activities that encourage optimal client engagement include:
    (a) *Attending*, or evoking full awareness of the "here-and-now" experience;
    (b) *Experiential search*, or articulating emergent, unclear inner experiences;
    (c) *Active expression*, or expressing and owning appropriate emotional responses to events;
    (d) *Interpersonal contact*, or allowing inner experience to be known by the other person;

(e) *Self-reflection*, or creating a meaningful narrative about one's experience; and

(f) *Carrying forward into action*, or transferring emerging understandings into daily life.

2. *Task Focus and Completion*—use of therapeutic markers to negotiate key tasks, help clients stay on task, and decide whether to return if sidetracked or switch to a more important task.

3. *Self-Development* (*choice and growth*)—therapists empower client responsibility by focusing on growth-oriented experiences (strengths, possibilities, self-caring, assertiveness), treating clients as "experts" on themselves, and collaborating on choosing and implementing tasks.

EFT shares the traditional humanistic values of experiencing, wholeness, growth, agency, self-determination, pluralism, equality, presence, authenticity, and an emphasis on the therapeutic relationship (Elliott *et al.*, 2004). However, instead of phenomenology, EFT takes a postmodern perspective based on modern emotion theory and a neo-Piagetian *dialectical constructivism* that suggests "facts" are …

> … a joint construction of the "things themselves" and one's knowing process …. [R]eality constraints (emotion processes being one) … limit our constructions. Thus, not all constructions fit the data equally well, although it does seem likely that several accounts … might end up being plausible or valid. … [T]he person [is thus seen] as a complex, ever-changing, organized collection of various part aspects of self, such as critic versus object of criticism, or thinking versus feeling, or self versus internalized other (Elliott *et al.*, 2004, pp. 36–37).

Problems in emotional regulation (*e.g.*, *emotional intelligence*; Barrett & Salovey, 2002) may result if different parts of the self are in conflict.

Emotion Theory

Emotion schemes are equivalent to Polster's community of selves or cognitive schema concepts, but emphasize the emotional and action aspects of schemas. Figure 8.1 illustrates the emotion scheme components of a trauma-induced fear. An emotion scheme is (a) triggered by a *perceptual-situational* appraisal of threat that results in (b) *symbolic-conceptual* interpretations such as "I could be attacked any moment," which leads to (c) related *bodily sensations and expression*, and (d) wishes or needs to be safe (*motivational-behavioral* action tendencies). The four components of an emotion scheme mutually influence each other in a reciprocal fashion.

Emotion schemes are neurological networks of dynamic, self-organizing plans, intentions, and goals triggered by environmental events. Self-organization of emotion schemes may be likened to *voices* "… sometimes speaking alone, but often speaking along with other voices, either in unison or in contradiction" (Elliott *et al.*, 2004, p. 26). This dialectic of many voices (or selves) is synthesized into the experience of a unified, continuous self by narratives each person constructs from direct experience and stories told by significant others (Greenberg & Van Balen,

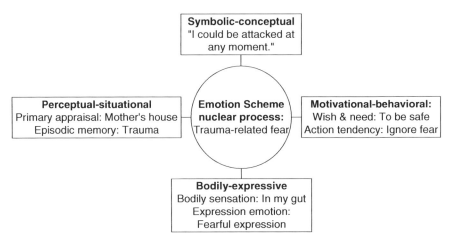

Fig. 8.1 Elements of a "trauma-related fear" emotion scheme. (R. Elliott, J. C. Watson, R. N. Goldman, & L. S. Greenberg, *Learning emotion-focused therapy*, p. 27; © 2004, American Psychological Association; reprinted with permission)

1998). EFT shares the post-modern emphasis on the role of narrative construction in change, but also suggests that reality shapes the emotion schemes underlying narratives. Dialog restructures the competing voices of dysfunctional emotion schemes into a narrative more in line with reality.

Figure 8.2 illustrates EFT's analysis of functional and dysfunctional emotional responding (Greenberg & Safran, 1987, 1989; Elliott *et al.*, 2004).

1. *Primary adaptive emotions* let people process complex situations rapidly and prepare them to respond adaptively; *e.g.*, flight to respond to fear or anger to defend against perceived violation. Therapists can say, "Take a moment and check inside to see if this is what you truly feel at rock bottom" to determine if primary emotions are being experienced.

2. *Maladaptive primary emotions* result when emotion schemes are activated that once were helpful, but fail to adapt to the person's current situation. The emotional response is over-generalized; *e.g.*, a sexually abused woman may respond with fear or disgust on her wedding night. Therapists can check if traumatic emotion schemes are activated by asking, "Does this feel like a response to what's happening now, or is it the way you've responded to things that have happened to you in the past? Is it a familiar, 'stuck' feeling?"

3. *Secondary reactive emotions* disguise or defend against difficult primary emotions a person is reluctant to experience; *e.g.*, boys are often taught it is unmanly to be emotional or cry, while girls are taught it is not ladylike to express anger. Inhibiting expression of primary emotions defends against changes in self-narratives and inhibits environmental awareness. Therapists can ask, "Do you feel anything else in addition to this first, strongest feeling?"

4. *Instrumental emotions* are not actually evoked by the situation, but are enacted emotions that influence others to meet the individual's needs; *e.g.*, "crocodile

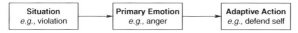

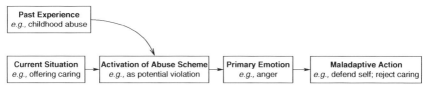

Fig. 8.2 Four forms of emotion response. (R. Elliott, J. C. Watson, R. N. Goldman, & L. S. Green-berg, *Learning emotion-focused therapy*, p. 30; © 2004, American Psychological Association; reprinted with permission)

tears" that elicit sympathy and satisfy unmet intimacy needs. The behavior may be deliberate, or so habitual the person is unaware of the underlying motive. To explore this, therapists might ask, "Are you trying to make a point or to tell someone else something with this feeling?"

Intervention in Emotionally Focused Therapy

Choosing the best intervention requires distinguishing among the four types of emotional responses. Primary adaptive emotions promote deeper exploration and constructive actions, but dysfunctional emotions create repetitious, stuck feelings (Elliott *et al.*, 2004). Clients are helped to explore negative emotions to access relevant emotion schemes to identify what they need or want and how to achieve it. Primary maladaptive emotions "highjack" responses that were appropriate in past traumatic situations, but not the current situation; *e.g.*, intimacy that evokes feelings of fear and victimization rather than love and caring in an abuse victim.

The origin and nature of maladaptive emotion schemes need to be explored, understood, so that new meanings may be constructed that respond more adaptively to current situations. Secondary reactive emotions are also empathically explored to discover the underlying primary emotion and the experiences that made it too uncomfortable to access. Instrumental emotions are examined for their interpersonal impact and the function they serve for the client.

Emotional Regulation EFT also addresses emotional regulation, the ability to tolerate emotional situations and respond effectively. Early attachment experiences affect the person's ability to self-soothe and maintain an optimal level of arousal for adaptive functioning (Cassidy & Shaver, 1999; Greenberg, 2002; Gross, 1999; Kennedy-Moore & Watson, 1999; see Chap. 7). Over-arousal disorganizes adaptive responses, under-arousal reduces motivation, and either interferes with good communication. Over-arousal can cause people to avoid primary emotions, while suppression of emotions such as anger may result in "emotional rebound" or over-reaction to minor situations. Table 8.2 describes interventions that help clients regulate emotions.

Kennedy-Moore and Watson (1999) note that appropriate emotional expression helps clients regulate arousal and cope with feelings, while it enhances self-understanding and social communication. However, extreme forms can be maladaptive. Intense expression of negative emotions can prolong arousal, interfere with clear thinking and awareness of self, and with coping with the environment. It can also alienate social support and evoke shame after the episode has passed. On the other hand, failure to express emotions leads to a lack of awareness of relevant cues and interferes with intimate relationships and coping with the environment. Suppressing emotions can also have physiological effects and result in physical symptoms.

Table 8.2 Emotional regulation interventions in emotionally focused therapy

To help clients access emotions …	To help clients contain emotions …
Encourage attention to bodily sensations that cue emotions	Help client observe and symbolize overwhelming feelings (imagine anxiety as a black ball in one's stomach to create a safe distance)
Help clients recall emotional situations that bring up particular feelings	Offer support and understanding; encourage client to seek support and understanding from others
Use vivid emotion cues, poignant words and images, in communicating with clients	Encourage clients to organize distressing emotions (rank-order their problems in a list)
Suggest clients act *as if* they feel a certain way in expressing an emotion (speaking in a loud, angry voice, shaking a fist)	Help clients self-soothe by relaxing or self-caring: "Try telling that critical part of yourself, 'It's okay to feel angry'"
Monitor arousal levels to maintain a sense of safety—critical for frightening emotions	Use distancing language or imagery (refer to client's anger as "it"—imagine locking it up in a closet)
	Explore activities that clients enjoy (listen to music)
	Help clients become aware and express emotions as they arise and decide what to do about them

Beginning and Ending Emotionally Focused Therapy

If clients seem anxious, EFT begins with a *state check* about the source of their feelings; perhaps they are unclear about their role as a client. If they are not anxious, EFT offers clients a choice about how to start; *e.g.*, "We have two main things we need to get done today: for us to talk about the nature of therapy, and for you to tell me about what your main issues are. Where would you like to start?" (Elliott *et al.*, 2004, p. 276). At some point, clients are given an introductory handout describing the nature of emotions, "They tell us what is important ... what we need or want, and that helps us figure out what to do. They [also] give us a sense of consistency and wholeness" (Elliott *et al.*, 2004, p. 274). The handout also describes therapeutic goals for maladaptive primary, secondary, and instrumental emotions, using lay terms.

Therapists also inform clients that everyone is unique, so *they* are the experts on their experience; that therapy is about discovering what works for them. They are asked to express any concerns they may have about therapy at any time, since therapists are not always aware of what does or does not work for the client. The structure of therapy is discussed and clients are encouraged to ask questions or give reactions. Therapists do a "state check" at the end of each session: "We have to end in a few minutes. Where are you right now?" "Do you have anything you'd like to tell me or ask me before we stop for today?" (Elliott *et al.*, 2004, p. 277).

Therapy Process Markers and Case Formulation

EFT therapists adopt humanistic principles in case formulation and avoid an "expert" role that could create an imbalance of power. Treatment plans encourage therapists to respond to the conceptualization, rather than the client's evolving self-presentation (*e.g.*, Rogers, 1951). EFT creates a more egalitarian relationship by emphasizing the client's expertise about their own experience and by on-going, collaborative formulation of goals, tasks, and procedures during each session. Importantly, case formulation is not done on an *a priori basis*, but as therapy unfolds. Therapists observe the client's moment-to-moment emotional processing style and any blocks to adaptive emotional processing. They note *process markers* that suggest ways to deepen exploration of problematic experiences in the here-and-now. Case formulation is tentative, based on observing the current moment and checked against the client's immediate experience. Rather than a context-free "history-taking," a problem's historical context is explored to discover the emotional relevance and meaning of past events.

Types of Markers

Elliott *et al.* (2004) describe five types of process markers that guide on-going case formulation as events unfold in session:

1. *Characteristic style markers*—indicate how clients allow others to treat them and how they treat themselves or others. They reflect emotion schemes that organize typical interpersonal relationship patterns; *e.g.*, self-invalidating *vs.* self-soothing; critical and blaming of others *vs.* nurturing and understanding; or allowing exploitation *vs.* setting boundaries.
2. *Mode of engagement markers:*
   (a) *Experiential engagement* with therapy is indicated by:
      i. Mindfulness or attending to internal feelings, meaning, intentions, wishes, fantasies, memories, or immediate sensations;
      ii. Searching to articulate complex, unclear, emergent, or idiosyncratic experience;
      iii. Expressing feelings in an immediate spontaneous manner;
      iv. Interpersonal contact, *e.g.*, awareness and acknowledgment of the therapist's prizing, attunement, or understanding of the client;
      v. Self-reflection or carrying forward (Gendlin, 1981) in which clients gain distance to reflect upon their experience and create new meanings, understandings, or intentions;
      vi. Action planning to translate new awareness into goals and appropriate strategies.
   (b) *Non-experiential engagement* occurs if clients are unaware of one or more elements of the relevant emotion scheme (see Fig. 8.1). To be good EFT candidates, they must learn to attend to missing components. Non-experiential engagement markers include:
      i. Acting out—attending primarily to the *motivational-behavioral* component;
      ii. Intellectualization—attending primarily to the *symbolic-conceptual* component;
      iii. Somatization—attending primarily to the *bodily-expressive* component;
      iv. Dissociation or conversion—neglecting the *perceptual-situational* component.
3. *Treatment Focus Indicators*—since EFT does not use a priori treatment plans to suggest how problems should be addressed, therapists check continuously for the client's most poignant or lively concern or for core meanings or primary emotions present in messages. Core issues develop across sessions as clients assimilate new material emerging from previous sessions and from living. As themes emerge, therapists empathically and tentatively formulate their understanding of tasks that may help clients explore an experience more fully if they agree.
4. *Task Markers*—the client struggles to express feelings or makes statements that indicate puzzling, intense feelings, or negative feelings toward self or others. These are markers for empathy; they must seem important enough to clients to motivate exploration of how their current situation relates to larger thematic life problems. Other markers for areas requiring deeper emotional processing include:

(a) Verbal markers:
   i. Rambling, disjointed narratives *vs.* concrete, specific, vivid language;
   ii. Rehearsed, third-person story-telling *vs.* poignant or powerful immediate experiencing;
   iii. Subtle nuances of meanings at the edge of the client's awareness, such as a tentativeness;
   iv. Timidity or vulnerability that may conceal underlying angry or defensive emotion schemes.
(b) Nonverbal markers:
   i. Repetitive, unconscious actions such as leg-swinging or finger-tapping;
   ii. Physiological reactions, such as blushing or sudden paleness;
   iii. Ambiguous facial expression or incongruent verbal and nonverbal communication;
   iv. Hesitations or inhibitions—going "blank" or becoming less fluent;
   v. Voice quality—focused, emotional, externalizing, or limited.

Voice quality indicates a client's depth of processing (Rice & Kerr, 1986). *Focused* voice is thoughtful, with slow, irregular pacing as clients explore their inner experience. *Emotional* voice, openly expressed emotion, crying, or raised voice can be rather inarticulate, but suggests a client is accessing primary emotion. In *external* voice, clients sound rehearsed and emotionally disengaged, telling an oft-repeated story (as if making a speech) that could as well be about someone else. Some clients may speak in a *limited*, constricted, overly soft, or fragile voice in order to distance themselves from their experience. A focused or emotional voice suggests a deeper processing of experience than is present with a limited or external voice.

Continuous Case Formulation with Task Markers and EFT Interventions

Therapists track the clients' evolving experience to formulate here-and-now interventions, avoiding a priori case formulation or an "expert" role. EFT interventions require the therapist's experiential presence, warmth and genuineness, a posture of respect, curiosity, prizing, and appropriate self-disclosure of the therapist's own experience of the relationship. Non-experiential interventions such as reassurance, suggestions, or interpretations are framed tentatively from a "non-expert" position to allow the client to judge their validity. However, the primary focus is on experiential interventions that are indicated by various task markers (see Table 8.3).

Empathic interventions involve reflection, affirmation, conjecture, checking for "goodness of fit," and observations about therapeutic process. Deeper experiencing is encouraged through process guidance: refocusing, exploring, experiential teaching, suggesting an experience is worthy of further exploration, or proposing tasks to evoke deeper experiencing. Figure 8.3 shows the stages of EFT, beginning

Table 8.3 Emotionally focused therapy interventions and task markers

Intervention	Task marker	Goals and techniques
Empathic exploration	Powerful, troubling, incomplete, or undifferentiated, global, abstract, and externalized experiences	Reflect problematic experience; encourage elaboration, differentiation, deepening and articulation; explore and clarify
Empathic affirmation	Vulnerability; painful emotions directed toward the self such as shame, guilt, hopelessness, or despair	Gentle, empathic understanding; metaphors reflecting prizing and hope→feeling understood and self-affirmation
Alliance formation	Beginning therapy	Create safe environment by empathic attunement, acceptance, openness, and prizing; collaborate on explicit agreement about goals and tasks
Alliance repair	Client is confrontational or hostile; withdrawn or self-conscious; misses sessions; "resistant"	Validate client's experience empathically; explore as a shared difficulty; raise withdrawal as an issue for mutual exploration
Clearing a space	Client is stuck, overwhelmed, or blank; somatic symptoms; numbness	Attend to inner experience: problems listed and set aside one at a time, metaphorically—problems are imagined to be in the distance or in a closet
Experiential focusing	Vague, stuck, unclear feeling that something is not right; a problematic, puzzling felt sense in the body	Clear space and attend inward with attitude of receptive waiting; compare labels that emerge with feelings until a "good fit" is found
Allowing and expressing experience	Difficulty in expressing feelings or answering feeling questions; external or constricted voice	Empathic warmth→safety to explore negative attitudes *re* feelings or signs of nervousness; teach labeling and appropriate expression of emotions
Systematic evocative unfolding	Unexpected, puzzling reaction to an event; client perplexed and disturbed, but does not understand why	Explore evoking details and vividly recreate all salient aspects of the event; then explore resultant emotional experience; empathic conjecture about possible meanings of puzzling feelings
Retelling traumatic experiences	Intense reaction to a traumatic event about which a story could be told (event, life disruption, night-mares); perhaps only the intense reaction	Propose rationale, negotiate task; explore pre-post-trauma experiences and reactions; encourage client to re-enter in imagination; help maintain safe "working" distance and create new meanings
Meaning creation	Experience is discrepant with a cherished belief: *e.g.*, just world, personal safety, trusting others	Clarify cherished belief with empathic exploration and conjecture; explore then *vs.* now and future values; explore needed modifications of belief

Table 8.3 (continued)

Intervention	Task marker	Goals and techniques
Two-chair self-evaluation split dialog	Severe self-criticism; split between a coercive, critical and punitive self *vs.* vulnerable parts of the self; decisional dilemma; tension	Give rationale for collaboration on task; separate, articulate and engage both sides in 2-chair dialog; differentiate and validate underlying values, feelings and needs for both sides of the split
Two-chair self-interruption split dialog	Client describes interrupting self or interrupts self in-session; burdened, blocked, or constricted feelings	Establish collaboration; separate, articulate, and create contact between self-aspects; promote awareness of how client interrupts self; support underlying values, feelings and needs
Empty chair unfinished business	Client blames, complains, expresses hurt, longing, or unresolved feelings about a significant other	Establish collaboration; evoke presence or a representation of other person; encourage 1st person empathic dialog with the other; explore secondary emotions; empathic affirmation of unmet needs

with establishing a therapeutic relationship and ending in helping clients be more aware of their inner experiences and make changes in their life.

A safe, collaborative relationship is established during the *premarker* stage. Stage 1 process markers begin a dialog about whether or how an issue should be explored. During stage 2, therapists evoke and empathically explore the emotional experience suggested by the task marker. Experiential teaching or empathic affirmation and exploration help clients fully access emotions and address interruptions or areas of avoidance. *Dialogical exploration* in Stage 3 deepens experiencing and helps clients become aware of internal or external voices that oppose full acceptance of feelings: *e.g.*, the therapist might help a client examine the validity of the belief that it is "unmanly" for men to be gentle. As clients explore the limitations of a restricting, critical voice, it may *soften* and allow access to previously subordinated voices or emotion schemes. This begins stage 4 as the client contacts relevant emotion schemes and the contexts, both current and historical, that allow them to resolve their problematic experience.

As clients gain new understanding of their problems in Stage 4, they may arrive at partial solutions with previously inaccessible options. Therapists help clients develop this new perspective by being alert to shifts in understanding. Increased awareness and insight allow clients to enter stage 5 with more adaptive, restructured emotion schemes. Stage 6 leads to full resolution and symptomatic relief as clients "carry forward" stage 5's improved experiential processing, incorporate new self-perceptions into their world-view, and commit to changes outside of therapy. Therapists serve as consultants during stages 5 and 6 as clients explore the implications and effects of their changed sense of self. These invariant stages of problem resolution provide a road map of intervention tasks and goals.

Fig. 8.3 The change process in emotionally focused therapy. (R. Elliott & L. S. Greenberg, Multiple voices in process-experiential therapy: Dialogues between aspects of the self. *Journal of Psychotherapy Integration, Vol. 7,* p. 234; © 1997, American Psychological Association; reprinted with permission)

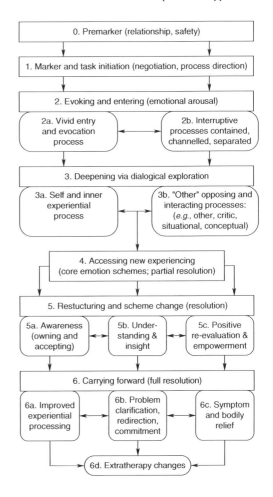

Empathic Exploration and Affirmation

Therapeutically, empathy functions to:

1. Help clients feel understood and supported, promoting a safe, effective working alliance;
2. Enable a dialectical, hermeneutic (contextualized) exploration and deconstruction of the meanings and intentions implicit in the client's assumptions, values, goals, narratives, and world-view;
3. Help clients understand and articulate their emotional experience, develop nonjudgmental, self-nurturing emotion-schemes, and learn to regulate their emotions.

Elliott *et al.* (2004) note that empathy is not just something one "does," but reflects the therapist's inner experience. Five mindfulness practices help facilitate empathic attunement:

1. *Letting Go*—set aside one's own value system to avoid preconceptions or premature closure; adopt a "not knowing" stance that tolerates ambiguity; respond to the client's subjective perceptions rather than an objective, "correct" interpretation of events.
2. *Entering*—project oneself into the role of the client; track the client's here-and-now experiencing and changes in mood or content (see Table 8.4).
3. *Resonating*—avoid agreeing or disagreeing; focus on one's own, visceral experience (*felt sense*), while listening to clients' descriptions of their experience; use that felt sense to understand and describe what clients feel; ask "fit" questions to check accuracy.
4. *Searching and Selecting*—empathic selection of the most poignant, lively, or important aspects of clients' narratives; distinguish between primary and secondary emotions; attend to the developing "edge" of client feelings in a tentative, exploratory fashion that supports client self-discovery and emphasizes their desire for change and growth.
5. *Grasping and Expressing*—speak succinctly with respectful, tentative, fresh, and evocative language to convey understanding; revise that understanding as clients give feedback; provide rationales for process-guidance tasks that may help deepen the client's experience.

Empathy also requires tracking the sequence of client experiences. Table 8.4 describes seven different levels of experiencing or *experiential tracks* that require different responses. Therapists shift attention to those aspects of experiencing the client is ready to explore more deeply. They search for process markers about personally relevant, powerful, troubling, externalized, or undifferentiated experiences that have been blocked. Therapists then clarify processes that interfere with deeper exploration and experiencing.

Therapists help clients deepen their experience by:

1. Turning client's attention toward the felt sense of internal bodily sensations;
2. Helping client vividly remember past occasions when similar feelings were experienced;
3. Exploring the "edges" of any unclear, confused, or unfinished experience;
4. Differentiating global, vague feelings by clarifying what they are *not*, and perhaps offering conjectures about what they *are*;
5. Empathic exploration of an emotion scheme's missing *perceptual-situational, bodily-expressive, symbolic-conceptual,* or *motivational-behavioral* components.

Deepening interventions help clients re-experience past events, attend to bodily experience, and articulate their experience until clarity, resolution, and closure are attained.

Empathic affirmation is used when voice or nonverbal markers suggest the client is fragile or vulnerable following a painful confession or experience of shame, hopelessness, despair, or exhaustion. Self-soothing is supported with gentleness, prizing, and careful pacing. The goal is to help clients fully experience painful emo-

Table 8.4 Therapeutic interventions as a function of client's experiential track

Intervention type	Client's experiential track→intervention
Empathic understanding	Main point is clear and poignant→Reflection of content; prizing
Evocative reflection	Feelings are expressed→Vivid imagery to deepen experience
Empathic exploration	Emerging feelings→Tentative, open-ended, focusing reflections
Process observation	Nonverbal signs→Note and help articulate unexpressed feelings
Empathic refocusing	Minimized/avoided feelings→Empathize with the pain/difficulty
Empathic conjecture	Implicit feelings→Conjecture, ask "fit" questions to check accuracy
Experiential formulation	Client is stuck→Guidance and rationale for tasks (*e.g.*, 2-chair)

tions, to "touch bottom" so that avoidance tendencies are extinguished and clients can express the need at the heart of their vulnerability.

Case Illustration

Tracey is a 20-year-old, European-American honor student and homecoming queen, who sought assistance at a large Midwestern university counseling center. She was immaculately dressed in designer clothing. [Dialog edited for brevity.]

Tracey:	I really bombed my Sociology exam today! If I keep that up, I can kiss my scholarship goodbye! [*external voice—an oft-told story; feelings are implicit*]
Therapist:	Sounds like you might have some real worries there. [*empathic focus on feelings*]
Tracey:	Yeah! I'd be letting down my sorority sisters and I dunno if I could keep up with my house expenses, if I lose the scholarship. [*externalized focus; implicit feelings*]
Therapist:	You're afraid you'll lose your friends, is that it? [*empathic conjecture; check for fit*]
Tracey:	Yeah … no … Oh, I don't know, I'm just so confused [*conjecture is off, but feelings are emerging as Tracey becomes more agitated and less rehearsed*]
Therapist:	Uh huh! [*following response, encouraging continued exploration*]
Tracey:	It just seems that everything is falling apart. [*emergent feelings*]
Therapist:	Things are hard, but it seems like something more than poor grades or scholarship. [*empathic exploration*]
Tracey:	Oh, it's just … I'm so mixed up … I just can't concentrate! [*becoming more agitated*]
Therapist:	Something has you so worried, you can't focus on your studies? [*conjecture; fit?*]
Tracey:	Yes! Well … it's my boyfriend … I thought we were going to get married, but now … I just don't know. [*closer to real problem, but feelings are still distanced*]
Therapist:	It's painful to think about, much less try to talk about it. [*empathize with difficulty*]

Tracey: I just love him so … and I thought he loved me! [*angry voice*]

Therapist: You sound really angry about this. [*process observation*]

Tracey: I hate that he just won't take "no" for an answer … he just keeps pushing and pushing and I get so upset and he won't stop! [*experiencing angry self*]

Therapist: That's not even respect, much less love! [*evocative reflection*]

Tracey: [*begins to cry*] I keep thinking something's wrong with me—why'm I such a prude? [*talking through sobs; feelings of vulnerable self emerge*]

Therapist: Part of you feels angry and unloved, and part of you worries that the problem is with you … and all of you is pretty confused. [*empathic understanding; affirmation*]

Tracey: Yeah! I just don't know where to go. [*stuck*]

Therapist: It seems clear to me why you would be upset with your boyfriend, but it's not so clear why you would then think something is wrong with you. Would you like to explore where that comes from? [*experiential formulation; process guidance*]

Tracey: [*softly crying*] I had a pretty bad experience in high school. [*exploring roots of bad feelings*]

[*Note that the therapist actively keeps the therapeutic interaction moving with relatively short interventions. Also note how the therapist formulates in vivo interventions by continuously tracking Tracey's experience for expressions of feeling or for missing elements in her narrative. Tracey's case is revisited below as it exemplifies other EFT interventions.*]

Focusing, Accessing, and Allowing Experience

EFT combines *allowing and expressing emotion*, derived from emotion theory (Greenberg & Safran, 1987; Kennedy-Moore & Watson, 1999) with Gendlin's (1981, 1996) techniques of *clearing a space* and *experiential focusing*. These interventions are especially useful with clients who are cut off from their emotions or become anxious and overwhelmed when they try to access inner experiences.

Clearing a Space Feeling overwhelmed and blank are the two markers for this intervention. Some clients experience themselves as the problem or feel overwhelmed by multiple concerns. In contrast, clients who feel blank over-distance themselves from problems with avoidant or numbing defenses and focus on inconsequential issues. They have difficulty identifying problems or core issues and often have psychosomatic symptoms. Therapists help these clients find a working distance that lets them address core experiences thoughtfully.

Clearing a space involves metaphors that create a *working distance* between the extremes of over-distancing or merging with problems. As an inconsequential or overwhelming thought occurs, clients are directed to imagine moving away and leaving that thought behind or to imagine the problem moving away, perhaps shut in a box or closet. Such metaphors are most helpful if framed in the client's own language. Clients are invited to *externalize* their problem with a metaphoric label, and then dialog and negotiate with it: *e.g.*, "What would you like to say to that inner critic who is depressing you?" This reduces self-blaming, creates a useful working distance, and invites collaboration in solving the problem. If clients find this process too difficult, labels make it easier to address an issue later. Clients feel safe and mindful of their experience as they identify and contain problems. Clearing a space self-soothes and allows salient concerns to emerge during experiential focusing.

Experiential Focusing Vague, global, nagging, externalized, or inarticulate inner feelings that something is "not right" are markers for this intervention. Clients are asked to adopt a curious, waiting stance and remain mindful of the puzzling experience. They clear a space and set aside extraneous thoughts, allowing time for a Gestalt to form. They then focus on the fit between the puzzling experience and emerging Gestalts or labels. Clients usually require minimal assistance, but if they seem stuck therapists may tentatively suggest a useful label.

When clients struggle for words, they are asked if any *felt bodily sensations* accompany their search. They are then encouraged to give "voice" to those feelings with sounds that feel appropriate even if no words come to mind. Groans, growls, and whimpers can all be helpful in narrowing the range of appropriate labels. Useful labels usually result in a sense of rightness or a *felt bodily shift.* If the shift fails to occur, therapists can ask "What *else* does this feel like?" or "What would it feel like if this feeling were resolved?" (Elliott *et al.*, 2004, p. 185).

As clients access a subordinated emotion scheme or voice during a felt shift, a "critical voice" may emerge and try to suppress the experience. Therapists suggest the critical voice be set aside for the moment and empathically support the new experience. Successful focusing allows clients to "carry forward" an understanding of this experience to dialog with the critical voice, and achieve resolution. Since clearing a space and focusing may be a novel experience, therapists need to stay attuned to the relationship. An alternative approach may be needed for clients uncomfortable with their bodies who find it difficult to focus on bodily sensations.

Allowing and Expressing Emotion Markers include signs of stopping, physically holding back, or constriction such as holding one's breath, or nonverbal signs of *emotional leakage* such as finger-tapping, foot-swinging, speaking in an external voice, or not attending to the emotional impact of a problem. Experiential interference or blockage may occur at any of the following five steps of emotional processing (Kennedy-Moore & Watson, 1999).

1. *Preconscious perceptual, emotional, or cognitive processing*: Clients must feel safe in a strong therapeutic alliance to unblock interference with experiential awareness and confront threatening feelings at this level. Once clients become aware of nonverbal markers and their lack of overt response, they are invited to clear a space and focus on the elusive experience. Systematic evocative unfolding with imagery that recreates the troubling situation may help.

2. *Conscious awareness of the emotional response*: Limitations in awareness often result from inattention to an emotional experience. Clients may seem confused or say they "don't know how they feel." Empathic evocative intervention, exploration, experiential focusing, and "awareness" homework may help identify problematic thoughts and feelings.

3. *Labeling and interpretation of reactions*: Clients who are unable to interpret or label their experience may be uncertain of their feelings, "I don't have the words." Empathic exploration, focusing, or systematic evocative unfolding may help them access and label their emotions.

4. *Negative attitude toward emotion*: Clients may judge their feelings unacceptable or shameful, especially early in therapy before they begin to feel safe. Negative attitudes, especially those based on powerful experiences or family and cultural values, need to be addressed before trying to increase emotional awareness. Empathic exploration or two-chair work can make negative attitudes explicit and facilitate exploration of their current validity.

5. *Desirability of revealing feelings in a given context*: If clients still think their emotions are unacceptable to others, secondary emotions may be involved. Exploring and expressing the underlying primary emotions may be more acceptable since, unlike secondary emotions, they are understandable responses to the environment.

Failure to express emotion can reflect implicit decisions at any one of these steps. A client's failure to express his feelings may not reflect avoidance, but rather a high tolerance for distress. Steps 4 or 5 reflect a conscious decision to suppress feelings, which may have fewer negative consequences than at earlier steps when decisions are made out of awareness. Suppression of an emotional response is seldom complete, since preconscious responses to stimuli may result in partial expression or *emotional leakage*.

Case Illustration (Continuation with Tracey)

Therapist: Do you see a connection between your bad experience in high school and feeling that something is wrong with you? [*empathic conjecture*]

Tracey: I'm just not the goody-goody everyone thinks I am! [*mournful; vulnerable; eyes down*]

Therapist: [*gently*] Part of you feels others might see you differently, if you were to reveal yourself more fully. Would it be safe doing that here? [*empathic affirmation; invite exploration*]

Tracey: Yeah, but I don't know where to start. There's just so much I'm all confused. It feels like everything is falling apart. [*slumped; crying less; seems hopeless; overwhelmed*]

Therapist:	With so many worries, it's hard to know what's most important. Would you like to try an experiment to see if we can clear away the less important things? [*clearing a space*]
Tracey:	I suppose! What do I do? [*crying stopped; makes eye-contact*]
Therapist:	Let's imagine we could take each of your anxieties one at a time and put them in that "anxiety closet" over there. Once all of those anxieties are over there, maybe you can focus better on what's most important to you. Could you try this? [*process guidance*]
Tracey:	It'd be nice to get all of this junk out of me! How do I start? [*agreement*]
Therapist:	Why don't you take the first worrisome thing that comes to mind, and just imagine yourself shoving it into your anxiety closet? [*guidance*]
Tracey:	That's easy! I'll just shove Steve [*boyfriend*] in there and he can just stay! [*grinning*]
Therapist:	What else? [*following response*]

[*Over the next few exchanges, Steve is followed into the closet by her Sociology professor and exam, her sorority sisters, and money concerns. Tracey is obviously amused by the process. Session 1 ends on a positive note, and the closet is "refilled" to begin session 2. Not all clients will find this process as easy as Tracey did. In such cases, it is necessary to explore the nature of their difficulty with them and either modify the procedure or try another approach.*]

Tracey:	I think the closet must be getting awfully full! [*laughs*] I don't know what else to put in there. My head's just a blank now—no more worries! [*moving from inward focus*]
Therapist:	Why don't you just sit there for a moment and enjoy that feeling of being able to look inside and not have worries. Perhaps something else'll come up. [*focusing guidance*]
Tracey:	[*long pause*] I don't think anything else is in there. [*blank*]
Therapist:	Maybe you could just take the time to tune in to how your body feels for a while—any tenseness, tightness, tingling, that sort of thing. [*focus on body awareness*]
Tracey:	[*long pause*] There's maybe like a knot in my stomach. [*felt bodily sense*]
Therapist:	As you focus on that knot, does it seem to say anything, or signal you? Maybe a noise? Anything that might put a label on that feeling? [*process guidance*]
Tracey:	Unnnh! Oh shit! I really never wanted to think about it again. I suppose … do I have to go there? [*moving out of phase 2—emotional blockage, motivated lack of awareness*]
Therapist:	It sounds like that last feeling inside is a really hard one. There's no need to explore anything, until *you* feel you're ready. [*empathic affirmation; allowing*]
Tracey:	It's not gonna get any easier. I think I kinda knew I'd have to face up to this …. [*small, constricted voice*] When I was 17 I had an abortion. [*step 3 process, labeling*]

Therapist: This was the bad thing that happened in high school … and it still seems to be full of hurt for you. [*empathic affirmation; allowing the emotion*]

Tracey: [*crying*] I'm just so ashamed. I don't deserve Steve. [*self-critical voice*]

Therapist: [*tentatively*] So somehow, I don't know, you feel unworthy of being loved? [*allowing*]

Tracey: [*sobbing; long pause*] If Daddy ever found out, he'd just kill me. [*critical voice?*]

Therapist: So your father doesn't know and it's scary to think of what'd happen if he did. What do you think would happen? [*empathic exploration*]

Tracey: [*crying*] I've always been his little girl. Mom said he'd be so disappointed if he knew.

Therapist: So your Mom was there for you, but she was concerned about your Dad's reaction? [*empathic exploration*]

Tracey: Yeah! I've always been able to talk with her and we decided it was best to keep it a secret between us. I couldn't bear for him to know what a slut I am. [*critical voice*]

Therapist: Could you take that feeling that your father couldn't accept your behavior and put it also in that closet for a bit? [*process guidance; set aside critical feelings*]

Tracey: I don't know … that's a hard one. [*long pause*]

Therapist: Is it over there now?

Tracey: Pretty much!

Therapist: Would you be willing now to imagine what your father might actually say if he knew? If you're willing, I'd like you to try an experiment. [*process guidance*]

Tracey: Oh! Well, I guess so, if you think I should? [*tentative*]

[*At some level, Tracey knows she has not resolved her abortion issues; she has internalized a critical voice, possibly father's, but perhaps mother's. This may have motivated avoidance of her father's reactions as well as her attempts at restitution by school achievements and extra- curricular activities. The therapist is preparing her for two-chair work, discussed below.*]

Reprocessing Problematic Experiences: Chair Work and Meaning Creation

Ultimately, the goal of psychotherapy is to help people process problematic experiences. Until now, the focus has been on bringing them into full awareness. The next step is to confront and master problematic experiences, or in behavioral terms, extinguish problematic responses.

Retelling Traumatic Experiences

The marker for retelling is any intense reaction or reference to a difficult or po-tentially frightening experience (Elliott *et al.*, 2004). Because post-traumatic stress disorder (PTSD) involves emotional numbing and avoidance, another marker is when clients minimize difficult events in some way. Critical parts of this interven-tion are:

1. *Pacing* the retelling so the client is not overwhelmed or re-traumatized;
2. *Elaborating the context* with concrete details, including what the client was feel-ing and doing before the event, what else was happening, who else was there, and what they saw, heard, felt, thought, and did at the time;
3. *Exploring intense reactions*, such as fear, helplessness, or self-recrimination. Retelling and re-experiencing traumatic events in a safe, supportive environ-ment helps extinguish conditioned fears and begins the process of creating new meanings to replace a victimization narrative.

Meaning Creation

Traumatic events, significant loss, abuse, injury, or illness all challenge cherished beliefs. Violation of cherished beliefs creates confusion, surprise, and an *emotional protest*. Clients are forced to re-examine their beliefs about invulnerability, ability to handle emergencies, the trustworthiness of others, or the *just-world hypothesis*: "only good things happen to good people, while bad things happen to bad people." Emotional protests, such as "I should've known better than to walk home alone," signal an implicit belief has been violated. Therapists first make the challenged belief explicit and clarify what expectations were violated. Empathic exploration of the belief's origins helps clients examine "then" and "now" attitudes: to re-evaluate the meaning of former beliefs, how valid the new beliefs are, and what they imply about needed life changes. Clients may also need to address emotional numbing.

Systematic evocative unfolding recreates the contextual cues associated with a trauma and helps alleviate PTSD's emotional numbing. Imagery allows clients to re-live a trauma and regain a sense of mastery by recovering suppressed emotional experience. However, care needs to be taken to prevent re-traumatization; if espe-cially intense feelings or self-blame are evoked, it may be necessary to interrupt the evocation of the traumatic experience with imagery of a safe place.

Two-Chair Work

Interpersonal conflict, decisional splits, and *conflict splits* are markers for two-chair work. Interpersonal conflicts include past or present conflicts with others, while decisional splits reflect difficulty choosing between opposing courses of ac-tion. *Self-evaluation* conflict splits involve implicit debates between a self-criti-cal voice and a vulnerable, experiencing voice. They include narratives rich with "oughts," "shoulds," "musts," and self-evaluations that reflect a demanding, critical voice. Sometimes, the vulnerable voice is only experienced as a felt bodily sensation such as heaviness, tension in the shoulders, or butterflies in the stomach. Such experiences may be *personified* by having the "butterflies speak" to the experiencing self. In *self-interruption* splits, even the felt bodily sense may be suppressed by an internalized critic; markers include sudden shifts or blockages in a narrative where clients lose the train of their thought.

Clients switch between different chairs as they role-play a dialog between the opposing voices. If clients are self-conscious about moving between chairs, they can be invited to role-play the alternative voices without physically moving. They are helped to symbolize both voices and look for valid points in each position: the experiencing voice may be trying to meet legitimate needs, while the critical voice may be protecting the client from potential disappointment or danger. Chairs are switched if a voice is clearly expressed or if one side dismissively shuts down the other voice (self-interruption splits); *e.g.*, when a headache restricts a client's exploration of an experience. Therapists should avoid favoring one voice over the other.

Typically, critical voices are dominant at first, but *soften* in a *felt shift* as the experiencing voice articulates its vulnerability. A compromise may be negotiated that keeps the client safe after the critical voice softens and becomes more accepting of the vulnerable self's needs. If a client drops out of the role-play and directs comments to the therapist, the therapist empathizes with the difficulty of the procedure and re-directs the client back to the role-play. The procedure is stopped if clients dissociate or become overwhelmed by overly intense emotions during two-chair work.

Empty Chair Work

Empty chair markers include unfinished business with significant others of unresolved feelings of hurt, longing, abuse, or trauma. Secondary emotional responses are another marker; *e.g.*, blaming or complaining to disguise painful primary emotions. Empty chair work lets clients resolve unfinished business with someone who has died or is unavailable, or confront abusers safely without risking re-victimization. Empty chair work may evoke powerful feelings that lead to self-interruption splits, which then require two-chair work as well.

Once clients realize the impact of unfinished business on their lives, they are asked to imagine a dialog with their significant other in the empty chair. Clients with religious or cultural taboos about "talking back" to elders may need additional support. Careful pacing is also important for clients who are fragile or those with overpowering feelings. Clients are helped to see how reactions that were adaptive in childhood may create problems in current relationships.

Since conflicts often re-enact childhood experiences, clients are encouraged to imagine what they can say now that they could not when they were small. Focusing or systematic evocative unfolding of contextualized images of early encounters lets clients make full emotional contact with their experience. They can then role-play the significant other with an adult's perspective. Therapists help clients differentiate between secondary and primary emotions and become aware of previously unmet needs. As therapists acknowledge the validity of those needs, clients are enabled to express the associated primary emotions.

Clients gain a better understanding of the significant other's actions as they shift roles and imagine the other's point of view. This shift in perception typically leads to softening of the critical voice that helps client let go of bad feelings and shift to a more positive view of the other, perhaps to forgive the other. Even if unable to forgive, the new understanding lets them stop holding themselves responsible for their abuse, abandonment, or inability to please the other.

Case Illustration (Conclusion with Tracey)

[*Two sessions have passed during which on-going conflicts with her boyfriend delayed two-chair work to address Tracey's avoidance of talking to her father about her abortion. After determining at the beginning of Session 4 that Tracey was avoiding going home, the therapist asks if she has any sense of where that avoidance is coming from.*]

Tracey: [*long pause*] Yeah! Remember a couple times ago you said I ought to tell my father about the abortion?

Therapist: I remember asking if you'd be willing to do an experiment, imagining what it would be like if you *were* to tell your father. [*clarification*]

Tracey: Oh! You mean I wouldn't actually have to tell him?

Therapist: Only if you decided that was something you wanted to do. It's not about what you *should* do, but what you *choose* to do. It sounds, though, like some part of you was hearing my suggestion as a "should." [*guidance; empathic exploration*]

Tracey: Huh! My whole life is a bunch of "shoulds."

Therapist: Where would you like to go now? [*giving choice*]

Tracey: Oh Jeez! I guess I can't put it off any more, huh? [*ambivalence*]

Therapist: Sounds like part of you just wants to forget about it, but that "shoulds" part thinks maybe it's necessary. [*empathic affirmation and exploration*]

Tracey: Yeah! I'm not looking forward to this .... How do I start?

Therapist: Perhaps you might start at the point where you were considering whether or not to tell your father you were pregnant. Would that be a possibility? [*guidance; giving choice*]

Tracey: Okay!

Therapist: How about imagining sitting down in one particular room in your home, with you sitting in this chair here, and your father sitting in that chair over there [*points*]. Can you get a clear picture of him sitting there in your mind's eye? [*process guidance*]

Tracey: [*pause*] Yes! I can see him.

Therapist: How might you begin telling him? What would you say? [*process guidance*]

Tracey:	[*pause*] Daddy, I've done something terrible. I'm so ashamed to tell you. [*starts to cry*]
Therapist:	[*gently*] So you just feel so ashamed. Go on! [*empathic reflection; following*]
Tracey:	I know you're going to hate me …. I'm …. I'm pregnant! [*crying; constricted voice*]
Therapist:	[*pause*] When you're ready, can you move to that other chair and imagine what he might say or do? [*self-interruption; process guidance*]
Tracey:	[*moves; long pause; looks at therapist*] He'd just be shocked and angry. [*out of role*]
Therapist:	[*gently*] Be your father! Tell Tracey how shocked and angry you are. [*role guidance*]
Tracey:	[*harsh voice*] How could you do such a stupid thing? I'm so angry! I'm really disappointed in you. [*resumes crying*]
Therapist:	Now move back to Tracey's chair. What do you want to say now? [*process guidance*]
Tracey:	[*moves; crying*] Daddy, please don't hate me. I love you and need you so much.
Therapist:	[*long pause until crying slows*] Now move back to the other chair. How does he reply? [*process guidance*]
Tracey:	[*long pause*] You're my little girl …. I expected more from you. [*softening*]
Therapist:	Switch chairs …. Tell him what you need from him. [*process guidance*]
Tracey:	[*long pause; small voice*] Please tell me you still love me, Daddy.
Therapist:	Switch again …. How does he answer you? [*process guidance*]
Tracey:	[*long pause; turns to therapist*] I think he'd …
Therapist:	[*interrupting*] No, have your Dad talk to you. [*process guidance*]
Tracey:	[*long pause*] Tracey … You know I'll always love you …. It's just so disappointing.
Therapist:	Switch again, and focus a bit on how you're feeling. [*long pause*] Can you share with me what you're thinking and feeling just now? [*process guidance; exploration*]
Tracey:	I guess I've always known he'd love me, no matter what …. I'm just so afraid that it would hurt him … but I've not really been able to talk with him since. [*partial resolution*]

[*As the session ended, Tracey indicated her intention to return home over the weekend to disclose her abortion to her father. The therapist explored this choice to ensure it was something she wanted, not just something she should do. The next session begins with the therapist asking an open question about what she wants to work on that day.*]

Tracey:	Well, I did it! I made my big confession and it didn't go at all as I expected. [*smiling*]
Therapist:	Oh? What happened? [*following*]

Tracey: Turns out he knew about it all along! It's just that after time passed, we
             didn't either of us know what to do about it .... He was more unhappy
             that we didn't seem able to talk or anything, more than he was upset
             about what I did. We hugged and talked and all that went so well!

Therapist: You must be so relieved that it worked out so well ... but did I hear
             that not *everything* went so well? [*empathic exploration*]

Tracey: Yah ... we got talking and realized last Friday was the 3rd anniver-
             sary for when the baby died .... It feels so weird ... here I've been all
             worried about myself and I've not even really thought about the baby.
             I don't like that in myself. [*self-evaluation about actions discrepant
             with her self-view*]

Therapist: Sounds like you've got some unfinished business with the baby.
             [*process marker*]

Tracey: Yeah ... it's really strange ... I've started having this same dream I
             kept having for so long after the abortion .... I'm at the abortion clinic,
             but I'm having the baby instead. I'm holding him in my dream and it
             feels so good and then something happens .... Sometimes the baby is
             gone and I don't know how ... sometimes I wake up. [*puzzled*]

Therapist: So it seems the abortion was pretty traumatizing on several levels ...
             the abortion itself, your worries over your father, and then the baby
             is gone as well. And now you're also feeling self-critical about your
             actions. Do you think your dream is trying to work all that out for
             you? [*Empathic affirmation and exploration*]

Tracey: It seems that way, doesn't it? Is there something else I need to do?

Therapist: Well, there are a couple things happening all at once here, I think
             need to be looked at one at a time: first there's the fact that the abor-
             tion and your actions afterwards don't seem to fit with the person you
             see yourself to be. Then, it sounds like you've got that unfinished
             business with the baby. Perhaps you'd like to start with reflecting on
             how you felt about yourself before and after the abortion? [*process
             markers; guidance*]

Tracey: Well, my folks are pretty religious and raised me to be a good Chris-
             tian ... and I think I was doing pretty good until things started get-
             ting so hot and heavy with me and Jerry [*baby's father*]. We really
             cared about each other and everyone thought we were going to end
             up together. It didn't seem so bad at the time ... and we only did it a
             few times, before ... well, before I got pregnant. [*focused voice*]

Therapist: So, before the abortion, you saw yourself as living pretty much
             up to your parent's standards ... and then afterwards? [*empathic
             exploration*]

Tracey: I guess the people at the clinic were okay, but I felt like I was just a
             piece of meat being processed ... and then there was nobody I could
             talk to ... [*beginning to tear up*]

Therapist: [*gently*] There was no one you could talk to .... [*following
             reflection*]

Tracey: No! Afterwards, Mom said "Thank goodness it's over and behind us. I don't want either one of us to have to go through that again." She meant well ... I know it was hard for her too ... and she just took charge and did everything ... it was all over within a week after I learned I was pregnant. [*tears flowing, blowing nose, and trying to stop crying*]

Therapist: It all happened pretty fast ... what were you feeling afterwards? [*empathic exploration*]

Tracey: We didn't have much time ... college was starting in a couple weeks .... I don't think I felt much of anything ... just got busy getting ready to leave home. [*crying stopped*]

Therapist: So, you just felt numb and there wasn't much time to feel or think about your experience ... life had to go on. Now that you're looking back on your experience, can you describe your feelings, both about the abortion and about yourself? [*exploration*]

Tracey: It feels awful ... the baby would just about be walking and talking now. [*crying again*] .... I know I'm not really a bad person ... but it was just such a terrible thing to have done. What chance did the baby have? How can I ever make it up? [*meaning protest*]

Therapist: You've never really had a chance before to grieve for the baby, or to create something meaningful out of such an important experience. [*marker for meaning creation*]

Tracey: What can I do now? There's nothing left of him! [*still crying*]

Therapist: If the baby were old enough to understand, and sitting in that chair over there, what would you want to say to him? [*process guidance for empty chair work*]

Tracey: [*long pause until crying slows; looks at chair*] I'm so sorry ... I wish I could've kept you and loved you and held you. [*deep sobbing; self-interruption*]

Therapist: If the baby could speak, what might he say? Move to his chair! [*process guidance*]

Tracey: [*moves; long pause; sobbing*] I wanted to live! Why couldn't I have a life too?

Therapist: [*gently*] Yes, he wanted to live too ... go ahead and shift back to the other chair. How might you answer him? [*process guidance*]

Tracey: [*moves; long pause; sobbing*] Oh, if I could only go back, I'd want you to live ... but it's too late ... I was too dumb to know better!

Therapist: Uh huh! You just didn't know better. Go on! [*affirmation reflection; following response*]

Tracey: [*long pause*] I know better now ... all I can do is try to do better ... maybe I could help other girls [*sobbing subsides; meaning creation*]

Therapist: Then, helping others could give your baby's life meaning? [*empathic exploration*]

Tracey: Yeah ... I need to think about that some more. [*thoughtful, focused voice*]

Therapist: It sounds like you may have a direction that might help give you some closure. As you look inside, is there still more that needs to be examined? [*process guidance*]

Tracey: [*long pause*] The baby never had a funeral … and I never talked to Jerry again … I think Mom told him and said not to call me again. I wonder what Jerry thought … it was his baby too!

Therapist: Yes, funerals are all about closure and reconnecting with our other loved ones. So, Jerry and you've never talked since, and he's not had any chance to grieve either? [*empathic exploration*]

Tracey: No … and it's funny, but every time I go home I'm reminded of Jerry. When we first started getting serious, he gave me this huge "thunder-egg," I think they call them geodes. It's been cut in half and the center is all these beautiful purple crystals. It's lining the path up to our house and I think of Jerry every time I see it. [*excited*]

Therapist: You sound excited. Can you share a little of what that's about? [*exploration*]

Tracey: It just came to me what I want to do! I want to have a funeral for the baby … I could make up the words I really want to say to the baby and to everybody. And I want Jerry and both our folks to be there. And the thunder egg, that's a part of Jerry and me … we could bury the egg since the baby's not there. [*full resolution; Gestalt formation*]

Therapist: That sounds like a plan that could be very meaningful for everyone involved. [*empathic affirmation*]

[*In her final session following spring break, Tracey came dressed casually for the first time. She reported that the funeral went pretty much as planned. Everyone, including Jerry and his parents attended, and it was a sad, bittersweet experience. She said she had had no more dreams since the funeral, and was doing well in her classes again. She said the chemistry was no longer there with Jerry, but that they and their families might be able to remain friends. She was ending her relationship with Steve. The Sociology exam grade turned out to be a C, but she thought she could still get an A in the course.*]

Integrative Implications

One of the dialectics between humanistic experiential therapies and other approaches is between *ad hoc* case formulation in response to the clients' here-and-now experience and more traditional a priori treatment planning. Critics view humanistic approaches as unstructured and susceptible to each therapist's idiosyncrasies. However, Tracey's case illustrates that experiential approaches can be focused on the here-and-now, but also highly structured. The here-and-now activity of most other therapeutic approaches seems rather unstructured compared to EFT.

The dialectic tension is between structured case formulation *during* therapy and structured treatment planning *before* therapy. A synthesis of these viewpoints requires reconciling concerns over idiosyncratic intervention and concerns that treatment plans distract from being fully present with clients. An analogy may be helpful: classical musicians practice extensively with detailed musical scores, but the mark of true artistry is the ability to be fully present in responding to cues from the other musicians and the audience. Psychotherapy also involves both science and art as empirically supported process interventions are shaped into individualized plans and sensitively applied in the therapeutic relationship. Since outcome is heavily influenced by the therapeutic relationship, EFT and other experiential therapies provide helpful guidance for critical moments. Elliott concludes his outcome review, "Process-directive humanistic therapies … appear to be particularly promising and should be more widely researched and used" (2001, p. 74).

Chapter Eight: Main Points

- Gestalt therapy is a holistic, humanist approach that assumes Gestalts will form to guide and motivate the best possible actions to meet people's needs as long as they attend to the *contact-boundary* between experience and the environment.
- Boundary defenses prevent full experiential contact and Gestalt formation when threatened:
  1. *Introjection*: uncritical incorporation of someone else's beliefs or viewpoint;
  2. *Projection*: the source of an experience is located not in the self, but in someone else;
  3. *Retroflection*: thoughts or feelings caused by others are experienced as caused by the self;
  4. *Deflection*: diminishing contact with humor, intellectualizing, politeness, distraction, *etc.*;
  5. *Confluence*: minimizing—feelings are suppressed to avoid conflict and please others.
- Gestalt therapists note when experiences are blocked and enquire whether clients would like to try an *experiment* that could allow them to regain contact with their full experience. Chair-work dialogs, exaggeration, and repetition are commonly used experiments.
- Polster suggests that there is no "true" self, but rather a *community of selves*. Enduring, compelling, articulated experiences that are central to the person's sense of identity result in *essential* selves, while more peripheral experiences create *member* selves. Good contact-boundaries result in a harmonious community of selves as new selves are integrated by:
  1. *Contact*: momentary loss of boundaries between self and other (introjection);
  2. *Configuration*: construing an experience to create harmony within the community of selves;
  3. *Tailoring*: accommodating discordant perceptions so an experience is harmonious with the community of selves.
- Clients become *stuck* when an essential self tailors perceptions so that full experiencing of a natural sequence is disrupted. *Storylines* then tend to have gaps

between cause and effect and be *loose* and disjointed as a result. Therapists help clients focus on connections within an experiential sequence that leads to *tightening* and the development of a Gestalt.

- Therapists strike a balance between empathy and experiential contact to help clients become comfortable contacting the rigid *I-boundaries* that limit experiential contact with actions, ideas, memories, or people that are perceived as threats. Empathy encourages *mutuality* or "we- ness" that helps boundaries become more permeable and increases experiential contact.
- EFT process researchers have identified critical incidents in therapy and the types of interventions that help clients to deepen their processing of those moments. Intervention principles are classified either as relationship- (empathic attunement, therapeutic bonding, or client task collaboration) or task-oriented (experiential processing, task focus and completion, or self-development—growth and choosing).
- Clients have problems when they avoid contact with one or more components of a current emotion scheme. Components include:
  1. *Perceptual-situational*: inattention to environmental cues;
  2. *Bodily-expressive*: inattention to bodily sensations (*felt sense*);
  3. *Motivational-behavioral*: inattention to wishes, needs, or feared situations;
  4. *Symbolic-conceptual*: beliefs incongruent with experience; *e.g.*, self-narratives that reflect other's ideas.
- Therapists intervene depending on which of four types of emotional response is expressed:
  1. *Primary adaptive emotions*: rapid, adaptive situational processing preparing individual to act;
  2. *Primary maladaptive emotions*: over-learned actions, no longer adaptive in current situation;
  3. *Secondary reactive emotions*: responses learned to mask "unacceptable" primary emotions;
  4. *Instrumental emotions*: responses reinforced by others' capitulation to expressed neediness.
- The goal is to help clients become aware of the adaptive primary emotion(s) underlying the maladaptive ones. Task markers, that suggest a need for empathic exploration include:
  1. *Verbal indicators*: rambling, disjointed, rehearsed, or third-person narratives;
  2. *Unconscious repetitive actions*: leg-swinging, finger-tapping, *etc.*;
  3. *Physiological reactions*: blushing, sudden paleness;
  4. *Hesitations or inhibitions*: going blank or becoming less fluent;
  5. Voice quality: externalized or constricted instead of focused or emotional voice.
- Once a safe relationship is established (*Premarker* stage), therapy proceeds in six stages:
  1. *Marker and task initiation*: identify marker, negotiate exploration, process guidance;
  2. *Evoking and entering*: vivid emotional arousal and containing interruptive processes;

3. *Deepening via dialogical exploration*: explore processes opposing inner experience (*critics*);
4. *Accessing new experiences*: explore poignant core emotion schemes and their implications;
5. *Restructuring and scheme change*: understanding, accepting, and re-evaluating experience;
6. *Carrying forward*: problem clarification, redirection, symptom relief, and extratherapy change.

- Some task markers and possible interventions include:

1. *Alliance formation/repair*: empathically validate/share responsibility for difficulties;
2. *Empathic exploration/affirmation*: empathically reflect/explore/clarify troubling experiences;
3. *Clearing space, focusing, expressing*: patiently focus on problem experiences one at a time;
4. *Evocative unfolding*: vivid recreation of contexts in which problematic experience occurred;
5. *Retelling/meaning creation*: review loss of *cherished beliefs* and explore alternative beliefs;
6. *Chair-work*: role-play both sides of internal or external conflicts/explore *unfinished business*.

Further Reading

Elliott, R. (2001). The effectiveness of humanistic therapies: A meta-analysis. In D. J. Cain & J. Seeman (Eds.), *Humanistic therapies: Handbook of research and practice* (Chap. 2, pp. 8157–81). Washington: American Psychological Association.

Elliott, R., Greenberg, L. S., & Lietaer, G. (2004). Research on experiential psychotherapies. In M. J. Lambert (Ed.), *Bergin and Garfield's Handbook of Psychotherapy and Behavior Change* (5th ed., pp. 493–539). New York: Wiley.

Elliott, R., Watson, J. C., Goldman, R. N., & Greenberg, L. S. (2004). *Learning emotion-focused therapy*. New York: Guilford Press.

Gold, E. K., & Zahm, S. G. (2008). Gestalt therapy. In M. Hersen & A. M. Gross (Eds.), *Handbook of clinical psychology* (Vol. 1, pp. 585–616). Hoboken: Wiley.

Polster, E. (1995). *A population of selves*. San Francisco: Jossey-Bass.

Polster, E., & Polster, M. (1973). *Gestalt therapy integrated*. New York: Brunner/Mazel.

Videos

Emotion-Focused Therapy Over Time, with Leslie S. Greenberg. Part of the American Psychological Association Psychotherapy in Six Sessions Video Series. Retrieved from http://www.apa.org/pubs/videos/4310761.aspx.

Psychotherapy with the Unmotivated Patient with Erving Polster. Psychotherapy.net. Retrieved from http://www.psychotherapy.net/video/Psychotherapy_Unmotivated_Patient.

Chapter 9
Humanism: Phenomenological Approaches

> *... I take very seriously the dehumanizing dangers in our*
> *tendency in modern science to make man over into the image*
> *of the machine, into the image of the techniques by which we*
> *study him.*
>
> Rollo May (1960, p. 4)

Chapter 8 described the dialectic between humanism and scientific modernism. Rollo May's quote captures humanist's concerns that a scientific modernist, objective analyses of human behavior fail to capture human capacities for self-reflection and transformation. These capacities include self-awareness, intentionality,, and agency, all emergent properties that cannot be reduced to component parts or observed from outside perspectives. Phenomenological and experiential theorists agree to this extent. Their dialectic revolves around the question, "Do clients need active assistance in the *process* of self-discovery or do they only need an empathic listener who strives to understand their inner world?"

Husserl's (1931) *phenomenological* method is a strategy for understanding another person's subjective experiences. Phenomenology is an epistemological alternative to scientific modernism designed to help observers avoid influencing clients' self-exploration inadvertently. Phenomenologists use empathic identification with the other person's core beliefs and values to understand their inner experience. Spinelli (1989) describes three steps in this process:

1. *Disciplined naïveté (Epoché)*: Therapists consciously suspend preconceived ideas, theoretical constructs, judgments, or assumptions to avoid imposing their own interpretations on a client's experience. Since categories inevitably frame perceptions, this is an ideal requiring therapists to develop awareness of their preferred categories and to avoid applying them inadvertently. Therapists take a position of disciplined naïveté, openness, and curiosity as they try to understand the client's categories, meanings, and experience of the world.

2. *Description of experience*: Therapists then *describe* rather than *explain* what they hear about the client's subjective experience in concrete, atheoretical terms. Discipline allows therapists to remain faithful to the client's concepts, understanding, and meanings without interpreting or substituting their own theory or categories.

D. K. Fromme, *Systems of Psychotherapy*,
DOI 10.1007/978-1-4419-7308-5_9, © Springer Science+Business Media, LLC 2011

3. *Equalization*: Therapists avoid assuming that any one reported experience is more important than any other. Each aspect of client experience is potentially as significant as every other aspect. Communicating accurate, empathic understanding allows clients to reflect further upon their own experience and achieve greater clarity. It also helps the therapist respond to the whole person rather than the person's "diagnostic" characteristics. Finally, equalization acknowledges that multiple perspectives are possible for any given experience: that clients are the ultimate experts on their subjective experience and thus the final arbiter for the accuracy of the therapist's understanding.

Instead of the active stance of the experiential therapist, existential and client centered therapists take a more passive, phenomenological stance. Both groups avoid categorizing people, but experiential therapists use categories to identify task markers and recommend interventions.

Outcome research suggests phenomenological approaches are at least as effective as cognitive-behavioral therapy (*e.g.*, Stiles, Barkham, Mellor-Clark, & Connell, 2008), but there is also support for the more active, experiential stance (*e.g.*, Elliott, Greenberg, & Lietaer, 2004). Unfortunately, perhaps because managed care rewards greater structure in treatment planning, a declining number of clinical psychologists report client centered or existential therapy as their preferred approach (Norcross, Karpiak, & Santoro, 2005). Nevertheless, these therapies address significant issues not covered by other approaches and are historically significant in the humanist tradition (Kirschenbaum & Jourdan, 2005).

Existential Therapy

Existentialists address the ultimate questions of human existence. They ask, "What is the purpose of a life that inevitably ends in suffering and death?" A major dialectic exists between postmodern perspectives that assume existential questions have no ultimate answers (*e.g.*, Yalom, 1980) and more optimistic religious or spiritual views (*e.g.*, Buber, 1976; May, 1969). Postmodernism suggests there are many possible answers to existential questions, while spiritual viewpoints focus on human capacities for goodness, growth, and love. All major world religions provide answers to existential questions, but a personal search is necessary for those who lack faith or are troubled by a lack of direction and meaning in their lives.

As modern society becomes increasingly secular, questions about life's meaning and suffering become increasingly challenging. Existential therapy helps people confront these questions and address the lack of purpose or meaning that can accompany an unexamined life. Existential therapists believe each person must find a personal meaning in life to cope with loss and suffering. Although suffering is inevitable, the attitude taken toward suffering is always under the individual's control. Viktor Frankl, a leading existential therapist, describes in *Man's Search for Meaning* (1963) how his commitment to help others as a physician allowed him to survive life in a Nazi concentration camp. Similarly, despite being crippled by amyotrophic lateral sclerosis (Lou Gehrig's Disease), the astrophysicist Stephen Hawking has explored the universe's origins. Frankl and Hawking illustrate how a meaningful life is possible in even the most limiting situations.

Existential therapy is based on a stance toward life, rather than a set of therapeutic principles. As such, its tenets can easily be integrated with other approaches. Developed by psychoanalysts (e.g., Binswanger, 1963; Boss, 1984; Frankl, 1963), interpretation is often used to help clients uncover disguised existential problems, but existentialism is equally compatible with experiential, cognitive-behavioral, and post-modern approaches.

Conceptual Framework

Although each person's experience is unique, Yalom (1980) suggests everyone faces questions posed by four universal *existential givens:*

1. *Groundlessness*: How can we know whether an action leads to desirable consequences or not in the absence of objective, external grounds for deciding?
2. *Isolation*: How can we truly know another person if everyone is ultimately isolated in their own subjective experience?
3. *Meaninglessness*: What is the meaning of life's struggle, if the ultimate consequences of our actions are unknowable?
4. *Death*: Why should we struggle with these issues since everyone dies anyway?

People's deepest fears or *existential anxieties* stem more from these questions than from the early childhood conflicts described by psychoanalysis. Despite this fundamental difference, most existential therapists share the psychoanalytic assumption that *insight* is necessary to let go of the defenses against these deepest concerns.

Western religions address fears of death by faith in an afterlife that reunites the person with loved ones. Scripture provides the grounds for decisions and serving God's will makes life meaningful. Such answers are seldom questioned in traditional societies with widely shared beliefs. However, in America's modern, secular, multicultural society, the answers of different faiths may seem to conflict with one another. This lack of consensus creates doubt and the need to confront existential questions more directly. Existentialists suggest that failure to confront the existential givens can result in symptoms.

Absurdity, Anxiety, Alienation, and Authenticity

Camus (1955) used *absurdity* to describe the universe's indifference to transcendent human aspirations for intimacy, meaning, and values. If the others' experience is ultimately unknowable, is meaningful intimacy a possibility? How can life have meaning if an action's consequences are unknowable making it impossible to make responsible choices? Even if that knowledge were possible, what meaning can a person's efforts have if they are soon forgotten after death? Is non-being the only reward for the pain, uncertainty, and suffering that comes with being?

Dread, panic, and overwhelming *existential anxiety* result when life's absurdity and the thought of eternal non-being are fully comprehended. Existential anxiety may be suppressed to avoid these overwhelming feeling, but complete repression of awareness creates its own set of problems. Repression creates further repression of other aspects of experience and leads to rigidity and *neurotic anxiety* in efforts to find authoritative guidance. The choice is existential anxiety and on the one hand and the development of neurotic anxiety or symptoms on the other. Confronting existential givens requires courage and is best accomplished in a supportive relationship that keeps awareness at tolerable levels.

Rigidity can lead to neurotic symptoms when traumatic experiences force awareness of mortality; *e.g.*, Skoog (1975) found that over 70% of his clients developed severe obsessive symptoms after death-related, security-disturbing experiences. Overwhelming, death-related experiences early in life can result in too few defenses against existential death anxieties; *e.g.*, Rosenzweig and Bray (1942) found that over 60% of clients diagnosed with schizophrenia suffered significantly more losses than other clinical groups or normal controls. At the other extreme, limited awareness can also lead to *neurotic guilt* once people realize how rigid avoidance of existential concerns has led to missed opportunities.

Neurotic anxiety leads to *alienation* from the three worlds of experience (Binswanger, 1963):

1. *Umwelt*, the natural world: buildings isolate people from nature; pre-packaged meats, nursing homes for the aged, sick, or disabled, and cosmetics to make the dead seem merely asleep all isolate people from the nature of death; loved ones do not die, but "go to a better place."
2. *Mitwelt*, the social world with other people: replacing concern and intimacy with others with materialistic values; *e.g.*, people pretend not to notice the homeless.
3. *Eigenwelt*, inner experience of self as an agent in the world: alienated from one's experience; prizing the "stiff upper lip" or treating self as a commodity to be marketed (*e.g.*, Fromm, 1955).

To live with *authenticity* in the face of absurdity and anxiety is the only alternative to alienation. With no external grounds for choosing how to act, every action is essentially an act of faith, but people act authentically only to the extent they remain aware of their natural, social, and inner worlds. Maddi's (2002, 2004) research on the related concept of psychological resilience or *hardiness* suggests that facing life with courage and realism protects people from harmful effects of stress. Maddi (1987) studied 400 executives when Illinois Bell Telephone downsized from 26,000 to about half that number. Over two-thirds of the remaining managers suffered performance and health problems in the following 6 years, including heart attacks, substance abuse, strokes, and depression. The other one-third showed hardiness, thrived in their positions, and remained healthy and enthusiastic. Three variables were critical:

1. *Challenge*: They saw crises as challenges rather than as threats.
2. *Control*: They believed they were able to choose or to influence events affecting them.
3. *Commitment*: They were committed to something self-transcendent, outside themselves.

Groundlessness

Maddi's hardy executives were committed to something meaningful, which gave them grounds for their decisions. They felt they could influence events, which they viewed as challenges and so had the courage to act authentically. Although groundlessness leads to anxiety, it is in dialectic tension with the *freedom* of the individual to choose how to act. Being aware of one's agency, able to act one way or another, is the basis of "response-ability." As freely choosing agents, people must find the courage to assume responsibility for their choices in order to live authentically. Even if an action's ultimate outcome were known in advance, there are no criteria for judging its "goodness" or "rightness." This is the dilemma in such truisms as the law of unintended consequences, or "You can't do just one thing."

It requires courage to maintain awareness of this uncertainty. Too often, people blunt awareness by holding someone or something else responsible for their actions. They blame fate, circumstances, or others and fail to see that they had a choice in the matter. But by avoiding responsibility or procrastinating, they create a world in which they are powerless. If they cannot influence events, then they are at the mercy of those events. Ironically, in avoiding existential anxiety, they create neurotic anxiety about an uncertain, potentially dangerous world over which they have no control. Frankl (1963) notes that even in concentration camp conditions, there is always a choice to view adversity either as a victim or as a test of one's courage, strength, and capacity to find meaning. Choosing to be a victim leads to neurotic anxiety and symptoms.

The *learned helplessness* literature (Seligman, 1992) illustrates how believing one has no influence over events can result in depression. Limited awareness of the ability to choose how to act also reduces awareness of emotions (*alexithymia*), associated with various somatization disorders (DeGucht & Heiser, 2003). Impulsive or compulsive disorders and depending on others to decide are other examples of problems in choosing and acting. In paranoid disorders, the responsibility for a choice or action is projected onto others. Existential therapy helps clients become aware of their feelings and their ability to choose how to act. But there is a double price to pay: not only must they confront existential anxiety and create personal guidelines for action, they must also confront existential guilt over the "roads not taken," the rejected alternatives.

Isolation

Yalom (1980) distinguishes three types of isolation:

1. *Interpersonal*: the loneliness that results from separation from others, cultural decline in a sense of community, or lack of adequate social skills to form and maintain relationships.
2. *Intrapersonal*: dissociation from inner experience; "oughts" or "shoulds" substitute for feelings.
3. *Existential*: inability to know others' inner experience or the outside world, except as filtered by perceptions, biases, beliefs, and past experience.

As Orson Scott Card, the novelist, poignantly framed the dilemma of existential isolation …

> … the tragedy of the individual is that the true cause of his behavior remains forever unknowable. And if we cannot know ourselves, true understanding of any other human being is permanently out of reach (1990, p. 273).

Yalom (1989) illustrates the unknowability of other's experience in the case of *Two Smiles*. His client, "Marie," smiled when a consulting hypnotherapist advised asking her oral surgeon how to distinguish between necessary pain that tells her how hard she should chew and unnecessary pain from her broken jaw. After the session, the consultant thought the smile indicated she had appreciated his suggestion. Yalom thought it was a cynical smile, since he knew Marie was angry at her surgeon's unwanted sexual attentions. But Marie reported she was embarrassed that the consultant might know about this and think badly of her working with the surgeon.

Existential isolation is inextricably related to the other existential givens: people die alone, are solely responsible for their choices, and author their own meanings. A dialectic exists between the autonomy of groundlessness and the need for intimacy that results from isolation. On the one hand, people seek fusion with others to escape the universal experience of isolation. On the other, their sense of autonomy and capacity for growth suffers exactly to the extent they become dependent on others to meet intimacy needs.

Existential philosophers (Buber, 1976; Fromm, 1956; Maslow, 1968; Yalom, 1980) believe that confronting isolation and groundlessness enables a viable compromise between intimacy and autonomy needs: a "need-free" *I-Thou* relationship. An I-Thou relationship is active loving, not a passive being loved—giving, not receiving. It is empathic, reciprocal, and self-transcending, viewing the partner's needs as meaningful as one's own. In contrast, most relationships are *I-it*, with others viewed as objects to serve one's needs. I-Thou relationships are ideals, approximated only in moments of deepest intimacy with the other.

Self-transcendence is not easily achieved and so other, less useful alternatives may be sought. Depending on others to make choices alleviates responsibility and gives an illusion of intimacy, but it requires a sacrifice of autonomy and constant vigilance to prevent the other from leaving. Some people submerge the self into a cause, into work, or some ideology instead. If that work is driven by neurotic anxiety to avoid confrontation with ultimate isolation, however, people may become "workaholics" or perennial seekers after causes. Others seek temporary self-transcendence compulsively with mind-altering drugs or sexual orgasm. What is needed is a therapeutic I-Thou relationship that gives clients the courage needed to confront their isolation.

Meaninglessness

Death and meaning form an existential dialectic: death gives urgency to life's meaning since there would no need to do anything today with infinite tomorrows. This dialectic raises the question of what meaning life could have, if one's best efforts end in death and soon are forgotten. In the face of this ultimate absurdity, the existential question becomes a quest for reasons to continue living. Existentialists suggest life is a search for meaning through self-discovery and authentic engagement with the world.

Most religions posit a *cosmic* meaning to life, reflecting an external, spiritual ordering of the universe. People of faith try to harmonize their actions with that spiritual ordering to give cosmic meaning to their lives. With no external grounds to order one's life, however, each religious faith has developed different sects, and modern science has further eroded cosmic belief systems. Table 9.1 lists the *secular* meanings that many use to replace or supplement cosmic meanings.

Each secular meaning is a type of self-transcendence, an engaging in something beyond the self for its own sake. Self-transcendence lets existential questions recede from awareness as the person actively engages the world. Boredom, cynicism, apathy, aimlessness, drug abuse, hyper-sexuality, risk-taking, or depression become likely without self-transcendent meanings. Compulsive striving for prestige, power, or material possessions replace meaningful pursuits.

For clients who lack meaning in their lives, Yalom (1980) encourages active engagement in life. Meanings develop dialectically from actions, just as one later pursues activities found to be meaningful. As mothers advise, "You never know if you'll enjoy it until you try it." Treatment goals for clients who lack meaning of life

Table 9.1 Yalom's (1980) categories of secular meanings

Category	Examples
Altruism	Leaving the world a better place; service to others
Cause	Dedication to something larger than ourselves
Creativity	Creating something novel, beautiful, or harmonious is its own justification
Self-actualization	Realizing innate potentials for knowledge, wisdom, beauty, love, and serenity
Self-transcendence	Turning from self-preoccupation to something outside oneself; *e.g.*, meditation

differ from the other existential givens, which emphasize awareness over action. *Action*, however, is a phenomenon of Western cultures, while *acceptance* is the goal of Eastern philosophies such as Buddhism. The *serenity prayer* is an interesting synthesis of this action *vs.* acceptance dialectic: "God grant me serenity to accept the things I cannot change; courage to change the things I can; and wisdom to know the difference."

Death

Death is the ultimate threat. People fear the process of dying, but even more frightening is the question of what, if anything, comes after death. Everyone has difficulty imagining non-being, the end of experiences and projects. Awareness of death starts early, with toddlers recognizing that something is different about dead animals or insects. Existentialists view childhood fears as defensive projections of death anxiety onto potentially avoidable "bogey-men" or monsters. Yalom (1980) suggests two types of defenses develop from childhood anxieties:

1. Specialness—death and injury happen to someone else;
2. Ultimate Rescuer—God or a powerful other will protect me.

If death anxiety defenses are optimally effective and not too rigid, adults typically develop *immortality projects* such as those in Table 9.2.

Panic, psychosis, or even suicide may result if defenses are inadequate and death anxiety overwhelms the person. If defenses are too rigid, people who adopt the specialness strategy may strive narcissistically for power or adulation, strive compulsively for superiority through Type A workaholism or heroics, or become aggressively controlling. Paranoid ideas of reference or grandiosity may develop. People who adopt the ultimate rescuer strategy may become passive, dependent, self-effacing, and self-sacrificing. If their efforts to retain the other's interest fail, they may try to coerce attention with anorexia, self-harm, or threats of suicide. They may have difficulty separating from abusive relationships. Existential therapists help clients modulate their anxiety as they confront the destructive consequences of avoiding awareness of non-being. Insight into death anxiety is a project only for long-term therapy. With limited time, therapy focuses on helping clients' defenses become less rigid or stronger as needed.

Table 9.2 Lifton's (1974) typology of immortality projects

Type of project	Description
Biological	Living on through one's descendants
Theological	Living on a higher, spiritual plane of existence
Creative	Living on through the impact of one's works
Eternal nature	One's body returns to nature, which is immortal
Experiential	Self-transcendence through intense living in the moment

The Nature of Human Problems

Human problems result from self-deception to avoid the anxiety of the existential givens. People seek ultimate rescuers or assume they are "special" to avoid the responsibility of acting on their own behalf. People who are special do not need to act, but may need a rescuer if they become a victim. These inauthentic responses to existential anxiety reduce the individual to an object unable to influence events, rather than an agent who chooses how best to respond to problems. Intractable problems in living are the consequence of seeing the self as an object at the mercy of events and unable to influence them.

Instead of an authentic self that confronts existential concerns directly and chooses how to act, the inauthentic self is caught in a web of self-deception. To live authentically is to be in a state of becoming, open to the myriad possibilities of each moment of existence. The inauthentic self instead is passive, rigid, and self-deceiving; it perceives agency in others and not the self, which leads to neurotic anxiety and symptoms; e.g., fear of reprisal by powerful "others" can lead to paranoid ideas; illness removes the somaticizers' need to make decisions or act. In addition to defending against existential concerns, symptoms effectively limit the ways others can respond politely. Despite being disguised, inauthenticity is noticed at some level by both self and others, which compounds neurotic anxiety with neurotic guilt, drives others away, and intensifies symptoms in an on-going vicious circle. Existential therapists rely on *intersubjective I-Thou* encounters rather than "techniques" and avoid treating clients as objects to be manipulated. I-Thou relationships facilitate clients in responding authentically with no need for self-deception.

Intervention in Existential Approaches

"Existentialism is not a system of therapy but an attitude toward therapy" (May, 1969a, p. 15). As May suggests, there are no uniquely "existential" interventions. Many existential therapists were trained in psychoanalysis and rely primarily on interpretation, dream analysis, analysis of transference, etc. However, instead of examining early childhood conflicts, existential analysts examine how clients cope with the givens of existence in the here-and-now therapeutic relationship. Entering the client's phenomenological world of immediate experience can transform any therapeutic system into an existential approach. European existential therapists focus more on the client's dread of facing existential givens; in contrast, Americans usually focus on a client's potential for growth and creating personally meaningful responses to existential concerns.

May's Existential Approach

Rollo May is the "grandfather" of American existential psychotherapy. His (1969b) case of Mrs. Hutchens illustrates the six principles of human nature guid-

Table 9.3 May's (1969b) characteristics of existential psychotherapy

Principle	Description
Phenomenal centeredness	Problems are understood as *continuing* efforts to protect the center of one's experience by limiting awareness of threats of non-being.
Courage for self-affirmation	Seeking therapy is a self-affirming act of courage to preserve centeredness without accepting limits to one's being.
Participation in relationship	The self can only be understood in terms of the need and possibility for people to participate in other's being despite risks to their centeredness.
Awareness leads to vigilance	The subjective side of centeredness is awareness, including vigilance for threats to centeredness and being.
Self-consciousness	Awareness of oneself as the being whose world is threatened, also allows awareness of alternatives—the basis of choice, freedom, and responsibility.
Anxiety and nonbeing	Awareness of one's own death and non-being leads to anxiety; the only alternatives are self-affirmation or self-denial with limited self-awareness.

ing his approach to existential therapy (see Table 9.3). Mrs. Hutchens, in her mid-thirties, has conversion symptoms of perpetual hoarseness. She tries unsuccessfully to present herself as a poised, sophisticated woman. She sought May's help after dismissing her previous therapist, who suggested she was over-controlled. Although severely limited by symptoms, this interpretation failed to appreciate how her hoarseness and self-control protected her centeredness: "If I opened up, if I communicated, I would lose what little space in life I have" (May, 1969b, p. 75). Still, her need for self-affirmation gave her the courage to continue seeking help in a new relationship.

Mrs. Hutchens' hoarseness and self-control reflected vigilant defense against threats to her center. Her previous therapist failed to appreciate her subjective experience of a direct attack on herself when her defenses were confronted. Mrs. Hutchens eventually learned that Dr. May would not threaten her centeredness and had the following dream:

> She was searching room by room for a baby in an unfinished house at an airport. She thought the baby belonged to someone else, but the other person might let her take it. Now it seemed that she had put the baby in a pocket of her robe (or her mother's robe), and she was seized with anxiety that it would be smothered. Much to her joy, she found that the baby was still alive. Then she had a strange thought, "Shall I kill it?" (May, 1969b, p. 80).

Mrs. Hutchens associated the airport with learning to fly at age 20, a self-affirming act of independence from her parents. The baby reflected the emergence of a still not completely accepted self-consciousness that may be too dangerous to let live. After a few more sessions, Mrs. Hutchens' emerging self-awareness let her consider if she should let her authoritarian parents know she joined another faith and left their church 6 years previously. Her anxiety over separating from her parents and making her own choices then led to fainting spells during therapy and fears she was going crazy. May (1969b) notes:

This is not surprising, for consciousness of one's own desires and affirming them involves accepting one's originality and uniqueness. It implies that one must be prepared not only to be isolated from those parental figures upon whom one has been dependent but at that instant to stand alone in the entire psychic universe as well (p. 81).

Mrs. Hutchens feared both taking responsibility for her choices and also standing in irrevocable isolation from her parents. Although May was largely responsible for bringing existentialism to the United States and adding an optimistic American view, Yalom's (1980) text provides perhaps the most accessible and comprehensive introduction to existential therapy. His analysis describes the ways existential concerns may overlap one another.

Yalom's Existential Approach

The primal source of existential anxiety is to realize that one must die. This ultimate life transition or *boundary condition* may also be triggered by other life transitions; *e.g.*, the death of a friend or family member is problematic for people at several levels, including grief over the loss of someone who appreciated their existence and reminders of their own mortality. As John Donne put it, "Ask not for whom the bell tolls, it tolls for thee." In addition to anxiety, however, such situations also create opportunities for life changes. In Dickens' *A Christmas Carol*, Scrooge changes only after the ghost of Christmas Future confronts him with the specter of his own death. In general, opportunities to explore existential concerns are found in anniversaries, births, and life transitions that bring to mind the next generation's arrival and the passage of years. Important decisions such as career and marital choices create anxiety related to groundlessness and responsibility, but they also eliminate other possibilities (existential guilt) and also elicit death anxiety. Yalom (1980) describes a number of techniques and therapeutic markers that therapists can use to help clients identify their underlying existential issues.

Death *vs.* Existence

As the ultimate boundary condition, death anxiety is often too challenging to confront directly. Except when external events force awareness, few people spend time contemplating their death. However, death is closely associated with the other existential givens: to be alive is to make choices (since "not choosing" is also a choice), to be ultimately alone, and to struggle to find meaning in life. As life transitions and boundaries are identified in therapy, dreams or other symbolic material, Yalom (1980) looks for themes of "specialness" or an "ultimate rescuer;" *e.g.*, his client, Marie, relied on her special beauty to attract a husband who would protect her and give meaning to her life.

Yalom uses a *disidentification* exercise to help people identify existential anxieties that the busyness of everyday life keeps out of awareness. Clients are asked to list eight answers to "Who am I?" and meditate on what life would be like if they relinquished each of those roles. Clients eventually come face-to-face with the existential givens as they eliminate the activities that fill their daily lives. Students of Buddhism recognize this procedure as the way to end suffering by giving up all desire. A similar exercise repeatedly asks clients to answer the question "What do I want?" Clients quickly end up calling out to "… absent parents, spouses, children, friends: 'I want to see you again;' 'I want your love;' 'I want to know you're proud of me;' 'I want you back—I am so lonely'" (Yalom, 1989, p. 3). Clients may also be encouraged to confront existential concerns by marking their current position with an "X" on a line extending from birth to death and meditate for five minutes on the meanings implicit in that line. Clients might be asked to write their epitaph and then imagine what people would say at their funeral. In group therapy, death anxiety may be confronted by calling out names from a hat. As each name is called, clients turn their chair to face away from the group and drop out of the discussion.

Groundlessness vs. Free Will

Groundlessness creates anxiety, but, paradoxically, also provides a sense of free will: if there were clear external grounds for making choices, there would be no reason to choose otherwise. The price of this freedom is the necessity to be responsible for one's choices and actions, not always an easy price to pay. Procrastination, indecisiveness, helplessness, dependency, "losing" control, or being driven by impulses or compulsions are all ways to avoid responsibility for choices. Clients must take responsibility for their problems, no matter how poignant or distressing the circumstances. There is nothing to change and no motivation to do so if clients attribute suffering to other people or circumstances.

Similarly, there is no need to change if a rescuer such as the therapist can be induced to be responsible for the change. When therapists feel burdened by their client's problems, it is likely their client expects to be rescued and has shifted responsibility to them. Responsibility avoidance markers include helplessness, blaming, explaining, agonizing over decisions, and saying "I can't." Therapists need to let themselves be maneuvered several times to see how clients maneuver them to support their avoidance. Once the relational pattern is clear, therapists can help clients become aware how they avoid responsibility and get others to support them. The therapist's warmth, acceptance, and empathy help build the trust and support clients need to confront how avoidance of responsibility has contributed to their problems.

Yalom (1980) emphasizes the importance of will in transforming choice into action. Helping clients become aware of their choices is not enough: choices must be realized by acting in the world. This requires will, which combines choice, commitment, and determination. May (1969c) suggests that wishes precede will. It is the wish that makes needs meaningful; e.g., wishes transform indiscriminate sexual needs into desire for a specific partner who is attractive and promises a meaningful relationship.

Rank (1945) suggests that emotions motivate acts of will during the expression or inhibition of impulses. Parents need to balance their response to a child's angry *counter-will* or resistance to limits: children's emotions become constricted if their impulsive acts are always punished. They may develop *positive will* and do what is required, but their constricted emotional repertoire prevents them from sustaining meaningful relationships. Conversely, if there are no limits on impulsive actions, then *will-power* fails to develop and children become impulse-ridden and antisocial. But if appropriate expression of impulses is allowed, children develop *creative will*, willing what one wants, and are able to act upon their wishes. Creative will mobilizes people's emotional life and allows them to realize meaningful choices.

Farber (1966) notes that many important choices are not made consciously and are only inferred after the fact. Although people are obviously responsible for their choice of partners, such choices are often experienced as "falling in love," something that happened to them. Conscious choices are directed toward specific objects or desired outcomes and can be influenced by exhortations to exercise will-power, effort, and determination. In contrast, unconscious choices cannot be influenced so directly. Farber (1966) notes that:

> I can will knowledge, but not wisdom; going to bed, but not sleeping; eating, but not hunger; meekness, but not humility; scrupulosity, but not virtue, self-assertion or bravado, but not courage; lust, but not love; commiseration, but not sympathy; congratulations, but not admiration; religiosity, but not faith; reading, but not understanding (p. 15).

Therapists help ambivalent clients with unconscious decisional anxieties explore the costs and benefits of change *vs.* staying the same. Reframing "not changing" as a decision may help them gain insight into how they create their own world in passive as well as active ways. Before clients are ready to move on, they may need to resolve neurotic guilt over opportunities missed due to inaction. Hermeneutic exploration of meaning helps clients understand how context, belief, and choice all influence one another. Yalom (1980) quotes Mark Twain on how contexts influence beliefs, "When I was seventeen I was convinced my father was a damn fool. When I was twenty-one I was astounded by how much the old man had learned in four years" (p. 350).

Isolation *vs.* Intimacy

Death, partings, and the necessity to make life-altering choices are all times when people need to confront the existential isolation of realizing no one else can fully appreciate their inner experience, fears, and loneliness. They may seek a surrogate parent, a guru, or ultimate rescuer for reassurance, but this requires attention to the rescuer's wishes and ignoring their own wishes or inner experience. Alienation from inner experience has the short-term advantage of suppressing awareness of existential isolation. However, the long-term effect is to create an It-It relationship in which the self and others are experienced as objects to be manipulated, not selves with independent, inner experiences capable of I-Thou relationships. It-It relationship markers include histories of disrupted relationships, promiscuity, narcissism, dependency, or obsessive conformity. Loneliness, depression, dissociation, or psychosis may result when It-It strategies fail. Interpersonal or intrapersonal isolation (self-alienation) are the only alternatives to confronting fears of existential isolation. Letting go of unrealistic hopes of fusion makes it possible to relate to the other without neediness, the hallmark of an I-Thou relationship.

A therapist's awareness and interest, and acceptance of ambivalence and constricted range of relatedness, all help clients confront their isolation and enter into an I-Thou relationship (Kaiser, 1965). Existential therapists are interested in the unique qualities of their clients' *being* in the here-and-now relationship as well as their potential for *becoming*. To minimize inequality, therapists seldom address issues of transference or counter-transference. Client self-disclosures require therapists to take responsibility for their own feelings and respond to clients with authentic, reciprocal self-disclosures that are sensitive to client feelings. They own their feelings: rather than "You bore me," they might say, "I'm not staying focused just now. Have you noticed me drifting?"

Initially, clients find it hard to reciprocate in the dual self-and-other perspective of an I-Thou relationship. However, as they experience their therapist's interest and acceptance, they become less defensive, begin to communicate freely, and are more open to the therapist's perspective. As they enter an I-Thou relationship, they also find the courage to confront existential loneliness. By entering into an authentic relationship, clients have already chosen to change.

Yalom (1980) suggests ways to help clients relate more authentically. Most importantly, therapists confront instances when clients ascribe responsibility for problems or meeting needs to someone else. Clients are asked to "reverse" excuses: instead of "I can't be with another person because of my drinking problem," they might be asked to say "I drink so I won't have to be with another person." Clients might also be asked to rate their "risk-taking" with others on a 1–10 scale and then to meditate on "What would happen if I moved it up a notch or two?" As clients develop trust in the therapist's genuineness, they are able to accept responsibility and confront existential loneliness. Although difficult, this path leads to the openness, selflessness, compassion, and empathy that I-Thou relationships require without needing anything else from the therapist.

Meaninglessness *vs.* Meaning

Yalom (1980) summarizes the existential position in a quote from the Indian philosopher, Bhaqway Shree Rajneesh, "Existence has no goal. It is pure journey." Even so, people always search for the meaning of their experiences, even in random patterns such as clouds or Rorschach blots. Nietzsche, the German philosopher, wrote "If we have our own why of life, we shall get along with almost any how." This statement reflects Western assumptions that life can have meanings that transcend death. Finding meaning in life thus serves to blunt existential anxieties surrounding freedom, isolation, and death.

Generally, meanings develop from actions and experiences valued by others in the individual's culture. Shared values help people coexist with each other and assuage feelings of isolation. As well as defining what is meaningful for a culture, values provide the grounds for making choices. In stable, traditional cultures existential issues are not typically a problem; but if rapid social change disrupts social norms and values (*social anomie*), then emotional problems and social disorder increase (Bernard, Gebauer, & Maio, 2006; Fromm, 1941). People are left with no grounds for deciding how they should act in changing societies with no consensus about what is valued or meaningful. Not surprisingly, people in modern society are uniquely vulnerable to existential concerns, especially if social anomie is combined with a life transition.

Sometimes, questions of meaning are obvious in a client's lack of direction in life; but even clients with apparently rich and full lives may lack a sense of fulfillment, while others restlessly engage in sensation-seeking. A search for meaning should be the focus of therapy for these clients. Unlike the other existential givens, awareness of life's ultimate meaninglessness creates feelings of emptiness or boredom rather than panic. Increased leisure increases empty feelings as people need less time for the necessities of survival and have more time to ponder existential questions. With problems of meaning, therapists focus less on increased awareness and more on action and helping clients discover their own personal meanings. As Yalom (1980) suggests:

> [W]hen it comes to meaninglessness, the effective therapist must help patients to look away from the question: to embrace the solution of engagement rather than to plunge in and through the problem of meaninglessness. The question of meaning in life is, as the Buddha taught, not edifying. One must immerse oneself in the river of life and let the question drift away (p. 483).

Therapists use *dereflection* to help clients become more engaged in life and less self-absorbed (Frankl, 1963). Dereflection directs questions of meaning to exploring self-transcendent activities and goals: creativity, seeking joyful life experiences and relationships, or a "heroic" stance toward suffering; *e.g.*, Candy Lightner, who lost her daughter to a drunken driver, modeled transcendence of unavoidable suffering with her advocacy group, *Mothers Against Drunk Driving*.

Because meaning develops from activities, not through reflection, therapy helps clients remove obstacles to engagement. Clients need to look away from unanswerable existential questions and make a leap of faith. The search for self-transcendent meanings is spiritual. It is also healthy. Southwick, Vythilingam, and Charney (2005) found that religion, spirituality, optimism, and altruism all enhance resilience to stress, depression, and anxiety. Maddi's (2004) existentially based psychoeducation program helped participants increase their hardiness and resilience to stress. Maddi's participants receive …

> … feedback about their efforts to improve their life circumstances and are taught how to use this sense of their effectiveness to deepen their hardiness attitudes of commitment, control, and challenge. They come to see themselves as (a) continually immersed in the world of people and events around them, (b) willing and able to try to influence the outcomes that are involved and (c) constantly learning in the process so as to grow in wisdom

for handling future situations. When the program is over, trainees leave with enhanced existential courage, which motivates them to choose the future rather than the past .... These attitudes lead to perceiving stressful circumstances as (a) normal provocations to development (challenge), (b) manageable (control), and (c) worth investing in (commitment) (pp. 294–295).

Case Illustration

Bugental (1999) wrote, "Case formulations can so easily become like butterflies impaled on pins and put in display cases." Existential therapists avoid treatment planning and prefer to work with the clients' continuous process of self-discovery. They focus how clients explore and utilize their abilities during therapy and then coach clients on expanding self-awareness and understanding. Yalom's (1989) case study, *In search of the dreamer*, illustrates the difficulty and value of responding authentically to clients who initially seem uninteresting.

Presenting Problems

Marvin, a 64-year-old, recently retired accountant, had suffered for the prior 6 months from migraine headaches subsequent to impotence during intercourse. He was referred to Dr. Yalom by a neurologist who could not control the headaches medically. Marvin reported rapid cycling mood changes over the past year, but noted that lithium did not control the mood swings. Marvin came prepared to defend the linkage of impotence and headaches with a 3-foot-long chart for the previous 4 months detailing ratings of sexual performance and the intensity and duration of subsequent migraines: "Sex is at the root of everything. Isn't that what you fellows always say? Well in my case, you may be right" (p. 230). He reports an extremely harmonious relationship with his wife with a wonderful sex life until the impotence and headaches developed. Marvin spoke in a rehearsed, pedantic manner, remaining detached from feelings about his symptoms. Marvin denied any connection between retirement and the headaches, saying "You've got to be kidding. This is what I've been working for—so I *can* retire." He also resisted attempts to explore his marriage noting that his wife, Phyllis, and he had little faith in psychiatry: "We've known two couples with marital problems who saw psychiatrists and both ended up in the divorce court" (p. 234).

Preliminary Recommendation

Before Yalom could give his recommendations at the third meeting, Marvin described a dream series requested by Yalom at their first meeting. One dream in particular seemed to suggest linkage between symptoms and retirement:

The ground under my house was liquefying. [*Metaphor for groundlessness subsequent to retirement?*] I had a giant auger [*Penis?*] and knew that I would have to drill down sixty-five feet [*his next birthday?*] to save the house [*Undo the groundlessness?*]. I hit a layer of solidrock, and the vibrations woke me up (p. 239).

Despite the intriguing nature of Marvin's dreams, Yalom felt that Marvin's lack of curiosity or psychological-mindedness and his resistance to deeper exploration argued against an uncovering therapy. Accordingly, he recommended that Marvin and his wife seek an 8 to 12 week course of behaviorally oriented marital therapy. Marvin said he would consider Yalom's idea and get back to him. A few days later, he scheduled another appointment, but came by himself as Phyllis refused to come. He acknowledged he had understated his problems with Phyllis; also his mood swings related to "difficulties with sex" had a 20-year history. His headaches were so bad the prior week he went to the emergency room for an injection. Nightmares also interfered with his sleep; Yalom asked him to put his notes aside and describe the dream in the present tense:

Therapy Process (Copyright © 1989 Irvin Yalom. Excerpts reprinted by permission of Basic Books, a member of the Perseus Books Group)

M: The two men are tall, pale, and very gaunt. In a dark meadow they glide along in silence. They are dressed entirely in black. With tall stovepipe hats, long-tailed coats, black spats, and shoes, they resemble Victorian undertakers or temperance workers. Suddenly, they come upon a carriage, ebony black, cradling a baby girl swaddled in black gauze. Wordlessly, one of the men begins to push the carriage. After a short distance he stops, walks around to the front, and with his black cane, which now has a glowing white tip, he leans over, parts the gauze, and methodically inserts the white tip into the baby's vagina.

Y: [*Amazed that Marvin could have such a dream.*] Why was the dream a nightmare? Precisely what part of it was frightening?

M: As I think about it *now*, the last thing—putting the cane in the baby's vagina—is the horrible part. Yet *not when I was having the dream*. It was everything else, the silent footsteps, the blackness, the sense of deep foreboding. The whole dream was soaked in fear.

Y: What feeling was there *in* the dream about the insertion of the cane into the baby's vagina?

M: If anything, that part seemed almost soothing, as though it quieted the dream—or rather, it tried to. It didn't really .... None of this makes any sense to me. I've never believed in dreams (pp. 242–243).

Yalom wants to stay with the dream, which seems to say that Marvin approaches death full of dread. Attempts to ward off this dread with sexuality are not enough. However, Yalom also felt it necessary to explore why, despite their idyllic marriage, Phyllis refused to help her husband by coming in even once. Marvin then described Phyllis' agoraphobia and fear of people visiting their house. He explained that they've not entertained at home for decades. Family visitors are taken to a restaurant and Marvin packs up his collection of political buttons to show interested parties elsewhere. If he were to break this rule, "It would be a month of Sundays before I got 'laid' again." Yalom reiterates that marital therapy would be the best course, but agrees to see Marvin alone twice weekly, warning him that painful thoughts may emerge. He begins by asking Marvin to associate to the last dream, to say anything that comes to mind. Marvin shakes his head and Yalom asks about the white-tipped cane:

M: [*smirking*] I was wondering when you'd get around to that! Didn't I say earlier you fellows see sex at the root of everything? [*Actually, Yalom thinks sex is defending against death!*]

Y: But it's *your* dream, Marvin. And your cane. You created it, what do you make of it? And what do you make of the allusions to death—undertakers, silence, blackness, the whole atmosphere of dread and foreboding? [*Not surprisingly, Marvin chooses to discuss sex.*]

M: Well, you might be interested in something sexual that happened yesterday afternoon—that would be about ten hours before the dream. I was lying in bed still recovering from my migraine. Phyllis came over and gave me a head and neck massage. She then kept on going and massaged my back, then my legs, and then my penis. She undressed me and then took off all her clothes [*Marvin nearly always initiated sex.*] At first, I wouldn't respond.

Y: How come?

M: To tell you the truth, I was scared. I was just getting over my worst migraine, and I was afraid I'd fail and get another migraine. But Phyllis started sucking my cock and got me hard. I've never seen her so persistent. I finally said, "Let's go, a good lay might be just the thing to get rid of tension"… [*pause*] I was doing pretty well, but just as I was getting ready to come, Phyllis said, "There are other reasons for making love than to get rid of tension." Well that did it! I lost it in a second.

Y: Marvin, did you tell Phyllis exactly how you felt about her timing?

M: Her timing is not good—never has been. But I was too riled up to talk. Afraid of what I'd say. If I say the wrong thing, she can make my life hell—turn off the sexual spigot altogether.

Y: What sort of thing might you say?

M: I'm afraid of my impulses—my murderous and sexual impulses …. Do you remember, years ago, a news story of a man who killed his wife by pouring acid on her? Horrible thing! Yet I've often thought about that crime. I can understand how fury toward a woman could lead to a crime like that.

Y: [*Alarmed that primitive feelings were being uncovered too quickly, Yalom switches to sex.*] Marvin, you said you're frightened also by your sexual impulses. What do you mean?

M: My sex drive has always been too strong. I've been told that's true of many bald men. A sign of too much male hormone. Is that true?

Y: [*Deflecting the distraction.*] Keep going.
M: Well I've had to keep it under rein all my life because Phyllis has got strong
      ideas about how much sex we will have. And it's always the same—two times
      a week, some exceptions for birthdays and holidays.
Y: You've got some feelings about that?
M: Sometimes. But sometimes I think restraints are good. Without them I might
      run wild.
Y: What does "running wild" mean? Do you mean extramarital affairs?
M: … I don't know what I mean, but at times I've wondered what it would have
      been like to have married a woman who wanted and enjoyed sex as much as
      me.
Y: What do you think? Your life would have been very different?
M: Let me back up a minute. I shouldn't have used the word *enjoy* a few minutes
      ago. Phyllis enjoys sex. It's just that she never seems to *want* it. Instead, she
      … dispenses it—if I'm good. These are the times I feel cheated and angry
      (pp. 246–248).

During the following weeks, Yalom encouraged exploration of retirement and the
marriage, but not to the degree that might destabilize the marriage or evoke unbear-
able death anxiety. Marvin became more cooperative, open, and mysteriously the
migraines disappeared. He continued to bring in dreams that expressed hope; *e.g.*,
a teacher looking for children interested in painting on a large blank canvas. Soon,
however, Marvin dreams about a heart transplant surgeon who is more concerned
about procedures than where the donor heart came from.

   Yalom understood this as a warning against being more interested in the dreams
than in Marvin and shifted his focus to Marvin's early life. An Oedipal situation
was revealed when Marvin was about seven and his mother banished his father
from her bedroom. The father soon left their lives altogether and Marvin became
his mother's constant companion and confidant. Phyllis was his first and only date.
Yalom noted that Marvin can be understood from three perspectives: existential, in
terms of death anxiety; psychodynamic, as intimacy and sexuality were associated
with catastrophic oedipal anxiety; and communicational, with the marital dynamic
disrupted by retirement. The dreams soon returned to core issues:

M: I saw a car with a curious shape, like a large, long box on wheels. It was black
      and patent-leather shiny. I was struck by the fact that the only windows were
      in the back and were very askew—so that you could not really look through
      them. [*His first association was* "It's not a coffin."]
Y: The car has no front windows, Marvin. Think about that. What comes to
      you?
M: I don't know. Without front windows you don't know where you're heading.
Y: How would that apply to you, to what you're facing ahead of you in your life
      now?
M: Retirement. I'm a little slow, but I'm beginning to get it. But I don't worry
      about retirement. Why don't I *feel* anything?

Y: The feeling is there. It seeps into your dreams. Maybe it's too painful to feel.
      Maybe the pain gets short-circuited and put onto other things. Look how often
      you've said, "Why should I get so upset about my sexual performance? It
      doesn't make sense." One of our main jobs is to sort things out and restore the
      feelings to where they belong (pp. 253–254).

Soon, Marvin started to have more explicit dreams about aging and death, including
a woman he had known 45 years previously. In the dream, "she looked up at me
and her face was a hideous mucous-filled skull" (p. 255). As fearful as that dream
was, Marvin reflected that the dream with the gaunt undertakers had the strongest
impact, perhaps it was a symbol he had been too temperate. He'd known for a
couple years he deadened himself all his life. He related that he followed a Psychology Today magazine article's suggestion one day to have a final conversation with
important people in his life. Despite imagining saying goodbye to his mother and
to his father, no feelings came, no matter how hard he tried to force them. He cried
that day in Yalom's office. A few days later, just beginning intercourse, he suddenly
said, "Maybe the doctor is right, maybe all my sexual anxiety is really anxiety about
death" and immediately ejaculated prematurely.

The next dreams reflected anxiety over becoming aware of too much too fast,
grief over lost opportunities, and that it may be too late to change life's course; *e.g.*,
he was climbing a mountain and heard his mother overtaking him with a message
that someone is dying; Marvin knew it was himself that was dying and woke in a
sweat. Over 6 months, Marvin had discovered a rich, but frightening inner world.
His initial enthusiasm became tinged with regret for the children he never had, the
father he never knew, the house that was empty of friends and family, and a life
work that might have had more meaning than making money. He also reported
more open and honest communication with Phyllis, talking in detail about his work
with Yalom. They joked with one another about receiving a two-for-one therapy
bargain.

She was struck by Marvin's regret over spending his life making money rather
than giving something back to the world. Phyllis said "if it were true for me, it was
true in spades for her—that she had led a totally self-centered life, that she's never
given anything of herself" (pp. 261–262). She especially regretted not seeing a fer-
tility doctor when they failed to have children. He described how Phyllis had become agitated by her own confrontation with mortality. One night he discovered her
kneeling and praying over and over, "The mother of God will protect me" (p. 262).
That night he had another significant dream:

M: There was a statue of a female god on a pedestal in a large crowded room. It
      looked like Christ but was wearing a flowing orange pastel dress. On the other
      side of the room there was an actress with a long white dress. The actress and
      the statue traded places. Somehow they traded dresses, and the statue got down
      and the actress climbed up on the pedestal. [*Marvin thought the dream meant he
      turned women into goddesses and would be safe only if he appeased them. That
      was why he dreaded Phyllis' anger and why she could offer relief with sex.*]

Y: You do grant her magical powers—like a goddess. She can heal you with just a smile, an embrace, or by taking you inside her. No wonder you take great pains not to displease her .... Sex becomes a life or death proposition .... No wonder sex has been difficult ....

M: So there are two issues. First, I'm asking sex to do something beyond its power. Second, I'm giving almost supernatural power to Phyllis to heal me or protect me ....

Y: There's something else that's important. Consider things now from Phyllis' side: if she, in her love for you, accepts the role of goddess that you assign her, think of what that role does to her own possibilities for growth. In order to stay on her pedestal, she was never able to talk to you about *her* pain—or not until very recently .... So in a sense she was following your unspoken wishes by not openly expressing her uncertainties, by pretending to be stronger than she felt. I have a hunch that's one of the reasons she wouldn't come into therapy ... she picked up on your wish that she *not* change. I also have a hunch that if you ask her now, she might come.

M: God, we are really on the same wavelength now. Phyllis and I have already discussed it and she is ready to talk to you (pp. 263–264).

Next session, Phyllis agreed she had to be solicitous toward Marvin most of the time, but that she also felt intellectually inferior to others because of her limited education. She also dreaded that people might ask her what she did. She felt the only thing she had to offer Marvin was sex. She also was disturbed by Marvin's retirement: not only might he "take over" the house, but he'd see how little she actually did during the day. She said she'd felt too old to change for the past 30 years, but seeing Marvin change had given her new courage.

The next few sessions reinforced their more open communication and provided guidance for how Phyllis could help Marvin's sexual functioning. The meaning of Phyllis' agoraphobia had already changed, so Yalom felt comfortable using a paradoxic injunction to help her move out of the house. He instructed Marvin to tell Phyllis every two hours, punctually, "Phyllis, please don't leave the house. I need to know you are there at all times to take care of me, and prevent me from being frightened" (p. 267). Both thought this was funny, but persevered. Phyllis was progressively more irritated with Marvin's repetition even though she knew he was merely following instructions; but began going to the library and shopping alone, venturing farther than she had in years.

At the one-year follow-up with Marvin, Yalom played the tape recording of their first session. Marvin's comment was "Who is that jerk, anyway?" He seldom had nightmares, his mood swings moderated, and although he occasionally was impotent, he brooded less about it and continued free from migraines. He had gone back to work, but as a real estate developer and manager. Phyllis had joined a women's therapy group to work on her social phobia and was enrolled in several college courses. Their relationship was still very good, but Marvin did feel ignored at times with all Phyllis' newfound activities.

Carl Rogers' Client Centered Therapy

Carl Rogers' *Client Centered Therapy* (1951) is a phenomenological approach that makes very few assumptions about client issues. Although existentialists avoid categorizing people, they respond selectively to signs of existential issues, which can reinforce client explorations of those categories. Instead, Rogers used the client's language to understand their experience in their own terms. He believed clients have the ability to solve their own problems, as long as they do not try to live up to others' expectations. Clients have access unavailable to anyone else about what troubles them, their needs, and the resources available to resolve their problems. The role of therapists is simply to be fully present in the here-and-now moment (*genuine*), listen with understanding (*empathy*), and be nonjudgmental and open to their client's experience (*warmth* and *unconditional positive regard*).

Rogers originally termed his approach *Nondirective Therapy* (1942), but later chose the term, client centered, following research by his colleague, Charles Truax. Truax (1966) found that clients notice which experiences interest their therapists, *e.g.*, emotions, and then explore those feelings in depth, with insight, and with an expressive style similar to the therapist. Despite efforts to avoid influencing client narratives, clients want guidance and quickly discern what the therapist considers important. Rogers also chose the term client centered to minimize the importance of nondirective techniques such as *reflection of feeling* and to highlight the importance of entering the client's experiential world with empathic understanding. Although techniques help therapists identify more closely with client experiences, the focus needs to be on understanding the client, not on how to gain that understanding. Later in life, Rogers expanded his theoretical interests to include education and international conflict resolution, which led him to describe his work with normal populations as *person centered.*

Conceptual Framework

Like other humanists, Rogers was concerned about normative research that categorizes people, but saw no contradiction between treating people as unique individuals and empirical tests of therapy process or outcome. His pioneering research led him to postulate six *necessary and sufficient* conditions for therapeutic facilitation of personality change (Rogers, 1957):

1. *Relationship*: At least two people are in a relationship meaningful to both; *e.g.*, *pretherapy* (Prouty, 2001) is a recent person-centered approach to help clients with psychotic symptoms, who are unable to communicate well enough to form meaningful relationships.
2. *Vulnerability*: Clients experience anxiety-provoking incongruities in their lives that motivate seeking and participating in therapy.

3. *Genuineness*: Therapists are in a state of congruence, self-acceptance that allows awareness of the therapist's own experience and other-acceptance that lets them identify empathically with their client's experience. The therapist's perceptions are then not distorted by disowned needs to present the self in an artificial way or to see the client in an inaccurate way. Instead, the therapist is comfortable in self-disclosure and willing to share inner feelings experienced in the here-and-now relationship.
4. *Unconditional Positive Regard*: Therapists experience clients with unconditional acceptance, as is, with no need for the client to be different. Acceptance is communicated with a warmth and genuineness that provides a corrective emotional experience for clients; this allows self-acceptance instead of trying to be what others need them to be. The therapist's consistent prizing and caring allows the client to be more self-accepting.
5. *Accurate Empathy*: Therapists enter into the client's experiential world of thoughts, feelings, and needs and communicate this awareness to the client while maintaining clear boundaries and sense of self. Although an initial reflection of a client's inner experience may be faulty, therapists use the client's feedback to continue to make reflections as accurately as possible. Only the client has direct knowledge of that inner experience.
6. *Perceptions of Genuineness*: Clients perceive the therapist's understanding and acceptance as a genuine human response. Client *perception* is critical: Bachelor (1988) found accurate empathy for some clients was shown by their therapist's cognitive understanding, while for others, it was shown by their therapist's *feeling with* them as they experienced strong emotion.

Research has focused on the "necessary and sufficient" conditions. Kirschenbaum and Jourdan (2005) conclude that decades of research have validated "… empathy, unconditional positive regard, and, possibly, congruence—as being critical components of effective therapy" (p. 37). They note these conditions are not always "sufficient" to determine positive outcomes, nor are they always "necessary" as good outcomes may occur even in their absence. The mixed results for congruence emphasize the importance of client perceptions and, in general, results based on client rather than observer ratings offer more support (Asay & Lambert, 2001).

Theory of Personality and Behavior

Rogers suggests, "Every individual exists in a continually changing world of experience of which he is the center" (1957, p. 483). This center or *phenomenal field* is the person's reality, but only part of it is conscious or symbolized in words. Over time, salient parts of the phenomenal field are differentiated into a *self-concept*. The organism's basic drive is to preserve, enhance, and *self-actualize* its inherent potential. Emotion is part of the holistic response to the individual's phenomenal field and facilitates self-preservation and self-actualization. Children's innate potential unfolds naturally and they will adapt well to their environment if physical needs are met and caregivers provide *unconditional positive regard*.

Unfortunately, caregivers may set *conditions of worth* that children must meet to gain the caregivers' positive regard. Some conditions are unavoidable as small children explore their environment, and endanger themselves or others. Children learn appropriate limits to their autonomy if this happens occasionally, but with constant disapproval or punishment they learn to ignore or distort their organismic experience and attend to what others desire. They introject what others seem to value into an *ideal self* and their immediate organismic experience is devalued.

Discrepancies between the organismic, real self and a perceived, ideal self may threaten a clients' self-organization. Resulting anxiety distorts self and other perceptions and makes it hard for clients to adapt to the real world. "Psychological maladjustment exists when the organism denies to awareness significant sensory and visceral experience, which consequently are not symbolized and organized into the gestalt of the self-structure" (Rogers, 1957, p. 510). In contrast, "Psychological adjustment exists when the concept of the self is such that all the sensory and visceral experiences of the organism are, or may be, assimilated on a symbolic level into a consistent relationship with the concept of self" (p. 513).

Therapeutic Intervention

Rogers had faith that humans were intrinsically good as long as there was no need to distort perceptions of reality to live up to an internalized ideal self. He saw health as the person's capacity to self-actualize inherent potentials and be *fully functioning*. Rogers' *growth* principle postulates that everyone has the ability to meet all their needs, given an accepting environment. Genuine unconditional positive regard and empathy that demonstrates the client's experience is understood are the necessary and sufficient conditions to facilitate that growth. Rogers suggested that therapists reflect and paraphrase client statements in order to maintain a nondirective, phenomenological stance. The therapist's goals are to:

1. Respond to expressed feelings, not content;
2. Clarify the client's feelings;
3. Accept the client's feelings.

Although still part of his approach, these goals focused more attention on technique than on entering the client's world. As a result, Rogers de-emphasized nondirective methods and shifted his emphasis to the effective therapist's core attributes of warmth, empathy, and genuineness.

Today, research supports their importance in facilitating the therapeutic alliance regardless of theoretical orientation (*e.g.*, Hubble, Duncan, & Miller, 1999). If clients perceive warmth, empathy, and genuineness, they are comfortable in the therapeutic relationship, have less need to conform to external standards, and are more open to their immediate organismic experience. Because life is only experienced in the present moment, client centered therapists focus on the client's immediate, *here-*

and-now experience. With continued positive regard, clients can then attend to their organismic experience and have less need to live up to an ideal self.

Pretherapy

Rogers' Wisconsin Project (Rogers, Gendlin, Kiesler, & Truax, 1967; Truax, 1970) examined therapist adherence to the core conditions of warmth, empathy, and genuineness in working with hospitalized patients diagnosed with schizophrenia. The results were disappointing, but patients with the most empathic therapists did show a trend toward reduced hospital time. Prouty (1990) suggested this poor showing reflected the difficulty of making meaningful contact with hospitalized patients, Rogers' first criterion for therapeutic change. The problems such patients have in making meaningful contact is illustrated by Haley's (1963) analysis of a dialog between two patients. He proposes that "schizophrenese" is a paradoxic way to communicate that communication is impossible, illustrating this with dialog between "Jones" and "Smith":

Jones: (*Laughs loudly, then pauses*) I'm McDougal myself. (This actually is not his name.)
Smith: What do you do for a living, little fellow? Work on a ranch or something?
Jones: No, I'm a civilian seaman. Supposed to be high mucka-muck society (p. 93).

Haley notes that Jones' apparent friendly overture is negated by his awkward laugh, tone of voice, and by using an alias: even the denial is denied! Smith's apparently friendly reply is disqualified by an unfriendly comment on Jones' size. He further disqualified their presence in a mental hospital by asking if Jones works on a ranch, thereby denying he is talking to a mental patient. Jones also denies he's a patient, stating he's a seaman and denies this saying he's high society.

Pretherapy (Prouty,1990, 2001) is an integration of Rogerian and Gestalt ideas that uses *contact reflections* to help therapists make contact with patients. Contact reflections are literal descriptions or duplications that "point at the concrete" of whatever clients present.

1. *Situational reflections* attempt contact with reality by describing what the client is doing, "John is looking out the window."
2. *Facial reflections* describe or interpret emotional expressions, "You look sad. I see tears."
3. *Word-for-word reflections* duplicate sentence fragments, isolated words, or sounds uttered by the client.
4. *Body reflections* begin with description, "Your arm is in the air" and are completed by the therapist assuming the same posture.
5. *Reiterative reflections* implement the *principle of recontact*. When any reflection elicits a response, the therapist repeats it, strengthening the communicative bond, "You just smiled when I said 'tree'" (Prouty, 2001, pp. 591–592).

Contact reflections help restore (a) *reality contact*, (b) *affective contact*, or awareness of the client's own feelings, and (c) *communicative contact*, which enables meaningful psychological contact. These functions are measured by *contact behaviors*, the degree to which patients talk realistically with another person about people, things, or events and express emotions in the body or face.

In the following illustration, Dorothy works with Prouty's student (G. Prouty, Humanistic psychotherapy for people with schizophrenia. In D. J. Cain & J. Seeman (Eds.), *Humanistic psychotherapies: Handbook of research and practice*, p. 594. © 2001 American Psychological Association. Reprinted by permission):

T: *"Dorothy" is a 65-year-old woman who is one of the more regressed women on X ward. She was mumbling something (as she usually did). This time I could hear certain words in her confusion. I reflected only the words I could understand. After about 10 minutes, I could hear a complete sentence.*

D: Come with me.

T: Come with me. *Word-for-word (WFW) reflection; the patient led me to the corner of the day-room. We stood there silently for what seemed to be a very long time. Since I couldn't communicate with her, I watched her body movements and closely reflected these.*

D: Cold. *The patient puts her hand on the wall.*

T: Cold. *WFW; I put my hand on the wall (Body Reflection--BR) and repeated the word. She had been holding my hand all along, but when I reflected her, she would tighten her grip. Dorothy would begin to mumble word fragments. I was careful to reflect only the words I could understand. What she was saying began to make sense.*

D: I don't know what this is anymore. The walls and chairs don't mean anything anymore. *Touching the wall; Reality contact, existential autism.*

T: You don't know what this is any more. The chairs and walls don't mean anything to you anymore. *WFW; Touching the wall, BR.*

D: *The patient begins to cry; Affective contact; Pause.*

D: I don't like it here. I'm so tired … so tired. *This time she spoke clearly: Communicative contact.*

T: You're so tired, so tired. *WFW; As I gently touched her arm, this time it was I who tightened my grip on her hand.*

D: *The patient smiled and told me to sit in a chair directly in front of her and began to braid my hair.*

Prouty (2001) reported success with pretherapy in several case studies, but controlled outcome research is still needed. He cites the closely related approach of the Soteria House projects in San Francisco and Berne, Switzerland, which have reported success in treating schizophrenia (*e.g.*, Mosher, Vallone, & Menn, 1995). Soteria Houses are small residential programs that train non-professional staff to "be with" clients, validating their experiences in nonjudgmental ways. Mosher and Menn (1978) describe six elements of Soteria House:

1. Positive expectations of learning from residents' behavior;
2. Flexible roles and relationships;

3. Sufficient residential time so patients can identify with staff's validation of their experience;
4. Staff is responsible to "be with" residents, with no expectation that they must "do" something;
5. Tolerance for "crazy" behavior with no need to control it;
6. Normalizing the experience of psychotic symptoms.

Although only 7–10% of residents received minimal levels of drugs, comparable discharge rates and lower relapse rates were reported, compared to standard drug treatment (Matthews, Roper, Mosher, & Menn, 1979).

Motivational Interviewing (MI)

William Miller based his Rogerian model of motivational interviewing (MI) on a series of studies evaluating behavioral self-control interventions (Miller, Taylor, & West, 1980). Their control groups received an initial assessment, advice, encouragement, and a self-help book. Finding no advantage for the behavioral interventions, they provided more behavioral training sessions and also measured counselors' empathy toward their clients. Again, behavioral self-control was no better than the control condition, but empathy ratings accounted for 67% of outcome variance at 6 months, 50% at 12 months, and 26% at 24-month follow-ups.

Inspired by these results, Miller and Rollnick (2002) developed client centered, process-directive interventions that favor *change* over *resistance* talk. MI is often used to motivate clients and prepare them for other therapeutic approaches. It is effective with treatment-resistant problems such as substance abuse, dual diagnosis, eating disorders, and encouraging clients to make health-related behavioral changes (Burke, Arkowitz, & Menchola, 2003). MI appears to be as effective as other approaches and usually requires less time (Hettema, Steele, & Miller, 2005).

Conceptual Framework

MI assumes clients are ambivalent about change since they experience their problems, *e.g.*, substance abuse, as solutions to other, more immediate problems. Problematic behaviors provide both gains and losses, so clients are in a classic approach-avoidance conflict (Dollard & Miller, 1950). Increasing approach tendencies by exhortation, persuasion, or advice only increases conflict and produces resistance. Reactance research (Brehm, 1966) suggests many people react oppositionally to advice, which they perceive as limiting their freedom. A less directive approach is required before difficult, reactant (resistant), or precontemplative clients are "ready, willing, and able" to benefit from therapy.

Self-perception theory (Bem, 1972) suggests people become committed to positions they defend. MI therapists accordingly use Socratic methods to evoke and reflect client statements that suggest readiness, willingness, ability, or commitment to change. Readiness, willingness, and ability all predict levels of commitment *vs.* resistance talk, but only commitment talk itself leads to changed behavior (Amrheim, Miller, Yahne, Palmer, & Fulcher, 2003). Therapists "roll with resistance talk," accept and frame it as natural ambivalence toward trying new things and giving up old ways. If clients have no need to resist pressures to change, it is easier for them to commit to change.

Client and Therapist Activities

MI uses Socratic questioning and empathic, reflective listening to establish a collaborative, working alliance and evoke the client's *intrinsic motivation* for change. MI therapists do not teach, argue, or persuade; instead, they support their client's autonomy and freedom to act upon their own values and goals. They help clients assess relative costs and benefits of changing or not changing problematic behaviors using a *decisional balance sheet* and make informed decisions; *e.g.*, an alcoholic client might note that drinking is relaxing and lets him socialize with friends, but has the potential costs of losing his family or damaging his health. On the other hand, abstention would lead to less family conflict and help with money problems, but would leave him with no way to handle stress and no venue for meeting with his friends.

Miller and Rollnick (2002) consider motivation an *interpersonal process* in which therapists respond selectively as clients *develop discrepancies* between the advantages of the *status quo vs.* changing. MI's goal is for clients to engage in any of four categories of *change talk*:

1. *Disadvantages of the status quo*: recognizing their current state or behavior is undesirable;
2. *Advantages of change*: recognizing positive benefits that might occur with change;
3. *Optimism for change*: confidence or hope in their ability to change;
4. *Intention to change*: desire, willingness, intentions, or commitment to making a change.

MI therapists are process-directive, encouraging talk about ambivalence, but are nondirective regarding decisions: clients decide whether to change and, if so, how and when.

The MI therapist's job is to reflect, intensify, and help clients resolve their ambivalence. Reasons for change and for resisting change are both acknowledged, but therapists give greater emphasis to the resistance side of this dialectic, encouraging clients to address the change side. "*It is the client who should be voicing the arguments for change*" (Miller & Rollnick, 2002, p. 22;emphasis in the original). MI therapists follow four general principles of intervention:

1. *Express empathy*—listen respectfully, normalize ambivalence, and communicate nonjudgmental understanding and acceptance of the client's experience;
2. *Develop discrepancy* between present circumstances and desired goals or values—reflect reasons for not changing so the client engages in change talk;
3. *Roll with the resistance*—never argue or oppose the client's position—arguing strains the alliance and encourages clients to engage in resistance talk;
4. *Support self-efficacy*—clients develop hope and faith they can make their desired changes.

Therapists avoid arguing for change; assuming the "expert" role; criticizing, shaming, or blaming; labeling; being in a hurry; or claiming pre-eminence for therapist aims or goals over the client's. More specifically, MI therapists use OARS interventions:

1. *Open questions*—encourage active, thoughtful responses rather than "yes" or "no";
2. *Affirmations* that avoid overly appreciative comments on a client's positive steps;
3. *Reflective statements* rather than questions that force clients away from their experience so they can answer—reflections *understate* change talk and *overstate* resistance so clients will argue more strongly for change and "resist" their resistance;
4. *Summarize* periodically what the client is saying.

Change talk is evoked with the *importance ruler* and open questions (Miller & Rollnick, 2002):

• *The importance ruler* asks clients to rate the importance to them of making a change on a scale from 0 to10; they usually do not answer "0" and can then be asked why they are at that number and not a zero. They can also be asked what is needed to go to a higher number.
• *Disadvantages of the status quo*, "How is your problem affecting your life?" "Has it interfered with your goals in life?"
• *Advantages of change*, "How would things be different if you changed?" What are some of the reasons you'd like to change?"
• *Optimism about change*, "What are your strengths that might help you change?" "What other changes have you made in your life? How did you succeed in that?"
• *Intention to change*, "What might you want to try? Would that be important to you?"

Direct affirmations build rapport and reinforce open exploration of the client's ambivalence. Therapists can comment on the client's resourcefulness in coping so long with their problems, acknowledge that just coming in is an important step that requires courage, and expressing pleasure in talking with them. Reflections are also affirming, in part because clients learn the therapist actively listens to what they are saying. Reflections are best formed as short and simple statements, rather than questions. Questions demand a response and may invite resistance talk, while statements just acknowledge understanding without interrupting the client's train of thought. Therapists do not "parrot" what clients say, but *continue the paragraph*, making their best guess about the probable meaning of statements that sometimes could be taken different ways.

Miller and Rollnick (2002) give an example of skillful reflections that *continue the paragraph*: (In R. W. Miller, & S. Rollnick, *Motivational interviewing: Preparing people to change* (2nd ed.), pp. 70–71. © 2002 by Guilford Press. Reprinted by permission)

C: I worry sometimes that I may be drinking too much for my own good.
T: You've been drinking quite a bit.
C: I don't really feel like it's that much. I can drink a lot and not feel it.
T: More than most people.
C: Yes. I can drink most people under the table.
T: And that's what worries you.
C: Well, that and how I feel. The next morning I'm usually in bad shape. I feel jittery, and I can't think straight through most of the morning.
T: And that doesn't seem right to you.
C: No, I guess not. I haven't thought about it that much, but I don't think it's good to be hung over all the time. And sometimes I have trouble remembering things.
T: Things that happen while you're drinking.
C: That, too. Sometimes I just have a blank for a few hours.
T: But that isn't what you meant when you said you have trouble remembering things.
C: No. Even when I'm not drinking, it seems I'm forgetting things more often, and I'm not thinking clearly.
T: And you wonder if it has something to do with your drinking.
C: I don't know what else it could be.
T: You haven't always been like that.
C: No! It's only the last few years. Maybe I'm just getting older.
T: It might just be what happens to everybody when they reach 45.
C: No, it's probably my drinking. I don't sleep very well, either.
T: So maybe you're damaging your health and your sleep and your brain by drinking as much as you do.
C: Mind you, I'm not a drunk. Never was.
T: You're not that bad off. Still, you're worried.
C: I don't know about "worried," but I guess I'm thinking about it more.
T: And wondering if you should do something, so that's why you came here.
C: I guess so.
T: You're not sure.
C: I'm not sure what I want to do about it.
T: So if I understand you so far, you think that you've been drinking too much and you've been damaging your health, but you're not sure yet if you want to change that.
C: Doesn't make much sense, does it?
T: I can see how you might feel confused at this point (pp. 70–71).

The therapist's last two comments summarize, then affirm, as well as reflect client statements. Therapists show they are listening and reinforce client statements with periodic summaries that link segments of change talk into a coherent narrative. There are three types of summaries:

1. *Collecting summaries* pull together key points in clients' change talk; asking "What else?" encourages them to correct any misperceptions and to continue exploring feelings.
2. *Linking summaries* help clients connect previously unrelated issues and explore ambivalent feelings by contrasting them, "On the one hand ... and on the other," or by asking "I wonder if those two things are related. What do you think?"
3. *Transitional summaries* summarize prior meetings, bridge topic or emphasis shifts, or review material at session's end. Transitional summaries develop focus and continuity within and across sessions, avoiding "problems of the week" that might otherwise occur. Asking "What have I missed?" reinforces client collaboration and allows needed corrections.

Prochaska and Norcross' (2002) Stages of Change theory influenced the development of MI's methods for motivating precontemplative, resistant clients. Readiness to change reflects both an affirmation of the need for change and of clients' confidence they can carry out the needed actions. MI therapists periodically assess the separate processes of being ready, willing, and able. Willingness is collaboratively assessed by co-constructing a list of reasons for change *vs.* maintaining the status quo. Clients then use 0–10 scales to rate the importance of change (not at all important, to extremely important) and confidence in their ability to make a change (not at all confident, to extremely confident). Since clients seldom choose 0, MI facilitates change and confidence talk by asking "Why aren't you at the zero point?" or "What would it take to go to a higher number?" Change talk is also facilitated by:

1. *Asking evocative questions*, "How might you go about this change?"
2. *Reviewing past successes* or times when the problem did not occur;
3. *Identifying strengths and supports* that may be useful;
4. *Brainstorming*, then reviewing which ideas seem most feasible and why;
5. *Reframing* "failures" as "tries";
6. *Asking hypothetical questions*, "Suppose you succeed and are now looking back. What happened that let you succeed?"

If clients are willing and able, readiness is assessed by presence of the following:

1. Decreased resistance and greater awareness of difficulties in the status quo;
2. Decreased discussion of problems;
3. Resolve—calmness about moving forward and perhaps regret over what is being given up;
4. Increased change, optimism, and intention talk;
5. Questions about change, asking for advice or examples of how it is done;
6. Envisioning life after the change has occurred;
7. Experimenting between sessions with possible change actions.

Once these elements are present, clients are ready for change and Phase 1 of MI has been completed. Phase 2, *strengthening commitment to change*, then *recapitulates* and summarizes current perceptions of the problem, the client's ambivalence, evidence for the importance of change (*e.g.*, health considerations), signs the client intends to change, and the therapist's assessment of the client's situation. Not all ambivalence may be safely behind the client even at this point. Clients should take the initiative in planning change to *strengthen* their commitment to change. Therapists must affirmatively answer two questions before giving advice: "Have I elicited the client's own ideas and knowledge about this subject?" and "Is what I am going to convey important to the client's safety, or likely to enhance the client's motivation for change?" (Miller & Rollnick, 2002, p. 131). MI suggests advice only be offered if clients ask directly or after asking permission: "I have an idea that may or not be relevant. Do you want to hear it?" MI therapists consistently honor client autonomy.

Nondirective approaches such as MI may seem more time consuming initially than others, but most of the work of therapy is already completed once Phase 1 of MI is completed. In Miller and Rollnick's (2002) simile, negotiating Phase 1 is "like climbing a mountain on snowshoes," while Phase 2 is "like skiing down the other side." More directive attempts to influence client readiness may require even more time and effort to overcome resistance. In actual practice, MI sessions typically take about 2–6 weeks to move to Phase 2. MI avoids interpersonal conflict by taking a consistent one-down position and never challenging the client. MI precepts strengthen the collaborative alliance and are often adapted as a precursor to other therapeutic approaches, especially for resistant clients with thematic problems.

Integrative Implications

Existentialists note that anxiety or guilt result when people fail to address the existential givens. It is likely that the existential givens give rise to universal needs: *e.g.*, anxiety over death leads to a superordinate need to maintain *integrity*, both physical and psychological; existential isolation leads to a need for *intimacy*; groundlessness leads to a need to act on one's own or *autonomy*; and the need to find meaning in one's life leads to a need for *competency*. Meeting these needs requires the participation and appreciation of others, making them essentially interpersonal needs. Several chapters refer to these needs, while their relation to a broader integrative perspective is further developed in Chap. 15.

As this chapter suggests, a subjective, phenomenological focus on understanding clients in their own terms can be very effective, perhaps because clients so seldom experience having another's undivided attention and acceptance. Understanding clients from the inside-out is an important complement to outside-in, objective approaches such as cognitive-behavioral therapy. However, the phenomenological tenet that clients need to be understood using only their own categories and concepts is likely an impossible ideal. Certainly, clients are more likely to understand and accept interventions framed in their own terms, but it may be naïve to suppose that therapists can avoid imposing their own concepts or categories. As Truax (1966) found, the values of clients who improve become more like their therapist's. Postmodern relational theorists (Chap. 14) suggest that every communication is co-created by the participants: even babies influence how mothers communicate with them. This being the case, it is probably better that the therapist's influence be thoughtful and purposeful rather than idiosyncratic. Therapy needs to be both inside-out and outside-in: the inner world of needs derived from the existential givens reflects the client's outer world of interpersonal relationships and *vice versa*.

Chapter Nine: Main Points

- Phenomenological therapies share a holistic, humanistic view of individuals whose uniqueness defies categorization. They differ from the closely related experiential therapies in also trying to avoid imposing any therapeutic constraints on what clients discuss.
- Husserl's (1931) phenomenology uses three methods to avoid such constraints:

  1. *Disciplined naïveté*: become aware and suspend one's own preconceived ideas, while being open to the client's categories, meanings, and experience.
  2. *Describe client's experience*: therapists describe, but do not try to explain the client's subjective world using concrete, atheoretical terms.
  3. *Equalization*: therapists empathically communicate their understanding and do not assume any one aspect of client experience is more important than any other.

- Existential therapists are attentive to client concerns about ultimate questions of death, meaning, grounds for deciding what is right, and the isolation of not directly knowing the other person's experience. Spiritually oriented existentialists have faith in humanity's goodness, capacity for growth, and love, while more skeptical therapists suggest each person must either answer existential questions on their own or accept religious answers as a matter of faith.
- Yalom (1980) identifies four universal *existential givens*:

  1. *Groundlessness*: There are no objective grounds for deciding what actions are right.
  2. *Isolation*: People are always apart from others, unable to share their subjective experience.
  3. *Meaninglessness*: Why should one strive, if the outcome of one's actions is unknowable?
  4. *Death*: Such struggle seems doubly meaningless, if we are doomed to die anyway.

- Life's *absurdity* in the face of these existential givens inevitably creates *existential anxiety*. Efforts to escape this anxiety may diminish awareness of inner experiences, causing *neurotic anxiety* and *alienation* from the self, others, and the natural world. The only viable alternative is to find the courage to confront life and its existential givens by living *authentically*, Maddi (1987) suggests authenticity involves experiencing crises as *challenges*, belief in one's ability to *control* or influence events, and *commitment* to something personally meaningful.

- If people engage in personally meaningful activities, they are generally not aware of existential anxieties, except in times of crisis or life transition. In the absence of personally constructed meanings in life, people may defend against existential anxiety by assuming they are *special* (death and injury happen to others) or depend upon an *ultimate rescuer* who will give life meaning, and protect, love, and give them guidance.
- Existential therapy is an attitude, not a set of techniques: the therapist's goal is to enter their clients' phenomenal world and help them contact, explore, and clarify their inner experience. In experiencing a therapist's understanding openness to their experience, clients find courage to examine their defenses and become centered. Inner experiences are one's only guide for deciding what is right and meaningful and engaging others in an I-Thou relationship. If a person's life is meaningful and has one or more I-Thou relationships, then death anxieties arise only in major life transitions and are bearable.
- Markers for existential givens that may be an issue and need exploration include:

  1. *Groundlessness*: Procrastination, dependency, impulsivity, compulsivity, "loss" of control.
  2. *Isolation*: Losing loved ones, loneliness, conformity, promiscuity, narcissism, dependency.
  3. *Meaninglessness*: Aimlessness, sensation-seeking, disengaged, obsessed.
  4. *Death*: Usually well-defended; explored only when client brings up death-related concerns.

- Client centered therapy assumes that an innate, *self-actualizing* growth potential automatically guides people into meaningful, socially desirable paths as long as they do not try to live up to someone else's *conditions of worth*. These may develop in children whose caregivers fail to provide *unconditional positive regard*, resulting in the person responding to an *ideal self* rather than the *organismic wisdom* of the *real self*.
- Client centered therapists promote growth in clients if six conditions of therapy are met:

  1. *Relationship*: Two people must be in a relationship meaningful to both of them.
  2. *Vulnerability*: Clients experience anxiety-provoking incongruence motivating therapy work.
  3. *Genuineness*: Congruence of therapist's self- and other-acceptance facilitates sharing of feelings in the here-and-now relationship.
  4. *Unconditional Positive Regard*: Therapists communicate a warm prizing of the client.

5. *Accurate Empathy*: Therapists maintain personal boundaries, but enter into clients' inner worlds and communicate accurate understanding and acceptance of that experience.

6. *Perception of Genuineness*: Clients perceive the therapist's warmth and understanding as a genuine human response.

- *Pretherapy*, implemented in the Soteria House programs, establishes the relationship needed for therapy with clients diagnosed with schizophrenia. Contact is established by:

1. *Situational reflections*: describe what the client is doing—"John's looking out the window."

2. *Facial reflections*: interpret or describe the client's facial expressions.

3. *Word-for-word reflections*: duplicate the client's sentence fragments, words, or sounds.

4. *Body reflections*: assume and describe the client's position and posture.

- MI recognizes clients' essential ambivalence toward change in their lives. It selectively focuses on *change talk* rather than on *resistance talk* by applying Rogers' client centered approach to precontemplative, non-motivated clients. It is often combined with other approaches at later stages of intervention. MI avoids resistance by not urging change, but instead wondering what will happen if change does not occur. Clients are encouraged to think about reasons to change, rather than defend the status quo.

- Desirable change topics include disadvantages of the status quo, advantages of change, optimism about change, and intention to change. Interventions include non-judgmental *empathy* with client's position and experience, *developing discrepancy* by reflecting reasons for *not* changing, *rolling with resistance* by never opposing the client's position, and *supporting self-efficacy* by encouraging the client's belief that change is possible. MI therapists avoid arguing, criticizing, labeling, hurrying, or pushing their own "expert" agenda.

- OARS interventions include *Open* questions, *Affirmation* of client's positive steps, *Reflective* statements rather than questions to encourage further client elaboration, and *Summarizing* key points the client has made, followed by "What else?" to encourage still further exploration. Summaries *collect* what has already been discussed, help clients form *links* among previously unrelated points, or provide *transitions* if there is a shift in emphasis or sessions begin or end. Transitions help sustain a focus both within and across sessions.

- In assessing readiness, willingness, and ability to change, clients rate their perceived ability to make changes and how important change is. Therapists enhance change talk by asking what is needed to move to higher ratings. Readiness is shown by increases in change talk, resolve, and optimism, asking advice, envisioning life after change, and decreased resistance.

- MI also includes questions to *evoke* change talk, review past successes or *exceptions*, identify *strengths, brainstorm, reframe* "failures" as "tries," and *hypothetical questions* that assume future success, asking clients what might have led to that success.

- MI's *Phase 2* begins once clients commit to change. Phase 2 *recapitulates* how the client's perceptions have changed, *strengthens* commitment to change, and assists implementation.

- Integrative therapists might usefully combine subjective inside-out and objective outside-in approaches. The inner world of needs that derive from the existential givens and the outer world of interpersonal relations that gratify them are two complementary ways of understanding the client's experience.

Further Reading

Bozarth, J. D., Simring, F. M., & Tausch, R. (2001). Client centered therapy: The evolution of a revolution. In D. J. Cain & J. Seeman (Eds.), *Humanistic psychotherapies: Handbook of research and practice* (pp. 147–188). Washington: American Psychological Association.

Miller, R. W., & Rollnick, S. (2002). *Motivational interviewing: Preparing people to change* (2nd ed.). New York: Guilford Press.

Yalom, I. D. (1980). *Existential psychotherapy*. New York: Basic Books.

Yalom, I. D. (1989). *Love's executioner and other tales of psychotherapy*. New York: Basic Books.

Videos

Carlson, J., & Kjos, D. (2000a). *Existential-humanistic therapy with Dr. James Bugental*. Boston: Allyn & Bacon.

Carlson, J., & Kjos, D. (2000b). *Person centered therapy with Dr. Natalie Rogers*. Boston: Allyn & Bacon.

Miller, R. W., & Rollnick, S. (1998). *Motivational interviewing* (Vols. 1–7). Albuquerque: Horizon West Productions.

Websites

Center for the Person Homepage: http://www.centerfortheperson.org/.

Existential Therapy Homepage: http://www.existential-therapy.com/Index.htm.

Chapter 10
Psychotherapy and Social Context

> *Personality is nothing more (or less) than the patterned regularities that may be observed in an individual's relations with other persons, who may be real in the sense of actually being present, real but absent and hence "personified," or illusory.*
>
> Carson (1969, p. 26)

Is personality a relatively stable structure within the person? Or is it a process that occurs between two or more people? If the latter, is that process actually between people or is it the person's *perception* of interpersonal interactions? Robert Carson's definition of personality, based on Harry Stack Sullivan's ideas, reflects the interpersonal pole of this dialectic. It proposes that personality only exists in relation to others in contrast to traditional concepts of personality as the structural basis of consistency in an individual's behavior. In part, the question is whether "personality" is relatively stable or is continuously influenced by others' actions.

This dialectic is part of a larger debate about social influences on personality; *e.g.*, Freud recognized the family as an important determinant, but believed personality to be largely fixed by about age six. In contrast, theorists in this and succeeding chapters focus on the influence of social forces throughout the individual's lifetime. Alfred Adler was the first to recognize how family members define and refine their roles within the family as children develop and noted that the emergence of democratic principles no longer supported traditional authoritarian parenting practices. He also shared Sullivan's interest in how clients influence therapists during treatment.

Developed nearly a century ago, Adler's theories are remarkably modern. His approach anticipates a number of contemporary therapeutic approaches and would be "integrative" except that he predates the others. Table 10.1 lists Adlerian concepts that have been incorporated into contemporary models. Although contemporary approaches developed in novel directions and added new ideas, the underlying similarities provide a basis for a modern re-integration. Among others, Adlerian therapy is compatible with ego analytic, social analytic, humanist, existential, cognitive, family systems, and postmodern narrative and feminist therapies (*e.g.*, Watts, 2003).

D. K. Fromme, *Systems of Psychotherapy,*
DOI 10.1007/978-1-4419-7308-5_10, © Springer Science+Business Media, LLC 2011

Table 10.1 Adlerian concepts incorporated in contemporary therapeutic models

Modern approach	Adlerian concepts that anticipate modern approaches
Ego analytic	People act intentionally on the basis of conscious, rational choices
Social analytic	Society affects parenting methods, which affect children's development
Humanist	Intentionality and self-actualization (striving for perfection—social interest)
Cognitive	Therapy confronts problematic, self-centered life styles (schemas)
Existential	Life styles must show concern for the greater social good to be meaningful
Positive psychology	Identify positive, healthy ways to solve life's love, work, and social tasks
Postmodernism	Life style goals are constructed by the person's choices (final fictionalism)
Feminist therapy	Gender roles are cultural constructions; everyone strives for perfection
Narrative	Stories we tell reveal life style goals; new goals may need to be constructed
Family systems	Birth-order influences family niches and roles available to a child
Child guidance	Adler established the first Child Guidance Clinics to teach parenting skills

Individual Psychology

Adler chose the label, Individual Psychology, to distinguish his idiographic, holistic view of the person from Freud's structural analysis of personality. Adler also emphasized social influences, suggesting each child must find his or her niche in the ecology of the family. In the larger context of society, he noted that the democratic values developed in the nineteenth and early twentieth centuries no longer supported authoritarian parenting practices. Other theorists emphasizing social processes included Fromm (1941, 1955) as well as Sullivan and Karen Horney, who focused on dyadic processes of personality.

Adler's emphasis on rationality is a dialectic alternative to Freud's theory of unconscious processes in personality, psychopathology, and psychotherapy. Folk psychology suggests people act rationally on intentions formed by beliefs and desires (Kashima, McKintyre, & Clifford, 1998). Similarly, Adler proposed that intentions and goals are constructed from beliefs (*fictional finalism*) to determine an individual's actions. His emphasis on social contexts, intentionality, and the construction of fictional goals aligns his approach with contemporary postmodern constructivist approaches (see Chap. 14).

Intentionality

Intentionality assigns responsibility for actions to the person rather than to external forces and coordinates behavior with the actions of others. Premack (1990) suggests that people are biologically prepared to read intentions into any self-propelled motion. Intentions reflect a *desire* for some goal plus the *belief* that a particular course of action will lead to that outcome. Desires are motivational, may be idle or impossible, and can be directed toward anything, while intentions refer to a commitment to act in a particular way. Desires and beliefs inform and limit reasoning about how best to realize intentions. For actions to be considered intentional, they must also be skillful: a novice golfer may "intend" a hole-in-one, but most observers would think such an eventuality was lucky rather than intentional.

Intentions coordinate human interaction by assigning meaning and responsibility for actions and events. For example, a meaningful life results from intentional actions that realize goals reflecting core principles of one's philosophy of life. Socialization then reflects the child's ascription to others of intentions "like me" in learning to interpret the intentions of others (Meltzoff & Brooks, 2001). Children learn to discriminate intentional bumps that are "meant" from accidental bumps, even though the behaviors may be the same. Actions are meaningful and responsibility is assigned when an action is intended. People are held legally responsible for the consequences of intentional acts or actions that *should* have involved intentionality: *i.e.*, in the case of accidents, only for those consequences that could have been "reasonably" foreseen.

Determining an actions' meaning requires sensitivity to historical and interpersonal contexts and is a necessary skill for social interaction. Insensitivity to such cues results in naïveté or gullibility, while oversensitivity can lead to a paranoid ascription of hostile intent where none exists.

Individual Psychology's Conceptual Framework

Perhaps more than any other approach, Individual Psychology holds clients responsible for their symptoms. For Adler, symptoms are goal-directed and reflect prior choices and actions. Because important *life style* choices can be made before language develops, problematic life style goals may need to be *confronted* in therapy. Once clients become fully conscious of their symptomatic goals, they can make more adaptive, responsible choices. Adler's conception of the motivational factors that determine life style choices evolved dramatically over his career.

While part of Freud's circle, Adler suggested everyone experiences some sense of *organ inferiority* that leads to compensatory efforts; *e.g.*, Adler developed his intellect to compensate for sickliness as a child. After breaking with Freud, Adler suggested organ inferiority can reflect any perceived lack and proposed *striving for superiority*, inherent tendencies toward growth and mastery of life challenges, as the basic motivation. His last motivational concept, *social interest*, aligned Adler with positive psychology (Snyder & Lopez, 2001). Social interest reframes striving for superiority as a positive way to find solutions to the life tasks of love, work, and community by becoming *useful*. In contrast, psychopathology is behavior that is socially *useless*.

Adler anticipated postmodern thought with in his concept of *fictional finalism* based on Vaihinger's (1925) "as-if" philosophy. Fictional finalism proposes that all human constructs are merely fictional opinions, including the goals that people strive for (finalism). Healthy people revise their fictions constantly to keep them useful, but disturbed people cling to their fictions regardless of the consequences.

Problems result from choosing fictional goals that lack social interest. Adler suggests that normal people act as if they could lose their money and take precautions against this possibility. In contrast, "neurotic" people act as if they were actually losing their money (anxiety) and psychotic individuals act as if it were already lost (delusions).

Children's Goals and Discouragement

Dreikurs (1968) systematized Adler's model relating a child's discouragement to goals that show progressively less social interest. Adler proposed that children's innate social interest encourages them to act constructively, but if this goes unrecognized, they become discouraged and feel they do not belong. Figure 10.1's dotted line "a" suggests that innately active children may choose goals and actions of decreasing social interest as they become more discouraged about feeling they belong. If acting helpfully does not gain a feeling of belonging, the discouraged child may try to be "special" and choose a mistaken goal to gain attention. They may strive for sports or academics success, but peers may shun them, recognizing their appeal to be special. If they fail to gain attention, they may become even more discouraged and escalate to being a *nuisance* to gain attention. If still unsuccessful, the active child may strive instead for the goal of power and be rebellious. If this does not work, the child's goal may shift to seeking revenge by acting in vicious ways. This progression illustrates how antisocial behavior might develop from abuse and neglect.

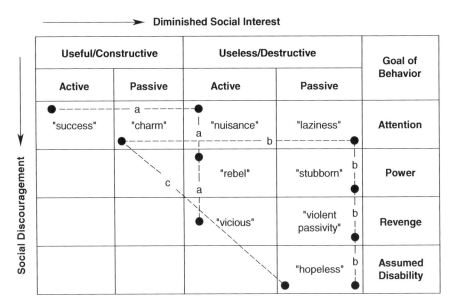

Fig. 10.1 Children's goals and discouragement. (R. Dreikurs, *Psychology in the classroom: A manual for teachers*, 2nd ed., p. 30. © 1968, Eva Dreikurs Ferguson; reprinted with permission.)

Temperamentally passive children show a different progression, as illustrated by lines "b" and "c" in Figure 10.1. Passive children may use charm to gain attention, but if this fails, some follow path "c" with feelings of hopelessness and develop symptoms to demonstrate an assumed disability to others. Others follow path "b" and dawdle lazily to gain attention. Continued failures lead to stubbornness to gain power, to a self-destructive, "violent passivity" (*e.g.*, self-harm) to exact revenge, and ultimately to hopelessness, symptoms, and assumed disability. Fortunately, children's mistaken goals are usually temporary, reflecting momentary discouragement.

Adler and Dreikurs' motivational approach notes that attention may reinforce misbehavior, but suggests that ignoring misbehavior leads to further discouragement and escalation of problem behavior rather than "extinction." Instead, children need encouragement. Metacommunication about the child's goals is the best way to resolve this double bind; *e.g.*, "I think you want to see if you're powerful enough to win this argument," reframes disputes with the stubborn child. Misbehavior is defused by identifying a child's goals correctly or "spitting-in-the-soup," which evokes a *recognition reflex*, a sheepish smile and a sidewise turn of the head.

The same behavior can serve different goals, so it is helpful to have other ways to identify goals besides the recognition reflex, which tends to disappear by adolescence. These include:

1. Giving the child attention and observing the consequences. If the child stops misbehaving, the goal was most likely to gain attention. Power goals are signaled when attention results in continued misbehavior as the child wants to learn who will win. If the goal is revenge, the child interprets attention as a sign of the adult's vulnerability and escalates the misbehavior. Assumed disability is indicated if the child becomes unresponsive to the environment and the effects of attention are random and unpredictable.
2. Although less reliable, the first clues to a child's goal are the observer's emotional reactions to the child's behavior; *e.g.*, irritation signals attention, anger indicates power, hurt reflects revenge, and hopelessness suggests assumed disability. These reactions form the basis for hypotheses about the child's goals, which are then verified either by observing the effect of attention or by suggesting the hypothesized goal to the child.

Society and Parenting

Adler was interested in the effect of society on the family as well as the effect of the family on the individual. He noted that the eighteenth and nineteenth centuries experienced revolutions in which authoritarian social orders were increasingly replaced by democratic values. As belief in a divinely ordained social hierarchy was overturned in the political arena, relationships in the family were also challenged; *e.g.*, the notion that all men are created equal was extended to include equality with women and Adler was an early supporter of women's suffrage. With men no longer viewed as divinely ordained masters of their families, authoritarian discipline of family members also came under question. Adler pointed to increased juvenile delinquency rates in Vienna at this time as evidence that authoritarian methods of discipline lacked credibility and proposed "democratic" child-rearing methods to help parents become more effective.

To meet this need, Adler established the first child guidance clinics and taught parents democratic child-rearing methods. *Systematic Training for Effective Parenting* (STEP; Dinkmeyer, McKay, & Dinkmeyer, 1997) and *Active Parenting* (Popkin, 1993) are widely adopted, modern Adlerian programs. Parents learn to encourage their child, using natural or logical consequences rather than evaluative methods of praise, rewards, or punishment that could encourage power struggles. *Encouragement* acknowledges actions, rather than consequences: instead of "I'm proud of your excellent report card," parents learn to say "I know how much effort these grades required. You have every reason to feel proud of your efforts."

Periodic *family councils* allow children a democratic voice in developing rules that affect them. Children generally view rules and their consequences as fair and reasonable when they help to develop them. Parents sometimes need to suggest less severe consequences than those that children propose. Everyone needs to be affected equally by rules: if the rule is that articles left on the living room floor go into a "Saturday" bag to be retrieved on Saturday, then that rule also applies to Mom and Dad. Children need to feel that family councils benefit them as well as their parents. Family councils held only for "disciplinary" reasons tend to be seen as punitive.

Punitive forms of discipline lead to power struggles, feelings of inferiority, and they model aggression as a means for solving problems. In their place, Adler proposed natural and logical consequences to minimize punishment's negative consequences. Parents often intervene in situations in which the *natural consequences* of the child's actions are sufficiently instructive; *e.g.*, it is better to allow siblings to learn on their own how to resolve arguments when they are small and less likely to inflict serious damage on one another. At least one child will resent externally imposed solutions and neither child is likely to learn to self-regulate their actions. Adults need to monitor potentially dangerous situations, but tolerate minor bumps and scrapes.

Logical consequences may be needed to protect a child who is at significant risk or if natural consequences are too distant in the future to be effective. If children see imposed consequences as logically related to misbehaviors, they are less likely to feel resentful or discouraged. Logical consequences work best when they are based on rules previously agreed upon by everyone during family council; *e.g.*, the rule might be no TV privileges until homework is completed. *Ad hoc* consequences for an unanticipated dangerous situation should be reviewed at the next family council. Because no one ultimately wins power struggles, parents need to walk away for the moment, ask for a family council, or metacommunicate about the conflict.

Life Style and the Family Constellation

Adler's *life style* concept encompasses a range of ideas; it reflects individual choices about how to think about the self, the world, and the people in it and allows

Table 10.2 Common birth order effects

Firstborn	Middle child	Youngest child	Only child
Undivided attention, then dethronement that may lead to feeling unloved	Never has undivided attention, rights of eldest, or privileges of youngest	Pampered and spoiled, never dethroned. Feels small and weak	Pampered and spoiled, never dethroned; undivided attention
Afraid of being pushed back; believes must gain superiority over siblings	Feels unloved, left out, and life is unfair: someone is always more advanced	Feels special, but not taken seriously and feels less competent than sibs	Feels incompetent as adults are more capable
Being right and in control is important. Works hard, is responsible and competent	Feels squeezed, unsure, and may push down sibs. Acts as if in race	Expects others to make decisions, take responsibility	Self-centered, enjoys attention, and expects service from others
Tries to please, help and protect others. May feel unloved and discouraged	Develops skills first child does not have and is adaptive; may rebel	Often gets own way and places others in service: is the "baby"	Relates better with adults than peers. Creative; demanding

for change more than most conceptions of personality. It includes goals the person has chosen, together with the unique constellation of perceptions and beliefs about how the world works and how goals can be achieved. The stories people tell about themselves, how they expect the world to treat them, and their earliest memories all reflect their life style. Early memories are recalled selectively because they are a metaphor for the person's life style.

Family atmosphere, reflecting parental style and support, and the family's structure or *family constellation* influence choices before language develops and make early life style choices difficult to change. Family structure, especially *birth order*, affects life style choices by limiting the roles available to a child (Adler, 1931; Dinkmeyer *et al.*, 1997; see Table 10.2). Oldest children enjoy a favored status until the second child is born and as a result often strive to regain parental attention by helping with the younger children. Firstborns thus tend to be responsible pleasers and leaders. Interestingly, most American presidents have been firstborn children. The middle child is born into a world in which parental attention is always divided. Second-born children may feel neglected, that they must strive harder be accepted in the family. As a result they tend to be competitive and may become rebellious when discouraged. As the baby of the family, youngest children tend to be spoiled, pampered, and charming, but may feel inferior to their older, more competent siblings. Perhaps as a result, youngest children may be very ambitious and surpass their siblings' accomplishments, but a combination of ambition, inferiority feelings, and discouragement may result in laziness and failure to achieve.

The only child receives undivided adult attention and learns to charm adults, but with no competition, may also be pampered and spoiled even more than a youngest child. Only children are apt to combine ambition with expectations of being served. If successful, they may be highly creative, because they had to learn how to entertain themselves; never competing with siblings, they may be lazy and easily discouraged. Adler realized these "tendencies" were subject to many other factors; *e.g.*, a youngest child 10 years younger than the next older sibling may have experiences more like that of an only child. A firstborn whose father is very competitive may have the experience of a middle child. In large families, middle children must cooperate to get their needs met, rather than depend on overextended parents and may be less competitive. Parents may have different expectations for an oldest girl than for an oldest boy. A chronically ill child may have experiences that have little to do with birth order. Therapists must determine how birth order, parenting styles, developmental experiences, socioeconomic factors, and emotional climate interact in their client's individual circumstances to influence unique life style choices.

Safeguarding and Neurotic Symptoms

Adler believed everyone develops feelings of inferiority at some time, if only because everyone begins life very small and inexperienced. Inferiority feelings generally become less important with maturity, but remain an essential part of the life style for the neurotic person. Neurotic symptoms develop as *safeguarding strategies* to protect individuals from feeling inferior, but also create a self-absorption that interferes with the development of social interest. Table 10.3 compares various safeguarding strategies with Freud's related ego defenses. *Excuses*, like rationalization, increase security feelings by allowing neurotic people to expect less of themselves. *Aggressive* strategies safely express hostility and defend against feeling inferior by depreciating others, blaming them for one's failures, or soliciting sympathy by blaming oneself or making others feel guilty. *Distancing* strategies protect against failure. Symptoms such as paralysis or amnesia allow the person to *move backward* and excuse failure to move forward in the world. *Standing still* involves less dramatic symptoms, *e.g.*, fatigue or insomnia that prevent meeting life demands. *Hesitation* includes obsessions, compulsions, or procrastination that prevents the completion of tasks, while *construction of obstacles* creates self-handicapping excuses such as over-drinking. These strategies all interfere with the life tasks of love, work, and contributing to society necessary to the person's innate needs for social interest.

Intervention Approaches

As in other approaches, Adlerians begin therapy by establishing a framework for the therapeutic relationship. Therapeutic contract parameters include fees, schedules, purpose of therapy, and limiting contact with the therapist between sessions to emergencies (Oberst & Stewart, 2003). By the second or third session, preliminary

Table 10.3 Adler's safeguards and Freud's defense mechanisms. (C. F. Monte & R. F. Sollod, *Beneath the mask: An introduction to theories of personality* (7th ed.), p. 176. © 2003, Wiley & Sons; reprinted with permission.)

Adlerian "safeguard"	Description	Comparable Freudian defense mechanism
Excuses	Neurotic symptoms used as reasons to escape life's demands, cannot perform one's best	*Rationalization* *Secondary gain*
Aggression	1. *Depreciation*: strategies for feeling superior by making others feel inferior, overvaluing self relative to others, or being overly solicitous of others' welfare as a way to control them	*Reaction formation* *Altruistic surrender* *Reversal*
	2. *Accusation*: unconscious feelings of deprivation lead to blaming others for one's own feelings of inferiority and frustration. Sometimes person blames fate	*Displacement* *Rationalization* *Projection*
	3. *Self-accusation* (guilt): blaming or cursing self, suicidal thoughts and acts sometimes to gain attention, sometimes as a displaced intention to really hurt someone else. Or sometimes self-blame is a way of punishing others by making them feel guilty	*Turning against self* *Reversal* *Asceticism*
Distancing	Reflects the basic neurotic conflict between feelings of inferiority and strivings for superiority	
	1. *Moving backward* by using symptoms to avoid social obligations, being helpless, "can't do anything"	*Fixation* *Regression*
	2. *Standing still* by refusing to do anything or participate in life, especially when demands are made	*Inhibition* *Regression*
	3. *Hesitation and procrastination* around a self-created difficulty and attempts to master it. Obsessions and compulsions	*Rationalization* *Undoing*
	4. *Constructing obstacles* by focusing on a symptom and blaming failure on it. Usually the least severe form of safeguarding because there is some success	*Rationalization* *Inhibition*

life style assessment should lead to tentative agreements on tangible goals, methods, treatment length, expectations for the client's participation, and the criteria that indicate the completion of therapy. Most importantly, therapists foster cooperation and give encouragement during the initial stage.

Therapists expect clients will feel threatened as they confront perceived inferiorities and safeguarding strategies, especially if they are on the verge of an important insight or change. The therapist's objectivity may be challenged if clients idealize the therapist or if passive-aggressive clients feel threatened and sabotage the therapist's efforts. Adler warns against evaluating therapy on the basis of perceived client progress due to such risks. Therapists can resist assaults on their self-esteem to the degree they adhere to therapeutic principles. If they gently address alliance ruptures, clients will experience them as steady and reliable in spite of efforts to test them. As Rogers suggests, clients who feel valued and accepted by their therapist eventually become able to value and accept themselves (Oberst & Stewart, 2003).

Table 10.4 Sources and types of information used to analyze life style

Source	Examples of types of information
Case history	Developmental, relationship, education, work, drug and medical problems
Interview questions	*The Question*: How would life change, if problem/symptom disappeared?
Observation	Posture, dress, expression of confidence, assertiveness, shyness, *etc.*
Psychological tests	Basic Adlerian Scales for Interpersonal Success-Adult (BASIS-A)
Family constellation	Birth order/spacing, parenting style, family atmosphere, and sibling roles
Early recollections	Repetitive themes and emotional tone of earliest childhood memories
Dreams	Recurrent themes reflect goals, obstacles, and suggest alternatives
Group interactions	Leadership, assertiveness, supportiveness, and empathy for others
Symptoms	Interpersonal consequences/goals of symptoms; who is impacted and how?

Assessing the Life Style

Life style narratives give unity, consistency, and meaning to the individual's actions and striving for superiority. It reflects the *private logic* of the *creative self* that integrates the person's interests and values into a unique interpretation of the world and leads to a *life goal*. Table 10.4 describes the types of data used in creating a unique, idiographic analysis of an individual's life style (Lombardi, 1973). As life style hypotheses are developed, they can be validated by convergences that occur among themes from the different types of data.

For example, George's history of vague somatic complaints has prevented him from working. He may have a life style of expecting others to take care of him. If he responds to the *Adlerian Question*: "How would things change if you miraculously became well tomorrow?" with, "Then I could work," chances are his goal is to avoid working; "Then I would feel better" would suggest his symptoms are medical in nature. Passivity and waiting direction from the therapist would lend further support for the goal of expecting others to serve him. High scores on the *going along* and *being cautious* scales of the BASIS-A inventory (Kern, Wheeler, & Curlette, 1993) and low scores on the *wanting recognition, taking charge,* and *social interest* scales would also support the hypothesis. A family atmosphere high in concerns about health, plus authoritarian, overly permissive, or overly involved parenting styles, and youngest or only birth order are likely. Early recollections and dreams may reflect themes of superiority/inferiority conflicts, trying to act but feeling paralyzed, or of illness, injury, and feeling loved when others took care of the client. In group therapy, clients might be passive and encourage others to "help" by acting helpless. Table 10.5 lists typical questions assessing family constellation and atmosphere.

The themes in the last question of Table 10.5 list possible life style niches. The available niches for younger children may be limited by those occupied by older siblings or a competitive parent. O'Phelan's (1977) factor analysis of a similar list confirmed Mosak and Sulman's (1971) assumption that niche themes constitute six

Table 10.5 Sample questions for assessment of family atmosphere and constellation

1. What was the nature of your parent's relationship? Quarrels? How resolved?
2. How did you react to the quarrels? What would you do? Did you take sides?
3. Did Dad enjoy his work? Did Mom hers? What were their favorite activities?
4. How were decisions made? Who had the most influence? Children involved?
5. How were the children disciplined? Who was punished the most? Your reaction? Siblings?
6. Who was Dad's most/least favorite child? Mom's most/least favorite child? Why?
7. Who is most like Dad? Mom? In what ways?
8. How and with whom did Dad spend free time? Mom? How about with you?
9. What general or particular ambitions did they have for each of you?
10. Among siblings, who took care of whom? Played together? Got along best?
11. Who started quarrels? What were they about? How were they resolved?
12. Among siblings (friends, if an only child) who was more or less like each of the following?

(a) Intelligent	(j) Selfish	(s) Attractive
(b) Hardest worker	(k) Sensitive, easily hurt	(t) Gregarious
(c) Best grades	(l) Good sense of humor	(u) Masculine
(d) Helpful around house	(m) Spoiled	(v) Feminine
(e) Conforming	(n) Idealistic	(w) Artistic
(f) Rebellious	(o) Materialistic	(x) Leader
(g) Trying to please	(p) Athletic	(y) Follower
(h) Critical of others	(q) Strongest	(z) Musical
(i) Considerate of others	(r) Weakest	

groups. Although Adler emphasized the uniqueness of each individual, these categories can serve as starting points in describing an individual's life style. Table 10.6 lists common life style factors; note that Factors 1 and 6 are unipolar, while Factors 2–5 describe opposing, bipolar life style patterns.

Insight

Once clients agree with a life style description, therapy shifts to examining how their problems are a natural extension of their life style. Insight includes intellectual understanding and experiential awareness of the ways moment-to-moment life style choices affect relationships and personal functioning. Confrontation, paradoxical

Table 10.6 O'Phelan's (1977) factor analysis of life style themes

Factor	Defining themes
1. Achievement	Intelligent, competitive, high standards, idealistic
2. Social skills	Spoiled, charming, demands and gets way *vs.* gets punished a lot
3. Gender	Strong, athletic, masculine *vs.* feminine
4. Right-wrong	Temper tantrums, rebellious *vs.* conformity, pleasing others
5. Safeguarding	Easily hurt, felt sorry for self *vs.* sense of humor, friends
6. Social interest	Helped around house, hard worker, considerate

intention, and "spitting-in-the-soup" (identifying mistaken goals) are typical Adlerian interventions (Oberst & Stewart, 2003).

Confrontation requires a safe, supportive relationship and focuses on inconsistencies in the client's life and self-presentation (Schulman, 1973). Therapists reflect their client's subjective experience empathically in clear, poignant terms that intensify the experience. They challenge mistaken beliefs with questions or exaggerations that highlight inconsistencies: "If you end all contact with your friends and family, stay home, and do nothing but housework, will your husband never lose his temper with you again?" Procrastinator's goals can be confronted by "Waiting until the last moment to prepare for exams seems to keep you safe from finding out if you have the ability to be an engineer." Destructive behavior may need direct confrontation, "You're going to lose your marriage and your job if you keep on drinking. You need help."

Spitting-in-the-soup makes a problem behavior less palatable by noting its self-defeating goal (Oberst & Stewart, 2003). If a dysfunctional behavior or its goal is made to seem childish or humorous, clients may be willing to explore alternatives. Children who are too "sick" to go to school may recover quickly if told they will need to stay in bed and would not be able to watch TV. Spitting-in-the-soup is only used with adults if there is a strong alliance and the therapist can predict the client's response. Resistant clients may respond to paradoxic interventions that encourage symptoms. Clients learn they can consciously control symptoms and increase their intensity or frequency. Because symptoms are effective ways to maneuver others only if they appear uncontrollable, this exercise effectively interferes with that goal. Similarly, predicting or requesting a relapse normalizes and inoculates clients against over-reacting to lapses.

Reorientation

In the last stage of therapy, reorientation helps clients commit to goals that express social interest and meet the life tasks of love, work, and community involvement. Clients learn to handle lapses and resist pressures from family or friends whose goals may be disrupted by the client's changed behavior. Interventions include Mosak's (1985) *pushbutton technique, catching oneself,* and *living as-if.* In the pushbutton technique, clients learn to relax and visualize a pleasant, self-affirming memory as if watching a movie. They note the resulting pleasant feelings and signal the end of the sequence by raising a finger. Next, they visualize a negative memory and again note their feelings and signal when the scene is over. Replaying positive memories and noting the return of positive feelings helps clients realize the degree of control they have over their feelings—that they can literally "push their own buttons" (Oberst & Stewart, 2003).

While the pushbutton technique can be used during any stage of therapy, the remaining interventions help clients implement new behaviors and resist pressures to resume old ones. Lapses happen because maladaptive behaviors are well-practiced and automatic and because significant others trigger or reinforce old patterns. Catching oneself involves becoming aware of situational or interpersonal triggers and learning either to avoid those situations or to respond more adaptively. At first, diaries help clients catch themselves after the fact, but noting time, place, and circumstances helps them become aware of relevant triggers; *e.g.*, a client may be particularly irritable after coming home after a long commute. After several repetitions, the client is able to anticipate this and choose how to respond, rather than react automatically. A reliable, sensitive partner or friend may also be able to help clients catch themselves early enough to change course in problematic sequences (Oberst & Stewart, 2003).

The as-if techniques of fantasy, imagery, and role-playing let clients practice adaptive ways of responding to old triggers. Clients begin either with guided-imagery or write a narrative visualizing the problem situation and the new response. Kelly's (1955) *fixed-role* technique helps clients practice new patterns of behavior. Clients write a self-description that therapists then revise positively: if a client describes herself as, "Betty is anxious, self-conscious, and lacks confidence," the therapist's revision might be "Elizabeth is energetic, self-aware, and sensitive." The revision is positive, within the client's range of possible selves, and the "new self" is emphasized by a new name. After discussion, the client role plays how to think, feel and act as if they were this new person. Once necessary adjustments are made, clients are encouraged to role play first with friendly outside acquaintances, moving to closer relationships as they gain confidence. They are asked not to share any hint of this experiment with their friends or family. After 3–4 weeks they are asked to revert to their original persona. In a successful intervention, they will find this difficult because they have assimilated aspects of the new persona.

Case Illustration

- *Background*: Elena is a 23-year-old, moderately obese Hispanic-American woman with an 11th-grade education, who lives alone and "feels tired and sluggish all the time." She says life has no more meaning and she "might as well be dead" since Carlos, her husband of 6 years, asked for a divorce and moved out 3 months ago. As a Catholic, she says she would never act on her suicidal thoughts. Her religion also forbids remarriage and "there is no reason to live with no husband or family." Elena dropped out of school at age 17 when she became pregnant and married Carlos. Unfortunately, a month later, she miscarried and was told she would not be able to have children. She reports that ever since, she has forced herself to get through each day. Life currently consists of work as a waitress, after which she comes home exhausted and sleeps 12–14 hours until time to get ready to work again. On off-days, she lays around the house watching TV, eating junk food, and feeling "sorry for myself." She has gained 10 pounds since the separation, adding to her distress since her weight was an issue for her husband. He also complained about her neglect of house-keeping, lack of interest in sex, and inability to make decisions on her own. She states that "Carlos left me because he said he was tired of taking care of everything and not getting anything in return." She has made no friends of her own since they moved to Los Angeles, and has limited contact with her family in Houston.

- *Diagnosis*: Axis I—Major depressive disorder; Axis II—Dependent personality disorder; Axis III—Infertility; Axis IV—Separation/divorce, no social support; Axis V—GAF = 45.
- *Family Constellation and Atmosphere*: Elena's father, Jorge, immigrated illegally, later bringing his wife, Maria, and eldest daughter, Anna, to the U.S. after receiving amnesty and a green card. Jorge followed fruit and vegetable harvests across the Southwest and California, until the birth of Miguel 4 years after Anna. He drank heavily after each paycheck and was physically abusive when Maria complained about the loss of needed finances. Although Maria was subservient and chronically depressed, after Miguel's birth she gave Jorge an ultimatum that she would return to Mexico with the family unless he found stable work and stopped the beatings. He then found construction work in Houston and the drinking and abuse became less frequent, but never disappeared. Elena was born 2 years after Miguel. Her earliest memories are hiding and being afraid her parent's arguments would result in someone being killed. She remembers being comforted by Anna after these events. She was closest to Anna who took care of Miguel and her when Maria was depressed. Miguel was the favored child and the most intelligent, having recently graduated from Rice University on scholarship. Elena was the baby and spoiled by the rest of the family. She was the weakest, most sensitive, and easily hurt, but also the most fun-loving and gregarious. She wishes she could be more like Anna, who is now happily married with four children, but feels she has nothing to offer anyone.
- *Life Style Summary*: Life is dangerous and beyond Elena's ability to handle on her own. She needs someone to protect and look after her. The only roles for a woman are to be a wife and mother. If you fail in these roles, there is nothing else to offer that has meaning, and you will be alone with no one to look after you.
- *Problem List*: 1. Suicidal Ideation; 2. Depression; 3. Lack of Goals and Purpose in Life; 4. Social Isolation; 5. Dependence.
- *Treatment Plan*:

    1. As Elena's suicidal risk is assessed as low to moderate, the treatment contract will include her agreement to remember the strictures of her religion and not to act on any suicidal impulse before discussing her feelings and alternatives with the therapist. The distinction between depression and grieving over her interrupted life will be the initial focus. She will be encouraged to express her sorrow for her loss, but also to increase enjoyable activities.
    2. Her depression partly reflects her narrowly defined life style and lack of purpose since her divorce prevents her from fulfilling the life goals of wife and mother. She will review times when she showed her fun-loving and gregarious aspects. Her self-description as weak and easily hurt will be reframed as "being gentle and sensitive." To expand available role models, she will be asked to list respected Hispanic and minority women and rank their similarity

with these characteristics. This information will then help Elena consider life goals and the steps necessary to achieve them; *e.g.*, a gentle, sensitive, gregarious, fun-loving woman, who misses not having children, might become a very good child-care provider. She will be encouraged to role-play "Elena Maria," who works with children on her off-days.

3. Elena's depression also partly reflects her current social isolation. A concurrent women's group will provide a temporary source of support, as well as provide a venue in which greater assertiveness can be encouraged. Individual therapy will address the decision whether to remain in Los Angeles or return to Houston to be near her family and their support. Although Mexican-American families traditionally provide the individual's primary social support, Elena appears to have been unusually dependent on others. Dependencies will be confronted as they occur in Elena's behavior or planning. In particular, her depression, hopelessness, and helplessness will be confronted as ways of enlisting the care of others.

Interpersonal Theory: Harry Stack Sullivan

The Interpersonal School of Psychoanalysis (Fromm, 1964; Horney, 1966, 1970; Sullivan, 1953a, b; Thompson, 1950) was a precursor to the modern interpersonal approaches discussed in this and the next chapter as well as family systems theory (Chap. 12) and intersubjective relational analysis (Chap. 14). Sullivan (1953a) recognized the parallels between Heisenberg's uncertainty principle (observing a sub-atomic particle alters its behavior) and the effects of therapists observing their clients. Sullivan held that therapeutic neutrality was impossible, that therapists inevitably influence clients through tone of voice and responding selectively to their narratives. He accepted Freud's position that therapy involves understanding and transforming the transference reaction, but conceptualized the therapist's role as a *participant-observer* rather than a passive *tabula rasa* on which clients project their fantasies. Participant-observers actively confront repetitive patterns that create problems for the client, but are aware that transference is also affected by the actual interactions of client and therapist.

Sullivan's most radical suggestion was that personality and psychopathology emerge from repeated interactions initially co-created by caretaker and child and then replicated later in life with other people. The idea that personality is an on-going co-creation anticipated both systems theory and postmodern emphases on contextual influences on behavior. Sullivan's ideas have had wide influence, leading to a number of "Neo-Sullivanian" interpersonal approaches.

If psychopathology occurs *between* people rather than *within* the individual, then therapists need no longer to rely only on interpretation or insight to facilitate change. The therapist's actions provide *corrective emotional experiences* (Alexander & French, 1946) that can directly influence transference behaviors. By reacting in ways that disconfirm client expectations, therapists provide an experience of relating to others in new ways. Interpretation then focuses on parallels between problems in therapy and the client's presenting problems. With a focus on the interaction process with the therapist and not just themselves, clients are helped to examine their own contributions less defensively.

Conceptual Framework

Sullivan's (1953a) *dynamism* concept resembles the modern concept of a schema. The most important dynamism, *personification*, is essentially an interpersonal schema, but with an added postmodern meaning. Personifications are constructions about self and others, including pets and inanimate objects; *e.g.*, people tell pets how nice they are or talk to a car that would not start as if these were persons. People personify others and then respond to that personification rather than the actual person. The *self-concept* is also a personification based on *reflected appraisals* of others, especially from repeated interactions with *significant others* such as primary caregivers.

Sullivan believed people have basic needs for *security* and *relationship*, but it is anxiety that needs would not be met that motivates most behavior. Children develop interpersonal strategies, a personality, to avoid overwhelming anxiety when being rejected or punished by their caregiver. Interpersonal strategies involve concepts of self and others that develop as caregivers meet the child's needs, *good-me* and *good-mother* personifications, or are rejecting or punitive, *bad-me* and *bad-mother* personifications. Sullivan anticipated object relations theory noting that children *dissociate* aspects of self and other to avoid being overwhelmed by anxiety; *e.g.*, they may feel helpless in the face of demands by powerful others part of the time, but feel loved and omnipotent at other times. The young child is unable to integrate good experiences of need satisfaction with bad experiences and anxiety, especially if caregivers communicate anxiety with uncoordinated, jerky, or unresponsive handling. *Not-me* personifications, dissociated from awareness, protect the self-system from being overwhelmed by extreme, terrifying experiences. *Selective inattention* to anxiety-arousing impulses or experiences defends against lesser levels of anxiety.

Sullivan (1953b) proposed a developmental model that complements both Erikson's psychosocial and Piaget's cognitive developmental stage theories. Sullivan described cognitive and psychosocial issues that develop during six stages of maturation:

1. *Infancy*: Characterized by preverbal *prototaxic* thought with largely disconnected, serial images. Vestiges of prototaxic thought persist in psychotic states, dreams, or when normal adults "woolgather." Prolonged deprivation or stress can lead to *apathy* or a *somnolent detachment* dynamism; today this is termed *failure to thrive*.

2. *Childhood*: Characterized by *parataxic* thoughts that associate events contiguous in time or space as in Piaget's (1952/1963) preoperational stage. Magical thinking dominates with poorly understood causal relationships. A *malevolent*

transformation, the sense one lives among enemies and must conceal any tenderness, can occur if the child's need for tender relationships with significant others results in teasing or humiliation. Play or *as-if* enactments let children practice appropriate grown-up and gender roles. Play may also be used defensively, *as if* the child were too busy to interact with anxiety-provoking others.

3. *Juvenile*: *Syntaxic thought*, based on *consensually validated* beliefs, progressively replaces parataxic thought. As magical and mistaken ideas become evident, others correct the child with socially accepted, consensually validated beliefs. During this period, relational needs extend beyond the immediate family and joining peer groups or *cliques* helps the child differentiate from the family. Paradoxically, this step toward individuation is also marked by slavish conformity to the group, in which children learn to *subordinate* their own immediate wishes and *accommodate* the needs of the group or authority figures in order to belong.

4. *Preadolescence*: Ideally, children form their first intimate relationship with a *chum* or non-familial *significant other*, often chosen from their peer group. Intimacy that develops before adolescence helps the child understand the difference between love and lust once puberty begins. The chum is also a trustworthy person who provides consensual validation and a sounding-board for ideas or questions that the child may have been too self-conscious to mention to others; *e.g.*, questions about sexuality or parataxic distortions.

5. *Early Adolescence*: Conflicts among security, intimacy, and sexual needs provoke anxiety and uncertainty about the teenager's sexual competency and attractiveness. Teasing about sexual changes and interests can be especially demoralizing for the developing self-system.

6. *Late Adolescence*: The full range of adult interpersonal behaviors is evidenced, but the individual may experience handicaps based on past developmental failures. The need to maintain self-respect in the face of negative reflected appraisals of others can lead to the development of the *mask* or social façade; this need to conceal needs and weaknesses may then prevent full integration and development of the self.

Communication Analysis: Social Reinforcement of Unconscious Processes

Modern interpersonal therapies are "Neo-Sullivanian" rather than a direct extension of Sullivan's approach. They typically share Sullivan's emphasis on the therapist as participant-observer: active participation in the therapeutic relationship that alternates with a more objective stance that observes salient aspects of the interaction process unfolding during therapy. Sullivan recognized that pure objectivity is impossible, given observer biases and the fact that any two people are likely to attribute different meanings to the same words. Like humanists, interpersonal therapists enter the client's phenomenal field, attend to verbal and nonverbal communications, and the here-and-now context in which the interaction develops. They differ from humanists by focusing on how the client and therapist co-construct the interactional process.

Ernst Beier's *Communication Analysis* (Beier, 1966; Beier & Young, 1998) integrates social learning theory with Sullivan's process-oriented approach. Beier suggests people unconsciously evoke emotions that limit how others respond to avoid feeling vulnerable or responsible; *e.g.*, acting helpless encourages significant others to be helpful and caring so that intimacy needs are met without risking rejection. Eventually, others resent this burden, an example of Mowrer's (1948) "neurotic paradox" in which clients suffer from the responses they evoke in others. Beier's approach also links Adler's emphasis on purposive behavior with Sullivan's interpersonal conception of problems.

Conceptual Framework

Beier and Young (1998) suggest that problems can occur if unconscious nonverbal, contextual, or paralinguistic communications are incongruent with an overt verbal communication. If there is incongruence, social convention encourages people to attend only to manifest content and latent messages may or may not be noticed. Table 10.7 illustrates the various outcomes if either the sender or the receiver is aware or unaware of a latent message. *e.g.*, rational, overt communication occurs if only one message is sent or both parties are aware of manifest and latent content. In contrast, an advertiser's persuasive message limits realistic appraisal of claims with cues of excitement and sexuality that create emotional rather than rational reactions by recipients. A client's neurotic, *evoking* message will result in a corrective emotional experience if the therapist becomes aware and is able to make the covert message overt.

Evoking Messages

Neurotic communication resembles a persuasive message, except neither sender nor receiver is aware of the latent message. If direct expression of feelings or needs results in punishment or rejection, children learn to send double messages: a con-

Table 10.7 Sending and receiving conscious and unconscious messages

Message awareness	Sender is *aware* of message	Sender is *unaware* of message
Receiver is *aware* of message	Overt communications based on awareness and reason	Therapeutic metacommunications can increase sender's awareness
Receiver is *unaware* of message	Persuasive communications that manipulate emotional climate	Evoking (neurotic) messages that manipulate emotional climate

ventional, manifest message that is socially acceptable and avoids vulnerability, and an unconscious latent message that *evokes* the desired response. They learn to *scan* others for *areas of vulnerability* in which the other person has strong feelings or unmet needs. Messages with a strong emotional impact constrict awareness in recipients, giving the sender greater control in the relationship. Once people are emotionally *engaged*, they typically respond in conventional, predictable ways that meet at least some of the individual's needs; *e.g.*, if a mother is caring only when her son is sick or hurt, he may learn to be "accident-prone."

Evoking messages are reinforced by (a) increased predictability of the other's response, (b) responses that meet at least some needs, and (c) allowing people to deny responsibility or vulnerability. People are victims of circumstance or the other person's actions, not their own. They avoid rejection or retaliation by keeping recipients unaware of the hidden needs in their communication. If they also remain unaware, they can deny responsibility for the message's outcome should their subterfuge be uncovered. Evoking messages create constrictive emotional climates that influence recipients to meet short-term client needs, but can have problematic long-term negative consequences of repeated interpersonal losses. Because they are unconscious, they are also difficult to modify. Therapists increase clients' awareness of evoking messages and provide extinction trials by not reinforcing latent demands implicit in the message.

Conventions

Interpersonal relations are largely governed by conventions such as taking turns in conversations, making "reasonable" requests politely, and expressing appreciation for favors. Social conventions bring predictability into human intercourse and allow interaction with a minimum of conflict. Because they evoke predictable responses, conventions are also useful for expressing feelings unconsciously. The manifest meaning of "thanks" is a friendly appreciation that is beyond reasonable criticism. But said sardonically, its latent message can express hostility in a way that protects the sender from retaliation—after all, who can object to being thanked! Conventions create recipient *blind spots* that make recognition or effective responses to latent messages difficult; *e.g.*, a husband who nicely offers to cook the meal after his wife has burned dinner may be surprised and defensive when she responds with anger. He fails to recognize the latent criticism that he could do a better job and his wife may be angry without fully realizing why.

Psychotic behavior demonstrates the power of breaking conventions. An agitated man who reports aliens are injecting him with drugs may induce bewilderment and fear in others; but he will probably not be held responsible for his statements or actions. Babbling nonsense syllables elicits sympathetic care from others and disguises a wish to be cared for as an infant. Clients may also use social conventions or symptom formation to disguise poor social skills. A significant body of research has linked psychopathology to poor skills in responding to social conventions (Fischetti, Curran, & Wessberg, 1977; Klerman & Weissman, 1993).

Extratherapeutic Incidents

Clients may use conventions or symptoms to disguise their vulnerability and discourage further discussion of sensitive issues. They make reasonable requests, asking the therapist to change appointment times, or make demands that would be insensitive to refuse. Exploration may reveal the latent message and disguised needs, especially when incidents occur after discussion of a sensitive issue. Therapists obviously should respond to client safety issues, but then explore latent meanings to avoid reinforcing problematic patterns of interaction. The therapist's emotional response is a useful indicator of evoking messages, but some are subtle enough to escape attention. Beier and Young (1998) recommend a consultant's review of therapy tapes and procedures if therapy is stuck to see if the client is using a therapist's blind spots. Table 10.8 summarizes their suggestions for following up extratherapeutic incidents.

Table 10.8 Suggested responses to extratherapeutic incidents

Incident	Description of typical situation
Appointment change	Client gives "convincing" reasons to make a change, such as family obligations or medical appointments that take precedence over therapy
Missed appointment	Unless client is at risk, ignore first miss; call after second miss to see if client is returning; third miss in a row requires written notice that therapy is terminated
Payment questions	Clients may feel being charged for services takes advantage of their weakness; may be entitlement or a "test of love." Change fees on basis of objective situation
Habitual gestures	Behavioral patterns that are easy to overlook: slouched posture, soft voice, constricted movements, speech habits ("Don't you know?"), *etc.*
Gifts to/from therapist	Gifts, compliments, client referrals, and trying to please all reflect disguised ways to express feelings. Requests ("Would you turn off the recorder?") solicit nurturance
Demands for service	Hard-to-refuse requests for phone consultation, change in therapy contract, or to extend time in a therapy session: latent messages need to be clarified
Vacations and interruptions	Therapist vacations require discussion. Office interruptions are minimized and therapist needs to be alert to the client's vulnerable feelings when they occur
Outside contacts	Information from other parties is shared with clients so therapist does not have to stop and think; however, trust issues are an inevitable part of the therapy process
Suicide calls	Responding to suicidal threat may increase future risk, so only serious threats are addressed; client may need referral to therapist who has not been manipulated
Terminating treatment	Request, threat, or demand to terminate may be attempts to punish therapist; if clients are ready, they will simply announce the fact and not need permission

Intervention Approach

For Beier and Young (1998), as in other process-oriented therapies, the influence of client communications on the here-and-now therapeutic relationship is more important than the choice of content. Often, clients choose content areas that reduce responsibility for their thoughts, wishes, or actions; *e.g.*, discussing dreams or free associations and linking problem behaviors to childhood experiences or past traumas all create distance from one's actions. Therapy content is problematic whenever *word cages* preclude the possibility of change, *e.g.*, Popeye's "I yam what I yam." Attributions that suggest that a problem is stable, caused by external forces, or otherwise beyond the client's control create traps that prevent change from even being considered.

Therapy begins when the therapist becomes aware of word cages or being emotionally engaged with the client. *Beneficial uncertainty* is created as the therapist *disengages* and fails to respond in predictable, socially conventional ways to the emotional climate evoked by the client. Awareness of the latent message helps therapists become aware of the nature of the client's motivation and fears—where the client *hurts*. The therapist disengages from evoking messages, avoids reinforcing problematic messages, and helps the client develop awareness of their pattern of interaction. As clients gain insight into their evocative patterns, they can explore more direct, less manipulative ways of communicating their needs; however, without beneficial uncertainty there is no pressure to change. Beneficial uncertainty provides the necessary motivation.

Evoking messages are identified by therapists becoming aware of their own emotional state. If therapists feel constricted, irritated, uncomfortable, frightened, pleased, or amused, then clients may have their needs met without being vulnerable and expressing them openly. Disengaging from evoking messages can be difficult, since clients have had a lifetime to master their unique style of emotional engagement and are usually quite astute at *scanning for areas of vulnerability*. Therapists may feel pressured to "fix" dependent clients and find they are working harder than the client. Young, inexperienced therapists can expect to have clients "innocently" inquire about credentials and experience. Conversely, clients may offer the stressed or upset therapist sympathy and advice or become still more challenging. Therapists may need personal therapy or consultation about a therapeutic impasse to become aware of their vulnerabilities.

In addition to word cages and emotional reactions, therapists note incongruent messages to learn where clients hurt. The intrinsic paradox of both communicating and disguising needs leads to unintended slips and contradictions. Hypotheses about client messages are tested by responding in unexpected ways to evoking messages and creating beneficial uncertainty. If a hypothesis is correct, then failure to reinforce an evoking message produces emotional arousal and clients redouble their efforts. If incorrect, non-reinforcement is a non-issue.

As noted earlier, clients use social conventions to take advantage of a therapist's social conditioning. Table 10.9 lists some evocative ploys clients use to alter the

Table 10.9 Common evocative ploys and associated conventions or meanings

Reciprocity	*[If I tell you all about myself, why don't you tell me all about yourself?]*
Emergency calls	*[This will show you care for me and then I will feel in control.]*
Politeness	"I wasn't irritable, I said 'good morning.'" *[excusing grouchy tone of voice.]*
Naïveté	"Gee, isn't it fun getting laid?" *["innocently" testing therapist's interest.]*
Word cages	"I am what I am;" "My feelings are overwhelming;" [status quo *is inevitable.*]
Compliments/gifts	*[I'm not worthy, but maybe my gifts are; Let's just be friends and not work.]*
Silence; confusion	*[If I wait long enough, perhaps you will rescue me.]*
Excuses	"I'm sorry I'm late with my payment." *[If you cared for me as a friend, you wouldn't charge me; I'm not sure I want to do this, anyhow!]*
Last minute ploy	"I know it's 5 minutes before the hour, but I've decided to leave my spouse!" *[Now I won't have to deal with unpleasant feelings and can just act out.]*

conventions or meanings associated with the treatment frame; *e.g.*, acting naïvely while behaving seductively allows clients to test the waters in a deniable way that avoids vulnerability. In each example, it is likely that a therapist would become emotionally and cognitively constricted and find it difficult to access alternative responses. Once beginning therapists recognize an evocative message they often adopt a "You can't get me" approach in the belief they should avoid emotional engagement or countertransference. The therapeutic response to an evoking message, a breach of the therapeutic frame, or an expression of transference is to allow it to continue until the therapist (a) is able to disengage emotionally, (b) has a history to review with the client, and (c) has tested hypotheses about the meanings implicit in the evoking message against other evidence. Therapists then respond in an unexpected, non-reinforcing *asocial* manner (see Table 10.10).

Timing and sensitivity to the client's current state are always important, but are essential with paradigmatic responses or in demonstrating the impact of an evoking message. Humorous exaggeration of an implicit message can often help clients

Table 10.10 Therapeutic disengagement and asocial interventions

Intervention	Description [example]
Delay	Generic response, used to gain time [*Mm-hm; Go on; Tell me more about ....*]
Reflection	Rephrase/clarify client comment [*He really hurt you with those words.*]
Probe	Explore hidden meanings [*If I don't agree with you, what would that mean?*]
Interpretation	Suggest meanings [*I wonder if you wait until the session is almost over to mention painful things, so you won't have to face your feelings?*]
Paradigmatic response	Exaggerate/dramatize client behavior [Client: *You only say you care cause it's your job;* Therapist: *Why would anyone care about you except for money?*]
Demonstrate the impact	Feedback about impact of message [Verbal: *I liked it when you touched my hand.*] [Video: *Allows client to observe own performances more objectively.*]

see there is no compelling reason to continue disguising their needs. If they fail to recognize the therapist's caring and humorous intent, however, they may experience paradigmatic responses as rejecting or threatening. Similarly, demonstrating the impact of an "accidental" touch to reveal an implicit sexual motive may be too threatening for clients who are insecure about their sexuality.

Therapists should expect to be emotionally engaged, blind-sided, surprised, and upset with their clients. It is impossible to respond to every evoking message, as they happen frequently. Rather, therapists choose when to intervene based on such criteria as:

1. Does this message breach the treatment frame or endanger the therapeutic process?
2. Is this a core issue for the client? Does it recur time and again? Does non-reinforcement result in extreme, emotional responses?
3. Is the client ready to accept a probe or hear an interpretation? Can I frame my response in such a way that the client can explore the issue at a conscious level?
4. Do I have time today to work through the issues an interpretation will bring up?

Responding to a breach of the treatment frame is critical, since failure to maintain boundaries confuses clients and reinforces problem behaviors. Boundaries establish the professional nature of the relationship and create a context to explore new responses as old ones are abandoned.

Case Illustration

Bill is a 37-year-old Anglo-American man whose moderate dysthymic symptoms began in late adolescence. He is underemployed as a part-time computer technician and still lives at home with his parents. Bill is a bright, charming, and articulate person who can be very engaging in his humorous descriptions of his shortcomings. His usual pattern is to start ambitious projects that somehow never come to fruition. This pattern first became apparent when he left a prestigious engineering college one semester prior to graduating. He stated he just lost interest in his studies, had trouble sleeping and concentrating, and decided it would be better to drop out than to fail and disappoint his family. His current plan is to open his own computer business using capital provided by his parents. The following dialog from Bill's third session shows how a communication analysis therapist might use beneficial uncertainty and reveal that progress may be more apparent than real.

B: [*smiling*] This past week has been great! I found my new shop and signed the lease.

T: Go on, tell me more. [*Is this progress or Bill's typical pattern of initial enthusiasm? The disengaged delay response avoids responding to Bill's mood and shifts responsibility to him to explore further.*]

B: Yeah, wow! I found this really neat location next to the CompUSA store. And I talked with their manager and she was really supportive and said a repair service next door would create great synergy!

T: Uh huh. [*A delay response that avoids reinforcing Bill's excited plea for approval.*]

B: [*pause*] Uh ... Yeah, my folks were really excited for me. They loaned me the money for the lease and are going to help me set up my books and all. Isn't that great?

T: It sounds as if you're hoping I'll approve of all you accomplished also. [*An asocial reflection that points to Bill's bid for approval by others without reinforcing that bid.*]

B: [*awkward pause*] Well ... uh, I've only had trouble sleeping one night this week and I've not been depressed at all. Things are finally looking up for me.

T: Uh huh. [*This asocial delay response avoids reinforcing Bill's attempts to gain approval, but it might have been more effective to reflect how his demands were escalating. After all, these are his presenting complaints and isn't he making good progress?*]

B: [*Silence; Bill's posture and facial expression all show dejection and hopelessness. The return of symptoms reflects the collapse of his pleas for approval and is a way to punish the therapist for not being more supportive.*]

T: I can see you're feeling really down just now. I'm guessing you're unhappy that I wasn't more excited when you talked about your new shop and how your symptoms were better. [*This asocial reflection of the session's here-and-now process potentially suggests that Bill might have other choices than to impress the therapist.*]

B: [*angrily*] Ah, what's the use? Nobody really cares. I think I'm getting better, but I'm just a hopeless case. I should just quit wasting your time.

T: [*shaking head and smiling*] Yeah, you poor guy. Here you were all excited and happy and your lousy therapist flushed all that down the toilet! [*The therapist uses a paradigmatic response that exaggerates Bill's collapse and threat to end therapy.*]

C: [*laughing*] You're right! You are a lousy therapist! I guess I just wanted you to appreciate all that I'd been doing—I never know what you're thinking and I wonder if you even like me. [*With consistent non-reinforcement, Bill experienced beneficial uncertainty and was able to let go of his manipulation and explore feelings that he normally avoided.*]

Note how Bill's failure to engage the therapist led to a collapse of his efforts to please his therapist and to threats of termination. If not for the therapist's asocial responses, it is likely he would continue his pattern of relying on other's judgments of whether he was worthy or not. The therapist's disengagement was essential to prevent reinforcement of the client's pattern of using symptoms to evoke care and support from others when conventional accomplishments were unsuccessful.

Integrative Implications

Although Adler's Individual Psychology is a useful therapeutic approach that anticipated many contemporary ideas, his theory has not been accepted as Freud's was and lacks empirical support. A literature search revealed only one supportive outcome study of Adlerian therapy (Rogner, 1994). One reason for this neglect is the incompatibility of Adler's rationalism with scientific modernism. Nevertheless, many Adlerian concepts now have empirical support thanks to research on self-regulation and social cognition theory. Past concerns about the validity of the intentionality concept are addressed by self-regulation and general systems theory, which provide ways to think integratively about humanistic and deterministic theoretical models.

Self-Regulation and General Systems Theory

Historically, intentionality was considered non-scientific because it was associated with *teleological* causation in which future events determine the present. Cognitive theorists, *e.g.*, Bandura (1986), now consider *beliefs* about the future to determine goal-directed behavior, which has resurrected interest in the concept of intentionality; *e.g.*, self-regulation theory describes how individuals adapt to changing circumstances to attain intended goals by covert rehearsal and self-regulating feedback loops. People continuously monitor on-going efforts to determine if they are likely to attain their goals or not; *e.g.*, a pianist might alter fingerings in a difficult passage (behavioral self-regulation), relax and mentally rehearse the desired phrasing (covert self-regulation), or close the window to shut out distracting noises (environmental self-regulation).

Although many goal-directed activities such as driving and talking can occur with little conscious awareness, conscious self-regulation involves three mutually influencing processes: forethought, performance or volitional control, and self-reflection (Schunk & Zimmerman, 1998; Zimmerman, 2000). Forethought involves goal setting and strategic plans about how to achieve the goal. It is influenced by self-motivational factors including the goal's intrinsic interest and self-efficacy and outcome expectancies (Bandura, 1997). Once goals and plans are set, actual performances are controlled by imagery, self-monitoring, self-instruction, and task strategies such as monitoring sub-goals or trial-and-error experimentation. Once a performance is completed, self-evaluation and attributions about causes of the outcome guide strategies for future performances: current performance is compared with past performances or the mastery of sub-goals to determine if any changes are necessary. Past performances or sub-goals prove more useful for individual performances than comparisons with others.

Self-regulated people value intrinsic satisfactions of jobs well-done more than extrinsic rewards (Bandura, 1997). If outcomes are unsatisfactory, they consider

Table 10.11 Powers (1973) hierarchic organization of behavioral self-regulation

Perceptual-cognitive processing levels	Error output when discrepancies occur between reference and perception values	Level reflects innate or developmental process
1. Intensity	Something happened	Innate/preconscious
2. Sensation	Light, sound, touch, taste. smell, pain	Innate/preconscious
3. Configuration	Color, shapes, phonemes, *etc.*	Innate/preconscious
4. Transitions	Change, motion, contrast, words	Innate/preconscious
5. Sequence	Perceived event, pattern, sentence, thought	Sensorimotor
6. Relationships	Concepts, causal attributions, intentions	Pre-operational
7. Programs	Strategies, beliefs, plans	Concrete operations
8. Principles	Values, heuristics, guiding concepts	Formal operations
9. Philosophy	World view, religious system, "Life Style"	Dialectical operations?

how to improve performance, while less self-regulated people react defensively to protect self-esteem by insuring there are external reasons for failure. Unfortunately, such self-handicapping interferes with the person's growth and leads to task avoidance, helplessness, or apathy.

General systems theory explains how self-regulation occurs without conscious awareness. A self-regulating system, *e.g.*, a thermostatic heating system, compares a *reference* value (r; the thermostat setting) with a *perceptual* value (p; the room temperature). If there is a discrepancy or *error* value (e), the system will automatically act to reduce that discrepancy (furnace turns on). In general, reference-perceptual errors ($r - p = $ e) activate appropriate subsystem(s) to reduce errors in self-regulating system. In complex systems such people, hierarchically organized subsystems regulate goal attainment.

Table 10.11 describes Powers' (1973) model in which each level of perceptual-cognitive processing provides a reference value to compare with the next lower-level perceptual value to determine if an error exists that requires action. The first four levels of this model are pre-conscious sensory-perceptual systems that monitor goal attainment at higher levels. Goals at the philosophy level are typically framed in general, abstract terms. They reflect core interpersonal and world-view schemas (Adler's life style), many of which develop before language and are only partly in awareness; *e.g.*, an oldest child who helps mother care for younger siblings may develop a "responsible" life style. As an adult, her life style provides the philosophical reference values by which she governs her life: she may value hard work and giving to others. The last column suggests a parallel between Powers' conscious levels and Piaget's (1952/1963) developmental stages plus a proposed *dialectical operations* stage.

Powers' philosophy level corresponds to Basseches' (1984) and Riegel's (1973) concept of a dialectical operations stage in which adults learn to accept contradiction as an integral aspect of reality and think more contextually. Carver and Scheier (2000) describe the reference values of philosophy and principle as goals of "being" that enter consciousness only if people fail to live up to these standards. Reference values at the subordinate "program" and "relationship" levels are "doing" goals, which require conscious awareness of the action "sequences" needed to implement higher-order goals. In this view, consciousness monitors objective progress toward the person's goals. Superordinate being or doing goals also reflect Piaget's (1952/1963) developmental stages; *e.g.*, infants develop control over sequential actions during the sensorimotor stage, integrate sequences into concepts, intentions, and cause-effect relationships during the pre-operational stage, and form beliefs and plans during concrete operations. General systems theorists (*e.g.*, Bailey, 2006; Miller, 1978) add subordinate biological and superordinate family and societal levels to hierarchic models of the person: *e.g.*, families set reference values or expectations about cooperation and household duties that regulate an individual's behavior in the family, while social norms for age-related, gender, and occupational roles govern family roles and interactions with the outside world.

Carver and Scheier (2000) suggest that, in addition to feedback loops that guide behavior, secondary loops monitor the *rate* at which error discrepancies increase or decrease. People experience pleasure and elation if movement toward a positive goal (deviation-reduction) is quicker than expected and depression if it is slower. Pleasure and elation are "cruise-controls" signaling no more effort is needed, while depression is a signal for increased goal-directed efforts. A second affective system is postulated for deviation-enlarging loops that signal the need to avoid or escape a negative situation. Successful avoidance (deviation-reduction) results in relief, but failures result in anxiety (deviation increases). Interestingly, this contradicts hedonic models that suggest people maximize pleasure and minimize pain. Carver and Scheier's (2000) data suggest that while people do strive to minimize pain, pleasure is a signal that no further effort is needed. This suggests human motivation is more complex than simple hedonism and helps explain why pleasure tends to be fleeting.

Intentionality and Interpersonal Relations as Integrative Concepts

The subject-object dialectic has been a recurring theme in psychological discourse—the role of internal and external processes as determinants of behavior. Together, Adler and Sullivan provide perspectives that help bridge this essential divide. The Adlerian therapist maintains an objective, coaching stance toward clients, but addresses the subjective pole by emphasizing their capacity for intentionality, choice of goals, life style, and self-direction. General Systems Theory has since addressed historical concerns that intentionality was not "scientific."

Sullivan's emphasis on therapists as participant-observers illustrates how tensions in the subject-object dialectic operate in practice: as participants, therapists co-create the therapeutic relationship, while as observers they step back to view what is happening objectively in the relationship. Neo-Sullivanian interventions are not limited to insight or learning, but have their greatest impact when therapists step back, disengage from emotional constriction evoked by use of conventions or blind spots, and thus provide a corrective emotional experience.

Both Adler and Sullivan anticipated many modern developments in psychotherapy, but only Adler is currently represented by an "Adlerian" school of therapy. This is due in large part to the lack of acceptance of his ideas, which were incongruent with foundational views of science until recently. In contrast, Sullivan's ideas have been developed in multiple directions, so that no "official" Sullivanian school of therapy exists. But the participant-observer concept led to the here-and-now process focus of humanistic, family, and group therapies as well as object relations and Neo-Sullivanian interpersonal therapies. Sullivan's conception of personality and psychopathology as interpersonal processes rather than static aspects of an individual also gave rise to applications of general systems theory such as family systems therapy.

Chapter Ten: Main Points

- In contrast to Freud's drive theory, Adler's constructivist approach proposed that people act on the basis of conscious intentions and goals constructed on the basis of their beliefs (*fictional finalism*). His emphasis on societal influences on parenting and family influences on the individual anticipated many modern ideas, including postmodernism's emphasis on social contexts, intentionality, and the construction of meanings.
- An individual's goals are adaptive if they fulfill the innate motive of *social interest*. If children fail to achieve their goals, they become discouraged and choose increasingly less adaptive goals, moving from seeking attention to power to revenge, and finally to develop symptoms that demonstrate their *assumed disability* to function adaptively. Withholding attention may extinguish maladaptive goal-directed behavior, but leads to even more maladaptive goals. Pointing out a child's goal elicits a *recognition reflex* and allows alternatives to be discussed.
- Authoritarian parenting styles are no longer supported by increasingly democratic societal values, so Adler developed the first child guidance clinics to teach more effective parenting. Parents are taught to encourage behavior with social interest and let *natural consequences* discourage misbehavior. Dangerous misbehaviors are given *logical consequences* that are clearly related to the misbehavior, so that children do not experience discipline as arbitrary. Family councils are useful ways to air problems and set logical consequences; but to avoid becoming punitive, children must feel that they have a voice and a stake in the outcomes.
- Each person makes choices about goals and how to view the self, others, and the world, which constitutes their *life style*. Life style choices are influenced by parental style and support (*family atmosphere*) and by *birth order*, which affects the available familial roles. Family structure and number and gender of siblings are also influential, but the general tendency is for firstborns to be responsible pleasers, middle children to be competitive, and youngest to be spoiled and dependent. Only children may combine elements of both firstborns and youngest children.
- The neurotic person fails to develop goals that have social interest and may *safeguard* against feelings of inferiority with *excuses* (symptoms), *aggression* (hostility, blaming others), or *distancing* (helplessness, avoidance, self-handicapping, *etc.*).

- Therapy begins by establishing collaboration and assessing the client's unique life style with a case history, family constellation, observing the relationship, and other measures such as early recollections, dreams, symptoms, psychological tests, and the *Adlerian Question*, "How would things be different if you miraculously became well tomorrow?" Life style hypotheses are cross-validated by congruence of difference types of data. Typical life style themes include social charm, achievement, social interest, and safeguarding.

- Confrontation, paradoxical intention (symptom prescription), and "spitting-in-the-soup" (pointing out self-defeating goals) then help clients gain intellectual *insight* and experiential awareness how their life style choices affect their current problems. The final, *reorientation* stage helps clients commit to goals with social interest. Interventions include *catching oneself* (being aware of old "triggers"), *living as-if* (role playing a more adaptive life style), and the *push-button* technique (guided imagery that helps clients manage emotional responses).

- Sullivan argued that personality and psychopathology are revealed in interpersonal behavior. People respond to internalized schemas or *personifications* of self and others, rather than directly to others. Concepts of a *generalized other* and a *self-concept* begin to differentiate as a means of controlling anxiety when the child's needs are not met immediately. The child *dissociates* aspects of self and other, especially if mother is also anxious, resulting in *good-me, bad-me, good mother*, and *bad mother* personifications. Extreme anxiety can produce a *not me* personification, while *selective inattention* controls lesser anxieties.

- Sullivan's model of social and cognitive development has six stages: 1. *infancy*, characterized by disconnected *prototaxic* thought; 2. *childhood*, with associative, magical *parataxic* thought, which may result in a *malevolent transformation* if the child experiences humiliation; 3. *juvenile*, in which parataxic distortions are corrected by *consensual validation* of beliefs by significant others and peer groups, leading to *syntaxic* thought; 4. *preadolescence*, in which a *chum* provides the first-loving peer relationship and helps the child recognize the difference between love and lust once puberty begins; 5. *early adolescence*, in which the child needs to resolve conflicts among security, sexual, and intimacy needs; and 6. *late adolescence*, in which a social façade or *mask* develops to maintain self-respect in response to negative *reflected appraisals* by others.

- Therapists who use Beier's Neo-Sullivanian *Communication Analysis* focus on latent nonverbal and contextual messages in client communications. If latent messages are kept out of both sender's and receiver's awareness, clients avoid vulnerability and responsibility. Such *evoking messages* rely on social conventions and induce emotionality to constrict receivers' awareness and response alternatives.

- Once therapists are aware of evoking messages and *word cages* that make change seem impossible, their *disengagement* from the expected response creates *beneficial uncertainty* in the client. With increased awareness of how they influence others, evoking messages are extinguished and clients are enabled to communicate needs more honestly and directly.

- Self-Regulation and General Systems Theory provide models that explain intentionality as a circular causality, feedback process in which perceptions are compared with reference or goal values. Discrepancies are fed back into the system until errors are corrected, as in thermostat-regulated heating systems. Powers' hierarchic model suggests that perceptions are compared against reference values based on higher-level subsystems; *e.g.*, *principles* establish the types of goals (reference values) that would be acceptable, and goals then determine possible plans.

Further Reading

Beier, E. G., & Young, D. M. (1998). *The silent language of psychotherapy: Social reinforcement of unconscious processes* (3rd ed.). Edison: Aldine Transaction Press.
Carlson, J., Maniacci, M. P., & Watts, R. E. (2005). *Adlerian therapy: Theory and practice.* Washington: American Psychological Association.
Dreikurs, R., Cassel, P., & Ferguson, E. D. (2004). *Discipline without tears: How to reduce conflict and establish cooperation in the classroom* (Rev. ed). Toronto: Wiley.
Oberst, U. O., & Stewart, A. E. (2003). *Adlerian psychotherapy: An advanced approach to Individual Psychology.* New York: Brunner-Routledge.

Website

Alfred Adler Institutes of San Francisco and Northwestern Washington. *Distance training in Classical Adlerian Psychotherapy.* Retrieved from http://ourworld.compuserve.com/homepages/HStein/

Videos

Carlson, J., & Kjjos, D. (2000). Adlerian therapy with Dr. James Bitter [Videotape]. Boston: Allyn & Bacon.
Carlson, J., & Kjjos, D. (2000). Adlerian therapy with Dr. Jon Carlson [Videotape]. Boston: Allyn & Bacon.

Chapter 11
Contemporary Interpersonal Approaches

> *The analyst cannot single-mindedly attempt to uncover the unconscious conflicts dating from the patient's past history, but must also be constantly attentive to the present analytic situation. He must constantly ask himself, "What important person from the patient's past am I being for him now, and what specific conflict is being played out?"*
>
> Fancher (1973, p. 178)

Fancher is describing transference, which transformed Freud's conception of neurosis and led to his consideration of the process of therapy in addition to the historical content of the client's early memories. The transference dialectic revolves around three questions:

- Should therapy focus on the historical antecedents of problematic patterns?
- Should it focus on those patterns as they are recreated in the client's current problems?
- Or should it confront the transference of those patterns into the therapy relationship?

Psychoanalysts historically treated transference either as a problem or as a pointer to underlying problems; in contrast, Sullivan viewed transference as an opportunity to confront here-and-now interpersonal process and provide a corrective emotional experience. Most modern psychodynamic and interpersonal therapists attend to all three alternatives, but differ in what they emphasize; *e.g.*, Beier (Chap. 10) focuses mostly on the therapy relationship. At the opposite pole, Gerald Klerman focuses almost exclusively on the client's current problems. Other theorists discussed in this chapter consider all three alternatives, but Edward Teyber emphasizes the therapy relationship, while Lorna Smith Benjamin focuses more on helping clients relate historical maladaptive patterns to current problems as they appear in therapy and elsewhere.

Therapeutic process is addressed differently by different approaches; *e.g.*, in Emotionally Focused Therapy (Chap. 8), process interventions help clients access blocked feelings that keep them from solving problems on their own. In interpersonal

D. K. Fromme, *Systems of Psychotherapy*,
DOI 10.1007/978-1-4419-7308-5_11, © Springer Science+Business Media, LLC 2011

therapies, process interventions modify the client's problematic interaction patterns as they occur. Cognitive-behavioral therapies have only recently begun to address process variables explicitly because it is difficult to create manuals that capture the here-and-now focus of process-oriented therapies; *e.g.*, Safran (1998) integrates experiential and interpersonal therapies and argues that therapy should focus on "hot" cognitions about emotionally significant interpersonal processes. Because it is so central to interpersonal theory, the following section discusses the process dimension in more detail.

Communication Theory: Process *vs.* Content

The Palo Alto group (*e.g.*, Bateson, 1972; Watzlawick, Beavin, & Jackson, 1967) were instrumental in applying General Systems Theory and Communications Theory (CT), to problems of clinical interest. Watzlawick *et al.* (1967) developed Sullivan's emphasis on nonverbal messages into a set of axioms about the nature of all communication:

1. It is impossible *not* to communicate in the presence of others. (Silence can be very powerful!)
2. Communication involves a verbal report of *content* and a nonverbal and contextual *process* or command that defines the relationship between two people; *e.g.*, "Hello" implies a relationship exists and demands a reply, especially if it is the boss speaking.
3. Content is governed by *syntax* and communicates *semantic* meanings verbally; process is not governed by syntax and instead unconsciously communicates the *pragmatic* function of the message nonverbally; *e.g.*, "I feel sick!" implies an expectation of being excused from one's usual responsibilities.
4. Process *commands* modify the meaning of content *reports*; they are a *metacommunication* about the overt *communication* that defines the nature of the communication and relationship; *e.g.*, context and nonverbal signals can transform an insult into "good-natured" teasing.
5. Participants arbitrarily *punctuate* cause and effect during a series of exchanges, which can lead to disagreement; *e.g.*, "I withdraw because you nag." "I nag because you withdraw."
6. Relationships are defined in part by punctuation sequences; overt metacommunication may enable change to occur: "We're stuck unless we find an alternative to 'nag-withdraw-nag....'"
7. Relationships are also defined in part by sequences of process commands; *complementary* relationships develop over time when one person regularly asserts control or direction in the relationship and the other person acquiesces; *symmetrical* relationships result if the other person responds with counter-assertions that define the relationship as one between equals: "Please take out the trash." "Yes, dear." *vs.* "I'll do it after you finish the dishes, dear."

8. Over time, relationships develop into self-regulating systems; should one person not respond with the expected complementary or symmetrical response, the other will act to re-establish the usual pattern: "If you won't take out the trash, I'll do it." "No! That's alright, dear, I'll do it."

Incongruence of content and process can lead to relationship problems, but can also be the source of humor; *e.g.*, the classic *double-bind* conflict is illustrated by the story of the mother who gave her son two shirts for Christmas. When she next saw him wearing one of the shirts, she asked, "So, you didn't care for the other one?" Double-binds are difficult to escape because people typically focus on a message's content and are less aware of contextual or nonverbal processes. Repeated double-bind experiences cause people to respond ineffectively since complying with one side of the demand automatically negates the other. This is a uniquely human problem since animals have only process commands to communicate their intentions such as growling to warn others to back off.

Blame and counter-blame cycles reflect punctuation problems in which each person views their own behavior as a reasonable response to the other's unreasonable behavior. People who alternate complementary and symmetrical interactions usually resolve their problems. However, repeated complementary interactions become difficult to alter; the intrinsic inequality means one party becomes controlling and over-functions, while the other becomes submissive and under-functions. People who under-function often suppress needs and feelings and *disqualify* their communication in order to preserve the status quo. They may refer to themselves in the third person or use vague, tangential, circumstantial, or confused language. In contrast, symmetrical relations may escalate into violence as each party tries to one-up the other in order to establish equality in their relationship. Symmetrical couples are often baffled by the petty nature of the content of their arguments, but the disagreement is not about problems such as who takes out the trash. The argument is about the underlying process of who has the right to set the rules in the relationship and that can be quite threatening.

A common element in punctuation problems and rigid interactions is a process in which each partner *invalidates* the other's communication. There is no problem if a statement elicits acceptance. Even rejection is not a serious problem, but just means that problem-solving and compromise are needed. But if messages are ignored or met with contempt and ridicule, the person's sense of self-worth is undermined. When people come for therapy, their self-esteem has been undermined by repeated invalidation of needs, wishes, and feelings. Empathic validation of their feelings and communication are crucial in providing a corrective emotional experience. Clients and well-meaning friends are usually not able to help resolve such problems because social conventions require them to respond to a message's content rather than its process. It is impolite to point out another's faux pas or implicit demands! Resolving communication problems caused by incongruent content and process messages requires metacommunication, *process comments* that bring incongruities into awareness. This is the essence of interpersonal therapy.

Interpersonal Process in Therapy

Teyber's (2006) Interpersonal Process Approach (IPA) integrates interpersonal theory (Sullivan, 1953a, b, 1964; Horney, 1966, 1970) with attachment and object relations theory and incorporates ideas from cognitive, experiential, and family systems approaches. Terms such as personification, maladaptive interpersonal pattern, internal working model, relational template, core belief, faulty expectation, emotion scheme, and cognitive schema are all different ways to express essentially the same concept. They reflect the efforts of different therapeutic systems to account for the long-term effects of children's early experiences with caregivers and how these currently impact relationship problems and the therapy process.

To understand an interpersonal schema, therapists examine childhood experiences, current problems, and the therapeutic process to determine recurring interpersonal patterns and the associated emotional reactions. They ask questions such as:

- Does the client elicit irritation, sympathy, boredom from others?
- How do they do this? Do they have tragic stories? Do they have a point or just wander about?
- What is their typical emotional reaction? Anxiety? Shame? Hostility?
- What beliefs support this reaction? Do they feel they're a burden to others? Unlovable? What do they expect from others? Rejection? What do they want? Love? Understanding?

Teyber (2006) brings answers to these questions together with well-validated concepts and interventions in creating an integrative interpersonal theoretical system that has great promise. Unfortunately, no outcome studies directly examine IPA's efficacy, but other, related interpersonal approaches have received empirical support.

Conceptual Framework

Following Sullivan and object relations theorists, Teyber (2006) assumes personality and human problems reflect current relationship patterns that developed from repeated interactions between infant and caregivers. Schemas are formed during these early attachment experiences that represent self-and-other interactions. Split schemas of *good-me, good-mother vs. bad-me, bad-mother* develop as caregivers are slow or unresponsive in meeting the infant's needs. With *good-enough* mothering that meets needs for safe limits and emotional security most of the time, children are eventually able to form secure attachments that integrate these dissociated elements into realistic self and other schemas reflecting both positive and negative experiences. As Fig. 7.1 suggested, good-enough, authoritative parenting leads to secure attachment, harsh discipline leads to anxious-avoidant attachment, warm, inconsistent discipline leads to anxious-ambivalent attachment, and neglectful parenting leads to disorganized attachment.

Family Influences

Parenting style is itself affected by the caregiver's own developmental history and by the family system that evolves between parents or with single parenting. If parents do not resolve insecure early attachments, their parenting style may reflect early avoidance, dependence, or disorganization. Such parents fail to differentiate and integrate realistic self and other schemas, which can result in *multi-generational transmission* of insecure attachments (Bowen, 1978; Beavers, 1982). Problems in family *structure*, especially *cross-generational alliances*, can also create serious problems by preventing a cohesive parental coalition that works together to support children and provide realistic limits (Minuchin, 1974).

Leaving home to establish a new family is a developmental challenge for newlyweds. In addition to setting up a new household, the couple must learn to accommodate to each other's habits and traits as well as balance *family loyalties* with each other and their respective families. Although there is wide cultural variation in levels of mutual involvement between generations, effective parenting needs either a cohesive couple or a single parent to establish an authoritative style of relating to their children. Problems occur if *coalitions* form between generations, *e.g.*, if grandmother and mother align themselves against father or if father and son align themselves against mother. Such *triangles* create power imbalances that lead to marital discord or enable a child to defy a triangulated parent. Cohesive marital coalitions or single parents that have healthy peer relations help children in several ways:

1. *Parents find it easier to establish consistent rules and limits:* Children learn to follow rules and accept reasonable authority if they cannot play one parent against the other. If father takes his son's side against mother, the child learns adult rules can safely be ignored and will likely have authority problems throughout his life. He learns to manipulate others rather than delay gratification and may have acting-out problems such as substance abuse. He may manipulate his therapist and expect special treatment—extended time, reduced fees, mid-week calls, *etc.*

2. *Children gain a realistic sense of self and their role:* Children gain an exaggerated sense of importance if a parent's primary emotional bond is with them. They fail to understand their limitations if allowed to make important decisions or support a parent's well-being. Despite feelings of grandiosity engendered by an adult role, they are likely to suffer anxiety and feelings of inadequacy since they are never able to meet their caretaker's needs fully. In therapy, they are apt to be "pleasers" and expect the therapist to respond in kind.

3. *They avoid being* parentified *and feeling overly responsible for others:* Children whose role is to take care of a parent's emotional needs become *parentified* and sacrifice their own needs. They are the parent's "best friend," but feel guilty about depending on others to meet their needs. Adult relationships are unstable because they worry about meeting their partner's needs, but are anxious and angered if the partner is not sufficiently available to them. They have poor boundaries, over-identify with others' problems, and may be intrusively controlling. Countertransference is likely in therapy, because parentified clients quickly discern what will make their

therapist feel competent, at least until therapists ask them about their feelings. This creates strong resistance in clients who have learned to ignore their own feelings.

4. *Children are enabled to differentiate and leave home successfully:* Differentiation can look very different in Anglo families who encourage individuation and in Latin or Asian families who encourage extended family ties. Every culture has the task, however, of helping children be free to be children and not suffer *separation guilt* over abandoning a parent when leaving home. Enmeshed children may feel guilt over successes, have trouble forming intimate relationships, may "fail to launch" or are chronically depressed. They may fear getting well in therapy and worry about no longer "needing" the therapist.

Ideally, family members are sufficiently *differentiated* from one another that each person is free to follow their own interests and ensure their needs are met. At the same time, the family needs to be sufficiently *integrated* to provide the support and structure necessary to support both intimacy and autonomy. Differentiation and integration fail in family triangles if two people are *enmeshed* or overly involved with one another in a cross-generational alliance and *disengaged* from a third member. This may be one parent and child against the other parent, but it could be grandparent and parent against the other parent, grandparent and child against parent, or other cross-generational alliances. However, it is equally problematic if the whole family is enmeshed with or disengaged from one another.

A child's needs for autonomy and individuation threaten over-involved, enmeshed families, while needs for intimacy and attachment threaten the emotionally, cut-off, disengaged family's structure. In both cases, rigid family structures prevent flexible movement between encouraging autonomy and offering emotional support as needed by the child. Parents in rigid families are relatively undifferentiated and may view their own intimacy or autonomy needs as unacceptable. They may then choose a boy or girl similar to themselves in important ways to express these unacceptable needs or feelings. By projecting unacceptable aspects of themselves onto the child, they gain vicarious satisfaction of needs while avoiding responsibility. The child then becomes the "problem" rather than themselves or the family's structure. The child's misbehavior, of course, is simply to express needs for intimacy and autonomy. As adults, the children continue the family history of poor differentiation with inflexible interpersonal coping strategies that fail to meet needs for intimacy, autonomy, and competency.

Inflexible Interpersonal Coping Strategies

In Teyber's (2006) model, rigid family structures result in unresponsive parenting, which causes insecure attachment and maladaptive interpersonal patterns; the resulting schemas or core conflicts may resurface in adulthood as repetitive, unsatisfactory relationships with significant others. Although everyone uses defensive coping in difficult situations, people with insecure attachments apply interpersonal strategies inflexibly in situations that arouse feelings or needs associated with core conflicts. Although these strategies were a necessary adaptation to problematic childhood relationships, they now prevent the adult from establishing intimacy, autonomy, or even competency in current relationships.

The goal of therapy is to help clients recognize when defensive coping strategies may be appropriate or necessary and when they interfere unnecessarily with relationships and prevent clients from having their needs met. To achieve this goal, Teyber (2006) suggests that therapists first identify the interpersonal patterns and feelings that constitute the client's core conflict and coping strategy. Once therapy clarifies how their coping strategy unintentionally creates problems in current relationships, clients can begin changing their relationship patterns in therapy and with significant others. Treatment plans and case conceptualizations are always "works in progress" as new information confirms or disconfirms hypotheses about core conflicts and coping mechanisms. Teyber (2006) uses Horney's (1970) interpersonal model to conceptualize the client's core conflicts, intrapsychic defenses, and interpersonal coping strategies.

Horney's Interpersonal Model

Teyber (2006) proposes a five-step model based on Horney's (1970) interpersonal theory to describe how insecure attachments block developmental needs and develop into core conflicts and inflexible coping mechanisms:

1. *Developmental trajectory:* children need a secure attachment that can provide a base for learning how to meet basic needs such as those for intimacy, autonomy, or competency
2. *Environmental block:* disengaged, authoritarian, or permissive parenting creates an insecure attachment that blocks the fulfillment of developmental needs
3. *Consequence:* a core conflict develops in which anxiety over unmet needs poses a threat to the child's need to maintain some level of connection with their caregiver(s)
4. *Compromise solutions:* insecurely attached children cope with anxiety related to their core conflict in two ways:

   (a) *Inflexible coping style:* the child learns to "rise above" unmet needs with an exaggerated interpersonal style that sacrifices other needs in the hope of maintaining connection with their caregiver by being "special"—three basic styles may be carried into adulthood:

      i. *Moving toward others:* rejection and punishment are avoided and attachments are maintained by pleasing others, even though needs for autonomy might be sacrificed
      ii. *Moving away from others:* avoiding and "not needing" others sacrifices intimacy and attachment, but provides a sense of superiority, independence, and self-sufficiency
      iii. *Moving against others:* aggressive dominance, competitiveness, and intimidation of others provides a sense of superiority that replaces intimacy and attachment needs

(b) *Turning against the self:* insecurely attached children learn to treat themselves in the same way they were treated by their caregiver—again, three
variants may carry into adulthood:

  i. *Reject self:* insecurely attached children introject the judgmental rejec-
     tion experienced from caretakers and feel contemptuous about their
     emotional needs ("I'm stupid!")
 ii. *Reject others:* they re-enact the same judgmental punitiveness toward
     others as their caregiver used with them—as adults, they may treat their
     children as they were treated
iii. *Elicit rejection from others:* they evoke harsh, punitive, or rejecting
     judgments from others that recapitulate early experiences (projective
     identification)

5. *Resolution of the core conflict:* compromise solutions inevitably fail, because the
   individual is overwhelmed by "tyranny of shoulds" that diminish the quality of
   life; because an entitled sense of "specialness" or "false pride" will eventually
   fail—it's impossible to please, avoid, or dominate everyone all the time; and
   because turning against the self or being special avoids, but does not resolve the
   client's core conflict; resolution is the goal of an IPA therapist

Clients block "dangerous" needs to manage anxiety in the same harsh, rejecting
way their caretakers used and take a neurotic, false pride in rising above those
needs to become "special" through self-sacrificing care for others, rugged independence, or superiority to others. These coping mechanisms result in broken relationships and emotional constriction, but also support the client's self-esteem, a
solution to earlier problems. This inevitable ambivalence means change requires
a strong, collaborative relationship to help clients confront the ways they perpetuate narcissistic childhood wounds and relinquish the "tyranny of shoulds" that
dominates their lives.

Interpersonal Process Intervention Principles

Therapeutic collaboration, the first principle of interpersonal therapy, provides a
corrective emotional experience (Alexander & French, 1946) as clients form strong
attachment bonds and discover their therapist does not respond as expected. Instead,
the second principle requires therapists to disengage from a client's attempts to recreate childhood patterns by making here-and-now *process comments* about strains
in their on-going relationship. The third principle is *client response specificity*, the
necessity for individualized interventions that consider the client's unique experiences and methods of coping with unmet attachment needs. Response specificity
precludes manualized interventions and requires therapists to ask themselves repeatedly if they are recreating a repetitive, problematic pattern or helping to create
a more adaptive relationship.

Developing an Internal Focus and Responding to Painful Feelings

The initial stages of interpersonal therapy (IPT) focus on establishing a collaborative relationship that *honors the client's resistance* and develops trust in the therapeutic relationship. Therapists then encourage an *internal focus* that brings painful feelings about unmet needs into awareness. The next step is to explore the relationships among unmet needs, problematic patterns in therapy, and in the client's current interpersonal relationships. It is at this point that hypotheses about blocked needs and inflexible coping patterns may be explored. Since clients determine therapy's content, therapists do not ask about childhood experiences, but explore the attachment origins of problems if these arise spontaneously in the client's narrative. Corrective emotional experiences are possible at each of these steps.

Therapists strive for a collaborative, working alliance by demonstrating it from the very beginning; *e.g.*, if clients experience conflict over taking the initiative in a relationship, they may have difficulty deciding what to talk about. A nondirective stance would only exacerbate the problem and perhaps drive the client away. A directive stance would just reinforce the problem. Teyber (2006) suggests beginning with a process comment about the client's difficulty in getting started and asking whether this is a common problem or unique to the current situation.

Process comments are intrinsically collaborative and neither directive or nondirective. They are essential for repairing strains or ruptures in the relationship and create *immediacy* by working in the moment. They redirect clients from externalizing their problems and bring them into the here-and-now, which increases the strength of the relationship. Empathic understanding of the client's experience also contributes to stronger collaboration.

Most clients have a history of disconfirming relationships, of not being heard or having their subjective experience invalidated. Empathic understanding provides a corrective experience by validating feelings and confirming that concerns are heard. Teyber notes it is particularly important for minorities, the poor, or victims of abuse to have their experience validated. Prejudice, oppression, and abuse are invalidating experiences that can leave victims feeling they have no voice and that no one cares. Validating feelings is not the same as agreeing with the client's interpretation of events. People may misconstrue events, but their resultant feelings are nevertheless valid given their understanding of what happened.

Clients may find it difficult to explore alternative explanations for events unless therapists first communicate acceptance and understanding of their feelings. Teyber (2006) also notes that "accurate empathy is not a stable personality characteristic of the therapist; it is an interpersonal process characterized by mutual exploration and collaboration" (p. 57). Effective therapists do not necessarily "get it right" all the time, but they check in and use their client's feedback to revise their understanding. Perhaps the most validating part of empathy for clients is to see the effort the therapist makes to understand their experience.

Since clients are always ambivalent about change, empathy and *honoring the resistance* are essential in maintaining a working alliance. Resistance is a sign that clients feel a threat and are reluctant to continue the on-going therapeutic process, but are unable to express this directly. After a first session, they may simply not show for their next appointment. In general, therapists should inquire toward the end of the first session about their clients' experience and if there are any concerns about either treatment or the therapist. Any hesitations or qualifications need to be explored: if the client says "I guess it's okay. I'll probably be here next week," there is a good chance everything is not *okay*. Therapists strengthen the therapeutic alliance by inviting clients to make their concerns known as they occur, taking those concerns seriously, and responding nondefensively to conflicts.

Ruptures of the therapeutic alliance typically occur in response to reenactments of core conflicts in therapy or resistance caused by feelings evoked by asking for help, exploring conflictual topics, or beginning to improve. Therapists honor resistance by accepting clients' reluctance to discuss a difficult topic, but then exploring their fears about what might happen; *e.g.*, clients may fear they might reveal perceived inadequacies and be rejected by the therapist or be overwhelmed by painful feelings if they continue. Clients are usually reassured and able to continue with the original topic if therapists show acceptance of fears of self-disclosure.

With repeated experiences of acceptance and empathic understanding, a safe *holding environment* is created that allows client to *focus inward* on painful and shameful feelings they have habitually avoided or externalized by blaming others. Therapists can collude with such externalization if they give advice, reassurance that things will work out, or make interpretations. Instead, therapists foster initiative and place the *locus of change* with the client. Clients gain a sense of self-efficacy and ownership for change if they look within themselves to uncover feelings that block their ability to make sense of problematic interactions. Therapists avoid an "expert" role and support the client's autonomy and initiative by using process comments or *self-involving statements* when clients appear stuck. They might say "I hear how you think others are feeling, but somehow I'm missing you. Could we talk about more about you? Perhaps about the difficulty you seem to have talking about your own feelings?"

Therapists obtain information to form and test hypotheses about a client's core conflicts in several ways. First, they look for obvious or subtle nonverbal signs that *track the client's anxiety* to identify topics or triggers for the anxiety and then make process comments that focus clients inward to explore their anxiety. Therapists empathize and let clients know that neither therapist nor client will be overwhelmed by the feelings, and that the pain's intensity will eventually lessen. They help clients realize they are no longer alone in their pain as they make full contact and share painful feelings. As clients stay with their feelings, especially recurrent ones, they often discover that their typical feelings have masked primary, but less acceptable emotions (see Chap. 8's discussion of primary and secondary emotions).

Teyber (2006) describes *affective constellations* or common patterns of emotions in which secondary emotions such as recurrent anger defend against shame, guilt, or anxiety evoked by an underlying sadness. Conversely, a recurrent sadness might defend against a primary emotion of anger that produces shame or guilt. Teyber suggests shame may be a *master emotion* (*e.g.*, Scheff, 1995) that clients reveal in self-descriptions as bad, stupid, or humiliated, or frequent use of shoulds, oughts, and musts. Clients defend against shameful sad or angry feelings by enacting their opposites or evoking shame in the other person.

Therapists may also learn about a client's core conflicts if they:

- Attend to repetitive, negative patterns in the therapeutic relationship and client narratives
- Collaboratively explore how such patterns affect therapy and current outside relationships, and
- Use process comments to change problematic patterns in the therapy relationship

For example, a self-involving process comment to give a corrective emotional experience when a client enacts a problematic pattern of hostility in therapy might be, "Ouch! That felt like another put down. We were talking earlier about your difficulties with your fiancée. Could she feel you are critical of her as I sometimes feel? Or am I just being over-sensitive? What do you think?"

Interpersonal Patterns and Solutions

Teyber (2006) recommends that therapists:

1. Identify recurring maladaptive interpersonal patterns
2. Respond in a way that differs from the usual pattern; and
3. Help clients generalize this new pattern into relationships with their significant others

Clients recreate problematic early relationships in three closely related ways: evoking messages or *eliciting maneuvers, testing behavior* to check if the therapist might provide a more helpful response than expected, and through *transference reactions.*

Eliciting maneuvers are enactments of inflexible coping styles that evoke a predictable response, avoid unwanted conflicts, and manage anxiety. Therapy is unproductive if a therapist's countertransference reaction complements the eliciting maneuver; *e.g.*, if therapists enjoy how pleasers treat them, withdraw from avoiders, or are competitive with intimidators. However, therapists can provide an unexpected beneficial experience and begin the change process if they recognize their countertransference pattern and disengage with self-involving process comments. Therapists need consultation or therapy to recognize their vulnerabilities and discriminate between informative, client-induced and unproductive, therapist-induced countertransference. Processing client-induced feelings moves therapy along, but a therapeutic impasse is likely if the feelings are primarily a reflection of therapist vulnerabilities.

Testing behavior is a growth-oriented response that explores the safety of the therapeutic relationship, whether it will reenact old patterns or perhaps begin to resolve them. An unexpected warm, accepting, and understanding therapist response can help clients question faulty beliefs about self and others. Clients teach therapists how best to intervene through such tests when they question old beliefs, explore feelings, or consider relevant new material. Conversely, they teach therapists how *not* to respond by externalizing, or acting weaker, more anxious, confused, or less collaborative in the relationship.

IPT rejects the psychoanalytic "blank screen" conception of transference. Instead, it takes the postmodern position that client actions are co-created with the therapist, based in part on the actual relationship and in part on distortions that reflect early attachment experiences. It is important that therapists acknowledge their own contribution to problematic interactions before seeking collaborative exploration of what else is involved. The goal is to:

1. Help the client explore potential misperceptions and other personal reactions to the therapist
2. Work collaboratively to explore how repetitive patterns (*e.g.*, experiencing the therapist as impatient when the therapist is not) disrupt the therapeutic relationship, and how the same pattern contributes to misunderstandings and problems with others; and
3. Work together to understand and change repetitive patterns with the therapist and with others

Recognizing transference distortions and relinquishing them in favor of more realistic perceptions in therapy is a precondition before new, more adaptive interpersonal skills can be generalized into relationships with significant others in the client's world.

Therapists must find an *optimal balance* between engaging the client in a reality-based, affectively significant therapeutic relationship and disengaging from client-induced transference reactions. They must recognize and appropriately address both sides of the client's ambivalence about changing *vs.* maintaining a hard-won comfort zone. As they repeatedly test the therapist and explore the consequences of transference and eliciting behaviors, clients find new ways of relating to the therapist. Paradoxically, change in conflictual relationships cannot occur until that conflict is re-experienced and then resolved in the therapy relationship. The therapist's challenge is to gain sufficient emotional distance from problematic relational patterns to be able to comment supportively about the process and prevent it from moving to its usual unhappy ending.

Therapy moves in a series of identifiable steps that begins when clients decide they have a problem that requires help and progresses as therapists:

1. Address concerns about seeking help or disloyalty to significant others;
2. Invite full expression of concerns, listen with respect, show understanding of the client's world view, and help solve some part of the difficulty, perhaps with relaxation training;
3. Establish a collaborative working alliance that creates a secure base and instills hope;
4. Focus clients' attention inward on their own needs or feelings rather than blaming others;
5. Help clients stop defending against core conflicts and begin to resolve their problems;

6. Recognize faulty assumptions and emotional themes that create repetitive relational patterns as these are re-enacted in therapy and in current problematic relationships;

7. Provide a corrective emotional experience by not responding as expected; and

8. Help clients generalize their new skills to relationships with significant others.

However, long-established patterns are not easily extinguished; it is not easy to apply new skills in all the contexts in which they are needed. In the final *working through* stage of therapy, therapists actively encourage clients to try new ways of responding. Clients now have confidence their therapist will respond affirmatively, rather than in the problematic patterns of the past. Although not essential, clients often become aware of the childhood origins of problem patterns at this time, if they have not already recognized them. Therapists help them try new behaviors in progressively challenging situations, first with casual acquaintances, then with supportive friends or mentors, possibly with parents or caregivers, and finally with significant others such as a spouse or children who were engaged in the presenting, problematic relationships.

This process often does not go smoothly so therapists collaboratively explore probable outcomes as clients try new behaviors with various parties. Disappointments are inevitable and so therapy tries to anticipate and help clients prepare to respond more effectively than on past occasions when unwanted responses occurred. Possible responses are role-played in therapy with the focus on how clients can modify their own response rather than to try to change the other person's behavior. Clients need to overlearn that they did not deserve mistreatment as children, they no longer need to participate in their own mistreatment, and they deserve respect now even if significant others in their lives are unable to provide such affirmation. Therapists help clients with grief work as they work through the hurt and disappointment if hoped-for reconciliations prove impossible. Those dreams need to be replaced with more realistic expectations that "some relationships can be different some of the time" (Teyber, 2006, p. 176).

The final stages of therapy are existential, requiring clients to replace the "specialness" of previous inflexible coping styles with a "Dream" or pursuits that give meaning to life as they look forward rather than being driven by the past. In many ways, clients must create a new "self" to replace the neurotic self that previously dominated their lives. The therapist's job is yet again to help clients focus inward for ideas about possible life paths that will be fulfilling and meet their needs for intimacy, autonomy, competency, and integrity. This period may see regression to old coping styles as separation anxiety or guilt results from leaving behind old, faulty attachment ties.

Termination and relinquishing the holding environment of the therapy relationship is the last existential challenge: to be autonomous in making one's own decisions with no guarantees and without the safety net of the therapist's support and presence. Termination occurs naturally when clients feel better and respond adaptively to old conflictual situations in and out of therapy and when significant others in the client's life notice and comment upon the changes. Therapists need to recognize and support the client's ambivalence about termination, to show appreciation of the client's new independence, while giving reassurance they are still available should the need arise. Unnatural terminations occur when a therapist or client is unable to continue for reasons unrelated to therapy such as moves or insurance limitations. In this case, angry, blaming, or distancing reactions are likely and must be addressed even though clients entered knowing therapy would be time-limited. In addition, it is important that clients both recognize the progress they made during the foreshortened therapy and review what still needs to be done and how that work will be accomplished. It is helpful to begin a "countdown" 2–3 weeks before either type of termination to ensure that termination issues are fully addressed.

Case Illustration (IPA's Six-Step Treatment Plan)

Statement of the Problem Ethan is a 36-year-old European-American who self-identifies as "bisexual, but I prefer guys cause they have fewer sexual hang-ups." He came to therapy at the insistence of his sales' supervisor at a large Southern California advertising agency, but agreed that "things have recently gone in the toilet." The precipitating incident occurred during lunch with a prospective client when he became enraged and verbally abusive when the client was reluctant to buy into a proposed advertising campaign. Since other clients had previously complained that Ethan was overbearing and arrogant, the supervisor said he should either seek therapy or a new job. Ethan said "I probably went over the top that time, but I was coming down from a coke high and the guy really irritated me. You wouldn't believe the cretins I have suck up to in this job." On questioning, Ethan also said his use of "uppers, downers, and booze" recently escalated since he lost his earlier "dream job." Previously, Ethan was a "talent manager" for a Hollywood agency that represented both established and early career movie actors. He was responsible for "keeping them entertained and out of trouble." Ethan arranged several parties each week on the agency's yacht and made sure "plenty of booze, drugs, and sex" were available for actors, producers, and financiers. He also had access to the yacht at other times for his own parties, attended by a wide circle of "beautiful people who really dug the scene, cause I had the boat, the drugs, and Hollywood's most gorgeous studs and broads. And I could have my pick of any of them. Then some fink ratted on me and I got busted for the drugs." Although indicted, Ethan was released following police errors with the chain of evidence, but he was still fired. He now works at a job that he feels is beneath him "for half the money and no perks." His sex life has suffered as well; he reports that his previous coterie of friends is so "shallow" they all dropped him. He finds the people at the gay bars he now frequents to be a "bunch of losers."

Diagnosis:
Axis I—Polysubstance dependence
Axis II—Narcissistic personality disorder
Axis III—No reported medical problems
Axis IV—Occupational problems
Axis V—GAF = 58

Developmental Context Ethan's father was a second-generation Polish-American, who worked for a large automobile manufacturer and was active in his local union. He was 29 when he married Ethan's mother, a fifth-generation Anglo-American who was then age 21. She was a college senior active in the Democratic party when they met and worked together to organize the local union members for an upcoming presidential election. Ethan reports their marriage was "made in hell" as his father was verbally abusive and his mother was depressed all the time. His father would leave home after dinner most evenings to drink with his union buddies, coming back belligerently drunk and waking the household with his swearing. Ethan's father first called him "queer" at age six after taking him to a football game in cold weather; Ethan cried about being cold and asked to go home. His father was an avid sports fan and could not understand why Ethan preferred books. His mother would reassure Ethan after one of his father's verbal attacks that he "was superior in intellect to his father, who is unable to appreciate the finer things in life." Ethan reports only one incident of serious physical abuse, which occurred when he was caught masturbating at about age 12. During the beating, which left serious bruises, his father repeatedly accused him of being "queer" and that only "homos" did that sort of thing. Ethan excelled in school, was active in community theater, and won a scholarship to college majoring in the dramatic arts. After graduation, he left for Hollywood expecting to have a successful career in the movies. He had little success in his auditions, which he attributed to casting directors being too unsophisticated to appreciate his "method" acting. After several years of odd jobs, he got a job with the talent agency where he quickly worked his way to his position as a talent manager.

Treatment Focus Ethan's core conflicts stem from an insecure avoidant attachment following his mother's unavailability during her depressive episodes and his father's emotional distancing from the family and later rejection of Ethan. Conflicting schemas developed from his identification with his mother's belief in his superiority to his father. This was reinforced by early successes in school and community theater; he also developed schemas reflecting his father's homophobia and rejection of Ethan's interest in academics and the arts. Ethan's compromise solution to his core conflicts has been to rise above his need for intimacy by moving against and rejecting others by demonstrating his superiority. His narcissistic hostility defends against the shame associated with Ethan's latent homophobia and sadness from the lack of any meaningful attachments in his life. He suffered a narcissistic injury when he failed to succeed as an actor in Hollywood; but his drug use and the glamour associated with his job as a talent manager helped preserve his sense of superiority until he lost that job. In his current advertising position he is no longer the gracious host of celebrities, but must ingratiate himself with prospective clients. His sex life also suffered a loss of glamour since he is now limited to acquaintances found at gay bars. This combination of narcissistic injuries has exacerbated his drug use, while the compromise solution of rejecting others has become prominent with repeated failures to demonstrate his superiority. He no longer is able to surround himself with people who appreciate his parties and help him feel one of the "beautiful people." Drugs and promiscuity provide little defense against his shame and sadness, so he now interacts in aggressive, hostile ways with most people. The initial stages of therapy must focus on developing collaboration and an inward focus to help Ethan become aware of how the drugs and his interpersonal process defend against his underlying sadness and shame, but also create a vicious circle that has led to successive failures.

Therapeutic Process Ethan has had three sessions. He began with derogatory remarks about the facilities and the therapist's competency, at the same time seeking admiration and approval. This process began to diminish as the therapist responded with process comments that bridge Ethan's work problems with the problems arising in therapy. Recognizing that Ethan's hostility and neediness are coming from a place of deep hurt has allowed the therapist to become less irritated and frustrated and to use self-involving statements to "wonder if others, perhaps clients or colleagues might have similar feelings." As a result, Ethan has become more engaged in therapy and able to see in part how he contributes to his outside problems. He still tests the therapist for signs of homophobia and is resistant to working on his substance abuse, but has indicated he would contact Alcoholics Anonymous about local meetings.

Goals and Interventions Ethan is now aware how his anger perpetuates many of his problems and is beginning to consider that drugs may also be a problem. The short-term focus will be to comment on his challenging or externalizing actions in therapy with the goal of helping Ethan commit to joining an AA group. As he is looks inward more, the focus will shift to examining Ethan's underlying sadness and shame. His latent homophobia can be explored as he tests the therapist's tolerance for homosexuality. Once Ethan begins to grieve over the absence of meaningful relationships in his life, therapy can explore his defenses of rejecting and competing with others. The collaborative mutuality of the therapy relationship can then be generalized to other relationships, perhaps first with clients and AA group members and later on with colleagues at work. The final stage of therapy will focus on helping Ethan explore his dreams and determine what would be desirable and realistic life goals.

Impediments to Change The two greatest risks in therapy are Ethan's continuing use of drugs and the anxiety he will experience as the therapist fails to reinforce his desire to be superior to others and is not driven away. Drug use will be addressed by asking Ethan to explore the costs and benefits of drug use and supporting Ethan's interest in attending AA meetings. Motivational Interviewing will help Ethan make his own decision to work on his drug use. The therapist needs to be sensitive to alliance strains as deeper issues are discussed. An important topic will be to explore how Ethan's relationships have ended in the past and to collaborate with him on how such ruptures might be avoided or repaired in the therapeutic relationship.

Interpersonal Reconstructive Therapy

Benjamin's (2006) Interpersonal Reconstructive Therapy (IRT) resembles IPA in integrating attachment theory with interpersonal, experiential, cognitive, and psychodynamic approaches to therapy. IRT's major differences are in targeting treatment-resistant clients and giving more emphasis to early attachment. IRT also incorporates the Structural Analysis of Social Behavior (SASB; Benjamin, 1974, 1978, 1996), discussed below, a three-dimensional variant of two-dimensional models of interpersonal behavior (Carson, 1969; Kiesler, 1983; Leary, 1957).

IRT is a long-term treatment for clients who do not respond to "treatment as usual." As in psychoanalytic theory, maladaptive behavior reflects internalized conflict; rather than Id/Superego conflicts, IRT examines conflicts among internalized attachment schemas that prevent clients from mobilizing more adaptive self-aspects. The restrictive part of the self is the "Regressive Loyalist" or "Red," a dominant self-schema that interferes with adaptive choices that might be made by the "Growth Collaborator" or "Green" part of the self. Benjamin believes that therapy must encourage the client's *will to change* by supporting the Growth Collaborator.

Case Formulation in Interpersonal Reconstructive Therapy

Developmental Learning and Loving (DLL) theory is the basis of IRT case formulation. Internalized models of interpersonal relationships (*Important Person Internalized Representation,* or *IPIR*) reflect early attachments with caregivers. Maladaptive interpersonal behaviors are based on IPIR schemas internalized through some combination of three *copy processes:*

1. Identification: to be like the IPIR, *e.g.*, rejecting others
2. Recapitulation: to act as if the IPIR will still be there, *e.g.*, by eliciting rejection from others
3. Introjection: to treat the self as the IPIR did, *e.g.*, rejecting the self

Note the parallels between Benjamin's copy processes and Teyber's compromise solutions of turning against the self. Copy processes describe how symptoms or thematic problems develop; *e.g.*, people diagnosed with dependent personality disorder recapitulate early attachment relationships in which they learned that being dutiful would gain approval from caregivers. Motivation in DLL theory derives from the *gift of love*, persisting efforts of Red patterns to gain love and psychologically join an IPIR by being loyal and copying its rules and values. In each copy process, clients follow their perception of the IPIR's rules and values.

Therapists can infer the nature of Red patterns from thematic problems in living, in the therapeutic relationship, in early childhood experiences, or by asking "What do you need? What would help?" Such questions explore motivation, not pathology; *e.g.*, Marie presented with panic symptoms, generalized anxiety, depression, and complaints of diarrhea. There was a long-term history of sexual and physical abuse of Marie, her siblings, and her mother by the father. She was the only one in the family who could deflect his abuse and she developed a pattern of being alert to signs of danger and protecting others that still continues. When asked what she needed, Marie replied, "I want to feel safe, and peaceful, and protected" (Benjamin, 2006, p. 37). Marie's anxiety symptoms recapitulate childhood experiences; her gift of love is to be loyal to her family role as if her father was still present and only she can prevent disaster. DLL case formulation helps form a coherent treatment plan about Marie's symptoms. As Marie does the difficult work of linking her attempts to gain closeness in current relationships with her wish for her IPIR's love, she may be able to relinquish that wish and no longer need to sacrifice herself in order to protect others.

Structural Analysis of Social Behavior

Benjamin (2006) suggests that IRT can be done effectively without use of the SASB, but it can help clients distinguish between concepts such as assertion and aggression. The SASB includes an *affiliation* dimension that mirrors the friendly-hostile dimension described in two-dimensional interpersonal models. Its *interdependence* dimension includes the dominance-submission factor of two-dimensional models as one pole of a dimension ranging from *enmeshment* or *control* to *emancipation* or *being free*. Dominance and submission are not opposites, but are complementary behaviors that both involve control. SASB's *focus* dimension has three levels: *interpersonal* actions directed toward *others*, toward the *self*, and an intrapsychic *introject* focus in which clients treat themselves with attitudes or actions incorporated from someone else. The three dimensions interact as follows:

1. *Other-focus* is the perspective used in two-dimensional models; it describes (*transitive*) actions directed toward another person. These actions can be either *friendly* or *hostile* and either *controlling* (enmeshment) or *giving autonomy* (emancipation) to the other.
2. *Self-focus* involves *intransitive* actions that only involve the actor and not others. The person either *submits* (enmeshment) or *remains apart* (emancipation) in friendly or hostile fashion.
3. *Introject-focus* is not interpersonal, but reflects intrapsychic processes: friendly *vs.* hostile *self-control* (enmeshment) or *letting-self-be* (emancipation); *e.g.*, hostile self-control involves guilt, doubt, or self-blame, while friendly self-control involves self-indulgence or nurturance. Hostile letting-self-be involves self-neglect or living in fantasy, while friendly letting-self-be involves self-satisfaction or self-acceptance.

Figure 11.1 illustrates the relationship between two-dimensional interpersonal circle (IPC) models and one way of arranging the SASB model. The face of Fig. 11.1 presents Fromme and O'Brien's (1982) model of interpersonal behavior and emotion, which corresponds to the "Controlling" pole of the SASB model's interdependence dimension. The IPC model's top half corresponds to the SASB "Controlling" and "Focus on Other" quadrant, in which others are treated either with hostile power or

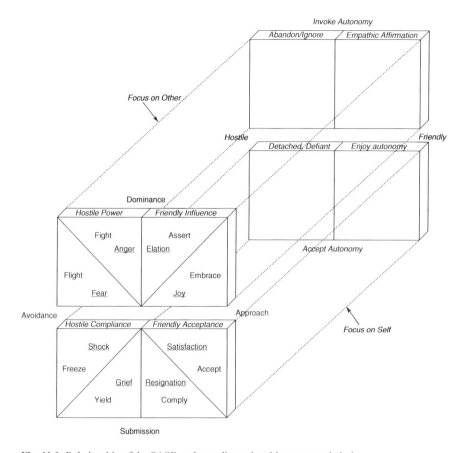

Fig. 11.1 Relationship of the SASB and two-dimensional interpersonal circles

friendly influence. The IPC model's lower half corresponds to the SASB's "Controlling" and "Focus on Self" quadrant, in which the individual responds to others with either hostile compliance or friendly acceptance. The SASB's emancipation pole, which has no parallel in two-dimensional models, is at the back of Fig. 11.1 and behaviors that allow autonomy for others (top half) or the self (bottom half) in either friendly or hostile ways. The overlap of two- and three-dimensional models allows comparison of research based on the respective approaches; *e.g.*, Gurtman reported results "… supportive of theoretical predictions for both the SASB and IPC models" (2000, p. 97).

Although the SASB produces complex interactions, therapists need ask only three questions to describe an interpersonal behavior, "Does it focus on the self or others? Is it friendly or hostile? Does it reflect control or give autonomy?" Benjamin (2006) is also developing parallel models for the emotions and cognitions predicted to accompany each of the SASB interpersonal dimensions. The SASB may be used to predict probable responses that a particular behavior may evoke

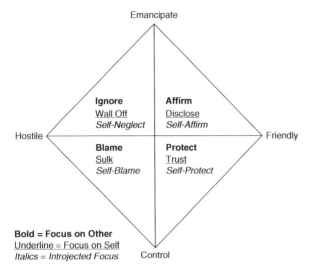

Fig. 11.2 Benjamin's (1996) SASB cluster quadrant model

in others, from the self, or in an introjected experience. The axes in Fig. 11.2 are the SASB dimensions of interdependence and affiliation, while different type faces describe the focus dimension. In general, emancipation, friendliness, and hostility evoke similar responses, while control evokes submission and other-focus evokes self-focus. These tendencies give the outcomes of interpersonal acts a degree of predictability that IRT therapists can use to understand a client's implicit goals and to respond in unexpected ways (Gurtman, 2000).

Table 11.1 illustrates relationship patterns and their probable effects. *Complementarity* describes common self-focus reactions to other-focused actions. Because this interpersonal pattern is so predictable, complementary relationships tend to be rather stable. Positive patterns develop if the focus on the other is friendly, but ignoring or blaming only lead to walling off or sulking. SASB also describes relationship patterns of *introjection, opposition, similarity*, and *antithesis*. Introjections

Table 11.1 SASB relationship patterns

Relationship pattern	Examples
Complementarity: adjacent **bold** and underlined pairs	**Ignoring**→Walling Off; **Blaming**→Sulking; **Affirming**→Disclosing; **Protecting**→Trusting
Introjection: adjacent **bold** and *italicized* pairs	**Ignoring**→*Self-Neglect*; **Blaming**→*Self-Blame*; **Affirming**→*Self*-Affirming; **Protecting**→*Self-Protecting*
Opposition: similar pairs 180° from one another	**Ignoring**→**Protecting**; **Blaming**→**Affirming**; **Affirming**→**Blaming**; **Protecting**→**Ignoring**
Similarity: identical pairs	**Ignoring**→**Ignoring**; **Blaming**→**Blaming**; **Affirming**→**Affirming**; **Protecting**→**Protecting**
Antithesis: complement of its opposite	**Ignoring**→Trust; **Blaming**→Disclosing; **Affirming**→Sulking; **Protecting**→Walling Off

are reactions to another's actions that are internalized as schemas if repeated often enough; *e.g.*, **ignoring** a child leads to introjection of *self-neglect*, while **protecting** leads to *self-protection*. *Opposition* occurs when someone responds unexpectedly to an action with the opposite response; *e.g.*, a therapist might respond to a client's **blame** with an **affirmation**, hoping to elicit the complementary response of disclosure. *Similarity* in responses is associated with maximal instability (an escalating *symmetrical* relationship); *e.g.*, **blame** leads to **blame** or sulking leads to sulking. Even similarities on the positive side of the quadrant result in instability: the expected response to **protection** is trust, not reciprocal **protection**. Finally, an *antithesis* response is the "complement of its opposite." This complicated relationship suggests interventions that might elicit client responses that are the opposite of what is occurring. If clients wall off the therapist, the opposite response, trust may be encouraged by a therapist's nurturant **protection**.

To summarize IRT theory, problematic internalizations of important persons (IPIRs) can produce problematic relationships later in life. To gain the IPIR's love and acceptance, clients try to live up to internalized demands with the copy processes of identification, recapitulation, or introjection. Because these problematic efforts are also attempted solutions, clients are ambivalent about therapy. The Green *growth collaborator* aspect of the self wishes to change and grow; but the Red *regressive loyalist* still hopes to please the IPIR by remaining loyal to the vision created by repeated early interactions.

Therapeutic Intervention

IRT's *core algorithm* consists of six *rules of engagement* (Benjamin, 2006, pp. 21–25):

Rule 1.	Work consistently from a baseline of accurate empathy.
Rule 2.	Support the growth collaborator more than the regressive loyalist—the loyalist's concerns need to be validated, but therapists need to align with the growth collaborator. Care must be taken that empathy does not reinforce the regressive loyalist.
Rule 3.	Relate every intervention to the DLL case formulation of interpersonal patterns.
Rule 4.	Seek specific, concrete, illustrative details about input (what happened), client response, and impact on the self, when clients present problematic encounters.
Rule 5.	Explore each problematic episode in terms of the ABC's: Affect, Behavior, and Cognition, "What did you feel? do? think?"
Rule 6.	Relate interventions from preferred theoretical perspectives to each of the following five steps of therapy: 1. Ensure the client's active collaboration in therapy; 2. Learn what the patterns are, where they come from, and what they are for; 3. Block maladaptive patterns to prevent still another enactment; 4. Enable the will to change to support Green's belief that there's a better way; 5. Learn new patterns: explore and practice new ways of relating interpersonally.

Effective empathic responses implement several of these steps simultaneously; *e.g.*, Jason's case conceptualization suggested that his childhood demonstrations of competence or vitality were criticized. His parents gave him the message that such displays were inconsiderate of his disabled, depressed brother. When Jason reported, "There is still a pesky part of me that is alive," the therapist summarized: "You want to be alive. To be alive, you must be loved. To be alive is to be pesky. To be pesky is to be not loved. Therefore, you cannot be alive" (Benjamin, 2006, pp. 75–76). This empathic response-supported collaboration (step 1), described patterns (step 2), blocked a maladaptive pattern (step 3), and addressed the "will to change" (step 4).

Steps of Therapy: Collaboration

Therapists invite collaboration with a learning speech that invites clients to decide about changing once they learn how to recognize problem patterns, where they come from, and what they accomplish. To collaborate, clients and therapists must agree that therapy is a learning process. They must let go of any preconceived need for catharsis or justice. Clients learn it is not enough just to express feelings, they must also relinquish expectations that blame will be assigned. A strong therapeutic alliance is necessary if clients are to hear when their therapist identifies maladaptive Red patterns. With a strong alliance and a growing attachment, clients begin to internalize and transfer early Red patterns onto the therapist. This internalization enables Green choices to be made when therapists confront Red patterns; *e.g.*, clients may ask themselves, "What would my therapist say now?"

As therapists become an IPIR, clients use adaptive Green strategies and make choices they hope will win the therapist's approval. Therapists reinforce such choices, but they soon fade unless they become normative and receive social reinforcement in the outside world. As clients become aware of choices between Green or Red patterns Therapists can give a *goals speech*. Green goals help clients affirm and disclose honestly to self and others in friendly and loving ways with a balance between control and compliance. Red goals encourage clients to engage in fewer hostile or attacking behaviors and less blaming or sulking, or control or submission.

A goals speech communicates IRT values and defines "normality" in a straightforward manner. Clients who cannot accept these values for cultural or other reasons are inappropriate for IRT. IRT uses empathic reflections to encourage collaboration and avoids interpretations that place the initiative with the therapist. Active effortful learning is more likely to be retained than passive learning. Interpretations can also lead to defensiveness or premature termination if clients are not ready to assimilate a new perspective. IRT directs therapy *process*, but not therapy *content*. Even a process directive is given only as a request to consider, so clients always control therapy's pace and direction.

Rule 2 of the core algorithm suggests that therapists respond preferentially to signs of Green rather than Red, but they occasionally need to empathize with a dominant Red perspective to maintain the relationship. Alliance ruptures can occur if Red perspectives are not heard. Once repaired, therapists can tentatively inquire about the client's openness to a Green perspective. In addition to sensitivity to perceived disconfirmations, treatment-resistant clients may have loose boundaries and ask personal questions, request outside social contacts, or conversely, be caustically critical of the therapist or therapy. As with every intervention, the DLL case formulation determines how best to respond. Therapists delay complying until they are clear that a request or comment does not reflect a Red pattern, but if it does, they help the client become aware of their underlying motives. *e.g.*, Benjamin (2006) described Lilly who just wanted to feel better without having to do any learning. The therapist used Lilly's case formulation to give her a glimpse of an alternative to her passive-aggressive Red pattern. Lilly's disappointment with life in general was related to her passivity and disappointment in therapy, "Let's talk about this conversation. You are giving me all of the initiative. If I drop the ball here, you are going to be disappointed again. If I don't come through with something different, you'll be hurt. You have given all the power to me" (Benjamin, 2006, p. 179).

Steps of Therapy: Recognizing and Blocking Maladaptive Patterns

IRT defines insight as the client's ability to identify:

1. Problematic (Red) patterns of inputs, responses, and impact on the self;
2. How those patterns copy the IPIR pattern; and
3. How wishes (gifts of love) motivate the patterns.

Therapists help clients identify Red patterns by empathizing more with their Green; *e.g.*, empathy for a passive-aggressive client's resentment of his boss' criticisms only reinforces his Red pattern; telling him he's repeating a Red pattern would be inflammatory; but empathizing with the disappointment his efforts went unappreciated might support a Green perspective that eventually such efforts could succeed. It is generally more helpful to empathize with primary emotions of vulnerability and disappointment than with defensive, secondary Red emotions (Elliott, 2001; Teyber, 2006). Once therapists identify current Red patterns, exploring childhood experiences can help clarify copy processes by identifying the client's motivating wish or gift of love.

Once clients gain insight into motivating wishes and copy processes, they have the ability to choose a more adaptive goal than their gift of love. Gifts of love may either copy childhood experiences directly or enact the opposite; *e.g.*, identification may be an attempt to gain love by being just like the IPIR or by being the exact opposite. Clients who internalize the opposite of their IPIR imagine an admission of wrong-doing that leads to making up and showing that they were loved after all. Similarly, clients can enact patterns that recapitulate the IPIR's rules and views, or enact the opposite. They look for acceptance on their own terms, to be loved "as is."

Insight into how current problems echo past relationships strengthens clients' *will to change*, their willingness to let go and choose Green patterns. While insight may be necessary for change, it usually is not sufficient. Non-responding clients have impaired attachments and poor working relationship models. They require a strong therapy relationship and time to learn new goals and practice new patterns of relating to others. Therapists resist the pull to become an IPIR substitute and meet client needs during this stage of therapy; instead they help clients learn ways to fulfill needs on their own.

Benjamin (2006) emphasizes the need for specific, concrete details to facilitate insight. A client's statement, "My mother never loved me," can have a variety of meanings. Without more details, this comment could reflect either mother's preference for another sibling, a childhood of unremitting abuse and neglect, or many other possibilities. As in all interpersonal approaches, it is useful to explore problems in the therapeutic alliance. Not only is there a chance for therapists to modify problematic patterns, but they also have the opportunity to observe directly how such difficulties develop. Similarly, family conferences can reveal problematic patterns and provide therapists a direct look at problematic antecedents and consequences.

For each problem clients present, therapists inquire about the details of persons and preceding events. Therapists then determine the ABCs, the affect, behavior, and cognitions that occurred in the situation. Similar past experiences are explored once clients describe a situation in detail. First, agreement is sought on the core algorithm of how the past has affected the present. If asking "Has this happened before?" fails to elicit linkages, then a general exploration of the past is attempted, "Let's talk about what it was like for you growing up." Dreams can also be explored for possible associations to current or past experiences. If insight does not develop from such exploration, most likely defenses are preventing recognition of patterns and underlying wishes. In the following, Harry shows unrealistic self-blame that leads to suicidal thoughts. Note how the therapist confronts distortions directly, but empathically.

Harry: You are sympathetic, but just because you only have information coming from me.

Therapist: OK. Let's look at the facts. The accountant found a bookkeeping error that had nothing to do with you. Right?

Harry: Right.

Therapist: There has been 100% turnover in the secretarial staff in an organization of 30-some people during the past year. Right?

Harry: Right.

Therapist: A consultant came and affirmed a number of your perceptions. Right?

Harry: Right.

Therapist: I invite you to challenge your filter. You may be right that you distort the facts. I believe, though, that the distortion is when the facts are friendly. I do not see that you could or would present a case on your own behalf—even when the facts support your position.

Harry: OK. I have not distorted those facts. And they do seem to show there is something wrong there besides me.

Therapist: So our biggest problem right now is your preference to grab the blame and threaten your life with it.

Here, the therapist reflects past statements that illustrate a pattern of "blame-grabbing." The focus is on the distortion process and its relation to the case formulation, rather than determining who is "right." Many distortions simply maintain Red patterns. Benjamin (2006) describes two patterns of distorted views of self and others dramatized in movies of the same name. The *Sunset Boulevard* syndrome (SBS) describes narcissistic patterns that result from early childhood adoration and catering by over-indulgent parents. The child comes to believe that the only effort necessary to have one's needs met is "to show up." When needs are not met immediately, tantrums may speed the process. If indulgence was also eroticized by inappropriate sexual stimulation, then SBS clients find it hard to abandon patterns of narcissistic passivity. The SBS client has difficulty utilizing therapy, since "boring" effort is required instead of the expected pattern of effortless excitement. The challenge is to help SBS clients discover that being strong and taking responsibility can be attractive rather than dangerous. Skills training may also be necessary since SBS clients typically never learn effective vocational or self-management skills.

The *Klute* syndrome occurs when maladaptive interactions are associated with pleasure from inappropriate eroticization, escaping otherwise intolerable situations, or both. Childhood sexual or eroticized physical abuse may lead to seeking repeated abusive relationships; *e.g.*, Tamara's gift of love to a psychologically rejecting family was a life of loneliness and rejection.

Tamara: I want to try to talk about the sexual fantasies. It is so hard to even
            think about. I told you that when I "come," I cry. You asked what it
            was about. I couldn't answer before, but it feels like the same feeling
            I have when somebody really cares about me. When people are good
            to me, I never expect someone to really be caring about me. Orgasm
            feels like I have been given something I am not supposed to have and
            can't expect to have again.
Therapist: It means you cannot have love, pleasure, dreams. That is not for you.
Tamara: Yes. For me, it is more like a starving person is grateful when some-
            body hands them a loaf of bread.

Tamara may need covert sensitization; *i.e.*, she might be asked to imagine normal, pleasurable scenes at the moment of climax. While this may initially interfere with the experience of orgasm, eventually the association of pain and pleasure should extinguish. Gradually, the fantasy can be introduced earlier during foreplay, until pain and pleasure are completely dissociated.

Nonresponders often engage in life-threatening or therapy-disrupting behavior that must be blocked before therapy can resume. Suicidal or homicidal thoughts are often final attempts at reconciliation by demonstrating an IPIR's power over the client. IRT helps clients see how their case formulation relates to self-destructive goals and enables them to choose more adaptive goals. They see how self-destructive behavior is a gift of love that aims for a desired proximity to an IPIR who was never fully available. This transforms underlying motivation for problematic ways of relating to the IPIR and allows more life-affirming Green choices. Clients learn self-talk to challenge Red perspectives and make life-affirming Green choices to self-manage and treat themselves better rather than to make suicidal or disruptive gifts of love.

Lapses are expected with any new behavior, so standard crisis management procedures are used (see Chap. 2) if self-management is not working. Crises are examined in terms of the case formulation since they may be a gift of love to a therapist who has become a substitute IPIR. Getting better would end the relationship, while crises keep clients close to their therapist. Crises are best handled on an out-patient basis since hospitalization can rupture the therapeutic alliance. Phone contacts are kept to a minimum to avoid reinforcing therapy-disrupting behavior and to avoid doing "long-distance" therapy. Once a crisis passes, it is normalized as a lapse rather than as a sign therapy is not working. Future crises are less likely if clients realize therapy stops during crisis management; they may also need to be reminded of the learning speech.

Therapists avoid crises by helping clients realize that success in therapy may threaten jealous IPIRs. Clients also develop lists of constructive activities such as calling a friend to be used if they are in crisis. Therapists encourage clients to save problematic thoughts for the therapy hour and to distract themselves at other times by isolating worries about past stressful events: *e.g.*, clients are reminded, "That was then. This is now." Therapists model the delay of stressful discussions by allowing decompression during a session's final 10 minutes with progress reviews and homework assignments.

Minor therapy disruptions such as late or missed appointments are considered in terms of the case formulation, with the therapist making necessary accommodations if there are objective reasons for schedule problems. The therapist might reschedule the client at times minimally disruptive for the therapist. Disruptions that reflect Red patterns are related to case formulations; *e.g.*, the therapists may note that Red choices to miss a session represent a loss for the Green's wish to get better. If missed or late appointments become too disruptive, then clients are invited to return to therapy once they are ready or able to rearrange their schedule. Therapists handle alliance ruptures such as anger toward the therapist by acknowledging their contribution to the rupture, but they also examine how the client's actions relate to the case formulation. If a client is so enraged that alliance ruptures are not resolved, then IRT is suspended and the therapist may suggest that the focus move to anger-management skills.

Not all clients respond to IRT. By 3–4 weeks symptomatic or disruptive behavior should be contained with only occasional lapses. Clients have the right to know that IRT does not seem to be working for them and symptom-oriented treatment may be indicated if awareness of the case formulation fails to help them begin to make Green choices within a few weeks.

Steps of Therapy: Enabling the Will to Change and Learning New Patterns

Benjamin (2006) relates the client's will to change to the stages of change (Prochaska & Norcross, 2002). Clients are at the precontemplation stage until they gain awareness of copy processes and gifts of love. Establishing a collaborative working alliance is a prerequisite for this necessary self-discovery process. Once clients become aware of linkages between present problems and past experience, they can begin to contemplate making Green choices.

To enable their will to change, clients must first contemplate the costs of their continuing failure to gain love and acceptance from their IPIR. Clients begin to differentiate from their wish for closeness to their IPIRs as they recognize their parents' limitations. They may or may not "forgive" their IPIRs, but do need to recognize that what happened is what happened and cannot be changed. Anger can be constructive if it enables distancing from the IPIR, but unresolved rage is a sign of frustration that the gift of love is still not working. Giving up cherished fantasies about "justice" or what "should have been" is the first step toward considering alternative goals. Clients develop compassion and tolerance for themselves as they gain distance from their wish for their IPIR's love. Therapists facilitate self-nurturance by encouraging clients to imagine how they would respond as adults to a child who had a similar experience. Clients alleviate feelings of guilt, shame, self-blame by taking this more tolerant stance toward themselves.

IRT's *action* stage begins as clients grieve for their loss of cherished fantasies for the love, acceptance, and protection they needed as children. Once they let go of their IPIR, they can internalize more supportive models such as the therapist or respected significant others. Clients develop goals and strategies suggested by their new role models during the action stage. Along the way, fears of change, of unfamiliar feelings, and of accepting responsibility for their choices must be faced. At this point, clients are aware of their Red patterns, their old fantasies, and the will to change is realized in the self-discipline needed to learn new ways of relating to others. That this is not easily accomplished on the first try introduces the *maintenance* stage in which clients learn to resist wishes to revert to old Red patterns when overwhelmed by fears of the unknown. Inviting a supportive significant other to a session can help clients tolerate ups and downs as they implement new patterns in their lives and lapses inevitably occur. Sasha exemplifies this emerging self-reconstruction. Note Sasha's reflectiveness and ability to make connections and actively disrupt her old patterns.

Sasha: I want to not have so much of "damaged-ness" be there. But it is really hard to stop it when it is happening.

Therapist: You have noticed a lot about your patterns this week, and you are even more aware you want to be free of old habits.

Sasha: Yes. I am going through stuff a lot faster than I used to. I cry intensely, but only for a short time. I am interested in turning this around. Even as stuff happens, I have a voice that says, "Well wait a minute." I try to think about what is happening and what I really want to do. Last night, my boyfriend stayed at work late and canceled our dinner plans. Instead of getting all unhinged, I just called a friend to make different plans. My evening really was quite pleasant.

IRT is eclectic in helping clients learn new patterns; *e.g.*, the SASB model may be used to illustrate a range of more flexible ways of responding in relationships, which are then combined with behavior therapy to teach stress management, assertion, communication, or conflict resolution skills. Therapists model and help clients practice the new behaviors using role plays. Experiential interventions such as chair-work are useful during the action and maintenance stages of therapy. Self-help groups provide further opportunities to practice new skills as well as support when lapses occur. When clients confront existential issues, however, IRT therapists become a reflective listener: choices about what is important to the client are always the client's responsibility. In summary, IRT is a structured set of interventions that help move nonresponders to a position where they can make more adaptive choices. Once the will to change has been mobilized, "treatment as usual" helps clients develop any needed skills.

Case Illustration (Summarized from Benjamin, 2006, pp. 2, 17–20)

- **Background:** Patsy is a 40-year-old, married woman, unspecified ethnicity, with two adult daughters and a son. She has been diagnosed with major depressive disorder for the past 6 years. During this period she attempted to separate from her physically abusive, alcoholic husband, repeatedly asking him to leave only to invite him back shortly afterward. She said, "I asked him back because I need somebody to love me. After another beating last week, my therapist told me to tell him to get his stuff out of the house. I was visiting my mother for the weekend and decided to kill myself on the way back. I don't want to live with him, and I don't want to live without him. Everybody thinks I am a fool." Patsy provides the sole support for the family, while her husband spends large sums on boats and motorcycles. He has lost many jobs and is no longer interested in working. She is tired of being the breadwinner and dislikes her job working for a controlling, unappreciative boss. Her suicidal ideation has escalated, despite treatment with Prozac and, more recently, Zoloft. She assaulted her daughters on several occasions, breaking wooden spoons on them or hurling them across the room. Her rages result from being a "clean freak." She has been particularly abusive toward her eldest daughter, who was defiant and refused to cry. The resulting injuries were serious enough to require medical attention and stitches. In contrast, her son deflects her anger by saying, "Don't be mad. I love you, Mom." Patsy reports that seeing him so scared is calming. After cognitive therapy focused on anger management, she reports she would never again attack one of her children. However, impulses to do so have been returning. She describes her rages as being out of control. "A thing goes off in my head. It gets hot. I want to lash out at whatever is nearest. I want to tear something."
- **Developmental History:** Patsy's mother was extremely clean, keeping the house "sterile." If she disapproved of some item of Patsy's clothing, she would rip it off, as Patsy has done with her children. Patsy reports her father was "crazy" and

very abusive toward her mother and the six children. Once he tied up her mother and whipped her. "When he hurts someone, his eyes sparkle." He appeared to delight in torturing family pets to the point of death. From infancy to age 10, Patsy was often punched or thrown into the closet. Even so, she remembers her father hugging her and being loving. She says all six children inherited their father's temper.

- *Diagnosis:* Axis I—Major depression, recurrent, with suicidal ideation; Axis II—Personality disorder NOS, with borderline features; Axis III—No diagnosis; Axis IV—Marital problems; Axis V—GAF=45.
- *Conceptualization:* Patsy has identified with both her mother and father. Being a "clean freak" and tearing things off are direct imitations of the mother. Similarly, Patsy's rages and violence copy her father, but she reports she does not believe she takes the same pleasure in hurting that her father did. Patsy reported she was harsher if her child refused to cry and more lenient if the child showed fear and love. This suggests that Patsy needs to be in control, feared, and loved, just as she related to her father with fear, obedience, and love. Her SASB interpersonal stance is primarily one of hostile control. Patsy's fantasy is to gain closeness to her father by her gift of love, to be just like him. This analysis is supported by the fact that Patsy was the sibling that took care of the father in his declining years. Her marriage to an abusive husband has also recapitulated the same relationship she experienced with her father. Like her father, Patsy's husband hugged her and told her she was loved. When he was present, Patsy experienced fewer rages toward her children. When her husband is not there, she needs to be more like her father in order to maintain proximity to her IPIR. Given these dynamics, it is not surprising that Patsy continues to invite her husband back into the home.
- *Intervention:* The case formulation will help Patsy understand how her efforts to gain psychic proximity to her parents have affected her relationships with her husband, children, and others. Patsy's Red patterns include needs for neatness, control, and love. When these are frustrated, she gains closeness to her mother by tearing clothing or to her father by becoming enraged and abusive. Empathy for the Red will be shown by sharing how understandable these patterns are, given her childhood experiences. Empathy for Green choices will focus on Patsy's concerns for her children, her desire to alleviate her depression, and the other costs that Red patterns have incurred. The therapist's interpersonal stance toward Patsy will be friendly autonomy, the antithesis to her typical hostile power stance; *i.e.*, the therapist will use openness and empathy to help Patsy grant friendly autonomy to others. Patsy will collaborate with the therapist to develop lists of alternative activities and self-talk for use when Red wishes surface. Once Patsy embraces Green choices and her will to change is engaged, cognitive-behavioral and experiential therapy will be used in Phase II of therapy. Goals of Phase II will be: 1. help Patsy make some long-term decisions about the viability of her marriage; 2. help Patsy explore other needed decisions, *e.g.*, whether or not to continue in a disliked job; and monitor for lapses and recurrence of depression or rages.

Interpersonal Therapy

Interpersonal Therapy (IPT; Klerman, Weissman, & Rounsaville, 1984; Weissman, Markowitz, & Klerman, 2007) is a brief, manualized therapy initially developed by Gerald Klerman and Myrna Weissman as an adjunct to medication in treating acute depression. Numerous randomized control studies support IPT's efficacy in treating depression. Recent research has adapted IPT to address a variety of other disorders including dysthymia, substance abuse, eating disorders, trauma, and some anxiety disorders. Each adaptation uses the same principles, but emphasizes different components of the method.

Loosely based on attachment theory and Sullivan's emphasis on the interpersonal origins of psychopathology, IPT agrees with behaviorists that therapy should focus on what maintains problems rather than what caused them historically. This facilitates a manualized approach that encourages research, but means that IPT does not focus on transference processes as is done in most other interpersonal approaches. Instead, IPT focuses on the interpersonal contexts affecting the development of social skills and stressors that lead to symptoms; *e.g.*, IPT suggests that depression results from the on-going effects of four factors: *grief, role disputes, role transitions*, and *interpersonal deficits*.

Conceptual Framework

IPT is conducted during 12–16 weekly one-hour sessions. The first two sessions focus on obtaining information to clarify and conceptualize the client's interpersonal problems, and then to explain the IPT approach. It concludes with an *interpersonal inventory* that describes the client's significant relationships and relates problems to one of four areas associated with depression. Sessions 3–14 address the identified interpersonal problems, using symptoms mostly to assess if treatment is working. Sessions 15–16 focus on termination and explore how current loss experiences compare with past losses.

Grief

IPT defines grief as a loss caused by death. If grief is a relevant concern, it is likely that normal grieving processes were interrupted. IPT facilitates mourning with empathic listening to clarify the client's relationship with the deceased and help the patient to move on eventually to develop new significant relationships.

Role Disputes

These conflicts occur when clients and significant others have different expectations about their relationship that seem impossible to resolve, resulting in hopelessness and depression; *e.g.*, serious conflicts arise if one partner believes love involves anticipating the other's needs and the other person believes in explicit communication about such matters. IPT would first assess the couple's interest in resolving their dispute: if they are willing to *renegotiate* their relationship to find a solution; if hostilities have reached an *impasse* and they no longer try to resolve their issues; or if the relationship is so damaged that *dissolution* is the only course left. If clients are willing to work on the relationship or re-open negotiations, IPT helps them assess unrealistic expectations or poor communication patterns and uses communication training, problem solving, or other techniques to resolve their disputes. If they are unwilling, then the focus is on how to help them move on and develop more satisfactory relationships.

Role Transitions

Roles change as relationships change, families grow, children develop, parents die, or as jobs change or require moving to new cities. Such changes are stressful and force people to create new routines, skills, and relationships. They are developmental crises that, if experienced as a loss, may lead to depression or other problems. IPT helps clients relinquish old roles, identify pros and cons of the new role, acquire new skills, and develop new supports.

Interpersonal Deficits

People who are isolated and have difficulty forming or maintaining relationships may have little to report on their interpersonal inventory. IPT focuses on how these clients relate to the therapist and their past relationships. Past relationships are reviewed for repetitive themes that can be linked to the client's isolation. IPT therapists also note problems such as dependency or hostility in the therapeutic relationship, help clients relate more effectively in therapy, and help them generalize this in forming new relationships and renewing old ones.

Intervention Techniques

IPT is a time-limited, structured approach that focuses on strengths and improving the client's coping skills and current relationships (Klerman *et al.*, 1984). The therapeutic relationship may be used to identify interpersonal deficits and model new ways of interacting; more typically, *supportive listening* and questions to *clarify* the client's issues are used. The focus is to help clients improve their current relationships and interpersonal skills, while little attention is given to defenses used in the past. Emotional *catharsis* is encouraged to help clients move past defensive stances, analyze communication problems, and then use role plays to try out new skills. Clients' self-efficacy and self-esteem is enhanced as they learn that needs are more likely to be met by others if expressed directly. IPT gradually fades the therapist's activity as clients are encouraged to take more responsibility in the therapy process. Therapists are empathic, warm advocates for their clients, but point out maladaptive behaviors that interfere with satisfactory relationships. The following case study illustrates typical IPT interventions.

Case Illustration (Summarized from Crowe and Luty, 2005)

- **Background:** X, a 42-year-old Australian woman with one adult son, divorced her husband after a violent marriage and was a volunteer in an experiment evaluating IPT's efficacy. X lives alone in her home. She has few friends other than her son's, but has enjoyed her past work with elderly people. X's depression followed a stressful series of events: her mother, with whom she was close, died from cancer 3 years previously; her father, a heavy drinker, died a year later, just as she was finally getting to know him; and a bitter conflict over her father's will with three half-siblings from his first marriage with whom she and her three biological siblings had a history of conflict throughout their childhood. She was also distressed by a series of "difficult" relationships with men since her divorce 15 years earlier and the lack of supportive, intimate relationships in her life. She presented with "low mood, loss of enjoyment, insomnia, loss of appetite," and described life as "crappy; what's the point of going on?" (p. 45). Her initial Beck Depression Inventory-II (BDI-II) score was in the severe range.
- **Diagnosis:** Axis I—Major Depression; Axis II—No diagnosis; Axis III—No diagnosis; Axis IV—Primary support group, occupational, and social environment problems; Axis V—GAF = 55.
- **Interventions:** X and the therapist agreed role disputes were her principal problem. Therapy helped X explore other relationships for parallels in how communication and relationship patterns perpetuated her disputes and related her symptoms to conflicting expectations about what the disputes might accomplish. Once these were clarified, the therapist used a variety of IPT and related techniques to modify communication patterns and expectations. The following quotes illustrate the active, directive IPT approach (Crowe & Luty, 2005, pp. 46–48):

  Seeking information—"What is he like as a person?" "What kinds of things do you do together?" "Would you want the relationship to be different?"
  Exploring parallels and linking them to current issues—"Has that happened to you in the past?" "Your tendency has been to rush and fix things." "Remember with your mom dying, things just took over and you didn't have time to really grieve." "Did it bring up issues for you, about the losses before? Are there similarities to your mom?" "You might be able to draw on things you have achieved in the past for what it was that worked."
  Exploring, naming, and changing relationship patterns—"I guess that demonstrates that you chose a backward step because you knew there would be

conflict." "Looking at different decisions, it might have been that you were trying to be all things to all people." "You have learned how not to compromise when probably what you need to do is practice compromise." "We have already talked about you being in the caring role; maybe it is not what you want to do ... you have overly stressed yourself and put yourself in situations of multi-tasking, but the future could be 'let me do what I want to do.'" "Perhaps you need to be clear about what you want for yourself, and that would make a difference."

Exploring problems and alternatives in communication patterns—"Is that giving him the message that you don't actually want to see him?" "I guess sometimes you don't really talk about how badly you feel about yourself." "So that is a kind of giving excuses sort of thing." "What does she [wife] need to be able to do to forgive you, do you think? What would you expect in that situation?" "Have you talked to her about it? What have you done about it?" "So you were direct with him, you were honest."

Providing support—"I see you have already made some fast steps ... you have come to some decisions just by exploring them ... more in terms of 'how helpful is this?'"

Exploring affect—"What about the fact that you have been hurt; what about dealing with that a little bit; do you see what I mean?"

Exploring options—"What were your choices; did you choose to retaliate or withdraw?"

Problem solving—"Let's look at what is going to be good for you and what is not, because that might help clarify the goal or what the need is." "That's the same ... thing with life decisions; you kind of narrow it down and start testing the waters, and if it doesn't work, it doesn't work."

Drawing analogies—"When you say you are not sure [what to do], it's like saying, I'm not sure about that color; what will I do? I will try that color, let's have a look, let's just see. Maybe I made the wrong decision or maybe I could go with that."

Challenging—"Is it really selfish? Following something you want to do, why should that be selfish just because other people say it is?"

- **The Client's Response:** X's BDI-II scores dropped to the moderate range by the second session, were in the mild range by the final 12th session, and the non-depressed range at the 3-month follow-up. As a child she learned to suppress her feelings and adopted the role of "responsible pacifier" to defend against family conflicts. Exploring her concerns about being "selfish" led to concerns about trusting and being "true" to herself vs. maintaining her pacifier role and trusting others. She was then able to practice more direct and assertive communication. In developing greater self-assurance, she went through several stages (quotes from pp. 48–52):

Struggles, losses, and being overwhelmed—"Most of our childhood was just spent trying to not be seen essentially, all we heard was a lot of yelling ... and screaming and the less you were noticed the better." "I tell you at that stage I still hadn't grieved for mum; death was fine, I don't know to be honest, I didn't really feel much, I wasn't feeling anything." "At the time, I thought keeping everything smooth was fine, I mean not just for me but for everyone, doing what I thought was best for all of us." "Before I always managed to survive but just recently I stopped [being able to survive], it is such a struggle."

Deconstructing—"A lot of the things I have chosen to do is because I don't want to be selfish." "I think a lot of things I do and why I make a lot of decisions is to oppose that I am just being selfish but it doesn't make me any happier." "I liked being free … it is a feeling where you have got to rely on yourself and it is just you against everything, just you with nature, and it is a great feeling. You have to rely on your own know-how, your own skill, strength." "I think maybe I have done my time; yeah, I am allowed to be selfish."

Connecting depression to relationships—"Maybe if I can't trust myself I can't trust other people." "A lot of them have been kind of a non-decision, I have to admit, but that is a decision in itself." "I thought keeping everything smooth was fine, I mean not just for me but for everyone … then I thought things have got to change, they've certainly got to change." "The thing that keeps ringing through is unless you are true to yourself … life ain't going to work. Now it is ringing through, it didn't ring through before; I didn't even hear anything before."

Practicing boundaries and communication—"I actually just said no, look I can't cope, I can't do it, I have other things to do; she was really nice, so that was alright." "I mean it is lovely that they all love you and want you there and need to see you, but it is kind of like a bit here, a bit there—you are just pulled in millions of directions. But I survived that too." "I am just going to have to be more honest with him and say definitely not. It is throwing me out; I really don't need to worry about having a relationship … I just didn't really know whether I wanted to be myself at that stage." "I just want time to be me."

Reconstructing a sense of self and her own needs—"Maybe it is just kind of a reaffirmation of the fact that it is OK to feel how I am feeling and you know, I am not such a drop-kick after all." "I was just thinking instead of giving all these other people my energy I could actually focus on myself." "I feel better, I was just thinking today, the situation hasn't changed, I just don't feel so bad about it …. I know that I am just feeling OK, it is feeling good, I am feeling like a person, I mean there are still things I need to think about like work and how I feel about that … but basically as a human being I am feeling OK, and it doesn't mean my life has changed."

Integrative Implications

Both interpersonal and experiential therapies confront here-and-now therapeutic process, but IPT focuses more on its behavioral consequences and experiential therapy more on the feelings that are produced. Process interventions provide clients with corrective emotional experiences and provide therapists with tools besides insight that interrupt problematic patterns of interpersonal behavior. Since affect, behavior, and cognition comprise the basic facets of any problem, approaches that address all three facets should have an advantage. In addition, it seems useful to address the historical attachment sources of treatment-resistant, thematic client problems as is done in IRT and psychodynamic therapies. An ideal therapeutic integration might include the moment-to-moment guidance of emotionally focused therapy, sensitivity to the client's misdirected interpersonal solutions or goals, interpersonal skills training, confrontation of distorted cognitions, and a framework to analyze the source of thematic, attachment-related problems. It seems desirable that therapists not only focus on a client's presenting problem, but also address the ways it affects the therapy relationship, and, if needed, its historical roots.

Chapter Eleven: Main Points

- *Process* refers to commands or metacommunications about the nature of a relationship, while *content* refers to the overt message or report in a communication. Relationships are defined in part by *punctuation*, arbitrary attributions of who caused what in an on-going sequence; and in part by a history of metacommunicative commands: sequences in which one person accedes to the demands of the other are *complementary*; *symmetry* refers to relationships in which each person attempts to maintain equal levels of power.
- The IPA suggests that problems develop when parenting and family structures fail to meet or block a child's needs. The resulting *core conflict* between maintaining attachment and having needs met results in anxiety that motivates two parallel *compromise solutions*: 1. *Rising above the unmet need* by moving toward, away, or against others; and 2. *Turning against the self* by rejecting self, others, or eliciting rejection.
- IPA provides corrective emotional experiences by developing an internal focus, responding to painful feelings, and empathically confronting maladaptive interpersonal patterns such as eliciting maneuvers, testing behavior, or transferences as these occur in the therapeutic relationship. IPA therapists collaborate with clients as they explore repetitive misperceptions and patterns, change patterns in therapy, and generalize change to outside relationships. Clients learn to replace inflexible coping styles with a "dream" that lets them look to the future rather than be driven by the past.
- IRT is a long-term approach integrating cognitive, behavioral, interpersonal, and psychodynamic approaches with attachment theory and Buddhist meditation practices. IRT encourages the *will-to-change* in treatment-resistant clients by mobilizing the Green *growth collaborator* self to resist the restrictive Red *regressive loyalist*.
- DLL proposes that early attachment experiences form IPIR or working models of interpersonal relationships. Problematic IPIR's affect current interpersonal relations through three copy processes: *identification, recapitulation,* and *intro-*

jection. The *gift of love* represents a client's persistent Red efforts to have attachment needs met.

- SASB describes three dimensions of interpersonal behavior: *affiliation* (friendly vs. hostile), *interdependence* (controlling—dominate/submit vs. giving autonomy), and *focus* (intransitive action toward self vs. transitive action toward others). The SASB describes the "pull" associated with any interpersonal behavior: *complementarity*—as when blaming elicits sulking; *introjection*—ignoring a child encourages self-neglect; *opposition*—emancipation contrasts with control; *similarity*—reflects maximal conflict, as when two people sulk; and *antithesis*—the complement of an opposite, used by therapists to elicit desired responses, *e.g.*, the "walled-off" client learns trust through the therapist's protection.
- IRT's *core algorithm* has six rules of engagement: 1. accurate empathy; 2. support growth collaborator; 3. intervene based on case conceptualization; 4. seek concrete illustrations of problem input, response, and impact; 5. explore each episode's **A**ffect, **B**ehavior, and **C**ognition; and 6. interventions follow the five steps of therapy.
- The five steps: 1. ensure active collaboration; 2. learn origin and function of patterns; 3. block maladaptive Red patterns; 4. support Green to enable will to change; and 5. explore and practice new patterns of relating.
- Sunset Boulevard Syndrome: Narcissism engendered by over-indulgence as child. Eroticized form is very hard to change. Client expects things to happen with no effort and finds therapy "boring." Client must learn that taking responsibility and being competent is attractive.
- Klute (masochism) Syndrome: Pain is imagined to be pleasurable as an escape from intolerable situations. Eroticization leads to repeatedly seeking abusive relationships. Covert sensitization, imagining pleasurable scenes during orgasm may help.
- IPT suggests depression results from 1. grief, 2. role disputes, 3. role transitions, and 4. interpersonal deficits. IPT uses a short-term, manualized intervention approach that focuses on client strengths to improve coping skills and current relationships. Emotional *catharsis* helps clients move past defenses and then use analysis of problems in communication and role plays to find more direct ways of addressing losses and problems.

Further Reading

Benjamin, L. S. (2006). *Interpersonal reconstructive therapy: Promoting change in nonresponders*. New York: Guilford Press.
Teyber, E. (2006). *Interpersonal process in psychotherapy: A relational approach* (4th ed.). Belmont: Thomson Brooks.
Weissman, M. M., Markowitz, J. C., & Klerman, G. L. (2007). *Clinician's quick guide to Interpersonal psychotherapy*. New York: Oxford University Press.

Video

Hinrichsen, G. A. (2007). Interpersonal psychotherapy for older adults with depression. American
       Psychological Association's APA Psychotherapy Videos. Retrieved from http://www.apa.org/
       videos/4310796.html

Chapter 12
Family Systems and Couples Approaches

> *Happiness is having a large, loving, caring, close-knit family in another city.*
>
> George Burns (1896–1996)

The quote by the late, great comedian, George Burns, alludes to the individual *vs.* family dialectic that exists both in families and in the field of psychotherapy. Every one experiences a tension between their need for autonomy and their need for intimacy: to differentiate an identity separate from one's family, but still remain connected with them. With a few exceptions, *e.g.*, Adler's child guidance clinics and the family focus of social workers, psychotherapy has focused on the individual during its first 50 years. The family was of interest only as experienced and internalized by the individual. Sullivan began the shift from a monadic to a dyadic focus when he conceptualized psychopathology as a process occurring between two people and ushered in the interpersonal school of psychotherapy. Problems with others develop from maladaptive caregiver and child interactions instead of being located in the "identified patient." Family theorists took the next step in the 1950s with a *triadic* focus. Instead of a monadic focus on problems within the person or a dyadic focus on what happens between client and therapist, they worked with at least three people in the room: therapist, child, parents, and perhaps other children or family.

Triadic approaches assign responsibility for a problem to the way maladaptive interaction patterns evolve in families, leading to a *scapegoat* or *identified patient* whose symptoms are thought to maintain family stability. Family theorists, notably Gregory Bateson and the Palo Alto group, developed communications theory (Chap. 11) and general systems theory to model how families with schizophrenic members function; *e.g.*, Jackson and Weakland (1959) described the *homeostatic* role of schizophrenic symptoms in maintaining family stability in the case of a young woman whose mother was helpless, father was sexually impotent, and both were unable to listen whenever she spoke decisively. Her parents could function normally only if she were indecisive. Whenever *family rules* were threatened, her symptoms intensified in a negative feedback loop that distracted her parents from their issues and helped maintain the *status quo*.

D. K. Fromme, *Systems of Psychotherapy,*
DOI 10.1007/978-1-4419-7308-5_12, © Springer Science+Business Media, LLC 2011

Mothers were no longer blamed for a child's problems and systems theory remained a dominant force until the 1980s. Feminist theorists were concerned that attributing problems to the family fails to hold domestic violence perpetrators responsible for their actions. Also, Anderson and Goolishian (1988) noted that systems therapists typically used confrontation to overcome resistance and failed to recognize a family's capacity for change. They advocated a postmodern view in which therapists *collaborate* with families to co-create new family rules and narratives rather than act as a critical, outside "expert" observer.

Many family therapists took a definite "us *vs.* them" stance, except a few like Nathan Ackerman and Virginia Satir who never lost sight of the person in the system. However, the pendulum may now have swung too far in the other direction: the postmodern focus on replacing "problem-rich" stories with "solution-rich" narratives tends to neglect the effect on the individual of family interactions. This dialectic between family connectedness and individual autonomy and the potential for their integration is the topic of this chapter.

Systems Approaches to Family Therapy

Early psychoanalytic thought created a long-standing bias against therapists becoming involved with a client's family members. Freudians and client-centered therapists alike felt that therapy must be a neutral territory where clients can feel safe to reveal their innermost thoughts and feelings, which typically involve their family. It was feared that family members' presence would inhibit free exchange and possibly cause re-traumatizing conflicts. Instead, they chose to focus on the internalized *perceptions* of family members believed to determine client problems, which are usually revealed only if therapists are seen as safe and trustworthy.

In contrast, family systems therapists focus on current relationship problems, especially those with the client's nuclear and extended family. They observe families "in action" to assess problems and intervene directly in the family process. Family therapists do not encourage clients to reveal their innermost thoughts about family members since it may in fact *not* be safe to return home after revealing secrets. Instead, they apply general systems theory, the topic of the next section, to make sense of observed problems in family systems.

Cybernetics and Family Systems Theory

Cybernetics, or general systems theory, suggests that all self-regulating systems follow the same principles; these are used to describe interaction processes in families:

1. *Recursion* (circular causality) regulates systems by feeding information from one part of a system back to other parts, just as thermostats regulate heating systems, marital problems may reflect poor feedback regulation; *e.g.*, a wife's

criticism of her husband's uninvolvement leads him to withdraw rather than express remorse as intended. Neither cause the problem, but influence each other reciprocally as *subsystems* of a couple's *suprasystem* in which withdrawal maintains both the husband's emotional equilibrium and stability in the relationship.

2. *Negative feedback* maintains systemic stability by *reducing* deviation or *error* between a standard *reference* value and an observed or measured value, *e.g.*, thermostat setting *vs.* thermometer reading. This causes *equifinality*, the tendency of systems to return to particular end states despite different initial states. Reference values are often set in hierarchically organized systems at the next higher level; *e.g.*, families develop rules that govern what is considered acceptable behavior.

3. *Positive feedback* disorganizes systemic stability by *amplifying* deviations from reference values, leading to *equipotentiality* or the tendency of systems to evolve or grow into different end-states despite identical initial states; *e.g.*, pointing a microphone at a loudspeaker creates an ever-increasing signal that can destroy the loudspeaker. Adaptive changes sometimes occur if clients are directed to enact their symptoms consciously, thereby destabilizing the defensive value of thinking they have no control over their symptoms.

4. Positive and negative feedback are not the same as praise or blame. In systems theory, they refer only to regulation or dysregulation in a system. Their value depends upon context; *e.g.*, discovering one is pregnant may be stabilizing for a 35-year-old married woman anxious over her "biological clock," but destabilizing for a 15-year-old unwed schoolgirl.

5. *Rules* specify, often implicitly, reference values for actions or roles that maintain a system. Observers infer rules from repeated patterns of systemic behavior; *e.g.*, if a child obeys only after mother screams, the rule is "I don't have to listen until she gets really angry!"

6. *Boundaries* are a system's gatekeeper, limiting interaction with other systems at the same or other levels of a hierarchy; *e.g.*, families set boundaries to limit what TV programs the children watch or with whom they may interact.

7. *Open vs. Closed Systems*: Boundaries that limit information and influence from other systems affect a system's ability to adapt to changing environments. The system's *channel capacity* may be overwhelmed if it is too open to outside influences and cannot adapt successfully to all its inputs. If a system is too closed, it does not have sufficient contextual information to adapt successfully to its environment.

8. *First-Order vs. Second-Order Change*: Systems evolve or are built to adapt to a specific range of environments. *First-order change* is a system's ability to adapt to those circumstances; *e.g.*, a couple agrees to a conventional division of roles in which the wife prepares the meals, but if she becomes ill the system adapts by her husband taking that responsibility or ordering out. *Second-order changes* in structure, rules, or openness allow a system to adapt to more extreme changes or to normal systemic wear and tear over time (*entropy*); *e.g.*, babies turn couples into family systems with new rules, roles, and boundaries, or else divorce is likely.

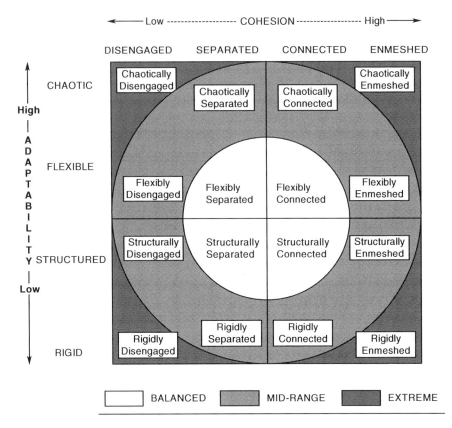

Fig. 12.1 Circumplex model of marital and family systems. (Reprinted from *Family Process*, 22, p. 71. By D. H. Olson, C. Russell, & D. H. Sprenkle. © 1983 by Wiley Press. Used with permission.)

Figure 12.1 illustrates how structural rules and boundaries in open *vs.* closed systems affect family *cohesion* or emotional bonding and family *adaptability* or flexibility in response to change. Families with balanced mid-range values of separation or connection and flexibility or structure are well-adjusted, but the extremes become progressively maladaptive; *e.g.*, families with little structure and few rules may respond to change in disorganized, chaotic ways, while those with rigid structures find it difficult to adapt at all. Disengaged families provide little emotional support for one another, while enmeshed families allow little autonomy for their members. Olson, Russell, and Sprenkle (1983) suggest clear family communications facilitate cohesion and adaptability.

Strategic Family Therapy

Haley (1963) and his wife, Madanes (1981) developed an influential version of strategic therapy based on the premise that families are not interested in "insight" or in changing life styles, they just want their problems to go away. Strategic therapists sidestep resistance in changing problematic family patterns since insight or willingness to change is unnecessary. In contrast to other approaches, therapists are responsible for change; they help family members relax instead of seeking collaboration. Typical interventions, based on Haley's earlier work in communication theory, include directives that alter the meaning of problematic sequences of family interaction. Both systemic problems and therapeutic directives involve inconsistencies among communications, contexts, and metacommunications that modify their meaning. *Double-binds* result if messages are important and inconsistencies are not addressed; *e.g.*, complying with the paradoxical demand **"IGNORE THIS SIGN"** is a classic "Catch-22" double-bind since the sign must be read before it can be ignored. Bateson and the Palo Alto group originally suggested double-binds are a "crazy-making" cause of schizophrenia. The modern view is that any deviant communication between two or more people, repeated often enough, can influence a range of symptoms, including schizophrenia in those who are vulnerable (*e.g.*, Velligan, Funderburg, Giesecke, & Miller, 1995).

Conceptual Framework

Strategic therapy suggests that family problems are caused by:

1. Covert metacommunications about power or who makes the rules governing a relationship
2. *More of the same* solutions that create positive feedback loops and exacerbate problems
3. Structural incongruities in which cross-generational alliances disrupt normal lines of authority
4. Covert attempts to maintain homeostatic stability by controlling or protecting a family member

Every interaction metacommunicates who is in charge of the relationship; a request, if repeated often enough, becomes a rule and part of the family's structure. Because rules evolve gradually outside of awareness, they are not discussed and their recipient may come to resent both rule and rule-maker without quite knowing why. A complementary relationship may result as one partner over-functions and the other under-functions. Alternatively, if the expectation was for a symmetrical or reciprocal relationship, arguments about apparently trivial matters result as the couple try to restore a more egalitarian relationship. Left unresolved, arguments become even more destabilizing as one partner withdraws to restore his or her intrapsychic balance. The result, unfortunately, is a *pursuer-distancer* interaction pattern that frustrates the active partner who is trying to resolve their differences.

Pursuit typically creates a positive feedback loop, a vicious circle with more-of-the-same distancing. To gain power in a symmetrical relationship, one partner may seek an alliance with a child or parent. Successful coalitions create stable systems, but are unsatisfactory if a cross-generational alliance usurps the parental coalition's authority: the parents may sacrifice marital intimacy, the excluded parent may disengage further from the family, and children may be placed in adult roles as surrogate confidantes. Stereotypical "in-law" problems result if the alliance is with the older generation. In either case, discipline breaks down as children learn to play off one adult against the other. Coalitions and vicious circles multiply until second-order change happens: either a divorce or symptoms that restore stability, but distract everyone in the family from the fact that needs are going unmet. Note that problem behaviors can be part of a negative feedback loop at one systemic level and part of positive feedback loop at other levels; *e.g.*, symptoms that stabilize a family system may also create a destabilizing vicious circle for an identified patient.

Intervention Techniques

Haley and Madanes see the entire family so they can observe patterns, infer hierarchic structures, and give *directives* that create adaptive second-order change by altering the meaning of problematic interactions. Only one therapist is present with the family so no one is confused about who is in charge, a problem typical of families burdened by cross-generational coalitions. Consultant(s) behind one-way mirrors offer suggestions about the family process and help the therapist maintain control of the session. Most families enter therapy with a mixture of guilt about the identified patient's problems, uncertainty about how safe family therapy will be, and fear that they will be blamed. This is particularly true in families when conflict has escalated to toxic levels. Thus, Haley devotes the initial interview's first few minutes to acting the genial host, greeting each member, and making them comfortable.

In the *problem* stage Haley asks each person how they see the family's problem, starting with the person who seems most disengaged, usually the father. Each member is treated as a resource, as someone who has important information and insight that may help the family. During this stage, interaction is *therapist-centered* and interruptions by other members are discouraged. Initial hypotheses about coalitions, hierarchies, and the function of symptoms are formed during this period, but not shared with the family. After each person has their say, the *interaction* stage begins by asking the family to discuss their problem among themselves. In this *family-centered* phase, the therapist confirms earlier hypotheses as they are enacted in the family discussion and continues to form hypotheses as new family processes are revealed. The goal is to identify the functions served by problematic interactions, cross-generational coalitions, power imbalances, and to see how well the parents work together and support one another. The final, *goal setting* stage defines the family's presenting problems and the desired changes in behavioral terms. Directives may be given at the first session, but are an essential part of subsequent meetings.

Directives are related meaningfully to observed problems using the family's own language and metaphors. Observing consultants help develop directives that fit the family's problems and communication style. "Directives may be simple or complex, straightforward or paradoxical, to be carried out in or out of the session. They may be an ordeal to be performed as a punishment if the problem occurs, or they can be pleasurable experiences" (Madanes, 1990, p. 214). Problem behaviors can be reframed positively with *descriptive* directives; *e.g.*, "Johnny must really love you guys. Every time you get into your pursue-distance routine, he hits his sister and, *voila*, you join in punishing him. He's willing to take his lumps just to keep you happy." This reframe helps defuse parental anger over Johnny's behavior and suggests the real problem is parental conflict.

Prescriptive directives usually involve homework for each family member, if only to remind others about their prescribed role. Influenced by his studies with the renowned hypnotherapist, Milton Erickson, Haley's *paradoxic injunctions* use resistance to create positive feedback loops that induce families to change. Paradoxic directives can take many forms:

- *Prescribe the symptom*: "Set aside 15 min at a set time in a set place each day; then be depressed so your husband can comfort you and tell you everything will be okay."
- *Restrain*: "It might be better to just let the kids fight it out. I'm afraid if they don't, you two may get into a donnybrook and who knows what would happen."
- *Predict a relapse*: "Well, it's good the hand-washing has lessened but it'll probably come back in full force next week."
- *Ordeals*: Madanes (1990) describes a woman who procrastinated on her dissertation despite believing she could reasonably write four pages a day. She also intensely disliked her step-sister. Madanes told her client there was a solution that she would not like, but it was not open to argument. Once the client agreed, Madanes said "Every day that you don't write four pages, I want you to write a $ 100 check to your sister and mail it to her with a note saying, 'With all my love,' or 'Thinking about you!'" (p. 22). After piteous pleas and some negotiation, the client agreed, finished the dissertation in a few months, and never sent any checks.

Paradoxic injunctions create a double-bind in which resistance means giving up symptoms, but compliance puts "uncontrollable" symptoms under conscious control and changes their meaning.

An advocate for playful metaphors, Madanes (1981) developed a *pretend* intervention in which a symptomatic family member pretends to have his or her symptom; then other family members pretend to help. She gives the example of the 5-year-old boy whose tantrums were out of control. When asked to demonstrate his tantrum, the boy puffed up his chest, declared he was the Incredible Hulk, and began screaming and kicking the furniture. Mother's demonstration of her usual reaction was a timid request to calm down and go to another room. Madanes then directed mother and son to pretend he was the Incredible Hulk and pretend to throw a tantrum while she walked him to his room. They were to pretend to close the door, hug, and kiss. She then had them reverse roles with mother pretending to have a tantrum and the boy giving her a hug and kiss. Finally, they were told to repeat this performance before and after school each day. The mother cancelled the following week's appointment saying he was now quite well-behaved. The meaning of the tantrum and its consequences were so changed by this directive, the mother and child were no longer able to continue with their previous patterns. Such pretending also involves a focus on nurturance instead of power, an important shift in Haley's and Madanes' thinking about their approach, which they now refer to as *strategic humanism*.

Multigenerational Approaches

Although Bateson, Haley, and the Palo Alto group introduced communications and systems theory into family therapy, their early thinking was dyadic and focused on interactions between a couple or a parent and child. Bowen (Anonymous, 1972; Bowen, 1978) was the first to expand family therapy to include *emotional triangles* and *families of origin*. His followers further broadened the contextual focus of multigenerational family therapy by including gender, ethnicity, family life-span, and broader socio-economic issues (*e.g.*, Carter & McGoldrick, 2005). Bowen's theory of family process relating an individual's experience to broader familial and social contexts was a major influence on family therapy. Although no direct outcomes studies exist, extensive research supports Bowen's association of the concepts of differentiation, triangulation, and multi-generational transmission with anxiety and symptoms (*e.g.*, Elieson & Rubin, 2001; Gehring & Marty, 1993; Skowron & Friedlander, 1998; Whitehouse & Harris, 1998).

Conceptual Framework

Bowen's principal concept is *differentiation of self*: the level of autonomy clients develop from attachment figures. Differentiated people reflect on situations and respond rationally rather than emotionally. Undifferentiated people respond to emotional pressure impulsively and are either *emotionally fused* with their family of origin or *emotionally cut-off* and unable to relate with them. Differentiation involves both intrapsychic and interpersonal processes: families as a whole may show emotional reactivity as an *undifferentiated family ego mass* reflecting fusion among family members. Family members in unstable, conflictual dyads typically try to *triangulate* a third person to take their side in conflicts. Triangles are everyday, unproblematic events if the triangle is temporary and the conflict is resolved, but if the conflict persists and a third person is triangulated, then all three experience anxiety; *e.g.*, if a mother habitually engages her child with complaints about her husband, father may become alienated from both of them, which further increases their anxieties and fears. Mother and child are fused, father is emotionally cut-off, and a lack of differentiation is transmitted to the younger generation.

Multigenerational transmission interferes with the differentiation of the child most fused with the parent's struggles. It makes that child more likely to develop symptoms than siblings who are less fused. Figure 12.2 illustrates *structural*

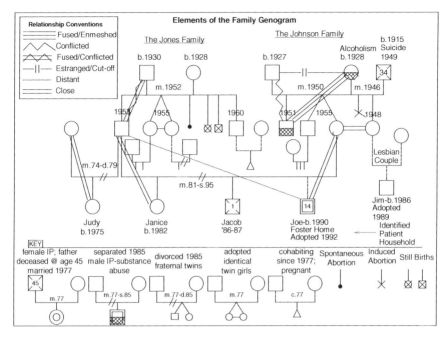

Fig. 12.2 An illustration of family genogram and relationship conventions

genogram symbols and conventions used to describe family relationships and the transmission of relational problems through the generations. It shows an identified patient, Joe, age 14, as adopted at age 2 by Mr. and Mrs. Jones (née Johnson) 5 years after the death at age 1 of their son, Jacob. Joe appears close to his adoptive mother, but her mother was an alcoholic enmeshed with an alcoholic son and estranged from her husband. Joe's adoptive father had a conflicted relationship with his father, is close to one of his daughters, but distant with Joe. A multigenerational therapist would explore the maternal grandmother's and paternal grandfather's current relationships with the Jones' family, the quality of Mr. Jones' relationship with his wife, and consider ways to involve him more with his adoptive son. The family may be quite relieved to see that problems are not just of their own making, but have a history through the generations.

In addition to influencing strategic and structural therapy, Bowen's followers continue to broaden the applications of multigenerational therapy. Foremost among these are Betty Carter and Monica McGoldrick who expanded Bowen's contextual emphasis to include developmental crises over the lifespan as well as the influence of the family's community and cultural experience (Carter & McGoldrick, 2005). They explore how open families are to the larger community: Do they have social support from involvement with friends and neighbors or with church or volunteer activities? Do they experience bias or prejudice based on gender, ethnicity, age, religion, sexual orientation, or disability, and do these stressors impact the family's ability to function?

Table 12.1 Adjustments to family life cycle stages. (Based on Duvall, 1977; Carter & McGoldrick, 2005)

Life cycle stage	Emotional adjustments	Necessary second-order developmental family changes
Leaving home: young adulthood	Accept emotional responsibility for self	Differentiate self from family of origin Develop intimate peer relationships Establish work and financial independence
Marriage: the new couple	Accept differences and commit to each other	Develop rules and marital system boundaries Realign relations with extended families and friends to include spouse
Becoming parents	Share primary attachment figure with someone else	Adapt to new members with new rules and systemic structures Join in child rearing, financial and household tasks Realign extended family relationships to include grandparenting roles
Children begin school	Accept less contact with children	Form extra-systemic contacts with schools, sports groups, *etc.* Shift in nature of parental roles—less contact with children
Families with teenagers	Accept more flexibility in teen's boundaries	Allow adolescent to move into and out of family system Refocus on midlife marital and career issues Begin shift toward caring for older generation
Launching children and moving on	Accept less contact with children and loss of parental role	Renegotiate marital system as a dyad Develop adult-to-adult relationships with grown children Deal with frailty, disability, or death of parents (grandparents)
Aging family members	Accept greater dependency on others, especially children	Adapt to physical decline: explore new family and social roles Support the central role of the middle generation Incorporate the elders' wisdom and experience Prepare for death of spouse, siblings, peers, and one's own death

Carter and McGoldrick (2005) emphasize stressors that result from normal development such as marriage, birth of a new baby, transitions to adolescence, leaving home, and aging as well as life events such as illness. Life cycle transitions (Table 12.1) require second-order change in family structures and roles and emotional adjustments for individuals; *e.g.*, new parents need to accept they will no longer have their partner's undivided attention, while negotiating a new set of rules for child care and household duties. Carter and McGoldrick (2005) propose that families can usually adapt to the *horizontal* stressors of life-span issues and other crises that occur at specific points in time. They can also adapt to *vertical* stressors that are always present including lack of differentiation or social stressors such as prejudice. However, if a family is simultaneously confronted with both vertical and horizontal stressors, their ability to adapt may be overwhelmed resulting in conflict or symptoms. It is at these times that families seek help.

Intervention Techniques

Just as well-differentiated people respond to situations rationally rather than emotionally, so is Bowenian therapy governed by theory rather than intuition. Therapists act as consultants or coaches who model differentiated rationality and note how undifferentiated family processes lead to fusion, triangulation, and unresolved conflicts. Well-differentiated therapists avoid triangulation and maintain an objective focus on the family's interaction processes. They avoid inappropriate helpfulness and encourage autonomy in all family members. It is autonomy that makes intimacy possible since undifferentiated people are emotionally reactive rather than having concern for each other's needs.

Therapy begins by taking a history of the presenting problem and its impact on each family member. *Process questions* directed toward individuals help them consider how they react to others in the family and how they might contribute to a problem; *e.g.* "When your wife raises her voice, how do you feel inside? What do you typically do in response? Does that help or make things worse?" Traditional Bowenian therapy channels communication through the therapist to minimize the emotional reactivity of direct interactions among family members. Bowen did not usually include children in session since they cannot be expected to be well-differentiated and their problems reflect the parents' lack of differentiation.

A three-generation genogram helps place family problems in context and reveals any problems transmitted to the younger generations. Such revelatory discoveries help family members disengage from guilty emotional reactivity to family problems. Bowen often used *relationship experiments* in which a motivated family member is coached to have conversations with emotionally fused or cut-off members of the family of origin, while remaining a differentiated, objective observer of process. Individual, family-focused sessions are still used by multicultural therapists today, but they are flexible on who is present at any particular session according to individual or family needs. Direct observation of family process is possible with the entire family present, perhaps including grandparents, while meetings with couples allows focus on marital or parental disagreements. Individual meetings let family members explore issues they are unable to address in front of others such as affairs, violence, or thoughts of divorce. Emotional reactivity is also less likely to disrupt individual sessions; couples sessions in particular may require that therapists block escalating arguments so problems can be explored rationally.

Structural Therapy

Just as strategic therapy assimilated Bowen's triadic thinking, Salvador Minuchin's structural therapy assimilated his ideas on differentiation. There was also cross-fertilization of ideas between Haley and Minuchin who worked together at the Philadelphia Child Guidance Center for several years beginning in 1965. Haley's cross-generational emphasis came from Minuchin who, in turn was influenced by

Haley's directive approach. All three approaches have been influenced by feminist and postmodern emphases on collaboration and the broader social contexts in which family dramas are embedded. Minuchin developed Bowen's ideas of triangles and family differentiation into a therapeutic model of family structures and guidelines that has influenced many family therapists.

Conceptual Framework

Family members interact in systematic ways that, with repetition, become expected or rule-governed structures about who interacts with whom for what purpose. These interaction patterns define the family's subsystems or *holons* and the boundaries of what actions are acceptable at what times and with whom: who makes or enforces decisions, who provides nurturance, what degrees of intimacy and spontaneity are acceptable, and all the other functions necessary to family functioning. Subsystems include the spousal, parental, and sibling holons with each ideally having its own distinct boundaries, rules, and roles.

Holons usually evolve spontaneously without reflection, which is problematic if the family cannot articulate concerns about burdensome roles or rules and negotiate mutually agreeable solutions. Adaptive spousal holons create boundaries that keep children from intruding in the marriage, while parental holons establish their authority over the children. Sibling boundaries are particularly important as parents need to know when to let them learn how to resolve disputes on their own and when to intervene and exercise parental authority.

Flexibility within predictable structures (see Fig. 12.1) is necessary for family holons to adapt to changing circumstances: marital roles must be renegotiated equitably when children are born and parental roles must adapt to children's changing developmental needs and abilities. Clear, firm, flexible boundaries provide the security children need as they grow, learn to deal with one another, and venture into the outside worlds of the neighborhood, school, and beyond. Such boundaries are *permeable*, allowing interactions among holons that encourage intimacy balanced with security, autonomy balanced with nurturance, and adaptability balanced with predictability.

Overly rigid boundaries limit communication and interaction, leading to disengagement, insecure autonomy, and poor adaptation to change. Stressors must reach extreme levels before disengaged families are able to act. Overly diffuse boundaries place no constraints on interaction, leading to over-involved enmeshment, lack of autonomy, and poor adaptation to change. Inability to act independently makes it difficult for enmeshed families to adapt to change.

While boundaries influence everyday interaction patterns, the family *hierarchy* determines who has the *power* to make decisions and who has the *responsibility* to carry out the work that maintains the family. Family hierarchies reflect *universal* patterns such as greater authority for the older generation and *idiosyncratic* patterns evolved by each family including *alignments* or coalitions; adaptive patterns might be a single-parent aligning with a grandparent to make decisions or provide guidance to the children. Less adaptive are *cross-generational triangulations* that align parent and child against the other parent. Although the child may appreciate the power of this new role, it comes at the cost of disloyalty and driving the other parent away. Coalitions often result in *reciprocal and complementary functions*; *i.e.*, one parent's disengagement causes the other to become over-involved and enmeshed with one or more children, which further reinforces the marital disengagement. Enmeshment may also lead to a reciprocal complementary reaction by the children in which one is the "good" child and the other is the "bad" child.

Intervention Techniques

Minuchin assumes families can solve their own problems as long as structural and communication problems do not interfere. The goal of therapy is to help families develop structures that foster clear communication, balance intimacy and autonomy, and support a parental hierarchy that sets limits flexibly according to the child's current developmental needs. Boundaries among marital, parental, and sibling holons should be clear and permeable to allow adaptation to vertical and horizontal stressors. Therapists alter family structures by joining the family in a position of leadership and then use that role to disrupt cross-generation coalitions and modify overly rigid or loose boundaries *as those processes occur* in the session. Structural genograms that map coalitions and boundaries help the family understand why past efforts failed to solve problems, while success at resolving past issues reinforces newly developed structures. Homework directives are also used to reinforce new boundaries and hierarchic structures and to help generalize new patterns of interaction and communication, in which therapists influence family structures temporarily by becoming part of the family; enactments, which can be spontaneous or staged to illustrate family structures and try out new interactions; unbalancing, as therapists shift alignments with different family members to disrupt a coalition or engage disengaged members; and constructing realities with positive reframes, reflecting Minuchin's early interest in postmodern constructionism. He also felt that technique for the sake of technique detracts from the spontaneity needed for effective therapy. In line with postmodern critiques and the overall movement of family therapy, Minuchin has moved from confrontation to a collaborative style, using humor, metaphor, and acceptance, but retaining his "expert" role. He gives the example of telling a father "he should be gentler with his daughter since 'his voice is strong, while hers is soft'" (Minuchin, Nichols, & Lee, 2007, p. 6). He now attends more to intrapsychic processes and uses nonverbal interventions, *e.g.*, asking people to move their chairs closer or away as a metaphor to strengthen or loosen family boundaries. He has also adopted a four-step assessment and intervention model:

1. *Open presenting complaints*: challenge family belief that the identified patient is the problem; focus on his or her strengths; reframe the problem's meaning;

explore different perspectives on how, when, and where symptoms occur; explore similarities and differences with other family member's problems; and explore the identified patient's perspective on both personal strengths and symptoms while other family members serve as a respectful audience.

2. *Highlight problem-maintaining interactions*: align with the family's desire to be helpful to encourage changes in family coalitions, boundaries, or hierarchy.
3. *Structural exploration of the past*: a recent addition to Minuchin's approach that explores how family-of-origin experiences determine the parent's typical patterns of interaction in the nuclear family, while the children serve as an audience.
4. *Explore alternative ways of relating*: therapists describe how the family is stuck, and invite collaboration on "who needs to change what—and who is willing or unwilling" (Minuchin *et al.*, 2007, p. 11).

Table 12.2 describes typical structural interventions and some of the more important concepts.

Table 12.2 Minuchin and Fishman's (1981) structural therapy interventions

Technique	Description
Spontaneity	With a clear plan, practice and experience, therapists forget about everything but the moment, and join the family confident that useful ways of intervening will present themselves
Families	Consider how family dynamics, structure, and meanings help or hinder therapy. Respect family meanings, but encourage openness to new meanings congruent with community values
Joining	Join family to encourage change in dynamics, structure, or meanings: *Distant* "expert" directs or observes, useful for enmeshment. *Median* position tracks dynamics, structures, or meanings in the family's stories; allows close or distant joining as needed. In *close* position, therapists use self for change and *confirm* each person's experience, especially those usually most disconfirmed
Planning	Plan how best to intervene by understanding the family's stressors and unique structure
Change	Confront family dynamics, structures, or meanings; focus on strengths, exceptions, not problems; externalize symptoms; re-punctuate causal chains; focus on what, when, or how, rather than why
Reframing	Immerse self in family meanings to find super-ordinate, positive reframes that encompass, but do not invalidate, existing meanings and their roots and connections to the family's past
Enactment	Spontaneous or requested enactments of problems yield more information than stories; ask for a "twist" to make it come out different this time; challenge old patterns, experiment with new ones
Focus	People have intractable problems because they do not sustain a focus on problems or focus on irrelevancies. Therapists *track* family process and decide where to direct focus, using selective attention, interpretation, reframes, or connecting disparate themes that help Gestalts form
Intensity	Strong feelings motivate searching for meaning and *therapeutic moments* when change becomes possible. Focus, reflection, repeating messages, and metaphor increase emotional intensity
Restructure boundaries	Change permeability of boundaries; strengthen enmeshed boundaries by assigning role of "silent observer" or increase permeability of disengaged boundaries with play and shared activities

Table 12.2 (Continued)

Technique	Description
Unbalancing	Therapists unbalance power, destabilize triangles, or alter boundary permeability by shifting alignments with family coalitions. They alternate alliances to validate each person's experience, but emphasize whoever is most disengaged; ignoring over-involved members is an advanced unbalancing technique used judiciously to avoid narcissistic injury
Complementarity	Challenge family's tendency to view problems linearly; use different punctuations to challenge attributions about family relationships
Constructing realities	Work within existing family realities/world views to develop broader, more adaptive constructions. Concrete imagery, apt metaphors, rituals, proverbs, paradoxes, religious stories, or scientific theory create alternative constructions of reality that can defuse toxic beliefs. Validating strengths of the family's current world view avoids resistance and maintains a sense of historical continuity
Paradox	Paradoxic injunctions circumvent resistance and change systems so symptoms are unnecessary. Effective injunctions are framed positively as part of a necessary family dance, with follow through to note compliance or defiance in case injunctions need to be modified
Strengths	Encourage family belief in their strength and abilities to solve problems: problems often begin as an adaptation and may be seen as "paradoxical" indications of strength. Avoid viewing family or its members as defective, which would perpetuate a self-fulfilling prophecy
Beyond technique	Techniques are meaningless without sensitivity to the moment: choose and practice techniques, but then forget them and focus on the family's here-and-now experience; trust your preparation

Although Minuchin (2007) agrees with postmodern emphases on collaboration, inner experience, and constructing new, adaptive meanings from old, problematic experiences, he is concerned the new narrative approaches fail to appreciate three important discoveries of family therapy: 1. family conflicts can cause psychological symptoms; 2. problems occur in interactions with others; and 3. problems reflect processes in the family as a whole as well as in individuals.

Case Illustration

This abridged summary illustrates Minuchin's four-step consultation with Alfred and Joan Pierce and their sons, Spencer, 11, and Tyler, 6 (Minuchin *et al.*, 2007, pp. 35–49). Spencer is diagnosed with ADHD and is taking Ritalin that has little effect on his exuberance, facial tics, or denial of being rude to his teacher. Minuchin begins with the younger child to set a light tone and discovers Tyler agreed with the family's perception that Spencer is the problem. In step 1, Minuchin noted the discrepancy of his pleasant, respectful conversation with Spencer and with reports of disrespect at school. Joan replied, "It's true that he can be respectful. People often tell me what a nice kid he is." As the adults spoke, Tyler provoked Spencer who responded in kind. Minuchin asked "Spencer, when you were talking to me you were an 11-year-old, but Tyler pulled you down to being a 6-year-old. How can you defend yourself from that?" Spencer saw he was not being blamed as Minuchin began to focus on interaction sequences as explanations. In response to Spencer's uncertainty about responding to Tyler, Alfred picked up on the idea Spencer needs to defend himself, while Joan maintained the family narrative that Tyler needs protection from Spencer, the first signs of parental disagreement.

Minuchin observed the family debating the boys' fights for a while and then asked Spencer if Tyler had other friends and could play with them without getting into trouble. Spencer replied that Tyler's friends seem to get mad at him. Asked about his own friends, he described a friend's small motorcycle in a relaxed, confident manner. Minuchin then turned to the parents and noted his surprise that such a bright, nice kid also misbehaves a lot. Joan acknowledged that Spencer is bright and does well at school. In step 2, Minuchin began to *highlight problem interactions* by acknowledging that parents know their children best, but expressing interest in how the problem is maintained.

Minuchin	I'm wondering why Spencer responds differently here than at home. What do you do at home? Can you think about that together, because it's strange that he should obey somebody he doesn't know but not his parents?
Joan	A counselor told us that Spencer needs a structured environment—structured meals, structured time to go to bed—but we haven't yet achieved that at home. [*Tyler kicked Spencer and Minuchin told him to move his chair.*]
Minuchin [*to Spencer*]	I wanted to help you, because Tyler is asking you to be 6 years old, and he's powerful. [*He then asked Joan and Alfred to continue discussing problems at home.*]
Joan	We frequently disagree. I'm stricter, and [*turning to Alfred*] and you don't back me up.
Alfred	Yes, I'm more the culprit. I sometimes contradict her when she tries to impose discipline. But I work late, and when I come home I want to be with my children and she wants them to go to bed.
Joan	But first you play golf, and then you come late and want to play with the children.
Alfred	So if I have a good time at golf, I shouldn't have time with my children?
Joan	But I'm with them all the time, and I need some time alone.
Minuchin	You seem to be always on duty. I just saw your husband respond to a request from Tyler, but you also responded, and then you looked at Spencer to be certain he wasn't feeling ignored.
Minuchin [*to Alfred*]	How can you help your wife relax? [*Helping one another makes a system.*]
Joan	I don't need his help.
Alfred	I can't help her, because she doesn't allow me to be a father.
Minuchin	How did she develop the idea she needs to monitor you when you're with the children?

Alfred	Probably I goofed up more than once.
Minuchin	So you have a contract she will over-function, while you goof off. [*Complementarity.*]
Alfred	It's a good contract for me, but it's not a good contract for her or the children.
Joan	I trust him to take the children biking, but not to go to public places. He's forgetful. He doesn't pay attention to the children…[*to Alfred*] You need to demonstrate that you're responsible.
Minuchin	So you're frequently angry at him. [*to Alfred*] How can you help your tired wife? [*Anger is reframed as fatigue, which opens possibilities for Alfred to meet his wife's needs.*]
Alfred	I try to discuss things with her, and usually the arguments are small: like "do you put jelly or peanut butter on the bread."
Joan	It's not that simple, and you always walk away and we never resolve anything.

(Reprinted from *Assessing families and couples: From symptom to system*, pp. 38–40. By S. Minuchin, M. P. Nichols, & W.-Y. Lee. © 2007 by Pearson Education. Used with permission.)

After a break for lunch, the consultation resumed with Tyler sitting on his father's lap and Alfred chatting with Spencer. After sending the children to play in the outer office, Minuchin began step 3, *structural exploration of the past*, by saying to Joan that her husband seemed to be a natural caregiver. At first dismissive, she then admitted she does not pay enough attention to the positive things Alfred does. Minuchin asks "Where did you learn to worry? Where did you learn to look at the negatives?" This elicited Joan's childhood fear of her alcoholic father and the lack of protection by her mother. Minuchin empathized with the difficulty of separating the hyper-alertness she learned around her father from her frustrations with her husband. She agreed and noted that while her husband did not drink to excess, he often called her "stupid" and had knocked her down on two occasions during arguments.

Minuchin immediately switches attention to Alfred, who denies anger problems but admits to pushing and knocking Joan down. Asked if that meant their arguments reflected only Joan's "distorted personality," Alfred acknowledged his passivity and withdrawal in the face of conflict.

Although pushed, he maintained he could not control his disengagement and passivity. Minuchin switched tactics and asked if there were parallels between Spencer's denial of disrespect toward his teacher and Alfred's interactions with Joan. Both Alfred and Joan agreed with this association.

Minuchin [*to Alfred*]	So when you become silent you're invisible and she's alone. Then she becomes a nag, and you've made her a nag. But you withdraw further, and she remains alone. [*Minuchin continues to help Alfred see his contribution to the family's problems. He then asks about the marital relationship and discovers it has been years since they've gone out alone or done anything romantic.*]
Minuchin [*teasing Alfred*]	So your juices are dry? [*turning to Joan*] Is he an interesting guy? Is he attractive?

Joan	I just want there to be less conflict in the house. I've stopped try-ing to change him.
Alfred	We never spend time together.
Minuchin	Would you like to marry her?
Alfred	Would I like to *marry*—my wife?
Minuchin	Yes. You're not married now. [*They clearly soften toward each other at this point.*]

(Reprinted from *Assessing families and couples: From symptom to system*, pp. 44–45. By S. Minuchin, M. P. Nichols, & W.-Y. Lee. © 2007 by Pearson Education. Used with permission.)

After exploring how they gave up trying to change each other years ago, Minuchin began step 4, *exploring alternate ways of relating*, with the whole family together again. At this point it was clear that Alfred and Joan understood better how their re-lationship problems were replicated in Spencer's behavior and were ready to work on changes. Their discussion was largely over the heads of the children, but the family interactions were definitely less polarized.

Experiential Therapy with Couples and Families

Whitaker (1976) and Satir (1972) pioneered experiential family therapy with emphases on spontaneity and communication. Whitaker's approach was anti-theo-retical, relying heavily on metaphor and humor. He used his unconscious, intuitive feelings about a family's dynamics to "seed the unconscious" with light-hearted comments that reframed family processes in new ways. If the reframe was mean-ingful, it would "take root" and eventually cause the family's dynamics to change. If not, light-heartedness made it easy for families to ignore the intervention. In one demonstration, Whitaker asked the disengaged father of a farming family, "So, when did you first realize you loved your tractor more than your wife?" Whitaker recognized the danger of relying solely on intuition and pioneered use of co-thera-pists to expand family perspectives and to check one other if a comment were more countertransferential than helpful. His approach is illustrated in the very readable book, *The family crucible* (Napier & Whitaker, 1978).

Satir saw troubled families as staying together out of duty, but emotionally "dead" due to low self-esteem. They hide feelings with dishonest communication and become *blamers, placators, super-reasonable*, or *act irrelevantly*. In her ap-proach, Satir (1972) helps family members:

1. Communicate their feelings about self and each other honestly
2. Respect each person's uniqueness by exploring issues and making decisions collaboratively
3. Acknowledge "differences" openly and use them to help each other grow

Her approach was not to change, but to join with people in exploring new, scary feelings and help them make their own decisions. Because neither Whitaker nor

Satir developed comprehensive theories or schools, experiential therapy was on the wane until emotionally focused couples therapy came on the scene.

Emotionally Focused Couples Therapy (EFCT): Conceptual Framework

EFCT is an adaptation by Susan Johnson and Leslie Greenberg of Greenberg's individual approach (see Chap. 8; Johnson & Greenberg, 1985). Johnson (1996, 2006) noted that previous approaches to couples therapy were hampered by the lack of a comprehensive theory of relatedness, which led to conceptual confusion: *e.g.*, the concept of enmeshment confounds caring and coercion, while *quid pro quo* contracts are more common in distressed than happy couples. EFCT fills this void by integrating attachment and family systems theory with the emotionally focused approach.

Attachment theory (Bowlby, 1973, 1982) suggests an infant's earliest learning experiences have pervasive effects in human problems. Attachment theory has extensive empirical support, based largely on Mary Ainsworth's use of the *strange situation* to measure types and levels of security in children (Ainsworth, Blehar, Waters, & Wall, 1978). When mothers leave their toddler with a researcher in a strange situation (the laboratory), they react with one of four types of attachment (Main & Solomon, 1990): secure, anxious-resistant, anxious-avoidant, or disorganized/disoriented (see Fig. 7.1). Fortunately, attachment schemas are sufficiently flexible that family members or significant others can modify more problematic patterns later. Hazan and Shaver (1987, 1994) provide evidence that analogous patterns occur in adults, with 25% describing their relationships with others in avoidant terms and 19% in anxious-ambivalent (anxious-resistant) terms.

Parenting style appears to interact with biological factors such as infant *temperament*, which is important in defining what constitutes sensitive, responsive parenting. Temperament is the *phenotypic* expression of genetics, intrauterine experience, and other biological factors such as premature delivery, illness, *etc.* Thomas and Chess (1977) identified temperament factors that influence further development, classifying infants as *easy, slow to warm up*, and *difficult* (easily upset and hard to soothe). It is not difficult to respond to an easy baby's needs and parenting style differences are relatively unimportant. Slow-to-warm-up babies need extra parental warmth, while difficult babies need both consistent discipline and warmth to develop secure attachments (*e.g.*, Vaughan & Bost, 2002). EFCT (Johnson, 2006) incorporates attachment theory by focusing on:

1. A couple's need to construct a relationship that provides a safe haven or secure base as they confront anxieties and difficult situations; without a secure base, learning new problem-solving or communication skills may be of little lasting value (Johnson & Greenberg, 1985);
2. The intrinsic traumatization of separation or isolation from an attachment figure, which leads to a fight/flight response that further separates the couple and creates a vicious circle;

3. Deconstructing cultural beliefs about independence that pathologize healthy dependency: a secure base of mutual dependency is necessary to become fully autonomous as an adult—it is rigid, global disengagement or emotional fusion that leads to problems;

4. Escalating vicious circles of distressed interactions as one partner demands or pursues and the other avoids or withdraws to avoid criticism or keep the peace; this pattern continues until the pursuer's anger and clinging transforms into depression and reciprocal detachment;

5. Depression and anxiety that follow relational distress, especially for those who have suffered earlier traumatic relational injuries such as childhood sexual abuse;

6. Regulating emotional expression of relational distress, anger, sadness, longing, shame, or fear, by increasing awareness of suppressed feelings or modulating out-of-control feelings;

7. Helping couples recognize and deconstruct engagement strategies that move from coercive preoccupation with the relationship to eventual "numbing out" or alternating back and forth;

8. Well-constructed definitions of a lovable self and trustworthy others, which generally evoke confirmation from others, but may be disconfirmed in a stressed relationship;

9. Transforming moments when the relationship feels unsafe into change events or *softenings*, which mark a newly vulnerable partner seeking confirmation from a newly accessible partner.

EFCT directly addresses critical complaining and distancing, which predicts relationship distress and divorce (Gottman, 1994). Vicious circles of blaming and avoidance escalate until the relationship is no longer the safe haven everyone needs to cope with external stressors. Instead, the relationship is a stressor that produces loneliness, anxiety, and depression. EFCT focuses on each partner's emotional struggle and fear of being vulnerable to still further hurt. As therapists validate their feelings, partners begin to discuss them in each other's presence and understand they suffer from an interactional pattern they have both constructed. Once one partner softens, becomes vulnerable, accepts his or her part in the process, and expresses hope for reconciliation, the other partner is enabled to soften as well and become less defensive. Reconciliation begins as they once more experience each other as a safe haven. Without that secure base, it is difficult for partners to commit to learning or using better communication or problem-solving skills.

Intervention Techniques

The goals of EFCT are to:

1. Validate attachment needs and fears to create a safe haven of emotional support;

2. Focus on emotions and communication of vulnerability to foster emotional responsiveness;

3. Create a collaborative alliance that makes the therapy room a safe haven;
4. Shape mutual accessibility by softening blaming and re-engaging the avoidant partner;
5. Focus on self-definition and redefinition by emotional communication with attachment figure;
6. Address relational injuries and shape attachment responses that redefine the relationship.

Research suggests EFCT is more effective than skill-building or other approaches: 90% of couples show some improvement after 10–12 sessions and 70–75% resolve their differences (Johnson & Greenberg, 1985; Johnson, Hunsley, Greenberg, & Schindler, 1999). Relapse rates are low with a trend toward improvement after termination (Johnson, S. M., Hunsley, J., Greenberg, L. S., & Schindler, D., 1999).

EFCT moves through three stages (Johnson, 1996):

1. De-escalation of relational distress as negative attack-withdraw cycles are labeled as the problem rather than one's partner;
2. Powerful bonds are created by shaping new cycles of responsiveness as withdrawn partners are re-engaged to state their needs and fears and critical partners are helped to ask in more compassionate ways to have their needs met;
3. Gains are consolidated into the couple's definitions of self, partner, and their relationship.

Table 12.3 lists EFCT interventions described by Johnson (2006). In general, therapists reflect on-going interactions, prescribe tasks that enact or clarify interaction problems, shape supportive patterns, and help couples explore attachment-related emotions and associated beliefs. They remain closely attuned to subtle nonverbal expressions or hesitations that suggest partners are suppressing emotions and help bring these into the open to foster more responsive interactions. They are alert to signs of *attachment injuries* that reflect traumatic abuse or betrayal experiences.

Case Illustration

(abstracted from Johnson, 2006, pp. 116–120): Jim and Louise, married 14 years with no children, were caught in a demand-withdraw cycle for years. Two years ago her mother died and Louise stopped pursuing and cut off intimate relationships. Both Jim and Louise describe insecure attachment histories in their own families. They sought help after a disastrous session with a previous therapist who agreed with Jim that Louise was too needy and dependent. Louise said "something snapped" and she "switched off" after this double betrayal. She was no longer willing to be vulnerable or pursue Jim, who switched from a disengaged style of interaction and became angry about "walking on eggshells and trying to meet Louise's expectations."

In the first phase of therapy, Johnson gave Louise time and reassurance to recover from the attachment injury she suffered in the previous therapy. They were

Table 12.3 Emotionally focused couples interventions

Intervention	Description and function
Emotion reflection	Track essential elements in each client's relational experience; clarify feelings about attachment issues; develop focus and build alliance
Validation	Frame client's experience as valid and acceptable; legitimize attachment needs; support exploring how clients construct their experiences and relationship; build alliance
Evocative responding	Open questions that expand circumstances, desires, and meanings implicit in emotions; facilitate reorganization of unclear, marginalized experience; encourage exploration
Heightening	Imagery, metaphor, enactment, or asking client to repeat statements clarifies emotional experience and how it is constructed; reorganize how clients respond to partners
Empathic conjecture	Clarify implicit message in client's experience or actions; formulate new meanings about interaction patterns that prevent engagement with partner: open to correction by client
Track, reflect, replay actions	Stop interaction, explore, and clarify key steps in interactional sequences; replay interactions so they may be restructured to create responsive, caring support
Reframe action as cyclic	Interpret problematic interactions as part of an interaction cycle, rather than blaming either partner; shifts meanings and fosters more positive perceptions of each other
Restructure interactions	After enacting and clarifying current patterns, ask couple to enact new ways of interacting, ask for support, express need rather than anger; creates new dialog and positive cycles

able to see how they were caught in a vicious circle and committed to trying to save their marriage. Louise was able to express her anger at Jim's detachment and labeling her as the "needy one." For a time, Jim held that he was naturally reserved, but with help began to recognize he felt "flooded and exhausted" from being so careful in their relationship. They became more hopeful and sharing and could begin the next phase of therapy to help Jim be more responsive and help Louise overcome her attachment injury. Jim was able to express his frustration at not knowing what to do—"how to give her what she wants" and his fear of disappointing and losing her. Johnson then asked,

Therapist: What is happening right now, Jim? Your voice sounds very calm, but you are talking slower and more and more "carefully," and you are rubbing your hands together all the time.

Jim: Am I? Well, maybe I'm learning, but I can't talk on an emotional level all the time you know. I can't be made over instantly into what I am not. I am who I am.

Therapist: And you are worried this may not be acceptable to Louise? (*He nods and his eyes fill with tears.*) Can you tell her about that? (*He shakes his head.*) That would be too hard? To tell her how—well—overwhelming it is—this fear of losing her and how it paralyzes you and makes it even harder to try to open up—is that OK? (*He nods in assent.*) Can you tell her, it's so hard to let you see my fear and confusion?

(Reprinted from S. M. Johnson, & V. E. Whiffen (Eds.), *Attachment processes in couple and family therapy*, pp. 117–118. © 2006 by Guilford. Used with permission.)

Jim is able to follow through in this pivotal moment and Louise responds with her first softening. Therapy then focused on helping Jim stay engaged and helping Louise process her anger, fear of being vulnerable, and the difficulty of taking the risk of being abandoned again. Jim acknowledged and validated her experience and expressed his remorse. At first, Louise refused Johnson's suggestion to let Jim comfort her, but after exploring her continued fear of vulnerability and Jim's expression of being "desperate" for her forgiveness, she was able to hear his remorse and acknowledge her own longing for him. She was then able to accept Jim's comforting and both acknowledged their need for reassurance and comfort. Louise noted how important it was to her to hear Jim acknowledge she had a "right to feel angry and hurt about the session where the injury occurred and the lack of intimacy in the relationship" (p. 119).

Attachment-Based Family Therapy

Although Emotionally Focused Therapy has been applied mostly to individuals or couples, family-based approaches such as Attachment-Based Family Therapy (ABFT; Diamond & Stern, 2006) have recently been developed to address family problems with older children. Diamond and Stern note that, as with younger children, secure attachment in adolescence depends on access to caregivers who provide safety and security. The difference is that adolescents can negotiate attachment needs verbally with caregivers. ABFT facilitates open conversation in the family that explores adolescent experiences of injustice or trauma and helps parents acknowledge their role in the rupture of attachment bonds. The goal is to help parents *contain* the adolescent's negative feelings without being fearful of abandonment or retaliation (*e.g.*, Winnicott, 1965).

ABFT combines emotionally focused attachment interventions with the goals of Herman's (1992) trauma recovery model: 1. restore sense of control; 2. establish safety; 3. tell the trauma story; 4. mourn losses; and 5. reconnect with self and community. Adolescents are helped to identify and clarify their attachment injury and are guided through these steps, while parents are helped to listen and acknowledge their child's story. ABFT begins with three preparatory tasks, followed by three phases of attachment reparation:

Preparation: A family session clarifies relational patterns; meeting individually helps prepare the adolescent to clarify grievances and be comfortable disclosing openly with parents; meeting individually with parents prepares them to listen nondefensively and share their story later:

1. *Build family's trust*; explore why the adolescent cannot ask for comfort from the parents

2. *Prepare adolescent to disclose*; alliance helps develop goals, trust, and clarify core conflicts
3. *Parental alliance*; explore parental stressors, losses, and their own attachment experiences

Attachment-Reparation: Summarize earlier sessions, describe session goals, reaffirm family's commitment to reparation, and express optimism and support:

1. *Adolescent disclosure* of anger and vulnerability over attachment rupture and his or her attributions about why the trauma occurred; parents listen but not allowed to defend;
2. *Parent disclosure* is now permitted to help their child understand circumstances surrounding the trauma more clearly, to acknowledge his or her experience, share their own vulnerability, and then apologize for their role;
3. *Parent-child dialog* helps family learn to communicate openly—about their reactions to each other's disclosures and the impact of the parent's apology; it helps the adolescent accept their apology, understand that ambivalent feelings are normal, and link symptoms and family conflicts to the attachment rupture.

Postmodern Family Approaches

All the family approaches discussed so far have been based upon a cybernetic systems point of view. However, family systems approaches were criticized in the 1980s by feminist theorists such as Rachel Hare-Mustin (1978) on the grounds that they:

1. Ignore historical, socio-economic, and political contexts that contribute to family dysfunction;
2. Reinforce patriarchal views of gender roles, power, autonomy, and connectedness;
3. Avoid blaming the mother as earlier approaches did, but still view dysfunctional families in terms of disengaged fathers and overinvolved mothers, ignoring the 200 year history that led to this normative pattern;
4. Attribute responsibility for problems to the family rather than individuals, which, in cases of domestic violence, abuse, or incest, suggests victims are as responsible as perpetrators.

Feminist critics take the postmodern stance that theories about human problems are arbitrary constructions that do not reflect any essential qualities of human nature. If problems are historical, cultural constructions, their influence can be deconstructed. Therapy should not blame families, but focus on cultural practices that exploit marginalized groups and privilege dominant groups.

Feminist therapies focus on gender and empowering women, topics covered in Chap. 13. However, their criticisms have dramatically altered family therapy practices and led to the evolution of multigenerational family therapy's inclusion of socio-cultural factors and to the focus in Minuchin's recent work and emotionally focused therapies on constructing new realities. Most family therapists today incorporate many feminist and postmodern ideas into their work with families and some have adopted purely postmodern approaches such as the narrative and solution-focused therapies discussed below.

However, as Minuchin *et al.* (2007) suggest, the dialectic pendulum may have swung too far by focusing solely on the narratives family members construct about themselves. It is one thing to recognize that family's problems do not occur in a vacuum; it is another to neglect the family as a unit whose interaction patterns lead to conflict and symptoms. Feminist critiques of family therapy as practiced from the 1960s through the 1980s were timely and needed, but there is no intrinsic barrier that divides postmodern and systems views; *e.g.*, the multigenerational approach includes cultural issues, while emotionally focused couples therapy examines how emotions affect narrative constructions. Also, there is nothing in systems theory that necessarily blames victims or excuses perpetrators; to clarify this claim it is necessary to deconstruct the three ways people use the term, *responsibility*:

1. To *explain* causal relations, *e.g.*, insecure attachment is *responsible* for impaired empathy for others, a prerequisite for efforts to prevent violence or abuse;
2. To *hold* perpetrators *responsible* for causing harm or breaking the law, the feminist's concern;
3. To *take responsibility* for one's actions, a goal of therapy that is unlikely to happen if clients feel blamed by the therapist or other attachment figures.

This chapter next reviews postmodern therapies, developed following the feminist critique, which can be used with either individuals or families. The remaining chapters of this book then explore how integrations of postmodern and systems approaches address human problems.

Narrative Therapy

White and Epston (1990) suggest the *ultimate truth stories* of modernist science *objectify* people and socialize them to compare themselves with others and define some actions as normal and others as abnormal. If validated by mental health professionals, they may define themselves with paranoid, schizophrenic, or other labels. Their unique, personal story is suppressed in favor of a dominant social narrative. *Externalization* can help people break free from internalized problem narratives about self and others: the client is not the "problem," but is encouraged to work with the therapist to "defeat" externalized problems. With this reframe, the client is no longer *held* responsible for being a problem, but is encouraged to *take* responsibility for overcoming the problem; *e.g.*, they describe the encopretic child, who worked together with his parents to defeat their common enemy, personified as "stinky-poo." White and Epston (1990) note that the use of personifications to externalize problems helps families:

1. Decrease unproductive conflicts over who is responsible for the problem;
2. Avoid guilt feelings that a problem continues despite their best efforts;
3. Cooperate in struggling against the problem to escape its influence in their lives;
4. Create new possibilities to retrieve their lives from the problem's influence;
5. Take a lighter, more effective, and less stressed approach to "deadly serious" problems;
6. Engage in dialogs rather than monologs about the problem (pp. 39–40).

White and Epston's (1990) *externalizing conversations* ask *relative influence* questions that help families confront how a personified problem affects their lives; *e.g.*, "How has [the problem] influenced your family's life and relationships with others?" They are curious how the family has impacted the "life" of the problem at various times and look for *unique outcomes* or exceptions to the dominant narrative when the family functioned in non-problematic ways. Stories of unique outcomes help families *deconstruct* objectified narratives of self and each other and *reauthor* their lives with *alternative stories* that contradict the dominant story of the problem. *Landscape of action* questions encourage family members to develop an alternative history that focuses on the actions and contexts in which unique outcomes occurred. *Landscape of consciousness* questions help them explore the meanings of those actions and unique outcomes, to question the dominant story, and to construct an alternative story. Epston (1994) wrote letters to the family summarizing case notes of the co-created, alternative story to keep it fresh in their memory and available to re-read or elaborate as necessary.

Solution-Focused Therapy

DeShazer's (1991, 1994) *solution-focused therapy* (SFT) is a constructivist approach that suggests problems are not necessarily related to solutions or vice versa; *i.e.*, problems do not have to be understood to be solved. SFT helps families create solution-focused narratives that replace problem-focused narratives. SFT therapists ask about enjoyable times and are interested in *exceptions* to the problem rather than stories about it. DeShazer suggested that exceptions to problems are non-random events embedded in contextual patterns that need to be described so they can then be prescribed.

When people used problem-oriented words such as "depressed," DeShazer would ask "What is happening when you use words like depression to describe your experience?" This questions the label's legitimacy, asks the family to describe problems concretely in ways that relabel their experience, and helps identify exceptions and therapeutic goals. Someone who says "I don't have the energy to go out any more" is asked about exceptions that might suggest more motivating activities. Exceptions are also identified by *scaling* questions that ask family members to rate problems on a scale from 0, how they felt when first calling for an appointment, to 10, how they would feel if the problem were gone. If they respond with a 3, they are asked how they improved from 0 to 3 in such a short time, followed by "What could you do to move to a 4 or 5?"

DeShazer (1991) encourages *progressive narratives* that move families toward workable goals that are 1. small rather than large; 2. salient to the family; 3. described in specific, concrete behavioral terms; 4. achievable within the practical context of their lives; 5. perceived by the family as involving their "hard work"; 6. involving new behavior(s) rather than the absence or cessation of existing behavior(s). The *miracle question* may help define workable goals:

> Suppose that one night there is a miracle and while you were sleeping the problem that brought you to therapy is solved: How would you know? What would be different? What will you notice different the next morning that will tell you that there has been a miracle? What will your spouse notice? (p. 115).

O'Hanlon's (1993) *solution-oriented* therapy is closely related to SFT, but emphasizes the family's experience and actions in addition to narratives. He *acknowledges*, respects, and validates the family's experience to create an attitude of *possibility* that solution and change are possible. Gale (1991) summarized solution-oriented therapy interventions as follows:

1. *Speaking the client's language*, the therapist joins by using family members' words, phrases, metaphors, and paralanguage or emotional tone so they feel understood
2. *Presupposing change* questions that ask when change will occur, not if it will
3. *Multiple-choice questions* with possible answers that move the family in desirable directions
4. *Therapeutic interruptions* that redirect conversation toward constructive goal-directed solutions
5. *Normalizing the problem* as an everyday phenomenon rather than as pathology
6. *Summarizing with a twist* to turn the preceding conversation in a solution-oriented direction
7. *Utilizing* the family's perspective rather than rejecting or disagreeing with their views; "building a bridge from where the client is now to the eventual goal" (O'Hanlon & Wilk, 1987, p. 133)
8. *Providing obvious solutions*, commonsense suggestions, alternative expressions, or behaviors
9. *Introducing doubt*, questioning assumptions and beliefs in which the problem is embedded
10. *Future focus* toward specific, concrete goals and anticipating barriers to success

Other Approaches

Most family therapists have been influenced by postmodern and systems thinking or both; but two important approaches remain close to their origins in individual therapy. David and Jill Scharff's work is representative of psychodynamic family therapy and cognitive-behavioral therapy is represented by four main groups: behavioral parent training, behavioral couples therapy, sexual dysfunction therapy, and cognitive-behavioral family therapies such as Functional Family Therapy. In staying close to their theoretical roots, these approaches rely more on linear than circular or constructivist ideas of causality, but they do focus on how family members influence one another. Despite less cross-fertilization of ideas among these approaches, most family therapists are sufficiently eclectic that they often borrow cognitive-behavioral techniques.

Object Relations Family Therapy

Scharff and Scharff's (1987) approach begins with the object relations' idea that anxiety associated with internalized, insecure attachment to caregivers interferes with integrated self and other concepts. Splitting defenses lead to projective identification in which negative feelings and dissociated self-aspects are transferred to significant others by actions that encourage others to respond in ways that confirm internalized object relations schemas. They may also introject positive aspects of the other, while projecting negative experiences onto the environment. Either way, interpersonal problems and symptoms develop as family members respond more to internalized images and projections than to each other's actual behavior.

The Scharff's goal is to create a secure holding environment (Winnicott, 1972) until family members can take over holding functions for each other and develop integrated self and other schemas. As families feel more secure, therapists interpret transference behaviors as these happen among family members or with the therapist and help each person rework fragmented object representations. Object relations family therapy is essentially individual therapy in a family context that allows transferences to be enacted and worked through directly in session. Unlike individual therapy, there is no need to generalize new insights to a possibly resistant family. The disadvantage is that the requisite sense of security may be hard to create.

Cognitive-Behavioral Couples and Family Therapy

Cognitive-behavioral couples and family therapy, like their individual cousins, rely heavily on conditioning and social learning principles. The main difference is the extent to which they also rely on Social Exchange Theory (Thibaut & Kelley, 1959), which includes the following ideas:

1. People strive to maximize rewards and minimize costs in relationships (*cost/ benefit ratio*);
2. Reciprocal giving and getting between partners trends to equilibrium over time;
3. Positive behavior elicits positive behavior; negative behavior elicits negative behavior;
4. Rewards are unique for each individual, which means interventions must be individualized;

5. Positive, satisfying relationships result when rewards are greater than costs;
6. Stable relationships depend on *comparison level for alternatives*—what options are believed to be available that might provide a more satisfactory relationship?

Gottman's (1994, 1996) research confirms many of these notions; *e.g.*, the ratio of positive to negative interactions is 5:1 in happily married couples, while the ratio is 0.8:1 with negative interactions prevailing in unstable marriages. Stable couples come in three types:

1. *Volatile* couples argue frequently, but are more romantic and affectionate than most couples;
2. *Validating* couples are less expressive but listen and acknowledge each other's viewpoint;
3. *Conflict-avoidant* couples are low on emotional expression, but focus on positive elements in their relationship and minimize negative elements that are seen as not open to change.

Gottman, Ryan, Carrere, and Erley (2002) found four factors predict 85% of divorces:

1. *Criticism*—attacking a spouse's character, more frequent among women;
2. *Defensiveness*—denying responsibility for problem behaviors;
3. *Contempt*—an insulting or abusive attitude toward the spouse;
4. *Stonewalling*—withdrawal and avoiding discussing problems, more frequent among men.

Other factors contributing smaller amounts of variance included emotional flooding, viewing problems as severe, disinterest in working problems out, living parallel lives, and loneliness. Interestingly, direct expression of anger was not a factor, probably because it is more likely to force resolution when marital disagreements occur.

As in individual cognitive-behavioral therapy, therapists accept the couple's or family's definition of the problem, but frame it in behavioral terms that can be observed and measured. Therapy begins by assessing baseline behaviors, often asking the clients to keep a diary of how often the problem occurs, its antecedents and consequences. Continued monitoring determines whether an intervention works or if modifications are needed. Interventions extinguish problem behaviors by modifying reinforcement contingencies and then shape and reinforce more complex, adaptive interactions. Couples or family members help develop lists of desirable reinforcers.

Cognitive-Behavioral Couples Interventions

Interventions include behavioral parent training, behavioral couples training, and conjoint marital therapy for sexual dysfunction. Parent training (*e.g.*, Patterson, 1971) teaches parents how to use operant techniques, shaping and reinforcing desired behaviors and extinguishing problem behaviors. Although the focus is on the child's problem behaviors, therapists work mostly with parents after observing family interactions and designing a program tailored to the family's specific needs;

e.g., Johnny throws a tantrum at the grocery check-out counter if mother doesn't buy him candy and she intermittently reinforces this to quiet him. Applying the Stimulus-Organism-Response-Contingency (SORC) model, it is noted that mother usually goes shopping just before lunch when Johnny is hungry. The intervention might be to shop after lunch and reinforce good behavior intermittently with candy or an opportunity to engage in a high-frequency behavior such as a video game (Premack Principle). Shaping, time-outs, or token economies might be used with more complex problems.

Behavioral couples therapy begins by rating problem behaviors and identifying strengths and weaknesses in the couples' relationship. Stuart (1969) suggests that couples be taught:

1. To express wishes and concerns clearly in behavioral terms;
2. Behavior exchanges (*e.g.*, contingency contracts or *quid pro quo*) to improve cost/benefit ratios by meeting each other's requests for changes in behavior or for something they desire;
3. To improve communication skills, *e.g.*, "I" language, "I worry when you're late coming home" instead of "you" language, "You're so inconsiderate not letting me know when you're coming."
4. To establish clear agreements about how to share power and make decisions;
5. Problem-solving strategies to resolve future conflicts and maintain therapeutic gains.

Contingency contracts and *quid pro quo* are clearly specified written agreements that specify who will do what, when, in exchange for what. *Quid pro quo* is more conditional, in that one party must complete an agreed upon task before the other party is obligated to fulfill their part of the bargain. Both interventions may also be used with older children who resist parental discipline or requests.

Conjoint marital therapy, developed by Masters and Johnson (1971), is premised on the idea that sexual dysfunction often reflects *performance anxieties* affecting arousal and orgasm. Following Wolpe's (1958) systematic desensitization approach, they developed *sensate focus* exercises that focus on relaxing and enjoying mutual touch with no expectations for intercourse. For couples with no medical or other marital problems, sensate focus removes pressures to perform, while mutual pleasuring is incompatible with anxieties that impair sexual performance. Kaplan (1979) noted that sexual problems also include sexual desire as well as arousal and orgasm problems. Kaplan helps clients resist negative thoughts and explore anxieties associated with sexuality, and then uses exposure techniques to extinguish the anxieties.

Functional Family Therapy

Functional Family Therapy (FFT; Alexander & Parsons, 1982; Sexton & Alexander, 1999) is effective for families of varied cultural backgrounds with youth at risk for delinquency. FFT creates a nonjudgmental relationship with all family members while examining the functional "pay-off" of problem behaviors for each person. In contrast with other cognitive-behavioral approaches, FFT considers problems from a systemic viewpoint that includes community variables. Its goal is to substitute adaptive behaviors that serve the same functions for family members as the maladaptive behaviors; *e.g.*, acting out may help a teenager feel more independent, anger his father sufficiently to derail marital conflicts, and protect mother from abuse, while keeping father engaged with the family. Therapeutic goals might be 1. to help the teenager find an after-school job that increases his sense of autonomy; 2. find ways for the father to engage his son in constructive activities, perhaps hunting or fishing; and 3. to help the parents communicate effectively and begin to support one another.

The first phase of FFT assesses risk factors of hopelessness and blaming, while forming alliances, reducing negativity, and improving communication among family members. Therapists validate each person's viewpoint and reattribute causes for problem behaviors with positive reframes. FFT's second phase implements an individualized treatment plan that addresses parenting and communication skills, negativity, and family relationship problems. Asking the family to monitor problem interactions allows the therapist to modify the treatment plan if needed. The final phase focuses on generalization of positive changes, attending to the family's access to community resources and social supports, and active case management to prevent relapse.

Integrative Implications

The postmodernism *vs.* cybernetic systems dialectic mirrors the subject *vs.* object and individual *vs.* family dialectics: postmodernism looks at how the individual's subjective reality is created and systems theory looks at how families actually interact with one another. As previous chapters discussed, the subject-object divide is basic. The most useful position for therapists is to maintain a dialectic tension between inner and outer worlds, to explore how one affects the other without privileging either. Similarly, it is important to explore the inevitable tension between the family and the individual, between the desire for closeness and intimacy on the one hand, and the desire for distance and autonomy on the other. In each case, one is not possible without the other: with no object, there is no subject; with no family, there is no individual; with no intimacy, there is no autonomy.

The question then is not *whether* the different approaches should be integrated, but *how*? Individual therapists who ignore the family system miss both the forces that create problems and those that maintain problems. Therapists who focus only on an individual's growth and neglect its impact on the client's family often contribute to unintended effects such as divorce and the dissolution of the family. Therapists who consider only family dynamics may unintentionally support an oppressive patriarchal system that impedes the growth of one or more family members. New models that combine both systems and postmodern thinking are now available, such as emotionally focused couples therapy and integrative postmodern approaches discussed in Chap. 14. Finally, therapists need to look beyond the individual-family dialectic and consider the sociopolitical context of problems as discussed by feminist and multicultural theorists, which is the topic of Chap. 13.

Chapter Twelve: Main Points

- *Family therapy* takes a triadic view that suggests parents and children develop systems or narratives that create and maintain problems. Interaction patterns in family systems are maintained by deviation-reducing *negative feedback* loops. If systems fail to adapt to changing environments, deviation-amplifying *positive feedback* loops cause change or systemic dissolution. Feminists criticized family-based explanations for treating both abuse perpetrator and victim as part of a systemic problem and for ignoring the origins of problems in social narratives and historical contexts. This led to a postmodernist *vs.* family systems dialectic, narrative-based therapies and an emphasis on collaboration in systems therapies.
- *Strategic therapy* uses directives to change the meaning of problematic family interactions, thereby creating positive feedback loops that change interactions. Directives send messages that differ at overt and covert levels: *e.g.*, directing a child to pretend to have a symptom and parents to pretend they are punishing the child changes the meaning of the interaction and creates possibilities for relating in other ways.
- *Multigenerational therapies* encourage *differentiation* from *triangulated*, fused relationships with family members. Genograms illustrate the generational transmission of problems, while process questions or experiments assess whether clients react rationally or emotionally with emotionally reactive members. The approach also focuses on *horizontal* lifespan or crisis stressors and *vertical* stressors such as lack of differentiation or socioeconomic factors such as prejudice, poverty, or oppression.
- *Structural therapists* influence families by joining them in a leadership position; observing or asking for enactments of problem sequences; reenactments of new patterns; unbalancing rigid structures by shifting alliances to separate enmeshed members or engage disengaged members; and constructing new realities that encourage clear, permeable boundaries among marital, parental, and sibling subsystems.
- *Emotionally focused couples therapy* helps distressed couples repair attachment injuries by validating their attachment needs and fears and by creating a safe haven that lets them soften and express needs constructively, while validating their partner's concerns. Therapists help couples de-escalate attack-withdraw cycles: they help withdrawn partners become more responsive and demanding partners ask more compassionately for support. *Attachment-based family therapy* is a related approach that repairs attachment ruptures for adolescents traumatized by family processes or negative experiences. They are coached to express their hurt,

while parents are coached to listen and then validate the child's feelings and apologize.

- *Narrative therapy* suggests people are *objectified* by *dominant cultural narratives*: they define themselves as normal or abnormal in comparison with others, especially if expert "helpers" confirm this view. *Externalization and personification* construct the problem as an "enemy" that harms the client and significant others. This absolves clients of responsibility for the problem, but engages them in taking responsibility to defeat it. *Alternative stories* that allow more choices are explored by asking about *unique outcomes* when problems did not occur.

- *Solution-focused* and *solution-oriented* therapies search for *exceptions* to problematic outcomes to construct solution-rich rather than problem-rich narratives. *Scaling questions* identify times when problems are less severe to explore actions or contexts that decrease problems or increase positive outcomes. The *miracle question* asks what concrete, specific differences would appear should the "problem" magically disappear overnight.

- Other approaches include object-relations family therapy in which transferences of distorted internalized attachment representations among family members are directly worked through in the family's presence. Cognitive-behavioral couples therapies rely on social learning methods to train parents to modify problematic child behavior with operant techniques; social exchange techniques of contingency contracting or *quid pro quo* create better cost/benefit ratios of positive to negative interactions in couples; and *sensate focus* exercises treat sexual dysfunction by replacing performance anxiety with mutual pleasuring. Functional family therapy identifies the function maladaptive behaviors serve families of at-risk youth. It then helps them find adaptive ways to serve those functions for each member.

Further Reading

Anonymous. (1972). Toward the differentiation of a self in one's own family. In J. L. Framo (Ed.), *Family interaction: A dialogue between family researchers and family therapists*. New York: Springer.

Minuchin, S., Nichols, M. P., & Lee, W.-Y. (2007). *Assessing families and couples: From symptom to system*. Boston: Allyn and Bacon.

Napier, A. Y., & Whitaker, C. A. (1978). *The family crucible*. New York: Bantam Books.

Nichols, M. P. (2009). *The essentials of family therapy* (4th ed.). Boston: Allyn & Bacon.

Videos

Alexander, J. F. *Functional family therapy*. Part of the Relationships APA Psychotherapy Video Series.

Angus, L. *Narrative Therapy*. Part of the Systems of Psychotherapy APA Psychotherapy Video Series.

Greenberg, L. S. *Emotionally focused therapy with couples*. Part of the Relationships APA Psychotherapy Video Series.

Heitler, S. *The angry couple: Conflict focused treatment.* Denver: TherapyHelp. http://www.
    therapyhelp.com/marriage.htm.
McDaniel, S. H. (2009). *Family therapy over time.* Part of the Psychotherapy in Six Sessions APA
    Psychotherapy Video Series.
McGoldrick, M. *The legacy of unresolved loss: A family systems approach.* The Multicultural
    Family Institute.

Websites

American Association for Marriage and Family Therapy: www.aamft.org/.
Bowen Center for the Study of the Family: www.thebowencenter.org/index.html
Minuchin Center for the Family: www.minuchincenter.org/http://www.multiculturalfamily.org/
    publications/videos/the_legacy_of_unresolved_loss.html

Chapter 13
Ecosystemic Issues and Approaches

> *DSM-Marginalization Version:* Privilege Disorder—*[T]hose*
> *who enjoy the unearned benefits accorded to them by virtue of*
> *living in a patriarchal, sexist, heterosexist, racist, Christian-*
> *oriented society. One of the main features of this disorder is to*
> *have privilege but claim not to know or feel it.*
>
> K. V. Hardy (2007)

Kenneth Hardy's tongue-in-cheek diagnostic category reflects postmodern and feminist concerns about labeling people for problems caused by socioeconomic forces or by the oppression of marginalized groups. It reflects a dialectic of individual or family *vs.* societal processes as explanations for psychopathology. *Ecosystemic* models examine the hierarchy of social forces that affect opportunities available for individuals and families. Uri Bronfenbrenner (1979) suggested a hierarchy of *macrosystems* to *microsystems* that mediate these influences, privileging White Anglo-Saxon Protestant (WASP) men, but oppressing less powerful groups. Bronfenbrenner's model described the environment's influence on children's development. He recognized that individuals affect the environment as well and that these mutual effects continue throughout a person's lifespan, the *chronosystem*.

Figure 13.1 divides environmental effects into cultural, political, economic, and relational categories. Bronfenbrenner's *macrosystem* level describes the broad environmental influence of cultural beliefs and customs, ethnic differences, economic conditions, and governmental policies. These influences evolve with shifts in global powers, climate, immigration, or conflicts such as those that arise when traditional or tribal cultures confront modern Western society. The *exosystem* refers to institutions such as religious denominations, corporations, school systems, or communities that implement the broad principles of the macrosystem and, while relatively stable, can change during an individual's lifetime. The *mesosystem*, changing from year to year, includes local establishments, churches, neighborhoods, employers, extended family, or hospitals and clinics that affect the individual directly. Immediate, daily influences on individuals occur at the *microsystem* level, which includes the nuclear family, peers, the media and doctors, lawyers, or therapists that are accessible if problems arise.

D. K. Fromme, *Systems of Psychotherapy,*
DOI 10.1007/978-1-4419-7308-5_13, © Springer Science+Business Media, LLC 2011

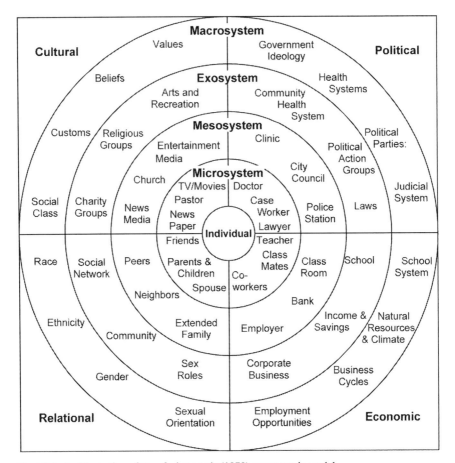

Fig. 13.1 An illustration of Bronfenbrenner's (1979) ecosystemic model

Privileged and Oppressive Ecosystems

Macrosystems and exosystems set the standards or reference values for the institutions and relationships that affect daily life, but are so broad-based they seldom
change except in response to large-scale forces. Recent events affecting American institutions, beliefs, and values include international terrorism, global warming, and the
civil rights movement. Civil rights were first articulated in the Declaration of Independence and the Bill of Rights. However, the social, political, and economic forces that
maintain the status quo are resistant to change and civil rights privileges were initially
restricted to white male land-owners. Only they had the right to vote. The pervasive,
eighteenth-century feudal mentality allowed figures such as Thomas Jefferson to see
no incongruence in owning slaves and believing "All men are created equal."

American history is marked by slow movement in realizing civil rights values;
e.g., the vote was first extended to free men, then to all men after slavery was abol-

ished, and eventually to women in the twentieth century. However, Jim Crow laws and continuing economic suppression of minority groups and women often made these rights more apparent than real. The civil rights movement of the 1950s and 1960s reaffirmed Jeffersonian ideals and Jim Crow laws were abolished; but economic and other forms of oppression, some subtle and some not so subtle, continue to affect minorities and women.

Among the more subtle forms are explanations for the intractable problems experienced by minorities and women created by white men; *e.g.*, The Moynihan Report (U.S. Department of Labor, 1965) suggested Afro-American problems were intractable due to unstable families that often lack a father. Psychiatric labels such as Dependent Personality Disorder, which occur more frequently in women, fail to acknowledge the economic dependency that leads to "symptoms" such as difficulty making decisions without reassurance, wanting others to take responsibility for major areas of life, avoiding disagreement for fear of loss of support, urgently seeking new relationships as old ones end, fear of being unable to care for self if left alone, and going to excessive lengths such as doing unpleasant things to obtain support from others.

American society was created by white men for the benefit of white men; unsurprisingly, they have difficulty recognizing their privileged status as other than "normal." Few white men are so underemployed they cannot provide financially for their family, but must leave home so their family can collect welfare assistance. Few white men fear a loss of financial support with poor prospects for employment if they are disagreeable or avoid unpleasant household duties. Few white men feel they must sacrifice career opportunities to advance those of their wives. Few white men need confront such concerns, which are "transparent" or hard to see. Instead, they blame the victims whose problems are seen to reflect individual or family weaknesses.

These cultural blinders are supported by institutions at the mesosystemic level such as the media, extended family, and the educational system, which reinforce stereotyped views of gender roles and minorities. The microsystem of friends and family also shape the individual's cultural values and beliefs, which are internalized as part of a modern, Western *referential self* (Landrine, 1992). The referential self reflects cultural values of individualism and autonomy that lead people to create a unique self fundamentally separate from outside influences. The referential self is the center of awareness and self-reflection, responsible for its behavior and relationships with other autonomous selves. However, self-definition means modern people can lose their religious beliefs and become vulnerable to existential concerns.

Landrine (1992) contrasts the modern referential self with the *indexical self* of traditional cultures and American minorities that is defined or "indexed" by relationships. Many white women have both modern and traditional perspectives; *e.g.*, they are more likely than their spouse to be concerned about maintaining family relationships and holiday traditions. Modern women are also expected to be autonomous, unless that conflicts with their spouse's needs.

Traditional people are defined by cultural roles and beliefs to see themselves having no needs or responsibilities separate from those of their family or community. They are sensitive to contexts and others' needs, and make sacrifices for the good of others. As a result, they are ready to be whatever the group needs them to be. They have duties and obligations, not rights; they experience shame if they fail in their role and may be cast out by their group.

Therapists may view such patterns as indicating a non-assertive, enmeshed, dependent person with a poorly integrated ego, who lacks social skills, self-respect, and self-reliance. The danger is twofold: first, to treat a cultural pattern as a problem and undermine the client's self-esteem; second, to lose the opportunity to raise awareness about societal problems and to recruit a potential social activist.

Feminism and Multiculturalism

Postmodern feminist and multicultural therapists (*e.g.*, Boyd-Franklin, 1983; Hare-Mustin, 1978; Sue, 1978) suggest that cultural practices are social constructions. Encouraged by the successes of civil rights activists, they suggested that many problems reflect social pathologies and that many problems of women and minorities might be *deconstructed* to create less oppressive practices. Instead of reinforcing the status quo with a focus on the individual, they encouraged therapists to consider how social privilege and oppression affect human problems.

Feminist and multicultural approaches are not independent therapeutic systems with specific techniques or interventions; rather they are an appeal to therapists of all theoretical persuasions to consider how societal oppression contributes to client problems. Despite civil and equal rights legislation, women and minorities are still affected by gender roles and racial prejudices that limit their economic opportunities. These limitations also impact individuals at mesosystemic and microsystemic levels; *e.g.*, the leading cause of death among Black youths is murder, while women are more vulnerable than men to sexual and domestic violence.

Freyd (1996) discusses the effects of *betrayal traumas* such as loss of trust in attachment figures following incest or domestic violence. Betrayal traumas can cause victimized children to dissociate as they try to stay connected with attachment figures. Feminists (*e.g.*, Root, 1992) suggest that constant exposure to media reports about such events leads to *insidious traumatization* and an increased vulnerability that exacerbates the distress associated with even mild forms of sexual harassment or racial prejudice. Sue *et al.* (2007) note that minorities typically experience lifelong *microaggression*, racial slurs, subtle insults (*e.g.*, assumptions that affirmative action "gave" a minority person their position), or invalidations (*e.g.*, assuming an Asian-American is an immigrant). Because microaggressions are subtle and covert, they create difficult situations for victims who feel insulted, but may not be sure exactly why.

Feminist and multicultural therapists help clients understand that feelings of unworthiness or insecurity resulting from culturally based invalidating encounters are not a personal failure. By externalizing the problem, they help clients find more adaptive ways to cope and perhaps become involved in social action to raise the general awareness of how oppression affects everyone. Even "privileged" people suffer from the climate of fear and disengagement from others that oppression creates.

With a few exceptions such as Brown (2008) and McGoldrick and Hardy (2008) integration of feminist and multicultural agendas has proven difficult; *e.g.*, internal disagreements divide feminists on the value of confronting male oppression, which may engender conflict rather than collaboration for gender equality (Guyer & Rowell, 1997). Williams and Barber (2004) describe a number of systemic barriers to the integration of feminism and multiculturalism:

1. Feminists focus mostly on healthy, heterosexual, middle-class white women.
2. Multiculturalists focus mostly on race and ethnic issues.
3. Both ignore the interaction of gender and ethnicity and lack theories to suggest how gender and ethnicity could be integrated with specific therapeutic interventions.
4. Mainstream therapists see both perspectives as "add-ons" to their own approach, but this has proved ineffective in the absence of a unifying theory.

Williams and Barber (2004) recommend the guiding principles, Power and Responsibility (PAR), be included as an integral part of every therapeutic approach:

1. Oppression or privilege is part of everyone's experience—privilege creates a false sense of superiority and social unrest, while oppression creates needless suffering.
2. Empower everyone to advocate responsibly for social justice, balancing individualism and communalism and giving equal importance to intimacy and autonomy in gender roles.
3. Therapy's goal should be to change oppressive conditions rather than adjusting to them; a client's pain or "paranoid" sensitivity may be adaptive.
4. Recognize that clients are strong, capable, and may not be the cause of their problem; value and learn from their experience with privilege or oppression.
5. Clients may need to change their response to oppression, but this is not enough; the ultimate goal is to broaden the client's view to include working for social change for the greater good, whether their experience was of privilege or of oppression.

In summary, the first step in conceptualizing client problems is to consider the role of privilege or oppression. Interventions that just address the individual's reactions only maintain underlying oppressive social conditions unless larger ecosystemic influences are addressed.

Minorities and Oppression in the United States

A major multicultural dialectic contrasts normative *etic* models that examine differences between ethnic groups with hermeneutic *emic* models that privilege the individual's own experience of his or her ethnicity. Cross-cultural questions were first raised by etic research that described the concerns of typical members of a group. However, therapists who rely on etic research may develop a false sense of cultural competence, since normative research ignores the variability of individuals *within* groups. Brown (2008) argues that an emic epistemology lets clinicians operate from a non-expert collaborative position in which clients are the experts on the effects of ethnicity and culture on their lives. Therapists are responsible for knowing how culture affects their own world view, which is not always easy. Monica McGoldrick (2008) noted she felt she was just an American with a "strange" family until visiting Ireland, "Patterns I had experienced all my life suddenly had a context: my family wasn't 'crazy,' I was just Irish!" (p. 103). An emic, hermeneutic approach requires therapists to examine the meaning of their clients' experience in its historical context, which is the emphasis of the following sections.

The African-American Experience

Slavery has been termed the African Holocaust with mortality estimates ranging from 25–100 million (Boyd-Franklin, 1983). Deaths occurred during capture, inhumane conditions in slave ships, and in reprisal for acts of rebellion. Education and traditional religious or tribal practices were forbidden, marriage discouraged (mating was arranged for "breeding" purposes), and families disbanded in slave auctions. Although many traditions and cultural beliefs were lost to be replaced by Christianity, the communalism of African cultures was actually enhanced by the disruption of nuclear families. The extended community banded together to provide each other with what support they could and this tradition continues to the present as does reliance on the church.

Despite political and economic advances between 1970 and 2000 that tripled numbers of middle-class Black families, 22.7% live below the poverty line. Average income is two-third that of whites and unemployment is twice as high (Mckinnon, 2003). At the microsystemic level, disempowered Black men may compensate by being "cool" or demanding "respect" through intimidation, which adds to a climate of fear that nourishes gang formation and Black-on-Black crime: 13.5% of Americans are Black, but they comprise 43% of murder victims with 93.1% killed by other Blacks (Black On Black Crime Coalition, 2009). Black men are eight times more likely to be incarcerated than whites, with about 12% in their twenties in jail. Jail is now a rite of passage for many Black men, but it also diminishes future employment opportunities.

The resulting climate of fear and despair also leads to disrespect and violence toward Black women and contributes to the fact that more than half are unmarried, single parents. The interaction of gender and race ensures that few Black women are able to support their families. Without support from African-American churches and the extended community, very few could manage at all. Because outside agencies are often part of the problem, non-Black therapists must expect to be tested extensively before trust is established. They then need to help clients access their most important resource, the extended family of friends, neighbors, and pastors.

The Black on Black Crime Coalition (2009) suggests a number of ecosystemic interventions:

1. Provide mentoring and support system interventions for released prisoners.
2. Conduct workshops for community organizations, churches, and other human service providers or organizations that help crime victims and their families.
3. Encourage involvement in neighborhood associations that promote economic development and provide crime prevention programs and resources.
4. Encourage involvement in developing youth activities in the schools or other groups and support media campaigns that increase awareness of the problems of Black youths.

The Native-American Experience

Ethnic cleansing and systematic genocide was introduced in the United States with Andrew Jackson's signing of the Indian Removal Act of 1830. From 1831 to 1838, about 60,000 members of the Cherokee, Choctaw, Chickasaw, Creek, and Seminole tribes were forcibly marched from their homes in Southern states to what is now Oklahoma. This freed over 25 million acres of land for whites to settle. It also removed the largest concentrations of Native Americans who survived the diseases and conflicts following European settlement from the Eastern United States. The forced march through winter conditions is now known as the "Trail of Tears" due to the thousands who died from disease, exposure, and starvation. In still another of a long line of broken treaties, choice parts of the Oklahoma Indian Territories were made available to white settlers in the 1889 land rush.

The Indian wars began with the 1622–1644 Powhatan conflicts, escalated during the 1830s, and ended with the Wounded Knee Massacre of several hundred Sioux in 1890. There were over 2,000 tribal groups, each with distinctive languages, traditions, and culture when Europeans first invaded the Americas. Today, the federal government recognizes 562 tribes, with 2.5 million people identifying themselves as Indian and another 1.6 million claiming part-heritage. The exact numbers decimated by disease, warfare, and destruction of a way of life will never be known, but Thornton (1990) cites 1980 U.S. Bureau of Census estimates that suggest Indian populations collapsed from 5 million to about 600,000 people by 1800.

Although warfare ended in 1890, cultural genocide has continued since 1879 with the forcible removal of children as young as 5 years old to government boarding schools. Although these schools still exist, forcible removal no longer occurs. Boarding schools continued earlier missionary school practices of suppressing Indian languages and culture. Generations were raised without nurturing family ties in overcrowded conditions with harsh discipline, forced labor, and emotional, physical, and sexual abuse. Curricula included:

1. English language immersion with punishment for speaking tribal languages.
2. Destruction of traditional garments and replacement with alien, Western clothing.
3. Braids and traditional hairstyles shaved and replaced with Western-style haircuts.

4. Forced physical labor to run the schools kitchens, stables, gardens, and shops.
5. Corporal punishment for infraction of rules or not following the work and school schedules.
6. Immersion in a Western educational curriculum with associated alien goals and philosophy.
7. Regimented, time-bound schedules (Tafoya & Del Vecchio, 2005, pp. 60–61).

DeBruyn and Heart (cited in Tafoya & Del Vecchio, 2005, p. 62) suggest Native American's problems are influenced by historical traumas. Treatment should include:

1. Discussion of the history of Native American genocide, boarding schools, and loss of cultural traditions to help clients recognize the impact of trauma and racism on their lives.
2. Providing a nonjudgmental, secure base to help clients manage the emotions that result.
3. Careful timing to modulate the impact of realizing the impact of multigenerational trauma, with frequent reminders of clients' achievements in handling powerful, negative feelings.
4. Encouraging access to traditional healers to engage in cultural healing ceremonies to facilitate working through unresolved feelings of anger and grief.

As with all clients, the goal is to empower clients to feel free to make choices congruent with their own values. One challenge with Native Americans is the variability in the degree they have maintained cultural ties, which can be well-developed in some tribal areas, but minimal in many urban areas; in other areas, "detribalization" has caused the entire mesosystem to lose its traditions. The issue for some clients is to build their trust in working with someone with different cultural values. For others, the issue is to help them rediscover and reconnect with their cultural base. In either case, inquiry should be made about tribal affiliations and the client's involvement in tribal culture. Therapists should then use tribal names in discussing cultural concerns, since Native Americans do not think of themselves as "Indians," but as Sioux, Hopi, *etc.* Therapists should also be sensitive to differences in nonverbal communication; *e.g.*, averted gaze may be a sign of respect, while extended silences might involve collecting one's thoughts or waiting for a sign that it is okay to speak. Most Indians retain traditional values of community over self and seek harmony with their surroundings rather than control. Careful inquiry into who is significant in their lives is necessary since, like African-Americans, they often have an expanded definition of their family.

The Latino Experience

Latinos also generally retain a strong attachment to traditional values of community before the individual, have an expanded definition of family, and are a heterogeneous group. They think of themselves as Mexican, Puerto Rican, or Cuban rather than Latino. "Hispanic" is a U.S. Bureau of Census term that reflects the Spanish culture's influence, but not the fact that Latinos may also have Indian or African heritage. Despite many differences, most Latinos are Roman Catholics, speak Spanish, are economically depressed, accept the Latino label as useful for shared political concerns, and some are also immigrants.

Many Mexican-Americans were living within the current boundaries of the United States before the Mayflower. The U.S. annexed territories from Texas to California following the Mexican-American war from 1846 to 1848, and although Mexicans were granted citizenship, they experienced harsh discrimination and are among the poorest groups today. Other Latinos may not have experienced oppression in the United States, but were driven to emigrate due to political or economic oppression in their homelands. Of the three largest groups, Mexicans (67% of Latinos) and Puerto Ricans (8.6%) emigrated for economic reasons, while most Cubans (3.7%) left after Castro's socialist revolution in 1959. Most Latino groups experience poverty, prejudice, and confrontation with the U.S. Immigration and Customs Enforcement (ICE) agency. However, many Cubans came with financial backing and were welcomed as a coup in the struggle with Communism.

Racial profiling is significant in ICE deportations with dark-skinned Mexicans more likely to be detained than light-skinned. As poor immigrants, often without legal documents, Mexicans have a unique set of challenges and strengths. Immigration itself causes disruption of family and cultural attachments, culture shock, and economic and political marginalization. They may experience prolonged family separations as the father migrates first and brings his family later, disrupting family structures both at departure and at reunion. Because some enter the U.S. illegally, Latinos may be asked to show their papers even if their ancestors pre-dated the Mayflower. As with other minorities that suffer discrimination, they have high rates of substance abuse, domestic or gang violence, teen pregnancies, and AIDS (Falicov, 2005).

Latino strengths include supportive family systems that expand to include isolated individuals. In contrast to Native and African-Americans, they have an uninterrupted religious and cultural heritage. Pride in heritage can help maintain self-esteem in the face of prejudice and discrimination; *e.g.*, Falicov (2002) found that those who retain their language and cultural ties are less likely to have psychological or substance abuse problems. Immigrants face a dilemma: if they live in a barrio and do not learn English, they preserve cultural ties, but remain marginal to the larger culture; if they assimilate and lose connections to their cultural heritage, they lose a way of defending self-esteem against prejudice. *Biculturalism* seems the best solution: bilingual, knowledgeable about both cultures, and able to move back and forth (Falicov, 2002; Rouse, 1992). Therapists should obtain a migration narrative detailing

> … how long the family has resided in the United States, who immigrated first, who was left behind, who came later or is yet to be reunited; what stresses and learnings were experienced by various family members here and there, and what strengths and resources they discovered (Falicov, 2005, p. 231).

Because Latino families rely heavily on one another, they are reluctant to ask outsiders for help. This reluctance is magnified if a family member lacks documentation. On the other hand, they are likely to be comfortable with family therapy that focuses on concrete, practical advice rather than feelings, *e.g.*, about separation trauma. The Latino copes with trauma by stoic endurance and striving to overcome rather than by exploring its emotional consequences.

Family therapy can help interpret cultural conflicts and encourage compromise for connection problems of separation or hierarchy problems when elders rely on children for English translation. Falicov (2005) suggests that therapists use culturally sensitive, indirect modes of communication such as metaphor, proverbs, or humor to address emotional issues. Given Latino culture's patriarchic nature, it is important to engage the father, remembering that *machismo* also refers to men's roles as providers and protectors of their family. Therapists need to be personal and enter into the extended family to be helpful, *e.g.*, creating a family-like atmosphere with coffee and snacks. Hartman and Laird (1983) suggest therapists help families construct an *ecomap* that explores issues of isolation, access to community resources, or cultural conflicts with Americanized children. Ecomaps use diagrams to show families how to address problems of housing, employment, or crime by accessing extended family, schools, and community agencies. As with other minorities, therapists help families recognize strengths and understand that their problems may reflect oppression rather than weakness.

The Asian Experience

Asian-Americans are extremely diverse, from 30 Asian countries, and the U.S. Bureau of Census now includes 21 Pacific Island groups in this category. Totaling 14 million citizens, including 1 million Pacific Islanders, Chinese (27%), Filipino (19%), Asian Indian (12%), Japanese (11%), Korean (11%), and Vietnamese (9%) comprise the largest groups. Most emigrated to escape economic oppression, but many Filipinos, Koreans, Vietnamese, and Cambodians came as war refugees. A recent wave of Chinese immigrants followed the political upheaval when Hong Kong reverted to China after 100 years of British administration. Like other minorities, Asian immigrants experienced racial prejudice, *e.g.*, the Chinese Exclusion Act of 1882 and Immigration Act of 1924 prevented wives from joining husbands who came for the Gold Rush of 1849 or to build the transcontinental railway system.

Many Chinese and Japanese are now third- or fourth-generation Americans, but are more likely to be asked "Where are you from?" than second-generation European-Americans. Most Japanese immigrated before 1924, but fresh waves of immigrants still come from other Asian countries, including Chinese who previously lived in Vietnam, Singapore, and elsewhere. "Mail-order brides" still come from the Philippines. Asking for a *migration narrative* can alert therapists to different Asian-American immigration experiences, level of acculturation, specific traumas experienced in moving, how many moves were made, and discrimination or other difficulties experienced upon arrival. Validating strengths in coping with these struggles removes stigmas associated with emotional problems and helps traditional Asian-Americans accept treatment.

Lee and Mock (2005a) note that Asian immigrants may be at different acculturation levels:

1. *Traditional Families*: recent arrivals from agricultural backgrounds or those who
   live in ethnic communities such as Chinatown, speak their native language, practice traditional rituals, and have limited interaction with mainstream American
   society. Father and eldest son may be the most important dyad in the family, with
   the spousal relationship secondary.
2. *Cultural Conflict*: these families may depend on acculturated children for their
   English and knowledge of American culture; but this creates a role-reversal and
   diminishes the authority of the traditional family patriarch. Conflicts also occur
   if one spouse arrived earlier, as in an arranged marriage with someone from the
   home country; *e.g.*, differences in facility with English and how things are done
   in America can be stressors.
3. *Bicultural Families*: may be second generation or professionals who were already
   bilingual and familiar with Western ways when they immigrated. Spouses share
   responsibility and authority and are less likely to live with the extended family.
4. *"Americanized" Families*: second or later generations who speak English primarily and have adopted Western individualism and egalitarianism; they may or
   may not identify with their Asian heritage.
5. *New Millennium Families*: couples with differing ethnic or racial backgrounds
   who struggle to integrate different cultural values, religious beliefs, traditions,
   and relational styles and forge a new identity.

Asian immigrants have diverse religious beliefs, including Catholicism, Protestant-
ism, Confucianism, Taoism, Buddhism, Hinduism, Shintoism, Islam, and animism.
They also speak 32 different languages, some with distinctly different dialects; *e.g.*,
most Chinatown Chinese speak Cantonese, but recent immigrants from China or
Taiwan speak Mandarin. Many other regional and ethnic dialects exist such as Toi-
shanese, Chiuchow, Shanghaiese, Taiwanese, Fukien, Hakka, and still others (Lee
& Mock, 2005b).

Despite this diversity, traditional Asian-Americans have patriarchic family structures, value the family over the individual, rely on the extended family to solve
problems, and are reluctant to share problems with outsiders. For many groups,
the family includes remembrance, respect and honor for ancestors and concern
for future generations. Asian-Americans also value stoic endurance of problems,
tend not to express opinions or emotions directly, but attend carefully to contextual
and nonverbal cues and allude indirectly to problems with metaphors or proverbs.
Therapists need to be aware that indirect responses are not signs of resistance or
dysfunction, but an essential part of cultures that value harmony in all things.

Among other suggestions, Lee and Mock (2005a) recommend that therapists:

1. Join the family through the decision maker, usually the father, and take care
   not to reinforce role reversals by asking other family members to interpret; professional interpreters are needed. Since work is valued over therapy, evening
   appointments may be necessary, especially if an interpreter is needed.

2. Explain what mental health professionals do and how they differ from physicians; present a knowledgeable expertise an immigrant might expect in consulting a village elder and enquire how their problem would be understood and treated in their native culture.

3. Maintain a polite, formal manner, but reinforce joining the family by greeting each person warmly, offering tea, and helping seat the elders. Appropriate self-disclosure about the therapist's heritage, family, and training can help strengthen the alliance, but lengthy data-gathering may lead to fears that information could be used politically against them.

4. Reframe mental health problems as attempts to solve difficult problems created by difficult situations; validating the family's efforts and strength in coping can offset strongly held beliefs that stigmatize emotional difficulties.

5. Establish credibility as an advice-giver: offer explanations for presenting problems, show familiarity and interest in their cultural background, and offer an intervention that gives some immediate relief.

6. Consider seeing adults and children separately so adults can discuss personal concerns without loss of face and children can express themselves and still maintain filial piety.

7. State goals in concrete, practical terms that reflect immediate problems and symptom-reduction, broken down into understandable, short-term subgoals. Homework is useful.

8. Validate family belief that the identified patient has a problem and its effect on the family, but focus on the problem, not the patient, to avoid scapegoating; reinforce family obligations to each other and their need to work together to solve the problem.

9. Take advantage of Asian respect for education and use psychoeducation to teach communication, problem-solving, behavior management, or conflict-resolution skills.

10. Reframe problems in positive terms and avoid confrontation; take advantage of extended family strengths, religious community support, obligations toward each other, work ethic, and parental sacrifice for their children's future; act as a teacher, advocate, mediator, and interpreter, but not as an interrogator.

In general, successful therapists become part of the extended family. Families may offer gifts of appreciation or ask therapists to future family celebrations. If clinicians wish to serve the Asian community, they need to accept such gestures as culturally embedded, while taking care not to become over-involved in dual relationships. Involvement with the larger community is perhaps the best solution—to be a "village elder" rather than a member of a particular family.

The Lesbian, Gay, Bisexual, Transgender Experience

With 2–10% of the population, the lesbian, gay, bisexual, transgender (LGBT) community faces unique challenges. Nealy (2008) notes that unlike other minority groups, LGBT couples lack access to over 1,100 federal rights associated with marriage; *e.g.*, LGBT couples with children are less likely to have health insurance, cannot file joint tax returns, which penalizes single-wage earner households, and surviving partners do not receive Social Security benefits.

"Coming out" requires strength and courage and can subject the individual to virulent and violent discrimination. Coming out may subject LGBT people to rejection and alienation from their family and support networks in contrast to other minorities who retain the support of family, cultural, and religious traditions. Clients often report childhood and adolescent isolation as they began to recognize their sexual orientation or gender identity was different and this difference was somehow shameful. They also realized their life path would be different from others, affect future partners, children, career, and religious life. There is no easily accessible community on whom they can rely as they navigate the many challenges once they let others know about their difference. LGBT suicide rates are two to three times that of their peers.

Coming out is a stressful, ongoing process that begins with first coming out to one's self, then to other LGBT individuals, family, friends, coworkers, and neighbors (Nealy, 2008). It is doubly difficult for the LGBT person from a traditional culture, where gender roles may be rigidly defined and homosexuality proscribed by both tradition and by religion. There is risk of family and network rejection and vulnerability to oppression both as an LGBT person and as a minority. Further complications arise if partners are at different stages of coming out and are not equally comfortable attending LGBT events. If the partners' families are at different stages of acceptance, there may need to be a choice between partner and family.

Transgendered people and their partners have an even more complex path to navigate, given their diversity: drag-queen, drag-king, female-to-male, male-to-female, pre-op, post-op, *etc.* Sex-change operations create unique problems for the children of married transsexuals and for their spouses who may need to confront their own sexual orientation. The English language lacks terms to describe these relationships and there are no traditional guidelines.

Nealy (2008) suggests that LGBT individuals and couples need therapists who:

1. Are nurturing, nondiscriminating, and sensitive to the diversity of LGBT relationships
2. Take steps to remedy gaps in their knowledge of LGBT problems and issues
3. Align with clients in recognizing "gender roles are by no means equitable, binary gender assumptions and roles are devastating to all of us—'masculine' men, 'feminine' women, and those somewhere in the middle" (Mollenkott, 2001, p. 74)
4. Acknowledge gender identity disorder (DSM-IV) as a stigmatizing, pathologizing label
5. Work with partners, children, parents, and siblings, so LGBT people do not need to choose between partner and family

Ecosystemic Interventions

Ecosystemic therapists assume that gender, race, and ethnicity are cultural constructs, while sexual orientation is biological. Cultural prejudices assert the opposite: that problems associated with gender, race, or ethnicity reflect biological inferiority, while LGBT people make a "lifestyle" choice. Ecosystemic therapists recognize that client problems often involve the oppression of women and minorities in contrast to white, heterosexual, middle-class, male privilege. Their goal is to help clients recognize their strengths in coping with the oppression-related, external causes of their problems. Ecosystemic therapists move beyond the therapy office to work collaboratively with community members to identify, understand, and engage in solving problems in the client/s community (Dale, 2008).

Ecosystemic therapists also help clients address immediate problems with individual, family, or psychoeducation approaches and with advocacy or consultation with other agencies. They recognize the diversity of client cultural issues and acculturation and the need to learn how their clients experience or cope with oppression. They also recognize that a therapist of the same ethnic background might be more helpful (Halliday-Boykins, Schoenwald, & Letourneau, 2005), but may not be readily available. Accordingly, they view the individual or the family as the expert on their cultural beliefs and traditions and collaboratively explore the nature of the presenting problems and its ecological roots. They use ecosystemic approaches such as *family networking* or *multisystemic therapy* whenever appropriate.

Family Networking

The modern European-American culture's emphasis on science and development has increased agricultural productivity, advanced medical cures, and raised material standards of living for many, but at a cost. An increasingly secular and mobile society has eroded traditional beliefs and practices such as reliance upon the extended family and community for assistance in times of trouble. It has created an existential vacuum in which families are increasingly isolated from the supports of religious beliefs and traditions. Groups such as the Native Americans have been hard hit by the loss of cultural traditions and have benefited very little from modern society's progress. Family networking literally *retribalizes* people whose loss of support from their community, extended family, and traditions has led to problematic behavior and symptoms as they experience difficulty in adjusting to stress or oppression.

Speck and Attneave (1973) suggest people are energized if retribalization renews old ties with their community. Renewed social support provides symptom-carriers with both direct, daily assistance in confronting problems and a renewed sense of self-worth as they see that many people *do* care about their welfare. Community members benefit by being part of a revitalized network available to each of them and by the self-esteem that comes from working toward goals that transcend the individual.

Family networking has not received the attention it might have, perhaps because Speck and Attneave (1973) used experiential and confrontation techniques typical of late 1960s encounter groups. However, the more collaborative techniques preferred today can also mobilize social networks and extensive research supports the importance of social support in adjusting to difficult situations; *e.g.*, Henrich and Shahar (2008) found that social support was a significant buffer against depression in Israeli youth subjected to terrorist rocket attacks. The following case illustrates many of Speck and Attneave's (1973) methods, but does not use confrontation or their encounter group techniques.

Case History

Lorene, a 35-year-old divorced Native-American mother of two children, was referred by her hospital-attending physician for psychological evaluation of her eating disorder. She was brought by ambulance to the hospital after her 16-year-old daughter, Laura, found her unconscious after returning from school. Upon admission, Lorene weighed 95 pounds, less than 75% of the ideal weight for a woman of 5′5″ height. She suffered from a life-threatening electrolyte imbalance with irregular heartbeat and swelling of her extremities. She did not remember when she last had a menstrual period, saying it was years ago and she had just "entered menopause early."

An advanced student therapist interviewed Lorene 2 weeks after hospitalization when her condition had stabilized and she had gained 5 pounds. She had binged and purged more or less continuously since being elected "princess" at a tribal pow-wow during her senior year in high school. Lorene said she was determined not to become fat like her mother and the older tribal women she knew. She married her Anglo-American high school sweetheart shortly after graduation and they moved to a tiny community of about 100 people near the oil fields where he had found work. Distance and both families' disapproval of the "mixed" marriage led to relations being cut off. Lorene says her marriage was fine until her second child, Larry, now 13 years old, was born. She said she gained too much weight during the pregnancy, began to diet and purge seriously, and then went through "early menopause." Her marital problems began at this time as she lost interest in sexual intimacy and they divorced 2 years later. Lorene and her children now subsist on food stamps and occasional child support payments.

Diagnosis

Axis I—Anorexia, binge/purge type; *Axis II*—No diagnosis; *Axis III*—Malnutrition; *Axis IV*—Economic and social environment problems; Axis V—GAF=25.

Intervention

The therapist and her supervisor agreed that usual treatment formats would not work due to the client's lack of insight and motivation, poverty, lack of transportation, and the 40-mile distance between her home and the hospital clinic. Accordingly, they decided to mobilize a support network for Lorene and her family. They held a conjoint family interview on a Saturday when Lorene's children were visiting her at the hospital. During this session, it was apparent that Laura was a parentified child who took major responsibility for the family's meals and her brother's care, since her mother was often too weak to get out of bed. The cotherapists explained that most families relied on their support systems when faced with problems, supports that Lorene and her family were missing. The family was interested in the idea of trying to create a support system by contacting all the neighbors and people they knew. With Lorene's permission, the therapists contacted her pastor, who readily agreed to host a meeting of potential supporters at the community church.

The next family session, on the day of Lorene's hospital discharge, developed a list of friends, family, and neighbors that included addresses of 75 households in the community phone book. A letter was written collaboratively to invite these people to an all-evening meeting hosted by the church to address Lorene's and her family's problems. After persuasion by her children, Lorene agreed the letter should indicate she had an eating disorder and that frequently food stamps ran out before the end of the month, which left everyone hungry.

On the appointed evening, 42 people joined Lorene, her children, and the cotherapists. Only Lorene's mother came from her family. Iced tea and refreshments initiated Speck and Attneave's (1973) retribalization phase of introductions and renewal of old acquaintances. After 30 minutes, the cotherapists introduced themselves and talked about how networks of caring people usually solve problems that defeat isolated families. They explained how social and media ideals pressure women to be thin and how this has led to an epidemic of eating disorders. They described how Lorene's eating disorder nearly ended in death by starvation; how in weak moments she would go through a week's worth of food stamps, feel ashamed, and then purge. This also left the family short of food at the end of the month.

The therapists asked the group to confront these problems, to be responsible for deciding what to do and then implement that decision. The cotherapists were there to facilitate discussion; *e.g.*, since large groups are unwieldy, they suggested the group divide into work groups of 6–8 people to brainstorm ideas to bring back to the whole group later. Generational differences were recognized with two groups in their twenties and thirties and the rest in their forties to sixties. This initiated *polarization*, a dialectic of ideas the whole group could discuss later. After small group discussion for 45 minutes, a refreshment break permitted informal talks before reuniting the whole group. Each of the seven work groups selected a speaker to join an "inner circle" of eight chairs. The eighth chair was for anyone in the outer circle to use temporarily if they had something to say. The Native American tradition of a *speaker's stick* was used to determine who had the floor: everyone was encouraged to limit speeches to 2 or 3 minutes and to yield the speaker's stick to anyone in the inner circle who raised their hand.

These procedures assured that activists were located in the inner circle and kept discussions orderly, a departure from Speck and Attneave's (1973) active encouragement of confrontation. Although they suggest that networking groups experience impasses that lead to frustration and depression before a *breakthrough* phase occurs, this did not occur in Lorene's network group, perhaps because collaboration was encouraged rather than confrontation.

Instead, the inner circle quickly came up with a number of workable suggestions with a few comments from the outer circle that led to a consensus forming rather quickly. The church pastor noted they needed someone to prepare the weekly church bulletin and offered Lorene a part-time job which she accepted. A neighboring rancher offered after-school work to Larry to feed and water his horses and occasionally muck the stables in return for spending money and freedom to ride the horses when his chores were finished. The younger work groups noted that Laura had had too much responsibility and, as a good student, she should focus on her studies and getting a scholarship for college. The church and neighborhood women all agreed they would work out a daily roster to visit the family at dinner-time to ensure there was food on the table and that Lorene was eating regularly.

The therapists congratulated the group on their solutions and admired their willingness to go out of their way to help Lorene and her family. They indicated they would be available for phone consultation if needed, would check back in 3 months to see how things were going, and tried to excuse themselves. The group decided, however, to give them a standing ovation and several commented they were not going "out of their way," but were excited to see their community come together and do something important. At the 3-month family interview, Lorene's weight had stabilized at 115 pounds, still too thin, but not life-threatening. She was enjoying her part-time job at the church and the extra money it brought. Laura proudly showed her acceptance letter offering a scholarship to the state university; and Larry, for the first time, took off his baseball cap in the therapists' presence to show how his hair had grown back. In focusing on Lorene, the therapists had failed to discover Larry coped with anxiety by pulling out hairs on the back of his head; they had thought nothing about a 13-year-old boy wearing a baseball cap backwards!

Multisystemic Therapy

Multisystemic therapy (MST; Henggeler, Schoenwald, Borduin, Rowland, & Cunningham, 2009) is based on Bronfenbrenner's (1979) theory of social ecology, which views individuals as nested within larger, hierarchically organized social systems. Changes in one part automatically influence changes in other parts of the ecosystem. Developed for delinquent youth and their families, MST considers risk factors at each systemic level: individual (poor verbal skills, attribution biases), family (lack of parental warmth or monitoring), peers (delinquent associates), schools (low achievement, chaotic environment), and neighborhoods (mobility, crime rate). It focuses in particular on two factors shown to mediate delinquent behavior: inconsistent caregiver discipline and association with deviant peers (Henggeler *et al.*, 2009).

MST has been found effective with delinquent youth, including those abusing drugs or in psychiatric crisis. At a cost of about $5,000 per family, MST improves family relationships and school attendance, while decreasing drug use, re-arrest rates (25–70%), and long-term institutionalization rates (47–64%; Aos, Phipps, Barnoski, & Lieb, 1999). Treatment completion rates of 97–98% suggest that MST is well-received by youths and their families. In randomized trials with juvenile sex offenders, MST was superior to cognitive-behavioral interventions with lower follow-up recidivism rates for sexual (8% *vs.* 46%) and nonsexual (29% *vs.* 58%) crimes. At an average of 8.9 years later, MST clients had 70% fewer overall arrests and 80% fewer days of incarceration (Borduin, Schaeffer, & Heiblum, 2009).

Conceptual Framework

MST helps caregivers, who have an immediate, consistent impact on their children's lives, alter delinquent behavior patterns and maintain positive treatment gains. Home-based treatment delivery strengthens caregiver support systems and addresses treatment barriers such as work schedules, unreliable transportation, or caregiver mental health. It also engages all family members, provides information about relevant family dynamics and resources, and avoids the negative effects of placing youths in group treatment with delinquent peers. MST focuses on family member strengths to build self-esteem, engage them in treatment, and as a lever to initiate change. It discourages labeling or disparaging comments at any systemic level. Problems are assessed in terms of the barriers that prevent needs from being met. Treatment adherence to MST's nine principles is strictly monitored:

Principle 1: Assessment delineates the fit between problems and their systemic context. Home-based assessment and interviews with extended family, teachers, case workers, *etc.*, identify the contexts or factors that initiate and maintain problem sequences. *Fit circles* diagram links among different systems and the youth's behavior and help therapists look beyond individual and family influences; *e.g.*, in the case below, no consequences followed "Mike's" verbal and physical aggression at school due to the lack of communication between school and family systems; also contributing were lack of supervision, alcohol present in the home, poor frustration tolerance, and delinquent peers. Each of these systemic influences requires intervention.

Principle 2: Interventions emphasize the positive, using systemic strengths to leverage change. Change occurs to the extent the youth's family members and social systems are actively engaged in treatment. This is especially important for family members whose own problems present barriers, or whose prior contact with social agencies and schools has been negative. Caregivers are more likely to collaborate if they see that therapists recognize their strengths and do not blame them for problems. Caregivers learn to monitor the youth's behavior, reinforce positive behavior, and ensure medications are taken as prescribed. Cognitive-behavioral therapy may be useful for cooperative youths with good verbal abilities.

Principle 3: Responsible family behavior is promoted and irresponsible behavior discouraged. Framing behavior as responsible or irresponsible helps families see how they influence the youth's problems. Conceptualizing problems in terms of behavior that can be modified, rather than a diagnostic condition, gives everyone greater confidence in the possibility of change.

Principle 4: Interventions focus on the present, are action oriented, and target specific, well-defined problems. It is easier to modify here-and-now situations than to change something that happened in the past. Historical factors do not explain how problems are currently maintained. Present-focused, action-oriented approaches facilitate ongoing assessment of interventions or needed revisions and provide opportunities to reinforce positive behavioral changes.

Principle 5: Interventions target behavioral sequences within and between system levels that maintain the identified problem. Problems do not occur spontaneously, but are the end result of a sequence of ecosystemic events. This view reduces blaming the child and expands the range of possible interventions. One factor contributing to Mike's problems was the lack of negative consequences for misbehaving that resulted from poor communication between his mother and teacher. Arranging a parent-teacher meeting could improve consistency and communication, avoid mutual blaming, analyze relevant problem contingencies, and brainstorm solutions.

Principle 6: Interventions fit the youth's developmental needs. Developmentally mature youths should be directly involved in the treatment program to prepare for independent living, while immature or developmentally delayed youths may need assistance from teachers and caregivers with social or learning skills. Caregiver abilities need to be considered; *e.g.*, foster parents or other community supports may be needed if grandparents lack stamina to be full-time parents.

Principle 7: Interventions require daily or weekly effort by family members, so that change occurs quickly and barriers are identified before caregivers become discouraged. Therapists also need to be available 24/7 to consult on problems that arise, especially while caregivers are learning to apply new contingencies and interventions. Organizational support for 3–6 family caseloads is essential to maintain this high level of therapist involvement.

Principle 8: Intervention effectiveness is continuously evaluated from multiple perspectives, with providers accountable for overcoming barriers to successful outcome. Different perspectives are essential, as youths may be unaware of their behavior's impact on others, teachers unaware of the home environment, and caregivers unaware of the school environment. Continuous monitoring allows immediate confrontation of barriers that could discourage families.

Principle 9: Interventions empower caregivers to address family members' needs across multiple systemic contexts and promote generalization and maintenance of treatment gains. Therapists avoid solving problems for the family. Instead, they teach parents problem-solving skills to overcome barriers and manage their child's behavior. They help clients discover community resources to manage the youth's (or their own) behavior. Informal support structures of family, friends, neighbors, and community or school programs are developed that eventually replace social agency supports (Letourneau, Cunningham, & Henggeler, 2002).

Case Illustration

Letourneau *et al.* (2002) discuss Mike, a 13-year-old African-American boy who was ordered into treatment after being convicted for burning down his family's garage. Mike explained that his fire-setting was an attention-getting prank that got out of control. He has a 2-year history of increasing verbal aggression at home and verbal and physical aggression at school. Mike lives with his mother, uncle (age 29), older brothers (19 and 20), and the older brother's pregnant girlfriend (18). They live in a low-income, high-crime neighborhood in which drugs are being sold. Mike denies substance abuse, but his mother notes his uncle and younger brother frequently drink. Mike's father had a history of significant substance abuse, is currently incarcerated, and has had no contact with the family in many years:

- *Assessment: Needs and Strengths*: Mike's teacher and probation officer were interviewed and his behavior observed in class. Mike had earlier been transferred into a class for children with behavioral problems and is being considered for expulsion due to noncompliant behavior and weekly fights. Classroom observation confirmed Mike's claim that his misbehavior was encouraged by friends. His teacher reports his verbal and physical aggression is easily provoked. The teacher was frustrated with Mike's mother after several missed appointments, but was unaware of her heavy work schedule. His probation officer sees Mike as likable and able to follow instructions. Strengths include Mike's attractive looks, verbal skills, and ability to relate well with adults. His mother works hard to meet Mike's and her family's needs. His uncle and brothers like him and express willingness to "do whatever it takes" to help him improve his behavior, especially toward his mother. Also, Mike's teachers like him and want to give him another chance now that he's actively involved in treatment. A neighborhood center is available for after-school activities.
- *Diagnosis*: Axis I—Adolescent antisocial behavior; Axis II—No diagnosis; Axis III—No diagnosis; Axis IV—Legal, social environment, and educational problems; Axis V—GAF = 58.
- *Conceptualization—Fit assessment*: Initial hypotheses about factors contributing to Mike's aggressive behavior included: (a) association with deviant peers who model and reinforce his actions; (b) school failure reflecting poor classroom management of special needs children; (c) weak behavioral contingencies reflecting lack of monitoring after school and poor communication between teacher and mother; (d) impulsivity; (e) Mike's need for attention; and (f) alcohol use. Classroom observation suggested aggressive behavior was especially likely on days following evenings with poor supervision. Unscheduled home visits revealed that Mike's uncle and 19-year-old brother were either drinking or absent on evenings they were supposed to be supervising. Also, Mike's breath smelled of alcohol: he was apparently sneaking his elders' alcohol into his room to drink. This alcohol intake appears responsible for the irritability and aggressiveness observed on subsequent days. Mike's goals are to have his own room and to return to a mainstream class. His mother's goals are also to return him to his regular class and for his verbal and physical aggression to stop. His teacher wants him to stop cursing and fighting at school and his probation officer wants him to engage in appropriate after-school activities with prosocial peers. His brothers and uncle want him to become less irritable and easily upset.
- *Interventions*:

  1. *Safety*. Because of the dangers of fire-starting, all flammable materials in Mike's home need to be removed or secured. Although the garage-burning

was likely a prank gone out of control, poor supervision of Mike could still place the family at risk.

2. Since Mike's alcohol use underlies other problems, it was collaboratively agreed that:

   (a) Mike's mother will throw out all alcoholic beverages and forbid them in the home; she will work with the therapist to develop the assertiveness skills necessary to enforce this rule.

   (b) The eldest brother and his girlfriend will provide after-school adult supervision 2 days a week; Mike will enroll for basketball at the local community center on the remaining days, with center rules to be reviewed by his new coach.

   (c) A plan structuring Mike's free time (homework, chores, play, curfew) will be posted on the refrigerator so everyone knows what he should be doing at any time; Mike's mother and the therapist will develop appropriate contingencies for responsible and irresponsible behavior (phone/TV privileges).

   (d) The therapist (eventually Mike's mother) will conduct random Breathalyzer tests; she will make random calls from work in the evening to check on his behavior with the responsible adult. His mother or eldest brother will record the frequency, duration, and intensity of verbal outbursts, reviewed weekly with the therapist to see if the plan needs changing.

3. The therapist will be available for emergency consultation to help the teacher develop appropriate classroom contingency management and Mike's mother will provide a same-day response for any disruptions. Mike's mother and teacher will meet to resolve any remaining conflicts in their relationship. A daily report card will monitor his behavior with inappropriate behavior resulting in response cost (time-out, public apology) and positive practice. Appropriate interactions with the teacher or peers will earn praise and points to be traded for privileges (library time to listen to music, extracurricular school activities, access to privileges at home). The principal will set guidelines for the changes needed for Mike to re-enter the regular classroom. Mike will be taught assertiveness skills to cope with peer pressure and self-talk to help defuse provocations. He will also learn ways to avoid high-risk situations, such as crowded hallways during free periods. Again, the therapist will be responsible for tracking each component of the home and school interventions to ensure compliance and to suggest changes if needed.

Community Mental Health

Treatment contexts contributing to human problems extend from the American mental health macrosystem to the therapist's office microsystem. Each level can perpetuate or alleviate problems at other levels. The Community Mental Health Act of 1964 envisioned a system that addressed a full range of mental health problems.

Newly developed psychoactive drugs held the promise of treating serious mental illness and avoiding the dependency created by long-term hospitalization. A system of community mental health agencies would provide:

1. *In-patient treatment* with drugs to stabilize seriously mental ill patients and prepare them to be released as soon as possible to ….
2. *Half-way houses* to provide intensive psychotherapy and support until patients could move from a sheltered living and rehabilitation environment to independent living, supported by ….
3. *Outpatient treatment* that would continue therapy until the patient was fully independent.
4. *Emergency treatment* to handle crisis situations would be available in all three settings.
5. *Consultation and education* would be provided to other human services agencies.

Unfortunately, this plan was never fully implemented or funded. Drugs did alleviate the most disturbing symptoms of serious mental illness and mental hospitals soon discharged the bulk of their clients. However, half-way homes were never adequately funded and local communities objected to placing them in their neighborhoods. Patient discharges are seldom coordinated with outpatient centers and the result is the current epidemic of homeless people. Their ranks have been increased by the lack of appropriate treatment for returning veterans with traumatic disorders and by families who have lost jobs and homes, but all are subject to hunger, the weather, the indifference of passersby, and to victimization. Most self-medicate with alcohol or street drugs that make their problems still more intractable.

Many who end up on the streets and do drugs commit crimes to support themselves and their habit. As a result, the prison system now warehouses the mentally ill instead of the state hospitals. Over the last three decades, prison populations grew at a rate seven times that of the general population. In state prisons, 73% of women and 55% of men have diagnosable mental illness; in the federal prisons, 61% of the women and 44% of the men; local jails, 75% of the women and 63% of the men. Only 1 in 3 received treatment in state prisons, 1 in 4 in federal prisons, and 1 in 6 of local jail inmates (James & Glaze, 2006). Over 3 million people, 1% of the population, are in jail, but Blacks are incarcerated at nearly three times the rate of Latinos and six to eight times the rate of whites (West & Sabol, 2009).

These data strongly suggest that the mental health and criminal justice systems are oppressive and harmful, especially for minorities. Therapists with an ecosystemic awareness need to move beyond the consulting room to educate and advocate for social change. Research needs to examine if society might be better served by prevention and treatment than by a costly prison system that incarcerates people at rates higher than any other nation. Research shows that serious mental illness can be treated successfully (*e.g.*, Hogarty, 2002), but a coordinated system to make its application available widely has yet to be created.

Power, Symptoms, and Ethics

For many clients, the therapeutic microsystem is one of the most intimate and powerful relationships in their lives. Clients share thoughts or secrets with the therapist they could never share with their immediate family. In addition to the inherent power differential of a distressed person seeking help from a professional, this intimacy makes clients uniquely vulnerable. Each helping profession has ethical principles designed to prevent abuse of this vulnerability. The end of this chapter presents Website links to such guidelines. Ethical codes help therapists avoid abusing their power and navigate complex situations where competing goals or interests make it difficult to decide on the best course of action. Perhaps the most important guideline is to consult with other professionals when in doubt. However, ethical codes do not fully explore the nature of the therapist's power to help or harm, which is the purpose of this section.

Clients seek help because they experience baffling, distressing symptoms that resist their efforts and those of significant others to make them go away. Clients are reluctant to give up theories about their symptoms that help make sense of a mystifying experience, but have not led to a satisfactory resolution. A common factor in all therapeutic approaches is to present a theory of symptoms and what to do about them that usually differs from the client's personal ideas. If therapy is to succeed, clients must be persuaded to adopt new explanations and relinquish their old ones. There are many theories to choose from, but they have implications that are not always recognized.

Some theories take the client's wish to make the symptom go away at face value and work to eliminate it without considering whether the symptom has any meaning. Biomedical approaches interpret symptoms as the result of disordered neurochemistry and give clients medication to relieve the symptoms. Clients are grateful if medication helps and relieved to have explanations that absolve them of responsibility, but the implicit message is that their symptoms mean something is wrong with them. Cognitive-behavioral approaches locate problems in the client's self-talk or in environmental contingencies, but also may not consider a symptom's meaning. Clients or significant others are expected to follow "expert" directives in these approaches, which reinforces their unequal status. Since their thoughts, feelings, or actions constitute the problem, their ideas may be seen as a hindrance rather than a help.

Symptom-removal strategies may be helpful if symptoms are an acute response to a situational stressor rather than a long-term theme in the person's life. They may also help if symptoms were a reaction to conditions that no longer exist, but now contribute to a self-maintaining vicious circle. Medication can also enable client collaboration in their treatment. However, if a symptom's meaning or function is not understood, its removal may have unintended effects; *e.g.*, divorce may result from assertiveness training that disrupts long-standing relational patterns in a marriage. If the function of the client's passivity had been understood, the divorce might have been averted by engaging the spouse in therapy.

In contrast, other approaches suggest symptoms have symbolic meanings that serve a function in the lives of clients and their families. Clients are the experts on their history, social supports, and inner experience. Their active collaboration is essential to unravel symptom meanings and functions; this enhances their sense of self-efficacy and helps equalize the balance of power in therapy. Symptoms are always a protest about difficult experiences, about oppression, trauma, the lack of a secure attachment base, or existential questions of life's meaning. They are a symbolic way to communicate experiences that are too dangerous and mystifying to put in words or whose origins are lost in preverbal experiences of early childhood. This is true even if biological vulnerabilities affect the symptom's form and extent.

For example, prophets or poets who heard voices were seen historically as divinely inspired. Today, auditory hallucinations or delusions are usually considered a sign of psychosis by the general public and professionals. However, many people hold false beliefs and receive a diagnosis only if they act upon their beliefs (Campbell & Morrison, 2007). Shawyer, Ratcliff, Mackinnon *et al.* (2007) found that subjects who accepted hallucinatory experiences without acting upon their demands had better overall functioning than those who rejected or acted upon them. It seems likely such experiences are more common than is usually believed and may not necessarily be associated with mental illness; it is the client's *reaction* to mystifying experiences, informed by modern beliefs, that creates distress (Morrison, 1997).

Therapists need to recognize their power to do harm with diagnoses that confirm a client's fear of "going crazy." Labeling a person, if accepted, can lead to depression, self-stigmatization, and stigmatization by others; *e.g.*, consider the nearly universal rejection by communities of having half-way houses in their midst. Labels also have the effect of reifying constantly changing, fluid processes as people confront new situations. Third-party payer diagnostic requirements confront clinicians with a dilemma: a diagnosis is necessary for treatment to proceed, but it can also transform a process into a stigmatizing condition. This dilemma is apt to be repeated as clients eagerly seek explanations for mystifying experiences. An interpretation can trigger an unforeseeable, negative sequence of events if it goes further than what clients have already considered (Orlinsky, Ronnestad, & Willutzki, 2004); *e.g.*, therapists' theoretical biases could lead to suggestions that disrupt significant attachment relationships.

A basic goal of therapy is to increase clients' options and help them choose wisely. This begins with the principle of *informed consent*, letting clients know the duration, costs, and the risks and benefits of various options for treatment or non-treatment. Limits to *confidentiality* need to be clear because they are sharing their most intimate experiences and are uniquely vulnerable. They should also be warned against reifying any diagnosis and asked to consider whether their distress is caused by their symptoms or by their interpretation of their symptoms. Finally, therapists should emphasize the client's expert knowledge of their own experience and explore the function of symptoms before deciding on their removal.

Integrative Implications

Pervasive effects of privilege and oppression may interfere with interventions at lower systemic levels and contribute to relapse if not addressed. This suggests that an ecosystemic assessment should be integral to any therapeutic approach. Ecosystemic assessment requires collaboration and reinforces cooperation with externalized explanations that counter feelings of shame or self-blame over having a problem. It encourages clients to find ways to counteract external pressures and to advocate for social change in their community. Internalized, attachment-related problems are placed in a perspective that helps clients understand why caregivers were not fully available and offers opportunities for forgiveness and reconciliation.

A functional, microsystemic analysis helps clients see how symptoms affect significant others who respond in ways that reinforce symptoms and create vicious circles. Clients are helped to find non-symptomatic ways to express their distress, whether the symptom maintains a family's status quo or provokes negative responses that create more distress. Ecosystemic interventions are not an alternative therapy, but should be an integral part of every therapeutic encounter. They are the definition of culturally competent therapy.

Chapter Thirteen: Main Points

- Ecosystemic theory suggests that historical, macrosystemic processes such as cultural, political, and economic conditions create social privilege and oppression. These are supported by institutions at intermediate levels that affect microsystemic, interpersonal relationships, the contexts in which symptoms develop.
- Privileged people seldom see their advantages, which pervade their experience. Privilege defines what is "normal" and people who lack those qualities are likely to be blamed for their problems rather than the oppressive conditions that pervade the experience of women and minorities.
- Privileged people are likely to have a *referential self* that emphasizes self-definition, individualism, and autonomy. Traditional values are often lost resulting in concerns about existential questions. Minority groups are more likely to have an *indexical self* defined in terms of mutual family and community roles and relationships. This creates a strong support system, but one that is cautious about admitting outsiders.
- Although feminist and multicultural theorists share a common world view and advocate for social change, they lack a unifying theory of therapeutic intervention and are divided by different emphases on the problems of middle-class white women *vs.* the problems of racial and ethnic minorities.
- Consequences of oppression such as economic inequality or overt prejudice are obvious, but more subtle *microaggressions* involving gender or ethnic stereotypes can have a cumulative, debilitating effect as well.
- Normative *etic* research first drew attention to cross-cultural problems, but ignores the subjective experience of individuals. Ecosystemic therapists adopt a hermeneutic *emic* stance that gives priority to the individual's interpretation of their experience. They ask clients to collaborate in exploring the socioeconomic and historic roots of problems.

- The African-American experience is defined by the historical oppression of slavery that destroyed cultural traditions and an ongoing prejudice that impacts opportunities for jobs and education, contributing to problems of poverty, substance abuse, and Black-on-Black crime. Imprisonment is a rite of passage shared by many Black youth. African-American strengths include the role of the church and a flexible, extended family support system.
- The Native-American experience is defined by genocidal wars and cultural suppression that destroyed many tribal traditions. Loss of cultural and tribal supports, together with ongoing discrimination, has led to problems of poverty and substance abuse. Some groups maintain tribal and extended family supports, but many have not and are especially vulnerable.
- The Latino experience is defined for many by migration to escape poverty only to find more poverty as well as discrimination. Immigration policies create an ongoing climate of fear of deportation as well as extended family separations. Strengths include intact cultural and religious traditions and a flexible definition of the extended family.
- The Asian-American experience is also defined in part by immigration, but some migrated for economic reasons and others as war refugees. They are a more diverse group than most other minorities, with many different languages and religious beliefs. Discrimination is less virulent than in the nineteenth and early twentieth centuries, but is still a universal experience. Therapy needs to consider the client's degree of acculturation, which varies from traditional to fully Americanized, especially in the second or third generations.
- The Lesbian, Gay, Bisexual, and Transgendered experience is typically one of shame over feeling different beginning in childhood, and of isolation from peers, family, and society. Coming out to self, family, peers, *etc.* requires strength and courage since it can lead to rejection and persecution. There are no cultural traditions to guide the process and most churches are apt to discriminate as well. Suicide rates are extremely high.
- Ecosystemic interventions help clients externalize problems as resulting from oppression rather than personal inadequacies. Family networking is useful if clients lack a supportive network of family or friends. Multisystemic therapy works with caregivers, schools, and other agencies to provide a strengths-oriented, nonjudgmental, and coordinated set of interventions that address how different systemic levels impact a client's problems.
- Although the Community Mental Health Act of 1964 proposed a coordinated program of services, it has never been fully funded or implemented. The result has been to move patients from mental hospitals to the streets or to prisons. Proven interventions are not used because of political and economic issues.
- A key ethical issue in psychotherapy is the power imbalance between therapist and client. Ethical codes provide guidance to avoid abuses, but do not address all the ways therapy can adversely affect or limit client choices; *e.g.*, diagnostic labeling may stigmatize clients, while failure to consider the meaning or function of symptoms as indirect communication can cause unintended, negative effects.

Further Reading

McGoldrick, M., & Hardy, K. V. (2008). *Re-visioning family therapy: Race, culture, and gender in clinical practice* (2nd ed.). New York: Guilford Press.

McGoldrick, M., Giordano, J., & Garcia-Preto, N. (2005). *Ethnicity & family therapy* (3rd ed.). New York: Guilford.

Videos

Brown, L. S. (2009). *Feminist therapy over time*. Part of the Psychotherapy in Six Sessions APA Psychotherapy Video Series. Washington: American Psychological Association.

Carlson, J., & Simms, W. F. (2005). *Working with Native Americans*. Governors State University, Communication Services. Washington: American Psychological Association.

Carlson, J., Parham, T. A., Snow, K., & VandenBos, G. R. (2005). *Working with African American clients*. Governors State University, Communications Services. Washington: American Psychological Association.

Comas-Diaz, L. (1994). *Ethnocultural psychotherapy*. Part of the Systems of Psychotherapy APA Psychotherapy Video Series. Washington: American Psychological Association.

Jean Lau Chin, J. L., & Jon Carlson, J. (2005). *Working with Asian American clients*. Governors State University. Washington: American Psychological Association.

Websites

American Association of Marriage and Family Therapists Code of Ethics: http://www.aamft.org/resources/lrm_plan/Ethics/ethicscode2001.asp

American Counseling Association Code of Ethics: http://www.counseling.org/Resources/CodeOfEthics/TP/Home/CT2.aspx

American Psychological Association Code of Ethics: http://www.apa.org/ethics/code2002.html

The Multicultural Family Institute: http://www.multiculturalfamily.org/

Chapter 14
Postmodernism and Integrative Therapies

Reality isn't what it used to be.

Anderson, 1990

*[A]ll human beings engage in storytelling about themselves,
creating the story they want to believe about themselves, the
story they actually believe about themselves, the story they want
others to believe about them, the stories they believe about
others, and the stories that they are afraid might be true about
themselves and others.*

Maps in a Mirror, Orson Scott Card, 1990

What is reality? Can it be known? Do people respond to reality? Or to their ideas about it? As Anderson (1990) suggests, postmodernism radically changes thinking about reality. Modernist assumptions that empiricism will eventually lead to a grand theory that accurately portrays essential qualities of reality accurately is challenged by a postmodern skepticism that suggests there always is more than one useful way to think about reality. This is especially true for human actions and thought whose limits are conditioned by evolving cultural practices and concepts. Orson Scott Card's quote suggests the possible constructions of reality by an individual are even more variable.

Despite epistemological differences between modernist cognitive therapy and postmodern approaches, both focus on client communications either to encourage more realistic thinking or more "solution-rich" narratives. Many of their differences disappear as cognitive therapy develops a more systemic view of reciprocal determination of cognition, affect, and behavior and a broader concern with contextual influences. The main remaining difference is the postmodern emphasis on the co-construction of the meaning of presenting problems and many cognitive therapists have adopted postmodern thinking in this respect as well (*e.g.,* Mahoney, 1996; Safran & Muran, 2000). Perhaps the most significant common factor among therapeutic approaches is their reliance on language and the therapeutic relationship to give clients a corrective experience by changing the meaning of their problems. Postmodern approaches differ from many others by making the role of language in creating narratives their point of departure.

D. K. Fromme, *Systems of Psychotherapy,*
DOI 10.1007/978-1-4419-7308-5_14, © Springer Science+Business Media, LLC 2011

In this respect postmodernism is closely related to the phenomenologist's entry into the client's world using language to clarify a problematic experience. The principal difference is the postmodern suggestion that therapist and client co-create the meaning of that experience. There are two main branches of postmodernist therapies. *Constructivism*, based on Kelly's (1955) personal construct approach, emphasizes individuals as the authors of the constructs, narratives, and meanings of their own lives. It has influenced contemporary psychoanalytic thinking (Mitchell, 1988; Spence, 1982), cognitive therapy (Guidano, 1995; Mahoney, 1996), systemic therapies (Anderson & Goolishian, 1992), and is the basis of solution-focused therapy (DeShazer, 1994) and narrative therapies (Chap. 12; Eron & Lund, 1996; White & Epston, 1990).

The other branch, *social constructionism* (Gergen, 1985; Harré & Gillet, 1994) examines how language, culture, and others' expectations influence a person's construction of meanings; *e.g.*, feminist and multicultural therapies examine how socio- political contexts construct oppressive gender and cultural roles (Chap. 13; Worell & Remer, 2003). They *empower* individuals to *deconstruct* unexamined assumptions about gender and race rather than accept the dominant discourse that problems reflect personal defects. This chapter reviews constructivist influences on therapies that emphasize narratives about relationships and on social constructionist influences on two integrative therapies.

Constructivism in Therapy

Constructivism resembles phenomenological approaches in its skepticism about normative diagnostic classifications that obscure the individual's unique qualities. Instead, it uses idiographic assessment to help clients articulate problematic experiences in useful ways and construct new meanings and courses of action. Assessment and therapy occur together as new meanings and narratives are co-constructed; *e.g.*, Jim may resent Linda's complaints about his failure to advance in his career. A constructivist therapist might help Jim construct a new narrative that includes Linda's subjective experience by asking him to think about what could cause her to be so anxious she would pressure him. The therapist might intensify Jim's experience by asking him to role play Linda, while the therapist role plays Jim to help him develop a broader understanding of Linda's anxieties and concerns for his well-being, changing how Jim interprets her actions and opening up new possibilities for their relationship.

Intersubjective Approaches

Intersubjective psychodynamic therapy is based on a postmodern focus on the continuous co-construction of subjective reality rather than interpersonal therapy's objective focus on how a client's actions impact the therapeutic relationship. Benjamin (1988) suggests children pass a critical developmental milestone once they realize mother has her own separate goals, intentions, and experiences. They develop an *intersubjective* world of awareness and empathy for the other's experience as well as an *intrapsychic* world of object relations. Instead of transference in which two people project their feelings on one another, intersubjective theory proposes continuous, bi-directional *mutual influences* between them. Aron (2001) suggests such influences may not be equal in parent-child or therapist-client relationships, but co-creation is so complete it is not possible to distinguish who contributed what to the meaning of an interaction.

The pre-Oedipal child's relationships with mother or father are dyadic (Aron, 2001). They become *triadic* in the Oedipal stage as concrete operations enable children to consider two different perspectives at the same time (Piaget, 1952/1963). This lets children recognize that mother and father have a relationship from which they are excluded. As children identify (mostly) with the same-sexed parent, they not only incorporate that parent's qualities but also the parent's *reflected appraisal* of them into their self-concept.

The self-concept reflects a dialectic tension between the reflected, intersubjective self as an object and an active, intrapsychic self as subject that constantly changes with changing contexts (Aron, 2001). Constantly changing, multiple selves conflict with the individual's need for a sense of self-constancy, which leads to the individual's construction of self as a continuous, consistent, and integrated *identity*. Intersubjective therapists engage clients in mutual exploration of each other's construction of subjective identity. They are interested in how clients construe the therapist and also share how they construe the client.

Constructivist Interventions

Laddering, based on Kelly's (1955) *personal construct* assessment and intervention methods, is similar to cognitive therapy's downward arrow technique and is used to explore intrapsychic meanings (Hinkle, 1965). Cognitive therapy's arrow points "down" to look for core schemas underlying a client's surface statements, while laddering moves clients "up" to look for *superordinate* constructs that frame client statements. Despite pointing in different directions, these metaphors are quite similar. The difference is that laddering questions recursively identify *bipolar* constructs, explore the client's reasons for preferring one pole over the other, and then explore superordinate constructs containing each pole; *e.g.*, recursive questions developed Bryce's ladder in Fig. 14.1. Bryce attributes his anxiety to "being a wimp." When asked what the opposite was, he replied "Someone who stands up for himself."

Therapist: So, rather than being a wimp, you'd choose to be …?
Bryce: I want to stand up for myself and not let others push me around.
Therapist: What would be the advantage for you if you stood up for yourself?

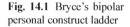
Fig. 14.1 Bryce's bipolar
personal construct ladder

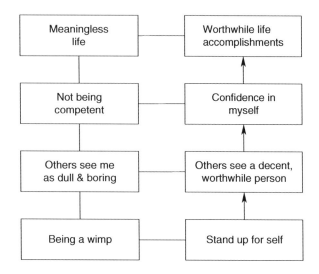

Meaningless life	Worthwhile life accomplishments
Not being competent	Confidence in myself
Others see me as dull & boring	Others see a decent, worthwhile person
Being a wimp	Stand up for self

Bryce: People could see that I'm a decent, worthwhile person.
Therapist: And the opposite of that is what?
Bryce: People think I'm dull and boring and don't want to be around me.
Therapist: How would being seen as decent and worthwhile by others help you?
Bryce: Maybe then I'd have more confidence in myself.
Therapist: And that contrasts with …?
Bryce: Not being competent.
Therapist: So, what would more competency do for you?
Bryce: I'd be able to accomplish something worthwhile with my life.
Therapist: If you accomplished nothing in your life, what would that mean?
Bryce: My life would be meaningless.

The superordinate properties of Bryce's presenting problem were revealed as he moved up the ladder. His initial complaint of not standing up for himself missed deeper existential concerns over the meaning of his life. Neimeyer and Bridges (2003) suggest ladders provide a framework that lets clients examine how core values are expressed, who exemplifies those values in their life, who supports their preferences, and how they make those preferences known. Clients are helped to explore difficulties in assigning values to different steps in the ladder and to consider if there might be positive connotations to some of the ladder's negative steps.

The *bow-tie* approach uses family therapy's *circular questioning* method to explore a couple's mutual intersubjective experiences (Procter, 1987). Penn (1982) describes circular questioning as a *double description* of perceptions by both parties in an interaction that provides a comprehensive view of the relationship. The "bow-tie" refers to the pattern resulting from diagrams of the mutual interactions among perceptions of both members of a dyad (see Fig. 14.2). Questioning begins with either party's self or other perceptions and continues until they agree the bow-tie accurately describes the relationship. In the following, Gene expressed his resentment over Linda's repeated complaint that he is not paying enough attention to their son, Andy.

Gene: She seems to think I have nothing better to do than play with Andy when I get home from work. She doesn't care that I've got to prepare for my sales contacts the next day. I could lose my job and all she can do is yell at me.

Therapist: Linda, would you care to clarify your concerns about Andy?

Linda: Yes! He doesn't realize we may lose our child. Andy is hanging out with a crowd that does drugs and Gene doesn't say a thing to him. He hides in his office or at work and we hardly ever see him.

Therapist: Gene, would you agree that you're spending more time away from home?

Gene: Well yes! It's the only place I can find peace and quiet to get my work done. What's at home except more arguments?

Therapist: Linda, would you agree you're pressuring Gene to spend more time with Andy?

Linda: It may be Andy's only chance. If we can't reach him now, we'll lose him altogether.

As Fig. 14.2 illustrates, Gene and Linda's actions reinforce each other's perceptions, but neither actually hears the other's concerns. Thus a vicious circle is created that will continue until they can appreciate the bow-tie's message and begin mutual exploration of each other's constructions of their relationship.

Cognitive-Experiential-Interpersonal Negotiation of Alliance Ruptures

Both interpersonal and intersubjective approaches emphasize the mutuality of relationships and the need for a therapeutic working alliance. Working alliance problems include disagreements about the *tasks* or *goals* of therapy or problems in the relational *bond* (Bordin, 1994). Therapists can address such problems directly or indirectly. Direct methods include *metacommunication* about procedural rationales to clarify misunderstandings about tasks or goals or to explore core relational themes

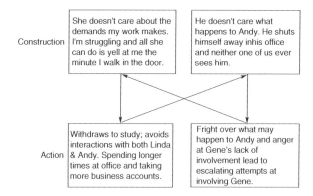

Fig. 14.2 Bow-tie illustration of intersubjectivity in Gene and Linda's conflict

in the case of alliance ruptures. Indirect approaches include *reframing* task or goal meanings by *allying with resistance* as in Motivational Interviewing, while corrective emotional experiences can repair a bond or *alliance rupture*; *e.g.*, by responding to a client's hostile or helpless behavior in unexpected ways (Beier & Young, 1998).

Jeremy Safran and Christopher Muran (Safran, 1998; Safran & Muran, 2000) analyze alliance issues from an integrative cognitive-experiential-interpersonal approach that focuses on intersubjectivity. They note that contexts determine whether an intervention is "good" or "bad." An expert therapeutic stance may antagonize resistant clients, but provide the structure that emotionally unstable clients need. Motivational Interviewing may help an ambivalent substance-abusing client, but seem frustrating and withholding to a dependent client. Working alliances are not created by technique, but facilitated by an empathic *participant-observer* (Sullivan, 1953b) who attends carefully to contexts and client reactions.

Mindfulness and the Working Alliance

Safran and Muran (2000) suggest that therapists strive for *mindfulness* or *beginner's mind* to maintain a participant-observer role with full awareness of intersubjective processes. This is similar to Freud's *evenly hovering attention* method and helps avoid an expert role that objectifies clients. Therapists set aside expectations, beliefs, or diagnoses to avoid confirmation biases. Therapists have the information they need to be aware of alliance ruptures and empathize as long as they suspend judgment and remain mindful of the here-and-now intersubjective process.

Mindfulness has three components: *direction of attention, remembering*, and *nonjudgmental awareness*. Attention involves letting go of preconceived ideas or concerns, creating an *internal space*, and then being curious about felt bodily experiences (Gendlin, 1996). Remembering requires therapists to recognize their attention will periodically be caught by a particular thought or feeling, remember their task, let go of the object of attention, and then return to an evenly hovering stance. Nonjudgmental awareness is essential for mindfulness, but just as something may catch their attention, therapists may become critical of themselves or of the client. Again, the process is to be aware of the judgmental position, let it go, and return to mindful acceptance. Mindfulness cannot be *intended*, so guilt over lapsed attention or critical feelings is its antithesis. Mindfulness only happens by considering such moments as another curious aspect of momentary experience and returning to an evenly hovering stance.

Transference and countertransference can be seen as judgmental concepts that objectify and prevent full awareness and acceptance of self and other. Instead of interpreting transference reactions, intersubjective therapists metacommunicate with clients about their mutual experiences and invite collaborative exploration. If an experience reflects a problematic interpersonal schema, *and* the client is ready to examine this self-state, then insight may be added to awareness. It is likely that the experience of mindful acceptance and discussion of their mutual experiencing of the relationship in nonjudgmental terms will provide an unexpected corrective emotional experience. Acceptance is dialectically related to change. Clients who hold judgments critical of self or others may create a vicious circle as they try to "solve the problem." Clients are enabled to change by the therapist's acceptance, which enables them to let go of judgments and be self-accepting.

Ruptures of the Therapeutic Alliance

Historically, ruptures of the therapeutic alliance were conceptualized as resistance in which clients oppose or subvert therapy. This is a "one-person" psychology that views clients as objects that require adjustment (Safran & Muran, 2000). Intersubjective therapists see ruptures as *therapeutic impasses* that emerge from conflicting self-states or interpersonal schemas evoked by client and therapist interactions. Working through impasses is the principal activity of therapy rather than an obstacle to be overcome. It allows therapist and client to perceive each other's subjectivity and recognize the other's needs. As long as the other is seen as an object, needs for relatedness are not being addressed. Working through impasses is not only the stuff of therapy, it is the stuff of everyday life.

Attachment research into affective attunement between mother and infant suggests that working through ruptures in relationships is an inevitable part of development and life. Tronick (1989) found that mothers oscillated between periods of attunement and misattunement to the infant's needs and feelings in both healthy and dysfunctional mother-infant dyads. Infants respond with a secondary emotion of anger when mother misreads their emotional states. Mothers in healthy dyads attune correctly to the secondary emotion and repair the relationship, but mothers in dysfunctional dyads fail to respond effectively to the secondary emotion and the infant does not have the experience that relational problems can be repaired. Without *good-enough* mothering, they do not learn that needs will be met eventually and form maladaptive interpersonal schemas (Teyber, 2006; Winnicott, 1965). Stern (1985) notes that affective attunement teaches infants how to experience and eventually to articulate the full range of emotional experience.

Therapeutic impasses provide the "royal road" to understanding core interpersonal schemas (Safran & Muran, 2000; Stolorow, Brandchaft, & Atwood, 1994). Schemas that underlie presenting problems also contribute to impasses. As client and therapist become aware of how they each contribute to the impasse, they both have the opportunity to learn and grow. Commonly occurring impasses suggest the nature of underlying schemas; *e.g.*, impasses that result from a therapist's frustration with a client's pervasive despair, bitterness, and cynicism or with another's pervasive neediness. By responding compassionately, therapists help clients articulate warded off feelings of hopelessness over unmet needs and learn they are not alone in their despair.

Metacommunication

Safran and Muran (2000) suggest the responsibility of therapists is to *survive* client enactments of expressed hostility, neediness, or hopelessness, and to *con-*

tain their own emotional response, which could reinforce the problem. This is done with mindful observing and not acting upon feelings elicited by the interaction. Once therapists gain enough distance to discuss their own feelings to avoid enacting them, they metacommunicate and collaboratively explore shared experiences with the client. The following summarizes Safran and Muran's (2000) general and specific principles of metacommunication.

General Participation and Orientation Principles:
1. *Frame observations tentatively:* Invite an exploratory dialogue—how interventions are phrased is at least as important as what is said.
2. *Convey message that impasses are shared experiences:* Both therapist and client are stuck; invite the client to join in exploring the shared dilemma.
3. *Do not assume impasses parallel other relationships:* Rather, explore whether an impasse reflects the therapist's issues, the client's, or their interaction. Remain open, avoid blaming, and let clients take responsibility for examining their role in the impasse. With no need to be defensive, they may be able to discover patterns on their own when they are ready.
4. *Emphasize own subjectivity:* Phrase comments with qualifiers such as "As I see it …," "It seems to me …," or "It felt to me as if …;" avoid an objectifying, expert role and help establish an egalitarian sharing of subjectivities that invites clients' corrective or explorative feedback.
5. *Encourage awareness, not change:* To advise change implies a criticism of what came before; encourage curiosity and an attitude of mindfulness to bring impasses into awareness.
6. *Base hypotheses on awareness of own feelings:* Observations not linked to the therapist's feelings may reflect preconceived ideas and risk further enactment of the impasse.
7. *Ground observations in here-and-now experience:* Feelings associated with emergent self-states emerge spontaneously, while observations based on prior experience may no longer be valid and are likely to be perceived as judgmental generalizations.
8. *Acknowledge how one's own actions contributed to an impasse:* This frees clients to articulate feelings that felt too risky to express; it models accepting responsibility, validates clients' perceptions, reinforces trust in their own judgment, and reduces the need to be defensive in examining their contributions.

General Attention and Focus Principles:
1. *Focus on the here-and-now:* It is easier to focus on the past because anxiety is experienced in the present; but this precludes corrective emotional experiences of learning that anxiety can be tolerated, conflicts resolved, and relationships repaired.
2. *Focus on the concrete and specific:* Primary emotions are always linked to specific events, while abstractions and generalizations reflect intellectualization; explore clients' abstract generalizations to see if they are disguised comments on the present—*e.g.*, "I avoid angry feelings" may be code for "I'm angry at you right now!"—therapists might respond to the overt statement with "Could you be avoiding some angry feelings just now?"

3. *Continuously monitor how close or distant one feels to the client:* Assess impending or existing ruptures and the client's depth of exploration; if clients feel safe, they can explore inner experiences nondefensively and the therapist feels close to the client; a sense of distance suggests misattunement to the client's experience.

4. *Evaluate how responsive clients are to an intervention:* Therapist misattunement is evidenced if clients agree too readily or make self-justifying, defensive, or minimal responses; active exploration reflects attunement and a collaborative working alliance.

5. *Explore how clients experience the intervention:* Especially if it does not sustain or deepen exploration; *e.g.,* "How did my comment just now feel to you? I have a feeling I wasn't helpful."

General Expectation Principles:

1. *Recognize that ruptures can occur in fractions of a second:* What emerges in the moment is always the point of departure for metacommunication; being stuck or other problems are not problems if they are recognized and therapists begin collaborative exploration with their client; self-disclose how the therapist experiences the strain.

2. *Resolution attempts may cause another rupture:* Even skillful metacommunication may be perceived as an implicit criticism when the flow of interaction is interrupted by a comment; *e.g.,* "I feel a distance between us just now" implies the client could be withdrawing; if that leads to further withdrawal, the new experience should be followed up, "I felt like my comment about distance created still more distance between us. Does that match with your feeling?"

3. *Similar impasses may happen repeatedly:* If an impasse reflects a problematic interpersonal schema, it will inevitably reappear in many therapeutic contexts; however, each new context contains new elements and possibilities that must be accessed in that moment and so recurrences are not a simple recapitulation.

4. *Expect to become discouraged during prolonged impasses:* Having no expectation of what may result from therapy is paradoxically freeing and allows a focus on what *is*, rather than what *might be*.

Specific Awareness Principles:

1. *Be aware of feelings, images, and fantasies:* Awareness of the responses that clients evoke is the basis of empathic understanding and metacommunication; if unsure where to begin, therapists might articulate their experience privately before acting upon it; however, mutual exploration of experiences during an impasse can be both diagnostic and therapeutic.

2. *Be aware of action tendencies:* It may be easier to recognize desired actions rather than associated feelings and this can also be a starting point for mutual exploration.

3. *Belated awareness of one's own actions:* If therapists become aware of a problematic situation after already acting, they disclose this awareness, apologize, and explore any possible rupture.

4. *Identify interpersonal markers:* Problematic reactions to clients are a marker to disengage and help clients explore their feelings and identify and explore problematic interpersonal patterns.

Specific Communication Principles:
1. *Disclose impact or acknowledge own role:* Self-disclosure of the relationship's experiential impact is the first step in addressing an impasse; acknowledging the therapist's contribution to the impasse prevents clients from feeling blamed, but it may be the therapist's revelation has nothing to do with the problem; collaboration can articulate the relational context and associated feelings, "I've been feeling inhibited the past few minutes and I don't know if it's anything to do with us. Would you be willing to help explore if it's related to our interaction?"
2. *Link feelings to interpersonal markers:* Explore relational contexts of possible links between the therapist's problematic experience and specific client behaviors, "I feel reluctant to make any comments here, because it seems to me you're very quick to dismiss anything I might suggest. Do you have any awareness of anything like this?" If the client is unaware of doing anything, it is important to back off, but leave open a possible return to the question if it occurs again; deeper exploration is possible if clients acknowledge the therapist's experience.
3. *Identify interpersonal marker and explore associated experiences:* Therapists identify actions or tone of voice without self-disclosing personal reactions, but inquire if the client is aware of the behavior or any feelings related to such behavior, "Your voice is getting so soft and hesitant. Can you share what's happening inside just now?"
4. *Disclose subjective experience or perception of the client:* Interventions that do not link the therapist's experience to client behavior or suggest the therapist's role need to be framed tentatively and works best if earlier ruptures have been worked through, "It feels like you're angry, but don't want to hurt my feelings. Does this match anything in your experience?" The purpose is to help clients reclaim dissociated self-state aspects.
5. *Explore possibly shared experiences:* Perceived parallels in the therapist's and client's actions are explored, "It seems like we're both being real careful of each other's feelings just now. How does it seem to you?" If clients disagree, ask for their perception.
6. *Track the client's reactions:* Explore the client's experience of interventions to see if they are perceived as blaming or critical, "I wonder how my comment felt to you just now?" Clients may not be comfortable expressing hurt or angry feelings and the therapist may need to speculate, "I wondered if you might have felt hurt by my comment?"
7. *Invite exploration of the therapist's impact:* Gain insight into therapist's own actions and clarify how the client construes the therapist, "Could you talk some about what you see me doing that might be keeping us stuck?" "What do you think is going on for me right now?"

Stage-Process Model of Alliance Rupture Resolution

Safran and Muran (2000) describe two types of ruptures: *withdrawal* and *confrontation or complaints*. Withdrawal markers that identify a need to begin resolving alliance ruptures include:

- *Denial*: client denies a feeling state such as anger that is manifestly present.
- *Minimal response*: client gives short, clipped answers to open-ended exploratory questions.
- *Shifting the topic*: client shifts focus from exploring an issue to something remote or unrelated.
- *Intellectualization*: discussing painful topic in detached, intellectualized manner.
- *Storytelling*: client explains an experience with overly elaborate or unrelated stories.
- *Talking about others*: client spends inordinate time talking about other people and their doings.

Confrontation markers include confrontations or complaints about:

- *Therapist as person*: *e.g.*, client attacks therapist's reserved manner as being passive.
- *Therapist as competent*: client finds therapist's comments useless and questions skills.
- *Activities of therapy*: client is irritated about relevance of questions about internal feelings.
- *Being in therapy*: client expresses doubts about continuing therapy.
- *Parameters of therapy*: client complains about inconvenience of therapy time, room, *etc.*
- *Progress in therapy*: client complains about lack of significant gains in therapy.

Most clients will use either withdrawal or confrontation most of the time, but may use either some of the time. Safran and Muran (2000) describe the stages and interventions needed to resolve withdrawal and confrontation ruptures separately since the client's experience is different in each.

Resolution Stages and Interventions for Withdrawal Ruptures:
1. *Withdrawal marker:* Therapists first must recognize the client's characteristic *response to the self* that evokes an engaged, or *embedded, response of the other* (Luborsky, 1984).
2. *Disembedding and attending to the rupture marker:* The therapist draws attention to the rupture and its relational context with an empathic attitude, curious about the client's experience and open to any negative feelings that emerge. Client autonomy or reluctance to discuss a topic are honored, especially with overcompliant clients, but the reluctance may be discussed so that both therapist and client can disembed to explore the impasse mutually. Disembedding follows two separate *experiencing* and *avoidance* pathways corresponding to Stages 3 and 4. The experiencing path explores the relational context of the rupture, while the avoidance path explores defensive processes that disrupt exploration of internal experiences. Resolution may involve a dialectic between experiencing and avoidance, so exploration can move back and forth between the various stages before underlying wishes are fully embraced in Stage 5.
3. *Qualified assertion:* Clients tentatively express underlying feelings or wishes such as anger or wishes for more autonomy or agency, but withdraw anxiously

(Stage 1) as relational intimacy needs are threatened; therapists facilitate exploration of a client's experience by:

(a) *Differentiating and exploring different self-states*: therapists acknowledge and empathize with both the wish and the resulting anxiety states that emerge.
(b) *Providing the client with feedback*: helping clients recognize how their anxiety defenses cause them to withdraw from the underlying wish.
(c) *Awareness experiments*: encouraging clients to role play saying the words associated with the wish, "Try saying, 'I want *more* from you' and see how it *feels*."

4. *Avoidance:* Often exploration of the experiencing pathway is blocked by defensive anxiety and clients continue to avoid feelings associated with either the *expected response of the other* or a self-critical or self-doubting *response to the self*. Empathy and exploration help resolve anxiety over possible abandonment or retaliation by the therapist; anxieties are validated as real since reassurance only distances clients from their experience. Self-doubt or self-criticism reflects the emergence of contradictory self-states, wish *vs.* denial of wish; clients are helped to explore both of these self-states. Alternating between experiencing and avoidance pathways deepens clients' exploration and enables resolution of their feelings about the alliance rupture.
5. *Self-assertion:* As the rupture is healed, clients become comfortable with underlying wishes; they accept responsibility for both wish and act and find ways to meet their own needs.

Resolution Model for Confrontation Ruptures: Confrontation ruptures can cause counter-hostility, impotence, or self-criticism in the therapist. To remain mindful and resolve confrontation ruptures, therapists must tolerate and contain client hostility. It helps to realize confrontation ruptures are aggressive self-protective responses; *i.e.*, clients may have learned that expressing needs for intimacy results in rejection or abandonment. They protect themselves by coercing or demanding others meet their needs, which then creates a vicious circle as others confirm the original fear of rejection. The goal for confrontation ruptures is to help clients tolerate their vulnerability. Again, the resolution stages begin with a marker.

1. *Confrontation marker*: Ruptures reflect a habitual *response of self* of angry demands and confrontation or complaints if needs are not met.
2. *Disembedding*: Therapists *reestablish internal space* and return to mindfulness after a hostile confrontation by noting their reactions to the alliance rupture. Giving feedback about the clients' impact empowers their sense of self and encourages exploration of the impasse. Therapists model how expressing painful or angry feelings can be discussed even though they are toxic. As clients express hostility directly, they take some responsibility for their actions; but indirect hostility may be mixed with withdrawal markers. To disembed from indirect hostility, therapists must help clients clarify and articulate explicitly the implicit demands and incongruities of their mixed confrontation and withdrawal, "It feels like you're protecting me from being overwhelmed by your anger."

3. *Explore construals*: Therapists validate the client's angry, hurt, or disappointed feelings and then explore more vulnerable feelings. As therapists acknowledge their contribution to an impasse and encourage clients to articulate how they construed the therapists' actions, clients become able to examine their own contributions without feeling blamed. This *unpacking* may resolve a therapeutic impasse, but in some cases it is necessary to move to the next stage.

4. *Avoidance of aggression*: In each stage, clients can experience anxiety or guilt secondary to their angry feelings. Mindful therapists explore the anxiety and guilt as well as angry feelings to avoid reinforcing clients' fears that others cannot tolerate their anger or self-assertion.

5. *Avoidance of vulnerability*: Clients may shift from avoiding angry feelings to avoiding the vulnerability they need to explore their inner experience. Therapists track and explore such shifts until clients can tolerate progressively longer periods of being vulnerable.

6. *Vulnerability*: Eventually, the warded-off primary emotions and unfulfilled wishes that underlie confrontational patterns emerge and clients are able to confront their fear of being rejected and isolated. The therapist's willingness to be present during their most difficult experiences helps clients feel nurtured, less isolated, and more compassionate toward themselves.

Case Illustration[1]

Joan is a 49-year-old, unemployed, socially isolated woman who alternates between a self-state of hostile, demanding skepticism and a somewhat vulnerable position; *e.g.*, after she framed her dilemma as backing off *vs.* hitting people on the head and indicated she had just backed off, the therapist asked, "What's that like for you?" She replied, "Well … I guess I start to feel compromised. It's like I have to allow myself to be brain-washed in order to be helped" (p. 166). In an early exchange, the therapist uses metacommunication to disembed from hostile confrontation.

J: I'm not interested in an abstract answer. I want a direct, concrete answer.

T: I'd like to answer your question, but my experience is that I feel so pressured that it's difficult for me to think clearly.

J: [T]hen say something that shows me how we're going to work so I can see what's going on.

T: See … even as you say that … I feel the same sort of pressure to perform.

J: Well, then say something meaningful.

T: I'd like to, but it feels to me like I'm trying and nothing I say satisfies you, so I feel at a loss.

J: Well, I don't want to give up.

---

[1] Adapted from *Negotiating the therapeutic alliance: A relational treatment guide,* pp. 165–166; 176–174. By J. D. Safran, & J. C. Muran. © 2000 by Guilford. Used with permission.

Here, the therapist's metacommunication about Joan's impact eventually led to a slight softening of her stance. After several months of work repeatedly visiting Joan's hopelessness over finding an alternative to her self-states of confrontation *vs.* compromise, the following exchange helped her work through the stages of alliance rupture and become more vulnerable.

J: We've been through this before and it's not getting us anywhere. [*Confrontation marker*]

T: Uh-huh, so it's feeling futile. [*Exploration of construal*]

J: Yeah. I can't afford to go on like this, doing nothing.

T: I hear a real sense of desperation in what you're saying.

J: Yeah, I guess so. I've been off work for a year and a half, and people are starting to wonder what the hell is wrong with me. And we've had some important sessions, but I still don't feel things changing.

T: Are you willing to tell me more about your feeling of desperation?

J: I don't know. I try not to think about it. [*Avoidance of vulnerability*]

T: What might happen? If you were to explore it more deeply with me right now?

J: I think I'd start to feel even more hopeless, and then I'd be weak and pathetic.

T: Uh-huh. So there's something very uncomfortable about going into your feelings of hopelessness with me?

J: Yeah, I'm not sure I trust you to be here for me (*voice begins to crack*). [*Vulnerability*]

T: What are you experiencing?

J: I feel sad.

T: Can you say anymore about your sadness?

J: I feel hurt and alone, and I don't know where to turn (*begins to sob*).

The authors note that prior sessions paved the way for this breakthrough, that little time was needed to disembed from a rather mild confrontation and shift to exploring her feelings of hopelessness. Despite one attempt to avoid vulnerability by questioning her trust in the therapist, she finally felt sufficiently safe to let down defenses and be open to her subjective experience. Safran and Muran (2000) provide useful principles and guidelines for exploring the therapist's and client's intersubjective experience that in many respects resemble Rogers' (1951) client-centered approach. The focus is less on therapist characteristics, however, and more on the process of staying centered in a mindful, nonjudgmental state; but the intersubjective approach has the same transtheoretical promise that Roger's approach has achieved. These principles are often made explicit in the following postmodern approaches that integrate both subjective and objective methods and have evidence for their efficacy with some of the most challenging clients.

Integrative Postmodernism: Functional Contextualism

Behaviorism may be considered the first wave of empirically based therapies, followed by the second wave of cognitive therapy. However, support for the components of cognitive therapy has not been strong. Dobson and Khatri found "… no additive benefit to providing cognitive interventions in cognitive therapy" (2000, p. 913). Third-wave, empirically based, postmodern *functional contextualism* also questions cognitive therapy's linear, mechanistic explanation that maladaptive cognitions cause maladaptive behavior. Instead of analyzing causal relationships, third-wave therapies examine the *functions* of behavior in a socioverbal (social constructionist) *context* (Hayes & Strosahl, 2004). They suggest that, despite its many advantages, language distances people from their immediate experience. People respond to the contexts of stories they tell about themselves and the world rather than the actual events or objects; they do what is expected by a culturally embedded narrative rather than responding directly to the environment.

Initial outcome studies on third-wave therapies report larger effect sizes than found in first- and second-wave cognitive-behavioral therapies (Bach & Hayes, 2002; Hayes, Masuda, Bissett, Luoma, & Guerrero, 2004; Linehan, Dimeff, Comtois, Welch, & Heagerty, 2002). Third-wave therapies include Action and Commitment Therapy (ACT; Hayes & Strosahl, 2005), Linehan's Dialectical Behavior Therapy (DBT; Linehan, 1993a, b), Functional Analytic Psychotherapy (Kohlenberg & Tsai, 1991), and Mindfulness-Based Cognitive Therapy (Segal, Williams, & Teasdale, 2002). They emphasize empirical verification of their methods in contrast to other postmodern therapies and integrate experiential, cognitive-behavioral, and other techniques into their approaches. DBT and ACT, perhaps the best supported, are discussed next.

Dialectical Behavior Therapy

Marsha Linehan developed DBT to work with chronically suicidal or parasuicidal (self-mutilating) clients, especially those diagnosed with Borderline Personality Disorder (BPD; Koerner & Linehan, 2002; Linehan, 1993a, b; Linehan, Cochran, & Kehrer, 2001). Research suggests that DBT is superior to "treatment as usual" in reducing parasuicidal behavior and substance abuse, while increasing treatment retention and overall functioning (Koerner & Linehan, 2000; Linehan, 2000; Linehan, Heard, & Armstrong, 1993; Linehan, Tutek, Heard, & Armstrong, 1994; Robins & Chapman, 2004). It has been adapted to treat eating disorders (Safer, Telch, & Agras, 2001), mentally ill offenders (McCann, Ball, & Ivanoff, 2000), depressed elderly clients (Lynch, 2000), domestic violence (Fruzzetti & Levensky, 2000), and posttraumatic stress disorder (Melia & Wagner, 2000). DBT procedures integrate cognitive-behavioral therapy with dialectical philosophy and Eastern meditation practices. DBT to help clients move from a chaotic lifestyle to one of sustained capacity for joy and self-awareness (Koerner & Linehan, 2002). Successful rehabilitative treatment may take from 1 to 3 years.

Conceptual Framework

Dialectic thinking appears several ways in DBT. First, there is the dialog of therapist and client as they co-construct the meanings and realities implied in the client's experiences. Second, DBT therapists note inconsistencies in narratives that reflect conflicting beliefs and dialog with the client to co-construct a more adaptive synthesis than the original, incompatible beliefs. Third, DBT tries to synthesize competing points of view among the client's significant others, to integrate caregiver perspectives or help family member achieve a broader perspective. Dialectic therapists expect people to have opposing views on situations that are important to them; it is that opposition that gives meaning to each perspective. It is a non-issue if two people share a perspective, but if one is jealous of the other, they must view their respective situations differently. This phenomenon exemplifies an axiom of dialectics: meaning occurs only in context. Nothing is "good" or "bad" in isolation; experiences are valued as a function of current and historical contexts. Assisting a disabled person has different meanings and values than assisting a dependent person. Finally, DBT incorporates dialectical tension into treatment by giving equal weight to accepting clients as they are and encouraging commitment to change (Hayes, & Strosahl, 2004). A DBT therapist validates and accepts a client's experiences, but then problem-solves to change problematic behaviors. Clients are taught mindfulness and distress tolerance to help them accept the most painful experiences, but are also taught interpersonal and emotional regulation skills.

DBT was developed for clients with a BPD diagnosis. Linehan's (1993a; Crowell, Beauchaine, & Linehan, 2009) biosocial BPD theory suggests that BPD reflects emotional dysregulation caused by biological vulnerability interacting with an invalidating environment. Genetic and prenatal factors, *e.g.*, substance abuse or a virus during pregnancy, can cause a child to be sensitive to emotional cues and have a long-lasting, intense arousal that interferes with cognitive functioning. The child finds it difficult to self-soothe, inhibit inappropriate mood-driven thoughts or actions, orient to salient environmental cues, or direct behavior toward long-term goals. Most caregivers find it challenging to soothe the distress of children with a difficult temperament. If they give up and become unresponsive, this invalidation of the child's needs interacts with emotional vulnerability to create a vicious circle: as the child's needs go unmet, emotional distress and angry cries increase, which leads caregivers either to distance themselves further from the child or to reinforce the child's emotionality intermittently by finding some way to relieve their distress. The consequences are that emotional dysregulation:

1. Spirals out of control and children never learn how to manage their emotions
2. Impacts self-regulation of cognitive functioning, impulsivity, and interpersonal relationships
3. Leads to neglect of problems, dysfunctional attempts to regulate affect, and vicious circles that lead to the behavioral extremes seen in clients with BPD

Gender biases mean that the ideas of girls and women are often invalidated and dismissed as "emotional." If family dynamics dismiss, criticize, or punish normative behavior and exacerbate these cultural biases, then children do not learn to trust their own experience. They have little opportunity to learn how to use feelings to interpret and respond appropriately to their environment. Instead, they learn to self-invalidate and depend on environmental cues to direct their actions. They may try to contain feelings until they can no longer inhibit them and then explode with an intensity that forces others to pay attention. Not only is emotional dysregulation exacerbated, they fail to learn effective interpersonal skills and how to solve problems. Emotional constriction of cognitive functions increases tendencies to think in all-or-none terms, which feeds back into emotional slights and exacerbates the temperamental impulsivity of BPD clients.

Interventions

DBT helps enhance client skills and motivation, generalize their skills to an environment that supports them, and enhance the abilities and motivation of therapists who work with BPD or other challenging clients. Skills training is done in structured, psychoeducational groups that teach mindfulness, emotional regulation, distress tolerance, self-management, conflict resolution, and interpersonal skills. Individual therapy enhances motivation, reinforces progress, and addresses factors that interfere with therapy such as comorbid symptoms, suicidal or parasuicidal behavior, or posttraumatic responses. Phone consultations available around the clock help clients generalize new skills as problems arise in their daily lives. Family sessions help structure environmental supports and weekly consultation groups provide support for therapists.

DBT is organized into four stages of treatment with goals associated with the four levels of borderline symptoms. Stage 1 targets the most serious problems (Koerner & Linehan, 2002):

(a) Credible risk of suicidal, homicidal, parasuicidal, or life-threatening behavior
(b) Behavior that interferes with therapy
(c) Behavior that seriously compromises the client's quality of life; and
(d) Behavioral skill deficits that interfere with making significant life changes

Individual therapy addresses therapy-interfering behavior such as nonattendance, non-collaboration, or actions affecting other clients. Quality-of-life issues focus on behavioral dysregulation issues that can result in a "crisis of the week" such as risky sexual or criminal behavior, relationship, work, housing, or financial problems.

So much time in individual therapy is typically devoted to crisis management that there is little opportunity to help clients learn more adaptive skills. Consequently, individual DBT therapists focus on client consultation and crisis management, while psychoeducation group trainers concentrate on new skills. If crises arise in group, the leader refers clients to their individual therapist for consultation. Weekly case consultation groups allow therapists to exchange support and technical advice with each other, to coordinate intervention strategies for their client, and to review developments.

Psychoeducation groups target skill deficits such as distress tolerance to help clients control life-threatening impulsive behavior; emotional regulation to reduce lability and intensity of angry outbursts; interpersonal effectiveness to address interpersonal fears of abandonment; and mindfulness to decrease identity confusion, emptiness, and cognitive dysregulation. Stage 1 is particularly difficult as it involves exposure to painful emotions. Stage 2 is for clients who have relatively stable daily lives but experience emotional numbing or vulnerability that prevents them from connecting with others without being retraumatized. Stage 3 targets "… self-respect, mastery, self-efficacy, a sense of morality, and an acceptable quality of life" (Koerner & Linehan, 2002, p. 327). Finally, Stage 4 resembles existential therapy as clients struggle to develop new meanings in a life not dominated by crisis. The ultimate goal is to help clients modulate emotional responses so they can self-soothe and be focused in the presence of strong emotion. They learn to inhibit inappropriate, mood-driven behavior, and strive for self-chosen goals (Linehan, 1993b).

DBT interventions communicate genuine caring and validate clients' concerns to implement an acceptance-change dialectic: acceptance is warm and empathic, while change interventions are more directive. *Communication style* interventions involve empathic acceptance, sprinkled with a change-oriented irreverence that encourages clients to take entrenched views less seriously and to consider other perspectives. The individual DBT therapist's *case management* acceptance strategies help clients change their environment, while phone consultations help clients try out new skills in the home environment. The consultation team also helps therapists balance acceptance and change in interventions. *Dialectical* strategies exaggerate extreme positions or inconsistencies between thoughts and actions to help clients consider alternatives.

Koerner and Linehan (2002) described the use of a dialectical strategy with a young woman who burned her arm with cigarettes to escape intense emotional pain. She was helped to reconsider her paradoxical position that burning herself was not "that bad this time" with the comment, "So what you're saying is that if you saw a person in a lot of emotional pain, say your little niece, and she was feeling as devastated as you were that night you burned your arm, you'd burn her arm with a cigarette to help her feel better?" (p. 720). Although she hesitated to give up something that gave her immediate relief, the client was certain it was not appropriate for others. Table 14.1 lists the dialectical strategies used in DBT.

Dialectical philosophy assumes all perspectives are partial and leave something out. DBT encourages clients to replace "either-or" thinking with a nuanced "both-and" position that includes more of their beliefs, values, and life situation. The *lemonade out of lemons* intervention describes how the Chinese ideogram for "crisis" combines the ideograms for "danger" and "opportunity" to illustrate that crises are more than just a problem. New solutions to problems may be found as clients gain a dialectical understanding of the dangers and opportunities in their situation. DBT also uses experiential techniques to help clients confront fears, cognitive techniques to challenge unrealistic beliefs, and behavioral interventions to manage environmental contingencies.

Psychoeducation homework is introduced with Fruzetti and Fruzetti's (2003) swimming metaphor, "The therapist, who is the coach, can teach the swimmer (patient) to swim in a calm pool (the therapist's office). But because the swimmer lives

Table 14.1 Dialectical behavior therapy strategies. (Reprinted from J. E. Fisher, & S. C. Hayes (Eds.). *Cognitive behavior therapy: Applying empirically supported techniques in your practice.* By A. R. Fruzzetti & A. E. Fruzzetti, p. 125. © 2003 by Wiley Press. Used with permission.)

Strategy	Description
Dialectical assessment	Assessment of behavioral patterns seeking answer to question: "What is left out of my understanding of this behavior?"
Balanced treatment strategies	Balancing acceptance and change strategies in session
Balanced treatment targets	Balancing acceptance of some targets and the targeting of others for change
Stylistic strategies	Balance of acceptance-oriented (warmth, genuineness) and change-oriented (directive, offbeat) styles
Dialectical thinking and behavior	Encouraging patient to move from either-or thinking to both-and thinking: Encouraging patient to respond in balanced ways
Metaphors	Using metaphors to help patients see alternative ways of thinking and responding
Observing paradoxes	Highlighting naturally occurring paradoxes in patient's life to facilitate letting go of extreme positions
Lemonade out of lemons	Encouraging patient to see that most problems afford opportunities as well. (Care taken not to minimize problems)

in the ocean, the swimmer needs to practice swimming there as well" (p. 127). In addition to its efficiency, a psychoeducation group format has several advantages compared to individual therapy (Linehan, 1993b). It:

1. Allows observation of problematic peer interactions that might not occur with a therapist;
2. Provides support and validation that cannot be dismissed as therapeutic professionalism;
3. Allows clients to learn from each other's experiences;
4. Attenuates the intensity of the client-group leader relationship and reduces idealization or devaluation that might interfere with learning; and
5. Gives clients a venue to practice new skills and learn how to give and accept support.

Skill modules include mindfulness, interpersonal effectiveness, emotional regulation, and distress tolerance. Clients usually stay in skills training for 1 year and go through each 8-week module two or more times. Weekly homework assignments are reviewed at the beginning of each meeting and problems analyzed if skills fail to work as expected. Since BPD clients often attend sporadically, they are told that regular attendance is expected. Missing four consecutive weeks of either group or individual therapy constitutes de facto termination. The only limit imposed if clients fail to do homework is to discuss how to shape homework assignments to increase their likelihood of being completed. Mindfulness is the first skill taught since it is part of the other modules.

Mindfulness Mindfulness is the first core DBT skill and is reviewed before each of the other skill modules (Linehan, 1993b). Clients learn there are three states of mind: *reasonable mind* that directs actions by reason and logic; *emotion mind* with momentary feelings that determine actions; and *wise mind* that brings together the reasonable mind's logical analysis and the emotion mind's intuitive knowing. Emotion mind brings love, passion, motivation, and meaning to one's life, but may result in short-term benefits at the cost of long-term negative effects. This is likely if clients fail to stop to think (reasonable mind) and act impulsively. Mindfulness helps clients balance reasonable mind with emotion mind to produce wise mind. It involves three "what" skills: *observing, describing,* and *participating*; and three "how" skills: *nonjudgmental stance, focusing on one thing in the moment,* and *being effective* or doing what works.

"The goal of mindfulness is to develop a lifestyle of participating with aware-ness" (Linehan, 1993b, p. 63). In contrast, mood-dependent, impulsive behavior reflects participation without awareness. As problems arise, mindfulness requires observing events as they occur with no attempt to alter them. Clients learn non-judgmental acceptance of things as they are in the moment with no attempt to avoid or prolong an experience. Describing develops self-control as clients learn to test their thoughts against their observed experience; *e.g.,* thinking one is unloved is not the same as actually being unloved. The final skill, participation, is the ability to act spontaneously without self-consciousness, to be effective without judging rightness. With practice, skilled performance allows the person to enter a mindful state of "flow" completely focused on the task at hand (Csikszentmihalyi, 1996). This may be contrasted with mindless experiences in which habitual actions are performed with no awareness later of what was done.

Interpersonal Effectiveness Skills This module provides assertiveness and problem-solving training to help clients cope effectively with interpersonal conflict, request legitimate needs to be met, and say "no" when necessary. Clients learn how to ask for change, while maintaining self-respect and their relationship. Although BPD clients can focus effectively on others' needs, they can have difficulty if their own needs or feelings are involved and their inability to tolerate distress drives others away. Nonjudgmental mindfulness and interpersonal skills need to be integrated to solve such problems. Clients also learn to challenge beliefs that interfere with their interpersonal effectiveness with more constructive beliefs and practice homework assignments in real-life situations. Clients are taught to:

1. Resolve conflicts before problems build up and to end hopeless relationships;
2. Balance priorities and demands and volunteer or ask for help if bored;
3. Balance wants and shoulds with enjoyable activities, to get others to take them seriously, and to say "no" to unwanted requests; and
4. Build mastery and self-respect by standing up for their beliefs and interacting competently rather than dependently with others.

The acronym DEAR MAN describes the DBT skill of assertion, while GIVE FAST describes the skill of maintaining both self-respect and the relationship:

	Describe (the situation)	(be)	Gentle
	Express (feelings or opinion)	(act)	Interested
	Assert (by asking or saying no)		Validate (the other's feelings)
	Reinforce (explain options and consequences)	(use an)	Easy manner
(stay)	Mindful	(be)	Fair
	Appear (confident)	(no)	Apologies
	Negotiate (give to get)		Stick (to values)
		(be)	Truthful

Clients record each day they actually practice homework assignments for these skills.

Emotion Regulation Skills The principal symptoms of BPD, emotional intensity and lability, cause others to invalidate the client's emotional experience, which leads to self-invalidation and denying emotions to regulate their existence. Alternatively, clients may feel that any attempt to self-regulate would be an admission they were wrong for feeling as they do. Nonjudgmental mindfulness can help clients accept the validity of their feelings and still self-regulate. Distress tolerance skills are also necessary as well as learning to:

1. *Identify and label emotions* in order to think about feelings. Clients are taught to observe and describe (a) events that elicited the emotion; (b) how they interpreted those events; (c) their physical, phenomenological experience; (d) how the feelings were expressed behaviorally; and (e) how the emotion affected other abilities such as clear thinking.
2. *Identify the emotion's functions* including motivation, communication with others, and validating how events are interpreted. Although interpretations are not always justified objectively, BPD clients still need to learn to accept and trust their own perceptions. Understanding the function of their feelings functions helps them consider other ways of meeting their needs.
3. *Reduce vulnerability to emotion mind*, especially with physical or environmental stress. Clients learn to regulate health behavior with adequate diets, sleep, exercise, and avoiding mood-altering drugs. Activities that develop a sense of mastery and self-efficacy are encouraged.
4. *Increase positive emotional events* by prescribing pleasurable activities each day and making needed life changes to help manage negative emotions. Clients are also encouraged to be mindful of positive events as they occur.
5. *Take opposite action* to change an overall experience by creating a new one rather than blocking a negative emotion; *e.g.*, it is hard to stay angry with someone while doing something nice for them. Clients also learn to relax, especially their face when tense or overwrought.

Distress Tolerance Skills Distress tolerance is a natural extension of nonjudgmental mindfulness. It helps clients confront painful experiences without avoidance or impulsive actions. They learn that they need to accept reality as it is before they can make meaningful changes in their life. Two dialectically opposed skills are taught: distraction to tolerate and survive immediate crises and mindful acceptance of life as it is in the moment (Linehan, 1993b). Survival skills to weather an immediate crisis until long-term solutions are developed, are organized by mnemonic,"Wise mind ACCEPTS," an acronym for:

	Activities (counter thoughts and feelings maintaining the negative emotion)
	Contributions (gifts refocus attention and enhance self-respect)
(making)	Comparisons (with those less fortunate recasts one's plight more positively)
(generate opposite)	Emotions (by opposite actions)
	Push away (leave the situation)
(distract with other)	Thoughts; or
(intense)	Sensations (*e.g.*, hold an ice pack)

These skills create a "holding environment" to help clients avoid actions they may later regret. Acceptance skills include considering the pros and cons of accepting reality as it is, self-soothing by being kind and nurturing to oneself, and learning to IMPROVE (the moment):

Imagery (that creates a safe, soothing retreat)
Meaning (*e.g.*, creating lemonade out of lemons)
Prayer (contrasting acceptance prayers with "Why me?" prayers)
Relaxing (as the body accepts the situation, so does the mind)
One (thing in the moment, "This too shall pass.")
Vacation (from adulthood—taking time for play)
Encouraging (oneself as one would with others)

As clients learn to tolerate distress, "radical" acceptance becomes possible. They learn that pain is not only ultimately unavoidable, but even necessary. It signals that something is wrong, encourages people to reach out to others who are in pain, and motivates necessary action. As the Buddha taught, suffering is pain plus the struggles that result from nonacceptance. With radical acceptance, suffering is relieved and pain becomes bearable.

Acceptance and Commitment Therapy

Steven Hayes' acceptance and commitment therapy (ACT; Hayes & Strosahl, 2004; Hayes, Strosahl, & Wilson, 1999) is a close relative of DBT. It is based on the pragmatic philosophy of *functional contextualism* (Biglan & Hayes, 1996), which suggests that to understand an event it is necessary to consider its function in a specific cultural, linguistic context; *e.g.*, the message of modern "feel good" culture is that painful experiences are unacceptable. People who experience strong levels of anxiety or depression are considered to have a "disorder." However, functional contextualism suggests that the "truth" value of any belief lies in its ultimate pragmatic utility.

By this criterion, first- and second-wave therapies are useful to the extent they help people live satisfying lives by controlling negative feelings; but attempts to suppress thoughts and feelings often have the paradoxical effect of increasing them. People find it difficult to comply when told *not* to think about "white bears" (Wegner, Schneider, Carter, & White, 1987). If suppressing negative feelings creates still more problems, the solution has become the problem! Another problem with first- and second-wave therapies is their lack of a theory of cognition to guide therapeutic intervention (Hayes, 2004), which led Hayes and his colleagues to develop *relational frame theory* (RFT; Hayes, Barnes-Holmes, & Roche, 2001).

RFT proposes that the core function of language is to describe relational frames among events such as "same as," "larger than," "before-after," "if A, then B." Relational frames are non-arbitrary properties of particular contexts and can be taught to animals. Language, however, permits an arbitrary contextual control of relational frames; *e.g.*, social convention says a dime is "larger than" a nickel, despite their physical sizes. Language creates relational frames such as rules and analogies that enable abstraction and formal logic systems and permit generalization about events from one context to other, novel contexts. Relational contingencies learned in one context are generalized by language to other contexts through relational frames. If the new context is sufficiently similar, such generalization is adaptive and helps solve novel problems. After many successful generalizations, however, the distinction between verbal thoughts and actual events may become blurred. *Cognitive fusion* occurs when thoughts dominate reality and people fail to distinguish between reality and the relational frames created by language; *e.g.*, people swallow their own saliva regularly, but most would balk at drinking it from a glass.

Conceptual Framework

Language's ability to describe temporal relationships enables anticipation, planning, delayed gratification, and problem-solving. It also encourages *cognitive fusion* with past hurts or future worries. Believing life is not worth living interferes with recognizing when positive events occur; such beliefs become self-confirming if they reduce efforts to relate with others and make life less intimate and meaningful. Psychopathology may be defined as the psychological rigidity caused by cognitive fusion and *experiential avoidance* (Hayes, Strosahl, Bunting, Twohig, & Wilson, 2004). Experiential avoidance occurs through suppression of painful feelings or thoughts, emotional numbing, dissociation, substance abuse, and by the avoidance of situations believed to cause painful feelings; *e.g.*, if students do not study for a test, failing only means they did not study and does not reflect on their abilities.

Unfortunately, relational frames such as "If I don't leave home, I won't become panicky" are self-amplifying. "Both suppression and avoidance based strategies will come to cue the feared or unwanted private event since they are based on (and thus strengthen) the underlying relational frames" (Hayes, Strosahl, Bunting *et al.*, 2004, pp. 27–28). Cultural or professional norms that suggest psychological pain is unhealthy only reinforce such problematic solutions. The DSM-IV-TR (APA, 2000) uses private events such as anxiety, depression, delusions, or suicidal thoughts to define many disorders, while first- and second-wave therapies are designed to eliminate such symptoms. In contrast, ACT questions whether the problem is the symptoms or if it is society's rules about symptoms. At best, a focus on symptoms distracts from helping clients create a constructive, rewarding life. At worst, trying to control symptoms may amplify them; *e.g.*, the harder one tries to go to sleep, the less likely it will happen.

Intervention Techniques

ACT creates psychological flexibility by bringing relational frames under appropriate contextual controls. Logic and language are used when effective, but direct experience is the final arbiter. The goal is to help clients act effectively in the pursuit of valued goals, even in the presence of distracting or painful experiences. Figure 14.3 describes six core interventions (acceptance processes are on the left and change processes on the right side).

Although discussed separately, they often overlap in actual practice and there is no set order.

1. *Acceptance* is nonjudgmental awareness of thoughts, feelings, and sensations as they occur. Experiential interventions such as mindfulness, empathy, and metaphors help clients become *willing* to accept feelings they have tried to avoid. *Creative hopelessness* teaches the futility of controlling private events. Messages to increase willingness to accept feelings include:

   - Although willingness is all-or-none, it applies to as many or few feelings as one chooses.
   - Willingness to accept is an alternative to emotional control and struggle.
   - It is necessary to decide what must be accepted in order to achieve what one values.
   - Expend effort on valued actions that can be controlled, not on experiences which cannot.
   - Willingness is a choice and an action, not a feeling, thought, or decision.
   - One does not have to want pain to be willing to accept it if it serves a valued goal (Strosahl *et al.*, 2004, p. 38).

2. *Defusion* helps clients become skeptical about their automatic interpretations of events, to differentiate between their thoughts and their experience of reality, and to undermine cognitive fusion (a) between an event and its evaluation or interpretations not intrinsic to the event; (b) with the imagined toxicity of painful events; (c) with the causal events that form the client's "story;" and (d) with expectations about the past or future. Defusion messages include:

   - Your mind is neither your friend, nor your enemy.
   - Thoughts and feelings do not cause behavior.
   - Who is responsible—the mind or the person?
   - The most dangerous thing about the past is that one's mind may make it into the future.

- Which is a more trustworthy guide to what works, your mind or your experience?
- Is it more important to be right, or to be effective? (p. 40).

3. *Contact with the present moment's* nonarbitrary contingencies is encouraged; therapists bring clients back if they are overly conceptual, evaluative, or focused on the past or future. This *mindfulness* helps clients defuse from the content of their stories. They also note interpersonal processes including nonverbal behavior, the function the client's stories are serving, the stories' impact on the therapeutic relationship, and their relation to outside problems. Key messages include:

- Life goes on now—it is not something that happens after problems are gone.
- There is as much living in a moment of pain as in a moment of joy.
- Would you be willing to notice what is going on within you and between us now?
- Thoughts and feelings may refer to past or future pains, but they are experienced from this moment's point of view (p. 43).

4. *Self-as-context* for an experience is the subjective "I" that gives the sense of an unbounded, immutable self. Self-as-context is open to the opportunities of each moment. The objective, *conceptualized self* evaluates narrative that describe past experience and future expectations. Messages that distinguish between these self-aspects are:

- You are not your thoughts, emotions, memories, or roles; thank your mind for the thought.
- There is a you that is not "thing like" that has been present all your life.
- When something is fearsome, notice who is noticing it.
- You are perfectly made to experience your own experience.
- The contents of your awareness are not bigger than you; you contain them.
- You are a safe place from which you can have experiences for what they are (p. 45)

5. *Values* provide guidance to choose goals that lead to a meaningful life. Clients who avoid unwanted experiences lose this sense of direction. They struggle for emotional control over "hot" events instead of learning to accept their experience. ACT messages that clarify valued directions for client's lives include:

- What do you want your life to stand for? And are you doing that now?
- What would you want your friends, family, and children to say at your funeral?
- In a world where you could choose a direction in your life, what would you choose?
- Values provide goals that change when achieved; values are guides that never change.
- Are you willing to do what needs to be done to move toward valued goals? (p. 47)

6. *Committed action* reflects ACT's ultimate aim of helping clients engage in behavior that serves intrinsically reinforcing, valued goals. The other five core processes remove barriers of fusion and avoidance and determine values that direct committed action. Clients commit to act in the face of perceived barriers and painful experiences even if only for short periods. Lapses become opportunities to discover any remaining barriers to commitment so that still larger, more elaborated patterns of action can be initiated. Journey metaphors are often used: "In climbing mountains, switchbacks may seem to take one the wrong direction, but are actually the only way to the top." Therapists help clients create valued goals and concrete action plans. Messages that sustain committed action include:

- Goals are just a process by which the process of living meaningfully becomes the goal.
- Behaving confidently is different from feeling confident.
- You are *response-able*.
- Notice the vitality of committed action, moving forward, and growing.
- Would you rather be "right" about your life's hopelessness or carry on with a commitment?
- Focus on building larger and larger patterns of effective action.
- If you slip, notice the pattern and return to your commitment.
- Can you keep moving toward what you value, even when obstacles surface? (p. 49)

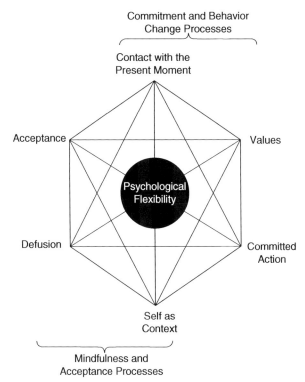

Fig. 14.3 Core ACT interventions (Reprinted from *A practical guide to acceptance and commitment therapy*, p. 7. By S. C. Hayes, & K. D. Strosahl (Eds.). © 2004 by Springer Science.)

ACT uses numerous techniques and metaphors to help clients confront problems that arise in session; *e.g.*, the *two scales* metaphor asks clients to visualize the imbalance of scales that measure their emotional discomfort and their willingness to feel. They are encouraged to consider increasing willingness since suffering is the product of unwillingness and pain. In general, clients are unwilling to experience pain until they have lost all hope it can be alleviated. This is why ACT has the core process goal of *creative hopelessness*, illustrated in the following dialog with an obsessive-compulsive client. Note the therapist's level of activity (Twohig, 2004):

T: Tell me some of the things that you tried to control the obsession.
C: I told myself that it was no big deal and that I could handle it.
T: How well did that work?
C: Seemed to make it a little easier.
T: But it sounds like the obsession was still there.
C: Yes.
T: So what did you do?
C: I tried to wait it out. I did other things, distracted myself, but in the end I had to give up because it was too much.
T: You have told me a lot of things you have tried to do, and it seems to me that you have tried to do just about everything that is logically there to be done. You've done all the obvious and reasonable things. You've thought hard, you've worked hard. You've looked for the angles. And now here you are in therapy once again … still trying. But you've come to me. I work for you. So it is my obligation to point something out: this isn't working, right?
C: I haven't figured it out yet.
T: Here is another way to say what you just said: even trying to figure it out isn't working so far.
C: Not yet.
T: Not yet. And even in that "not yet" I hear "but it will. Surely it will." What if it won't? What if this whole thing is a setup?
C: A setup?
T: Don't you smell a rat here? It doesn't make sense. You're an intelligent person. You've worked on this problem. Sometimes it even seemed to be getting better. And yet, here you are in therapy again. Isn't it true *in your experience*, although it doesn't seem that it *should* be this way, that the more you've struggled with these obsessions and urges—the more you have tried to get rid of them—the more difficult it has become. They don't seem to respond to conscious control. As you have run away or escaped, the obsessions haven't gotten smaller, they have gotten bigger.
C: I don't know how to get rid of them. I'm hoping you can help. How should I get rid of them? What am I doing wrong?
T: Those are important questions because they show what has been going on, but let's not get off on that issue quite yet. Let's start with what you know directly. You feel stuck.

C: Right.

T: It is not clear what to do next, but it doesn't seem like there is a way out.

C: Exactly.

T: So I'm here to say "you are stuck. There is no way out." Within the system in which you have been working there is only one thing that can happen: what has been happening. Just consider that as a possibility. Look, you know it hasn't been working. Now let's consider the possibility that it can't work. It isn't that you aren't clever enough, or don't work hard enough. It's a setup. A trap. You're stuck.

C: So I'm hopeless. I should give up. Why am I coming in here?

T: I don't know. But right now it's to try to see what hasn't been working. Anyway, I didn't say you are hopeless, I said *this* is hopeless. This whole thing that has been going on. This struggle that practically has you strangled is hopeless. And, yeah, if a struggle is hopeless, it is time to give up on that struggle. It is a hopelessness, but a creative kind of hopelessness. If we give up on what hasn't been working, maybe there is something else to do.

C: Then what should I do?

T: Well … first let's start from here. If this whole thing is a trick, a trap, we need to open up to that so that something different can happen. You came in here expecting some kind of trick, something to do, some solution I might have. You've been trying to find the solution, you can't find it, and maybe I have it. But maybe these so-called solutions are actually part of the problem. And check and see if this isn't so; maybe this isn't true for you but just look and see if it is: *deep down* you don't believe that there is a trick. If I brought out one more clever idea from a therapist, part of your mind would be going "oh, yeah. Sure." Your direct experience says this situation is hopeless. Your mind says that of course there is a way out. There has got to be a way out. So which do you believe: your mind or your experience?

ACT Case Formulation

In contextual analysis, therapists try to understand how clinical complaints function differently for different clients (Hayes, Strosahl, Luoma, Varra, & Wilson, 2005b). The ACT therapist reviews childhood and traumatic history to discover the functional contexts and purposes served by cognitive fusion and experiential avoidance. The functional organization of historical processes determines how clients currently face situations. Intense traumas that occur before an awareness of the self-as-context develops may interfere with psychological flexibility, the client's ability to defuse painful feelings, stay in the present moment, and commit to valued ends. Rather than symptomatic relief, ACT aims to restore psychological flexibility so clients can pursue valued goals. ACT case conceptualizations involve a five-step[2] review of each core process:

---

[2] Adapted from *A practical guide to acceptance and commitment therapy,* pp. 65–68. By S. C. Hayes, & K. D. Strosahl (Eds.). © 2004 by Springer Science.

1. *Analyze scope and nature of presenting problem*. The six core processes may not be involved with acute, situational symptoms that may only need a skills acquisition program. But presenting problems often involve fusion, avoidance, or values and need to be recast in these terms; *e.g.*, clients with an anxiety disorder want to reduce anxiety. The Adlerian question "What would change if your problem went away?" usually elicits a positive life goal: "I'd be able to find work" or "I'd be able to have a long-term relationship." ACT formulations suggest it is possible to work toward these goals in the presence of negative feelings: the problem is not a painful feeling, but fusion with the idea one's goals cannot be attained if one has problems. Client formulations are not challenged until the history is fully understood since bad feelings may also reflect on-going abusive relationships or other environmental problems.

2. *Assess factors affecting client's motivation for change*. Are clients aware of their behavior's long-term consequences so they can consider suspending old patterns and trying new ones? Motivational barriers may include:

   • *History of being right following rules*: Defusion strategies pit being "right" against costs to vitality; mindfulness or self-as-context work reduce attachment to the conceptualized self.
   • *Entanglement with unworkable strategies*: Creative hopelessness undermines improperly targeted change strategies.
   • *Fusion with belief that change is not possible*: Review costs of belief in not pursuing life goals; behavioral experiments to see if even small changes can occur.
   • *Fear of the consequences of change*: Accepting feared experiences, clarifying values, and teaching committed action, choice, and decision.
   • *Change threatens the conceptualized self*: Defusion strategies rewrite maladaptive beliefs about the self; values clarification examines the costs of self-defeating beliefs.
   • *Dominance of conceptualized past or future*: Experiential exercises to contact the moment and "just noticing" exercises to observe without belief or disagreement to defuse thoughts.
   • *Positive short-term consequences*: Creative hopelessness about long-term goals and values clarification of costs *vs.* benefits of short-term gratifications; *e.g.*, substance abuse.
   • *Social support for avoidance and fusion*: Families and institutions may reinforce problems of trauma or disabled clients; values clarification can help illuminate the cost of not changing.

3. *Assess factors promoting psychological inflexibility*. Assess strength and contextual control of inflexibility; mindfulness, acceptance, values clarification, or defusion are useful. Psychological flexibility barriers include:

   • *Experiential avoidance*: Unacceptable thoughts, feelings, sensations; low intimacy.
   • *Behavioral avoidance*: With what activities does the problem interfere?
   • *Poor persistence or self-control*: Procrastination, impulsivity, under-performance, poor health behavior.

- *Internal emotional control strategies*: Excessive self-monitoring; negative self-instructions or self-distractions; dissociation.
- *Behavioral emotional control strategies*: Substance abuse, compulsive behavior, over-eating, suicidal, or parasuicidal behavior.
- *Weak life direction*: Lacks values, involvement with family and friends, leisure activities, or spiritual practices; avoidance or fusion has led to abandoning important goals.
- *Fusion with evaluative thoughts and concepts*: Judgmental, critical toward self or others; overuse of "insight" or "giving reasons."

4. *Assess factors promoting psychological flexibility*. Assess exceptions to inflexibility. Before building on a potential strength, ensure it has not been used to avoid or resulted in negative outcomes; *e.g.*, wallowing in negative feelings. The goal is to discover skills or experiences that have the potential to give clients a head start. Examples include:

- Prior mindfulness or spiritual practice, human potential workshops, *etc.*
- Experiencing success through "letting go" of urges or self-defeating thoughts; *e.g.*, stopped smoking, attended Alcoholics Anonymous, or grieved the loss of a loved one.
- Times when the client felt intensely alive and in contact with strong negative feelings.
- Reducing a situation's negativity of by seeing its irony or by laughing at oneself.
- Taking a painful course of action because it involved something the client valued.
- Prior experience with setting goals and taking step-by-step action to implement them. Prior experience with changing one's course to a more positive life direction.

5. Develop *treatment goals and relevant interventions*. Distinguish process and outcome goals since client and therapist goals may be initially disparate. Outcome goals are client decisions, but the processes needed to achieve them derive from the therapist's professional training. Therapy clients often believe their failed strategy for controlling anxiety just needs "tweaking" to be effective. Once legitimate outcomes are collaboratively developed such as intimacy in relationships or being productive, therapists select process goals. Interventions include:

- *Generate creative hopelessness*: Help clients accept that the current strategy is not working.
- *Expose the non-toxic nature of private events*: Acceptance and defusion change beliefs about the danger of facing feared situations; *e.g.*, rapidly repeating a word or short phrase that describes an avoided experience quickly renders it meaningless.
- *Understand that emotional control is the problem*: Clients experience the paradoxic effects of emotional control.
- *Generate experiences of self-as-context*: Clients learn mindfulness to experience the self-as-context, the "I" that contains and is greater than any unpleasant memory or reaction.

- *Make contact with the present moment*: Mindfulness permits contact with reinforcers, while worry (conceptualized futures) prevents contact.
- *Explore values*: If clients lack a substantial set of values or are out of touch with them.
- *Engage in committed action based on chosen values*: Client lacks motivation to confront pain or is not living a generally consistent, productive life.

Table 14.2 describes the 6×5 matrix resulting from core processes and case formulation steps. There is always a significant overlap among the factors that contribute to client problems, so Hayes, Strosahl, Luoma *et al.* (2004) do not fill in all possible matrix cells in analyzing possible interventions; however, overlapping factors help identify intervention targets that should have the most impact.

Act Assessment

Traditional outcome measures may be inappropriate to assess ACT goals, since they typically reflect the form (frequency or intensity), but not the function of a symptom; *e.g.*, Bach and Hayes (2002) found that psychotic clients who learned to accept their symptoms reported more hallucinations and delusions than patients who received treatment as usual, but rehospitalization rates were 50% less and they were less likely to report believing their symptoms. ACT process goals are best measured by ratings of belief in symptoms or willingness to experience symptoms while acting effectively. The Acceptance and Action Questionnaire has received preliminary support as a valid measure of acceptance and committed action (Hayes, Strosahl, Wilson *et al.*, 2004). Recent developments of values assessment measures may be viewed on the Association for Contextual Behavior Science website (see below).

ACT and Substance Abuse

Hayes and Strosahl (2005) review applications of ACT procedures for a number of clinical problems including affective, anxiety, posttraumatic stress disorders, chronic pain, serious mental illness, and substance abuse. Hayes, Wilson, Gifford, *et al.* (2004) found that ACT in combination with methadone was more effective than methadone alone in treating opiate abuse. Wilson and Byrd (2004) note that treatment-resistant substance abusers often come from chaotic, abusive, or neglectful families that provided few opportunities to learn the interpersonal, conflict resolution, and problem-solving skills needed to pursue valued goals. Failure and humiliation then lead to fusion with a defective conceptualized self. "Recreational" drugs provide intrinsic positive reinforcement as well as the negative reinforcement of escape, which makes it difficult for substance abusers to renounce an experiential avoidance tactic that reduces their pain successfully. A vicious circle of still more failure occurs as dependence on drugs alienates friends and

Table 14.2 ACT case formulation matrix. (Reprinted from *A practical guide to acceptance and commitment therapy*, pp. 62. By S. C. Hayes, K. D. Strosahl, J. Luoma *et al.* (Eds.) ©2004 by Springer Science.)

Sources of psychological flexibility	Presenting problem analysis (core questions)	Analysis of motivational factors	Factors that contribute to psychological inflexibility	Factors that contribute to psychological flexibility	Treatment implications
Acceptance	What private experiences (thoughts, feeling, memories, sensations) is the client unwilling to have? What patterns of avoidance are in place? Can the client "make room" for experience in an undefended, nonjudgmental way?				
Defusion	Is the client overly attached to beliefs, expectations, right-wrong, good-bad evaluations of experience? Does the client confuse evaluations and experience?				
Contact with the present moment	Does the client exhibit ongoing, fluid tracking of immediate experience? Does the client find ways to "check out" or get off into their head? Does the client seem pre-occupied with past or future or engage in lifeless story telling?				
Self-as-context	Can client see a distinction between provocative and evocative content and self? Is client's identity defined in simplistic, judgmental terms (even if positive), by problematic content, or a particular life story?				
Contact with values	Can client describe personal values across a range of domains? Does client see a discrepancy between current behaviors and values? Does client describe tightly held but unexamined goals (*e.g.*, making money) as if they were values?				
Patterns of committed action	Is client engaged in actions that promote successful working? Does client exhibit specific, step-by-step pattern of action? Can client change course when actions are not working? Are there chronic self-control problems such as impulsivity or self-defeating actions?				

family and impairs job performance. Tolerance and the need for larger dosages to prevent withdrawal create still another vicious circle that complicates treatment.

Substance abusers referred by the court or their families may present with disengagement, sullen compliance, or angry defiance. The first step in building a collaborative alliance is to validate clients' resentment at being coerced into a situation not of their choosing (see Table 14.3). Values assessment also encourages collaboration as clients choose goals reflecting their own values: family, intimacy, parenting, friends, work, or education (see Appendix B). Time may be needed to build adequate trust as therapy helps clients translate values into concrete goals. Treatment plans address expected barriers and lapses so that clients are realistic and not discouraged by perceived failures. Creative hopelessness over past behavior encourages clients to consider ways to work for valued goals. The metaphor "How often does a child have to fall down before one gives up on their ability to walk?" helps clients recommit after a failure. Some substance abusers are consumed with guilt over the harm they have done to others when intoxicated. Cognitive fusion with self-condemnation interferes with making concrete or symbolic restitution to victims, but therapists can help clients value the concern for others that is embedded in that self-condemnation. As concerns shift to victims, therapeutic goals focus on restitution or to honor victims by making a commitment to serve others.

Many therapists adopt a "tough love" policy, accepting clients only after detoxification and sending them home when intoxicated. This policy retains clients with the best prognosis, but gives the neediest still one more message about their "hopelessness." Detoxification is stressful, so combining it with therapy provides an opportunity to teach clients about committed action in the face of negative experiences. The response to clients who come to therapy intoxicated should consider both the degree of intoxication and the context in which it occurred. With severe addiction, meeting a client who is somewhat intoxicated may be the only way the therapist can initiate contact. If intoxication levels are sufficiently high to impair meaningful communication or if the client is capable of abstaining, then clients are sent home after reaffirming the therapist's commitment to work with them and their sorrow at this missed opportunity. At the next session, the primary focus is on the costs of intoxication for the client.

Case Illustration[3]

- *History*: Tim is a 30-year-old Caucasian American with a history of polysubstance abuse, major depression, and suicidal ideation dating back to adolescence. Suicidality is exacerbated by major crises such as the breakup of his marriage and is the reason he entered treatment. Assessment of drug use (Appendix B) indicated shifts among types of drugs, degree of usage, and mode of administration. Tim's

---

[3] Adapted from S. C. Hayes, & K. D. Strosahl (Eds.). *A practical guide to acceptance and commitment therapy,* pp. 163–178. By K. G. Wilson & M. R. Byrd. © 2004 Springer Science.

Table 14.3 ACT substance abuse interventions. (Reprinted from S. C. Hayes, & K. D. Strosahl (Eds.). *A practical guide to acceptance and commitment therapy*, pp. 175–176. By K. G. Wilson & M. R. Byrd. © 2004 Springer Science.)

Clinical issue	Recommended ACT response
Treatment is mandated or coerced	• Defuse objections to treatment as an obstacle to effective work • Defuse both compliance and defiance • Values intervention—find a value that can be agreed upon as a basis for a therapeutic contract. For example, self-determination, making therapy a choice as a therapeutic value
Relapses and slips	• Defuse thoughts and feelings of failure, and especially around past failures, and thoughts of "permanent" or "ultimate" failure • Reconnect to values and link exposure and defusion to values • Do discrimination training to contrast the experienced vitality of values-driven suffering in defusion and exposure exercises with suffering experienced while trying to suppress thoughts and feelings of failure
Fear of commitment (*e.g.*, to living sober or to other values)	• Distinguish commitment as an object or an outcome from commitment as a process • Commitment is not to the outcome. Commitment is to the process. In essence, the commitment is to commit and recommit as many times as is necessary. Does one give up on a child that is learning to walk because it falls down? • Distinguish belief from assumption. Beliefs come and go; however, we can choose our assumption even as belief waxes and wanes
Client says that they do not care about anything	• Get present in an experiential exercise to "not caring about anything." Ask if the client could choose to be someone who cared or not, what they would choose. If they choose no, work on self-determination as a value (see above) • If they choose yes, ask "What if this therapy could be about creating a space where caring or valuing was a choice?"
Client is convinced that they are irretrievably bad: "I haven't told you everything." "Some things are so bad they cannot be told."	• Empathize. Therapist should get in psychological contact with the level of isolation the client is experiencing. "It must be so painful for you, so isolating." • Client and therapist should use experiential exercises to make contact with and defuse the client's altogether human longing to be known and accepted • Defuse "must" be able to tell in order to know if one is acceptable • Make it clear that there is no special virtue in telling or not telling. The question is, "What value is served by telling?" • Ask; "What if our work here could be about creating a space where even the most horrific things could be told, if telling could make a difference in what you value?"
Irreversible losses or harm caused (*i.e.*, loss of parental rights, vehicular manslaughter)	• Use experiential exercises to get psychologically present to the pain • Defuse content that emerges in exercise • "What if part of what we do here is to find a way to honor the loss or harm? • If the loss could guide activity you could value, what things, event very small things might you do this day that could honor the loss?" • Do discrimination training around vitality involved in even the smallest honoring of the loss as contrasted with the lack of vitality of working to suppress thoughts of the loss

Table 14.3 (continued)

Clinical issue	Recommended ACT response
Client comes to therapy intoxicated	• Intervention should be sensitive to the meaning of the intoxication and whether it is the first time, or one of many • The meeting should not be business as usual and the intoxication ought to be noted at minimum. Bear in mind that people in the addict's life have both ignored intoxication and rejected the client in anger over it. Take a moment to get present to the different reactions the client has gotten to intoxication in the past • If first time, to the extent possible, get present to the cost. This must be done in a thoroughly nonjudgmental way • With some severely addicted individuals, meeting them at some level of intoxication may be our only opportunity to intervene • With the client who is capable of coming to sessions clean, the therapist should allow their own feelings of vulnerability and incompetence to be present in the meeting. Make the therapist's sadness and ongoing, unremitting commitment apparent, and then send the client home
Therapist is angry with the client	• Take a moment of silence. Ask the client to focus on her or his breathing. The therapist should use this time to become mindful of anger, noting thoughts, images, memories, and bodily sensations as they emerge (therapist defuses own anger) • Therapist should try to make contact with the value and vulnerability underlying the anger. • Therapist may note the anger that occurred and ask client about previous experiences where a person working for or with them became angry • Therapist should make their unremitting commitment apparent in this exchange

use of drugs to increase a sense of belonging with his drug-use cohort, manage social discomfort, and avoid an increasingly painful world has diminished their original positive reinforcement value. Vicious circles caused by substance abuse include unreliable commitments to work and family, with problems at home interfering with work and vice versa. Tim became progressively estranged in two marriages and from his parents. Sue, his last wife, recently restricted contact with their 9-year-old daughter, Olivia, because of the child's distress at his many broken promises. His unreliable work performance has restricted him to menial levels of employment. Drugs have become his only means of coping with these repeated disappointments. Values assessment (Appendix B) revealed that his relationship with his daughter is a core value. Tim realizes how toxic his behavior is for his daughter, which serves to increase his self-loathing. When asked to imagine in detail Olivia's distress at waiting on the porch when her daddy fails to show up, Tim said, "I feel sick. I hate this. I feel this way whenever I talk to Sue. She kicks my ass, and I get mad, but I know I deserve it. I feel this way whenever I think about Olivia. She doesn't deserve this" (p. 166). The therapist asked what Tim would choose if the choice was between continuing his current patterns or feeling ten times worse than he was feeling in that moment in order to have a *possible* meaningful relationship with Olivia. While Tim did not like the choice, he chose Olivia. Even a potential relationship with her was worth confronting painful experiences.

- *Diagnosis*: Axis I—Polysubstance abuse (R/O dependence); major depression with suicidal ideation; Axis II—no diagnosis; Axis III—no other medical condition; Axis IV—estranged from family; lack of social support; occupational level is depressed by drug use; Axis V—GAF = 35.

- *Conceptualization*: Tim turned to drugs for a number of reasons—self-medication for his depression, to cope with social anxiety, to be a part of his clique, and for the initial pleasures they provided. Vicious circles developed as Tim increasingly relied on drugs to avoid negative feelings resulting from deteriorating relationships with family, friends, and work as he became progressively unreliable. Tim's cognitive fusion with the belief he is defective, unworthy of love, and hopeless reinforces this pattern of experiential avoidance. He is also fused with the idea that negative feelings are intolerable and only drugs can provide relief.

- *Plan*: Assessment revealed that Tim's relationship to his daughter, Olivia, is a core value. He has made an initial commitment to accept painful feelings as a possible way to achieve the valued goal of connecting with his daughter. This will be addressed repeatedly to help him maintain his commitment to work toward becoming a safe, reliable father for Olivia. A list of goals related to reconnecting with her will be developed, together with action plans and barriers that may be expected. One goal might be to buy a dozen stamped and addressed post cards to be sent weekly with a message beginning, "Hi Olivia. Just thinking about you today and wanted to write to tell you how much I love you." A probable barrier is Tim's reliance on other drug users for social support. Identified barriers can also serve to reinforce creative hopelessness about the ultimate value of drug usage. Lapses will be predicted and the metaphor of the child learning to walk used to help Tim recommit after each lapse. Lapses will provide opportunities to explore the cognitive fusion and negative feelings that triggered experiential avoidance. Lapses will also be used to reinforce creative hopelessness about the value of drugs in avoiding negative feelings. There will be an on-going focus on the steps needed in order to convince his wife, Sue, he is fit to resume contact with Olivia; *e.g.*, Tim has avoided reminders of Olivia by not carrying a picture of her. He will be encouraged to carry her picture and use it as a focus in therapy to reflect on past painful experiences such as being asked to leave the home. Her picture can also be used as a focus to help Tim explore Olivia's experience empathically. The therapist will note nonverbal signs of tension, difficulty, or avoidance as Tim engages in these exercises. As problematic thoughts and feelings arise, they will become a focus for defusion so Tim can stay present in the moment. Since responsible fathers provide child support, the plan will include problem solving with Tim to develop skills needed to improve his employment situation. Renewing visitation will provide opportunities to explore problems that may occur during the visit as well as an important outcome measure; *e.g.*, if Olivia is hesitant, Tim may have renewed thoughts about his worthlessness that need to be defused. Progress will be assessed by Tim's ability to stay drug-free and follow through with action plans.

Integrative Implications

Postmodernism's assertion that all knowledge is a construction alleviates questions about integrating therapeutic systems with different assumptions. It also ends the prospects of developing a single, unified theory of behavioral change, the holy grail of integrative therapy. The preceding chapters illustrate the diversity of integrative systems that have been proposed and, given all the possible combinations, many other systems are likely to follow. Nevertheless, postmodernism has led to interesting convergences in all the major schools of thought, including psychodynamic, cognitive, experiential, and family systems. Contemporary practitioners are more cognizant of the intersubjective nature of the therapeutic relationship and of the role of language as common factors in therapeutic construction of new meanings.

A new common factor is to understand therapy as the meeting of two subjectivities who co-create meaningful and helpful narratives for clients. The fact that all theories leave out important aspects of human experience provides a dialectical impetus to integrate parts of each of the major approaches into a coherent whole. Emotionally focused therapy, DBT, and ACT are all examples of this movement toward broader, more encompassing visions of human behavior. Inevitably, these therapeutic systems are also partial and will lead to further efforts to combine their insights into still more comprehensive systems.

Chapter Fourteen: Main Points

- Postmodernist approaches include *constructivism*, which focuses on the individual's unique constructions of meanings, and *social constructionism*, which focuses on the role of culture and language in shaping and limiting the construction of meanings.
- *Intersubjective* theory suggests infants develop *intersubjective awareness* that mother has needs and ideas that are different from their own. This helps children recognize other's intentions and coordinate interactions. The Oedipal period involves the child's awareness of a *triadic* relationship in which the parents share experiences unique to themselves. In identifying with the same-sexed parent, children incorporate not only ideals and values, but the parent's *reflected appraisal*, which becomes part of their self-concept.
- Relational therapists are more interested in the client's optimal functioning than in symptom removal, but are willing to be directed by client preferences. Differences among relational approaches are reflected in theories about transference

with interpersonal therapists trying to be as objective as possible in a *participant-observer* stance, while intersubjective analysts see the therapy relationship as an intersubjective, *co-created mutual influence.*

- Constructivist assessment and interventions are continuous, on-going co-creations between therapist and client. *Laddering* resembles CT's downward arrow and involves recursive questioning of constructs and their contrasting opposites to elicit the client's superordinate constructs. The *bow-tie* method uses *double description* or *circular questioning* to describe the self-sustaining vicious circles that result from a couple's conflicting constructions and actions.
- Ruptures occur repeatedly in the therapeutic alliance and are problematic only if they go unresolved. If resolved, the client gains a corrective emotional experience that relationship problems can be worked through if approached directly. Therapists maintain a *mindful* position to *disembed* from emotional engagement, *metacommunicate* about their own experience of a rupture, and invite clients to share their subjective experience of the rupture.
- DBT is a long-term rehabilitative therapy designed for parasuicidal or suicidal clients with a Borderline Personality Disorder (BPD) diagnosis. It integrates mindfulness and dialectical philosophy with cognitive-behavioral therapy. DBT balances inconsistencies in clients' beliefs, opposing viewpoints of significant others, and accepting negative feelings with a commitment to change. It helps clients recognize that "good" and "bad" exist only in a particular context. Therapists validate their clients' experiences, while helping them solve problems.
- Invalidating environments interact with temperamental vulnerability to produce the emotional dysregulation found in BPD. This creates vicious circles that result in interpersonal, cognitive, behavioral, and self-concept dysregulation. Attempts to regulate affect such as avoidance or suicidality lead to *splitting*, alienation, impulsivity, and unstable relationships.
- DBT prioritizes four levels of problems: 1. life-threatening behavior; 2. therapy-disrupting behavior; 3. behavior compromising quality of life; and 4. behavioral skill deficits. Skill deficits are addressed during group skills training, while individual therapy targets the other priorities. Individual therapy focuses on motivation, crisis management, and phone consultations to help clients generalize skills to real-life situations. Weekly group consultations between individual and group therapists help prevent burn-out and ensure conformity with treatment protocols.
- DBT alternates warm, empathic acceptance with more directive problem-solving and change. *Communication style* strategies alternate empathic acceptance with a more challenging, irreverence. *Case management* strategies support clients as they try new skills outside of therapy. *Dialectical* strategies exaggerate antithetical client positions to encourage syntheses.
- Group skills training modules address typical BPD skill deficits. *Mindfulness* helps clients observe their experiences nonjudgmentally in order to reduce both splitting and impulsivity. *Interpersonal effectiveness* teaches conflict

resolution, assertiveness, balancing demands and priorities, and self-respect by standing up for one's beliefs. *Emotion regulation* helps clients accept their feelings without being impulsively driven. *Distress tolerance* helps them accept unavoidable negative experiences without avoidance maneuvers or pushing away others.

- Acceptance and Commitment Therapy (ACT) is based on *functional contextualism*: a behavior's function reflects the contexts of culturally influenced stories people construct about themselves and the world. ACT helps free people from *cognitive fusion* with problematic stories in order to work toward valued goals. *Relational frames* such as "same as" or "larger than" are powerful tools to predict and manage real-world outcomes, but cognitive fusion occurs if distinctions between relational frames and the real world are lost.

- Psychopathology reflects psychological inflexibility that results from cognitive fusion and the suppression of painful thoughts and feelings or avoidance of feared situations or *experiential avoidance*. Vicious circles result when attempts to control experiences fail or amplify them.

- ACT involves six core processes to help clients *accept* both positive or negative experiences and *commit* to actions that will realize valued goals: 1. *Acceptance* interventions encourage *creative hopelessness* about avoidance strategies and *willingness* to tolerate distress; 2. *Defusion* teaches clients to discriminate between thoughts and reality and to be skeptical of automatic thoughts; 3. *Contact with the present moment* teaches mindfulness of the present moment and brings clients back if they are overly conceptual; 4. *Self-as-context* helps clients distinguish between their *conceptualized* self and the "I" that is larger than and contains self-thoughts and painful experiences; 5. *Values* help clients discover what is important in their lives once culturally derived goals are *defused*; and 6. *Committed action* helps clients choose value-based goals and commit to actions that realize those goals.

- ACT case formulation works from a matrix of the six core processes and the five steps in analyzing presenting problems: 1. *Analyze scope and nature of presenting problem*; 2. *Motivational analysis*; 3. *Factors contributing to Psychological Inflexibility*; 4. *Factors contributing to Psychological Flexibility*; and 5. *Treatment implications*.

- ACT outcomes are measured by ratings of willingness to experience symptoms and commit to carrying out action plans for valued goals. Traditional outcome measures focus on symptom removal or suppression, which is contrary to ACT's aims.

- Intervention programs address a number of clinical problems including substance abuse. Working with treatment-resistant substance abusers includes defusing objections to mandated treatment; defusing thoughts of failure after lapses; values assessment for discouraged clients who "don't care;" defusing a negative conceptualized self; accepting and grieving for losses experienced and created for others; working with intoxicated clients even during detoxification; and disembedding therapists from anger about client resistance or lapses.

Further Reading

Hayes, S. C., & Strosahl, K. D. (2004). *A practical guide to acceptance and commitment therapy*. New York: Springer Science.

Linehan, M. M. (1993a). *Cognitive-behavioral modification of borderline personality disorder*. New York: Guilford Press.

Linehan, M. M. (1993b). *Skills training manual for treating borderline personality disorder*. New York: Guilford Press.

Luoma, J. B., Hayes, S. C., & Walser, R. D. (2007). *Learning ACT: An acceptance and commitment therapy skills-training manual for therapists*. Oakland: New Harbinger.

Safran, J. D., & Muran, J. C. (2000). *Negotiating the therapeutic alliance: A relational treatment guide*. New York: Guilford Press.

Video

Hayes, S. C. Acceptance and Commitment Therapy. Part of the Systems of Psychotherapy APA Psychotherapy Video Series.

Websites

ACT: http://www.contextualpsychology.org/act
DBT: http://behavioraltech.org/index.cfm

Chapter 15
Epigenetic Systems: A Meta-Integrative Model of Human Functioning and Therapy

The Blind Men and the Elephant

[S]ix men of Indostan ... went to see the elephant
(Though all of them were blind) ...
That each by observation might satisfy his mind.

The First approached the Elephant ...
Against his broad and sturdy side ... and began to bawl
"God bless me! But the elephant is very like a wall!"

The Second, feeling of the tusk
Cried, "Ho! What have we here? ...
This wonder of an Elephant is very like a spear!"

The Third approached the animal ...
The squirming trunk ...happening to take:
"I see," quoth he, "the Elephant is very like a snake!"

The Fourth reached ... and felt about the knee:
"What this ... wondrous beast is like is ... plain," quoth he;
"Tis clear enough the Elephant is very like a tree!"

The Fifth, who chanced to touch the ear,
Added: "... Deny the fact who can,
This marvel of an Elephant is very like a fan!"

The Sixth no sooner had begun
About the beast to grope,
Than, seizing on the ... tail, ... quoth, "[T]he Elephant is very
like a rope!"

And so these men of Indostan
Disputed ... each ... his own opinion ... stiff and strong,
Though each was partly in the right, and all were in the wrong!
(Abridged from *John Godfrey Saxe*,
American Poet, 1816–1887)

Saxe's metaphor admirably captures the present model's thesis that the major therapeutic systems each focus on different facets of the human condition. Questions over the legitimacy of integrating therapeutic systems with incompatible assumptions, which have impeded past integrative efforts, are addressed by Safran's (1998)

D. K. Fromme, *Systems of Psychotherapy,*
DOI 10.1007/978-1-4419-7308-5_15, © Springer Science+Business Media, LLC 2011

postmodern perspective that all world views are partial, inadequate representations of the world. He recommends instead a "… superordinate worldview that views all worldviews as partial and inadequate in nature and recognizes the importance of viewing reality from the perspective of multiple lenses" (p. 265).

An existential divide exists between modernist objectivist approaches that emphasize what is observable and humanist phenomenological approaches that emphasize subjective inner experiences. In practice, both rely heavily on dialog, client report, and behavioral observation. They differ in that phenomenology gives greater emphasis to client reports, while objective approaches emphasize observation. This dialectic of an inside-out focus on inner experience and an outside-in focus on observed behavior is itself part of a larger dialectic of the interpersonal and ecosystemic contexts that influence the individual's actions. This chapter is an example of a comprehensive approach that incorporates all these factors.

Dialectical constructivism (Greenberg & Pascual-Leone, 2001) suggests that the meanings of therapeutic narratives emerge from dynamic interactions between an individual's experience and reality as limited by linguistic, interpersonal, environmental, and cultural contexts. Mascolo, Craig-Bray, and Neimeyer's (1997) *epigenetic systems theory* (EST) exemplifies this perspective and also provides an integrative framework for human functioning and intervention. Epigenesis describes how systems interact with historical and environmental contexts to create unexpected, *emergent* properties organized at new levels of complexity. Emergent properties cannot be explained by properties of lower levels since they are non-linear products of events evolving in particular historical and environmental contexts. Emergence is a *multifinal* process in which systems develop unpredictably in dynamically changing contexts that co-determine their "final" state. Slight environmental or historical variations can produce dramatically different phenotypes even with identical genotypes when only one identical twin develops schizophrenia. Epigenesis describes a synthesis of the nature *vs.* nurture dialectic.

Mascolo *et al.* (1997) postulate a systemic hierarchy beginning with a *biogenetic* level of genetic, cellular, and organ system interactions. The *personal-agentic* level of the individual evolves from the biogenetic level and in turn leads to *dyadic-relational* and *cultural-linguistic* levels. Not coincidentally, each level corresponds to a major therapeutic modality: biomedical, individual, interpersonal-family systems, and postmodern-ecosystemic. The biogenetic level describes processes such as the differentiation of the 7-week embryo into male or female, dependent upon ambient testosterone levels. If these are high enough, embryos develop as a male even with XX chromosomes. Biogenetic processes interact with the environment to create meanings at the personal-agentic level; *e.g.,* a neural network previously activated by an intentional state initiates actions in the environment that realize the individual's goals.

The personal-agentic level describes interactions of person and environment. Although neural networks mirror a person's actions, emergent principles of meaning, intentionality, and agency require another level of explanation. The personal-agentic level is the focus of cognitive, experiential, and psychodynamic therapies. It views people as agents who construct their own meanings. Biological need initiates action, but the specific action is determined by meanings the person constructs about the nature and value of the need, which then determines the person's goals and subsequent actions; *e.g.,* a client may learn to construe sexual feelings negatively. Instead of seeking a sexual partner, the client may satisfy intimacy needs by developing symptoms that invite nurturance from significant others and disguise the nature of the underlying impulse. Constructions at the personal-agentic level are influenced not only by the individual's experience, but also by dyadic-relational and cultural-linguistic processes. In general, meanings are constructed through interaction with others or the environment through learning that occurs in a social context and reflects the concepts available in the person's culture.

The dyadic-relational level reflects the interpersonal and interactional construction of meaning. Dyadic behavior is an emergent process that occurs in ever-changing contexts and is not reducible to either person's actions. Most interactions involve *continuous processing communications* in contrast to *discrete state communications* (Fogel, 1993). Discrete messages such as e-mails occur when one cannot respond until the other person completes a message. It is possible to discriminate among sender, receiver, message, and to assign the responsibility for meanings to one or the other parties. In face-to-face interactions, however, such distinctions are unclear as each party anticipates what the other will say and responds not only to the message but also to the anticipation. Both continuously anticipate and alter their communications, co-regulating each other's participation. The resultant meanings are so completely co-created that it is impossible to say who was a "sender" and who a "receiver." Imposing a linear ordering of cause and effect is merely an arbitrary punctuation of events (Watzlawick, Beavin, & Jackson, 1967). Co-created meanings are not identical for both parties, but are an epigenetic product of each person's prior experiences and their unique contexts including differing moods or goals. *Co-regulated coordination* describes the shaping and integration of each person's personal-agentic meanings and actions into the novel emergent properties of the dyadic relationship.

The cultural-linguistic level describes how cultural contexts and language shape meanings at the dyadic-relational level, and recursively, how dyadic-relational discourses ultimately shape culture and language over time. Language and culture provide meanings that precede an individual's existence and shape his or her adjustment to society. Mascolo *et al.* (1997) postulate that the construction of meaning always involves *situated interpretive activity*:

1. Human actions always involve interpretation of the meaning of their resultant effects;
2. Interpretation is always about the consequences of motoric or symbolic actions;
3. Activity is always situated in a particular context that involves other people or has been structured by prior actions of others—action is thus a property of a *person-in-a-context*;
4. A situated activity means that every action is unique to a specific context; this implies that there is no unified "self," only "self-states" that emerge in particular situational contexts.

People, nevertheless, strive to construct self-narratives that unify the meaning of various self-states and make life more predictable. Language and culture also coordinate actions with others in meeting mutual needs. Feminist, multicultural, and ecosystemic therapies act at this level; *e.g., deconstructing* cultural practices that exploit or limit people's opportunities and potential.

EST implies that people are normally in a state of "flux" responding to constantly changing circumstances. However, it does not address personality or continuity in a person's actions across different situations. Stability can be accounted for by several factors. First, temperamental factors evoke typical reactions from caregivers with easy babies receiving more positive attention than difficult babies. There is also environmental continuity as most of the child's experiences happen at home with the same caregivers and in repeated situations that share *functional equivalence*: *e.g.,* daily meals, elimination, sleep, play, and repetitive, age-related demands. Repeated interactions shape neurological networks into cognitive-emotional- interpersonal schemas as the child responds in predictable ways across similar situations. Such schemas also help make different situations functionally equivalent as new situations are assimilated into existing schemas (Piaget, 1936/1963). With maturity, people may also select their own environments and seek the familiar rather than the strange. Finally, both EST and dialectical constructivism (Greenberg & Pascual-Leon, 2001) suggest people and their significant others co-construct self-narratives that assimilate self-states into a relatively coherent pattern and ignore self-states that do not fit the narrative.

However, some people have problems coordinating actions with others to have their needs met. The environment evokes subjective self-states that cannot be ignored, but feel "alien" to their self-narrative and they develop symptoms or act in problematic ways; *e.g.,* clients who learn to suppress anger may depend on people who take advantage of their passivity. Symptoms may be their only way to express self-states elicited by unmet needs or hurt feelings. Therapy gives *voice* to suppressed self-states, co-constructs and *reauthors* self-narratives in optimistic and competent ways, and helps clients find adaptive ways to meet their needs.

An Epigenetic Systems Model of Human Development and Functioning

As discussed previously, postmodernism suggests human phenomena may always be described in multiple ways, making a unified theory impossible in principle. The integrative therapies discussed in prior chapters illustrate how different choices lead to a proliferation of models, but also suggest that more comprehensive views may lead to more effective interventions. The present model assumes each major school of psychotherapy emphasizes a facet of human functioning that should be included in a comprehensive approach. Figure 15.1 illustrates an EST model of human functioning based on 12 widely adopted therapeutic approaches and the facets of human functioning that are especially emphasized by each.

The epigenetic model incorporates aspects of human functioning emphasized by different approaches. At the cultural-linguistic level, ecosystemic therapies

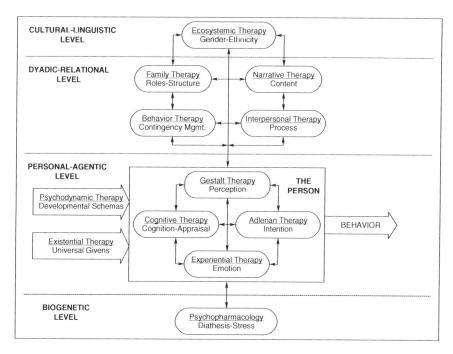

Fig. 15.1 Therapeutic and epigenetic human systems

(Chap. 13) focus on "outside-in" political, socio-economic, ethnic, gender, and community contexts that create or limit opportunities for a happy, productive life; *e.g.,* poor single-parent families living in high-crime neighborhoods with inadequate schools may need help in coping with the external sources of their problems. Until such issues are addressed, interventions at lower levels may be less effective or provide only temporary benefits. In general, ecosystemic processes provide the conceptual categories people use to understand their world, shape the forms that family structures may take, and determine whether an individual will be marginalized and suffer oppression or will have a privileged status in society.

The dyadic-relational level is also an objective, "outside-in" level that includes family structures and roles, narratives about presenting problems and solutions, relationships with significant others, and reinforcements available in the immediate environment. Shaped by ecosystemic processes, the family (Chap. 12) in turn shapes the narratives people tell about themselves. Interpersonal relationships (Chap. 11), especially with family members, help meet an individual's needs and reinforce adaptive behavior (Chap. 4). As Fig. 15.1 suggests, dyadic-relational systems strongly influence one other: narratives both reflect and reinforce family roles and structures; narratives arise from interpersonal dialogs that shape family structures and reinforce actions that meet individual needs for intimacy or autonomy. These systems collectively shape the personal-agentic level as individuals develop a unique sense of self in relationship to others and learn how to meet interpersonal needs. They correspond to Bronfenbrenner's (1979) microsystemic level, which comprises the individual's immediate environment of relationships, ideas, and resources.

The personal-agentic level focuses on subjective "inside-out" processes, the focus of most individual therapies. In Fig. 15.1, the box labeled "The Person" includes cognition (Chap. 5), intention (Chap. 10), and perception and emotion (Chap. 8). These subsystems coordinate inputs from other epigenetic levels with interpersonal schemas (Chap. 11) to form perceptual Gestalts. Core interpersonal schemas are themselves shaped by psychosocial development and the existential givens (Chaps. 6, 7 & 9). Current needs, shaped by biogenetic processes (Chap. 3) and schemas shaped by historical experiences in meeting needs also inform the intentions and plans resulting from Gestalt formation. The following sections present integrative frameworks describing personal-agentic functioning and influences from other epigenetic levels.

Motivation: Interpersonal Needs and Self-Determination Theory

Sheldon, Elliot, Kim, and Kasser (2001) suggest several reasons to posit psychological needs as basic explanatory concepts. Relatively few *genotypic* needs help explain many functionally equivalent *phenotypic* behaviors, suggest strategies to help clients meet needs, and integrate motivation with personality functioning. The present model assumes that human needs reflect the existential challenges of death, isolation, groundlessness, and meaninglessness; *e.g.,* the overarching need for *integrity* is challenged by the awareness that death is inevitable.

To maintain integrity, humans, like many other social animals, must connect with others to meet physiological and safety needs. The need for *intimacy* and attachment (Bowlby, 1982) evolved to ensure the social connections necessary to maintain integrity. But other people are not always available and their motivation to stay connected is ultimately unknowable, which results in feelings of isolation. The pleasures of intimacy are the "carrot," but fears of isolation are the "stick" that maintains attachment bonds. Intimacy can provide a secure base that can sustain feelings of wholeness and integrity for varying periods of time. Inevitably, others are sometimes unavailable, unresponsive, or controlling, which leads to the need for *autonomy* and confidence in one's independent ability to maintain integrity and ensure that needs are met.

This dialectic of intimacy and autonomy parallels Bakan's (1966) influential analysis of interpersonal motives into *communion* and *agency* needs. The distinction may also be seen in Clark and Beck's (1991) conception of sociotropic and autonomous depression types in which intimacy and autonomy needs, respectively, are frustrated. Bakan (1966) concluded:

> ... [there are] fundamental modalities in the existence of living forms, agency for the existence of an organism as an individual, and communion for the participation of the individual in some larger organism of which the individual is a part. Agency manifests itself in

self-protection, self-assertion, and self-expansion; communion manifests itself in the sense of being at one with other organisms .... Agency manifests itself in the urge to master: communion in noncontractual cooperation (pp. 14–15).

Bakan suggests here that mastery or competency is a form of agency manifest in communal cooperation. The present model also incorporates this integrative idea.

Striving for autonomy and independence both threatens intimacy needs and requires the individual to decide what to do next with no external grounds on which to base a decision. Paradoxically, attempts to maintain integrity through autonomy result in still other challenges to the individual's integrity and sense of wholeness. The intimacy-autonomy dialectic is eventually resolved in part as the person develops *competency* in something meaningful to others, something with social interest (Adler, 1929/1964). The need to be competent in something meaningful, of course, brings its own challenge as the person struggles with ultimate questions of meaning and meaninglessness. This struggle for meaning is the ultimate search for integrity: self-actualization in a search for truth, beauty, and wisdom (Maslow, 1971). To summarize, the present model proposes a superordinate need for integrity that underlies the dialectically opposed needs of intimacy and autonomy; the individual then resolves this tension by developing a need for competency.

Different lines of research support the importance of these needs. Cognitive dissonance research (*e.g.,* Gibbons, Eggleston, & Benthin, 1997) suggests people reduce inconsistencies between beliefs and actions to maintain psychological integrity. Literature on attachment and loneliness supports the importance of intimacy needs (*e.g.,* McGuire & Clifford, 2000; Duggan & Brennan, 1994), while the *reactance* literature on limitations to freedom of action supports the importance of autonomy (*e.g.,* Brehm, 1966). The *self-efficacy* literature suggests people need to feel competent to perform the necessary actions before seeking a goal (*e.g.,* Bandura, 1997).

Ryan and Deci's (2000) *self-determination theory* is closely aligned with this analysis. Self-determination theory postulates that autonomy, competence, and relatedness or intimacy are the innate needs that motivate and direct interpersonal behavior; *e.g.,* Sheldon, Elliot, Kim, and Kasser (2001) asked American and South Korean college students to describe the most satisfying event that occurred in their lives during the past week, month, or semester. Analysis of their responses indicated that themes of autonomy, competence, and relatedness were consistently among the top four of ten needs that were rated. Themes of positive self-esteem were typically rated the highest. This was not predicted by self-determination theory, but is congruent with an assumption that integrity is an intrinsic need.

Concerns that high autonomy ratings might be an artifact of individualistic societies were addressed by Chirkov, Ryan, Kim, and Kaplan (2003), who found that autonomy was associated with well-being in subjects from South Korea, Russia, and Turkey, as well as the United States. They note that autonomy refers to the belief that actions are self-determined, whether directed to the individual's or the group's goals. In related research, LaGuardia, Ryan, Couchman, and Deci (2000) demonstrated that attachment security and positive relationships with self and others are associated with success in meeting autonomy, competence, and relatedness needs. The current model assumes that attachment security mediates success or failure in meeting interpersonal needs and the development of well-being or problems in living.

Cognitive-Experiential Self-Theory (CEST) and Personal-Agentic Processes

Epstein's (1990, 2003) CEST is a model of personal-agentic functioning that assumes people process information through two parallel, interacting conceptual systems: an emotion-based, preconscious, *experiential* system and a conscious rational system. CEST also assumes the existence of four needs similar to the four basic needs described in the preceding section (see Table 15.1 for areas of agreement in the two models).

Support for CEST's assumptions is found in a number of research literatures (Epstein, 2003).

The experiential system automatically creates implicit schemas about self, others, and the world at large through classical, instrumental, or vicarious conditioning of repetitive patterns and emotionally significant events. Schemas are organized hierarchically, from broad, abstract views of self or others as worthy or unworthy, to narrow, context-specific schemas. Generalized schemas of self-worth, others' trustworthiness, or the nature of the world are not usually in conscious awareness, but are experienced in the form of vague *vibes* or good or bad feelings; *e.g.,* vibes of uneasiness may signal the need to slow down and use rational processing. Narrow schemas are encoded as images, metaphors, or narratives organized into more general emotional networks on the basis of need gratification and frustration. They are easily modified in contrast to generalized schemas, whose abstractness ensures stability as new experiences are assimilated. However, if generalized schemas are sufficiently invalidated, the profound disorganization of an acute psychotic episode may result (Epstein, 2003).

In contrast to the experiential system's effortless, holistic operation, the rational system is based on slower, conscious verbal learning that uses more cognitive resources and relies on logical analysis rather than experience to solve problems. The rational system makes causal analysis, long-term planning, and the imagination of new realities possible. It can adapt to novel environments and may be needed to retrain an experiential system reacting to generalized schemas no longer adaptive in the current situation. On the other hand, the experiential system reacts quickly

Table 15.1 Agreement in meaning of basic needs in CEST and current model

Basic needs	CEST needs	Realm of agreement
Intimacy	Relatedness	Need for proximity to significant other
Autonomy	Pleasure principle	Intrinsic motivation, free from external constraint
Competency	Self-enhancement	Need to experience self as worthy of esteem and love
Integrity	Conceptual coherence	World is predictable and controllable

in complex, hard to classify situations that resist analysis such as empathizing with another person's perspective. Emotionally significant events automatically evoke associations among past experiences and present needs, plans, and goals to make executive decisions, guide current actions, and give them passion and color.

Interactions of the two systems include experiential biases that influence rational thought and the rational system's ability to correct errors made by the experiential system. Heuristics, mental shortcuts (Tversky & Kahneman, 1974), and past experience guide the experiential system, but are subject to various biases; *e.g.,* a situation may be interpreted in ways that are *self-enhancing* and support competency needs or confirm prior expectations and support needs for integrity and coherence (*assimilative bias*). Biases operate even if the current environment differs from earlier experience and a schema is no longer adaptive. People also engage in *self-verifying* behaviors that provoke others to act in ways that confirm maladaptive beliefs and fail to recognize how their implicit beliefs have influenced the interaction.

As Epstein (2003) notes, "… failure to recognize the operation of one's experiential system means that one will be controlled by it" (p. 167). Although biases are hard to change, therapy can assist the rational system in three ways to: 1. dispute maladaptive thoughts; 2. provide corrective emotional experiences; and 3. use imagery, fantasy, or narratives for vicarious corrective experiences. Problems develop when people generalize childhood experiences in which needs were thwarted to their current situation; *e.g.,* if self-esteem needs are frustrated, people develop *sensitivities* to any threat to self-esteem and respond with *compulsions*, rigid behaviors designed to protect them from vulnerable sensitivities.

Epstein (2003) illustrates the transmission of sensitivities and compulsions from one generation to the next with the case of Ralph. Ralph was much brighter than his siblings, but rather than being esteemed for his competency, his mother would become upset as his accomplishments evoked her own childhood schemas of being outshone by siblings. As an adult, Ralph was sensitive to any sign he was unlovable or unworthy, for which he compensated by working compulsively to succeed in business. Nevertheless, he continued to feel depressed, resented his family when his wife praised the children, accused them of not loving him, and spent even more time at work. This, of course, led to self-verification of his beliefs as his family became increasingly alienated by his avoidance and hostility. To forestall his wife asking for a divorce, he announced he would seek a divorce himself. Ralph was greatly pleased and vowed to be more attentive to his family when his wife said she wanted more than anything for them to work to save their marriage. Epstein (2003) notes these good intentions may be hampered by Ralph's lack of awareness of how his experiential system has influenced his behavior.

Developmental Stages and Tasks

CEST describes personal-agentic processes, but does not detail the development of their content. Personal-agentic content includes input from other epigenetic levels, past experience in meeting needs or protecting the self as encoded in interpersonal schemas, and the current situation. Gestalts or self-states form as people interact with the environment and succeed or fail in meeting their needs. The experiential system organizes emotionally significant or repeated experiences into interpersonal schemas, Polster's (1995) essential selves, which internalize the standards of significant others. What begins as a simple recognition of differences between self and others develops eventually into a system of essential selves that relate internalized standards from parents or peers to on-going situations to satisfy basic interpersonal needs. Children also internalize narratives, stories that significant others tell about them, into this self-system. As adults, integrity needs lead people to create new narratives that resolve the inevitable inconsistencies that arise in these stories.

The present model relates Piaget's (1936/1963) cognitive developmental theory to an expansion of Erikson's (1950) psychosocial theory. Table 15.2 describes developmental tasks at the personal-agentic level and associated influences of other epigenetic levels as a function of Piaget's stages. A *dialectical operations* stage adds a postmodern awareness of contextual influences and inevitable change to Piaget's stages (Basseches, 1984; Perry, 1968; Riegel, 1973). The model assumes a need for increasingly sophisticated skills in each cognitive stage to meet the interpersonal needs described by self-determination theory (Deci & Ryan, 1985). These skills include Erikson's (1950, 1968) psychosocial tasks and others that epigenetic theory suggests: developmental tasks at the personal-agentic level are influenced by temperament and maturation at the biogenetic level; ethnic, gender, and socioeconomic factors at the cultural-linguistic level; and relationships with family and significant others at the dyadic-relational level; *e.g.,* in traditional cultures, mothers or eldest daughters provide most of a child's care, while fathers, nannies, or daycare workers may be involved in modern cultures. Even though researchers disagree on many details of Piaget's model (*e.g.,* Baillargeon, 1993), it seems clear that Piaget's cognitive stages reflect qualitatively different ways of understanding the world; *e.g.,* current evidence suggests that the boundaries between developmental stages are fuzzier and there is a greater variability when various milestones are reached than Piaget believed (1936/1963).

Transitions from one stage to the next are not necessarily the same for different domains of experience; *e.g.,* it is doubtful that the 6-year-old Mozart functioned at the formal operations level in any area other than music. Also, there may be momentary fluctuations from one mode of thinking to another; *e.g.,* "wool-gathering" represents a temporary regression to sensorimotor functioning. Finally, culture significantly affects the degree to which more abstract, formal operations are achieved so that industrialized cultures need these skills much more than agrarian societies (Gardner, 1995).

The epigenetic model assumes children find their own unique solutions to satisfy needs for integrity, intimacy, autonomy, and competency as a function of their cognitive abilities at each developmental stage. At each stage, cognitive and physical developments enable children to develop increasingly sophisticated psychosocial skills to meet their needs. The solutions children find to meet needs at each stage form the basis of further development in succeeding stages (*epigenesis*). Underly-

Epigenetic Hierarchy	Self-Determination Theory: Needs	Cognitive Stages and Developmental Tasks & Influences (*Erikson's Psychosocial Tasks Indicated in Italics*)				
		Sensori-Motor	Preoperational Stage	Concrete Operations	Formal Operations	Dialectical Operations
Cultural-Linguistic Level		Ethnic Group	Socioeconomic Status Neighborhood	School Church	College Business	Social Security Medicare
Dyadic-Relational Level		Parents Caregivers	Siblings Neighbors	Chum Peer Cliques	Partner Nuclear Family	Extended Family
	Intimacy	*Trust* *Mistrust*	Peer Relations Egocentricity	Mutuality Selfishness	*Intimacy* *Isolation*	
Personal-Agentic Level	Autonomy	*Autonomy* *Shame*	Emotional Regulation	Social Roles Parental Fusion	*Identity* *Diffusion*	*Integrity* *Despair*
	Competency	Attentional Coordination	*Initiative* *Guilt*	Industry Inferiority	*Generativity* *Stagnation*	
Biogenetic Level		Temperament	Health and Maturation	Timing of Puberty	Sexual Orientation	Aging Health

Fig. 15.2 Epigenetic levels and stages of cognitive and psychosocial development

ing needs for integrity motivate a self-actualizing search for growth, exploration, and testing the limits of what is possible, yet safe. Safety is initially a function of secure attachment with caregivers, but this also serves to gratify intimacy needs. Integrity needs then motivate differentiation of self from other and autonomy as caregivers are sometimes slow in meeting the child's needs. Increased autonomy threatens needs for intimacy, a conflict resolved by the development of competency needs that are reinforced as caregivers mirror their delight in the child's accomplishments.

Sensorimotor Stage

The experiential system is dominant during Piaget's (1936/1963) preverbal, sensorimotor stage as infants form schemas for objects, recurring events, and self and other relationships. Psychosocial development begins with Erikson's trust stage as infants form attachment bonds with caregivers. The caregivers' own experiences in receiving care influence how responsive they are to the child's needs, while the child's temperament decides how difficult that job will be. Even caregivers with insecure attachments may be responsive enough to ensure secure attachments with "easy" temperament infants, but easily upset, hard-to-console, "colicky" infants may challenge even the most securely attached caregiver.

Object relations theory suggests that optimal levels of caregiver unresponsiveness help infants differentiate self from others, a necessary precursor for agency and autonomy. Infants develop interpersonal schemas about how lovable they are in response to caregiver love and mirroring, and about others' trustworthiness in response to caregiver lapses. The precursor competency skill of *coordination of joint attention* (*e.g.,* Tremblay & Rovira, 2007) develops in interactions with caregivers together with needs for intimacy and autonomy. Infants first attend closely to care-givers' eyes and then follow their gaze to begin the process of recognizing what is important in the environment and what may be ignored. Pointing reinforces this skill and associates relevant objects and action sequences with words as infants develop schemas of their environment. Language facilitates mature *object permanence* and prepares the child to learn the skills of the preoperational period. Children are now competent communicators and recognize what is important in their world.

Preoperational Stage

Language skills facilitate the preoperational cognitive task of learning about causal relations among actions, events, and objects. The child's exploration of the world is facilitated by secure caregiver attachment and by economic factors that determine the safety and amenities available in the child's home and neighborhood. Economic factors also affect diet, health, and maturation rates, which determine how competently children explore their world and interact with peers and siblings. With secure attachments, a distinct sense of self, and basic communication skills, children expand their range of attachment objects during this period to include ex-tended family members, neighbors, and parallel play with peers. With increased separation from caregivers, children must learn to *self-regulate* emotional distress, which is facilitated by their on-going learning about intentions and causes.

Skills associated with interpersonal needs develop in complementary ways: new attachment figures require greater self-regulation and autonomy, which requires new competencies in understanding causality and intentionality. Children who un-derstand causality can act with foresight about probable consequences, the essence of *initiative*. They also learn how their actions affect others and develop an under-standing of others that permits distinctions between intentional and unintentional actions. Preoperational children are less likely to cry after a bump if they decide it was unintentional and not a threat to attachment security. As they learn about others' intentions, they become less egocentric and aware that others may have dif-ferent perceptions of an event. Children develop a theory of mind by the end of the preoperational period and recognize that others have needs and intentions that must be considered. This allows more interactive play with peers and permits a level of autonomy and self-regulation that prepares them for the extended separations re-quired by formal schooling.

Concrete Operations Stage

With well-developed theories of mind, causes, and intentions, children now have a rational system that enables them to think logically about the world. They under-stand others have different perceptions about events and learn to anticipate what those might be. This enables children to form meaningful peer relationships that meet needs for attachment and to be more autonomous and less dependent on their family. In most developed societies, schools require children to be *industrious*, to learn to follow more and more complex classroom programs. They also provide a large pool of socially diverse peers with whom children learn skills of *social subordination* and *mutuality* (Sullivan, 1953b). They learn to accept their teachers' authority and to subordinate their own desires in order to accommodate the peer group's requirements for acceptance.

Peer groups also provide a venue of peers that help children learn to relate as equals rather than hierarchically as they do with adults or siblings. Paradoxically, the characteristic conformity to peers' standards during this stage is an essential step toward greater autonomy from parental controls. Children seek their peers' esteem by being part of the group, while distancing themselves from apparent need for their parents. Interactions with peers teach children to be leaders or followers and socialize them into male or female roles.

Ideally, children become *chums* with a peer from their clique toward the end of this stage. Chums provide the first opportunity for a mutual *I-Thou* relationship in which the chum's needs are as important as the child's own needs (Sullivan, 1953b). Chums let children experience a mature form of intimacy prior to puberty when hormones may confuse love and lust—unless an early puberty derails this process. Supported by increased cognitive abilities, this intimacy permits a sharing of confidences that helps children correct associative distortions about the world acquired earlier through experiential learning. It also prepares children to understand another person's point of view more fully, the beginning of formal operations.

Formal Operations Stage

Until this stage, behavior is largely determined by external forces such as temperament, attachment security, or socio-economic pressures. However, internal processes become more important as formal operations mark the beginning of abstract thinking, planning, and imagining possible future selves (Cross & Markus, 1994; Markus, 1977). People with formal operations analyze problems into relevant components and use the scientific method and logical reasoning to find solutions. People can now imagine how the world *might* be, create new realities, and choose their own destiny. This is the basis of individualism, a self-created, autonomous sense of identity (Landrine, 1992) and why people feel pride or guilt over success or failure. People with formal operations abilities also develop a sense of identity from long-term relationships or accomplishments in meeting needs for intimacy and competency. It is thus likely that people use formal operations skills to meet needs for intimacy, identity, and generativity as opportunities arise rather than in sequential stages as Erikson (1950, 1968) proposed.

In modern, individualistic societies, a sense of identity is formed by choosing among possible life narratives. A *diffuse* or *foreclosed* identity results if people fail to make such choices and let events determine life's course (Marcia, Waterman, Matteson, Archer, & Orlofsky, 1993). However, the freedom to choose that characterizes modern secular society also requires the individual to confront existential givens instead of relying on the answers suggested by religion or tradition. Marriage and family meet needs for intimacy and competency for some people, but marrying too early can foreclose options. Autonomy needs are met to the extent people feel they have chosen their life course, even if they make sacrifices for their family's welfare as often happens in traditional societies. Generativity and competency needs are usually met through work, raising a family, and providing for the next generation's future.

Dialectical Operations

There is increasing evidence that cognitive development does not always stop with formal operations (*e.g.,* Kramer, Kahlbaugh, & Goldston, 1992). A number of researchers suggest that formal operations are inadequate for problems that are affected by numerous hard-to-define variables (Arlin, 1975; Basseches, 1984; Commons & Richards, 2003; Kramer *et al.,* 1992; Riegel, 1973). Kramer *et al.* (1992) suggest a postformal cognitive development that moves from thinking in absolutes, to recognizing that knowledge is relativistic and eventually to a dialectic awareness. As people mature, they are less likely to see causality as linear and universal; instead they recognize that each person or situation is unique. Decisions are made pragmatically rather than on the basis of abstract ideals. Some people also develop a dialectical evolutionary perspective in which they understand that changes in one part of a system necessarily evoke emergent changes in all other parts. Dialectic thinking is less about solving problems and more about finding answerable problems in complex, "fuzzy" situations.

The present model views dialectical operations as an integration of the experiential system's ability to respond intuitively to complex situations with the rational system's ability to make real-world evaluations of the pragmatic utility of intuitive ideas. This creates a level of wisdom more easily achieved by individuals who internalize meaningful self-narratives of being loved and contributing to others. Because life experiences have satisfied needs for intimacy, autonomy, and competency, they are free to address transcendent needs for integrity evoked by awareness that death may be near. At this stage, integrity needs are essentially spiritual and are expressed in a quest for unity in one's life narrative and with loved ones.

Problems in Living

The epigenetic model uses the term "problems in living" rather than psychopathology to avoid suggesting that problems are somehow inside the person. Ecosystemic or cultural-linguistic contexts create many of the problems people experience and either exacerbate or mitigate the rest; *e.g.,* stressors that overwhelm an isolated, unemployed person may be easily handled by a middle-class, financially stable person who understands how to access community resources and has practical and

emotional support from friends. Ethnic or gender discrimination can limit educational, occupational, and economic opportunities and create a stressful, possibly
harassing work environment. Poverty means stress in meeting expenses, living in
high-density, high-crime areas, frequent moves requiring significant life changes,
and poor health care.

Such stressors disrupt dyadic-relational functioning as families try "more of the
same" solutions and become either rigid or disorganized in adapting to overwhelming circumstances. Without a safe haven to meet attachment needs, family members
become disengaged and avoidant or enmeshed and anxious and either intimacy or
autonomy needs go unmet. When vertical ecosystemic and family stressors coincide
with horizontal life cycle or traumatic stressors, the result is apt to be single-parent
families, teen pregnancies, domestic violence, substance abuse, or psychological
symptoms. The present model suggests one way to integrate concepts from several
theoretical frameworks into a comprehensive view of the objective behaviors and
subjective experiences of human problems.

The Development of Human Problems

The diathesis-stress hypothesis assumes that personal-agentic and biogenetic-
level factors predispose certain individuals to be particularly vulnerable to stressors
exceeding their adaptive abilities. Personal-agentic factors include schemas encod-
ing the individual's attachment experiences. Biogenetic factors include genetics,
maternal health during pregnancy, temperament, and physical health, all interacting
with dyadic-relational variables to influence attachment experiences. It is difficult to
be responsive to the needs of easily upset, hard to console children. Children who
are chronically ill or have limited attention spans and high activity levels present
still further challenges. If a caregiver's resources are already strained by familial or
ecosystemic stressors, only the most resilient can meet children's attachment needs
responsively. If the caregiver's own attachment needs are unmet, the stage is set for
the next generation's insecure attachment and vulnerability. Biogenetic diatheses not
only create vulnerabilities, but often lead to interpersonal stressors that interact addi-
tively with other familial and ecosystemic stressors (e.g., Monroe & Simons, 1991).

Attachment security is a dynamic process that fluctuates with the caregiver's
current ability to be responsive to the child's basic needs. Improved caregiving by
significant others in the child's life can overcome earlier insecurities, but critical
psychosocial skills may, nevertheless, have been affected. Psychodynamic theory
suggests that ineffective interpersonal skills acquired earlier in development have
the greatest impact, affecting skill development at later stages. The timing of attachment insecurities as a function of cognitive development may therefore influence
the type of problems the individual experiences.

The epigenetic model assumes attachment problems during the sensorimotor period are encoded in memory by the experiential system as a felt bodily sense (vibes).
When preverbal schemas are activated in adulthood, the person either misperceives
a situation as a threat or is unable to identify a source for the threat. Experiential

methods are useful to bring vibes into awareness where they can be labeled and challenged. Problematic schemas are represented in images and associations by the experiential system during the preoperational period and are also hard to label or challenge when activated later in life. By the concrete operations stage, the rational system is sufficiently developed that attachment problems are more easily recalled. It may still be difficult to challenge maladaptive beliefs, however, since they tend to be formed in absolute, black-and-white terms during this period. People are only able to use logical reasoning to challenge faulty beliefs and take multiple perspectives if their attachment problems develop primarily during formal operations. Attachment problems developing during this time with only minor influences from earlier periods are likely to respond to short-term interventions. Those based on the earlier stages may require more extended interventions to engage the rational system in challenging the vibes and associations of preverbal schemas.

Insecure attachment schemas are influenced by the cognitive stage in which needs go unmet, the specific needs that are thwarted, and the child's attempts to satisfy some needs even at the expense of others. Interpersonal theory (Horney, 1970; Teyber, 2006) describes the basic strategies children use, while schema theory (Young, Klosko, & Weishaar, 2003) describes how the resulting schemas affect adult problems. Children with anxious, preoccupied attachments may sacrifice their autonomy needs and move toward caregivers as they try to achieve closeness. As adults, they are self-sacrificing, have impaired autonomy, and fear abandonment or rejection. Children with avoidant, dismissive attachments sacrifice intimacy needs, maintaining a lonely autonomy as they move away from others. As adults, they may be pessimistic, hypercritical, vigilant, emotionally inhibited, and punitive toward others. Insecure children who are attractive, forceful, or have athletic or academic gifts may instead behave narcissistically or competitively, moving against others to demonstrate their superiority and competence. As adults, they have problems with limits, entitlement, self-discipline, and tend to exploit others.

Disorganized, fearful attachments create conflict between an anxious preoccupation with a caregiver and anxious avoidance because the caregiver is threatening as well as nurturing. Conflicted schemas that split self-other images into a good-self/bad-self and good-mother/bad-mother form early in the sensorimotor or preoperational period before the rational system can make distinctions such as sometimes good, sometimes bad. Problems may involve any of the basic interpersonal needs and defensive strategies. Table 15.2 suggests the diagnostic labels given to typical problems that develop if needs go unmet during a particular development stage. The most problematic patterns are associated with disorganized attachment during the sensorimotor stage: if the child were more preoccupied

Table 15.2 Problems as a function of interpersonal needs and cognitive development

	Sensorimotor	Preoperational	Concrete operations	Formal operations
Intimacy	Borderline	Histrionic	Dependent	Generalized anxiety
Autonomy	Schizoid	Paranoid	Avoidant	Panic; Agoraphobia
Competency	Antisocial	Narcissistic	Compulsive	Obsessive-compulsive

with intimacy needs than threat, then a borderline pattern of seeing self or others as all-good or all-bad is likely with the attendant swings in mood. If the caregiver were sufficiently threatening or unresponsive, then other people would be viewed as dangerous or unavailable and result in schizoid avoidance of others. If the child discovered that angry, aggressive outbursts were the only way to get needs met, the stage could be set for antisocial patterns of interaction. Problems at later stages are less likely to be associated with fearful, disorganized attachments, but can still be quite serious if they develop before the rational system matures. By formal operations, problems are more likely to reflect situational stressors that result in acute anxiety or mood symptoms rather than maladaptive interpersonal patterns.

The Dynamics of Human Problems

People are seldom aware of cultural-linguistic, dyadic-relational, or biogenetic influences on interpersonal problems and so attribute responsibility for symptoms or conflict to an *identified patient* (IP). Family members usually fail to recognize the historical antecedents or their own contributions to problematic patterns. Instead, EST assumes external factors are mostly responsible for the development and maintenance of problems. People often internalize responsibility for problems, but as active agents they can challenge internalized schemas and environmental influences.

Experiential and rational systems are both involved as people and their significant others co-construct conceptions of self, others, and the world at large. People first internalize problematic caregiver experiences at preverbal levels and, as the rational system develops, internalize narratives that significant others and peers tell about them. These experiences and narratives create core cognitive schemas about self-worth, the trustworthiness of others, and how just or safe the world is. Subsequent events then activate schemas that resemble the current situation and focus attention on environmental elements relevant to needs: *e.g.,* integrity needs focus attention on information supporting schema-related beliefs (*confirmation bias*) and competency needs focus attention on information that enhances self-esteem (*self-serving bias*).

Environment, schema, and emotional state interactions form Gestalts that help people meet needs or cope with situations that threaten needs. Needs and emotional states focus perceptual processes on relevant information, activate interpersonal schemas and memories, and form appropriate goals and intentions. Muran (2001) describes interpersonal schemas as cognitive-affective structures that "… evoke innate expressive-motor responses that serve adaptive functions and form the core for the development of subsequent emotional experience …. They serve a communicative function in that they continually orient the individual to the environment and the environment to the individual" (p. 349). However, this process fails if schemas are no longer relevant and the individual defends against non-existent threats.

Wachtel (1967) describes three perceptual-cognitive dimensions of attention deployment that serve either to orient people or defend the self-system against threatening information: broad *vs.* narrow attentional span, scanning *vs.* fixation, and global *vs.* articulated perceptions. When relaxed, people tend to focus broadly with no particular focus on any one part of their environment. They scan the environment for items of interest, but do so in an undifferentiated, global manner. As need-relevant information becomes available, emotional arousal increases and the Inverted-U law (Yerkes & Dodson,1908; see Fig. 2.1) begins to operate: people focus more narrowly, fixate on relevant cues, and develop an articulated perception of their situation. But if sufficient threat is present, emotional arousal moves past optimal levels and attention is fixated so narrowly on so few aspects of the situation that articulated views are no longer possible and the person can no longer function adaptively. Although maladaptive, a narrow fixation on irrelevant information serves as an "ego defense" by reducing the person's awareness of threats in the environment. In its extreme form, this attentional constriction can lead to an inability to meet any of the basic needs, to the disorganization of the cognitive-affective-intentional system and psychosis. The result is "a state of non-being, a void in which there are neither pleasant nor unpleasant feelings" (Epstein, 2003, p. 163).

To summarize, the epigenetic framework provides a framework describing interactions among the factors that influence problems in living and also suggests possible avenues for intervention. At the cultural-linguistic level, socio-economic factors compound the problematic effects of prejudice and oppression mediated by cultural narratives about different ethnic groups. The dyadic-relational level is affected by cultural narratives that define the stories families tell about themselves and by socio-economic factors that determine the resources they have to solve problems. These in turn interact with biogenetic factors to determine the individual's attachment style and ability to develop the psychosocial skills necessary to meet basic needs. Inadequate skills influence problems at the personal-agentic level such as internalized schemas that bias perceptions of self, others, and the world and rising above basic needs. The following case illustrates the interaction of these factors in the case of Lani.

Case Illustration: Epigenetic Case Conceptualization

History and Presenting Problems Lani Kimura is a husky, 28-year-old, unmarried man of Hawai'ian and Japanese ancestry on his mother's side, but his paternity is uncertain. Lani's classical Polynesian appearance suggests his father was a native Hawai'ian. He was joined in the initial interview by members of his household, his maternal aunt and uncle, Pualani and Robert Gurwich, and maternal grandmother, Anela Kimura. The Gurwich's children are no longer at home with two sons in the U.S. Navy and a daughter in graduate school on the mainland. Mr. Gurwich has middle-European ancestry and was the principal spokesperson for the family. He works as a security guard, having retired as a naval petty officer to have more time with his family following his father-in-law's death 12 years ago in an industrial accident. He was concerned that Lani took after his mother, Kailani Kimura, who dropped out of school at age 15 due to promiscuity and drugs and was disowned by her father "… as a disgrace to the family's honor." Mrs. Gurwich took custody of Lani at age three after discovering her sister in a drug-induced stupor and the child malnourished, filthy, and covered with bruises. She noted that Lani was mute and appeared developmentally delayed when he first came to their home; but he seemed to come out of his shell during the following year and her biggest concern was his tendency to become over-friendly with strangers. She said Lani always preferred being around adults growing up, disliking the rough-and-tumble play of his older cousins. He was diagnosed with attention deficit disorder and attended special education classes where he performed poorly and dropped out of school his Junior year. His mother has had only sporadic contacts since and currently is in court-mandated drug treatment.

The presenting problem was Lani's alcohol abuse, which culminated a week earlier when Lani became drunk at a party, passed out in the bathroom, destroyed the toilet as he fell on it, and caused significant water damage to his host's home before he was discovered. Mr. Gurwich said this was just another example of Lani's irresponsibility and drinking problem. He is giving Lani an ultimatum "to shape up or ship out." Lani's typical routine is to sleep in, catch rides to the beach in the afternoon, and be invited to a party that evening. The family was in agreement that, although Lani has no close friends, he has a wide range of acquaintances who are happy to have him at parties thanks to his inexhaustible fund of Hawai'ian songs and virtuosity on the ukulele. Mrs. Kimura said she began teaching Lani all the old songs and how to play the ukulele when he was about eight, because she was worried that although he always seemed happy, he did not seem to have any friends. Now, she wonders if she created his problems. This prompted one of the few spontaneous remarks by Lani who said that his grandma was the only one who really cared about him and music was all he had. He was sorry he messed up his host's home, but was only trying to have some fun. Mr. Gurwich responded angrily that all Lani cared about was having fun, but he was tired of supporting him and thought it was well past time he found a full-time job. Mrs. Gurwich said that Lani has had a number of jobs as a musician at local clubs since dropping out of high school, but is invariably fired for getting drunk and making a scene.

Diagnosis Axis I—Alcohol Dependence; Rule out Attention Deficit Disorder without hyperactivity; Axis II—Personality Disorder NOS, with avoidant, dependent, and narcissistic features. Axis III—None. Axis IV—Occupational problems; Family conflict; Lack of outside social support. Axis V—GAF = 45.

Conceptualization The Hawai'ian culture suffered greatly after contact with the West, with devastating loss of population from disease and suppression of religious traditions by missionaries. Immigration by multiple ethnic groups and intermarriage further diluted their culture. Hawai'ians were marginalized in their own land, which led to a legacy of poverty and alcoholism. At the same time, movies and tourism romanticized their music and dance and portrayed the Hawai'ians as a carefree people living in the moment. In many ways, Lani and his mother personify these forces. His mother did not cope with tensions between Japanese and Hawai'ian traditions and was disowned by her father, while Lani is threatened with a similar fate by his ex-navy, Caucasian foster father. It is likely both Lani and his mother rebelled against the authoritarian strictures of their father figures. Lani's aunt and grandmother are less judgmental, but seem reluctant to contradict Mr. Gurwich. One hypothesis is that they form a coalition with Lani whose symptoms may help balance the family's power structure. Lani and his grandmother appear close, but whether their relationship is enmeshed or not may reflect differing cultural standards: appropriate from a traditional Hawai'ian perspective, but perhaps enmeshed from the perspective of a retired naval petty officer.

At the dyadic-relational level, his mother's neglect and abuse created a disorganized, fearful attachment style that still affects Lani's interpersonal relationships. With the exception of his grandmother, interpersonal relationships are superficial and distant; he enjoys parties, but mostly for the drinks and as the center of attention. Supported by his competency as a musician, this suggests Lani "rises above" intimacy needs and takes "neurotic pride" in being free to play and do his own thing. His desire to be free may also reflect the rather authoritarian styles of his grandfather and foster father; it is noteworthy that Lani dropped out of school about a year after his grandfather's death and his foster father came to live full-time in the home. The diagnosis of attention deficit disorder (apparently without hyperactivity) and Lani's placement in special education as a child may reflect biogenetic factors resulting from his mother's drug use during pregnancy. It is also consistent with a disorganized attachment style: neglect and abuse can produce high levels of anxiety and arousal that lead to habitual patterns of narrow, fixated, and unarticulated perceptions of the world.

At the personal-agentic level, Lani uses avoidance of intimacy or emotional sharing to manage maladaptive schemas (Young *et al.*, 2003) in the disconnection/ rejection domain of abandonment, emotional deprivation, and defectiveness. Schemas of dependency and impaired self-discipline are similarly managed by avoiding responsibilities or new challenges. Lani's "care-free" style may in part reflect cultural expectancies and internalized prejudice. However, his avoidance of intimacy, new challenges, and responsibility also reflects disconnection schemas that were adaptive ways to cope with neglect and abuse as a toddler, but now prevent emotional engagement with others. Lani's diagnosis of attention deficit disorder and his affable, gregarious style masked his psychosocial problems during his school years, which only became apparent as an adult with his drinking and inability to hold a job.

The appeal of the older, "classical" personality theories was their comprehensive view providing therapists with a road map of where to go when it was unclear what to do next in real-world practice. Psychoanalytic theory has been particularly important in this respect, but grand theories have proved difficult to support with empirical methods. As a result, most theorists have focused their inquiries to more limited, researchable areas; *e.g.*, although it is hard to find empirical support for object relations theory as a whole, research has demonstrated that its core concept of attachment security affects nearly every area of human functioning. The EST model represents one way to integrate a number of empirically based integrative theories and therapeutic approaches in order to provide the comprehensive view of human functioning clinicians need when therapeutic processes are fuzzy and unclear.

To summarize epigenetic systems, cultural-linguistic and ecosystemic factors determine the material, economic, conceptual, and familial resources available to the individual as they negotiate with others at the dyadic-relational level to have basic interpersonal needs met. These factors interact with biogenetic temperament to determine how challenging a new-born will be for caregivers. Together, these interactions determine the security of attachment that results as caregivers respond to an infant's needs. Insecure attachment interacts with the stage of cognitive development (verbal *vs.* preverbal) and unmet intimacy, autonomy, or competency needs (self-determination theory) to create schemas about self, others, and the world that encourage the child to move toward, away, or against others. If no corrective experiences occur, adults will enact maladaptive schema patterns as described by Young's (1999) schema therapy.

Epigenetic Systems and Treatment Planning

Figure 15.3 illustrates the relationships among epigenetic levels, presenting problems, and therapeutic factors. All four epigenetic levels affect client problems, but the dyadic-relational level determines the process of therapy and the personal-agentic level determines its narrative content. The diagram suggests that therapy changes both therapist and client just as client and therapist characteristics affect and are in turn affected by therapeutic process and content. Therapeutic outcomes feed back to epigenetic factors that affect the client, which in turn influence the presenting problem. The epigenetic approach can thus be seen as an integration of integrative therapies, a *meta-integration* of ecosystemic, family, interpersonal, personal-agentic, and biogenetic therapies that address the various facets of individual functioning (see Fig. 15.1). EST is a meta-integration of

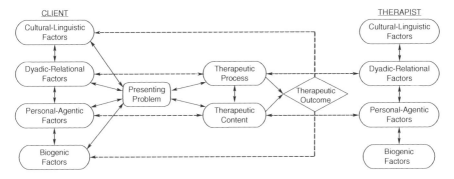

Fig. 15.3 Epigenetic treatment flowchart for chronic, interpersonal problems

empirically based integrative part-theories and therapeutic systems that address parts, but not all of the factors affecting human functioning and problems. As discussed above, EST case conceptualization of client strengths and problems links epigenetic levels to attachment theory, cognitive and psychosocial development, cognitive-experiential-self theory, self-determination theory, Teyber's (2006) theory relating the blockage of unmet needs to interpersonal behavior, and Young's (1999) schema therapy classification of maladaptive schemas. These are essential parts of case conceptualization.

Treatment planning is organized by the PACC approach (Woody, Detweiler-Bedell, Teachman, & O'Hearn, 2003) to help case conceptualization fit the client's unique characteristics, including readiness for change (see Table 2.2) and acceptance and commitment therapy's (ACT) analysis of personal-agentic factors (see Fig. 14.3); *e.g.,* poorly functioning clients may need biomedical interventions, while precontemplative clients may need motivational interviewing to encourage commitment to change. The rational and experiential systems of contemplative clients may require defusion, mindfulness to confront painful experiences, or values clarification to support committed action.

Client and therapist continuously co-construct treatment plans that analyze problems in ways that fit with the client's world view. Goals, methods for achieving them, and ways to measure their attainment (*e.g.,* the OQ-45) are agreed upon. Because understandings of strengths and problems are continuously co-created, conceptualizations and treatment plans require regular revision. Treatment plans clearly favor the objective side of the subject-object dialectic. Explicit, collaborative treatment plans have several virtues: they ensure active client involvement and understanding of the therapy contract, which enhances commitment to treatment; they clarify and provide new, non-blaming ways of thinking about presenting problems; and by making their ideas explicit, therapists avoid reacting to clients on the basis of unconsidered biases. However, the client's and therapist's intersubjective experiences are equally important: EST therapists assume that the therapy process will evoke the appropriate reactions automatically if conceptualizations and treatment plans are useful. Therapists can then set aside treatment plans and be fully present with the client once therapy begins.

To summarize, conceptualizations and treatment plans integrate client information from the various epigenetic levels. Case conceptualizations are hypotheses about how these variables affect the client's functioning. Plans require updating as new information confirms or disconfirms the conceptualization. Rather than an impossible *tabula rasa,* therapists make their current perceptions of the client as explicit as possible before each session and then put those perceptions aside to be fully present with the client. Ideas emerge "spontaneously" as Gestalts as therapists follow the client's current concerns if treatment plans are relevant; if not, they follow the client and revise their plan later. In general, symptom removal or problem-resolution is the goal for short-term problems that have only recently interfered with the pursuit of valued aims. The goal for long-term problems is to identify systemic factors and internalized schemas that maintain problems and interfere with meaningful pursuits.

Intervention Principles

The first principle of EST intervention builds on the fact that therapy always begins at the dyadic-relational level and on research indicating the centrality of the relationship for therapeutic outcomes (Orlinsky, Ronnestad, & Willutzki, 2004). Intersubjective theory suggests that clients and therapists co-construct a constantly changing, dynamic interpersonal reality (Safran & Muran, 2000). A need for integrity leads clients to seek themes that unify momentary self-states and experiences into coherent self-narratives (Aron, 2001), while therapists help clients construct self and other narratives that help meet previously denied basic needs in constructive ways. The co-construction of new, more helpful narratives creates a synthesis of the client's beliefs and values with the therapist's ideas. The guiding principle is to maintain a dialectic tension between an objective, systemic view of the client's situation and a subjective, phenomenological view of the client's self-states as new intersubjective narratives are co-constructed. Equal weight is given to the client's problematic constructions and the therapist's possibly fallible conceptualizations. Emotionally focused therapy (EFT; Greenberg, 2002) describes empirically based markers that indicate when clients are struggling with experiences that are not fully accessible. Similar markers are noted by Safran and Muran (2000) for strains or ruptures in the therapeutic alliance. The interventions suggested for these markers constitute the primary focus for therapists implementing this first principle.

A common factor in all psychotherapy systems is to avoid resistance by externalizing problems clients and their families locate in the client. The second epigenetic principle asks clients about ecosystemic, multigenerational family, and biogenetic factors as well as repetitive dyadic-relational patterns and unhelpful narratives. Externalizing responsibility for problems to other epigenetic levels lets clients and families break free from cycles of blame and withdrawal and work collaboratively. It addresses factors that could cause personal-agentic interventions to fail and creates contexts in which strengths in overcoming external stressors become salient instead of weaknesses. Therapists teach their clients that they are responsible only for getting better, not for having problems.

The third epigenetic principle gives equal weight to factors that contribute to the client's problems and to strengths and exceptions to problems. Postmodern therapies are right in suggesting that an exclusive focus on problems can be discouraging, while recognition of strengths and exceptions to problems instills hope in the possibility of change. This may suffice for acute, situation-specific problems, but the effect of each epigenetic level on chronic, thematic problems must be examined to prevent relapse once treatment concludes. A corollary of this principle is to begin therapy by assessing the historical and ecosystemic contexts of presenting problems and times when exceptions to the problem occurred.

Principle four incorporates transtheoretical suggestions about facilitating client participation in therapy (Beutler & Clarkin, 1990; Prochaska & DiClemente, 1984): *e.g.,* motivational interviewing techniques help low distress, precontemplative clients become aware of their problem's impact on self and others, while clients who resist directives respond better to nondirective or paradoxical interventions (see Chap. 2).

Epigenetic Treatment Planning and Intervention

Treatment planning relates epigenetic principles and systemic levels to the client's unique situation. As in any approach, the first step is to conduct risk analyses for suicide, substance abuse, psychosis, and the client's ability to self-care (see Chap. 2). Thorough risk analyses assess whether biogenetic factors indicate hospitalization or pharmacological intervention. Other biogenetic factors are assessed with a careful history of illnesses and medication usage.

Therapists next assess cultural-linguistic factors by asking clients:

- What is their ethnic identity? Do they identify with a minority group? If not, are they fully acculturated to the majority culture or are they bi-cultural?
- What language is spoken in their home? Are they fluent in English? Is a therapist available who matches their ethnicity or speaks their primary language?
- Have they recently immigrated or are they a member of a minority group that has been oppressed historically? Have they experienced prejudice? If so, how did they cope with it?
- Do they hold traditional communalist or modern individualist values? For example, how important is religion in their life? Church? Would they rather their children be independent or respectful?
- How connected are they with extended family, neighbors, or other support structures?
- How do they contribute to their community? How often? What would they like to do to help others if they had the opportunity?
- What community agencies have they contacted? What has that experience been like? How about schools? Recreational groups? Courts or judicial system?
- What is their neighborhood like? Do they feel safe? How about the police?
- Have they experienced any recent upheavals in their lives? Work? Accidents? Traumas?
- What is their work? How rewarding is it? Does the income meet basic needs? Enough to enjoy some extras? Do they have hobbies or participate in sports or community activities?
- What is most meaningful for them? Have they considered what goals they'd like to achieve? What barriers either prevent thinking about goals or might interfere with their attainment?

Therapists explore with clients how ecosystemic and cultural-linguistic factors affect their presenting problems and how they might cope with them or make use of community resources or the therapist's assistance. Intervention is guided at this level by multisystemic therapy principles (Henggeler, Schoenwald, & Borduin, 2009; Chap. 13). If the client lacks an adequate social support network, Speck and Attneave's (1973) networking approach is used.

Dyadic-relational assessment/intervention focuses on nuclear and family-of-origin relationships and other relationships significant in the client's life; *e.g.,* friends, work colleagues & supervisors, pastor, teachers, doctors, or previous therapists.

A three-generation family genogram may help clients with chronic symptoms or interpersonal problems see the historical roots of their problem. Questions that may clarify dyadic-relational patterns include:

- Who has been affected by the presenting problem(s)? What has been their response? How do they contribute to the problem? How do they help with it?
- What was going on when they decided to seek therapy? Whose idea was it? Had anything happened previously? Life transition events: marriage, birth, death, graduation, *etc.*?
- When did the problem begin? Does it resemble any past problems? When is the problem less problematic? How did they manage that?
- Who is most responsive, providing emotional support? Practical support? Who depends on them? Are they satisfied with these relationships? If not, what are the specific problems?
- Who was most responsive and nurturing when they were growing up? Were there other children, and if so, who was most favored? Why?
- Who else in the family (three generations) has had problems? What kind? Are there coalitions? Anyone disengaged? Who gets things done? What are the family's strengths?

Conceptualizing family dynamics helps: 1. assess problem chronicity and whether long-term treatment is needed; 2. avoid blaming individuals for the problem; 3. avoid destabilizing relationships as clients become more autonomous; and 4. identify contextual influences that help or hinder generalization of new interpersonal skills. Family therapy (*e.g.,* Minuchin, Nichols, & Lee, 2007) is indicated if problems occur primarily in the family or with a child, or are maintained by family dynamics. Interpersonal therapy is used with long-term thematic problems or as an adjunct to family therapy. Strategic (Madanes, 1981), narrative (White & Epston, 1990), or cognitive-behavioral therapies (Beck, 1967; Meichenbaum, 1977) are brief interventions effective with acute situational or symptomatic problems.

EST therapists begin with an intersubjective exploration of cultural-linguistic and dyadic-relational influences on the presenting problem, giving equal weight to objective behavior and subjective experience and to strengths and weaknesses. Therapists accommodate the client's resistance to suggestions by being more or less directive. Motivational interviewing is used for clients with low symptom distress or poor motivation. Therapists help clients explore their experiential system with one of the experiential therapies and focus on alliance ruptures that result from therapist misunderstandings or client misperceptions (Safran & Muran, 2000). After examining the therapist's contributions, clients may choose to explore if misperceptions relate to their presenting problem or long-term interpersonal patterns. The therapist's moment-to-moment therapeutic choices are guided by the task markers identified in Greenberg's (2002) emotionally focused approach (see Table 8.4) or Safran and Muran's (2000) markers of alliance ruptures.

EST therapists help clients explore attempts to gain psychological proximity to early attachment figures (Benjamin, 2006) or rise above unmet needs (Teyber,

2006). As patterns are identified in current or past problems or in the alliance, therapists use Young's (1999) system of classification to help clients explore the underlying interpersonal schemas. Personifying and externalizing problematic schemas (White & Epston, 1990) may help clients gain the distance necessary to address their problems more objectively. At this point, clients may already have some relief from their presenting problem; if not, the stage is set to introduce the principles and goals of ACT (Hayes & Strosahl, 2005).

ACT provides an integrative framework that accommodates intervention principles and goals found in other approaches. ACT's emphasis on values, committed action, and accepting that which cannot be changed is congruent with humanistic orientations such as existential therapy, motivational interviewing, and EFT, which facilitates contact with the present moment. Cognitive-behavioral, psychodynamic, interpersonal, and schema therapies all describe interventions that facilitate cognitive defusion.

Expertise with each of these approaches is ideal, but its lack does not prevent beginners from adopting an EST approach. Epigenetic therapists have some options. Essential EST skills include an ability to assess ecosystemic, family, and biogenetic factors and either intervene at appropriate levels or make referrals. EST therapists use cognitive-behavioral techniques to address situational problems or help clients who lack interpersonal skills. The nondirective skills of motivational interviewing complements cognitive-behavioral therapy's directive intervention style in working with unmotivated clients. It also helps therapists develop intersubjective awareness, which is necessary to maintain the therapeutic alliance after misunderstandings. This skill set prepares therapists to work effectively with most clients, but may be insufficient for those with long-standing thematic problems (Beutler, Consoli, & Lane, 2005). As therapists gain confidence with these widely used approaches, additional skill sets can be learned.

Expertise with ACT and EFT (Greenberg, 2002) give both an objective and a subjective perspective for intervening in thematic problems. ACT provides an objective framework for conceptualizing client problems and therapy goals that can build on cognitive-behavioral skills, while EFT provides moment-to-moment guidance for helping clients explore problematic experiences in greater depth. Since thematic problems involve internalized schemas, the epigenetic therapist's next skill set would be schema therapy (Young *et al.* 2003). Integrating cognitive-behavioral and experiential therapies, schema therapy adds a classification system that identifies common patterns of interpersonal problems. An interpersonal or psychodynamic therapy would complete an optimal skill set with training in how to explore attachment securities and provide a corrective emotional experience. The following illustrates an EST treatment plan for Lani Kimura.

Case Illustration: Epigenetic Treatment Planning

- *Strengths. Lani*: talented musician with extensive knowledge of Hawai'ian songs; *Grandmother Kimura*: Lani's only close relationship; knowledgeable about

Hawai'ian folklore; possible resource for developing Hawai'ian elders' mentorship and support system for Lani; *Mr. Gurwich:* family patriarch; willing to set limits on Lani's behavior; *Mrs. Gurwich:* appreciates husband's position, but is supportive of Lani.

- **Biogenetic Intervention.** Medical support with a *benzodiazepine* drug is needed to help Lani withdraw from alcohol dependence. Lani may be genetically predisposed for alcohol abuse as he does not appear to have many hangover effects. He may need an aversive drug such as *disulfram* (Antabuse) to help prevent relapse; motivational interviewing to encourage Lani's continued use of this drug: and evaluation for adult attention deficit disorder in case medication or behavioral routines might help him focus better.

- **Ecosystemic Intervention.** The destabilization of Native Hawai'ian culture and Lani's lack of cultural role models other than his grandmother exacerbate his problems. One goal is to develop a network to mentor Lani in the native traditions in which he has already shown interest and support his efforts to gain steady employment. Lani's grandmother or a church with strong Hawai'ian traditions may be useful resources. Ideally, Lani will find employment as a musician in a setting that does not emphasize alcohol consumption; *e.g.,* employment opportunities for a musician steeped in Hawai'ian tradition might be found at the Polynesian Cultural Center, a major tourist attraction in Oahu affiliated with the Mormon Church.

- **Dyadic-Relational Intervention.** Two to four family sessions are recommended to reframe Lani's problems as a result of an insecure attachment after early childhood abuse and the lack of a social network to support Lani's interest in the Hawai'ian culture and help him gain appropriate employment. Lani's grandmother and aunt would be encouraged to assist him in developing this network. The family, especially Mr. Gurwich, will be encouraged to help Lani develop routines to support a more structured lifestyle, stay with his detoxification program, and explore broader aspects of Hawai'ian culture and employment opportunities. Discussion of Lani's attachment difficulties will provide an opportunity to explore the family's interest in reconnecting with his mother now that she is in a drug rehabilitation program. This will also allow Lani to explore the traumatic feelings that followed separation from his mother.

- **Personal-Agentic Intervention.** Motivational interviewing can help Lani evaluate costs of his current lifestyle, *e.g.,* possible homelessness, against the benefits of a more structured lifestyle without alcohol. Once a working alliance is established and Lani expresses optimism and intention to change, therapy will shift to ACT assessment of values, especially his interests in the Hawai'ian culture and whether he is interested in working toward employment that would support those interests. Schema therapy will address Lani's disconnection schemas and the lack of intimacy in his life. The relationship between these schemas, his early abuse, and his avoidance close relationships will be explored, especially as he shows interpersonal distancing in the therapy relationship. Lani's feelings about his mother and any possible reconciliation will be relevant here. Emotionally focused and ACT interventions will help Lani stay mindful and in contact with the present moment as he explores uncomfortable feelings, an essential step since one of his defenses is to be affably vague and distracted. Lani's self-narrative is a series of undifferentiated, unrelated, mostly unhappy incidents. Lani will be able to create a more differentiated and integrated self-narrative that will give his life the direction and continuity it currently lacks as he becomes more aware of his inner experience, its roots in his childhood, and his cultural heritage. The ultimate goal is to help Lani find employment in a valued area and to be comfortable in emotionally meaningful relationships, especially with his family and members of his newly created social network.

Integrative Conclusions

An integrated psychotherapy that eliminates the proliferation of approaches is an idea based on the scientific modernist assumption that scientific methods will eventually give an accurate picture of the human condition. However, postmodern philosophers question the possibility of such an outcome. A single model of human functioning necessarily neglects the changing contexts in which human development occurs. Postmodernists envision a constantly changing marketplace of therapeutic models in which choices among approaches are made on the basis of empirical evidence, clinical effectiveness, cost-efficiencies, and pragmatic considerations. In the absence of a singular vision, perhaps the more interesting question is how broad or how narrow should a theoretical approach be?

In a search for rigorous methods, psychological research has focused on increasingly narrow questions "… with a parallel increase in parsimonious and modest models created *ad hoc* without any conceptual connection or empirical link with each other" (L'Abate, 2009, p. 780). The lack of an integrative framework makes it difficult to apply research findings to the unique situation of an individual client, a major reason for the researcher-practitioner gap. Theories such as psychoanalysis or behaviorism continue to be important because they give practitioners this necessary framework. What is needed is a framework that integrates factors overlooked by the pioneering theories and is sufficiently well defined that its major concepts are testable.

The epigenetic systems approach is a framework for integrating integrative therapies and conceptualizing influences on human problems identified by the major therapeutic approaches. The developmental model is based on empirically supported component theories and observable processes that can be assessed empirically. Figure 15.1 illustrates how each of the factors necessary to explain human development and functioning has been a principal focus for one or more of the major therapeutic approaches. Organizing them into a hierarchy of systemic levels and suggesting how they interact provides a comprehensive framework for considering which elements are relevant for a particular client. Several empirically supported "connecting" theories describe linkages among those elements; *i.e.,* an expanded self-determination theory (Deci & Ryan, 1985) describes the motivational system, while cognitive-experiential self-theory (Epstein, 1990, 2003) links the model's subjective and objective components and connects motivation with emotional and cognitive processes.

Figure 15.2 suggests that cognitive development influences individuals at each epigenetic level, especially psychosocial development of the skills ensuring that interpersonal needs are met. The relation of neo-Piagetian developmental cognitive levels to interpersonal needs also provides an expanded view of psychosocial tasks. Failure to develop adequate psychosocial skills to meet interpersonal needs results in psychological vulnerabilities that interact with other epigenetic stressors and vulnerabilities to create symptoms and problems in living. This diathesis-stress model of problem development includes influences from each epigenetic level and incorporates attachment theory (Bowlby, 1973, 1982) and schema theory (Young *et al.,* 2003) in describing the dynamics of problems at the personal-agentic level.

Finally, Fig. 15.3 illustrates the epigenetic influences of clients and therapists on the process and content of therapy. An intersubjective stance mends ruptures of the therapeutic alliance as they occur and weights therapist and client perceptions equally. Therapists maintain a balanced dialectical tension between noting clients' objective behavior and their subjective experience. Treatment plans targeting objective aspects of client problems are balanced by attending closely to immediate client experiences as they arise in therapy. Problems are balanced with an equal focus on client strengths. Attention is given to the client's motivation, readiness to change, ability to accept directions, and functional impairment (*i.e.,* symptomatic *vs.* thematic problems). The epigenetic framework further guides treatment planning by focusing the therapist's attention first on the external levels of biogenetic, cultural-linguistic, and dyadic-relational factors that contribute to the client's problems. Only then does the therapist help client's explore how these factors are internalized at the personal-agentic level. Although expertise in a number of therapeutic systems is required to work with the full range of problems, only a subset of skills are needed to work with symptomatic problems. As therapists gain skills in emotionally focused and ACT interventions, they may begin working with thematic problems.

Postmodern philosophy suggests that there are no "ultimate" theories, only those found more or less useful in the current marketplace of ideas. The epigenetic model's primary virtue is its comprehensive nature, incorporating some of the most useful ideas from all of the major systems of psychotherapy. Although based largely on empirically supported concepts and interventions, it has not been subjected to empirical tests as an overall system. It also demands more training of therapists than other, less comprehensive approaches. Ultimately, its value will be determined in the marketplace. If it stimulates other attempts at developing more inclusive theories, it will have proved to be a useful counterweight to current trends of narrowly focused theories that intervene with narrowly defined problems.

Chapter Fifteen: Main Points

- The *epigenetic systems* approach integrates postmodern and general systems or cybernetic thinking in a hierarchical model of biogenetic, personal-agentic, dyadic-relational, and cultural-linguistic influences on the construction of meanings and actions.

- The *biogenetic* level describes the interactions of genetic, cellular, and organ systems and their influence on higher level systems to create the sensorimotor basis of action and the construction of meanings at higher levels. Psychopharmacological interventions are used.
- The *personal-agentic* level involves the interaction of cognitive, affective, and intentional systems in the individual's construction of unique meanings and actions, constrained by inputs from biogenetic and dyadic-relational levels. Postmodern, cognitive, psychodynamic, and experiential therapies intervene at this level.
- The *dyadic-relational* level reflects communication between dyadic partners as each anticipates the other's response, co-regulates the other's participation, and co-creates the meanings and actions that flow from their relationship. Because personal-agentic and bio-genetic influences on the meaning creation processes are unique to each individual, the respective meanings that evolve in a relationship are not identical, even though co-created. Behavioral, interpersonal, family, and intersubjective therapies operate at this level.
- The *cultural-linguistic* level describes how culture and language shape the meanings and actions available to individuals. Feminist therapies deconstruct cultural or linguistic meanings that limit a person's opportunities, while ecosystemic therapies intervene directly at this level.
- The epigenetic systems model implies people are in constant *flux* as constantly changing environments elicit different self-states. Dialectical constructivism helps explain personality or *stability* of self-states by suggesting that relatively stable self-narratives are co-created with significant others. Together with regularly repeated environmental situations and experiencing one's body as continuous in time, such narratives provide for relative stability in self-perceptions and in how others perceive the individual.
- Ecosystemic and family systems constitute a hierarchy of contexts in which individuals strive to have needs met. Needs for integrity, intimacy, autonomy, and competency evolved from the existential realities that every human being faces: death, isolation, groundlessness, and meaninglessness. Infant temperament interacts with responsiveness of caregivers to influence developmental processes that result in the individual's core schemas of self, others, and world view.
- Schemas reflect the recursive influence of cognitive, affective, conative (intentional), and perceptual-motor systems in determining actions that meet the individual's needs, given the opportunities and limitations available in the environmental context. This holistic process may be described either from the individual's subjective, phenomenological viewpoint or from an objective viewpoint of an observer of the individual's interpersonal relationships.
- The meaning of a situation is a dialectic construction resulting from the point of contact between subjective and objective worlds, between emotional experience and interpersonal dialogs; *i.e.*, meaning is constructed both from experience and from the narratives co-created with significant others as people reach out and meet each other's needs. Schemas reflect meanings created by recurring or emotionally significant events.
- Interpersonal schemas develop around strategies appropriate to the individual's stage of cognitive development. There are qualitative differences in both the

child's understanding of events in the world and in the form that its needs take as a function of cognitive stage. Intimacy needs develop from needs attachment for caregivers in the sensori-motor stage, from attachments with peers during preoperational play, and from attachment with a chum during the concrete operations stage. With formal operations, intimacy that recognizes the needs and perspectives of the other becomes possible. Similarly, autonomy moves from individuation, to self-awareness, to learning social roles in one's clique, to acquiring self-determination and the ability to choose among foreseeable outcomes. Competency develops from language and parental mirroring, to identification with parental strength, to social comparison and industry, and finally to generativity. A possible adult stage of dialectical operations is proposed with integrity needs of self-transcendence and spirituality.

- Schemas reflect momentary environmental or intentional activation of neurological networks. Neuronal connections are either strengthened or weakened dependent on whether a schema results in needs being met or not. Because networks can be combined in myriad ways, there are many possible interpersonal schemas. An operational self-state (an *I*) reflects one's subjective, on-going awareness in the world. A representational self-state (a *me*) occurs when people observe or think about themselves. Potential self-states not relevant to immediate needs are normally dissociated, which helps provide a unitary sense of self. However, important self-states may become defensively dissociated after a trauma, degrading the sense of an integral self and making it difficult to access those self-states. In general, the sense of a unitary, continuous self reflects of interaction of the normal dissociation of less relevant self-states and the dialectical construction of a self-narrative through interpersonal dialogs.

- Secure attachment is most likely with infants born with easy dispositions. With slow to warm up, and especially with difficult temperaments, caregiving that is responsive to the infant's needs is necessary. *Authoritarian* (structured, emotionally distant) parenting tends to produce anxious avoidant attachment (aloofness). Inconsistent (*laissez faire*), but emotionally available care tends to produce anxious resistant attachments (dependent). Inconsistent and distant (neglectful or abusive) parenting tends to produce disorganized or disoriented attachment (fearful, conflicted, odd, or dazed).

- Healthy functioning occurs if people can access self-states useful in meeting needs in most situations. If needs are blocked, schemas may develop to minimize the associated threat and compensatory schemas may be formed. If intimacy or competency needs are consistently blocked, the person may rise above the unmet need and take neurotic pride in autonomy (moving away). Blocked autonomy or competency needs may cause pride in one's capacity for intimacy through self-sacrifice for others (moving toward). Blocked intimacy or autonomy needs may result in pride in competency or superiority to others (moving against).

- Many difficulties are directly related to self-states produced by environmental stressors. As long as stressors do not activate maladaptive interpersonal schemas, difficulties are typically overcome. Professional help may be needed if a vicious circle develops with significant others and attempts to resolve a problem further impedes the ability to meet each other's needs. If neurotic or thematic schemes are elicited, then intensive therapy to modify problematic schemas with corrective emotional experiences may be required. In general, problems are a reflection of the perspective one has. A solution for one person may be a problem for another. Alternatively, short-term solutions may prove to be long-term problems.

- The EST therapist follows four principles in relating to the client and developing a treatment plan that addresses all four epigenetic levels: The principles are to 1. relate intersubjectively with clients, attending to emotional or relational markers; 2. begin by addressing biogenetic and cultural-linguistic contributions to presenting problems; 3. give equal weight to client strengths and problems; and 4. incorporate transtheoretical findings to select interventions or theoretical approaches that best match the client's problems, situation, and world view.

Further Reading

Deci, E. L., & Ryan, R. M. (1985). *Intrinsic motivation and self-determination theory in human behavior*. New York: Plenum.

Epstein, S. (2003). Cognitive-experiential self-theory of personality. In T. Millon & M. J. Lerner (Eds.), *Comprehensive handbook of psychology: Personality and social psychology* (Vol. 5, pp. 159–184). Hoboken: Wiley.

Mascolo, M. F., Craig-Bray, L., & Neimeyer, R. A. (1997). The construction of meaning and action in development and psychotherapy: An epigenetic systems approach. *Advances in Personal Construct Psychology, 4,* 3–38.

Appendices

Appendix A: Initial Interview & Treatment Planning Tools

1: <u>PERSONAL DATA FORM</u>

NAME:_____ AGE:_____ SEX:_____
        (last)   (first)   (middle)

ADDRESS:_____EDUCATION:_____
        (street; PO Box #)   (years/degree)

_____
     (city)   (state)   (zip code)

OCCUPATION:_____EMPLOYER:_____

PHONE: (WORK)_____(HOME)_____OK to ID Agency? ☐ YES ☐ NO

BEST TIMES TO PHONE:_____SCHEDULE MEETINGS:_____
      (days of week; time of day)   (days of week; time of day)

IN CASE OF EMERGENCY CONTACT:

NAME:_____PHONE:_____

ADDRESS:_____

FAMILY PHYSICIAN:_____PHONE:_____

ETHNIC HERITAGE: ☐ European ☐ Asian ☐ African ☐ Hispanic ☐ Native American
☐ Multi-ethnic/Other (please specify)_____

CITIZENSHIP:
☐ US born ☐ US naturalized ☐ Green Card ☐ Temporary Visa ☐ Undeclared status

Citizen of _____Years in US _____

ENGLISH PROFICIENCY:
☐ Native speaker ☐ Fluent ☐ Can express self ☐ Express basic ideas ☐ No English

Please identify first language:_____Other languages:_____

FAMILY INFORMATION: Names, ages, & relationship of those living at home.

_____
_____
_____
_____
_____

OTHER CLOSE FAMILY: Extended family (e.g., grandparents, etc.)_____
_____
_____

RELIGIOUS PREFERENCE (optional): ☐ Fundamental Protestant ☐ Other Protestant
☐ Catholic ☐ Jewish ☐ Islamic ☐ Agnostic ☐ Atheist ☐ Other (specify)_____

D. K. Fromme, *Systems of Psychotherapy,*
DOI 10.1007/978-1-4419-7308-5, © Springer Science+Business Media, LLC 2011

SIGNIFICANCE OF SPIRITUAL VALUES IN HOME: ☐ Central to our home ☐ Very important
☐ Uncertain and unsettled   ☐ A real conflict/problem for us   ☐ There when we need them

MILITARY EXPERIENCE: Branch:_____ Rank:_____Service

Dates:_____

Service related problems:_____
_____

LEGAL PROBLEMS: ☐ none ☐ divorce proceedings ☐ child custody ☐ misdemeanor charge
☐ felony charge ☐ on probation/parole ☐ here by court-order ☐ other (please specify problem)
_____
_____

DESCRIPTION OF CURRENT PROBLEM:
1. Reason for coming at this time (if the problem involves people other than yourself, please give
their names and relationship to you).
_____
_____
_____
_____
_____

2. PRIOR TREATMENT (Names/dates seen by previous therapists/hospitals):_____
_____
_____
_____

3a. I hope that therapy will help me: ☐ Reduce stress   ☐ Explore/Understand Problem
☐ Resolve problem ☐ Learn to live with chronic problem ☐ Personal Growth ☐ Unsure

3b. After therapy, I expect my problems to be: ☐ Completely resolved ☐ Mostly resolved
☐ Well on the way to resolution ☐ something I know how to resolve ☐ Unresolved

3c. I expect therapy to last _____ sessions: ☐ 1-5 ☐ 6-10 ☐ 11-25 ☐ 26-52 ☐ Over 52

3d. I expect the likelihood my problems will be solved in the near future is: ☐ Very good
☐ Good ☐ Uncertain ☐ Poor ☐ Very poor

RATING OF THE CURRENT PROBLEM:
1. The pain and distress caused by my problem is:
☐ very mild ☐ mild ☐ moderate ☐ severe ☐ very severe

2. The pain and distress caused for others by my problem is:
☐ very mild ☐ mild ☐ moderate ☐ severe ☐ very severe

3. My problems are caused by factors which are in the control of:
a. myself: ☐ entirely ☐ mostly ☐ partly ☐ slightly ☐ not at all
b. my spouse: ☐ entirely ☐ mostly ☐ partly ☐ slightly ☐ not at all
c. others: ☐ entirely ☐ mostly ☐ partly ☐ slightly ☐ not at all

COMMON PROBLEMS: Please rate each of the following problems, using the scale below.
This area is: Not = Not a problem for me
               Rare = Rarely a problem for me
               Some = Sometimes a problem for me
               Freq = Frequently a problem for me
               Cons = Constantly a problem for me

Not Rare Some Freq Cons
1. ☐ ☐ ☐ ☐ ☐ Thoughts of committing suicide or harming myself
2. ☐ ☐ ☐ ☐ ☐ Fears I may harm someone
3. ☐ ☐ ☐ ☐ ☐ Other intrusive thoughts, obsessions, or compulsions
4. ☐ ☐ ☐ ☐ ☐ Fears I may be losing my mind
5. ☐ ☐ ☐ ☐ ☐ Loss of appetite, especially recently
6. ☐ ☐ ☐ ☐ ☐ Major weight change
7. ☐ ☐ ☐ ☐ ☐ Vomiting
8. ☐ ☐ ☐ ☐ ☐ Waking in the middle of the night and then not sleeping
9. ☐ ☐ ☐ ☐ ☐ Difficulties getting to sleep
10. ☐ ☐ ☐ ☐ ☐ Panic Attacks
11. ☐ ☐ ☐ ☐ ☐ Physical Abuse
12. ☐ ☐ ☐ ☐ ☐ Sexual Abuse
13. ☐ ☐ ☐ ☐ ☐ Emotional Abuse
14. ☐ ☐ ☐ ☐ ☐ Recent major loss (e.g., death) for which I still grieve

PERSONAL STRENGTHS/WEAKNESSES: Please rate each of the following using the scale below.
This area is a: Maj = Major Strength for me
Mod = Moderate Strength for me
Neut = Neutral: Neither a strength nor a weakness
Mod = Moderate Weakness for me
Maj = Major Weakness for me

Strength   Weakness
Maj Mod Neut Mod Maj
1. ☐ ☐ ☐ ☐ ☐ Relationship with my spouse/significant other
2. ☐ ☐ ☐ ☐ ☐ Sexual life
3. ☐ ☐ ☐ ☐ ☐ Relationship with other family members
4. ☐ ☐ ☐ ☐ ☐ Relationship with my friends
5. ☐ ☐ ☐ ☐ ☐ Relationship with others at work/school
6. ☐ ☐ ☐ ☐ ☐ Ability to count on friends & family when I need them
7. ☐ ☐ ☐ ☐ ☐ Ability to meet people and make friends
8. ☐ ☐ ☐ ☐ ☐ Emotional stability/lack of mood swings
9. ☐ ☐ ☐ ☐ ☐ Ability to meet situations calmly, without undue worry
10. ☐ ☐ ☐ ☐ ☐ Ability to handle frustrations without losing my temper
11. ☐ ☐ ☐ ☐ ☐ Energy level and interest in things
12. ☐ ☐ ☐ ☐ ☐ Physical health and well-being
13. ☐ ☐ ☐ ☐ ☐ Physical strength
14. ☐ ☐ ☐ ☐ ☐ Self esteem/liking for myself as a person
15. ☐ ☐ ☐ ☐ ☐ Physical appearance
16. ☐ ☐ ☐ ☐ ☐ Weight
17. ☐ ☐ ☐ ☐ ☐ Competence/know how
18. ☐ ☐ ☐ ☐ ☐ Ability to think things through clearly
19. ☐ ☐ ☐ ☐ ☐ Ability to communicate clearly
20. ☐ ☐ ☐ ☐ ☐ Ability to work hard and get things done
21. ☐ ☐ ☐ ☐ ☐ Money situation
22. ☐ ☐ ☐ ☐ ☐ Ability to play, to let go and have fun
23. ☐ ☐ ☐ ☐ ☐ Sense of responsibility and commitment to others
24. ☐ ☐ ☐ ☐ ☐ Work/job outlook
25. ☐ ☐ ☐ ☐ ☐ Purpose and meaningfulness of my life
26. ☐ ☐ ☐ ☐ ☐ Independence and self-sufficiency

2: Syracuse University Suicide or No-Harm Contract
(Accessed 8.14.2006)
http://suedweb.syr.edu/chs/OnlineField/suicide/contract.htm

I, _____ agree not to kill myself, harm myself, or attempt to kill myself

for the time period beginning now _____ until _____.

I agree to come to my next appointment on _____ at _____ with _____.

I agree to get rid of things that I have thought about using to kill myself.

I agree to call the crisis numbers on the crisis card given to me today by _____
should I have the urge to kill or harm myself.

I realize that this contract is part of my therapy contract with my counselor at _____.

Signature of Client   Signature of Counselor

Date and Time

Appendix B: Therapeutic Intervention Tools

Substance Abuse and Impact on Values Worksheets

Comprehensive Substance Involvement Worksheet: Part I

Write down a history of your drug use (alcohol too, of course). On the worksheet write your age, types of drugs used, frequency of use (# of times per week, month), and how used (smoke, eat, inject, etc.). Include a section for the following substances:

1. Alcohol
2. Marijuana
3. Hallucinogens (LSD, mushrooms, peyote, etc.)
4. Depressants (Xanax, Valium, barbiturates, etc.)
5. Stimulants (speed, cocaine, ecstasy, ephedrine, etc.)
6. Inhalants (glue, gasoline, Pam, etc.)
7. Opiates (heroin, Vicodin, codeine, OxyContin, Percodan, etc.)

Begin with the first time you remember using any mood altering substance no matter how little of the substance was used. It is important that you be painstakingly thorough in the task. Use the following format:

Stimulants

Age	Quantity	How Used
12 years-15 years	Amphetamines 2-3 tablets/6-8 x per year	Oral
16 years	A few lines of cocaine/about 4 x that year	Snorted
17 years	About ¼ gram of cocaine/about e-6 x per week	Snorted/some smoked
	Etc.	

This may well seem like a long and difficult task. It is. It really is doable though. Just pick a substance and work your way through from first use to present. Take your time. If you find yourself unable to remember for one substance, or time period, switch to another and work on that for a while. Sometimes working on another area will help you remember more about the one you are having trouble with. If, in the end, you find that you simply cannot remember for certain substances or time periods, make your best estimate. Your thoroughness with this task will have an important impact on the effectiveness of your treatment.

Comprehensive Substance Involvement Worksheet: Part II

This section should be completed after completing Part I. Write down any problems or things in your life that were associated with using in each of the listed areas. If there were no consequences, write "none." However, we would encourage you to list consequences event though they may have been small. For example, you may not have been fired from a job, but you may have gone to work hung-over and been less effective in your work as a result. This need not have been ineffectiveness that others noticed. What is important is whether you see yourself as having been less effective. Number each section and keep the 11 areas separate from each other as much as possible. What we are looking for here is any cost of using. Pay special attention to places where, as a result of using (or drug seeking) you did things that violate your personal values (concealing, rationalizing, being secretive, being violent, etc.). Give *descriptions of specific events in each area.*

1. Intimate relations (wives/husbands/girlfriends/boyfriends)
2. Family (include family of origin and your own children)
3. Friends (Changing to using friends, isolating, conflict over drug use)
4. Education/training (fail to start, perform poorly, or quit school training program)
5. Occupation/employment (lost jobs, chronic unemployment)
6. Legal problems (include all arrests and their outcomes—conviction or not, incarceration, probation, parole, fines, living secretively)
7. Physical/health problems
8. Engaging in dangerous/risk taking behaviors
9. Recreation
10. Spirituality/religious practice
11. Taking advantage of treatment

(Reprinted from S.C. Hayes, & K.D. Strosahl (Eds.) *A practical guide to acceptance and commitment therapy*, pp. 160-161. By K.G. Wilson & M.R. Byrd. © 2005 Springer Science. Used with permission).

Bibliography

Abramowitz, J. (1996). Variants of exposure and response prevention in the treatment of obsessive-compulsive disorder: A meta-analysis. *Behavior Therapy, 27,* 583–600.

Achenbach, T. M. (1992). *Manual for child behavior checklist/2-3 and 1992 profile.* Burlington, VT: University of Vermont, Department of Psychiatry.

Adler, A. (1929/1964). *Social interest: A challenge to mankind.* New York: Capricorn Press.

Adler, A. (1931). *What life should mean to you.* New York: Putnam.

Ainsworth, M., Blehar, M., Waters, E., & Wall, S. (1978). *Patterns of attachment.* Hillsdale, NJ: Erlbaum.

Alexander, F., & French, T. M. (1946). *Psychoanalytic therapy.* New York: Ronald Press.

Alexander, J. F., & Parson, B. V. (1982). *Functional family therapy.* Pacific Grove, CA: Brooks/Cole.

Alford, B. A., & Beck, A. T. (1997). *The integrative power of cognitive therapy.* New York: Guilford Press.

Alloy, L., Abramson, L., Hogan, M., Whitehouse, W., Rose, D., & Robinson, M., et al. (2000). The Temple-Wisconsin cognitive vulnerability to depression project: Lifetime history of Axis I psychopathology in individuals at high and low cognitive risk of depression. *Journal of Abnormal Psychology, 109,* 403–418.

Alloy, L., Kelly, K. A., Mineka, S., & Clements, C. M. (1990). Comorbidity of anxiety and depressive disorders: A helplessness-hopelessness perspective. In J. D. Maser & C. R. Cloninger (Eds.), *Comorbidity of mood and anxiety disorders* (pp. 499–543). Washington, DC: American Psychiatric Association.

Ambady, N., & Rosenthal, R. (1993). Half a minute: Predicting teacher evaluations from thin slices of nonverbal behavior and physical attractiveness. *Journal of Personality and Social Psychology, 64,* 431–441.

American Academy of Child and Adolescent Psychiatry. (2007). Practice parameter for the assessment and treatment of children and adolescents with attention-deficit/hyperactivity disorder. *Journal of the American Academy of Child and Adolescent Psychiatry, 46,* 894–921.

American Psychiatric Association. (1980). *Diagnostic and statistical manual* (3rd ed.). Washington, DC: Author.

American Psychiatric Association. (2000). *Diagnostic and statistical manual* (4th ed., text revision). Washington, DC: Author.

American Psychological Association. (2002). Ethical principles of psychologist and code of conduct. *American Psychologist, 57,* 1060–1073.

American Psychological Association Presidential Task Force. (2006). Evidence-based practice In psychology. *American Psychologist, 61,* 271–285.

Amrhein, P. C., Miller, W. R., Yahne, C. R., Palmer, M., & Fulcher, L. (2003). Client commitment language during motivational interviewing predicts drug use outcomes. *Journal of Consulting and Clinical Psychology, 71,* 862–878.

Anchin, J. C., & Kiesler, D. J. (Eds.). (1982). *Handbook of interpersonal psychotherapy*. New York: Pergamon Press.

Anderson, H., & Goolishian, H. (1988). Human systems as linguistic systems: Preliminary and evolving ideas about the implications for clinical theory. *Family Process, 27*, 371–394.

Anderson, H., & Goolishian, H. (1992). The client is the expert: A not-knowing approach to therapy. In S. McNamee & K. J. Gergen (Eds.), *Therapy as social construction* (pp. 25–39). Newbury Park, CA: Sage.

Anderson, W. T. (1990). *Reality isn't what it used to be*. New York: Harper/Collins.

Anonymous (1972). Toward the differentiation of a self in one's own family. In J. L. Framo (Ed.), *Family interaction: A dialogue between family researchers and family therapists* (pp. 111–166). New York: Springer.

Anthony, M. M., & Swinson, R. P. (2000). *Phobic disorders and panic in adults: A guide to assessment and treatment*. Washington, DC: American Psychological Association.

Aos, S., Phipps, P., Barnoski, R., & Lieb, R. (1999). *The comparative costs and benefits of programs to reduce crime: A review of national research findings with implications for Washington State, Version 3.0*. Olympia, WA: Washington State Institute for Public Policy.

Arlin, P. K. (1975). Cognitive development in adulthood: A fifth stage. *Developmental Psychology, 11*, 602–606.

Aron, L. (1996). *A meeting of minds: Mutuality in psychoanalysis*. Hillsdale, NJ: Analytic Press.

Aron, L. (2001). Intersubjectivity in the analytic situation. In J. C. Muran (Ed.), *Self-relations in the psychotherapy process*. Washington, DC: American Psychological Association.

Asarnow, J. R., Emslie, G., Clarke, G., Wagner, K. D., Spirito, A., Vitiello, B., et al. (2009). Treatment of SSRI-resistant-depression in adolescents: Predictors and moderators of treatment response. *Journal of the American Academy of Child and Adolescent Psychiatry, 48*, 330–339.

Asay, T. P., & Lambert, M. J. (1999). The empirical case for the common factors in therapy: Quantitative findings. In M. A. Hubble, B. L. Duncan, & S. D. Miller, Scott D (Eds). *The heart and soul of change: What works in therapy*. (pp. 23–55). Washington, DC: American Psychological Association.

Asay, T. P., & Lambert, M. J. (2001). Therapist relational variables. In D. J. Cain & J. Seeman (Eds.), *Humanistic therapies: Handbook of research and practice* (pp. 531–557). Washington, DC: American Psychological Association.

Asay, T. P., Lambert, M. J., Gregerson, A. T., & Goates, M. K. (2002). Using patient-focused research in evaluating treatment outcome in private practice. *Journal of Clinical Psychology, 58*, 1213–1225.

Ayllon, T., & Azrin, N. (1968). *The token economy: A motivational system for therapy and rehabilitation*. New York: Appleton-Century-Crofts.

Bach, P., & Hayes, S. C. (2002). The use of acceptance and commitment therapy to prevent the rehospitalization of psychotic patients: A randomized controlled trial. *Journal of Consulting and Clinical Psychology, 70*, 1129–1139.

Bachelor, A. (1988). How clients perceive therapist empathy: A content analysis of "received" empathy. *Psychotherapy: Therapy, Research, and Practice, 25*, 227–240.

Baer, R. A. (2003). Mindfulness training as a clinical intervention: A conceptual and empirical review. *Clinical Psychology: Science and Practice, 10*, 125–143.

Bailey, K. D. (2006). Living systems theory and social entropy theory. *Systems Research and Behavioral Science, 22*, 291–300.

Baillargeon, R. (1993). The object concept revisited: New directions in the investigation of infant's physical knowledge. In C. E. Granrud (Ed.), *Visual cognition and perception in infancy* (pp. 265–315). Hillsdale, NJ: Erlbaum.

Bakan, D. (1966). *The duality of human existence*. Boston: Beacon Press.

Baker, E. K. (2003). *Caring for ourselves: A therapist's guide to personal and professional well-being*. Washington, DC: American Psychological Association.

Ballard, C., Hanney, M. L., Theodoulou, M., Douglas, S., McShane, R.,Kossakowski, K., et al. (2009). The dementia antipsychotic withdrawal trial (DART-AD): A long-term follow-up of a randomised placebo-controlled trial. *Lancet Neurology, 8*, 151–157.

Bandura, A. (1965a). Influence of models' reinforcement contingencies on the acquisition of imitative responses. *Journal of Personality and Social Psychology, 1,* 589–595.

Bandura, A. (1965b). Vicarious processes: A case of no-trial learning. In L. Berkowitz (Ed.), *Advances in experimental and social psychology* (Vol. 2, pp. 49–91). New York: Academic Press.

Bandura, A. (1986). *Social foundations of thought and action: A social-cognitive theory.* Englewood-Cliffs, NJ: Prentice-Hall.

Bandura, A. (1997). *Self-efficacy: The exercise of control.* New York: Freeman.

Barlow, D. H. (Ed.). (2007). *Clinical handbook of psychological disorders: A step-by-step treatment manual.* New York: Guilford Press.

Barlow, D. H., & Craske, M. G. (2000). *Mastery of your anxiety and Panic (MAP-3).* Boulder, CO: Graywind.

Barrett, L. F., & Salovey, P. (Eds.). (2002). *The wisdom in feeling: Psychological in emotional intelligence.* New York: Guilford Press.

Bartholomew, K. (1990). Avoidance of intimacy: An attachment perspective. *Journal of Social and Personal Relationships, 7,* 147–178.

Bartlett, F. C. (1932). *Remembering.* Cambridge: Cambridge University Press.

Basseches, M. (1984). *Dialectical thinking.* Norwood, NJ: Ablex.

Bateson, G. (1972). *Steps toward and ecology of the mind.* New York: Dutton.

Beavers, W. R. (1982). Healthy, midrange and severely dysfunctional families. In F. Walsh (Ed.), *Normal family processes* (pp. 45–66). New York: Guilford Press.

Beck, A. T. (1963). Thinking and depression: I. Idiosyncratic content and cognitive distortions. *Archives of General Psychiatry, 9,* 324–333.

Beck, A. T. (1967). *Depression: Clinical, experimental, and theoretical aspects.* New York: Harper & Row.

Beck, A. T., & Beck, J. S. (2005). *Cognitive therapy for challenging problems: What to do when the basics don't work.* New York: Guilford Press.

Beck, A. T., Emery, G., & Greenberg, R. L. (1985). *Anxiety disorders and phobias: A cognitive perspective.* New York: Basic Books.

Beck, A. T., Epstein, N., Brown, B., & Steer, R. (1988). An inventory for measuring clinical anxiety. *Journal of Consulting and Clinical Psychology, 56,* 893–397.

Beck, A. T., & Freeman, A. (1990). *Cognitive therapy of personality disorders.* New York: Guilford Press.

Beck, A. T., Rush, A., Shaw, B., & Emery, G. (1979). *Cognitive therapy of depression.* New York: Guilford Press.

Beck, A. T., Steer, R. A., & Brown, G. (1996). *Manual for beck depression inventory—II.* San Antonio, TX: Psychological Corporation.

Beck, A. T., Weissman, S., Lester, D., & Trexler, L. (1974). The measurement of pessimism: The hopelessness scale. *Journal of Counseling and Clinical Psychology, 42,* 861–865.

Bedi, R. A. (2001). Prescriptive psychotherapy: Alternatives to diagnosis. *Journal of Psychotherapy in Independent Practice, 2,* 39–60.

Beier, E. G. (1966). *The silent language of psychotherapy: The social reinforcement of unconscious processes.* Chicago: Aldine.

Beier, E. G., & Young, D. M. (1998). *The silent language of psychotherapy: Social reinforcement of unconscious processes* (3rd ed.). Edison, NJ: Aldine Transaction Press.

Beitman, B. D. (1987). *The structure of individual psychotherapy.* New York: Guilford Press.

Beitman, B. D., Soth, A. M., & Bumby, N. A. (2005). The future as an integrating force through the schools of psychotherapy. In J. C. Norcross & M. R. Goldfried (Eds.), *Handbook of psychotherapy integration* (2nd ed., pp. 65–83). New York: Oxford University Press.

Bellack, A. S., & Hersen, M. (Eds.). (1985). *Dictionary of behavior therapy techniques.* New York: Peragamon Press.

Belle, S. H., Burgio, L., Burns, R., Coon, D., Czaja, S. J., Gallagher-Thompson, D., et al. (2006). Enhancing the quality of life of dementia caregivers from different ethnic or racial groups: A randomized, controlled trial. *Annals of Internal Medicine, 145,* 727–738

Bem, D. J. (1972). Self-perception theory. In L. Berkowitz (Ed.), *Advances in experimental social psychology* (Vol. 6, pp. 1–62). New York: Academic Press.

Benjamin, J. (1988). *The bonds of love*. New York: Pantheon.

Benjamin, L. S. (1974). Structural analysis of social behavior. *Psychological Review, 81*, 392–425.

Benjamin, L. S. (1978). Structural analysis of differentiation failure. *Psychiatry: Journal for the Study of Interpersonal Process, 42*, 1–23.

Benjamin, L. S. (1996). *Interpersonal diagnosis and treatment of personality disorders* (2nd ed.). New York: Guilford Press.

Benjamin, L. S. (2006). *Interpersonal reconstructive therapy: Promoting change in nonresponders*. New York: Guilford Press.

Bennet, T. L., Davalos, D. B., Green, M., & Rial, D. (Eds.). (1999). Addressing executive functioning and cognitive rehabilitation in the treatment of schizophrenia. *Rehabilitation Psychology, 44*, 403–410.

Berlyne, D. E. (1960). *Conflict, arousal, and curiosity*. New York: McGraw-Hill.

Bernard, M. M., Gebauer, J. E., & Maio, G. R. (2006). Cultural estrangement: The role of personal and societal value discrepancies. *Personality and Social Psychology Bulletin, 32*, 78–92.

Bernstein, R. J. (1992). *The new constellation: The ethical-political horizons of modernity/postmodernity*. Cambridge, MA: MIT Press.

Beutler, L. E. (1983). *Eclectic psychotherapy: A systematic approach*. New York: Pergamon.

Beutler, L. E. (2000). *Empirically based decision making in clinical practice. Prevention & Treatment, 3*(1), Article 27, Retrieved September 1, 2000, from http://www.apa.org

Beutler, L. E. (2006). Personal communication, May 6th.

Beutler, L. E., & Clarkin, J. F. (1990). *Systematic treatment selection: Toward targeted therapeutic Interventions*. New York: Brunner/Mazel Publishers.

Beutler, L. E., Consoli, A. J., & Lane, G. (2005). Systematic treatment selection and prescriptive psychotherapy. In J. C. Norcross & M. R. Goldfried (Eds.), *Handbook of psychotherapy integration* (2nd ed., pp. 121–146). New York: Oxford University Press.

Beutler, L. E., Consoli, A. J., & Williams, R. E. (1995). Integrative and eclectic therapies in practice. In B. Bongar & L. E. Beutler (Eds.), *Comprehensive textbook of psychotherapy: Theory and practice* (chap. 15, pp. 274–292). New York: Oxford Press.

Biederman, J. (Ed.). (2004). Diagnosing and treating ADHD in adults. *Journal of Clinical Psychiatry, 65*(Suppl. 3), 3–44.

Biglan, A., & Hayes, S. C. (1996). Should the behavioral sciences become more pragmatic? The case for functional contextualism in research on human behavior. *Applied and Preventive Psychology: Current Scientific Perspectives, 5*, 47–57.

Binswanger, L. (1963). *Being-in-the-world: Selected papers of Ludwig Binswanger*. New York: Basic Books.

Bion, W. (1962). *Learning from experience*. London: Heinemann.

Black On Black Crime Coalition. (2009). *Black on black crime statistics*. Retrieved July 31, 2009, from http://www.hhscenter.org/bonbstat.html

Bregnhøj, L., Thirstrup, S., Kristensen, M. B., Bjerrum, L., & Sonne, J. (2007). Prevalence of inappropriate prescribing in primary care. *Pharmacy World and Science, 29*, 109–115.

Boekaerts, M., Pintrich, P. R., & Zeidner, M. (Eds.). (2005). *Handbook of self-regulation*. San Diego, CA: Academic Press.

Bordin, E. (1994). Theory and research in the therapeutic working alliance: New directions. In A. O. Horvath & L. S. Greenberg (Eds.), *The working alliance: Theory, research and practice* (pp. 13–37). New york: Wiley

Borduin, C. M., Schaeffer, C. M., & Heiblum, N. (2009). A randomized clinical trial of Multisystemic Therapy with juvenile sexual offenders: Effects on youth social ecology and criminal activity. *Journal of Consulting and Clinical Psychology, 77*, 26–37.

Borkovec, T. D., & Newman, M. G. (1998). Worry and generalized anxiety disorder. In A. S. Bellack & M. Hersen (Series Eds.) & P. Salkovskis (Vol. Ed.), *Comprehensive clinical psychology: Clinical formulation and treatment* (Vol. 6, pp. 439–459). Oxford, UK: Elsevier Science.

Boss, M. (1984). *Existential foundations of medicine and psychology*. New York: Jason Aronson.

Bowen, M. (1978). *Family therapy in clinical practice*. New York: Jason Aronson.

Bower, G. H. (1983). Affect and cognition. *Philosophical Transactions: Royal Society of London, Series B, 302,* 387–492.

Bowlby, J. (1973). *Attachment and loss: Vol. II. Separation: Anxiety, and anger*. New York: Basic Books.

Bowlby, J. (1982). *Attachment and loss: Vol. 1. Attachment* (2nd ed.). New York: Basic Books.

Boyd-Franklin, N. (1983). Black family life styles: A lesson in survival. In A. Swerdlow & H. Lessinger (Eds.), *Class, race, and sex: The dynamics of control*. Boston: G.K. Hall (with Barnard College Women's Center).

Bozarth, J. D., Simring, F. M., & Tausch, R. (2001). Client-centered therapy: The evolution of a revolution. In D. J. Cain & J. Seeman (Eds.), *Humanistic Psychotherapies: Handbook of research and practice* (pp. 147–188). Washington, DC: American Psychological Association.

Bozarth, M. A., & Wise, R. A. (1984). Anatomically distinct opiate receptor fields mediate reward and physical dependence. *Science, 224,* 501–511.

Bracy, O. L. (1986). Cognitive rehabilitation: A process approach. *Cognitive rehabilitation, 4,* 10–17.

Brehm, J. W. (1966). *A theory of psychological reactance*. New York: Academic Press.

Breuer, J., & Freud, S. (1893–1895/1955). Studies on hysteria. In J. Strachey (Ed. & Trans.), *The standard edition of the complete psychological works of Sigmund Freud* (Vol. 2). London: Hogarth.

Bromberg, P. M. (1993). Shadow and substance: A relational perspective on clinical process. *Psychoanalytical Psychology, 10,* 147–168.

Bronfenbrenner, U. (1979). *The ecology of human development*. Cambridge, MA: Harvard University Press.

Brown, L. S. (2008) *Cultural competence in traua therapy: Beyond the flashback*. Washington, DC: American Psychological Association Press.

Buber, M. (1976). *I and thou* (W. Kaufman & S. G. Smith, Trans.). New York: Simon & Schuster.

Bucher, B., & Lovaas, O. I. (1968). Use of aversive stimulation in behavior modification. In M. R. Jones (Ed.), *Miami symposium on the prediction of behavior, 1967: Aversive stimulation* (pp. 77–145). Coral Gables, FL: University of Miami Press.

Büchner, L. (1855/2007). Force and matter or principles of the natural order of the universe: With a system of morality based thereon. Whitefish, MT: Kessinger Publications

Bugental, J. F. T. (1999). *Psychotherapy isn't what you think: Bringing the psychotherapeutic engagement into the living moment*. Phoenix, AZ: Zeig, Tucker, & Theisen, Inc.

Buhler, A. (2004). Screening for alcohol-related problems in the general population using CAGE and DSM-IV: Characteristics of congruently and incongruently identified participants. *Addictive Behaviors, 29,* 867–878.

Bulik, C. M., Sullivan, P. F., Carter, F. A., McIntosh, V. V., & Joyce, P. R. (1998). The role of exposure with response prevention in the cognitive-behavioural therapy for bulimia nervosa. *Psychological Medicine, 28,* 611–623.

Burke, B. L., Arkowitz, H., & Menchola, M. (2003). The efficacy of motivational interviewing: A meta-analysis of controlled clinical trials. *Journal of Consulting and Clinical Psychology, 71,* 843–861.

Campbell, M. L. C., & Morrison, A. P. (2007). The relationship between bullying, psychotic-like experiences and appraisals in 14–16-year olds. *Behaviour Research and Therapy, 45,* 1579–1591.

Camus, A. (1955). *The myth of Sisyphus and other essays*. New York: A.A. Knopf.

Cantor, N., & Mischel, W. (1977). Traits as prototypes: Effects on recognition memory. *Journal of Personality and Social Psychology, 35,* 38–48.

Caplan, T. (2005). First Impressions: Treatment considerations from first contact with a groupworker to first group experience. *Groupwork, 15,* 44–57.

Cardemil, E. V., & Battle, C. (2003). Guess who's coming to therapy? Getting comfortable with conversations about race and ethnicity in psychotherapy. *Professional Psychology: Research and Practice, 34,* 278–286.

Card, O. S. (1990). *Maps in a mirror*. New York: Tor Books—Tom Doherty Associates

Carrera, M. R., Ashley, J. A., Parsons, L. H., Wirsching, P., Koob, G. F., & Janda, K. D. (1995). Suppression of psychoactive effects of cocaine by active immunization. *Nature, 378,* 727–730.

Carson, R. C. (1969). *Interaction concepts of personality.* Chicago: Aldine.

Carson, R. C. (1982). Self-fulfilling prophecy, maladaptive behavior, and psychotherapy. In J. C. Anchin & D. J. Kiesler (Eds.), *Handbook of interpersonal psychotherapy* (pp. 64–77). New York: Pergamon Press.

Carter, B., & McGoldrick, M. (2005). The expanded family life cycle: Individual, social, and family perspectives (3rd ed.). Boston: Allyn & Bacon.

Carver, C., & Scheier, M. F. (2000). On the structure of behavioral self-regulation. In M. Boekaerts, P. R. Pintrich, & M. Zeidner (Eds.), *Handbook of self-regulation* (pp. 41–84). San Diego, CA: Academic Press.

Cassidy, J., & Mohr, J. J. (2001). Unsolvable fear, trauma, and psychopathology: Theory, research, and clinical considerations related to disorganized attachment across the life span. *Clinical Psychology: Science and Practice, 8,* 275–298.

Cassidy, J., & Shaver, P. R. (Eds.). (1999). *Handbook of attachment: Theory, research, and clinical applications.* New York: Guilford Press.

Cautela, J. R., & Kearney, A. J. (Eds.). (1993). *Covert conditioning casebook.* Belmont, CA: Brooks/Cole.

Center for Disease Control. (2007). Percentage of adults who where current, former or never smokers, overall and by sex, race, Hispanic origin, age, education and poverty status. Retrieved June 21, 2008, from http://www.cdc.gov/tobacco/data_statistics/tables/adult/table_2/htm

Chambless, D. L. (1998). Empirically validated treatments. In G. P. Koocher, J. C. Norcross, & S. S. Hill (Eds.), *Psychologist's desk reference* (pp. 209–218). New York: Oxford University Press.

Chambless, D. L., & Hollon, S. D. (1998). Defining empirically supported therapies. *Journal of Consulting and Clinical Psychology, 66,* 7–18.

Cheung, A. H., Zuckerbrot, R. A., Jensen, P. S., Ghalib, K., Laraque, D., & Stein. R. E., GLAD-PC Steering Group. (2007). Guidelines for adolescent depression in primary care (GLAD-PC): II. Treatment and ongoing management. *Pediatrics, 120,* 1313–1326.

Chirkov, V. I., Ryan, R. M., Kim, Y., & Kaplan, U. (2003). Differentiating autonomy from individualism and independence: A self-determination theory perspective on internalization of cultural orientations and well-being. *Journal of Personality & Social Psychology, 84,* 97–109.

Clark, D. A., & Beck, A. T. (1991). Personality factors in dysphoria: A psychometric refinement of Beck's, Sociotropy-Autonomy Scale. *Journal of psychopathology and Behavioral Assessment, 13,* 369–388.

Clarke, D. D. (2007). *They can't find anything wrong! : 7 keys to understanding, treating, and healing stress illness.* Boulder, CO: Sentient Publications.

Cohen, J. (1962). The statistical power of abnormal-social psychological research: A review. *Journal of Abnormal and Social Psychology, 65,* 145–153.

Cohen, J. (1977). *Statistical power analysis for the behavioral sciences* (2nd ed.). New York: Academic Press.

Commons, M. L., & Richards, F. A. (2003). Four postformal stages. In J. Demick & C. Andreoletti (Eds.), *Handbook of adult development.* New York: Plenum.

Cooley, C. H. (1909). *Social organization.* New York: Scribner's Sons.

Costello, E. J., Copeland, W., Cowell, A., & Keeler, G. (2007). Service costs of caring for adolescents with mental illness in a rural community, 1993–2000. *American Journal of Psychiatry, 164,* 36–42.

Craske, M. G., & Barlow, D. J. (2001). Panic disorder and agoraphobia. In D. H. Barlow (Ed.), *Clinical handbook of psychological disorders* (3rd ed., pp.1–59). New York: Guilford.

Cross, S. E., & Markus, H. (1994). Self-schemas, possible selves, and competent performance. *Journal of Educational Psychology, 86,* 423–438.

Crowell, S. E., Beauchaine, T. P., & Linehan, M. M. (2009). A biosocial developmental model of borderline personality: Elaborating and extending Linehan's theory. *Psychological Bulletin, 135,* 495–510.

Crowe, M., & Luty, S. (2005). The process of change in Interpersonal Psychotherapy (IPT) for depression: A case study for the new IPT therapist. *Psychiatry, 68*, 43–54.

Cox, B. J., Endler, N. S., Lee, P. S., & Swinson, R. P. (1992). A meta-analysis of treatments for panic disorder with agoraphobia: Imipramine, alprazolam, and in vivo exposure. *Journal of Behavior Therapy and Experimental Psychiatry, 23*, 175–182.

Csikszentmihalyi, M. (1996). *Creativity: Flow and the psychology of discovery and invention.* New York: Harper Collins.

Cunningham, C. E., Bremner, R., & Boyle, M. (1995). Large group community-based parenting programs for families of preschoolers at risk for disruptive behaviour disorders: Utilization, cost effectiveness, and outcome. *Journal of Child Psychology and Psychiatry, 36*, 1141–1159.

Curtis, R. C., & Hirsch, I. (2003). Relational approaches to psychoanalytic psychotherapy. In A. S. Gurman & S. B. Messer (Eds.), *Essential psychotherapies: Theory and practice* (2nd ed., pp. 69–106). New York: Guilford Press.

Dale, G. (2008). The single practitioner and community engagement: Bridging the gap between practice and social action. *American Psychologist, 63*, 791–797.

Darley, J. M., Fleming, J. H., Hilton, L. L., & Swann, W. B. (1988). Dispelling negative expectancies: The impact of interaction goals and target characteristics on the expectancy confirmation process. *Journal of Experimental Social Psychology, 24*, 19–36.

Davidson, P. R., & Parker, K. C. H. (2001). Eye Movement Desensitzation and Repreocessing (EMDR): A meta-analysis. *Journal of Consulting and Clinical Psychology, 69*, 305–316.

Deci, E. L., Koestner, R., & Ryan, R. M. (1999). A meta-analytic review of experiments examining the effects of extrinsic rewards on intrinsic motivation. *Psychological Bulletin, 125*, 627–668.

Deci, E. L., & Ryan, R. M. (1985). *Intrinsic motivation and self-determination theory in human behavior.* New York: Plenum.

Deci, E. L., & Ryan, R. M. (1991). A motivational approach to self: Integration in personality. In R. Dienstbier (Ed.), *Nebraska Symposium on Motivation: Vol. 38. Perspectives on motivation* (pp. 237–288). Lincoln: University of Nebraska Press.

Deci, E. L., & Ryan, R. M. (2000). The "what" and "why" of goal pursuits: Human needs and the self-determination of behavior. *Psychological Inquiry, 11*, 319–338.

De Gucht, V., & Heiser, W. (2003). Alexithymia and somatization: A quantitative review of the literature. *Journal of Psychosomatic Research, 54*, 425–434.

de Koning, P., & de Kwant, A. (2002). Dutch drug policy and the role of social workers. In S. L. A. Straussner & L. Harrison (Eds.), *International aspects of social work practice in the addictions* (pp. 49–68). Binghamton, NY: Haworth Social Work Practice Press.

Dennett, D. C. (2003). *Freedom evolves.* New York: Viking Press.

Derogatis, L. R. (1994). *The SCL-90-R: Administration, scoring, and procedures manual* (3rd ed.) Minneapolis, MN: National Computer Systems.

DeRubeis, R. J., & Crits-Christoph, P. (1998). Empirically supported individual and group psychological treatments for adult mental disorders. *Journal of Consulting and Clinical Psychology, 66*, 37–52.

DeRubeis, R. J., Tang, T. Z., & Beck, A. T. (2001). Cognitive therapy. In K. S. Dobson (Ed.), *Handbook of cognitive-behavioral therapies* (2nd ed., pp. 349–392). New York: Guilford Press.

DeShazer, S. (1991). *Putting difference to work.* New York: Norton.

DeShazer, S. (1994). *Words were originally magic.* New York: Norton.

Diamond, G. S., & Stern, R. S. (2006). Attachment-based family therapy for depressed adolescents. In S. M. Johnson & V. E. Whiffen (Eds.), *Attachment processes in couple and family therapy* (pp. 191–212). New York: Guilford Press.

DiClemente, C. C. (2003). *Addiction and change: How addictions develop and addicted people recover.* New York: Guilford.

Dinkmeyer, D. Sr., McKay, G. D., & Dinkmeyer, D. Jr. (1997). *The parent's handbook.* Circle Pines, MN: American Guidance Service.

Dobson, K. S., & Khatri, N. (2000). Cognitive therapy: Looking backward, looking forward. *Journal of Clinical Psychology, 56*, 907–923.

Dollard, J., & Miller, N. E. (1950). *Personality and psychotherapy: An analysis in terms of learning, thinking, and culture*. New York: McGraw-Hill.

Donnelly, J. (1984). Cultural relativism and universal human rights. *Human Rights Quarterly, 6,* 400–419.

Downing, J. N. (2004). Psychotherapy practice in a pluralistic world: Philosophical and moral dilemmas. *Journal of Psychotherapy Integration, 14,* 123–148.

Dreikurs, R. (1958). *The challenge of parenthood* (Rev. ed.). New York: Duell, Sloan, & Pearce.

Dreikurs, R. (1968). *Psychology in the classroom: A manual for teachers* (2nd ed.). New York: Harper & Row.

Duggan, E. S., & Brennan, K. A. (1994). Social avoidance and its relation to Barholomew's adult attachment typology. *Journal of Social and Personal Relations, 11,* 147–153.

Duman, R. S., Heninger, G. R., & Nestler, E. J. (1997). A molecular and cellular theory of depression. *Archives of General Psychiatry, 54,* 597–606.

Duncan, B. L., Miller, S. D., & Wampold, B. (Eds.). (2009). *The heart and soul of change* (2nd ed.). Washington, DC: American Psychological Association.

Durant, W. (1957). *The reformation*. New York: Simon and Schuster.

Duvall, E. (1977). *Marriage and family development*. (5th ed.). Philadelphia: Lippincott.

Eels, T. D. (Ed.). (1997). *Handbook of psychotherapy case formulation*. New York: Guilford Press.

Eich, E. (1995). Searching for mood-dependent memory. *Psychological Science, 6,* 67–75.

Elieson, M. V., & Rubin, L. J. (2001). Differentiation of self and major depressive disorders: A test of Bowen theory among clinical, tradition, and internet groups. *Family Therapy, 29,* 125–142.

Elkins, I., Shea, M. T., Watkins, J. T., Imber, S. D., Sotsky, S. M., Collins, J. F., et al. (1989). National Institute of Mental Health Treatment of Depression Collaborative Research Program: General effects of treatments. *Archives of General Psychiatry, 46,* 971–982.

Elliott, R. (2001). The effectiveness of humanistic therapies: A meta-analysis. In D. J. Cain & J. Seeman (Eds.), *Humanistic therapies: Handbook of research and practice* (chap. 2, pp. 57–81). Washington, DC: American Psychological Association.

Elliott, R., & Greenberg, L. S. (1997). Multiple voices in process-experiential therapy: Dialogues between aspects of the self. *Journal of Psychotherapy Integration, 7,* 225–239.

Elliott, R., & Greenberg, L. S. (2002). Process-experiential psychotherapy. In D. J. Cain & J. Seeman (Eds.), *Humanistic psychotherapies: Handbook of research and practice* (pp. 279–306). Washington, DC: American Psychological Association.

Elliott, R., Greenberg, L. S., & Lietauer, G. (2004). Research on experiential psychotherapies. In M. J. Lambert (Ed.), *Bergin and Garfield's handbook of psychotherapy and behavior change* (5th ed., pp. 493–539). New York: Wiley.

Elliott, R., Watson, J. C., Goldman, R. N., & Greenberg, L. S. (2004). *Learning emotion-focused therapy*. New York: Guilford Press.

Ellis, A. (1962). *Reason and emotion in psychotherapy*. New York: Stuart.

Ellis, A. (1972). Rational-emotive therapy. In R. Jurjevich (Ed.), *Direct psychotherapy: 28 American originals* (Vol. 1). Coral Gables, FL: University of Miami Press.

Ellis, A. (1990). Is rational-emotive therapy (RET) "rationalist" or "constructivist"? In A. Ellis & W. Dryden (Eds.), *The essential Albert Ellis* (pp. 114–141). New York: Springer.

Ellis, A. (1991). The revised ABC's of rational-emotive therapy. *Journal of Rational-Emotive and Cognitive-Behavior Therapy, 9,* 139–172.

Ellis, A. (1995). *Better, deeper, and more enduring brief therapy*. New York: Brunnel/Mazel.

Ellis, A. (1999). *How to make yourself happy and remarkably less disturbable*. San Luis Obispo, CA: Impact.

Ellis, A. (2003). Early theories and practices of rational emotive behavior theory and how they have been augmented and revised during the last three decades. *Journal of Rational-Emotive & Cognitive-Behavior Therapy, 21,* 219–243.

Emmelkamp, P. M. G., Krijn, M., Hulsbosch, A. M., deVries, S., Schuemie, M. J., & Van Der Mast, C. A. P. G. (2002). Virtual reality treatment versus exposure in vivo: A comparative evaluation in acrophobia. *Behavior Research and Therapy, 40,* 509–516.

Emslie, G. J., Rush, A. J., Weinberg, W. A., Kowatch, R. A., Hughes, C. W., Carmody, T., et al. (1997). A double-blind, randomized, placebo-controlled trial of fluoxetine in children and adolescents with depression. *Archives of General Psychiatry, 54,* 1031–1037.

Enns, C. Z. (2004). *Feminist theories and feminist psychotherapies: Origins, themes, and diversity* (2nd ed.). New York: Haworth.

Epstein, S. (1990). Cognitive-experiential self-theory. In L. Perviin (Ed.), *Handbook of personality theory and research: Theory and research* (pp. 165–192). New York: Guilford Press.

Epstein, S. (2003). Cognitive-experiential self-theory of personality. In T. Millon & M. J. Lerner (Eds.), *Comprehensive handbook of psychology: Personality and social psychology* (Vol. 5, pp. 159–184). Hoboken, NJ: Wiley.

Epston, D. (1994). Extending the conversation. *The Family Therapy Networker, 18,* 30–37, 62–63.

Erdelyi, M. H. (1988). Repression, reconstruction, and defense: History, and integration of the psychoanalytic and experimental frameworks. In J. Singer (Ed.), *Repression: Defense mechanism and cognitive style* (pp. 1–31). Chicago: University of Chicago press.

Erikson, E. H. (1950). *Childhood and Society.* New York: Norton.

Erikson, E. H. (1964). *Insight and responsibility.* New York: Norton.

Erikson, E. H. (1968). *Identity: Youth and crisis.* New York: Norton.

Erikson, E. H. (1977). *Toys and reason.* New York: Norton.

Erikson, E. H. (1978). *Adulthood.* New York: Norton.

Ernst, M., Zametkin, A. J., Matochik, J. A., Jons, P. H., & Cohen, R. M. (1998). DOPA decarboxylase activity in attention-deficit/hyperactivity disorder adults: A [flourine-18]flourodopa positron emission tomographic study. *Journal of Neuroscience, 18,* 5901–5907.

Eron, J. B., & Lund, T. W. (1996). *Narrative solutions in brief therapy.* New York: Guilford Press.

Evans, P. D., & Edgerton, N. (1990). Life events as predictors of the common cold. *British Journal of Medical Psychology, 64,* 35–44.

Fairbairn, W. R. D. (1952). *Psychoanalytic studies of the personality.* London: Tavistock.

Falicov, C. J. (2002). Immigrant family processes. In F. Walsh (Ed.), *Normal family processes: Growing diversity and complexity* (3rd ed., pp. 280–300). New York: Guilford Press.

Falicov, C. J. (2005). Mexican families. In M. McGoldrick, J. Giordano, & N. Garcia-Preto (Eds.), *Ethnicity & family therapy* (3rd ed., pp. 229–241). New York: Guilford Press.

Fancher, R. E. (1973). *Psychoanalytic thought: The development of Freud's thought.* New York: W.W. Norton

Farber, L. (1966). *The ways of the will.* New York: Basic Books.

Feldman, L. B., & Feldman, S. L. (2005). Integrating therapeutic modalities. In J. C. Norcross & M. R. Goldfried (Eds.), *Handbook of psychotherapy integration* (2nd ed., pp. 362–381). New York: Oxford University Press.

Fenton, L. R., Cecero, J. J., Nich, C., Frankforter, T. L., & Carroll, K. M. (2001). Perspective is everything: The predictive validity working alliance instruments. *Journal of Psychotherapy Practice & Research, 10,* 262–268.

Ferenczi, S. (1952). *Selected papers of Sandor Ferenczi.* New York: Basic Books.

Festinger, L. (1957). *A theory of cognitive dissonance.* Evanston, IL: Row, Peterson.

Fick, D. M., Cooper, J. W., Wade, W. E., Waller, J. L., Maclean, J. R., &. Beers, M. H. (2003). Updating the Beers criteria for potentially inappropriate medication use in older adults. *Archives of Internal Medicine, 163,* 2716–2725.

First, M. B., Spitzer, R. L., Gibbon, M., & Williams, J. B. W. (1996). *Structured Clinical Interview for Axis I DSM-IV Disorders Research Version—Patient Edition* (SCID-I/P, ver. 2.0). New York: New York State Psychiatric Institute, Biometrics Research Department.

Fischetti, M., Curran, J. P., & Wessberg, H. W. (1977). Sense of timing. *Behavior Modification, 1,* 179–194.

Florida Department of Law Enforcement. (2008). Drugs identified in deceased persons by Florida medical examiners. Retrieved June 23, 2008, from http://www.fdle.state.fl.us/publications/examiners/2007drugreport.pdf

Foa, E. B., & Meadows, E. A. (1997). Psychosocial treatments for post-traumatic stress disorder: A critical review. In J. Spence (Ed.), *Annual review of psychology* (Vol. 48, pp. 449–480). Palo Alto, CA: Annual Review.

Fogel, A. (1993). Developing through relationships. Origins of communication, self, and culture. Chicago: University of Chicago Press.

Fonagy, P., Steele, M., Steele, H., Leigh, T., Kennedy, R., Mattoon, G., et al. (1995). Attachment, the reflective self, and borderline states: The predictive specificity of the Adult Attachment Interview and pathological emotional development. In S. Goldberg, R. Muir, & J. Kerr (Eds.), *Attachment theory: Social, developmental, and clinical perspectives* (pp. 233–278). Hillsdale, NJ: Analytic Press.

Foucault, M. (1967). *Madness and civilization*. London: Tavistock.

Frank, J. B., Weihs, K., Minerva, E., & Lieberman, D. Z. (1998). Women's mental health in primary care. Depression, anxiety, somatization, eating disorders, and substance abuse. *Medical Clinics of North America, 82,* 359–389.

Frank, J. D., & Frank, J. B. (1991). *Persuasion and healing* (3rd ed.). Baltimore: Johns Hopkins University Press.

Frankl, V. E. (1963). *Man's search for meaning*. New York: Simon and Schuster.

Freud, A. (1936/1966). The ego and mechanisms of defense (Rev. ed.). *The writings of Anna Freud* (Vol. 2). New York: International Universities Press.

Freud, A. (1965). Normality and pathology in childhood. *The writings of Anna Freud* (Vol. 4). New York: International Universities Press.

Freud, S. (1917/1957). Mourning and melancholia. In J. Strachey (Ed.), *The standard edition of the complete psychological works of Sigmund Freud* (Vol. 14, pp. 240–263). London: Hogarth Press.

Freud, S. (1923/1961). The ego and the id. In J. Strachey (Ed.), *The standard edition of the complete psychological works of Sigmund Freud* (Vol. 19, pp. 3–68). London: Hogarth Press.

Freud, S. (1924/1953). *A general introduction to psychoanalysis*. New York: Permabooks.

Freud, S. (1933). *New introductory lectures on psychoanalysis*. New York: Norton.

Freud, S. (1933/1964). The dissection of the psychical personality. In J. Strachey (Ed.), *The standard edition of the complete psychological works of Sigmund Freud* (Vol. 22, pp. 57–81). London: Hogarth Press.

Freud, S. (1938). The history of the psychoanalytic movement. *The basic writings of Sigmund Freud*. New York: Modern Library, Random House.

Freud, S. (1954). The origin of psychoanalysis: Letters of Sigmund Freud to Wilhelm Fliess, drafts and notes, 1887–1902. In M. Bonaparte, A. Freud, & E. Kris (Eds.), *The life and work of Sigmund Freud* (Vols. 1–3). New York: Basic Books.

Freyd, J. J. (1996). *Betrayal trauma: The logic of forgetting abuse*. Cambridge, MA: Harvard University Press.

Friedrich, C. J. (Ed.). (1954). *The philosophy of Georg Wilhelm Hegel*. New York: Modern Library.

Fromm, E. (1941). *Escape from freedom*. New York: Avon.

Fromm. E. (1955). *The sane society*. New York: Holt, Rinehart, & Winston.

Fromm, E. (1956). *The art of loving*. New York: HarperCollins.

Fromm, E. (1964). *The heart of man*. New York: Halpern Row.

Fromme, D. K., & O'Brien, C. S. (1982). A dimensional approach to the circular ordering of the emotions. *Motivation and Emotion, 6,* 337–363.

Froyd, J., & Lambert, M. J. (1989). *A survey of outcome research measures in psychotherapy research*. Paper presented at the meeting of the Western Psychological Association, Reno, NV.

Fruzzetti, A. R., & Fruzzetti, A. E. (2003). Dialectics in cognitive and behavior therapy. In W. O'Donohue, J. E. Fisher, & S. C. Hayes (Eds.), *Cognitive behavior therapy: Applying empirically supported techniques in your practice* (chap. 21, pp. 121–128). Hoboken, NJ: Wiley.

Fruzzetti, A. E., & Levensky, E. R. (2000). Dialectical behavior therapy for domestic violence: Rationale and procedures. *Cognitive and Behavioral Practice, 7,* 435–447.

Gale, J. E. (1991). *Conversation analysis of therapeutic discourse: The pursuit of a therapeutic agenda*. Norwood, NJ: Ablex.

Garb, H. N. (2005). Clinical judgment and decision making. *Annual Review of Clinical Psychology, 1,* 67–89.

Gardner, H. (1995). The development of competence in culturally defined domains: A preliminary framework. In N. R. Goldberger & J. D. Veroff (Eds.), *The culture and psychology reader.* (pp. 222–244). New York: New York University Press.

Garfield, S. L. (2003). Eclectic psychotherapy: A common factors approach. In J. C. Norcross & M. R. Goldfried (Eds.), *Handbook of Psychotherapy Integration* (pp. 169–201). New York: Oxford University Press.

Gehring, T. M., & Marty, D. (1993).The family system test: Differences in perception of family structures between nonclinical and clinical children. *Journal of Child Psychology and Psychiatry, 34,* 363–377.

Gendlin, E. T. (1981). *Focusing* (2nd ed.). New York: Bantam Books.

Gendlin, E. T. (1996). *Focusing-oriented psychotherapy: A manual of the experiential method.* New York: Guilford Press.

George, C., Kaplan, N., & Main, M. (1996). *Adult Attachment Inventory* (3rd ed.) Unpublished manuscript, University of California at Berkeley.

Gergen, K. (1985). The social constructionist movement in modern psychology. *American Psychologist, 40,* 266–275.

Gibbons, F. X., Eggleston, T. J., & Benthin, A. C. (1997). Cognitive reactions to smoking relapse: The reciprocal relation between dissonance and self-esteem. *Journal of Personality and Social Psychology, 12,* 184–195.

Gilbody, S., Bower, P., Fletcher, J., Richards, D., & Sutton, A. J. (2006). Collaborative care for depression: A cumulative meta-analysis and review of longer-term outcomes. *Archives of Internal Medicine, 166,* 2314–2321.

Gilmer, W. S., & Kemp, D. E. (2006). STAR*D: What have we learned thus far? *International Drug Therapy Newsletter, 41,* 75–82.

Gold, E. K., & Zahm, S. G. (2008). Gestalt therapy. In M. Hersen & A. M. Gross (Eds.), *Handbook of clinical psychology* (Vol. 1, pp. 585–616). Hoboken, NJ: Wiley.

Goldfried, M. R., & Davison, G. (1994). *Clinical behavior therapy* (Rev. ed.). New York: Wiley.

Gordon, D. E., & Efran, J. S. (1997). Constructivism and the deconstruction of clinical practice. In T. L. Sexton & B. L. Griffin (Eds.), *Constructivist thinking in counseling practice, research, and training* (pp. 101–110). New York: Teachers College Press.

Gottman, J. M. (1994). *Why marriages succeed or fail.* New York: Simon & Schuster.

Gottman, J. M. (1996). *What predicts divorce?* Hillsdale, NJ: Erlbaum.

Gottman, J. M., Ryan, K. D., Carrere, S., & Erley, A. M. (2002). Toward a scientifically based marital therapy. In H. A. Liddle, D. A. Santisteban, R. F. Levant, & J. J. Bray (Eds.), *Family psychology: Science based intervetnnions* (pp. 147–174). Washington, DC: American Psychological Association.

Greenberg, J., & Mitchell, S. A. (1983). *Object relations in psychoanalytic theory.* Cambridge, MA: Harvard University Press.

Greenberg, L. S. (2002). *Emotion-focused therapy: Coaching clients to work through their feelings.* Washington, DC: American Psychological Association.

Greenberg, L. S., & Pascal-Leone, J. (2001). A dialectical constructivist view of the creation of personal meaning. *Journal of Constructivist Psychology, 14,* 165–186.

Greenberg, L. S., Rice, L. N., & Elliott, R. (1993). *Facilitating emotional change: The moment-by-moment process.* New York: Guilford Press.

Greenberg, L. S., & Safran, J. D. (1987). *Emotion in psychotherapy.* New York: Guilford Press.

Greenberg, L. S., & Safran, J. D. (1989). Emotion in psychotherapy. *American Psychologist, 44,* 19–68.

Greenberg, L. S., & Van Balen, R. (1998). The theory of experience-centered therapies. In L. S. Greenberg, J. C. Watson, & G. Lietaer (Eds.), *Handbook of experiential psychotherapy* (pp. 28–58). New York: Guilford Press.

Grenyer, B. F. S., & Luborsky, L. (1996). Dynamic change in psychotherapy: Mastery of interpersonal conflicts. *Journal of Consulting and Clinical Psychology, 64,* 411–416.

Guay, D. R. (2006). Rasagiline (TVP-1012): A new selective monoamine oxidase inhibitor for Parkinson's Disease. *American Journal of Geriatric Pharmacotherapy, 4,* 330–346.

Guidano, V. E. (1995). Constructivist therapy: A theoretical framework. In R.A. Neimeyer & M.J. Mahoney (Eds.), *Constructivism in psychotherapy* (pp. 93–108). Washington, DC: American Psychological Association.

Gurtman, M. (2000). Interpersonal complementarity: Integrating interpersonal measurement with interpersonal models. *Journal of Counseling Psychology, 48,* 97–110.

Guyer, L. T. and Rowell, L. L. (1997) Gender, social constructionism, and psychotherapy: Deconstructing feminist social constructions. In T. L. Sexton & B. L. Griffin (Eds.), *Constructivist thinking in counseling practice, research, and training* (pp. 58–73). New York: Teachers College Press.

Haley, J. (1963). *Strategies of psychotherapy.* New York: Grune & Stratton.

Hall, K. L., & Rossi J. S. (2003). Informing interventions: A meta-analysis of the magnitude of effect in decisional balance stage transitions across 43 health behaviors. *Annals of Behavioral Medicine, 25*(Suppl.), 180.

Halleck, S. (1979). *Politics of therapy.* New York: Jason Aronson.

Halliday-Boykins, C. A., Schoenwald, S. K., & Letourneau, E. J. (2005). Caregiver–therapist ethnic similarity predicts youth outcomes from an empirically based treatment. *Journal of Consulting and Clinical Psychology, 73,* 808–818.

Hamilton, N. G. (1989). A critical review of object relations theory. *American Journal of Psychiatry, 146,* 1552–1560.

Hardy, G. (2007). Researchers and practitioners working together: Process studies at a research center. *Psychotherapy Bulletin, 42,* 22–24.

Hardy, K. V. (2007, March 16). *Towards a new vision of psychotherapy.* Keynote address presented at the Psychotherapy Networker Symposium, Washington, DC.

Hare-Mustin, R. T. (1978). The problem of gender in family therapy theory. *Family Process, 26,* 15–27.

Harlow, H. F., & Harlow, M. K. (1966). Learning to love. *American Scientist, 54,* 244–272.

Harré, R., & Gillet, R. (1994). *The discursive mind.* Thousand Oaks, CA: Sage.

Harris, M. B., & Bruner, C. G. (1971). A comparison of a self-control and a contract procedure for weight control. *Behavior Research in Therapy, 9,* 347–354.

Hartman, A., & Laird, J. (1983). *Family-centered social work practice.* New York: Free Press.

Hartmann, H. (1939/1958). *Ego psychology and the problem of adaptation.* New York: International Universities Press.

Hashimoto, R., Takei, N., Shimazu, K., Christ, L., Lu, B., & Chuang, D.-M. (2002). Lithium induces brain-derived neurotrophic factor and activates TrkB in rodent cortical neurons: An essential step for neuroprotection against glutamate excitotoxicity. *Neuropharmacology, 43,* 1173–1179.

Hawkins, E. J., Lambert, M. J., Vermeersch, D. A., Slade, K. L., & Tuttle, K. C. (2004). The therapeutic effects of providing patient progress information to therapists and patients. *Psychotherapy Research, 3,* 308–327.

Hayes, S. C., Barnes-Holmes, D., & Roche, B. (Eds.). (2001). *Relational frame theory: A Post-Skinnerian account of human language and cognition.* New York: Plenum.

Hayes, S. C., Masuda, A., Bissett, R., Luoma, J., & Guerrero, L. F. (2004). DBT, FAP, and ACT: How empirically oriented are the new behavior therapy technologies? *Behavior Therapy, 35,* 35–54.

Hayes, S. C., & Strosahl, K. D. (2004). *A practical guide to acceptance and commitment therapy.* New York: Springer Science.

Hayes, S. C., Strosahl, K. D., Bunting, K., Twohig, M., & Wilson, K. G. (2004). What is acceptance and commitment therapy? In S. C. Hayes & K. D. Strosahl (Eds.), *A practical guide to acceptance and commitment therapy* (pp. 1–29). New York: Springer Science.

Hayes, S. C., Strosahl, K. D., Luoma, J., Varra, A. A., & Wilson, K. G. (2004). ACT case formulation. In S. C. Hayes & K. D. Strosahl (Eds.), *A practical guide to acceptance and commitment therapy* (pp. 59–73). New York: Springer Science.

Hayes, S. C., Strosahl, K. D., & Wilson, K. G. (1999). *Acceptance and Commitment Therapy: An experiential approach to behavior change.* New York: Guilford.

Hayes, S. C., Strosahl, K. D., Wilson, K. G., Bissett, R., Pistorello, J., Toarmino D., et al. (2004). Measuring experiential avoidance: A preliminary test of a working model. *Psychological Record, 54,* 553–578.

Hayes, S. C., Wilson, K. G., Gifford, E. V., Bissett, R., Piasecki, M., Batten S. V., et al. (2004). A preliminary trial of twelve-step facilitation and acceptance and commitment therapy with polysubstance-abusing methadone-maintained opiate addicts. *Behavior Therapy, 35,* 667–688.

Hazan, C., & Shaver, P. (1987). Romantic love conceptualized as an attachment process. *Journal of Personality and Social Psychology, 52,* 511–524.

Hazan, C., & Shaver, P. (1994). Attachment as an organizational framework for research on close relationships. *Psychological Inquiry, 5,* 1–22.

Hegel, G. W. F. (1830/1991). *The Encyclopaedia Logic: Part 1 of the Encyclopaedia of Philosophical Sciences,* trans. T. F. Geraets, W. A. Suchting, & H. S. Harris. Indianapolis: Hackett.

Henggeler, S. W., Letourneau, E. J., Borduin, C. M., Chapman, J. E., Schewe, P. A., & McCart, M. R. (2009). Mediators of change for multisystemic therapy with juvenile sexual offenders. *Journal of Consulting and Clinical Psychology, 77,* 451–462.

Henggeler, S. W., Schoenwald, S. K., Borduin, C. M., Rowland, M. D., & Cunningham, P. B. (2009). *Multisystemic therapy for antisocial behavior in children and adolescents* (2nd ed.). New York: Guilford Press.

Henrich, C. C., & Shahar, G. (2008). Social support buffers the effects of terrorism on adolescent depression: Findings from Sderot, Israel. *Journal of the American Academy of Child & Adolescent Psychiatry, 47,* 1073–1076.

Henry, C. A. (2007). Limit setting and projective identification in work with a provocative child and his parents: A revisiting of Winnicott's "Hate in the countertransference." *American Journal of Psychotherapy, 61,* 441–457.

Herman, J. L. (1992). *Trauma and recovery.* New York: Basic Books.

Hettema, J., Steele, J., & Miller, W. R. (2005). Motivational Interviewing. *Annual Review of Clinical Psychology, 1,* 91–111.

Hilsenroth, M. J., & Cromer, T. D. (2007). Clinician interventions related to alliance during the initial interview and psychological assessment. *Psychotherapy: Theory, Research, Practice, Training, 44,* 205–218.

Hinkle, D. (1965). The change of personal constructs from the viewpoint of a theory of implications. Unpublished dissertation, Ohio State University—Columbus.

Hoffman, S., & Rosman, L. (2003). "Procrustean psychotherapy" or differential therapeutics: Teaching treatment selection to trainees. *Journal of Contemporary Psychotherapy, 33,* 341–347.

Hogarty, G. E. (2002). *Personal therapy for schizophrenia and related disorders: A guide to individualized treatment.* New York: Guilford Press.

Hogarty, G. E., Anderson, C. M., Reiss, D. J., Kornblith, S. J., Greenwald, D. P., Ulrich, R. F., et al. (1991). Family psychoeducation, social skills training, and maintenance chemotherapy in the aftercare treatment of schizophrenia. II. Two-year effects of a controlled study on relapse and adjustment. *Archives of General Psychiatry, 48,* 340–347.

Hogarty, G. E., & Flesher, S. (1999a). Developmental theory for a cognitive enhancement therapy of schizophrenia. *Schizophrenia Bulletin, 25,* 677–692.

Hogarty, G. E., & Flesher, S. (1999b). Practice principles of cognitive enhancement therapy for schizophrenia. *Schizophrenia Bulletin, 25,* 693–708.

Hogarty, G. E., Greenwald, D., Ulrich, R. F., Kornblith, S. J., Dibarry, A. L., Cooley, S., et al. (1997). Three-year trials of personal therapy among schizophrenic patients living with or independent of family: II. Effects of adjustment of patients. *American Journal of Psychiatry, 154,* 1514–1524.

Horney, K. (1966). *Our inner conflicts.* New York: Norton.

Horney, K. (1970). *Neurosis and human growth.* New York: Norton.

Horvath, A. O., & Greenberg, L. S. (1989). Development and validation of the Working Alliance Inventory. *Journal of Counseling Psychology, 36,* 223–233.

Howard, K. I., Moras, K., Brill, P. L., Martinovich, Z., & Lutz, W. (1996). Evaluation of psychotherapy: Efficacy, effectiveness, and patient progress. *American Psychologist. 51,* 1059–1064.

Hubble, M. A., Duncan, B. L., & Miller, S. D. (1999). *The heart and soul of change: What works in therapy.* Washington, DC: American Psychological Association.

Humphreys, K., & Klaw, E. (2001). Can targeting nondependent problem drinkers and providing internet-based services expand access to assistance for alcohol problems? A study of the moderation management self-help/mutual aid organization. *Journal of Studies in Alcohol, 62,* 528–532.

Hunkeler, E. M., Katon, W., Tang, L., Williams, J. W., Kroenke, K., Lin, E. H. B., et al. (2006). Long term outcomes from the IMPACT randomised trial for depressed elderly patients in primary care. *British Medical Journal, 332,* 259–263.

Hunsley, J., & DiGiulio, G. (2002). Dodo bird, phoenix, or urban legend? The question of psychotherapy equivalence. *Scientific Review of Mental Health Practice, 1,* 11–22.

Husserl, E. (1931). *Ideas: General introduction to pure phenomenology* (W. R. Boyce Gibson, Trans.). New York: Macmillan.

Hyman, R. B., Feldman, H. R., Harris, R. B., Levin, R. F., & Mallory, G. B. (1989). The effects of relaxation training on clinical symptoms: A meta-analysis. *Nursing Research, 8,* 216–220.

Insel, T. R. (2008). Beyond efficacy: The STAR*D trial. Retrieved June 24, 2008, from http://www.nimh.nih.gov/about/director/publications/beyond-efficacy-the-stard-trial.shtml

Irwin, M. R. (2008). Human psychoneuroimmunology: 20 years of discovery. *Brain, Behavior, and Immunity, 22,* 129–139.

Isabella, R. A. (1993). Origins of attachment: Maternal interactive behavior across the first year. *Developmental Psychology, 64,* 605–621.

Iwata, B. A., Dorsey, M. F., Slifer, K. J., Bauman, K. E., & Richman, G. S. (1982/1994). Toward a functional analysis of self-injury. *Journal of Applied Behavior Analysis, 27,* 197–209. (Reprinted from *Analysis and Intervention in Developmental Disabilities, 2,* 3–20, 1982).

Jackson, D. D., & Weakland, J. H. (1959). Schizophrenic symptoms and family interaction. *Archives of General Psychiatry, 1,* 618–621.

Jacobs, L. (1989). Dialogue in Gestalt theory and therapy. *The Gestalt Journal, 12,* 25–67.

Jacobson, E. (1938). *Progressive relaxation.* Chicago: University of Chicago Press.

Jacobson, N. S., & Margolin, G. (1979). *Marital therapy: Strategies based on social learning and behavior exchange principles.* New York: Brunner/Mazel.

Jacobson, N. S., Martell, C. R., & Dimidjian, S. (2001). Behavioral activation treatment for depression: Returning to contextual roots. *Clinical Psychology: Science and Practice, 8,* 255–270.

Jacobson, N. S., & Truax, P. (1991). Clinical significance: A statistical approach to defining meaningful change in psychotherapy research. *Journal of Consulting and Clinical Psychology, 59,* 12–19.

James, D. J., & Glaze, L. E. (2006). *Mental health problems of prison and jail inmates. NCJ 213600.* Washington, DC: National Criminal Justice Reference Service.

James, W. (1902/2002). *The varieties of religious experience.* New York: Routledge.

Javitt, D. C., & Coyle, J. T. (2004). Decoding schizophrenia: A fuller understanding for signaling in the brain of people with disorder offers a new hope for improved therapy. *Scientific American, 290,* 48–56.

Johnson, S. M. (1996). *The practice of emotionally focused marital therapy: Creating connection.* New York: Brunner/Mazel.

Johnson, S. M. (2006). A guide for couple therapy. In S. M. Johnson & V. E. Whiffen (Eds.), *Attachment processes in couple and family therapy* (pp. 103–123). New York: Guilford Press.

Johnson, S. M., & Greenberg, L. S. (1985). The differential effects of experiential and problem solving interventions in resolving marital conflicts. *Journal of Consulting and Clinical Psychology, 53,* 175–184.

Johnson, S. M., Hunsley, J., Greenberg, L. S., & Schindler, D. (1999). Emotionally focused couples therapy: Status and challenges. *Clinical Psychology: Science and Practice, 6,* 67–79.

Joint Commission on Mental Illness and Health. (1961). *Action for mental health.* New York: Basic Books.

Jones, E. E., & Nisbett, R. E. (1971). *The actor and the observer: Divergent perceptions of the causes of behavior*. Morristown, NJ: General Learning Press.

Jones, K. M., & Friman, P. C. (1999). A case study of behavioral assessment and treatment of insect phobia. *Journal of Applied Behavior Analysis, 32*, 95–98.

Julien, R. M., Advokat, C. D., & Comaty, J. E. (2008). *A primer of drug action* (11th ed.). New York: Worth Publishers.

Kaiser, H. (1965). *Effective psychotherapy: The contribution of Hellmuth Kaiser* (L. Fierman, Ed.). New York: Free Press.

Kaplan, H. S. (1979). *Disorders of sexual desire and other new concepts and techniques in sex therapy*. New York: Brunner/Mazel.

Karasu, T. B. (1986). Specificity vs. nonspecificity. *American Journal of Psychiatry, 143*, 687–695.

Karasu, T. B. (1992). The worst of times, the best of times: Psychotherapy in the 1990s. *Journal of Psychotherapy Practice and Research, 1*, 2–15.

Kashima, Y., McKintyre, A., & Clifford, P. (1998). The category of the mind: Folk psychology of belief, desire, and intention. *Asian Journal of Social Psychology, 1*, 289–313.

Katerndahl, D. (2005). Variations on a theme: The spectrum of anxiety disorders and problems with DSM classification in primary care settings. In P. L. Gower (Ed.), *New research on the psychology of fear* (pp. 181–221). Hauppauge, NY: Nova Science Publishers.

Kazdin, A. E. (1977). Assessing the clinical or applied importance of behavior change through social validation. *Behavior Modification, 1*, 427–452.

Kazdin, A. E. (2008). Evidence-based treatment and practice: New opportunities to bridge clinical Research and practice, enhance the knowledge base, and improve patient care. *American Psychologist, 63*, 146–159.

Keck, P. E., & Susman, J. (2003). Introduction: Foundational treatment for bipolar disorder. *Journal of Family Practice* (Suppl. March), 4–5.

Keen, E. (1998). *Drugs, therapy, and professional power: Problems and pills*. Westport, CT: Praeger Publishers.

Kegan, R. (1982). *The evolving self*. Cambridge, MA: Harvard University Press.

Kelly, G. (1955). *The psychology of personal constructs*. New York: Norton.

Kennedy-Moore, E., & Watson, J. C. (1999). *Expressing emotion: Myths, realities, and therapeutic strategies*. New York: Guilford Press.

Kern, R. M., Wheeler, M. S., & Curlette, W. L. (1993). *BASIS-A inventory interpretive manual: A psychological theory*. Highlands, NC: TRT Associates.

Kernberg, O. F. (1965). Notes on countertransference. *Journal of the American Psychoanalytic Association, 13*, 38–56.

Kernberg, O. F. (1976). *Object-relations theory and clinical psychoanalysis*. New York: Jason Aronson.

Kernberg, O. F. (1984). *Severe personality disorders: Psychotherapeutic strategies*. New Haven: Yale University Press.

Kessler, R. C., Berglund, P., Demler, O., Jin, R., Merikangas, K. R., & Walters, E. E. (2005). Lifetime prevalence and age-of-onset distributions of *DSM-IV* disorders in the National Comorbidity Survey replication. *Archives of General Psychiatry, 62*, 593–602.

Kiesler, D. J. (1983). The 1982 interpersonal circle: A taxonomy for complementarity in human transactions. *Psychological Review, 90*, 185–214.

Kirsch, I., Deacon, B. J., Huedo-Medina, T. B., Scoboria, A., Moore, T. J., Johnson, B. T. (2008). Initial severity and antidepressant benefits: A meta-analysis of data submitted to the Food and Drug Administration. *PLoS Medicine, 5*, e45.

Kirsch, I., Moore, T. J., Scoboria, A., & Nicholls, S. S. (2002). The emperor's new drugs: An analysis of antidepressant medication data submitted to the U.S. Food and Drug Administration. *Prevention & Treatment, 5*. Retrieved December 5, 2003, from http://journals.apa.org/prevention/volume5/pre0050023a.html

Kirschenbaum, H., & Jourdan, A. (2005). The current status of Carl Rogers and the person-centered approach. *Psychotherapy: Theory, Research, Practice, Training, 42*, 37–51.

Klein, D. F., Zitrin, C. M., Woerner, M. G., & Ross, D. C. (1983). Treatment of phobia II. Behavior therapy and supportive psychotherapy. *Archives of General Psychiatry, 40,* 139–145.

Klein, M. (1935/1975). A contribution to the psychogenesis of manic-depressive states. In R. Money-Kyrle (Ed.), *The writings of Melanie Klein* (Vol. 1, pp. 262–289). New York: The Free Press.

Klein, M. (1957/1975). Envy and gratitude. In R. Money-Kyrle (Ed.), *The writings of Melanie Klein* (Vol. 3, pp. 176–235). New York: The Free Press.

Klerman, G. L., & Weissman, M. M. (Eds.). (1993). *New applications of interpersonal therapy.* Washington, DC: American Psychiatric Press.

Klerman G. L., Weissman, M. M., & Rounsaville, B. J. (1984). *Interpersonal psychotherapy for depression.* New York: Basic Books.

Koerner, K., & Linehan, M. M. (2000). Research on dialectical behavior therapy for borderline personality disorder. *Psychiatric Clinics of North America, 23,* 151–167.

Koerner, K., & Linehan, M. M. (2002). Dialectical behavior therapy for borderline personality disorder. In S. G. Hofman & M. C. Tompson (Eds.), *Treating chronic and severe mental disorders* (pp. 317–342). New York: Guilford Press.

Kohlenberg, R. J., & Tsai, M. (1991). *Functional analytic psychotherapy: Creating intense and curative therapeutic relationships.* New York: Plenum.

Kohler, W. (1959). *Gestalt psychology.* New York: New American Library of World Literature.

Kohut, H. (1971). *The analysis of the self: A systematic approach to the treatment of narcissistic personality disorders.* New York: International Universities Press.

Kohut, H. (1977). *The restoration of the self.* New York: International Universities Press.

Kohut, H. (1984). *How does analysis cure?* Chicago: University of Chicago Press.

Kopta, S. M., Howard, K. I., Lowry, J. L., & Beutler, L. E. (1994). Patterns of symptomatic recovery in psychotherapy. *Journal of Consulting and Clinical Psychology, 62,* 1009–1016.

Kramer, D. A., Kahlbaugh, P. E., & Goldston, R. B. (1992). A measure of paradigm beliefs about the social world. *Journal of Gerontology, 47,* 180–189.

Krause, K.-H., Dresel, S. H., Krause, J., Kung, H. F., & Tatsch, K. (2000). Increased striatal dopamine transporter in adult patients with attention-deficit/hyperactivity disorder: Effects of methylphenidate as measured by single photon emission computed tomography. *Neuroscience Letters, 285,* 107–110.

Kuhn, T. S. (1970). *The structure of scientific revolutions* (2nd ed.). Chicago: University of Chicago Press.

L'Abate, L. (2009). In search of a relational theory. *American Psychologist, 64,* 779–788.

LaForge, R., & Suczek, R. F. (1955). The interpersonal dimensions of personality: III. An interpersonal check list. *Journal of Personality, 24,* 94–112.

La Guardia, J. G., Ryan, R. M., Couchman, C. E., & Deci, E. L. (2000). Within-person variation in security of attachment: A self-determination theory perspective on attachment, need fulfillment, and well-being. *Journal of Personality & Social Psychology, 79,* 367–384.

Lambert, M. J. (1992). Psychotherapy outcome research. In J. C. Norcross & M. R. Goldfried (Eds.), *Handbook of psychotherapy integration* (pp. 94–129). New York: Basic Books.

Lambert, M. J. (2004). *Bergin and Garfield's handbook of psychotherapy and behavior change* (5th ed.). New York: Wiley.

Lambert, M. J., & Burlingame, G. M. (1996). *Outcome Questionnaire (OQ-45.2).* Stevenson, MD: American Professional Credentialing Services LLC. www.oqfamily.com.

Lambert, M. J., Garfield, S. L., & Bergin, A. E. (2004). Overview, trends, and future issues. In M. J. Lambert (Ed.), *Bergin and Garfield's handbook of psychotherapy and behavior change* (5th ed., pp. 805–821). New York: Wiley.

Lambert, M. J., & Ogles, B. M. (2004). The efficacy and effectiveness of psychotherapy. In M. J. Lambert (Ed.), *Bergin and Garfield's handbook of psychotherapy and behavior change* (5th ed., pp. 139–193). New York: Wiley.

Lambert, M. J., Whipple, J. L., Bishop, M. J., Vermeersch, D. A., Gray, G. V., & Finch, A. E. (2002). Comparison of empirically-derived and rationally-derived methods for identifying patients at risk for treatment failure. *Clinical Psychology and Psychotherapy, 9,* 149–162.

Lampropoulos, G. K., & Dixon, D. N. (2007). Psychotherapy integration in internships and counseling psychology doctoral programs. *Journal of Psychotherapy Integration, 17,* 185–208.

Landrine, H. (1992). Clinical implications of cultural differences: The referential versus the indexical self. *Clinical Psychology Review, 12,* 401–415.

Lane, R., & Baldwin, D. (1997). Selective serotonin reuptake inhibitor-induced serotonin syndrome: Review. *Journal of Clinical Psychopharmacology, 17,* 208–221.

Laroche, M.-L., Charmes, J.-P., Nouaille, Y., Picard, N., & Merle, L. (2006). Is inappropriate medication use a major cause of adverse drug reactions in the elderly? *British Journal of Clinical Pharmacology, 63,* 177–186.

Lavoie, K. L., & Barone, S. (2006). Prescription privileges for psychologists: A comprehensive review and critical analysis of current issues and controversies. *CNS Drugs, 20,* 51–66.

Lazarus, A. A. (1967). In support of technical eclecticism. *Psychological Reports, 21,* 415–416.

Lazarus, A. A. (1971). Where do behavior therapists take their troubles? *Psychological Reports, 28,* 349–350.

Lazarus, A. A. (2005). Multimodal therapy. In J. C. Norcross & M. R. Goldfried (Eds.), *Handbook of psychotherapy integration* (2nd ed., pp. 105–120). New York: Oxford University Press.

Leahy, R. L., & Holland, S. J. (2000). *Behavioral techniques.* Appendix A in *Treatment plans and interventions for depression and anxiety disorders* (pp. 1–18). New York: Guilford Press.

Leary, T. (1957). *Interpersonal diagnosis of personality: A functional theory and methodology for personality evaluation.* New York: Ronald Press.

LeDoux, J. (1996). Emotional networks and motor control: A fearful view. *Progress in Brain Research, 107,* 437–446.

Lee, E., & Mock, M. R. (2005a). Asian families: An overview. In M. McGoldrick, J. Giordano, & N. Garcia-Preto (Eds.), *Ethnicity & family therapy* (3rd ed., pp. 269–289). New York: Guilford Press.

Lee, E., & Mock, M. R. (2005b). Chinese families. In M. McGoldrick, J. Giordano, & N. Garcia-Preto (Eds.), *Ethnicity & family therapy* (3rd ed., pp. 302–318). New York: Guilford Press.

LeFever, G. B., Arcona, A. P., & Antonuccio, D. O. (2003). ADHD among American schoolchildren: Evidence of overdiagnosis and overuse of medication. *The Scientific Review of Mental Health Practice, 2,* 49–60.

Lehman, A. F., Steinwachs, D. M., Dixon, L. B., Postrado, L., Scott, J. E., Fahey, M., et al. (1998). Patterns of usual care for schizophrenia: Initial results from the Schizophrenia Patient Outcomes Research Team (PORT) Client Survey. *Schizophrenia Bulletin, 24,* 11–20.

Letourneau, E. J., Cunningham, P. B., & Henggeler, S. W. (2002). Multisystemic treatment of antisocial behavior in adolescents. In S. G. Hoffmann & M. C. Tompson (Eds.), *Treating chronic and severe mental disorders: A handbook of empirically supported treatments* (pp. 364–381). New York: Guilford Press.

Levensky, E. R. (2003). Motivational interviewing. In W. O'Donohue, J. E. Fisher, & S. C. Hayes (Eds.), *Cognitive behavior therapy: Applying empirically supported techniques in your practice* (chap. 38, pp. 252–260). Hoboken, NJ: Wiley.

Levenson, H. (1995). *Time-limited dynamic psychotherapy: A guide to clinical practice.* New York: Basic Books.

Levitsky, A., & Perls, F. S. (1970). The rules and games of Gestalt therapy. In J. Fagan & I. Shepherd (Eds.), *Gestalt therapy now* (pp. 140–149). New York: Harper & Row (Colophon).

Levy, K. N., Meehan, K. B., Kelly, K. M., Reynoso, J. S., Weber, M., Clarkin, J. F., et al. (2006). Change in attachment patterns and reflective function in a randomized control trial of transference-focused psychotherapy for borderline personality disorder. *Journal of Consulting and Clinical Psychology, 74,* 1027–1040.

Lewin, K. (1948). *Resolving social conflicts: Selected papers on group dynamics.* New York: Harper.

Lifton, R. J. (1974). The sense of immortality: On death and the continuity of life. In R. J. Lifton & E. Olson (Eds.), *Explorations in psychohistory* (pp. 271–287). New York: Simon & Schuster.

Lindsley, O. R., Skinner, B. F., & Solomon, H. C. (1953). *Studies in behavior therapy* (Status report 1). Waltham, MA: Metropolitan Sate Hospital.

Linehan, M. M. (1993a). *Cognitive-behavioral modification of borderline personality disorder.* New York: Guilford Press.

Linehan, M. M. (1993b). *Skills training manual for treating borderline personality disorder.* New York: Guilford Press.

Linehan, M. M. (2000). The empirical basis of dialectical behavior therapy: Development of new treatments vs. evaluation of existing treatments. *Clinical Psychology: Science and Practice, 7,* 113–119.

Linehan, M. M., Cochran, B. N., & Kehrer, C. A. (2001). Dialectical behavior therapy for borderline personality disorder. In D. H. Barlow (Ed.), *Clinical handbook of psychological disorders* (3rd ed., pp. 470–522). New York: Guilford Press.

Linehan, M. M., Dimeff, L. A., Comtois, S. K., Welch, S. S., & Heagerty, P. (2002). Dialectical behavior therapy versus comprehensive validation therapy plus 12-step for the treatment of opioid dependent women meeting criteria for borderline personality disorder. *Drug and Alcohol Dependence, 67,* 13–26.

Linehan, M. M., Heard, H. L., & Armstrong, H. E. (1993). Naturalistic follow up of a behavioral treatment for chronically parasuicidal patients. *Archives of General Psychiatry, 50,* 971–974.

Linehan, M. M., Tutek, D. A., Heard, H. L., & Armstrong, H. E. (1994). Interpersonal outcome of cognitive behavioral treatment for chronically suicidal borderline patients. *American Journal of Psychiatry, 151,* 1771–1776.

Loeser, J. D., Butler, S. H., Chapman, C. R., & Turk, D. C. (Eds.). (2001). *Bonica's management of pain* (3rd ed.). Philadelphia: Lippincott, Williams, & Wilkins.

Lombardi, D. N. (1973). Eight avenues of life style consistency. *Individual Psychologist, 10,* 5–9.

London, P. (1988). Metamorphosis in psychotherapy: Slouching toward integration. *Journal of Integrative and Eclectic Psychotherapy, 7,* 3–12.

Lord, C. G., Ross, L., & Lepper, M. (1979). Biased assimilation and attitude polarization: The effects of prior theories on subsequently considered evidence. *Journal of Personality and Social Psychology, 37,* 2098–2109.

Lovaas, O. I., & Favell, J. E. (1987). Protection for clients undergoing aversive/restrictive interventions. *Education & Treatment of Children, 10,* 311–325.

Lueger, R. J. (2002). Practice-informed research and research-informed practice. *Journal of Clinical Psychology, 58,* 1265–1276.

Luborsky, L. (1984). *Principles of psychoanalytic psychotherapy: A manual for supportive-expressive treatment.* New York: Basic Books.

Luborsky, L. (1997). The core conflictual relational theme: A basic case formulation method. In T. D. Eels (Ed.), *Handbook of psychotherapy case formulation.* (pp. 58–83). New York: Guilford Press.

Luborsky, L., & Crits-Christoph, P. (1998). *Understanding transference: The core conflictual relational theme method* (2nd ed.). Washington, DC: American Psychological Association.

Luborsky L., Rosenthal, R., Diguer, L., Andrusyna, T. P., Berman, J. S., Levitt, J. T., et al. (2002). The Dodo bird verdict is alive and well—mostly. *Clinical Psychology: Science and Practice, 9,* 2–12.

Luborsky, L., Singer, B., & Luborsky, E. (1975). Comparative studies of psychotherapies: Is it true that "Everybody has won and all must have prizes"? *Archives of General Psychiatry, 32,* 995–1008.

Luria, A. (1961). *The role of speech in the regulation of normal and abnormal behaviors.* New York: Liveright.

Lutz, W. (2003). Efficacy, effectiveness, and expected treatment response in psychotherapy. *Journal of Clinical Psychology, 59,* 745–750.

Lutz, W., Martinovich, Z., & Howard, K. I. (1999). Patient profiling: An application of random coefficient regression models to depicting the response of a patient to outpatient psychotherapy. *Journal of Clinical Psychology, 67,* 571–577.

Lutz, W., Martinovich, Z., Howard, K. I., & Leon, S. C. (2002). Outcomes management, expected treatment response, and severity-adjusted provider profiling in outpatient psychotherapy. *Journal of Clinical Psychology, 58,* 1291–1304.

Lynch, T. R. (2000). Treatment of elderly depression with personality disorder comorbidity using dialectical behavior therapy. *Cognitive Behavioral Practice, 7,* 468–477.

Lyons, L. C., & Woods, P. J. (1971). The efficacy of rational-emotive therapy: A quantitative review of the outcome research. *Clinical Psychology Review, 11,* 357–369.

Lyons-Ruth, K. (2008). Contributions of the mother-infant relationship to dissociative, borderline, and conduct symptoms in young adulthood. *Infant Mental Health Journal, 29,* 203–218.

Madanes, C. (1981). *Strategic family therapy.* San Francisco: Jossey-Bass.

Madanes, C. (1990). *Sex, love, and violence: Strategies for transformation.* New York: Norton.

Maddi, S. R. (1987). Hardiness training at Illinois Bell Telephone. In J. P. Opatz (Ed.), *Health promotion evaluation* (pp. 101–115). Stevens Point, WI: National Wellness Institute.

Maddi, S. R. (2002). The story of hardiness: Twenty years of theorizing, research, and practice. *Consulting Psychology Journal, 54,* 173–185.

Maddi, S. R. (2004). Hardiness: An operationalization of existential courage. *Journal of Humanistic Psychology, 44,* 279–298.

Mahler, M. S. (1968). *On human symbiosis of the vicissitudes of individuation.* New York: International University Press.

Mahoney, M. J. (1971). The self-management of covert behavior: A case study. *Behavior Therapy, 2,* 575–578.

Mahoney, M. J. (1980). Psychotherapy and the structure of personal revolutions. In M. J. Mahoney (Ed.), *Psychotherapy process: Current issues and future directions* (pp. 157–180). New York: Plenum.

Mahoney, M. J. (1996). Constructivism and the study of complex self-organization. *Constructive Change, 1,* 3–8.

Main, M., & Cassidy, J. (1988). Categories of response to reunion with the parent at age six: Predictable from infant attachment classifications and stable over a 1-month period. *Developmental Psychology, 24,* 415–426.

Main, M., & Goldwyn, R. (1998). *Adult attachment scoring and classification system.* Unpublished manuscript, University of California at Berkeley.

Main, M., & Hesse, E. (1990). Parent's unresolved traumatic experiences are related to infant disorganized attachment status: Is frightened or frightening parental behavior the linking mechanism? In M. T. Greenberg, D. Cicchetti, & E. M. Cummings (Eds.), *Attachment in preschool years* (pp. 181–182). Chicago: University of Chicago Press.

Main, M., & Solomon, J. (1990). Procedures for identifying infants as disorganized/disoriented during the Ainsworth Strange Situation. In M. T. Greenberg, D. Cicchetti, & E. M. Cummings (Eds.), *Attachment in the preschool years* (pp. 121–160). Chicago: University of Chicago Press.

Maj, M., Pirozzi, R., Magliano, L., & Bartoli, L. (1998). Long-term outcome of lithium prophylaxis in bipolar disorder: A 5-year prospective study of 402 patients at a lithium clinic. *American Journal of Psychiatry, 155,* 30–35.

Mang, S., Weiss, H., & Schalke, B. (1993). Psychosomatic and somatopsychic aspects of myasthenia gravis: A critical review of the literature. [German]. *Zeitschrift fur Klinische Psychologie, Psychopathologie und Psychotherapie, 41,* 69–86.

Marcia, J. E. (1980). Identity in adolescence. In J. Adelson (Ed.), *Handbook of adolescent psychology* (pp. 159–187). New York: Wiley.

Marcia, J. E., Waterman, A. S., Matteson, D. R., Archer, S. L., & Orlofsky, J. L. (1993). *Ego identity: A handbook for psychosocial research.* New York: Springer-Verlag.

Markus, H. (1977). Self-schemata and processing information about the self. *Journal of Personality and Social Psychology, 35,* 63–78.

Masters, W. H., & Johnson, V. E. (1970). *Human sexual inadequacy.* Boston: Little, Brown.

Myers, D. G. (2001). *Psychology* (6th ed.). New York: Worth.

Malia, K. B., Bewick, K. C., Raymond, M. J., & Bennett, T. L. (1997). Brainwave-R: Cognitive strategies and techniques for brain injury recovery: Executive functions (therapist and client workbook). Austin, TX: PRO-ED.

Marengell, L. B., Suppes, T., Ketter, T. A., Dennehy, E. B., Zboyan, H., Kertz, B., et al. (2006). Omega-3 fatty acids in bipolar disorder: Clinical and research considerations. *Prostaglandins Leuokot Essential Fatty Acids, 75*, 315–321.

Marmor, J. (1971). Dynamic psychotherapy and behavior therapy: Are they compatible? *Archives of General Psychiatry, 24*, 22–28.

Marshall, E. (2000). Epidemiology: Duke study faults overuse of stimulants for children. *Science, 289*, 721.

Martin, B. K., Clapp, L., Alfers, J., & Beresford, T. P. (2004). Adherence to court-ordered disulfiram at fifteen months: A naturalistic study. *Journal of Substance Abuse Treatment, 26*, 233–236.

Mascolo, M. F., Craig-Bray, L., & Neimeyer, R. A. (1997). The construction of meaning and action in development and psychotherapy: An epigenetic systems approach. *Advances in Personal Construct Psychology, 4*, 3–38.

Masi, M. V., Miller, R. B., & Olson, M. M. (2003). Differences in dropout rates among individual, couple, and family therapy clients. *Contemporary Family Therapy: An International Journal, 25*, 63–75.

Maslow, A. H. (1968). *Toward a psychology of being*. New York: Van Nostrand.

Maslow, A. H. (1971). *The farther reaches of human nature*. New York: Viking Press.

Masson, J. M. (1984). *The assault on truth: Freud's suppression of the seduction theory*. New York: Farrar, Straus, & Giroux.

Matthews, M., Roper, M., Mosher, L., & Menn, A. (1979). A non-neuroleptic treatment for Schizophrenia: Analysis of the two-year postdischarge risk of relapse. *Schizophrenia Bulletin, 5*, 322–333.

May, R. (1969a). *Existential psychology* (2nd ed.). New York: Random House.

May, R. (1969b). The emergence of existential psychology. In R. May (Ed.), *Existential psychology* (2nd ed.). New York: Random House.

May, R. (1969c). The bases of existential psychotherapy. In R. May (Ed.), *Existential psychology* (2nd ed.). New York: Random House.

May, R. (1969d). *Love and will*. New York: Norton.

McCann, R. A., Ball, E. M., & Ivanoff, A. (2000). DBT with an inpatient forensic population The CMHIP forensic model. *Cognitive and Behavioral Practice, 7*, 447–456.

McCarthy, K. S., Gibbons, M. B. C., & Barber, J. P. (2008). The relation of rigidity across relationships with symptoms and functioning: An investigation with the Revised Central Relationship Questionnaire. *Journal of Counseling Psychology, 55*, 346–358.

McDougle, C. J., Stigler, K. A., & Posey, D. J. (2003). Treatment of aggression in children and adolescents with autism and conduct disorder. *Journal of Clinical Psychiatry, 64*(Suppl. 4), 16–25.

McGoldrick, M. (2008). Finding a place called "home". In M. McGoldrick & K. V. Hardy (Eds.) *Re-visioning family therapy: Race, culture, and gender in clinical practice* (2nd ed., pp. 97–113). New York: Guilford Press.

McGoldrick, M., Giordano, J., & Garcia-Preto, N. (2005). *Ethnicity & family therapy* (3rd ed.). New York: Guilford.

McGoldrick, M., & Hardy, K. V. (2008). *Re-visioning family therapy: Race, culture, and gender in clinical practice* (2nd ed.). New York: Guilford Press.

McGuire, S., & Clifford, J. (2000). Genetic and environmental contributions to loneliness in children. *Psychological Science, 11*, 487–491.

McKinnon, J. (2003). *The Black population in the United States: March 2002*. Current Population Reports, Series P20-541. Washington, DC: U.S. Bureau of the Census.

McWilliams, N. (1994). *Psychoanalytic diagnosis: Understanding personality structure in the clinical process*. New York: Guilford Press.

McWilliams, N. (2004). *Psychoanalytic psychotherapy: A practitioner's guide*. New York: Guilford Press.

Meddin, J. (1982). Cognitive therapy and symbolic interactionism: Expanding clinical potential. *Cognitive Therapy and Research, 6*, 151–165.

Meehl, P. E. (1954). *Clinical vs. statistical prediction*. Minneapolis, MN: University of Minnesota Press.

Meehl, P. E. (1962). Schizotaxia, schizotypy, schizophrenia. *American Psychologist, 17,* 827–838.

Meichenbaum, D. (1969). The effects of instructions and reinforcement on thinking and language behaviors of schizophrenics. *Behavior Research and Therapy, 7,* 101–114.

Meichenbaum, D. (1977). *Cognitive-behavior modification.* New York: Plenum Press.

Meichenbaum, D. (1986). Cognitive-behavior modification. In F. H. Kanfer & A. P. Goldstein (Eds.), *Helping people change* (3rd ed., pp. 346–380). New York: Pergamon Press.

Meichenbaum, D. (1992). Evolution of cognitive behavior therapy: Origins, tenets and clinical examples. In J. K. Zeig (Ed.), *The evolution of psychotherapy: The second conference* (pp. 114–128). New York: Brunner/Mazel.

Meichenbaum, D. (1996). Stress inoculation training for coping with stressors. *The Clinical Psychologist, 49,* 4–10.

Melia, K., & Wagner, A. W. (2000). The application of dialectical behavior therapy to the treatment of posttraumantic stress disorder. *National Center for Posttruamatic Stress Disorder Clinical Quarterly, 9,* 6–12.

Meltzoff, A. N., & Brooks, R. (2001). "Like me" as a building block for understanding other minds: Bodily acts, attention, and intention. In B. F. Malle, L. J. Moses, & D. A. Baldwin (Eds.), *Intentions and intentionality: Foundations of social cognition* (pp. 171–191). Cambridge, MA: MIT Press.

Menditto, A. A. (2002). A social-learning approach to the rehabilitation of individuals with severe mental disorders who reside in forensic facilities. *Psychiatric Rehabilitation Skills, 6,* 73–93.

Messer, S. B. (2001). Assimilative integration [Special issue]. *Journal of Psychotherapy Integration, 11,* 1–154.

Messer, S. B. (2003). A critical examination of belief structures in integrative and eclectic psychotherapy. In J. C. Norcross & M. R. Goldfried (Eds.), *Handbook of psychotherapy integration* (pp. 130–165). New York: Basic Books.

Michalak, E. E., & Lam, R. W. (2002). Breaking the myths: New treatment approaches for chronic depression. *Canadian Journal of Psychiatry, 47,* 635–643.

Mickelson, K. D., Kessler, R. C., & Shaver, P. R. (1997). Adult attachment in a nationally representative sample. *Journal of Personality and Social Psychology, 73,* 1092–1106.

Miklowitz, D. J., Otto, M. W., Frank, E., Reilly-Harrington, N. A., Wisniewski, S. R., Kogan, J. N., et al. (2007). Psychosocial treatments for bipolar depression: A 1-Year randomized trial from the systematic treatment enhancement program. *Archives of General Psychiatry, 64,* 419–427.

Miller, A. (1986). *Thou shall not be aware.* New York: Meridian.

Miller, A. G., McHoskey, J. W., Bane, C. M., & Dowd, T. G. (1993). The attitude polarization phenomenon: Role of response measure, attitude extremity, and behavioral consequences of reported attitude change. *Journal of Personality and Social Psychology, 64,* 516–574.

Miller, J. G. (1978). *Living systems.* New York: McGraw-Hill.

Miller, R. W., & Rollnick, S. (2002). *Motivational interviewing: Preparing people to change* (2nd ed.). New York: Guilford Press.

Miller, R. W., Taylor, C. A., & West, J. C. (1980). Focused versus broad spectrum behavior therapy for problem drinkers. *Journal of Consulting and Clinical Psychology, 48,* 590–601.

Miller, S. D., Hubble, M. A., & Duncan, B. L. (Eds.). (1996). *Handbook of solution focused brief therapy.* San Francisco: Jossey-Bass.

Miltenberger, R. G. (2008). *Behavior modification: Principles and procedures* (4th ed.). Belmont, CA: Brooks/Cole.

Minuchin, S. (1974). *Families & family therapy.* Cambridge, MA: Harvard University Press.

Minuchin, S., & Fishman, H. C. (1981). *Family therapy techniques.* Cambridge, MA: Harvard University Press.

Minuchin, S., Nichols, M. P., & Lee, W.-Y. (2007). *Assessing families and couples: From symptom to system.* Boston, MA: Allyn and Bacon.

Mitchell, S. A. (1988). *Relational concepts in psychoanalysis.* Cambridge, MA: Harvard University Press.

Mobius, H. J. (2003). Memantine: Update on the current evidence. *International Journal of Geriatric Psychiatry, 18*(Suppl. 1), 47–54.

Mollenkott, V. R. (2001). *Omnigender: A trans-religious approach*. Cleveland: The Pilgrim Press.

Monroe, S. M., & Simons, A. D. (1991). Diathesis-stress theories in the context of life stress research: Implications for the depressive disorders. *Psychological Bulletin, 110*, 406–425.

Monte, C. F., & Sollod, R. F. (2003). *Beneath the mask: An introduction to theories of personality* (7th ed.). New York: Wiley.

Morrison, J. (1997). *When psychological problems mask medical disorders: A guide for psychotherapists*. New York: Guilford Press.

Mosak, H. H. (1985). Interrupting a depression: The pushbutton technique. *Individual Psychology, 4*, 210–214.

Mosak, H. H., & Sulman, B. H. (1971). *Life Sytle Inventory*. Chicago: Alfred Adler Institute.

Mosher, L., & Menn, A. (1978). Community residential treatment for schizophrenia: Two-year follow up. *Hospital and Community Psychiatry, 29*, 715–723.

Mosher, L. R., Vallone, R., & Menn, A. (1995). The treatment of acute psychosis without neuroleptics: Six week psychopathology outcome data from The Soteria Project. *International Journal of Social Psychiatry, 41*, 157–73.

Moreno, J. (1946). *Psychodrama*. Boston: Beacon Press.

Mowrer, O. H. (1948). Learning theory and the neurotic paradox. *American Journal of Orthopsychiatry, 18*, 571–610.

Mowrer, O. H. (1950). *Learning theory and personality dynamics*. New York: Arnold Press.

Muran, J. C. (2001). A final note: meditations on "both/and". In J. C. Muran (Ed.), *Self-relations in the psychotherapy process*. Washington, DC: American Psychological Association.

Napier, A. Y., & Whitaker, C. A. (1978). *The family crucible*. New York: Bantam Books.

Nathan, P. E., & Gorman, J. M. (Eds.). (1998). *A guide to treatments that work*. New York: Oxford University Press.

Nealy, E. C. (2008). Working with LGBT families. In M. McGoldrick & K. V. Hardy (Eds.) *Re-visioning family therapy: Race, culture, and gender in clinical practice* (2nd ed., pp. 289–299). New York: Guilford Press.

Neimeyer, R. A., & Bridges, S. K. (2003). Postmodern approaches to psychotherapy. In A. S. Gurman & S. B. Messer (Eds.), *Essential psychotherapies: Theory and practice* (2nd ed., pp. 272–316). New York: Guilford Press.

Nelson, R. O., & Hayes, S. C. (1986). The nature of behavioral assessment. In R. O. Nelson & S. C. Hayes (Eds.), *Conceptual foundations of behavior assessment* (pp. 3–41). New York: Guilford Press.

Nezu, A. M., & Nezu, C. M. (Eds.). (1989). *Clinical decision making in behavior therapy: A problem solving perspective*. Champaign, IL: Research Press.

NICHD Early Child Care Research Network. (1997). The effects of infant child care on infant-mother attachment security: Results of the NICHD study of early child care. *Child Development, 68*, 860–879.

Nichols, M. P. (2009). *The essentials of family therapy* (4th ed.). Boston: Allyn & Bacon.

Nicholson, B., & Passik, S. D. (2007). Management of chronic noncancer pain in the primary care setting. *Southern Medical Journal, 100*, 1028–1036.

Norcross, J. C. (1986). Eclectic psychotherapy: An introduction and overview. In J. C. Norcross (Ed.), *Handbook of eclectic psychotherapy* (pp. 3–24). New York: Brunner/Mazel.

Norcross, J. C. (1990). Commentary: Eclecticism misrepresented and integration misunderstood. *Psychotherapy, 7*, 415–421.

Norcross, J. C., Beutler, L. E., & Clarkin, J. F. (1998). Prescriptive eclectic psychotherapy. In R. A. Dorfman (Ed.), *Paradigms of clinical social work* (Vol. 2, pp. 289–314). Philadelphia, PA: Brunner/Mazel.

Norcross, J. C., & Goldfried, M. R. (Eds.). (2005). *Handbook of psychotherapy integration* (2nd ed.). New York: Oxford University Press.

Norcross, J. C., Karpiak, C. P., & Santoro, S. O. (2005). Clinical psychologists across the years: The division of clinical psychology from 1960 to 2003. *Journal of Clinical Psychology, 61*, 1467–1483.

Norcross, J. C., & Newman, C. F. (1992). Psychotherapy integration: Setting the context. In J. C. Norcross & M. R. Goldfried (Eds.), *Handbook of psychotherapy integration* (pp. 3–46). New York: Basic Books.

Nezu, A. M., & Nezu, C. M. (Eds.). (1989). *Clinical decision making in behavior therapy: A problem-solving perspective.* Champaign, IL: Research Press.

Nezu, A. M., Nezu, C. M., & Lombardo, E. (2004). *Cognitive-behavioral case formulation and treatment design: A problem-solving approach.* New York: Springer Publishing.

Oakhill, J., Garnham, A., & Johnson-Baird, P. N. (1990). Belief bias effects in syllogistic reasoning. In D. J. Bilhooly, M. T. G. Keane, R. H. Logic, & G. Erdos (Eds.), *Lines of thinking* (Vol. 1, pp. 125–138). Chichester, UK: Wiley.

Oberst, U. O., & Stewart, A. E. (2003). *Adlerian psychotherapy: An advanced approach to Individual Psychology.* New York: Brunner-Routledge.

Ogden, T. (1986). *The matrix of the mind.* Norvale, NJ: Aronson.

O'Hanlon, W. H. (1993). Possibility therapy: From iatrogenic injury to iatrogenic healing. In S. Gilligan & R. Price (Eds.), *Therapeutic conversations* (pp. 3–17). New York: W.W. Norton.

O'Hanlon, W. H., & Wilk, J. (1987). *Shifting contexts: The generation of effective psychotherapy.* New York: Guilford Press.

O'Leary, K. D., & Wilson, G. T. (1987). *Behavior therapy: Application and outcome* (2nd ed.). Englewood Cliffs, NJ: Prentice-Hall.

Olson, D. H., Russell, C., & Sprenkle, D. H. (1983). Circumplex model of marital and family systems: VI. Theoretical update. *Family Process, 22,* 69–83.

O'Phelan, M. L. (1977). Statistical evaluation of attributes in Adlerian life style forms. *Journal of Individual Psychology, 33,* 203–212.

Orlinsky, D. E. (2006). Comments on the state of psychotherapy research (As I see it). *Psychotherapy Bulletin, 41,* 37–41.

Orlinsky, D. E., Ronnestad, M. H., & Willutzki, U. (2004). Fifty years of psychotherapy, process-outcome research: Continuity and change. In M. J. Lambert (Ed.), *Bergin and Garfield's handbook of psychotherapy and behavior change* (5th ed., pp. 307–389). New York: Wiley.

Othmer, E., & Othmer, S. C. (1994). *The clinical interview using DSM-IV: Vol. 1: Fundamentals.* Washington, DC: American Psychiatric Press.

Pagnin, D., de Queiroz, V., Piini, S., & Cassano, G. B. (2004). Efficacy of ECT in depression: A meta-analytic review. *Journal of Electroconvulsive Thrapy, 20,* 13–20.

Pardridge, W. M. (2003). Blood-brain barrier drug targeting: The future of brain drug development. *Molecular Interventions, 3,* 90–105.

Patterson, G. R. (1971). *Families: Application of social learning to family life.* Champaign, IL: Research Press.

Paul, G. L. (1969). Behavior modification research: Design and tactics. In C. M. Franks (Ed.), *Behavior therapy: Appraisal and status* (pp. 29–62). New York: McGraw-Hill.

Paul, G. L., & Lentz, R. J. (1977). *Psychosocial treatment of chronic mental patients: Milieu versus social-learning programs.* Cambridge, MA: Harvard University Press.

Paul, G. L., & Menditto, A. A. (1992). Effectiveness of inpatient treatment programs for mentally ill adults in public psychiatric facilities. *Applied & Preventive Psychology, 1,* 41–63.

Paul, G. L., Stuve, P., & Menditto, A. A. (1997). Social-learning program (with token economy) for adult psychiatric inpatients. *The Clinical Psychologist, 50,* 14–17.

PDM Task Force. (2006). *Psychodynamic Diagnostic Manual.* Silver Spring, MD: Alliance for Psychoanalytic Organizations.

Pelios, L., Morren, J., Tesch, D., & Axelrod, S. (1999). The impact of functional analysis methodology on treatment choice for selfo-injurious and aggressive behavior. *Journal of Applied Behavior Analysis, 32,* 185–195.

Penn, P. (1982). Circular questioning. *Family Process, 21,* 267–279.

Pepper, S. C. (1942). *World hypotheses.* Berkeley, CA: University of California Press.

Persons, J. B., & Tompkins, M. A. (1997). Cognitive-behavioral case formulation. In T. D. Eels (Ed.), *Handbook of psychotherapy case formulation* (pp. 314–339). New York: Guilford Press.

Perls, F. S. (1947). *Ego, hunger, and aggression.* London: Allen & Unwin.

Perls, F. S. (1969). *Gestalt therapy verbatim*. Moab, UT: Real People Press.

Perls, F. S. (1970). Four lectures. In J. Fagan & I. Shepherd (Eds.), *Gestalt therapy now* (pp. 14–38). Palo Alto, CA: Science and Behavior Books.

Perls, F. S., Hefferline, R. F., & Goodman, P. (1951). *Gestalt therapy*. New York: Julian Press.

Perls, L. (1976). Comments on new directions. In E. W. L. Smith (Ed.), *The growing edge of Gestalt therapy* (pp. 221–226). New York: Brunner/Mazel.

Perry, W. G. (1968). *Forms of intellectual and ethical development in the college years*. New York: Holt, Rhinehart and Winston.

Petersen, T. J. (2006). Enhancing the efficacy of antidepressants with psychotherapy. *Journal of Psychopharmacology, 20*(Suppl. 3), 19–28.

Phares, E. J., & Chaplin, W. F. (1997). *Introduction to personality* (4th ed.). New York: Addison Wesley, Longman.

Piaget, J. (1952/1963). *The origins of intelligence in children*. New York: Norton.

Piazza, C. C., Fisher, W. W., Hanley, G. P., LeBlanc, L. A., Worsdell, A. S., Lindauer, S. E., et al. (1998). Treatment of pica through multiple analyses of its reinforcing functions. *Journal of Applied Behavior Analysis, 31*, 165–189.

Pine, F. (1985). *Developmental theory and clinical process*. New Haven, CT: Yale University Press.

Pizer, S. A. (2001). The capacity to tolerate paradox: Bridging multiplicity within a self. In J. C. Muran (Ed.), *Self-relations in the psychotherapy process* (pp. 111–130). Washington, DC: American Psychological Association.

Polster, E. (1987). Escape from the present: Transition and storyline. In J. K. Zeig (Ed.), *The evolution of psychotherapy* (pp. 326–340). New York: Brunner/Mazel.

Polster, E. (1995). *A population of selves*. San Francisco: Jossey-Bass.

Polster, M. (1987). Gestalt therapy: Evolution and application. In J. K. Zeig (Ed.), *The evolution of psychotherapy* (pp. 312–325). New York: Brunner/Mazel.

Polster, E., & Polster, M. (1973). *Gestalt therapy integrated*. New York: Brunner/Mazel.

Popkin, M. (1993). *Active parenting today*. Atlanta, GA: Active Parenting.

Powers, W. T. (1973). *Behavior: The control of perception*. Chicago: Aldine.

Premack, D. (1965). Reinforcement theory. In D. Levine (Ed.), *Nebraska symposium on motivation* (Vol. 13). Lincoln, NE: Nebraska University Press.

Premack, D. (1990). The infant's theory of self-propelled objects. *Cognition, 36*, 1–16.

Prochaska, J. O., & DiClemente, C. C. (1984). *The transtheoretical approach: Crossing the traditional boundaries of therapy*. Homewood, IL: Dow Jones-Irwin.

Prochaska, J. O., & DiClemente, C. C. (2005). The transtheoretical approach. In J. C. Norcross & M. R. Goldfried (Eds.). *Handbook of psychotherapy integration* (2nd ed., pp. 147–171). New York: Oxford University Press.

Prochaska, J. O., & Norcross, J. C. (2002). Stages of change. In J. C. Norcross (Ed.), *Psychotherapy relationships that work: Therapist contributions and responsiveness to patients* (pp. 303–313). New York: Oxford University Press.

Prochaska, J. O., & Norcross, J. C. (2007). *Systems of psychotherapy: A transtheoretical analysis* (6th ed.). Belmont, CA: Thomson Brooks/Cole.

Prochaska, J. O., Velicer, W. F., Fava, J., Ruggiero, L., Laforge, R., Rossi, J. S., et al. (2001). Counselor and stimulus control enhancements of a stage matched expert system for smokers in a managed care setting. *Preventive Medicine, 32*, 23–32.

Procter, H. G. (1987). Change in the family construct system. In R. A. Nemeyer & G. J. Neimeyer (Eds.), *Personal construct therapy casebook* (pp. 153–171). New York: Springer.

Prouty, G. (1990). Pre-therapy: A theoretical evolution in the person-centered/experiential psychotherapy of schizophrenia and retardation. In G. Lietaer, J. Rombauts, & R. Van Balen (Eds.), *Client-centered and experiential psychotherapy in the nineties* (pp. 645–658). Leuven, Belgium: Leuven University Press.

Prouty, G. (2001). Humanistic psychotherapy for people with schizophrenia. In D. J. Cain & J. Seeman (Eds.), *Humanistic psychotherapies: Handbook of research and practice* (pp. 579–601). Washington, DC: American Psychological Association.

Raimy, V. C. (1950). *Training in clinical psychology*. New York: Prentice Hall.

Rank, O. (1945). *Will therapy and truth and reality* (J. Taft, Trans.). New York: A.A. Knopf.

Rankin, H., Hodgson, R., & Stockwell, T. (1983). Cue-exposure and response prevention with alcoholics: A controlled trial. *Behaviour Research and Therapy, 21*, 435–446.

Regier, D. A., Farmer, M. E., Rae, D. S., Locke, B. Z., Keith, S. J., Judd, L. J., et al. (1990). Comorbidity of mental disorders with alcohol and other drug abuse: Results from the epidemiologic catchment area study. *Journal of the American Medical Association, 264*, 2511–2518.

Reich, W. (1949). *Character analysis*. New York: Orgone Institute Press.

Reinblatt, S. P., & Riddle, M. A. (2007).The pharmacological management of childhood anxiety disorders: A review. *Psychopharmacology, 191*, 67–86.

Reinecke, M. A., & Freeman, A. (2003). Cognitive therapy. In A. S. Gurman & S. B. Messer (Eds.), *Essential psychotherapies: Theory and practice* (2nd ed., pp. 224–271). New York: Guilford Press.

Reinecke, M. A., & Rogers, G. (2001). Dysfunctional attitudes and attachment style among clinically depressed adults. *Behavioural and Cognitive Psychotherapy, 29*, 129–141.

Resick, P. A., & Schnicke, M. K. (1993). *Cognitive processing therapy for rape victims: A treatment manual*. Newbury Park, CA: Sage.

Rice, L. N., & Greenberg, L. S. (1984). *Patterns of change: Intensive analysis of psychotherapy process*. New York: Guilford Press.

Rice, L. N., & Kerr, G. P. (1986). Measures of client and therapist vocal quality. In L. Greenberg & W. Pinsof (Eds.), *The psychotherapeutic process: A research handbook* (pp. 73–105). New York: Guilford Press.

Riegel, K. F. (1973). Dialectical operations: The final period of cognitive development. *Human Development, 16*, 346–370.

Rimm, D., & Masters, J. (1974). *Behavior therapy*. New York: Academic Press.

Robins, C. J., & Chapman, A. L. (2004). Dialectical behavior therapy: Current status, recent developments, and future directions. *Journal of Personality Disorders, 18*, 73–89.

Rogers, C. R. (1942). *Counseling and psychotherapy*. Boston: Houghton-Mifflin.

Rogers, C. R. (1951). *Client centered therapy*. Boston: Houghton-Mifflin.

Rogers, C. R. (1957). The necessary and sufficient conditions of therapeutic personality change. *Journal of Consulting Psychology, 21*, 95–103.

Rogers, C. R., & Dymond, R. (1954). *Psychotherapy and personality change*. Chicago: University of Chicago Press.

Rogers, C. R., Gendlin, E. T., Kiesler, D. J., & Truax, C. B. (1967). The findings in brief. In C. Rogers (Ed.), *The therapeutic relationship and its impact: A study of psychotherapy with schizophrenics* (pp. 73–93). Madison: University of Wisconsin Press.

Rogner, J. (1994). One year after the end of an analytical Adlerian psychotherapy: I. Comparison with persons who begin psychotherapy. *Zeitschrift fur Individualpsychologie, 19*, 191–202.

Root, M. P. P. (1992). Reconstructing the impact of trauma on personality. In L. S. Brown & M. Ballou (Eds.), *Personality and Psychopathology: Feminist reappraisals* (pp. 229–265). New York: Guilford.

Rosen, C. S. (2000). Is the sequencing of change processes by stage consistent across health problems? A meta-analysis. *Health Psychology, 19*, 593–604.

Rosen, G. M., Lohr, J. M., McNally, R. J., & Herbert, J. D. (2000). Power Therapies, miraculuous claims nd the cures that fail. In M. J. Schott & S. Palmer (Eds.), *Trauma and post-traumatic stress disorder* (pp. 134–136). London: Cassell.

Rosenthal, R., & Jacobson, L. (1968). *Pygmalion in the classroom*. New York: Holt, Rinehart, & Winston.

Rosenzweig, S. (1936/2002). Some implicit common factors in diverse methods of psychotherapy. (Reprinted in *Journal of Psychotherapy Integration, 12*, 5–9).

Rosenzweig, S., & Bray, D. (1942). Sibling death in anamneses of schizophrenic patients. *Psychoanalytic Review, 49*, 71–92.

Rouse, R. (1992). Making sense of settlement: Class transformation, cultural struggle, and transnationalism among Mexican migrants in the United States. In N. G. Schiller, L. Basch, & C. Blanc-Szanton (Eds.), *Towards a transnational perspective on migration: Race, class, ethnicity, and nationalism reconsidered* (pp. 22–55). New York: New York Academy of Sciences.

Rowbotham, M. C., Twilling, L., Davies, P., Taylor, K., Mohr, D., & Reisner, L. (2003). Oral opioid therapy for chronic peripheral and central neuropathic pain. *New England Journal of Medicine, 348,* 1223–1232.

Rudd, M. D., & Joiner, T. E. (1998). The assessment, management, and treatment of suicidality: Toward clinically informed and balanced standards of care. *Clinical Psychology: Science & Practice, 5,* 135–150.

Rummelhart, D. E., Smolensky, P., McClelland, J. L., & Hinton, G. E. (1986). Schemata and sequential thought processes in PDP models. In J. L. McClelland & D. E. Rummelhart (Eds.), *Parallel distributed processing: Explorations in the microstructure of cognition* (Vol. 2, pp. 7–57). Cambridge, MA: MIT Press.

Russell, D. E. H. (1986). *The secret trauma: Incest in the lives of girls and women.* New York: Basic Books.

Ryan, R. M., & Deci, E. L. (2000). Self-determination theory and the facilitation of intrinsic motivation, social development and well-being. *American Psychologist, 55,* 68–78.

Sachs, G. S. (2003). Decision tree for the treatment of bipolar disorder. *Journal of Clinical Psychiatry, 64*(Suppl. 8), 35–40.

Sachs, G. S., Grossman, F., Ghaemi, S. N., Okamoto, A., Bowden C. L., et al. (2002). Combination of a mood stabilizer with risperidone or haloperidol for treatment of acute mania: A double-blind, placebo-controlled comparison of efficacy and safety. *American Journal of Psychiatry, 159,* 1146–1154.

Sachs, G. S., Nierenberg, A. A., Calabrese, J. R., Lauren B., Marangell, L. B., Wisniewski, S. R., et al. (2007). Effectiveness of adjunctive antidepressant treatment for bipolar depression. *The New England Journal of Medicine, 356,* 1711–1722.

Sachse, R., & Elliott, R. (2001). Process-outcome research on humanistic therapy variables. In D. J. Cain & J. Seeman (Eds.), *Humanistic therapies: Handbook of research and practice* (pp. 83–115). Washington, DC: American Psychological Association.

Safer, D. L., Telch, C. F., & Agras, W. S. (2001). Dialectical behavior therapy for bulimia nervosa. *American Journal of Psychiatry, 158,* 632–634.

Safran, J. D. (1998). *Widening the scope of cognitive therapy: The therapeutic relationship, emotion, and the process of change.* Northvale, NJ: Aronson.

Safran, J. D., & Greenberg, L. S. (1982). Cognitive appraisal and reappraisal: Implications for clinical practice. *Cognitive Therapy and Research, 6,* 251–258.

Safran, J. D., & Messer, S. B. (1998). Psychotherapy integration: A postmodern critique. In J. D. Safran (Ed.), *Widening the scope of cognitive therapy* (chap. 13, pp. 269–290). Northvale, NJ: Aronson.

Safran, J. D., & Muran, J. C. (2000). *Negotiating the therapeutic alliance: A relational treatment guide.* New York: Guilford Press.

Sairanen, M., Lucas, G., Ernfors, P., Castrén, M., & Castrén, E. (2005). Brain-derived neurotrophic factor and antidepressant drugs have different but coordinated effects on neuronal turnover, proliferation, and survival in the adult dentate gyrus. *Journal of Neuroscience, 25,* 1089–1094.

Sanderson, W. C., DiNardo, P. A., Rapee, R. M., & Barlow, D. H. (1990). Syndrome comorbidity in patients diagnosed with a DSM-III-R anxiety disorder. *Journal of Abnormal Psychology, 99,* 308–312.

Sarason, I. G., Sarason, B. B., & Pierce, G. R. (1990). *Social support: An interactional view.* New York: Wiley.

Satir, V. M. (1972). *Peoplemaking.* Palo Alto, CA: Science and Behavior Books.

Scharff, D. E., & Scharff, J. S. (1987). *Object relations family therapy.* Northvale, NJ: Aronson.

Schatzberg, A. F., Haddad, P., Kaplan, E. M., Lejoyeux, M., Rosenbaum, J. F., Young, A. H., & Zajecka, J., et al. (1997). Possible biological mechanisms of the serotonin reuptake inhibitor discontinuation syndrome. *Journal of Clinical Psychiatry, 58*(Suppl. 7), 23–27.

Scheff, T. J. (1995). Shame and related emotions [Special issue]. *American Behavioral Scientist, 38*(8), 1053–1059.

Schmidt, N. B., Joiner, T. E., Young, J. E., & Telch, M. J. (1995). The Schema Questionnaire: Investigation of psychometric properties and the hierarchical structure of a measure of maladaptive schemata. *Cognitive Therapy and Research 19,* 296–321.

Schottenbauer, M. A., Glass, C. R., & Arnkoff, D. B. (2005). Outcome research on psychotherapy Integration. In J. C. Norcross & M. R. Goldfried (Eds.), *Handbook of psychotherapy integration* (2nd ed., pp. 459–493). New York: Oxford University Press.

Schulman, B. H. (1973). *Contributions to individual psychology.* Chicago: Alfred Adler Institute.

Schultz, W. (2002). Getting formal with dopamine and reward. *Neuron, 36,* 241–263.

Schunk, D. H., & Zimmerman, B. J. (1998). *Self-regulated learning: From teaching to self-reflective practice.* New York: Guilford Press.

Scott, J., Palmer, S., Paykel, E., Teasdale, J., & Hayhurst, H. (2003). Use of cognitive therapy for relapse prevention in chronic depression: Cost-effectiveness study. *British Journal of Psychiatry, 182,* 221–227.

Segal, Z. V., Williams, J. M. G., & Teasdale, J. D. (2002). *Mindfulness-based cognitive therapy for depression: A new approach to preventing relapse.* New York: Guilford.

Seidel, L., & Walkup, J. T. (2006). Selective serotonin reuptake inhibitor use in the treatment of the pediatric nono-oobseeive-compusleve disorder anxiety disorders. *Jounral of Child and Adolescent Psychopharmacology, 16,* 171–179.

Seligman, M. E. P. (1992). *Helplessness.* New York: Freeman.

Seligman, M. E. P. (1995). The effectiveness of psychotherapy: The *Consumer Reports* study. *American Psychologist, 50,* 965–974.

Seligman, M. E. P., Abramson, L. Y., Semmel, A., & von Baeyer, C. (1979). Depressive attributional style. *Journal of Abnormal Behavior, 88,* 242–247.

Sexton, T. L., & Alexander, J. F. (1999). Functional family therapy: Principles of clinical intervention, assessment, and implementation. Henderson NV: RCH Enterprises.

Sexton, T. L., & Griffin, B. L. (Eds.). (1997). *Constructivist thinking in counseling practice, research, and training* (Foreword). New York: Teachers College Press.

Shadish, W. R., Matt, G. E., Navarro, A. M., Siegle, G., Crits-Christoph, P. et al. (1997). Evidence that therapy works in clinically representative conditions. *Journal of Consulting and Clinical Psychology, 65,* 355–365.

Shapiro, D. (1956). *Neurotic styles.* New York: Basic Books.

Shapiro, D. A., & Shapiro, D. (1982). Meta-analysis of comparative therapy outcome studies: A replication and refinement. *Psychological Bulletin, 92,* 581–604.

Shapiro, F. (1995). *Eye movement desensitization and reprocessing: Basic principles, protocols, and procedures.* New York: Guilford Press.

Shapiro, F. (2001). *Eye movement desensitization and reprocessing: Basic principles, protocols, and procedures* (2nd ed.). New York: Guilford Press.

Shawyer, F., Ratcliff, K., Mackinnon, A., Farhall, J., Hayes S. C., & Copolov, D. (2007). The voices acceptance and action scale (VAAS): Pilot data. *Journal of Clinical Psychology, 63,* 593–606.

Shedler, J. (2010). The efficacy of psychodynamic psychotherapy. *American Psychologist, 65,* 98–109.

Sheldon, K. M., Elliot, A. J., Kim, Y.-M., & Kasser, T. (2001). What is satisfying about satisfying events? Testing 10 candidate psychological needs. *Journal of Personality and Social Psychology, 80,* 325–339.

Sheldon, R. C. (2000). Cellular mechanism in the vulnerability to depression and response to antidepressants. *Psychiatric Clinics of North America, 23,* 713–729.

Shoham, V., & Rohrbaugh, M. J. (1999). Beyond allegiance to comparative outcome studies. *Clinical Psychology: Science and Practice, 6,* 120–123.

Singer, E. (2004). The master switch. *New Scientist, March 6,* 34.

Skoog (1975). Cited in J. Meyer, *Death and neurosis* (p. 47). New York: International Universities Press.

Skowron, E. A., & Friedlander, M. L. (1998). The role of differentiation of self in marital adjustment. *Journal of Counseling Psychology, 45,* 235–246.

Slife, B. D. (2004a). Theoretical challenges to therapy practice and research. In M. J. Lambert (Ed.), *Bergin and Garfield's Handbook of psychotherapy and behavior change* (5th ed., pp. 493–539). New York: Wiley.

Slife, B. D. (2004b). Taking practice seriously: Toward a relational ontology. *Journal of Theoretical and Philosophical Psychology, 24,* 157–178.

Snyder, M. (1982). Self-fulfilling stereotypes. *Psychology Today, July,* 60–68.

Snyder, C. R., & Lopez, S. J. (2001). *Handbook of positive psychology.* New York: Oxford University Press.

Sohn, E. (2002, August 19). The gene that would stay still. *U.S. News & World Report.* Retrieved from www.usnews.com/usnews/culture/articles/020819/archive_022328_2.htm

Southwick, S. M., Vythilingam, M., & Charney, D. S. (2005). The psychobiology of depression and resilience to stress: Implications for prevention and reatment. *Annual Review of Clinical Psychology, 1,* 255–291.

Speck, R. V., & Attneave, C. L. (1973). *Family networks.* New York: Random House Pantheon Books.

Spence, D. P. (1982). Narrative truth and theoretical truth. *Psychoanalytic Quarterly, 51,* 43–69.

Spiegler, M. D., & Guevremont, D. C. (2003). *Contemporary behavior therapy* (4th ed.). Pacific Grove, CA: Brooks/Cole.

Spinelli, E. (1989). *The interpreted world.* London: Sage.

Sroufe, L. A. (1988). The role of infant-caregiver attachment in development. In J. Belsky & T. Nezworski (Eds.), *Clinical implications of attachment* (pp. 18–38). Hillsdale, NJ: Erlbaum.

Stampfl, T. (1976). Implosive therapy. In P. Olsen (Ed.), *Emotional flooding.* New York: Aldine.

Stanton, M. D. (2004). Getting reluctant substance abusers to engage in treatment/self-help: A review of outcomes and clinical options. *Journal of Marital & Family Therapy, 30,* 165–182.

Steiner, H., Saxena, K., Chang, K. (2003). Psychopharmacologic strategies for the treatment of aggression in juveniles. *CNS Spectrums, 8,* 298–308.

Steinman, M. A., Landefeld, C. S., Rosenthal, G. E., Bertenthal, D., Sen S., & Kaboli, P. J. (2006). Polypharmacy and prescribing quality in elders. *Journal of American Geriatric Society, 54,* 1516–1523.

Stern, D. N. (1985). *The interpersonal world of the infant.* New York: Basic Books.

Stevens, J. (1971). *Awareness: Exploring, experimenting, experiencing.* Moab, UT: Real People Press.

Stiles, W. B., Barkham, M., Mellor-Clark, J., & Connell, J. (2008). Effectiveness of cognitive-behavioural, person-centred, and psychodynamic therapies in UK primary-care routine practice: Replication in a larger sample. *Psychological Medicine, 38,* 677–688.

Stolorow, R., Brandchaft, B., & Atwood, G. (1994). *Psychoanalytic treatment: An intersubjective approach.* Hillsdale, NJ: Analytic Press.

Stricker, G. (2005). Perspectives on psychotherapy integration. *Psychotherapy Bulletin, 40,* 8–11.

Stricker, G., & Gold, J. (2003). Integrative approaches to psychotherapy. In A. S. Gurman & S. B. Messer (Eds.), *Essential psychotherapies:Theory and practice* (2nd ed., pp. 317–349). New York: Guilford Press.

Strosahl, K. D., Hayes, S. C., Wilson, K. G., & Gifford, E. V. (2005). An ACT primer: Core therapy processes, intervention strategies, and therapist competencies. In S. C. Hayes & K. D. Strosahl (Eds.), *A practical guide to acceptance and commitment therapy* (pp. 31–58). New York: Springer Science.

Strong, S. R., & Claiborn, C. D. (1982). *Change though interaction: Social psychological processes of counseling and psychotherapy.* New York: Wiley.

Strupp, H. H., & Anderson, T. (1997). On the limitations of therapy manuals. *Clinical Psychology: Science and Practice, 4,* 76–82.

Stuart, R. B. (1969). An operant-interpersonal treatment for marital discord. *Journal of Consulting and Clinical Psychology, 33,* 675–682.

Substance Abuse and Mental Health Administration (2008). 2006 National survey on drug use and health: Detailed tables. Retrieved December 5, 2008, from http://www.oas.samhsa.gov/NSDUH/2k6NSDUH/tabs/Sect1peTabs1to46.htm#Tab1.17A

Sue, D. W. (1978). Eliminating cultural oppression in counseling: Toward a general theory. *Journal of Counseling Psychology, 25,* 419–428.

Sue, D. W., Capodilupo, C. M., Torino, G. C., Bucceri, J. M., Holder, A. M. B., Nadal, K. L., et al. (2007). Racial microaggressions in everyday life: Implications for clinical practice. *American Psychologist, 62,* 271–286.

Sullivan, H. S. (1953a). *Conceptions of modern psychiatry.* New York: Norton.

Sullivan, H. S. (1953b). *The interpersonal theory of psychiatry.* New York: Norton.

Sullivan, H. S. (1964). *The fusion of psychiatry and the social sciences.* New York: Norton.

Svartberg, M., & Stiles, T. C. (1992). Predicting patient change from therapist competence and patient-therapist complementarity in short-term anxiety-provoking psychotherapy. *Journal of Consulting and Clinical Psychology, 60,* 304–307.

Swann, W. B., & Read, S. J. (1981). Self-verification processes: How we sustain our self-conceptions. *Journal of Experimental Social Psychology, 17,* 351–372.

Syracuse University (2006). Suicide or No-Harm Contract. Retrieved August 14, 2006, from http://suedweb.syr.edu/chs/OnlineField/suicide/contract.htm

Szatmari, P. (1992). The epidemiology of attention-deficit hyperactivity disorders. *Child and Adolescent Psychiatry Clinics of North America, 1,* 361–372.

TADS Team. (2007). The Treatment for Adolescents with Depression Study (TADS): Long-term effectiveness and safety outcomes. *Archives of General Psychiatry, 64,* 1132–1144.

Tafoya, N., & Del Vecchio, A. (2005). American Indian families: An overview. In M. McGoldrick, J. Giordano, & N. Garcia-Preto (Eds.), *Ethnicity & family therapy* (3rd ed., pp. 43–54). New York: Guilford Press.

Teyber, E. (2006). *Interpersonal process in psychotherapy: A relational approach* (4th ed.). Belmont, CA: Thomson Brooks/Cole.

Thibaut, J., & Kelley, H. H. (1959). *The social psychology of groups.* New York: Wiley.

Thomas, A., & Chess, S. (1977). *Temperament and development.* New York: Brunner/Mazel.

Thompson, C. (1950). *Psychoanalysis: Evolution and development.* New York: Grove Atlantic Monthly Press.

Thompson, R. A. (1993). *The brain: A neuroscience primer* (2nd ed.). New York: Freeman.

Thornton, R. (1990). *American Indian holocaust and survival: A population history since 1492.* Norman, OK: University of Oklahoma Press.

Tremblay, H., & Rovira, K. (2007). Joint visual attention and social triangular engagement at 3 and 6 months. *Infant Behavior & Development, 30,* 366–379.

Trimboli, F., & Farr, K. L. (2000). A psychodynamic guide for essential treatment planning. *Psychoanalytic Psychology, 17,* 336–359.

Tronick, E. Z. (1989). Emotions and emotional communication in infants. *American Psychologist, 44,* 112–119.

Truax, C. B. (1966). Reinforcement and nonreinforcement in Rogerian psychotherapy. *Journal of Abnormal Psychology, 71,* 1–9.

Truax, C. B. (1970). Effects of client-centered therapy with schizophrenics: Nine years pretherapy and nine years posttherapy hospitalization. *Journal of Consulting and Clinical Psychology, 35,* 417–422.

Turner, E. H., Matthews, A. M., Linardatos, E., Tell, R. A., & Rosenthal, R. (2008). Selective publication of antidepressant trials and its influence on apparent efficacy. *New England Journal of Medicine, 358,* 252–260.

Tversky, A., & Kahneman, D. (1974). Judgment under uncertainty: Heuristics and biases. *Science, 185,* 1124–1135.

Twohig, M. P. (2004). *ACT for OCD: Abbreviated treatment manual.* Retrieved May 9, 2005, from The Acceptance and Commitment Therapy website: http://www.acceptanceandcommitmenttherapy.com/docs/ACT for OCD Abbreviated Treatment Manual.doc

U.S. Department of Health and Human Services. (1999). *Mental health: A report of the surgeon general.* Rockville, MD: U.S. Department of Health and Human Services.

U.S. Department of Health and Human Services. (2003). *President's New Freedom Commission on Mental Health, final report.* Publication SMA 03-3832, National Institute of Mental Health.

U.S. Department of Labor (1965). The Negro family: The case for national action. Office of Planning and Research. Retrieved September 22, 2010 from http://www.dol.gov/oasam/programs/history/webid-meynihan.htm

Vaihinger, H. (1925). *The philosophy of "As-if": A system of the theoretical, practical, and religious fictions of mankind.* New York: Harcourt, Brace, & Company.

van IJzendoorn, M. H., Schuengel, C., & Bakermans-Kranenburg, M. J. (1999). Disorganized attachment in early childhood: Meta-analysis of precursors, concomitants, and sequalae. *Development and Psychopathology, 11,* 225–249.

van Rijswijk, E., Borghuis, M., van de Lisdonk, E., Zitman, F., & van Weel, C. (2007). Treatment of mental health problems in general practice: A survey of psychotropics prescribed and other treatments provided. *International Journal of Clinical Pharmacology, Therapy, and Toxicology, 45,* 23–29.

Vaughan, B. E., & Bost, K. (2002). Attachment and temperament: Redundant, independent, or interacting influences on interpersonal adaptation and development. In J. Cassidy & P. R. Shaver (Eds.), *Handbook of attachment theory, research, and clinical applications* (pp. 198–225). New York: Guilford Press.

Velligan, D. I., Funderburg, L. G., Giesecke, S. L., & Miller, A. L. (1995). Longitudinal analysis of communication deviance in the families of schizophrenic patients. *Psychiatry, 58,* 6–19.

Vestergaard-Poulsen, P., van Beek, M., Skewes, J., Bjarkam, C. R., Stubberup, M., Bertelsen, J., & Roepstorff, A. (2009). Long-term meditation is associated with increased gray matter density in the brain stem. *Neuroreport, 20,* 170–174.

Vickrey, B. G., Mittman, B. S., Connor, K. I., Pearson, M. L., Della Penna, R. D., Ganiats, T. D., et al. (2006). The effect of a disease management intervention on quality and outcomes of dementia care: A randomized, controlled trial. *Annals of Internal Medicine, 145,* 713–726.

Volkow, N. D., Fowler, J. S., Wang, G.-J., & Swanson, J. M. (2004). Dopamine in drug abuse and addiction: Results from imaging studies and treatment implications. *Molecular Psychiatry, 9,* 557–569.

Von Bertalanffy, L. (1950). An outline of general systems theory. *British Journal of Philosophical Science, 1,* 134–165.

Wachtel, P. L. (1967). Conceptions of broad and narrow attention. *Psychological Bulletin, 68,* 417–429.

Wachtel, P. L. (1977). *Psychoanalysis and behavior therapy: Toward an integration.* New York: Basic Books.

Wachtel, P. L. (1987). *Action and insight.* New York: Guilford Press.

Wachtel, P. L. (1997). *Psychoanalysis, behavior therapy, and the representational world.* Washington, DC: American Psychological Association.

Wachtel, P. L., Kruk, J. C., & McKinney, M. K. (2005). Cyclical psychodynamics and integrative psychodynamic psychotherapy. In J. C. Norcross & M. R. Goldfried (Eds.), *Handbook of psychotherapy integration* (pp. 172–195). New York: Oxford University Press.

Walsh, B. T., Seidman, S. N., Sysko, R., & Gould, M. (2002). Placebo response in studies of major depression: Variable, substantial, and growing. *Journal of the American Medical Association, 287,* 1840–1847.

Wampold, B. E. (2001). *The great psychotherapy debate: Models, methods, and findings.* Mahwah, NJ: Erlbaum.

Wampold, B. E., Mondin, G. W., Moody, M., Stich, F., Benson, K., & Ahn, H. (1997). A meta-analysis of outcome studies comparing bona fide psychotherapies: Empirically, "all must have prizes". *Psychological Bulletin, 122,* 203–215.

Wang, P. S., Berglund, P., Olfson, M., Pincus, H. A., Wells, K. B., & Kessler, R. C. (2005). Failure and delay in initial treatment contact after first onset of mental disorders in the National Comorbidity Survey replication. *Archives of General Psychiatry, 62,* 603–613.

Wason, P. C. (1960). On the failure to eliminate hypotheses in a conceptual task. *Quarterly Journal of Experimental Psychology, 12,* 129–140.

Watson, D. L., & Tharp, R. G. (1997). *Self-directed behavior: Self-modification for personal adjustment.* Pacific Grove, CA: Brooks/Cole.

Watson, J. B. (1924/1930). *Behaviorism*. New York: Norton Press.

Watts, R. E. (Ed.). (2003). *Adlerian, cognitive, and constructivist therapies*. New York: Springer.

Watzlawick, P., Beavin, J. H., & Jackson, D. D. (1967). *Pragmatics of human communication: A study of interactional patterns, pathologies, and paradoxes*. New York: Norton.

Weakland, J. H., Fisch, R., Watzlawick, P., & Bodin, A. (1974). Brief therapy: Focused problem resolution. *Family Process, 13*, 141–168.

Wegner, D. M., Schneider, D. J., Carter, S. R., & White, T. L. (1987). Paradoxical effects of thought suppression. *Journal of Personality and Social Psychology, 53*, 5–13.

Weissman, A. N., & Beck, A. T. (1978). *Development and validation of the Dysfunctional Attitude Scale: A preliminary investigation*. Paper presented at the meeting of the American Educational Research association, Toronto. Cited in DeRubeis, R. J., Tang, T. Z., & Beck, A. T. (2001). Cognitive therapy. In K. S. Dobson (Ed.), *Handbook of cognitive-behavioral therapies* (2nd ed., pp. 349–392). New York: Guilford Press.

Weissman, M. M., Markowitz, J. C., & Klerman, G. L. (2007). *Clinician's quick guide to interpersonal psychotherapy*. New York: Oxford University Press.

Wells, M. G., Burlingame, G. M., Lambert, M. J., & Hoag, M. J. (1996). Conceptualization and measurement of patient change during psychotherapy: Development of the outcome questionnaire and youth outcome questionnaire. *Psychotherapy: Theory, Research, Practice, Training, 33*, 275–283.

Werry, J. S., & Quay, H. C. (1971). The prevalence of behavior symptoms in younger elementary school children. *American Journal of Orthopsychiatry, 41*, 136–143.

Westen, D. (1998). Unconscious thought, feeling, and motivation: The end of a century-long debate. In R. F. Bornstein & J. M. Masling (Eds.), *Empirical perspectives on the psychoanalytic unconscious* (pp. 1–43). Washington, DC: American Psychological Association.

West, H. C., & Sabol, W. J. (2009). *Prison inmates at midyear 2008-Statistical tables. NCJ 225619*. Washington, DC: National Criminal Justice Reference Service.

Westermann, M. A. (2004). Theory and research on practices, theory and research as practices: Hermeneutics and psychological inquiry. *Journal of Theoretical and Philosophical Psychology, 24*, 123–156.

Whitaker, C. A. (1976). The hindrance of theory in clinical work. In P. J. Guerin (Ed.), *Family therapy: Theory and practice* (pp. 154–164). New York: Gardner Press.

White, M., & Epston, D. (1990). *Narrative means to therapeutic ends*. New York: Norton.

White, R. (1960). Competence and the psychosexual stages of development. In M. R. Jones (Ed.), *Nebraska symposium on motivation* (Vol. 8, pp. 97–141). Lincoln: University of Nebraska Press.

Whitehouse, P. J., & Harris, G. (1998). The intergenerational transmission of eating disorders. *European Eating Disorders Review, 6*, 238–254.

Wikipedia (n.d.). *Chemical synapse*. Retrieved December 14, 2009 from http://en.wikipedia.org/wiki/Chemical_synapse

Williams, E. N., & Barber, J. S. (2004). Power and responsibility in therapy: Integrating feminism and multiculturalism. *Journal of Multicultural Counseling and Development, 32*, 390–401.

Wilson, G. T., & Davison, G. C. (1971). Processes of fear reduction in systematic desensitization: Animal studies. *Psychological Bulletin, 76*, 1–14.

Wilson, K. G., & Byrd, M. R. (2004). ACT for substance abuse and dependence. In S. C. Hayes & K. D. Strosahl (Eds.), *A practical guide to acceptance and commitment therapy* (pp. 153–184). New York: Springer Science.

Winnicott, D. W. (1949). Hate in the countertransference. *International Journal of Psycho-analysis, 30*, 69–75.

Winnicott, D. W. (1965). *The maturational process and the facilitating environment*. New York: International Universities Press.

Winnicott, D. W. (1972). *Holding and interpretation*. New York: Grove Press.

Wise, D., & Rosqvist, J. (2006). Explanatory style and well-being. In J. C. Thomas, D. L. Segal, & M. Hersen (Eds.), *Comprehensive handbook of personality and psychopathology: Personality and everyday functioning* (Vol. 1, pp. 285–305). Hoboken, NJ: Wiley.

Wise, R. A. (2004). Dopamine, learning, and motivation. *Nature Reviews: Neuroscience, 5*, 1–12.

Wolf, M. M. (1978). Social validity: The case of subjective measurement or how applied behavior analysis is finding its heart. *Journal of Applied Behavior Analysis, 11,* 203–214.

Wolpe, J. (1958). *Psychotherapy by reciprocal inhibition.* Stanford, CA: Stanford University Press.

Woody, S. R., Detweiler-Bedell, J., Teachman, B. A., & O'Hearn, T. (2003). *Treatment planning: Taking the guesswork out of clinical care.* New York: Guilford Press.

Worell, J., & Remer, P. (2003). *Feminist perspectives in therapy: Empowering diverse women.* New York: Wiley.

Yalom, I. D. (1980). *Existential psychotherapy.* New York: Basic Books.

Yalom, I. D. (1989). *Love's executioner and other tales of psychotherapy.* New York: Basic Books.

Yerkes, R. M., & Dodson, J. D. (1908). The relation of strength of stimulus to rapidity of habit-formation. *Journal of Comparative Neurology and Psychology, 78,* 459–482.

Young, J. E. (1990). *Cognitive therapy for personality disorders.* Sarasota, FL: Professional Resources Press.

Young, J. E. (1994). *Young Parenting Inventory.* New York: Cognitive Therapy Center of New York.

Young, J. E. (1995). *Young Compensation Inventory.* New York: Cognitive Therapy Center of New York.

Young, J. E. (1999). *Cognitive therapy for personality disorders: A schema-focused approach* (Rev. ed.). Sarasota, FL: Professional Resources Press.

Young, J. E., & Brown, G. (1990). *Young schema questionnaire.* New York: Cognitive Therapy Center of New York.

Young, J. E., & Brown, G. (2001). *Young schema questionnaire: Special edition.* New York: Schema Therapy Institute.

Young, J. E., & Gluhoski, V. L. (1996). Schema-focused diagnosis for personality disorders. In F. W. Kaslow (Ed.), *Handbook of relational diagnosis and dysfunctional family patterns* (pp. 300–321). New York: Wiley.

Young, J. E., Klosko, J. S., & Weishaar, M. E. (2003). *Schema therapy: A practitioner's guide.* New York: Guilford Press.

Young, J. E., & Rygh, J. (1994). *Young-rygh avoidance inventory.* New York: Cognitive Therapy Center of New York.

Young, J. E., Weinberger, A. D., & Beck, A. T. (2001). Cognitive therapy for depression. In D. Barlow (Ed.), *Clinical handbook of psychological disorders* (3rd ed., pp. 264–308). New York: Guilford Press.

Yontef, G. M. (1993). *Awareness, dialogue and process: Essays on Gestalt therapy.* Highland, NY: Gestalt Journal Press.

Zahm, S. G., & Gold, E. K. (2002). Gestalt therapy. In M. Hersen & W. H. Sledge (Eds.), *Encyclopedia of psychotherapy* (Vol. 1, pp. 863–872). New York: Academic Press.

Zeigarnik, B. (1927). On finished and unfinished tasks. In W. D. Ellis (Ed.), *A source book of Gestalt psychology* (pp. 300–312). New York: Humanities Press, 1967.

Zimmerman, B. J. (2000). Attaining self-regulation: A social cognitive perspective. In M. Boekaerts, P. R. Pintrich, & M. Zeidner (Eds.), *Handbook of self-regulation* (pp. 13–39). San Diego, CA: Academic Press.

Zito, J. M., Safer, D. J., dosReis, S., Gardner, J. F., Magder, L., Soeken, K., et al. (2003).Psychotropic practice patterns for youth: A 10-year perspective. *Archives of Pediatric and Adolescent Medicine, 157,* 17–25.

Zuckerman, M. (1999). *Vulnerability to psychopathology: A biosocial model.* Washington, DC: American Psychogical Association.

Author Index

D. K. Fromme, *Systems of Psychotherapy,*
DOI 10.1007/978-1-4419-7308-5, © Springer Science+Business Media, LLC 2011

Subject Index

A

ABCs (Antecedent; Belief; Consequence), 138, 139, 166, 349, 352

Absurdity, 265, 266, 269, 295

Acceptance, 12, 15, 16, 20, 23, 112, 139, 140, 151, 156, 165, 177, 201, 223, 227, 231, 234, 242, 244, 270, 274, 276, 285, 291, 294, 296, 297, 326, 331, 337, 338, 347, 349, 351, 355, 379, 413, 417, 434, 435, 446–448, 450–467, 481

Acceptance and commitment therapy (ACT)
  functional contextualism, 450–468
  relational frame theory, 451

Accommodation, 142, 166, 354

Acculturation, 410, 411, 414, 426, 492

Activity scheduling, 125, 144

Adaptive functioning, 40, 204–208, 221, 238, 485

Agency, 17, 235, 263, 267, 271, 342, 343, 409, 419, 439, 470, 474, 475, 479

Alcoholics anonymous, 56, 95, 162, 344, 458

Alienation, 51, 126, 150, 164, 181, 202, 238, 265–267, 275, 276, 296, 374, 413, 461, 466, 477

Alliance ruptures, 307, 351, 354, 433–443, 493

Analgesics, 76, 79, 81, 85–87, 103

Antidepressants, 7, 17, 22, 64, 71–85, 87–89, 96, 102

Antipsychotics, 71, 73, 80, 82–86, 90–92, 96, 102, 128, 210

Anxiety, 18, 34, 64, 106, 138, 175, 199, 226, 265, 302, 332, 374, 417, 431, 484

Anxiety (existential *vs.* neurotic), 266, 267, 271, 295, 296

Anxiolytics, 64, 73, 75, 87, 88, 154

Applied behavioral analysis, 114–125, 133

Areas of vulnerability, 317, 319

Assertiveness, 15, 39, 106, 107, 127–129, 131, 134, 165, 180, 235, 308, 313, 361, 421, 423, 448, 467

Assimilation, 166

Attachment patterns
  anxious, 218
  avoidant, 218
  disorganized, 218
  secure, 218

Attention, 38, 39, 48, 51, 76, 79, 81, 92, 98, 99, 102, 106, 114–116, 119–122, 124, 125, 130, 133, 157, 173, 177, 209, 211, 213, 219, 225, 228, 230, 231, 238, 245, 268, 270, 275, 286, 294, 302, 303, 305, 307, 318, 326, 340, 356, 359, 376, 380, 383, 414, 419, 420, 425, 432, 434, 437, 439, 445, 450, 472, 479, 483, 485–488, 495, 497

Authenticity, 181, 182, 234, 235, 265–267, 269, 271, 276, 278, 296

Autism, 85, 123, 184, 185, 288

Automatic thoughts, 42, 141, 142, 144–148, 157, 167, 168, 467

Avoidance, 15, 26, 27, 107–109, 112, 115, 126, 138, 144, 146, 152–155, 163, 168, 189, 214, 218, 219, 244, 246, 249, 251, 252, 254, 266, 274, 289, 324–326, 333, 386, 439–442, 449, 451, 456–458, 460, 461, 464–467, 477, 484, 485, 488, 495

B

Behavioral activation, 125–127, 134, 143, 167

Behavioral diary, 123, 145

Behavior modification, 106, 114–125, 127–131

Behavior therapy, 15, 34, 36, 38, 56, 106, 356

Beneficial uncertainty, 319, 321, 322, 327

51751378R00315

Made in the USA
Lexington, KY
05 September 2019